Canada's

ণ্ড • ৯

Critical essays on 15 Canadian films

Cross / Cultures

Readings in the Post/Colonial Literatures in English

56

Series Editors:

Gordon
Collier
(Giessen)

Hena
Maes-Jelinek
(Liège)

Geoffrey
Davis
(Aachen)

Rodopi

Amsterdam – New York, NY 2002

Canada's Best Features

 » • «

Critical essays on 15 Canadian films

Edited by

Eugene P. Walz

The paper on which this book is printed meets the requirements of "ISO 9706:1994, Information and documentation - Paper for documents - Requirements for permanence".

ISBN: 90-420-1209-9 (bound)
©Editions Rodopi B.V., Amsterdam – New York, NY 2002
Printed in The Netherlands

Table of Contents

Acknowledgements and List of Figures | vii

Notes on Reference Procedure | ix

Introduction | xi

1 CHRISTINE RAMSAY ಬಂ
Canadian narrative cinema from the margins:
'The nation' and masculinity in *Goin' Down the Road* | 3

2 JIM LEACH ಬಂ
Double vision: *Mon oncle Antoine* and the cinema of fable | 27

3 TOM MCSORLEY ಬಂ
The Apprenticeship of Duddy Kravitz
Or, the anxiety of influence | 51

4 ANDRÉ LOISELLE ಬಂ
Michel Brault's *Les Ordres*: Documenting the reality
of experience and the fiction of history | 73

5 PETER MORRIS ಬಂ
Canadian gothic and *Les bons débarras*:
The night side of the soul | 99

6 BLAINE ALLAN ಬಂ
The Grey Fox afoot in a modern world | 117

7 SUZIE SAU-FONG YOUNG ಬಂ
"Forget Baudrillard": The horrors of 'pleasure' and
the pleasures of 'horror' in David Cronenberg's *Videodrome* | 147

8   BART TESTA ❧

The decline of frivolity
and Denys Arcand's *American Empire* | 175

9   BRENDA AUSTIN-SMITH ❧

"Gender is irrelevant": *I've Heard
the Mermaids Singing* as women's cinema | 209

10   ANGELA STUKATOR ❧

Pictures of age and ageing
in Cynthia Scott's *The Company of Strangers* | 237

11   THOMAS WAUGH ❧

Home is not the place one has left:
Or, *Masala* as 'a multi-cultural culinary treat'? | 255

12   GEORGE TOLES ❧

Drowning for love:
Jean-Claude Lauzon's *Léolo* | 275

13   WILL STRAW ❧

Reinhabiting lost languages:
Guy Maddin's *Careful* | 305

14   CATHERINE RUSSELL ❧

Role playing and the white male imaginary
in Atom Egoyan's *Exotica* | 321

15   ELUNED JONES ❧

Reconstructing the past:
Memory's enchantment in *The Red Violin* | 347

JOHN SCHOLES WITH GORDON COLLIER AND GENE WALZ ❧

Canadian film: A select annotated bibliography | 363

Contributors | 381

Acknowledgements and List of Figures

[handwritten annotations:] 5 Quebec (incl. Duddy) ; 5 English Can. ; 2 Women directed ; 1 co-pro.

———————————— ଓ

Stills courtesy of Cinematheque Ontario Film Reference Library and (marked *) the National Film Board of Canada. Cast identification reading from left to right.

1   *Goin' Down the Road* (Don Shebib, 1992) – Doug McGrath (Pete); Paul Bradley (Joey); Jayne Eastwood (Betty).   1

2   * *Mon oncle Antoine* (Claude Jutra, 1971) – Jacques Gagnon (Benoît); Jean Duceppe (Antoine).   25

3   *The Apprenticeship of Duddy Kravitz* (Ted Kotcheff, 1974; produced by John Kemeny) – Zvee Scooler (grandfather); Richard Dreyfuss (Duddy Kravitz).   51

4   *Les ordres* (Michel Brault, 1974) – Hélène Loiselle (Marie Boudreau).   73

5   *Les bons débarras* (Francis Mankiewicz, 1980; produced by Claude Godbout and Marcia Couëlle) – Marie Tifo (Michelle); Charlotte Laurier (Manon).   97

6   *The Grey Fox* (Phillip Borsos, 1982; produced by Peter O'Brian) – David Petersen (Louis Colquhoun); Richard Farnsworth (Bill Miner); Wayne Robson (Shorty Dunn).   115

7   *Videodrome* (David Cronenberg, 1983; produced by Claude Héroux) – James Woods (Max Renn); Deborah Harry (Nicki Brand).   145

8   *Le déclin de l'empire américain* (Denys Arcand, 1986; produced by René Malo and Roger Frappier) – Yves Jacques (Claude); Geneviève Rioux (Danielle); Pierre Curzi (Pierre); Dorothée Berryman (Louise); Dominique Michel (Dominique); Daniel Brière (Alain); Rémy Girard (Rémy).   173

9   *I've Heard the Mermaids Singing* (Patricia Rozema, 1987; produced by Alex-
     andra Raffé and Patricia Rozema) – Sheila McCarthy (Polly Vandersma).   207

10   * *The Company of Strangers* (Cynthia Scott, 1990) – Alice Diabo (Alice); Con-
     stance Garneau (Constance); Winfred Holden (Winnie); Cissy Meddings
     (Cissy); Mary Meigs (Mary); Catherine Roche (Catherine); Beth Webber
     (Beth).   235

11   *Masala* (Srinivas Krishna, 1991; produced by Camelia Frieberg and Srini-
     vas Krishna) – Zohra Segal (Grandma Tikkoo); Saeed Jaffrey (Lallu Bhai);
     Madhuri Bhatia (Bibi).   253

12   *Léolo* (Jean–Claude Lauzon, 1992; produced by Lyse Lafontaine and Aimée
     Danis) – Lorne Brass (Fernand's enemy); Yves Montmarquette (Fernand);
     Maxime Collin (Léolo).   273

13   *Careful* (Guy Maddin, 1992) – Gosla Dobrowolska (Zenaida); Kyle Mc-
     Culloch (Grigorss).   303

14   *Exotica* (Atom Egoyan, 1994) – Mia Kirshner (Christina); Bruce Greenwood
     (Francis).   319

15   *The Red Violin* (François Girard, 1998; produced by Niv Fichman) – Jason
     Flemyng (Frederick Pope); Greta Scacchi (Victoria Byrd).   344

ᘉ

Notes on Reference Procedure

—————————————————————— ℘

℘   In the grouped listings of film reviews in the bibliographical section of each essay, review titles have been omitted if they consist of nothing more individual than the title of the film in question. Compare

> John Hofsess, "The End of the Road: Don Shebib's Time of Illusion is Over," *Weekend Magazine* (28 February 1976): 16–20

with

> John Hofsess, *Take One* 2:6 (July–August 1969 [publ. July 1970]): 19–20

– where the review title was simply *"Goin' Down the Road."*

℘   In the reviews section, the sequence is chronological, not alphabetical by author.

℘   Some of the books referred to in the essays and footnotes also occur in the Select Bibliography at the back of this book, where full details can be found; references to such books in the essays are therefore abbreviated, with the additional indicator of the arrow-symbol (⇨).

> Harcourt, Peter. "Men of Vision: Some Comments on the Work of Don Shebib," *Cinema Canada* 32 (November 1976): 35–40; repr. in ⇨Feldman & Nelson, ed., *Canadian Film Reader*, 208–17.

> ⇨Hofsess, John. *Inner Views*, 67–79.

℘   In the Filmography section at the end of each essay, it is to be understood that the format is 35mm; only other formats (16mm etc) are explicitly included. In the interest of completeness, the detailed filmographical information heading each essay specifies 35mm and colour where this is the case; elsewhere, all films listed are to be understood as being in colour, unless otherwise indicated. Compare, from the essay on Donald Shebib, these three entries for feature films:

> 1969   *Good Times Bad Times* (director, cinematographer and editor; 35 mins., 16mm)

1970   *Goin' Down the Road* (*En roulant ma boule*, or: *La Route de l'ouest*, or: *Le voyage chimérique* ; 87 mins., 16mm)

1971   *Rip-Off* (director and co-editor; 89 mins.)

Here, *Rip-Off* is 35mm; and all three features are in colour. In the following two entries under short films and television work, change of format has been made explicit; "TV" indicates videotape format:

1977   *The Fighting Men* (CBC for *For the Record*; 75 mins., 16mm/TV; theatrical release 1978, 35mm)

1986   *Summits of Glory* (with Wendy Wacko; 120 mins., TV)

&   It is to be generally understood that the film listings register involvement as director; further functions by a given director are indicated as "+ screenplay," "+ co-cinematographer," etc.

&

Introduction
What Is Canadian Cinema?

—————————————— ɛ꜡

Our first English-Canadian feature

T HE TRIUMPH OF CANADIAN CINEMA." That was the title chosen by
Seth Feldman, Robarts Chair in Canadian Studies at York University
and one of the country's preeminent film scholars, for a series of screenings
and lectures in Toronto during the fall and winter of 2000–2001. For a nation
whose home-grown films have perennially accounted for less than three
percent of its theatrical screen-time, the word "triumph" may seem
hyperbolic, fanciful, even un-Canadian. Yet in the forty years that feature
films have been a recognizable part of the national dream (or at least
national politics), Canadian cinema has come a long, long way. The fact that
it continues to survive at all must itself be viewed as heroic.

While Canada's filmmakers have not become global celebrities of the
caliber of pop musicians Celine Dion and Shania Twain or even novelists
such as Margaret Atwood, Carol Shields and Michael Ondaatje, they have
gained, if not renown, then at least international recognition. And their films
have won many awards and attracted sympathetic audiences around the
world, particularly over the past ten years.

Only a dedicated group of film buffs and/or industry insiders and/or
academics paid much attention to Canadian films before 1984. In that year,
the Toronto Festival of Festivals (now called The Toronto International Film
Festival) programmed the first major retrospective of Canadian films. As
part of that retrospective, the film festival's organizers polled as many of the
aforementioned buffs, insiders and academics as it could. In an era when
theorists thunderously belittled "canonization," the festival published a top-
ten list of Canadian films. In 1993 the festival repeated the exercise. With
these top-ten lists as guides, this anthology, *Canada's Best Features*, was
compiled.

The wider world began to notice Canadian films when Denys Arcand
garnered two awards at the Cannes Film Festival in the late 1980s – the
International Film Critics' Prize in 1986 for *Le Déclin de l'empire américain* and

the Jury Prize in 1989 for *Jésus de Montreal*. Almost simultaneously, the Museum of Modern Art in New York staged a two-month series of films entitled "O Canada." A massive retrospective, "Les cinémas du Canada," held at the Centre Georges Pompidou in Paris in 1993 was the next step, unprecedented in the exposure it provided; seventy feature films and scores of shorts were screened, and a commemorative anthology of critical essays focusing on films from the various regions of the country accompanied the screenings. This event served notice that Canada had amassed a significant enough body of work that the film industry could be taken seriously.

Two years later an American film journal, *Post Script*,[1] devoted an entire issue to Canadian film; it proved to be so successful that a second issue on the same subject was published in 1998. More significantly, the Society for Cinema Studies, an international association of film professors, researchers and students, made "Cinema in Canada" the central focus of its annual conference in May 1997. Never before had a national cinema other than the USA been the subject of such intense examination. That same year, 1997, Atom Egoyan, Canada's most honoured contemporary filmmaker, dominated the Cannes Film Festival, winning the International Film Critics' Prize, the Ecumenical Prize, and the Grand Prize for *The Sweet Hereafter*. Clearly, Canadian films and filmmakers had arrived.

A cinema without much history

In 1957, twenty-four-year-old Sidney J. Furie directed his first feature film, *A Dangerous Age*, in Toronto. A low-budget quasi-documentary, it told the story of teenage lovers who flee to the USA to get married and, chastened by authorities there, return to Canada and the wishes of their parents. Given theatrical release in England and the USA, *A Dangerous Age* failed to find a distributor in Canada despite favourable notices at the Venice and Cannes Film Festivals. When his second feature, *A Cool Sound from Hell* (1958), was also snubbed by Canadian distributors, Furie packed up his ambitions and moved to England. There he lamented to the press: "I wanted to start a Canadian film industry, but nobody cared."[2]

---

[1] See the Annotated Filmography at the end of this book for listings of both *Post Script* issues, for *O Canada*, and for *Les cinémas du Canada*.

[2] Quoted in Wyndham Wise, ed. *Take One's Essential Guide to Films and Filmmakers in Canada* (Toronto: Take One, 1999): 116.

Furie's decision to make a Canadian feature film came out of nowhere. Ten years earlier, the Film Producers Association of Canada, expecting the government to impose restrictions on American film profits in Canada similar to those enforced by France, Italy, Australia and other countries, was poised to expand into feature filmmaking from the modest documentaries and promotional films that were their stock-in-trade. Hollywood, however, was not about to relinquish a penny of the $17 million it earned in Canadian movie theatres that year. American studios did not want rival producers to get a foothold in what they considered to be part of their domestic market. Shrewdly, the Motion Picture Association of America (MPAA) proposed a "Canadian Co-operation Project." It effectively eliminated the possibility of independent Canadian feature films for ten years.

The MPAA "co-operated" by promising to film some features in Canada and by agreeing to introduce Canadian sequences and subjects into Hollywood films and to make more short films, newsreels, and radio broadcasts about Canada.[3] Few features were made over the course of the agreement. And references to Canada in American films, as Pierre Berton detailed in his book *Hollywood's Canada*, were laughably and insultingly inaccurate.

Quebec, during roughly this same period, proved no great threat to Hollywood. "Co-operation," therefore, was unnecessary. As a result, modest feature-film companies sprang up. From 1944 to 1953 nineteen French-language films were made in Quebec. Determinedly Roman Catholic in characters and themes, the films were meant, as the 1946 shareholders report for Renaissance Films stated, "to propagate all our teaching: familial, pedagogic, professional, social, political, aesthetic, and religious."[4] Many of these films were popular throughout the province; some of them were recorded in French and English; and some of them made a profit for their investors.

All of these Quebec films suffered from melodramatic scripts and clumsy, plodding direction. Even the best of them were, in Pierre Véronneau's resonant phrase, "suffocated by Catholic values of penitence, atonement, forbearance, and self-sacrifice."[5] This is especially the case with *La Petite Aurore l'enfant* (1951). Enormously successful, perhaps because of its implied political metaphor about victimization, it tells the tale of a ten-year-

---

[3] Maynard Collins, "Cooperation, Hollywood and Howe," *Cinema Canada* 56 (June–July, 1979): 34–36.

[4] Quoted in Pierre Véronneau, "The first wave: 1944–53," *Cinema Canada* 56 (June–July, 1979): 43.

[5] Véronneau, "The first wave," 46.

old girl who is beaten, burned and tormented by her coldhearted step-
mother. Her father is too weak-willed to intercede, and even the noble
village priest intervenes too late to save the little girl's life.

The only other noteworthy film from this brief ascendency of Quebec
cinema is *Tit-coq* (1953), based on a successful play about a soldier who is
drafted into the war and loses his girlfriend to another man while he is at the
front. As Quebec was against conscription during World War II, its success
at tapping into the strong emotions of the local populace (again on the theme
of victimization) is readily apparent. Still, when television arrived, even this
was not enough to prevent the quick disappearance of feature filmmaking in
the province.

Before these nineteen films were produced, Quebec cinema was virtually
non-existent. Only a few feature films were made, mainly propaganda films
by priests. The situation in the rest of Canada was not much better.

The first Canadian feature film, *Evangeline* (1913), was produced at the
same time as initial features elsewhere in the world. Shot on locations
throughout Nova Scotia by the Canadian Bioscope Company of Halifax on a
substantial budget, *Evangeline* was based on a narrative poem by the American poet Henry Wadsworth Longfellow and directed and acted by Americans. It was both a critical and a popular success, but it did not generate
additional movie projects of any note. Canada lacked the infrastructure, the
financing, and the talent – more abundant to the south – to sustain a national
film industry. With its stock of Americans in pivotal roles, *Evangeline* also
underlines from the very beginning a continuing Canadian problem: just
what is a Canadian film?

That question did not seem to bother the one flamboyant and tempo-
rarily successful personality of the Canadian silent-film era. Ernest Shipman
knew what he wanted: films based on local Canadian stories, shot in the
Canadian regions in which the stories were set, and financed by regional
Canadian backers. Called "Ten-Percent Ernie" because of the commission he
took at the outset of each filmmaking endeavour, Shipman travelled west to
east across Canada, producing seven feature films. The most famous of his
productions was the first, *Back to God's Country* (1919). Highlighted by a
nude scene by lead actress and principal creative force on the film, Ernie's
wife, Nell, and an advertising campaign that asked: "Is the nude rude?",
Back to God's Country had almost everything: bears, lumberjacks, Mounties,
whaling schooners, a blizzard, a chase involving dog-sleds, and a rescue by
a vicious dog softened by the heroine's affection. It returned three-hundred-

percent profit to its Calgary investors and allowed Shipman to set up similar production companies in Winnipeg, Ottawa, Sault Ste. Marie, and St. John, none of which were as successful. By 1924 Shipman had fled Canada. Producer-driven feature films were not to be part of the Canadian cinematic landscape again for sixty years.

With Shipman as the larger-than-life exception, Canadian feature films in the early decades of the twentieth century were mostly amateur productions and almost entirely "one-offs" – films with a box-office response that was so meagre that their producers quickly went out of business. Only one film truly stands out – *Carry on Sergeant!* (1928). Written and directed by the British cartoonist Bruce Bairnsfather, *Carry on Sergeant!* is the story of a First World War soldier from Hamilton, Ontario who leaves a wife behind, is involved in the gas attack at Ypres, falls in love with a French barmaid and dies in battle. Billed as the first Canadian epic film, it was an expensive failure, disappearing after a few Ontario screenings despite its more than competent production values. Its realistic depiction of war and its pessimistic ending, seen by some as its truly Canadian qualities, likely contributed to its demise.[6]

Other noteworthy feature films made in Canada in the 1920s and 1930s were Canadian in theme and setting only. Chief among them were the fictionalized documentaries *Nanook of the North* (1922), *The Silent Enemy* (1930), and *The Viking* (1931). All three of them were made by filmmakers from outside Canada who felt compelled to make a film because of their romantic admiration of the hardy peoples they lived with – the Inuit, the Ojibway, and the seal-hunters of Newfoundland. Poverty, hardship, isolation and snow connect them all, along with the main characters' stubborn will to survival, a quality that would resurface in films forty years later.

Also of dubious Canadian pedigree were the so-called "Quota Quickies" of the 1930s. During this period (1928–37), a British law made it mandatory that a certain quota of films shown in that country be of British or Commonwealth origin. Nineteen low-budget features were produced by Canadian companies, most of them in Victoria, B.C. They had the look and feel of transplanted Hollywood B-movies, generic in subject-matter and often staffed by Americans (including a young Rita Hayworth). Audiences treated these cheap evasions of the law with indifference and disdain. They did not even generate any spin-off films with more recognizable Canadian content.

---

6 Peter Roffman, *The Story of Carry on Sergeant!* (Toronto: Ontario Film Institute Monograph, 1979).

Because Canada's entire feature-film output from 1913 to 1960 barely equalled the output of a single Hollywood studio in any average *year*, and because most pre-1960 features disappeared completely or languished unseen in well-meaning archives, Canadian film history even now has been a second-hand, paper history, passed on through written accounts but rarely experienced.

The National Film Board of Canada

Stymied in the production and distribution of indigenous feature films, Canadians have excelled in the areas of short documentaries and animation. This has particularly been the case since the establishment of the National Film Board of Canada (NFB) in 1939. With the British documentarian John Grierson as its first film commissioner, the NFB followed a 'realist' and 'nationalist' agenda, focusing on short films that showed Canada to Canadians and Canadians to the rest of the world. Grierson was opposed to the Hollywood model of spectacle and fantasy, preferring practical, factual films that alerted the citizenry to the social and political issues affecting their daily lives. Because the establishment of the NFB coincided with the outbreak of World War II, Grierson's documentary beliefs found their perfect expression in wartime propaganda. His policies were to remain in effect even after Grierson departed under the cloud of a Cold War scandal and his successors expanded the NFB's repertoire to include routine information documentaries such as *Fish Spoilage Control* (1956) and social-science films such as *Feelings of Anxiety* (1947) and *Who Will Teach Your Children?* (1948). Most of these films were screened through the alternative distribution system that the NFB set up (in church basements, community centres and schoolrooms) and underlined the NFB's liberal humanist orientation while reinforcing its sober 'classical' style.

After the advent of television in 1952, the NFB remained the dominant face that Canada saw in its cinematic mirrors and presented to the film-viewing public around the world. Its documentaries and animated films were shown on television and circulated widely, winning awards at festivals both at home and abroad. More importantly for the present anthology, the NFB gave rise to the feature-film industry as we now know it, producing several films that have long been viewed as the originators of the new wave of Canadian features made in the 1960s. It continued to make feature films into the 1990s and has supported or contributed to many others that were not part of its production mandate.

The new wave of Canadian features

As the Hollywood Studio System crumbled throughout the 1950s, Canadian filmmakers were anxious to add their voices to the revivification of cinema that was going on around the world. Concerted or not, efforts to create Canadian feature films were centred mainly on filmmakers associated with the NFB. With Sidney Furie's misfortunes still vividly fresh, two twenty-year NFB veterans launched feature film projects.

In 1959 Julian Roffman, former director of military training documentaries during the Grierson era, completed a self-produced crime film called *The Bloody Brood*. Although it failed to find much of an audience, it did encourage him enough to make Canada's first and only 3-D movie (five years after the fad had passed). *The Mask* (aka *Eyes of Hell*) was a horror film that enjoyed fairly wide distribution in the United States. A year later in 1962 Budge Crawley, long-time contract director for the NFB and one of the more colourful characters in Canadian film history, produced the quirky *Amanita Pestilens*, uncategorizable and pretty much unseen until cable television picked it up thirty years after it was completed.

Often overlooked in histories of Canadian film, Roffman's and Crawley's features in no way participated in the "realist" aesthetic promulgated by the NFB and defined by many as the governing approach to national cinema. These three films more properly fit into what has been termed "Canuxploitation" films – cheap, generic products aimed at trans-border B-movie or drive-in theatre crowds.[7] Canuxploitation films form a constant undercurrent in both English Canada and Quebec, swelling at certain points to near-tidal proportions.

More determinedly "Canadian" were two semi-documentary features begun in 1961 and completed in 1963. *The Drylanders*, an NFB production that fit smugly into the mandate to show Canada to Canadians, was the story of Saskatchewan farmsteaders who settled the land in 1907 and went bankrupt in the "Dirty Thirties." Written by Winnipeg radio dramatist M. Charles Cohen (who would later script the breakthrough US television

---

[7] See Paul Corupa, "Canuxploitation! Goin' Down the Road with the Cannibal Girls that Ate Black Christmas. Your Complete Guide to the Canadian B-movie," *Broken Pencil* 11 (Fall 1999): 12–17.

series *Roots*) and directed by Donald Haldane (who went on to direct Disney features), *The Drylanders* was an earnest if plodding depiction of Canadian prairie life. Livelier by far and influenced as much by François Truffaut and the French nouvelle vogue is *A tout prendre*. Directed by NFB veteran Claude Jutra and semi-autobiographical in content, it tells the story of a young interracial couple in Montreal, her pregnancy and his abandonment of her after his brief homosexual fling. With Jutra himself and his former lover Johanne Harrelle playing the lead roles, *A tout prendre* is notable as much for its frankness and elan as for the precedent it set as the first award-winning, independently produced Quebec feature film.

Two other NFB features, both released in 1964, are more often cited as the progenitors of the new wave of Canadian features, perhaps because they more accurately reflected the nascent "baby boomer" ethic of the times and conformed to the realist aesthetic of many critics.[8] Both *Le Chat dans le sac* and *Nobody Waved Goodbye* focus on adolescent males who are discontented with their middle-class values and end up unsatisfied in their quest for answers and romantic relationships. *Le Chat dans le sac*, written, directed, and edited by Gilles Groulx had a more immediate impact. It captured perfectly the Quiet Revolution taking place in Quebec at the time, questioning through its protagonist the province's past and its place in confederation. *Nobody Waved Goodbye* began as a Unit B documentary about suburban teenage malaise.[9] Directed by Don Owen, who had worked as a cinematographer on several direct cinema films,[10] and produced by the legendary Tom Daly, this disarming portrait of a boy in conflict with his family became a fictionalized feature by default more than by design. From a short outline rather than a script, it expanded by improvisation and incremental requests

---

[8] See Peter Harcourt, "The Years of Hope," in ⇨Seth Feldman & Joyce Nelson, ed. *Canadian Film Reader*, 139–43.

[9] In the early 1950s, the NFB underwent a structural re-organization which created four new units (A, B, C, D). Unit B, with Tom Daly as executive producer, was made up of young filmmakers, animators and experimentalists and had the broadest mandate of the four units. The classic article on Unit B is Peter Harcourt's "The Innocent Eye," *Sight and Sound* 34.1 (Winter 1964–65): 19–23 (repr. in ⇨Feldman & Nelson, ed. *Canadian Film Reader*, 67–76).

[10] Direct cinema, cinéma direct, or simply "le direct" was what the French documentary NFB unit called their style of cinéma verité. New lightweight cameras, high-speed film stock, and portable synchronized-sound equipment encouraged these filmmakers to shoot on location with minimal scripts. See Peter Wintonick's feature-length documentary *Cinéma Verité: Defining the Moment*, made in 2000.

for additional footage. Because it was panned by Canadian critics on its
initial release and then accepted after favorable reception in New York, *Nobody Waved Goodbye* also became a temporary paradigm for the insecurity of
Canadian audiences and critics.

Similar to *Le Chat dans le sac* and *Nobody Waved Goodbye* in both subject
and style and in fact preceding them chronologically are two less highly
regarded and often overlooked films from Quebec and British Columbia. At
sixty-four minutes, *Seul ou avec d'autres* barely qualifies as a feature-length
film. Improvised on ideas suggested by students at the University of Montreal and financed by their student association, the film traces the course of a
love-affair against the typical background of 1960s campus life. It is more
notable for the crew of filmmakers enlisted to assist the students; directors
Denis Héroux and Denys Arcand, cinematographer Michel Brault, editors
Gilles Groulx and Bernard Gosselin and soundman Marcel Carrière all went
on to have distinguished careers. They brought to *Seul ou avec d'autres* a
familiarity with direct cinema techniques that made the staged documentary
more memorable than its clichéed storyline might otherwise have merited.
In Vancouver Larry Kent focused on similar storylines and settings for *The
Bitter Ash* (1964) and *Sweet Substitute* (1964). Low budget, semi-improvised
films, their unabashed depiction of sexuality made them popular and financial successes if not critical hits.

The films that were made and the responses of critics and audiences at
this early stage were less significant, however, than the creation of a federal
commission in 1963 on "The Possible Development of a Feature Film Industry in Canada." Buoyed by the modest successes perhaps of the above-
mentioned films and by the national fervor of Expo 67 and Canada's centen-
nial celebrations, the government set aside $10 million per year for the pro-
duction of distinctly Canadian films. In doing so, it not only instituted the
means but also the policies, and, implicitly, a kind of government-sponsored
"studio" signature, that are in operation to this day.

The filmmakers that were best equipped to take advantage of the
government-sponsored Canadian Film Development Corporation (CFDC)
were those already at work in the film business, employed either by the NFB
or by the CBC (Canadian Broadcasting Corporation). During the first years
of the CFDC's operations Quebec filmmakers hit their stride quicker than
their English-Canadian colleagues. Six major directors emerged: Paul Almond, Gilles Carle, Jean Pierre Lefebvre, Claude Jutra, Michel Brault, and
Denys Arcand.

Paul Almond burst on the scene with the eerie and elliptical *Isabel* (1968), the first of a trilogy of English-language films starring Geneviève Bujold. *Isabel*, the story of a young woman who returns to the Gaspé region and the haunting secrets of her family, won four Canadian Film Awards (at the time called "Etrogs"), and Almond was compared favorably with the best European directors (Dreyer, Bergman, Resnais), establishing a connection that still persists in Quebec. With *The Act of the Heart* (1970) and *Journey* (1972), films that were increasingly murky and abstract, Almond's career faltered. Credited with establishing an "art cinema" for Canada, Almond has since been unable to match the success of his first film. This is not uncommon in all of Canada because perceived failures and fallow periods are much more devastating to a filmmaker's career than elsewhere.

A director with a more sustained career arc is Gilles Carle. Upon completing *La vie heureuse de Léopold Z.* (1965), a 69-minute NFB comedy about a harried snowplough operator on Christmas Eve, Carle moved to the private sector and became one of the key figures in Quebec cinema from the late 1960s to the early 1980's. Beginning with *Le viol d'une jeune fille douce* (1968), the tale of a young Montreal woman, pregnant and unwed, who goes in search of her baby's father, has an affair with a Moroccan and watches as her three thuggish brothers beat up an innocent man whom they decide is their sister's defiler, Carle made a series of dark and funny features, most notably *Red* (1969), *Les mâles* (1970), *La vrai nature de Bernadette* (1971), his most famous and likely his best, *La tête de Normande St–Onge* (1975), and *L'ange et la femme* (1977). Like Almond's films, Carle's focused on female protagonists caught in a society whose traditional values were fast disappearing, if not already gone. Not just an auteur but a total filmmaker, because he scripted and edited many of the films he directed, Carle turned to more elaborate productions in the 1980s, some based on famous novels – *Fantastica* (1980), *Les Plouffe* (1981), *Maria Chapdelaine* (1983) and the television series *Le crime d'Ovide Plouffe* (1984). Of the early Quebec filmmakers, he maintained a level of excellence and audience-pleasing consistency that was unmatched.

Carle's main competition for cinematic supremacy at the time was Jean Pierre Lefebvre. A poet and critic as well as a director and screenwriter, Lefebvre began in 1965 with *Le révolutionnaire*, an ironic portrait of the naivety of youthful revolutionaries. He followed that with a complete change of pace – *Il ne faut pas mourir pour ça* (1966), an amusing look at a day in the life of a pleasantly eccentric bachelor. After two years at the NFB (1967–69, where he not only continued making features but also assisted several young directors in starting theirs), he left to form his own company, Cinak, dedicated to low-budget films beholden to neither government nor industry nor political ideologues. *Un succès commercial ou Québec My Love ou Struggle for Love* (1969), for instance, was shot in two days at a cost of $25,000 and is an unflinching exploration of sex, pornography, and violence in Quebec. Although he has directed complicated, plot-driven stories, notable the noirish *On n'engraisse pas la cochons à l'eau claire* (1975), about a doomed undercover drug cop, he is mainly noted for his gentle, poetic studies of character and the carefully observed details of everyday living. Chief among them are *Les dernières fiançailles* (1973), a touching portrait of the final three days of an aging farm couple, *L'amour blessé* (1975), a minimalist look at one night in the life of a divorcée, *Le vieux pays où Rimbaud est mort* (1977), a visually stunning and politically unfashionable story about a Quebecker's travels through France and his realization of the toll that colonialism has exacted on Quebec, *Avoir 16 ans* (1979), about a high-schooler's change from rebellion to resignation conveyed visually through rigidly composed images and a precise structure, and *Les fleurs sauvages* (1982), winner of the Cannes International Critics Prize, an examination of three generations of a family sharing a summer cottage for a week. No Canadian director has a body of work as extensive (over twenty features), varied or attractive as Lefebvre. Because his films are so understated, they often pass below the radar of top-ten lists, unjustly so.

Michel Brault and Claude Jutra are two Montreal filmmakers whose names will forever be linked in Canadian film history. They met at university, where they collaborated on two self-made amateur films and then, beginning in 1956, worked together at the NFB as leading practitioners of the cinema direct movement. As feature film directors, their output is relatively small but their stature and influence is undeniable.

In addition to the already-mentioned *A tout prendre*, Jutra directed only five other Quebec feature films: *Wow* (1969), *Mon oncle Antoine* (1971), *Kamouraska* (1973), *Pour le meilleur et pour le pire* (1975) and *La Dame en couleurs* (1985). Such was the state of the Quebec and Canadian film industries at the time that he was forced to accept English-language projects outside Quebec. Unfortunately, only two of them merit any mention – the disappointing adaptation of Margaret Atwood's *Surfacing* (1980) and the CBC television drama *Dreamspeaker* (1977), a return to the themes of lost innocence and betrayal of his best films *Mon oncle Antoine* and *Kamouraska*, a period-costume drama based on a Quebec novel whose large, for its time, budget (over $900,000) was only justified by Jutra's stellar reputation.

Mon oncle Antoine has consistently been rated as the best Canadian film of all time. It is a reputation that has its share of cavillers who carp about its apparent structural weakness and political hesitancy. But as Jim Leach points out in the second essay in this anthology, it is a film of both nostalgic charm and dark power which "builds on the interplay between its roots in a specific Quebec community and its concern with aspects of human experience that transcend time and place." Somewhat indebted to the films of Jutra's friend François Truffaut, *Mon oncle Antoine* may not quite be Canada's *Citizen Kane*. But it can surely hold its own next to *Les quatre-cents coups* and other masterpieces of European new wave cinema.

Michel Brault, whose subtle yet expressive cinematography illuminates the interior and exterior life of the small mining town in *Mon oncle Antoine*, has a filmography as extensive as anybody in Canada. All but five of his credits as a director are for documentary films, however, and his feature film credits are mainly as a cinematographer. In 1963 he co-directed *Pour la suite du monde* with Pierre Perreault; this feature-length documentary re-creation of the abandoned tradition of beluga whaling on an island in the St. Lawrence River is considered by many to be one of the most important Quebec films ever made.[11] So Brault was, as Andre Loiselle says in his essay on *Les Ordres*, "arguably better suited than any other cinéaste to make the definitive film on the October crisis." Brault's decision to transform true stories of the consequences of the War Measures Act of 1970 into a work of cinematic art comparable to Franz Kafka's, Jean–Luc Godard's, and Ingmar Bergman's led to a firestorm of controversy. His artistic ambition and credentials did not prevent cultural critics and political ideologues from taking him to task for, ironically, overgeneralizing and trivializing the cause of Quebec separatism. *Les ordres* did win the award for best direction at Cannes, however, as well as a handful of other accolades.

Still, Brault's film was not as successful as the early films of Denys Arcand or, predictably, the "maple syrup porn" films *Valerie* (1969) or *Deux femmes en or* (1970), soft-core, Canadian sex features made by Denis Héroux and Claude Fournier. Arcand, director of a documentary that was deemed

---

[11] *Pour la suite du monde* was voted Canadian film of the year in 1964 and was Canada's first official entry at the Cannes Film Festival. See David Clandfield, "From the Picturesque to the Familiar: Films of the French Unit at the NFB (1958-1964)," *Take Two: A Tribute to Film in Canada*, ed. Seth Feldman (Toronto: Irwin, 1984): 112–24.

so inflammatory that it was suppressed for years by the NFB, began his career as a narrative film director with three cynical crime dramas that attempted to wed European art cinema with Hollywood genres. Although *La maudite gallette* (1972), *Réjeanne Padovani* (1973) and *Gina* (1975) were moderately successful, Arcand abandoned theatrical features for the next ten years.

While Quebec films proliferated in the late 1960s and early 1970s, filmmakers in the rest of Canada did not fare as well. In 1968 the NFB released two English-language "features": *The Best Damn Fiddler from Calabogie to Kaladar* (49 minutes), Peter Pearson's gritty portrait of a rural ne'er-do-well and his family's struggles with poverty, and *The Ernie Game*, Don Owen's ambitious but baffling follow-up to *Nobody Waved Good-bye*. After this a prolonged silence. That's what makes *Goin' Down the Road* (1970) such a stunning achievement.

Don Shebib went to film school in California and served as editor for B-movie king Roger Corman before returning to Canada to begin *Goin' Down the Road* in 1969. Shot on a minuscule budget but aided immeasurably by the hand-held camera-work of Richard Leiterman (cinematographer on the classic verité documentaries *A Married Couple* by Allan King and *High School* by Frederick Wiseman), Shebib's "buddies on the road" movie is a funny and sensitive portrait of Maritimers in mythic Toronto. It quickly became a touchstone film, maintaining its continued staying power, as Christine Ramsey explains, "because of the uncanny precision with which it captures and demonstrates how English Canada constructs nation, sees culture, and experiences its sense of social self."

Such was the impact of *Goin' Down the Road* that it not only ensured funding for several more Shebib features, among them the under-rated *Between Friends* (1973), but it also made his scriptwriter Bill Fruet one of the early success stories in English-Canadian cinema with two other award-winning films: *Wedding in White* (1972) which he also directed and *Slipstream* (1973). These films, plus *The Rowdyman* (1972) and *Paperback Hero* (1973), were the central exhibits in a widely held but myopic theory (first advanced by Margaret Atwood and championed by Robert Fothergill in his influential essay "Coward, Bully or Clown"[12]) that Canadian films were rife with lovable male losers.

---

[12] Robert Fothergill, "Coward, Bully or Clown: The Dream Life of a Younger Brother," in ⇨Seth Feldman & Joyce Nelson, ed. *Canadian Film Reader*, 234–50.

Although every one of these films is unmistakably, determinedly Canadian in its characters, setting, and themes, they also participate in movie genres that transcend national boundaries. At the top of the heap of this generational "border-blurring," to use Tom McSorley's apt term, is *The Apprenticeship of Duddy Kravitz*, a film that underlines the subtle and persistent problems associated with both movie making and film criticism in Canada. For, as McSorley indicates, despite its initially positive reviews as well as "its famous Canadian literary source [Mordecai Richler's classic novel], its Canadian financing, and its Canadian box-office success," *Duddy Kravitz* has been unjustly neglected by serious critics and scholars until now. Because its director has been such an internationalist and directed iconic Hollywood features (*First Blood* and *North Dallas Forty*) and its main characters were played by American actors (Richard Dreyfuss, Jack Warden, and Randy Quaid), its pedigree seems tainted. Like "a colonial gesture to the acknowledged and unassailable film power" of Hollywood, *Duddy Kravitz* raises as many difficult, nervous questions about Canadian cinema as it answers.

The tax shelter boom years

These questions would dominate the critical landscape for the next ten years. For, the same year that *Duddy Kravitz* was released marked the beginning of the Capital Cost Allowance (CCA) period. In order to encourage more production in Canada, the federal government provided a 100% tax write-off for investment in films that satisfied certain "Canadian-content" requirements. The legislation had the desired effect; from three features in 1974, production increased to 66 feature films in 1979 with total expenditures of over $100 million. Unfortunately, many of the films were Canadian in name only with New Orleans-born Bob Clark dominating the Canadian scene with thinly disguised, Hollywood-style genre pictures fronted by American actors: *Black Christmas* (1974), *Murder by Decree* (1979), *Tribute* (1980), *Porky's* (1981), *Porky's II* (1982), and *A Christmas Story* (1983). *Porky's*, a crude teen sex-comedy set in Florida, has the dubious distinction of being Canada's top money-making film of all time. Several well-known European directors also cashed in on the tax-credit scheme: Ján Kadár with *Lies My Father Told Me* (1975), Claude Chabrol with *Violette Nozière* (1978), Louis Malle with the much-admired *Atlantic City* (1980), Claude Lelouch with *A nous deux* (1979), and Jean–Jacques Annaud with *Quest for Fire* (1982).

The CCA did have a beneficial effect on the industry, however, raising the profile of Canadian film and establishing an infrastructure of experienced craftspeople. And more than a few outstanding films were produced. Among them are *J.A. Martin, Photographe* (1977) by Jean Beaudin, *Who Has Seen the Wind* (1977) by Allan King, *Outrageous!* (1977) by Richard Benner, *Silent Partner* (1978) by Daryl Duke, *Ticket to Heaven* (1981) and *The Terry Fox Story* (1983) both by Ralph Thomas. Financially profitable if less aesthetically pleasing films included *Meatballs* (1978) by Ivan Reitman (who then moved to Hollywood to direct and produce blockbuster comedies), *Prom Night* (1980) by Paul Lynch, *Heavy Metal* (1981), with supervising director Gerald Potterton employing many famous Canadian animators, and *Strange Brew* (1983) by Dave Thomas and Rick Moranis of SCTV fame.

Three of Canada's most important directors began their careers during this period: Francis Mankiewicz, Phillip Borsos, and David Cronenberg. That the three of them came to their directing careers via strikingly different routes is a testament to the growth of the Canadian film industry in little more than a decade.

Although Francis Mankiewicz is the nephew of Hollywood icons Herman (*Citizen Kane*) and Joseph (*All About Eve*) Mankiewicz, he was not given special access to the business because of his name. Nor does there seem to be a family sensibility. Born in China of missionary parents, Francis Mankiewicz studied filmmaking in London and worked his way up in the business as cameraman and assistant director on small Montreal films and features. Although his first feature films were self-scripted, he reached filmmaking maturity when he linked up with gifted collaborators: screenwriter Réjean Ducharme and cinematographer Michel Brault. *Les bons débarras*, released just after the 1980 Quebec referendum, has been read – fortuitously but mistakenly – as an allegory of Quebec nationhood. Its real power lies in its "bad seed" fairytale qualities. In Peter Morris's analysis, it "begins deceptively as a naturalistic tale of the dispossessed, but develops inexorably into tragedy, a quasi-mythic tale of evil and of survival above all else."

Phillip Borsos came to make his debut feature, *The Grey Fox*, because of the dovetailing of several outside forces. In the early 1970s, the NFB established a regionalization policy whereby production offices would be opened across Canada.[13] The pilot project was established in Vancouver, and it was

---

[13] For an insider's look at the regionalization of production offices at the NFB, see Ronald Dick, "Regionalization of a Federal Cultural Institution: The Experience of the

with the assistance of this NFB office that Borsos completed three short documentaries — *Cooperage, Spartree* and *Nails,* done in the same evocative visual style and with the same themes as *The Grey Fox.* With an ambitious producer, Peter O'Brian, who actually wanted to make a culturally responsible film with CCA backing, and working in a region that the CFDC felt was under-represented, Borsos still struggled to fund his masterful film about a local Canadian legend, Bill Miner. Blaine Allan points out that this movie, among its many other merits, participated in a cultural phenomenon of that time: the depiction of "solitary [American] males who, while in Canada, wield influence and indelibly imprint their lasting presence on the Canadians they touch before they steal away, implicitly or explicitly, back to the USA." In other words, part of the movie's success can be attributed to the fact that it was read as a metaphor on Canadian–American relations.

Although Borsos is from a different region and culture from Mankiewicz, both directors have several things in common. Both died tragically young, and before this both felt compelled to abandon their cinematic roots; Mankiewicz made an English-language TV-movie (*Love and Hate*) and Borsos turned to Hollywood-style productions. In a country with so few filmmaking options at the time, the temptations were enticing.

If there is any Canadian filmmaker that hardly needs an introduction, it is David Cronenberg, except perhaps *as* a Canadian. Although he produces almost all of his films in Canada with Canadian crews and is an undisguised Canadian chauvinist, Cronenberg's films transcend nationalism because of their genre and auteurist qualities. After his initial experimental films, two features, *Shivers* (1975) and *Rabid* (1977), produced by Ivan Reitman established his signature "beware of the body" themes and imagery. Because of their scandalous storytelling methods and their popularity, the CCA-funded features *The Brood* (1979) and *Scanners* (1981) provoked heated debates among reviewers and politicians not only about the arm's-length programme itself but also about the idea of a government-funded movie industry. *Videodrome* (1983) did little to mollify Cronenberg's many critics, although it is one of his most "Canadian" films (with its references to Marshall McLuhan and Toronto's CITY-TV) and one of his more accessible works with, as Suzie Jau–Fong Young argues, its unusually feminist sympathies. *Videodrome* seems to have turned things around for Cronenberg. In 1983 The Toronto International Film Festival mounted a complete retrospective of his

National Film Board of Canada 1965–799," in Gene Walz, ed. *Flashback: People and Institutions in Canadian Film History* (Montreal: Mediatexte Publications, 1986): 107–34.

films, and the following year an anthology of essays about his career, *The Shape of Rage*, was released.[14] Since then he has established a truly international reputation as both a media presence and a director of increasingly chilling tales of evolutionary glitches and societal dysfunction. His films not only test the limits of what it is to be a Canadian movie but what it is to be human as well.

The Telefilm years

In 1984 the Canadian Film Development Corporation (CFDC) changed its name to Telefilm Canada, a switch that was both symbolic and substantive; it symbolized the new realities of the television/movie/video industry, and it signalled stricter controls over producers who, during the CCA period, were more adept at procuring funds than at finishing creditable films or launching them in the marketplace. That same year, Atlantis Films won an Oscar for best short drama for *Boys and Girls*, based on an Alice Munro story, and began a slow rise to its current prominence with a series of science-fiction shows aimed at cable tv. Rock Demers launched *The Dog Who Stopped the War*, directed by Andre Melançon, the first in a long series of popular, family-oriented "Tales for All." One year later, producers Denis Héroux and John Kemeny of International Cinema Corporation (ICC) linked up with Robert Lantos and Stephen Roth of RSL Productions to form Alliance Entertainment Corporation. Today, Alliance–Atlantis, merged in 2000, is the most powerful production company in Canada.

Despite these new developments, the NFB was still a major influence on the Canadian feature film. It assisted indirectly in many films, especially those made in the Maritimes and on the prairies, that might otherwise not have been completed. Editing and processing services, promotion and distribution help, and/or "end-money" were provided for such diverse features as *Crime Wave* (1985) by John Paizs, *The Adventures of Faustus Bidgood* (1986) by Andy and Michael Jones, *Loyalties* (1986) by Anne Wheeler, *Life Classes* (1987) by Bill MacGillivray, and *Tales from the Gimli Hospital* (1988) by Guy Maddin, to name but a few of the more celebrated. Many of the major films of the 1980's were NFB productions or co-productions. Most notable are *Anne Trister* (1986) by Léa Pool, *Pouvoir Intime* (1986) by Yves Simoneau, *Un zoo la nuit* (1987) by Jean–Claude Lauzon, *Jésus de Montreal* (1989) by Denys

---

14 Piers Handling, ed. *The Shape of Rage: The Films of David Cronenberg* (Toronto: Academy of Canadian Cinema/General, 1983).

Arcand, *The Boys of St. Vincent* (1992) by John N. Smith, and four films included in this anthology: *Le déclin de l'empire américain* (1986), *I've Heard the Mermaids Singing* (1987), *Company of Strangers* (1990), and *Leolo* (1992). It is these films that prompted the Museum of Modern Art in New York to conclude that "recent Canadian films have a resiliency, a willingness to risk and explore, a sense of place, and often a sense of humour that travels well."[15]

If one filmmaker can be singled out from this list as the preeminent filmmaker of this era, it is Denys Arcand. After a hiatus from feature filmmaking of ten years, during which time he worked in television and completed a documentary so discomfitting to the NFB that they suppressed it for five years, Arcand returned with two witty, popular and widely acclaimed movies: *Le déclin de l'empire américain* and *Jésus de Montreal*. *Le déclin*, a critique of Quebec politics and academia, was as unexpected as it was original. "Sophisticated dialogue movies," as Bart Testa points out, "and dramas placed within an elite or intellectual setting, are unheard of in Canadian filmmaking, English or Québécois alike." By comparing it to Hollywood's *The Big Chill*, Testa shows how unstinting Arcand was in his criticism, a quality he was to retain in his most successful film *Jesus of Montreal*, an equally sardonic attack on religion, among many other things.

Even darker in his vision and more haunting in his themes and imagery is the former "bad boy" of Quebec filmmaking Jean–Claude Lauzon. He exploded onto the film scene with *Un zoo la nuit*, a bracing combination of crime genre and graphic quasi-autobiography. *Léolo*, his only other feature, has all the intimate details of a personal coming-of-age story along with the mystical imagery of a bizarre fable. In his essay George Toles confesses: "I can think of no film that lays greater stress on the body's peculiar and relentless demands for obedience than *Léolo*, but Lauzon's vision of the corporeal life neither celebrates nor grieves over our common servility." Toles's essay details Lauzon's aesthetically mesmerizing account of a young boy's attachment to his "strangely cursed family" and his wish to escape from it.

Two other feature films from this era that are examined in this anthology, *I've Heard the Mermaids Singing* and *Company of Strangers*, are the culmination of political developments at the NFB that date back to the early 1970s and the founding of the Women's Studio, Studio D, by Kathleen Shannon. Committed to ensuring equal representation of the sexes among crew members on all NFB projects as well as to the making of films by, for,

---

[15] Adrienne Mancia, "O Canada, L'amour du cinéma from North to South," *O Canada* (New York: The Museum of Modern Art, 1989): 3.

and about women via Studio D, the NFB trained scores of craftspeople and launched dozens of directorial careers.

Patricia Rozema was not the first woman director of an NFB feature, but *I've Heard the Mermaids Singing* was one of the break-out hits for women's cinema in Canada. In Brenda Austin–Smith's estimation, it is not a strongly feminist statement, for it is more concerned with "the validation of private dreams and private vision" than with "direct and sustained criticism of dominant class, social and sexual relations that many so-called women's films embody." But *Mermaids* was a first feature and it clearly struck a chord both at home and abroad. It was one of only a handful of Canadian films to quickly (or ever) turn a profit.

Cynthia Scott, whose Studio D documentary *Flamenco at 5:15* won an Oscar in 1983, ascended to feature film directing via in a slightly different route. She was a member of a small group of people in the NFB's head-quarters in Montreal participating in an Alternative Drama Programme. Not as doctrinaire as the Dogma 95 group in Denmark, the filmmakers of the Alternative Drama Programme wished to return to the "realist" aesthetic of Unit B and *Nobody Waved Good-bye*. Scott, Giles Walker and John N. Smith made seven low-budget features that focused on social issues (gender, race, crime, poverty, age) with non-actors playing themselves in natural situations that could be shaped into dramatic narratives. Scott's contribution, *Company of Strangers*, is the story of seven elderly women and their injured female bus-driver who are trapped in the woods when their bus breaks down. With improvised action, conversations captured with two-camera coverage, and personal photographs from the women's youth and middle years, the film does more than just paint vivid portraits of their lives. "Collectively," according to Angela Stukator, "the women's stories function as a disquisi-tion on the process of female ageing, on the coexistence of past and present, and on the experience of physical deterioration and the intractability of death." While this does not sound like the stuff that feature films are made of, the film won over audiences around the world, becoming one of the most unlikely, most unexpected hits of all time.

Not all women directors of feature films were confined to the NFB, how-ever. The 1980s and 1990s witnessed an unprecedented flowering of films by Canadian women. The list of important films in both official languages is not inconsiderable. The artist and experimental filmmaker Joyce Wieland led the charge with her portrait of the Group of Seven artist Tom Thompson in *The Far Shore* (1976). Other films of particular note include *Mourir à tue-tête*

(1979) by Anne Claire Poirier, *La Femme de l'hotel* (1984) and *Anne Trister* (1986) by Lea Pool, *Sonatine* (1984) and *Deux actrices* (1993) by Micheline Lanctôt, *My American Cousin* (1985) by Sandy Wilson, *Bye Bye Blues* (1989) and the made-for-television movie *The Diviners* (1993) by Anne Wheeler, *Sam and Me* (1991) and *Fire* (1997) by Deepa Mehta, *Double Happiness* (1994) by Mina Shum, and *Kissed* (1997) by Lynne Stopkewich.

The films of Mina Shum (a Chinese–Canadian) and Deepa Mehta (an Indo-Canadian) underline another tendency of the Telefilm era – feature films that reflect Canada's multicultural mosaic. While some have complained that this simply indicates that Telefilm is increasingly politicized, funding so-called "hyphenated-Canadians" and novices to boot, this can just as easily be seen as a Canadian variation on what Hollywood calls "niche-marketing" by an organization intent on replenishing the directorial talent pool with fresh new faces. Besides Shum and Mehta, Telefilm has brought such "ethnic" or "diasporic" filmmakers as Stephen Williams, Midi Onodera, Clement Virgo (*Rude* and *Love Come Down*) and Srinivas Krishna into the international spotlight. Krishna's film *Masala* (1991) is a perfect example of how far these diasporic films stray from the Canadian film stereotype of Griersonian realism and stretch the formerly acceptable limits of influence beyond Hollywood genres and European auteurism. Tom Waugh traces *Masala's* origins to "Krishna's fascination with Masala movies [Bombay commercial cinema], with Bollywood spectacle, and his absorption of their glitz, energy and eclecticism." This is what accounts for "the rich and irreverent narrative excess of *Masala*, its exuberance in confronting sexual, cultural, and political taboos – above all its reckless surfing along the interface of ethnoscape and mediascape."

In the mid-1980s, provincial governments across Canada also got involved in the film business, setting up arm's-length operations to fund local film projects. The Ontario Film Development Corporation (OFDC) was established in 1986; this, along with Telefilm's Feature Film Fund instituted that same year, gave rise to what some have called "the Toronto New Wave," a group of young filmmakers in open rebellion against both the realist tradition and the tax shelter cliches of previous years.[16]

Atom Egoyan, now Canada's most famous director, is the Toronto New Wave's most visible director and was the chief beneficiary of the new provincial and federal largesse. An Armenian–Canadian born in Cairo and

---

[16] Cameron Bailey, "Standing in the Kitchen All Night: A Secret History of the Toronto New Wave," *Take One* 9.28 (Summer 2000): 6–11.

relocated to Toronto from British Columbia as a youth, Egoyan began his feature filmmaking career in 1984 before OFDC was founded but completed six features, culminating in *Exotica* (1994), by the time OFDC was terminated in 1995. All of Egoyan's films focus on the "complex structure of memory, family, and representation," to use Catherine Russell's succinct phrase. In her analysis, *Exotica* marks a transition point for Egoyan because of its change in performance style and its far less frequent incorporation of video footage, and this has been amply borne out by his subsequent films.

Almost as important to this new Toronto-centric sensibility are two film-makers who have both worked with Egoyan. Bruce McDonald, editor on Egoyan's *Family Viewing* (1987), moved Canadian cinema more closely to the American independent model of youth-oriented fare with three brash, fun-ny, rock 'n roll movies – *Roadkill* (1991), *Highway 61* (1992) and the sadly neg-lected *Hard Core Logo* (1996) as well as *Dance Me Outside* (1994), a comedy set on a First Nation's reserve. A performer in *Exotica* and in *Highway 61*, Don McKellar is perhaps the most ubiquitous of the entire Toronto group, not only because of his acting but also because of his screenwriting – on three of McDonald's four features as well as two by François Girard (*Thirty-two Films about Glenn Gould* and *The Red Violin*). But it is his directorial-debut film *Last Night* (1998) that can serve perhaps as the epitome of the Toronto new wave. Contrasted by many reviewers with the Hollywood blockbuster *Armaged-don*, it has been read as a prototypically Canadian statement because of its modest and ironic approach to the end of the world.

Regionalization of the NFB's production facilities across Canada had established filmmaking communities in Halifax, Winnipeg, Edmonton and Vancouver by the late 1970s. So-called "magic realism" films from Nova Scotia such as *Margaret's Museum* (1996) by Mort Ransen, *The Hanging Garden* (1997) by Thom Fitzgerald, and *New Waterford Girl* (2000) by Allan Moyle built on the film profile created there by Bill McGillivray. In Mani-toba, a Cultural Industries Development agreement (CIDO) established in 1987 provided funds for local filmmakers to expand on nostalgic rural stories such as *Who Has Seen the Wind* and *Why Shoot the Teacher?* (both 1977) with the award-winning films *The Last Winter* (1991) by Kim Johnston and *Bordertown Café* (1992) by Norma Bailey. More importantly, CIDO allowed the local film co-op, the Winnipeg Film Group, to move into feature films. The result was a series of "prairie postmodern" films that were prized by festivals and cult audiences around the world. John Paizs's *The Three World's of Nick* (1983) and *Careful* (1987), amusing pastiches about boy-men bewildered by the world, launched the deadpan prairie movement, but the films of Guy Maddin have gained much more widespread attention and acclaim. In their weird appropriation of obscure genres – for instance, the Icelandic saga in *Tales from the Gimli Saga* (1988) and the Bavarian Mountain film in *Careful* (1992) – Maddin's films not only "challenge interpretation," as Will Straw demonstrates, they also "have proved even more resistant to distinctly Canadian traditions of critical analysis." More so than anyone else, Guy Maddin has stretched the boundaries of what is "allowable" in Canadian feature films. In many ways, "his insistence," to again quote Will Straw, "that his main allegiances are generational, rather than national or regional," underscores the elusiveness of boundaries in the so-called post-national era.

Canadian films in the global economy

The 1990s began with two of the costliest epic movies in Canadian history – *Bethune: The Making of a Hero* (1990), the story of a controversial Canadian physician in Mao's China directed by Phillip Borsos, and *Black Robe* (1991), Australian director Bruce Beresford's adaptation of Timothy Findlay's novel about a Jesuit priest among the Hurons. Before the decade and the century ended three more epics had been produced: *Agaguk/Shadow of the Wolf* (1993 – at $31 million the most expensive Canadian film ever made), *The Red Violin* (1998), and *Sunshine* (1999). All five of these films were co-productions with international financing, casts, and crews. Individually and collectively they testify to the maturation of the Canadian film industry.

The Red Violin, with its extensive time frame, multiple stories, and around-the-world settings, is the most ambitious Canadian film ever – and the second biggest box-office hit (behind, sadly, *Porky's*). This despite the fact that it is a serious and subtle costume drama. El Jones's interpretation uncovers not just the major themes of memory and desire but of faith, faith "that the past could somehow be collected, that everyone could return in some form to reclaim the violin, that no part of the past would become lost or go missing." While *The Red Violin's* sobriety and seriousness link it inextricably to Canadian film history, it otherwise seems only incidentally Canadian, despite its pivotal setting in present-day Montreal, which, because of Samuel L. Jackson and the international cast assembled there, could just as easily been New York or Los Angeles. That in itself signals a new direction in Canadian film; it can not only hold its own in the global marketplace but it can participate in filmic dialogues that transcend the merely nationalistic.

This new-found freedom has recently manifested itself in other ways. In 1996 a film version of *Long Day's Journey into Night* directed by Peter Wellington won four Canadian film awards; one year later Atom Egoyan's *The Sweet Hereafter* was named best Canadian film. What is most significant about them is that these Canadian films were made from American sources, a world-famous play and a best-selling novel. In 1999, the Icelandic–Canadian and former documentarian Sturla Gunnarsson transformed Rohinton Mistry's novel (a Governor-General's award-winner) *Such a Long Journey* into a stunning feature film. This reverses a dispiriting practice of major Canadian properties (Margaret Atwood's *Handmaid's Tale*, Michael Ondaatje's *(The English Patient*, Carol Shields's *Swann*, to name but a few) being bought and produced outside their country of origin. With Alliance-Atlantis, Canada's premier production and distribution company, purchasing options on more Canadian novels, the film industry looks poised for greater heights.

This is not to say that Telefilm, as the major funder/arbiter of what gets produced in Canada, has abandoned smaller-scale productions or its usual constituencies. Films from regional filmmaking centres as far-flung as Nova Scotia (*Margaret's Museum* by Mort Ransen), British Columbia (*Kissed* by Lynne Stopkewich), Alberta (*waydowntown* by Gary Burns), and even Igloolik, Nunavut (*Atanarjuat* by Zacharias Kunuk – which won the Golden Camera Prize in 2001 at Cannes) have graced screens around the world, expanding the country's repertoire of distinctive, personal, local-colour films. Films by the gay Toronto filmmaker John Greyson – *Zero Patience* (1994), *Lilies* (1996), and *Uncut* (1998) – continue to garner awards.

Quebec remains a unique film production centre. *La Florida* (1993) by George Mihalka, *Louis 19, le roi des ondes* (1994) by Michel Poulette, and *Les Boys* (1997) by Louis Saia are ample evidence that Quebec has lost neither its talent nor its taste for lowbrow, money-making comedies. It also produces the most consistently artful and intriguing films virtually every year. Witness: *Un histoire inventée* (1990) by Andre Forcier, *La Sarrasine* (1992) by Paul Tana, *Octobre* (1994) by Pierre Falardeau, *Le Confessionnal* (1995) and *Nô* (1998), both by Robert Lepage, *Emporte-moi* (1999) by Léa Pool and *Maelstrom* (2000) by Denis Villeneuve. If there is an oversight in the present anthology, besides the omission of Jean–Pierre Lefebvre and Gilles Carle, it is in accommodating only one of these major Quebec films from the past ten years.

One of the Quebec directors whose name is conspicuous by its absence from this list is Denys Arcand, creator of two of the best films from the late 1980s. Arcand did direct two feature films during the past decade, *Love and Human Remains* (1964) and *Stardom* (2000), both of them in English and neither of them worthy of many people's top-ten lists. It would be too facile to see in this that Arcand is a casualty of his own overreaching, a victim of the urge to abandon his culturally familiar backyard for the post-national world of the global cinematic marketplace. For Arcand was not the only eminent Quebec filmmaker to accept an English-language project. Yves Simoneau, Léa Pool, and Robert Lepage have recently done so as well. And English-Canadian filmmakers have also stepped out of their comfortable niches. Patricia Rozema recently wrote and directed *Mansfield Park*, a feature film that looked far more like a British Masterpiece Theatre production than a homey Canadian film; Atom Egoyan's last film, *Felicia's Journey* was hardly Canadian and his next, *Ararat*, is a drama about the Armenian holocaust in Turkey. Even Guy Maddin, maker of quirky and experimental "prairie postmodern" films, has opted for a dance version of *Dracula* for his next project.

Films such as these recall the taxonomic dilemmas of the notorious tax-shelter era. Then a film's Canadianness was often a matter of mysterious determinants inaccessible to most audiences (Telefilm financing, a Canadian production company, and a points system for cast members and crew). To the question "what is a Canadian film," there is a simple answer: a film financed in Canada (mainly by Telefilm), made by a required number of Canadians but not necessarily for Canadians or in/about Canada. This is to distinguish it from a film like *Agnes of God* (1985) made in Quebec about a local Catholic nun by ardent Canadian nationalist Norman Jewison but financed by a Hollywood studio. Exceptions only include, apparently, films by David Cronenberg (even *Naked Lunch* and *M. Butterfly*) or films like *The Terminator* sanctioned by Geoff Pevere.[17]

---

[17] Geoff Pevere, "Ghostbusting: 100 Years of Canadian Cinema, or Why My Canada Includes *The Terminator*," *Take One* 12 (Summer 2000), repr. in Wyndham Wise, ed. *Take One's Essential Guide to Films and Filmmakers in Canada* (Toronto: Take One, 1999): 4–13. Pevere proposes that Canadians lay claim to all Hollywood films with expatriate Canadian producers, directors, writer and/or actors – such as James Cameron (*The Terminator* and *Titanic*), Ivan Reitman, Jim Carrey, Michael J. Fox, Margot Kidder, et al. Taken to its logical conclusion, all MGM films made through 1957 would be "Canadian," since Louis B. Mayer spent most of his formative years (to age 18) in Saint John, New Brunswick; likewise all Mack Sennett comedies, since he lived outside Montreal until age 18.

Cronenberg and filmmakers of the past decade (and Pevere!) present a formidable challenge to the would-be definer of Canadian cinema. Twenty-five years ago when Canadian films were the almost exclusive domain of young white males working within limited budgets usually under the auspices of the NFB or some other constraining government bureaucracy, definitions and paradigms were relatively easy. Canadian cinema was realistic and unslick, personal if not auteurish, in some way a coming of age story about an inadequate male. Today, at the beginning of the twenty-first century, no inclusive paradigms exist. This is not just a matter of the "two solitudes," Quebec and English Canada; it's because of the wide-ranging idiosyncracies, extreme geographic diversity, and irregularly developed talents of Canadian filmmakers spread from Newfoundland to British Columbia and Nunavut to Southern Ontario and now also filming outside the country.

What is Canadian cinema? It's now realistic and fantastic, big budget and small-time, crude and polished. It's conventional and bizarre, generic and hermetically personal, plot-driven and character-oriented. It's male and female, gay and straight, chaste and pornographic. It's about interior states and exterior worlds. It may still be seen by only three percent of the population and be more appreciated on the festival circuit than in the cineplex. But it is growing and changing, and its virtues and variety are now being recognized around the world.[18]

recognition - Charles Taylor?

---

[18] As proof of the growing importance of Canadian film, there are at least three new anthologies of essays now about to go to press: one on NFB documentaries, one on English-Canadian cinema since 1980, and one on Canada's "hidden" cinemas.

FIGURE 1

Goin' Down the Road (Don Shebib, 1992) – Doug McGrath (Pete);
Paul Bradley (Joey); Jayne Eastwood (Betty).

1 Goin' Down the Road (Don Shebib, 1970)

Production: produced 1969, released 2 July 1970. Evdon Films, with the participation of the Canadian Film Development Corporation. **Director:** Don Shebib. **Producer:** Don Shebib. **Screenplay:** William Fruet, from a story by Don Shebib, William Fruet. **Cinematographer:** Richard Leiterman. **Editor:** Don Shebib. **Music:** Bruce Cockburn. **Titles:** Film Opticals. **Sound:** James McCarthy with re-recording by Clarke Da Prato. **Colour, 87 mins., 16 mm.**

Cast: Doug McGrath (Pete), **Paul Bradley** (Joey), **Jayne Eastwood** (Betty), **Cayle Chernin** (Selina), **Nicole Morin** (Nicole), **Pierre La Roche** (Frenchy), **Ted Sugar, Don Steinhouse** and **Ron Martin** (boys at plant), **Max Jones, Fred Zimmerman, Mary Black, Ivor Jackson, Ralph Stroh, Dennis Bishop, Stuart Marwick, Sheila White, Stan Ross.**

Synopsis: Pete and Joey, two single Maritime buddies, leave a very bleak Cape Breton, Nova Scotia in a beat-up Chevrolet convertible seeking high-paying jobs and the good life in Ontario. A flat tire and snubs by suburban Toronto relatives do not deter them. They land in the glittering commercial strip of Yonge Street in downtown Toronto, but their naive excitement and high hopes quickly dissipate.

After spending their first nights in a seedy men's hostel, they find a run-down apartment. Pete answers an ad for a job in advertising, but is humiliated in the interview and slowly comes to the painful realization that with no education and few marketable skills he is no better off in Toronto than he was on the east coast. He takes a factory job with Joey, stacking crates of pop-bottles, and spends his time drinking with other displaced Maritimers and fantasizing about middle-class women who are totally inaccessible to him. Tensions mount between the two friends when Betty, the waitress Joey is seeing, becomes pregnant. Betty and Joey marry, leaving Pete for their own apartment which they have furnished on credit. But when the two men are laid off from work, Betty and Joey's dream is repossessed. The three end up in another seedy dive, Betty is forced to quit work, and Pete and Joey are reduced to delivering flyers door-to-door in the cold Canadian winter. Their financial and emotional desperation reaches a peak when they attempt to steal two carts full of groceries in order to enjoy a decent Christmas dinner. The plan backfires when a clerk chases them; they beat him and leave him unconscious, if not dead, in the icy parking lot. The bond between the friends is re-established, however, as Joey reluctantly agrees to abandon Betty and flee the police with Pete. The film ends with the two Easterners continuing on the road, heading west, toward a very uncertain, but certainly less deluded, future.

ℭ

Canadian narrative cinema from the margins

'The nation' and masculinity in *Goin' Down the Road* *

──────────────── ℰↃ

Christine Ramsay

Our first English-Canadian feature

R EVIEWERS IN POPULAR NEWSPAPERS, magazines and film journals have praised *Goin' Down the Road* both as the product of a quintessentially Canadian imagination and as a quality fiction film. At the time of its release, Dane Lanken of the Montreal *Gazette* wrote:

> Until now, there has never been a made-in-Canada movie that was good enough to make people – here and elsewhere – sit up and notice that there is real movie-making talent right here at home. The breakthrough is *Goin' Down The Road*, a low-budget saga about two down-and-out Maritimers who journey to Toronto in search of big-money jobs and the Good Life. It's a well-made movie, humorous at times, touching and poignant at others; at no time meaningless or dull.[1]

The Toronto Star's Jim Beebe continued in the same vein:

> *Goin' Down The Road* [...] is the first real English-Canadian movie. Not a semi-documentary, not an art film, not an embarrassing piece of double-bill fare, but a real movie. And best of all, the fact that it is Canadian is almost irrelevant; it is an excellent picture by any standard.[2]

───────────────

* Thanks to the *Canadian Journal of Film Studies* for permission to reprint this article. It is a partial reproduction and reworking of the original which appeared in Volume 2, numbers 2-3, 1993, a special double issue on nation. The research for this work was funded by the Gerald Pratley Award, established by Telefilm Canada and the Ontario Film Development Corporation and administered by the Film Studies Association of Canada.

[1] Dane Lanken, "Finally – The Great Canadian Movie," *Gazette* (Montreal; 8 August 1970): 38.

[2] Jim Beebe, "*Goin' Down the Road* a great Canadian movie," *Toronto Star* (3 July 1970): 24.

In *MacLean's*, Kaspars Dzeguze expressed his delight that

> it *is* Canadian, though not excessively so (no Mounties or Eskimos). Moreover, the story has an authenticity beyond the settings and details that make it specifically Canadian.[3]

Dzeguze is pointing here to the film's thematic debt to the path Maritimers have historically cut on their journey to the centre, Toronto, and then 'out west' as Canada's source of cheap migrant labour. Robert Fulford (under his pseudonym of Marshall Delaney) placed the film hopefully and excitedly as

> the beginning [...] not only of a new independent talent in feature film-making but perhaps also of an era in which English-speaking Canadians, like French Canadians and scores of other peoples around the world, will finally be able to make a cinema of their own.[4]

Martin Knelman agreed that with the appearance of *Goin' Down The Road* "we began to see the glimmerings of a truly Canadian cinema."[5] And Piers Handling saw it as seminal: "*Goin' Down The Road* seemed to be our first step, tentative perhaps, but opening the floodgates to self-expression."[6]

Since its release in the summer of 1970, the film has indeed been widely heralded as the landmark of the beginning of English-Canadian national cinema. Its continuing status in the 1980s was signaled by a famous parody on SCTV starring John Candy, Joe Flaherty, and Jayne Eastwood (reprising her film role), a skit perhaps more widely known than the film itself. In 1992, *Goin' Down the Road* was selected by the National Art Gallery as one of seven fiction films to mark the 25th anniversary of Telefilm Canada, the federal government's film-funding agency.[7] Four years later it was chosen by Canada Post to be one of the ten films honoured with postage stamps to commemorate one hundred years of cinema in Canada.

Canonized as a classic, *Goin' Down the Road* has proven to be *the* benchmark of Don Shebib's filmmaking career, and according to most critics Shebib has never been able to live up to the promise of this first feature. *Satan's Choice* (1966), *Good Times, Bad Times* (1970), *Between Friends* (1973), *Second Wind* (1976), *Fish Hawk* (1979), *Heartaches* (1981) and, unaccredited, *Running*

---

[3] Kaspars Dzeguze, "Go and see *Goin' Down the Road*. You'll help Don Shebib pay for his new sports car, and encourage him to make more movies," *Maclean's* (September 1970): 73.

[4] Marshall Delaney [Robert Fulford], "Two Losers, Lost in Cold Toronto," *Saturday Night* (July 1970): 25.

[5] ⇨Martin Knelman, *This Is Where We Came In*, 11.

[6] Piers Handling, *The Films of Don Shebib* (Ottawa: Canadian Film Institute, 1978): 3.

[7] See "25 Years of Telefilm," *Globe & Mail* (22 May 1992): C2.

Brave (1983), to mention a few of his more notable productions, all share *Goin' Down the Road*'s concern with male friendship / bonding. While they do get some notice in classes on Canadian cinema, they remain relatively unknown minor works in most critical assessments of the director's oeuvre.

Given Shebib's film education in southern California and his love for American director John Ford, *Goin' Down the Road* could also be read generically. Geoff Pevere, English Canada's foremost film and popular-culture critic, has a well-documented attachment to the movie; he sees it as fitting perfectly into the "deluge of downer/buddy/road movies" unleashed in North America after the phenomenal success of *Easy Rider* in 1969.[8] Interesting comparisons could certainly be drawn between *Goin' Down the Road* and its American 'buddy' counterparts of the time – films like *Midnight Cowboy* (1969), *Butch Cassidy and the Sundance Kid* (1969), *Little Fauss and Big Halsy* (1970), *Two Lane Blacktop* (1971), *Pocket Money* (1972), and *Scarecrow* (1973). And, of course, there is the precursor to all of them, John Ford's *The Grapes of Wrath* (1939). What I want to focus on here, however, is not neo-auteurism, nor comparative genre analysis across national cinemas (as fruitful and revealing as these approaches might be), but on a critical evaluation of the film's continuing celebration as one of Canada's greatest films.

Imagining English Canada and mapping its margins

My interest in *Goin' Down The Road* has less to do with its exemplification of what are seen as the typical aesthetic markers of a film's traditional 'Canadianness' (ie, stark, if not 'depressing' social realism; documentary flavour; eccentric and off-beat characterizations; contemplative treatment of the landscape) than with the way the social and personal concerns of foregrounded marginality in the English-Canadian nation as an imagined community

---

[8] Pevere makes reference to *Goin' Down the Road* in three articles written recently: "On the Roads: Caught in the Headlights of a Cinematic Genre," *Canadian Forum* 71.811 (July–August 1992): 19–20; "Detour: Down the Road with Don Shebib;" and "On the Road Again: The Making and Unmaking of a Canadian Classic," *Take One* 8 (Summer 1995): 6–13. Pevere is well-known for his stint as host of the Canadian Broadcasting Corporation Radio's *Prime Time* programme in the early 1990s (the "boring Canadians" joke among academics is that he was eventually pushed out because what he was doing was too interesting), his current work as host of TV Ontario's *Film International*, and his involvement in the Toronto International Film Festival and the local Toronto film community. An important recent work by Pevere with Greig Dymond is ⇨*Mondo Canuck*, which includes references to both *Goin' Down the Road* and Don Shebib.

inhabit the text.[9] I suspect *Goin' Down The Road* enjoys the status it does because of the uncanny precision with which it captures and demonstrates
how English Canada constructs nation, sees culture, and experiences its
sense of social self around an acute awareness of diversity, the decentred
centre, the periphery, the margins.[10]

In *The Imaginary Canadian*, Tony Wilden explores the Canadian imagination in terms of our history of "colonization" and "victimization." He asks:

> Through what kind of communication, in what context, do we want to identify
> postcolonial Canada in order to avoid using blindly the dominant Western
> colonialist codes of domination, individualism, and negation of other?[11]

---

[9] For Benedict Anderson in *Imagined Communities: Reflections on the Origin and Spread of
Nationalism* (New York: Verso, 1983), each nation is fundamentally just that: an "imagined
community" (15–16). Nation is imagined because its citizens will never individually come
in contact with, let alone know, each other; nevertheless, they live together mentally in an
image of shared communion. To see yourself as a citizen of Canada, for example, you
have to be able to manage the paradox of remembering a constructed, imaginary commonality by forgetting such things as class conflict, regionalism, and linguistic differences.
The case of Canada is interesting and complex because regionalism is actually foregrounded and then disavowed in the assertion of a unified national Canadian identity. As
part of the image of shared communion, invented traditions (such as flags and anthems)
are created and re-created where nothing exists, or something else existed, in order to
preserve this fiction of an eternally unified nation. For example, we have the entry of
Newfoundland into confederation in 1949, which required a shift from a traditional flag
and anthem and allegiance to a new set of traditions demanded by Canada. The nation
thus imagines signs and limits for itself in its drive for absolute independence and autonomy controlled by the centre. But at the same moment, the nation imagines sovereignty
and freedom for itself and must incorporate and/or dominate its peripheries. In this way
the nation is imagined as a "community" of "horizontal brotherhood," even though
actual conflicts, inequalities, and exploitation abound.

[10] For Homi K. Bhabha in "DissemiNation: Time, Narrative, and the Margins of the
Modern Nation," in *Nation and Narration*, ed. Bhabha (New York: Routledge, 1990): 291–
322, these imagined communities we call nations get developed, represented and narra-
tivized in unique and culturally specific ways through a field of historically determined
textual strategies. The nation as an imagined community works to fill the voids and emptinesses it creates for the margins by turning the loss into metaphors, narratives, representations which work to empower the controlling centre. In this way, centres construct
affiliation to "stable" social knowledge through cultural activity – through texts. Thus, to
understand how the nation is imaginatively produced, it becomes essential to study what
Bhabha calls "the complex strategies of cultural identification and discursive address that
function more or less overtly in the name of 'the people' or 'the nation' and make them
the immanent subjects and objects of a range of social and literary narratives" (292).

[11] Tony Wilden, *The Imaginary Canadian* (Vancouver: Pulp Press, 1980): 113.

Clearly, however, these codes are complicated and complex. They cannot just simply be "avoided." They operate through the very structures of class, culture and gender which have historically been used (even in 'multicultural' Canada) to imagine and inflect the Western nation as a cohesive community of horizontal brotherhood.[12] And, under the fraternal ideology of national democracy, these structures in fact often function largely for the controlling centre to cover up marginality and difference – to order and contain the diversity of the group.[13]

Certainly, the assertion of 'the nation' as this kind of ideal, colonialist, ordered centre to be gained can be seen to operate in the Canadian imagination (ie, in this case around the signs of the Maple Leaf, the Mounted Police, the CPR, or Stompin' Tom Connors); yet that centre is clearly also premissed on an unusually overt, if often only symbolic, deference to the margins (multiculturalism, regional diversity; the *possibility* of a South Asian–Canadian Mountie wearing a turban[14]). Thus, the imagined community in post-colonial Canada is a self-conscious product of both centre and margins as oppositional forces, and many of our textual representations can be seen, not only to embody, but to foreground the two elements of this dynamic.

---

[12] Anderson, *Imagined Communities*, 16.

[13] Central to the phenomenon of national identity is an impulse to mastery in the face of uncertainty, contradiction, heterogeneity and difference. In *Theories of Nationalism* (London: Duckworth, 2nd ed. 1983), Anthony Smith writes that "every society has to face the familiar 'problem of meaning' in its various aspects. For this end, if for no other, an image of the total order of the universe is built up" (236). Western societies have historically addressed the problem of social and personal identity through the concept of 'the nation' as an ideal image of an ordered universe. Traditionally, the nation has been that place where the collective and individual questions of belonging get 'solved,' sewn-up, stabilized. The nation fixes limits, both physical and metaphysical, to secure identity.

This traditional concept of the nation, however, is from the very start unstable because "the nation" always represents an ideological struggle to guarantee certain meanings and achieve a hegemonic identity around those meanings in the face of heterogeneity and difference: other, competing meanings and identities are always part of the social purview. There is no such thing as a neutral and transparent or absolute 'nation' that easily and naturally provides a source of identity for all members of a society and makes their lives meaningful.

[14] A controversy raged in Canada in the early 1990s over whether Sikhs in the Royal Canadian Mounted Police should be allowed to replace the official uniform's standard hat (known by such epithets as the "smokey" or "lemon squeeze") with their traditional turban. In May 1995 the Federal Court of Appeal "upheld the right of Mounties to wear turbans while on duty." (See Daryl Slade, "Court OK's RCMP Turban," *Calgary Herald* [1 June 1995], B1.)

In *The Empire Writes Back*, Ashcroft, Griffiths and Tiffin suggest two ways in which colonial and postcolonial literary texts can be read: as metaphor and/or as metonymy. According to Ashcroft et al., the metaphoric impulse in textual interpretation is a centralizing impulse that produces idealized knowledge. They write that "Metaphor has always, in the Western tradition, had the privilege of revealing unexpected truth."[15] Metaphor, associated with symbolism and romanticism, generates an imaginative social "identity and totality" and can be said to produce the "national truth" through concentrated signs like the Maple Leaf and the Mounted Police. On the other hand, reading a text metonymically fragments it, producing separation and difference through signs like the image of a turbaned Mountie. Metonymy, associated with realism, generates a field of complex relationships that foreground paradox, social conflict, and the fact that in the metaphoric construction of the nation as a "naturally" totalistic whole, it is really only highly selected parts that are being chosen to stand for the national whole while other parts are coerced, disavowed, disallowed, or ignored. For Homi Bhabha, this distinction (and, I would add, play) between metaphor and metonymy is central to the reading of postcolonial texts, although he privileges the latter as more intellectually complex and critically fruitful:

> His point is that the perception of the figures of the text as metaphors imposes a universalist reading because metaphor makes no concessions to the cultural specificity of texts. For Bhabha it is preferable to read the tropes of the text as metonymy, which symptomatizes the text, reading through its features the social, cultural, and political forces which traverse it.[16]

A survey of the critical literature on *Goin' Down The Road* reveals that the film has predominantly been given the totalizing, universalist, metaphoric type of reading (in Margaret Atwood's *Survival*, in John Hofsess's *Inner Views*, and in Robert Fothergill's "Coward, Bully, or Clown: The Dream-Life of a Younger Brother," for example) and it goes something like this.

Atwood's "thematic guide" was first presented in 1972, but its "survival" premiss quickly became the canonized habit of English-Canadian cultural criticism. Her contention is that the Canadian national identity rests on a preoccupation with survival – personal and cultural. Moreover, in the face of the utopian American dream and the 'will to win' that fuels it, the scarcely surviving colony we call English Canada has developed a despairing 'will to

---

[15] Bill Ashcroft, Gareth Griffiths & Helen Tiffin, *The Empire Writes Back: Theory and Practice in Postcolonial Literatures* (London/New York: Routledge, 1989): 51.

[16] Ashcroft, Griffiths & Tiffin, *The Empire Writes Back*, 52.

lose,' and according to Atwood this negativity is manifested through gender in the way we construct heroes as crippled 'victims' and 'losers.' She writes:

> And just to round things out, we might add that the two English Canadian feature films (apart from Allan King's documentaries) to have had much success so far, *Goin' Down The Road* and *The Rowdyman*, are both drama-tizations of failure. The heroes survive, but just barely; they are born losers, and their failure to do anything but keep alive has nothing to do with the Maritime Provinces or 'regionalism.' It's pure Canadian, from sea to sea.[17]

In no uncertain terms Atwood sets up a metaphoric reading of *Goin' Down The Road* as the standard cinematic representation of the types of people and the set of social relations that determine a colonized Canada. For Atwood, the film is simply an allegory for her assumption that, in Canadian cultural representations, Canadian men are always imagined as victims and losers. In Tony Wilden's formulation, this prototypical image of the Canadian male as victim/loser translates across the terms of gender identity into the even broader notion of Canada as a "feminized" nation.[18]

Hofsess and Fothergill pick up Atwood's lead wholeheartedly in their readings of the film and so become complicit with the metaphoric/ allegoric assertion that men's losing and victimization (vis à vis an American stan-dard of fantastic masculine heroism) is not only all that goes on for *all* men in Canada, but it is also all that goes on imaginatively in *Goin' Down the Road*. Working closely from Atwood, Fothergill asserts that Canadians live in a perpetual relationship of "younger brotherhood" to American will, know-how, and mastery. "Radically inadequate," especially in "relation-ships with women," he writes, "the unprepossessing English Canadian male appears on the screen in several guises, which I have labeled Coward, Bully, and Clown."[19] He goes on to situate both Pete and Joey firmly in the coward and clown camps, wherein the coward is pusillanimous (sensitive, vul-nerable and mild, yet gutless) and the clown is irresponsible (refusing to assert the proper manly/masculine qualities of a self-determining [hetero-sexual] male adult):

> Joey [...] has a good deal of the Coward about him. Bewildered by big-city life, and with a tendency to get maudlin drunk, he finally runs out on the whole mess, leaving a pregnant and newly-evicted wife to fend for herself.

---

[17] ⇨Margaret Atwood, *Survival*, 34, 35.

[18] Wilden, *The Imaginary Canadian*, 111.

[19] Robert Fothergill, "Coward, Bully, or Clown: The Dream-Life of a Younger Brother," in ⇨Feldman & Nelson, ed., *Canadian Film Reader*, 235–36.

> When times are good, Joey and his friend Pete [...] caper about with childish irresponsibility, drinking and frolicking in a fashion that is likable enough but rather trying to the women who have to put up with it. Pete's repertoire includes a humiliatingly unsuccessful attempt to ingratiate himself with a sexy French lady, Nicole Morin. In their antics, the Canadian male as Coward can be seen shading into another incarnation: the Clown.[20]

Hofsess continues in the same vein, noticeably indignant that Shebib's and other Canadian directors' male characters are always victims and losers in comparison to the ways in which the symbols of masculinity south of the border are glamourized (read: metaphorical) absolutes, even as they confront death:

> Even when people fail in American films, they do so spectacularly, and in terms that are larger than life so that they seem heroic in spite of death. Their failure has been *glamorized*, whereas in Canadian films, the characters are usually grubby and more-than-a-little dumb. They just can't cope, they're pathetic even when (in a number of Québécois films) they rebel and shoot it out with authorities.[21]

For Hofsess, this failure on the nation's part to imagine and assert "mastery" is "unerotic," "repressive," and downright "gloomy."[22] He shows no understanding whatever of the fact that the lack of glamour or the presentation of characters who can't cope might be an intentional or at least meaningful strategy on the part of the filmmaker to question authority or the ability of a certain social structure and its dominant set of relations to function for its people. He seems to want Shebib to forego what I will later argue is clearly Shebib's textual foregrounding of metonymic realism, complexity and paradox in order to make "more *forceful* films": films "about stronger egos and more confident people, people who can because they think they can"[23] that would construct a more positive metaphoric representation of Canada.

But, in a more complicated, metonymic sense, and so, ironically, on another level, isn't that just what Pete and Joey *are* in *Goin' Down The Road*? People who *can* because they think they can? In simple terms, Pete and Joey leave Cape Breton because, as "Canadians," they think they can – they are under the impression that they can succeed where other Canadians have succeeded. Toronto promises to bring them, as Dane Lanken put it, "big-

---

20 Fothergill, "Coward, Bully, or Clown," 237.
21 ⇨John Hofsess, *Inner Views*, 77.
22 ⇨Hofsess, *Inner Views*, 78.
23 ⇨Hofsess, *Inner Views*, 79.

money jobs" and "the Good Life." But in reality it is a life that is available only to certain well-scrubbed Canadians – especially well-educated WASP males, like the advertising executive who will interview and humiliate Pete. Pete and Joey "fail," "rebel," and steal groceries for Christmas, not because of some abstract, flawed masculine "Canadian essence," but because of real regional, class, cultural, and gender differences in the structure of "the democratic nation" called Canada. My point is that the metaphoric readings of Canadian masculine identity in *Goin' Down The Road* that Atwood, Fothergill and Hofsess offer are incomplete and have clear limitations that another kind of reading might redress. A metonymic reading could perhaps take up the cultural specificities the film elaborates as a social text about difference, symptomatizing it as a complex network of conflicting relationships that clearly points to the existence of the social, cultural and political forces that traverse it and determine its heroes.

A metonymic reading of *Goin' Down The Road* might go something like this: The marginality of Pete and Joey that is so disturbingly negative to Atwood, Fothergill and Hofsess, while perhaps not the most enviable position to be in from the perspective of the centre, is not only or merely "bad." For Bhabha, marginality – or, as he calls it, "minority discourse" – is *the* necessary condition for serious contemplation of paradox and the "perplexity" of daily national life; for penetration and exposure of the fissures in the centre; for critical analysis of the metaphoric whole we call 'the nation,' and the (divisive) structures of region, class, culture, and gender that are variously managed and contained in order to "hold it together." He writes:

> Minority discourse [...] contests genealogies of 'origin' that lead to claims for cultural supremacy and historical priority. Minority discourse acknowledges the status of national culture – and the people – as a contentious, performative space of the perplexity of the living in the midst of the pedagogical representations of the fullness of life. Now there is no reason to believe that such marks of difference – the incommensurable time of the subject of culture – cannot inscribe a 'history' of the people or become the gathering points of political solidarity. They will not, however, celebrate the monumentality of historicist memory, the sociological solidity or totality of the society, or the homogeneity of cultural experience.[24]

Contemplation of the "perplexity of the living" in the midst, not of American but of *Canadian* romantic, symbolic, "pedagogical representations of the fullness of life": this is the quality that emerges, I think, in a text like Don

---

[24] Bhabha, "DissemiNation," 307–308.

Shebib's *Goin' Down The Road*. Here, the Canadian centre is not unconditionally stable. The margins are foregrounded as its enabling condition, its cheap migrant labour, for example. But in order for someone at the centre to actually get the "big-money jobs" and live the "Good Life," someone on the margins is forced to give more, take less, and feel inferior. *Goin' Down The Road* foregrounds and calls attention to the differences of region, class, culture, and gender that separate people as subjects of culture – that contribute to make some people "winners" and others "losers" within "the nation." In other words, *all* men are not victims and losers in Canada or in the film, any more than *all* American men, in reality or representationally, are heroes and winners. Perhaps the difference is that the Canadian imagination is simply more culturally predisposed to contemplate life from the margins and to appreciate the paradox of enabling conditions wherein seeming oppositions, like centre and margins, are so inextricably entwined.

Peter Harcourt describes the narrative mode of Canadian cinema as a visual, connotative, contemplative mode "that touches upon fable, that *implies* more than it says."[25] *Goin' Down The Road* does indeed imply more than it says; it is not about dominant psychological and social identities so much as it is about the gaps, spaces and fissures in between pedagogically prescribed metaphoric identities. *Goin' Down The Road* imagines the problems of trying to imagine Canada as a national community of heroic, hypermasculine men.

Goin' Down the Road, I would argue, is about the problems of national definition in English Canada: in particular, the problems created by Toronto's status at the centre of Canada's social and personal identity and economic prosperity, as seen from the peripheral perspective of two marginalized Canadian men. As Pete and Joey attempt to move from the margins to the centre, cultures clash and male egos take a beating. Thus, our national concern, if not obsession, with the problems of successfully creating an imagined community is negotiated in and through this text as a site of regional, class, cultural, and gender conflict.

From the aerial view of Cape Breton as Canada's beautiful eastern shore that opens the film, Shebib quickly cuts to the cultural and economic specificity of Cape Breton as one of Canada's most depressed and marginalized regions. As the song in voice-over ironically states, "It must get better the far enough I go," a montage of landscapes, towns and people

---

[25] Peter Harcourt, "Introduction" (reprinted from *Film Canadiana 1975-1976*), in ⇨Feldman & Nelson, ed., *Canadian Film Reader*, 372.

attest that it could not get worse. From lyrical contemplation of broken spaces – the gaps between the unused train rails, rotting fishing boats, and dead streets of Cape Breton – the film moves its male protagonists across borders of region, class, and culture to the centre of Toronto, to the glass towers of the advertising industry (one of Bhabha's national strategies of "cultural identification" and "discursive address") that makes the centre seem accessible to those on the margins.

With the conviction that "It's all right here – all you have to do is go out and get it," Pete applies for a job in an advertising firm, not only because he has seen lots of car commercials "down home" and "enjoyed them," but most importantly because he believed them. Of course, he has neither the education, cultivation, nor style to 'make it' in the centre, and the film makes this clear. But his Eastern Canadian working-class origins mean several things beyond the simple metaphoric contention that he is a 'loser' and a victim of American imperialism. Pete's origins are used by Shebib to indicate the differences between the Maritimes and Canada's imperial centre, Toronto. In the job interview scene, for example, it is directly revealed that higher education was not only unavailable to Pete but also unnecessary in order for him to perform the only available Maritime work in the canneries, on the docks, or in the mines of Cape Breton.

Pete's very being visibly annoys and disgusts the condescending big-city ad executive whose middle-class livelihood ironically consists in creating the fantasy of belonging for people like Pete. In reality, of course, Pete is repeatedly excluded from the world of the fashionable and cultured middle-class women who listen to classical music and read books, and whom advertising has convinced him are desirable and trained him to desire. Finally, in an effort to retrieve some sense of identity and belonging, Pete and his companions indulge in ribald Eastern forms of fun and entertainment (step dancing, men dancing with men, back slapping, and general adolescent drunkenness and carrying-on); but they are quickly derided, humiliated, and deemed publicly unacceptable by the barman as representative of the forces at the centre which articulate and police the reserve associated with some kind of 'true' English-Canadian identity.

While Joey blindly tries to fit in to the middle-class English-Canadian dream by getting married and consuming on credit a houseful of furniture he saw advertised on the back of *TV Guide*, Pete is reflective enough to see that he and Joey just don't belong. Their sense of their rightful Canadianness is naive and mistaken – in Bhabha's formulation, it is a false metaphor that never intended to fill the voids and emptinesses it has created for them as citizens of the margins.

For, as Shebib himself has noted, Maritimers are "foreigners" in Toronto, "as much as the Italians."[26] It is Shebib's frankness about marginality – his concern with the borders and boundaries operating just on the edge of visibility, in both his film and in the Canadian collective consciousness – that, I think, touches a nerve in and speaks to the many Canadians who have seen the film because it touches on the problems and complexity of the Canadian imagined community as de-centred centre. In an interview with P.M. Evanchuk, Shebib says:

> The basic premise of *Going Down The Road* was to make a film about people that most others would not like. The young twenty to twenty five year old hip kids that went to see the film wouldn't spend the time of day speaking to those Newfies and neither would I, but they liked them in the film.[27]

Here, Shebib directly reveals his own and other Canadians' obvious lack of belief and faith in the metaphoric strength and cohesiveness of the Canadian imagined community. Moreover, the bigger joke is that there are so many Canadian 'others' to be concerned with that even Shebib gets confused. Shebib calls them "Newfies," but Pete and Joey are Nova Scotians! As any self-respecting citizen of Eastern Canada will tell you, and in no uncertain terms, no Newfoundlander would deign to be called a Maritimer, and no Maritimer a Newfoundlander. In any case, the point is clear that hip Torontonians at the centre of Canada love "eccentric Easterners" on the big screen, but not in their living rooms. In *Goin' Down The Road* Pete and Joey are used to display – to make intelligible – differences within the "strong and cohesive" Canadian imagined community, but from the peripheral perspective of the margins, and thus suggest that the reasons for marginality are not simply 'innate' but are buried deeply in regional, class, cultural and gender struggles. Indeed, as things get progressively worse because of regional, class and cultural tensions, sexual difference comes to the fore: Pete, as the dominant male, is called upon to play the traditional masculine gender role of breadwinner for the pseudo-family of Joey, Betty and himself. But what he plays, instead, is Eric Satie on the phonograph. In what I think is perhaps the most moving moment in the entire film, Shebib captures Pete's dejection, resignation and emasculation in extreme close-up. Ultimately, what this

26 Lanken, "Finally – The Great Canadian Movie," 35.
27 P.M. Evanchuck, "An Interview with Don Shebib," *Motion* (March–April 1973): 14.

scene effects is a lyrical visual impression of the incredible dissonance between what is imagined as the "Good Life" for all Canadians and Pete's lived reality. As Harcourt writes, this is what makes it such a powerful exemplification of Canadian life:

> The films of Don Shebib add up to a statement about life that seems appropriate to us as Canadians. His characters, especially his men, convey a vision of some better kind of life that might be possible elsewhere but *should* be possible here. Whether this is seen in class or cultural terms, this insight is real for us, for many of us, living here in Canada.[28]

The insight Shebib offers is that what *should* be possible in Canada for Pete and Joey as Canadian men (that sublime vista of opportunity from Bona Vista to Vancouver Island imagined through the symbolism of popular song) and what *is* possible (that sorry lack of opportunity revealed through the metonymic realism of this popular film) are clearly two different things. Like region, class, and culture, gender is another sign of difference in *Goin' Down The Road* that the metaphoric reading would try to suppress. The film is not simply an allegory of Canada as a nation of feminized men: victims and losers. Again, it would be more fruitfully interpreted metonymically, as a text that sees complexity and renders it visible – that foregrounds the centre/margin dynamic at work in gender identity as well as in national identity. It is a text that contemplates and interrogates the problems inherent in masculine identity, male social roles, and men's relationship to women, and that refuses to ignore the way the fantasy of masculinity as "imagined community" so often erupts in violence.

As men, Pete and Joey originally imagine and construct themselves as empowered beings – as conquering heroes who, although they are from the margins, can penetrate the centre and win its spoils simply *because* of their maleness, their masculinity. Moreover, their sense of mastery is rooted in two basic assertions – sexual prowess and social power. Rolling into Toronto means that Pete and Joey will both kick ass and get some. As they compete for priority with the car ahead of them on the freeway, they carry on a laughing, typically 'masculine' exchange: "Beep the horn ... Come on, move it ya' bum ... Look out Toronto, here we come, all the way ... Hide y'er daughters. Lock the doors ... Cause we're about to drop our drawers."

Almost immediately, however, this fantasy of empowerment and independence is deflated and their emasculation begins. They wind up at the Sal-

---

[28] Peter Harcourt, "Men of Vision: Some Comments on the Work of Don Shebib," in ⇨Feldman & Nelson, ed., *Canadian Film Reader*, 217.

vation Army hostel, where Pete's dream of social power ("a job in an office, some chick for a secretary, company car, and my name on the door. Why not?") is in certain conflict with their lived reality. Enthusiastically immersed in their men's dream of independence and autonomy through prestige jobs and cars, they are oblivious to the roomful of silent, lonely, alcoholic, and emasculated men who surround them. As Joey reads the newspaper aloud to Pete in voice-off, "Hey, look at this, you can even phone somebody if you're lonely," Shebib's camera lingers on the face of one of these men whose loneliness is clearly unappeased by such big-city gimmicks.

This face attests ironically to both men's failure to achieve the masculine fantasy of total independence and autonomy, and to the paucity of that fantasy: after all, as the masculine ideal insists on denying men social connectedness for the sake of the myth of supreme heroic autonomy, this kind of pathetic isolation is often their fate.

Shebib uses the hostel residents metonymically, to expose the kind of suffering and degeneration that could very well be in store for Pete and Joey. Thus Shebib contemplates a broader insight that seems lost on Atwood. 'Losing' and 'victimization' are not presented here as a causal metaphor for Canadian masculinity as much as they are presented as the consequences of the disappointment necessarily embedded in a particular definition of masculinity which works to prove male power and omnipotence. Indeed, Atwood is clearly mistaken in her sweeping reading of the film which contends that Pete and Joey's failure as men has "nothing to do with the Maritime Provinces or 'regionalism'," and everything to do with their innate Canadian maleness.

Clearly, other Canadian men in the film are not victims and losers: the ad executive who tells Pete to go back home and get his high school diploma, the bottling factory foreman who monitors their every move, the guy in the bar who humiliates them are all empowered to some extent, or at least more powerful than Pete and Joey. Thus, in *Goin' Down The Road* Pete and Joey are marked as marginal because of regional, class, and cultural differences, and this marginality informs the film's representation of gender – their masculinity – as well.

The woman in the classical record store and the woman reading the book in the picnic scene on Toronto island are further signs of Pete's emasculation. Not only can he not dominate the woman he sexually objectifies, he cannot get near the women he idolizes. Shebib shoots the scene to clearly contrast the idealized, aloof, cultured reader with Betty and Selina, chattering mindlessly and in curlers, in order to show Pete's frustration at his failure to properly master the middle-class objects of his desire. Since he can't win by mastering relationships with women, he demands that Joey retreat with him, back into the adolescent fantasy of masculine empowerment, autonomy and independence through drinking and carousing.

Joey responds enthusiastically to Pete's frustration and suggests a night out, "Just the two of us. No broads. No nothing." But Joey, of course, can no longer retreat so easily into fantasy. Betty is pregnant, and so Joey's sexual choice is made for him: marriage and a family. As we have seen, however, it is Pete who is called upon to perform the man's role of breadwinner when Betty can no longer work and Joey slides into lethargy and depression. Unable to fulfil their masculine role and provide for the dependent woman on the salary that comes from sweating as a pin-boy in a bowling alley or delivering flyers door-to-door, their quiet desperation turns to petty crime and violence.

Knelman writes insightfully on the significance of the grocery store 'robbery' in terms of the issues the film has so subtly negotiated:

> In fact the picture is practically a case-study of how people get to be criminals. Uprooted because of the country's failure to make one region as prosperous as another, they find themselves stripped of the social customs and institutions that have always given them their bearings. In the big city, the dream that lured them away from home – the prospect of material heaven suggested by slick magazines and TV commercials – proves to be cruelly beyond their reach. They can't blend into the background; out of their element, they're forced to exist as freaks in a ghetto culture for displaced Maritimers.[29]

But theirs is not the commanding and gratuitous violence typical of male mastery and the American spectacle of empowered masculinity; rather, it springs out of a pathetically bungled attempt to just get some food for Christmas dinner by, as the song aptly names them, "two victims of the rainbow." Indeed, Pete and Joey as imagined in *Goin' Down The Road* are not merely two prototypical Canadian male losers; they are better understood metonymically, as marginalized parts of the Canadian whole.

The failure of Pete and Joey to win the centre is thus, at the same moment, a victory of exposure. The way their failure is imagined exposes the flaws in what Peter Morris calls Atwood's "canonical" assumption that the terms "victims" and "losers" are always associated and interchange-

---

[29] ⇨ Knelman, *This Is Where We Came In*, 101.

able.[30] Morris's point is that one can clearly be a victim without innately being a loser, and a loser without being a victim. In Shebib's film, Pete and Joey are imagined as marginalized victims of the centre, without being judged, on the film's own terms, as 'losers' because of it. In this film, that is, there is an empathetic engagement with marginality that, one could argue, becomes a dominant quality of many subsequent English-Canadian films:

> Several critics have remarked that Canadian movies seem to be consistently about victims and losers; and undeniably, there is a measure of defeat in these tales about the ways people faced with cultural deprivation try to compensate, and the prices they pay when their ways out fail. Yet there is also often a kind of noble stubbornness – sometimes funny and sometimes touching – about plain people who, faced with a world that requires something more complicated than plainness for survival, still refuse to surrender their dreams.[31]

Indeed, twenty-odd years later, with Bruce McDonald's *Highway 61* (1991) or Bruce Sweeney's *Live Bait* (1995), English-Canadian films are continuing to be produced that imagine 'the nation,' regionalism and the ideal of omnipotent, empowered white masculinity from the margins. With McDonald, for example, the provincial border has become international, and the Canadian hero perhaps even more 'emasculated' and feminized. Yet, in Pokey Jones as the perennial Canadian male 'loser' (ie, the guy who can't play the trumpet, whose car is his best friend, who is reluctant to shoot a chicken) there are clearly human qualities (such as a well-meaning generosity and subdued competence) to be desired, celebrated and admired. With Sweeney, the borders defining identity become intraprovincial (suburban Vancouver versus the wilderness of B.C. cottage country) and intergenerational (youth versus age) as the unemployed, cynical, sexually dysfunctional 22-year-old Trevor MacIntosh nevertheless charms and endears us by finding love with a 65-year-old installation artist. Interesting comparisons of 'the nation,' regionalism, and masculinity are there to be drawn between *Goin' Down The Road* and newer films like *Highway 61* and *Live Bait*. But that, of course, would be the subject of another essay.

৪০

---

[30] Peter Morris, "In Our Own Eyes: The Canonizing of Canadian Film," *Canadian Journal of Film Studies* 3.1 (Spring–Summer 1994): 27–44, here 37.

[31] ⇨Knelman, *This Is Where We Came In*, 114.

Masculinity and nation

In *Imagined Communities*, Benedict Anderson writes that "in the modern world everyone can, should, will 'have' a nationality, as he or she 'has' a gender."[32] Between the modern nation and dominant masculine gender identity there exists a common metaphoric impulse to power and mastery. Masculinity, like "the nation," is an imagined community that seeks for itself the ideal, ordered stability of the centre in order to contain the threats of difference, disorder and death from the margins. Omnipotent masculinity is 'imagined' because it does not exist in 'reality' as a quality of maleness. Masculinity, as the imaginative assertion of an eternally stable phallic identity (an identity based in an ethic of male power and domination) means men (and women) live mentally in the phallic image of a shared communion around empowered maleness. In "The Construction of Masculinity and the Triad of Men's Violence," Michael Kaufman writes:

> Masculinity is power. But masculinity is terrifyingly fragile because it does not really exist in the sense we are led to think it exists, that is, as a biological reality – something real that we have inside ourselves. It exists as ideology; it exists as scripted behavior; it exists within 'gendered' relationships [...] The presence of a penis and testicles is all it takes. Yet boys and men harbor great insecurity about their male credentials. This insecurity exists because maleness is equated with masculinity; but the latter is a figment of our collective, patriarchal, surplus-repressive imaginations.[33]

Masculine identity, like national identity, is not an innate, natural, eternal characteristic of men; rather, it is a product of imagination, a fantasy, a historical construction based in an economic, political and cultural power nexus that is open to historical change, hence always potentially unstable, fragile and insecure. To see yourself as a modern 'man' within a 'nation,' then, you have to be able to manage the paradox of remembering and asserting a constructed, imaginary, phallic commonality of "real men living in horizontal brotherhood" by forgetting the reality of male vulnerability, the perpetual threat of disempowerment from the margins, the very real conflicts between individual men and groups of men (involving region, class, culture), and the facts of sexual difference and social heterogeneity. And you have to invent traditions, like Canadian football, where absolutely nothing exists.[34]

---

[32] Anderson, *Imagined Communities*, 14.

[33] Michael Kaufman, "The Construction of Masculinity and the Triad of Men's Violence," in Kaufman, ed., *Beyond Patriarchy* (Toronto: Oxford UP, 1987): 13–14.

[34] I am referring, of course, to the recent crisis of patronage in the Canadian Football

Like nation, masculinity imagines exclusivity and highly defined limits for itself in its drive for absolute autonomy. Like nation, masculinity is about the drawing-up of borders and the myth of complete independence from others, while asserting complete rights, sovereignty and freedom for itself in dominating and mastering others. And finally, like nation, the imagined community of men under what Kaufman calls masculine "ideology" suffers great emotional pain and human sacrifice in the name of brotherhood, fraternity, and 'equality.'

Clearly, then, the parallel between 'the nation' and masculinity around the impulse to mastery becomes obvious: masculinity is a site of struggle between connection and independence just as nation is a site of struggle between community and homogeneity. In the nation known as English Canada, Shebib's *Goin' Down The Road* can be read as perhaps the originary and standard narrative cinematic representation of the way we, in constructing geographic, social and personal identity, have been more prone to foreground the struggle between centre and periphery – homogeneity and difference – from the perspective of the margins.

I put *Goin' Down The Road* forward as a valuable Canadian cinematic text because it lets the problems with 'the nation' and masculinity show. Arguing against Atwood, Hofsess and Fothergill, I think that this kind of 'minority discourse' should not merely be judged a bad thing that promotes negativity in our self-perception; rather, it should be celebrated and studied for what it offers as a "performative space"[35] for the representation of our social self – for what it offers as a lived text that makes intelligible to us, as English-Canadians, from the position of the margins, the unique way we have historically faced the problems of social and personal identity through the Western concepts of 'the nation' and omnipotent masculinity.

ಬ

Filmography

Features

1969   *Good Times Bad Times* (+ cinematographer, editor; 35 mins., 16mm)
1970   *Goin' Down the Road* (*En roulant ma boule*, or: *La Route de l'ouest*, or: *Le voyage chimérique*; 87 mins., 16mm)

League in the 1990s, particularly in Ottawa, the nation's capital, where controversial municipal subsidies, not the purchase of tickets by the public, have been keeping the Rough Riders "alive."

[35] Bhabha, "DissemiNation," 307.

1971	*Rip-Off* (+ co-editor; 89 mins.)
1973	*Between Friends* (+ co-editor; 91 mins.)
1976	*Second Wind* (+ editor; 93 mins.)
1978	*Fish Hawk* (*Old Fish Hawk*; released 1979; 97 mins.)
1981	*Heartaches* (released 1982; 105 mins.; video release 90 mins.)
1983	*Running Brave* (106 mins.; the film is listed under the fictitious name "D.S. Everett"; Shebib had his name removed over a dispute about the editing)
1987	*The Climb* (+ screenplay; 90 mins.)
1988	*Men of Steel* (91 mins.)
1992	*Change of Heart* (96 mins.)
1994	*The Ascent* (96 mins.)

Short films and television work

1961	*The Train* (+ cinematography, editor; 13 mins., 16mm)
1962	*The Duel* (+ cinematography, editor; 10 mins., 16mm)
1962	*Joey* (+ cinematography, editor; 27 mins., 16mm)
1962	*Dementia 13* (+ cinematography, editor; 81 mins.)
1963	*The Terror* (+ cinematography, editor; 81 mins.)
1963	*Revival* (+ cinematography, editor; 10 mins., 16mm)
1963	*Reparations* (unfinished; 16mm)
1964	*Surfin'* (+ co-cinematography, co-editor; 25 mins., 16mm)
1964	*Eddie* (40 mins., 16mm)
1964	*Autumnpan* (60 mins., 16mm)
1965	*Satan's Choice* (screenplay, editor; 28 mins., 16mm)
1966	*A Search for Learning* (+screenplay; 13 mins., 16mm)
1966	*Allan* (22 mins., 16mm)
1966	*David Secter* (+cinematography, editor; CTV for *This Land is People*; 14 mins., 16mm/TV)
1966	*June Marks* (+ cinematography, editor; CTV for *This Land is People*; 15 mins., 16mm/TV)
1966	*Christalot Hanson* (+ cinematography, editor; CTV for *This Land is People*; 15 mins., 16mm/TV)
1967	*Basketball* (+ editor; 24 mins., 16mm)
1967	*Everdale Place* (+ editor; CTV for *This Land is People*; 22 mins., 16mm/TV)
1967	*San Francisco Summer 1967* (+ co-cinematography, co-editor; CBC for *The Way it Is*; 59 mins., 16mm)
1967	*Satan's Choice* (CBC for *The Way it Is*; 8 mins., 16mm)
1968	*Unknown Soldier* (+ cinematography, editor; CBC for *The Way it Is*; 7 mins., 16mm)
1968	*Stanfield* (CBC for *The Way it Is*; 20 mins., 16mm)
1968	*Graduation Day* (+ cinematography, editor; CBC for *The Way it Is*; 8 mins., 16mm)
1972	*Born Hustler* (+ editor; CBC for *Telescope*; 25 mins., 16mm)
1974	*Winning is the Only Thing!* (CBC for *Gallery*; 24 mins., 16mm)
1974	*Mrs. Gray* (CBC for *Of All People*; 22 mins., 16mm)
1974	*We've Come A Long Way Together* (+ co-editor; 29 mins., 16mm)
1974	*Once Upon a Time in Genarro* (+ co-screenplay; CBC for *The Collaborators*; 50 mins., 16mm)

1974   *Deedee* (CBC for *The Collaborators*; 48 min 16mm)
1975   *The Canary* (CBC for *Performance*; 45 mins., 16mm)
1977   *Old Man Reever* (+ co-editor; CBC for *This Monday*; 40 mins., 16mm)
1977   *The Fighting Men* (CBC for *For the Record*; 75 mins., 16mm/TV; theatrical release 1978, 35mm)
1978   *Holiday for Homicide* (CBC; 16mm/TV)
1982   *By Reason of Insanity* (CBC; 16mm/TV)
1984   *Slim Obsession* (CBC; 16mm/TV)
1986   *Summits of Glory* (with Wendy Wacko; 120 mins., TV)
1990   *The Little Kidnappers* (with James Margellos; 100 mins., TV)
1994   *The Pathfinder* (104 mins., TV)
1999   *Code Name: Eternity* (TV series)

Bibliography

Screenplay

Fruet, William. *Goin' Down the Road*. Toronto: Phoenix Film, [1970].
——. "Goin' Down the Road," intro. William Fruet, in ⇨Douglas Bowie & Tom Shoebridge, ed. *Best Canadian Screenplays*, 17–81.

Books

Allan, Blaine. "The Films of Don Shebib," undergraduate thesis, Queen's University, 1976.
Handling, Piers. *The Films of Don Shebib*. Canadian Film Series 2. Ottawa: Canadian Film Institute, 1978.

Interviews and statements

Anon. "The Talk of the Town: McLuhan's Child," *New Yorker* 46.40 (21 November 1970): 47–49.
Collins, Alan, & Joe Medjuck. "Toronto Letter," *Take One* 1.10 (June 1968): 34–36.
Evanchuck, P.M. "An Interview With Don Shebib," *Motion* (March–April 1973): 10–14.
Gathercole, Sandra. "Just Between Friends: Don Shebib Talks With Sandra Gathercole," *Cinema Canada* 10–11 (October 1973–January 1974): 32–36.
Pittman, Bruce. "Shebib Exposes Himself," *Cinema Canada* 81 (February 1982): 18–21.
Shebib, Don. "Art is Like Baseball. For the Great Canadian Anything, Don't Build From the Top Down," *Globe & Mail* (9 October 1976): 6.

Articles, essays and sections in books

Fothergill, Robert. "Coward, Bully, or Clown: The Dream-Life of a Younger Brother," in ⇨Feldman & Nelson, ed., *Canadian Film Reader*, 234–50.
Handling, Piers. "Canada's Ten Best," *Take One* 6 (Fall 1994): 22–31.
Harcourt, Peter. "Men of Vision: Some Comments on the Work of Don Shebib," *Cinema Canada* 32 (November 1976): 35–40; repr. in ⇨Feldman & Nelson, ed., *Canadian Film Reader*, 208–17.
⇨Hofsess, John. *Inner Views*, 67–79.

Pâquet, André. "Goin Down the Roads of Canadian Cinema," *Skoop* 13.2 (1972): 32–37.
Pevere, Geoff. "On the Road Again: The Making and Unmaking of a Canadian Classic," *Take One* 8 (Summer 1995): 6–13.
Ramsay, Christine. "Canadian Narrative Cinema from the Margins: 'The Nation' and Masculinity in *Goin' Down the Road*," *Canadian Journal of Film Studies* 2.2–3 (1993): 27–49.
Reid, Alison. *Richard Leiterman* (Ottawa: Canadian Film Institute, 1978): 57–61.

Reviews

John Hofsess, *Take One* 2:6 (July–August 1969 [publ. July 1970]): 19–20; Pat Annesley, "'Big Time' Metro Told in Movie," *Toronto Telegram* (18 June 1970): 66; Martin Knelman, "Clutch Player Gets Film on the Road," *Globe & Mail* (20 June 1970): 22; Jim Beebe, "*Goin' Down the Road* a Great Canadian Movie," *Toronto Star* (3 July 1970): 24; Clyde Gilmour, "Human Tale of Two Drifters in Toronto," *Toronto Telegram* (3 July 1970): 41; Martin Knelman, "*Goin' Down the Road*: A Giant Step for Canadian Film," *Globe & Mail* (4 July 1970): 24; Marci McDonald, "Cabbagetown Background Helps Two Actors Create a Realistic New Movie," *Toronto Star* (4 July 1970): 33; Gerald Pratley, *Variety* (22 July 1970): 20; Robert Fulford, "Two Losers, Lost in Cold Toronto," *Saturday Night* (July 1970): 25; repr. ⇨Robert Fulford, *Marshall Delaney at the Movies*, 40–42; Dane Lanken, "Finally – The Great Canadian Movie," *Gazette* (Montreal; 8 August 1970): 35; Luc Perreault, "Réponse torontoise au défi québécois," *La Presse* (14 août 1970): 31; David Allnutt, "The Underdogs Get Their Day – On Film," *Montreal Star* (15 August 1970): 13; Paul King, "The Best Canadian Movie Yet is About Maritimers in T.O.," *Star Weekly* (15 August 1970); Dane Lanken, "*Goin' Down the Road*: A Film to be Savored," *Gazette* (Montreal; 15 August 1970): 38; Gordon Stoneham, "First Feature is a Hit," *Ottawa Citizen* (15 August 1970): 21; Jean-Pierre Tadros, "'Viens, mon amour,' lui dit il ... Et la Société de développement accourut," *Le Devoir* (15 août 1970): 12; Kaspars Dzeguze, "Film Success, Prospects Soar," *Globe & Mail* (18 August 1970): 11; Nick Yanni, *Motion Picture Daily* (30 September 1970): 4; Kaspars Dzeguze, "Go and See *Goin' Down the Road*: You'll Help Don Shebib Pay for his New Sports Car, and Encourage Him to Make More Movies," *Maclean's* 83.9 (September 1970): 73, 75; Sid Adilman, "*Goin' Down the Road* – All the Way to an Award," *Toronto Telegram* (5 October 1970): 45; Stefan Kanfer, "Sound Sleeper," *Time* 96 (Canada; 26 October 1970): 112–13; Pauline Kael, "Men in Trouble," *New Yorker* 46.37 (31 October 1970): 130–31, 135; repr. Kael, *Deeper into Movies* (Boston MA: Little, Brown, 1973): 171–72; Robert Claude Bérubé, *Séquences* 62 (octobre 1970): 36–37; Joseph A. Gelmis, "A Realistic Road," *Newsday* (October 1970): 7A; Arlene Gould, *Performing Arts in Canada* 7.3 (Fall 1970): 48; Alex Keneas, "Canadian Dream," *Newsweek* 76 (2 November 1970): 112; Peter Schjeldahl, "One Very Much for the Road," *New York Times* (8 November 1970): 13, 20; Robert Hatch, *The Nation* 211.15 (9 November 1970): 477–78; Dilys Powell, "Gloomsday," *Times* (London; 14 November 1971): 37; repr. (with prefatory note on reception outside North America) in ⇨Douglas Fetherling, ed., *Documents in Canadian Film*, 135–39; Stephen Handzo, *Village Voice* 15.50 (10 December 1970): 75–76; Guy Hennebelle [as G.H.], *Cinéma 71* 157 (juin 1971): 153; Gerald Pratley, in Peter Cowie, ed., *International Film Guide 1971* (London: Tantivy Press; New York: A.S. Barnes, 1971): 95; Victoria Wegg–Prosser, *Monthly Film Bulletin* 39.459 (April 1972): 72; Raymond Lefèvre [as R.L.], "*En roulant ma boule*," *Image et Son* 263–64 (septembre–octobre 1972): 95; Nat Shuster, "*Goin' Down the Road*: A Worthwhile Journey," *Motion* (July–August 1973): 30; John Hofsess, "The End of the Road: Don Shebib's Time of Illusion is Over," *Weekend Magazine* (28 February 1976): 16–20; Robert Fulford [as Marshall Delaney], "Nothing But Heartaches: Despite All His

Troubles, Don Shebib Persists in Bringing a Gritty Honesty to His Films," *Saturday Night* 97:3 (March 1982): 61–62; Bruce Bailey, "Elusive Don Shebib Isn't Too Sure Which Road He Wants to Go Down," *Gazette* (Montreal; 28 May 1982): C1; Peter Wilson, "Film-Maker Who's No Flag-Waver," *Vancouver Sun* (3 November 1984): D4; Elissa Barnard, "Shebib Recommends *Goin' Down the Road*," *Halifax Chronicle Herald* (14 December 1984): 2, ⇨Eleanor Beattie, *A Handbook of Canadian Film*, 149–51; Geoff Pevere, "On the Roads: Caught in the Headlights of a Cinematic Genre," *Canadian Forum* 71:811 (July–August 1992): 19–20; Jamie Kastner, "'I'm the Softest Guy in the World,' Says Shebib," *Toronto Star* (30 May 1993): D1, D7; Geoff Pevere, "Detour: Down the Road with Don Shebib," *Canadian Forum* 72.821 (July–August 1993): 24–25.

ଚ

FIGURE 2

Mon oncle Antoine (Claude Jutra, 1971) – Jacques Gagnon (Benoît);
Jean Duceppe (Antoine).

2 Mon oncle Antoine
(Claude Jutra, 1971)

Production: produced 1970, released in Montréal 19 November 1971. A production of the National Film Board of Canada. **Director:** Claude Jutra. **Producer:** Marc Beaudet. **Screenplay:** Clément Perron, adapted by Claude Jutra and Clément Perron. **Cinematographer:** Michel Brault. **Editors:** Claude Jutra and Claire Boyer. **Music:** Jean Cousineau.

Sound: Claude Hazanavicius. **Colour, 104 mins., 35 mm.**

Cast: Jacques Gagnon (Benoît), **Lyne Champagne** (Carmen), **Jean Duceppe** (Antoine), **Olivette Thibault** (Cécile), **Claude Jutra** (Fernand), **Lionel Villeneuve** (Jos), **Hélène Loiselle** (Mme Poulin), **Monique Mercure** (Alexandrine), **Dominique Joly** (Maurice)

Synopsis: In a small Québec mining community "not so long ago," Jos Poulin loses his job at the asbestos mine after an altercation with an English-speaking foreman. He leaves his family on their isolated farm and goes to find work at a logging camp. At the village store, Benoît lives with his uncle Antoine and aunt Cécile and assists Fernand, the manager. He also helps in the family undertaking business and is an altar boy at the local church. On Christmas Eve, the villagers gather at the store for the annual unveiling of the manger scene. Benoît flirts with Carmen, who also lives at the store and, along with Maurice, his fellow-worker, spies on Alexandrine, the wife of the village notary, as she tries on a new girdle. Later, he and Maurice throw snowballs at the mine owner, who is driving a sled through the streets throwing cheap gifts to the children. On the Poulin farm, the eldest son dies, and Antoine and Benoît make the journey to the farm with a coffin. During the return journey, Antoine succumbs to the effects of the gin he has been imbibing since they set out, and the coffin falls from the sled. Benoît is unable to retrieve the coffin on his own and returns to the store, where he finds Cécile in bed with Fernand. Meanwhile, unaware of his son's death, Jos has left his new job to be with his family at Christmas. Fernand returns to the farm with Benoît, who, looking through the front window, sees the entire Poulin family gathered around the coffin, which Jos has presumably retrieved from the road.

∞

Double vision

Mon oncle Antoine and the cinema of fable

———————— ℬ

Jim Leach

In celebration

I N JUNE 1970 the National Film Board (NFB) threw a party for the
people of Thetford Mines to mark the completion of shooting for a new
feature film directed by Claude Jutra. Many of the guests had appeared in
the film as the inhabitants of a small mining town in the region some time in
the recent past. A reporter from *Le Devoir* who was at the event described an
atmosphere of "enthusiasm" and "euphoria," and suggested that the lives of
the people had been deeply affected by "something marvellous and mysterious."[1] When *Mon oncle Antoine* was released in 1971, it was greeted with
similar enthusiasm by most spectators. It swept the Canadian Film Awards
for that year and quickly established itself as one of the major achievements
of Canadian cinema. After being voted the best film ever made in Québec in
a poll of film critics by *Séquences* magazine in 1980, it was honoured as the
best Canadian film in similar polls conducted by the Toronto Festival of Festivals in 1984 and 1993.

Although the film's success may be attributed to its apparently nostalgic
depiction of childhood and a less complicated past, its power stems from
darker currents which trouble the deceptively simple surface. These disturbing elements are fairly obvious in the experience of viewing the film but
tend to fade in the memory. *Mon oncle Antoine* has thus been praised for its
'charm' and also occasionally attacked for its alleged failure to do justice to
the historical period in which it is set. The few dissenting voices also point to
apparent weaknesses in the film's structure and, in so doing, draw attention
to what I see as a kind of 'double vision' that allows the film to create powerful effects of identification while simultaneously offering a critical perspective on its own cultural context. By examining the tensions surrounding the

---

[1] *Le Devoir* (6 juin 1970).

film's treatment of history, I will try to suggest how it builds on the interplay between its roots in a specific Québec community and its concern with aspects of human experience that transcend time and place.

The tensions to which I am referring can be traced back to the production process. As the report in *Le Devoir* on the Thetford Mines party reminded its readers, the region was trying to come to terms with its 'tragic' past when working conditions in the mines led to an epidemic of asbestosis. In response to these conditions, the asbestos mines had been heavily involved in the early stages of the political struggle that brought about the Quiet Revolution. When Jutra arrived to make his film, however, the community was concerned that it should not contribute to the bleak image of the area's past found in a number of earlier films, most notably Arthur Lamothe's *Poussière sur la ville* (1965).[2] In making his new film, Jutra had evidently helped restore a sense of community despite what *Le Devoir*'s reporter called the "suspicious eye" of people who were tired of being cast in the role of victims.

When the party was over, however, the filmmakers found that the NFB did not share the enthusiasm of the people of Thetford Mines. The film was scheduled for release just before Christmas 1970 – appropriately enough, since most of the action takes place on Christmas Eve, but it was not shown to the general public until November 1971. The problem was apparently a technical one which led Sidney Newman, the newly appointed NFB Commissioner, to request the re-shooting of two sequences.[3] Any doubts about the film must have been reinforced when it was rejected by the Cannes Film Festival, and the NFB seems to have been surprised by its success at the Canadian Film Awards in September 1971. Martin Knelman has suggested that, but for this success, the NFB may not have released the film at all.[4]

The success of *Mon oncle Antoine* helped to revive the faltering career of Claude Jutra, whose contribution to the emergence of a new Canadian cine-

---

[2] Lamothe's film is an adaptation of André Langevin's novel of the same title first published in 1953 and thus deals with a period quite close to that in which *Mon oncle Antoine* is set. The novel has been translated as *Dust Over the City* (Toronto: McClelland & Stewart, 1974). The "Quiet Revolution" refers to the movement by which Québec adopted modern political and technological ideas after decades of rule by the conservative Union Nationale Party whose policies received strong support from the Catholic Church. This process is often seen as beginning with the election of a Liberal government in 1960, but Pierre Trudeau traced its roots back to the strike by asbestos miners in 1944; see his *La Grève de l'amiante* (Montréal: Editions du jour, 1970).

[3] ⇨Gary Evans, *In the National Interest*, 208.

[4] ⇨Martin Knelman, *This Is Where We Came In*, 51.

ma with *A tout prendre* (1963) had been eclipsed by the attention paid to Gilles Groulx's *Le chat dans le sac* and Don Owen's *Nobody Waved Goodbye*, both released in 1964.[5] Although the new Canadian cinema had its roots in documentary and Jutra had been involved in the development of 'direct cinema' at the NFB in the 1950s, his films always pushed against the constraints of documentary realism. *Mon oncle Antoine* was the first of a series of films – to be followed by *Kamouraska* (1973), *Pour le meilleur et pour le pire* (1975), and *La Dame en couleurs* (1985) – that explore the relations of history and memory in Québec culture. None of the later films was a commercial or critical success, and Jutra spent many years in virtual 'exile,' working on English-language productions outside Québec. In 1986, the acclaimed director of *Mon oncle Antoine* committed suicide by drowning, his own memory ravaged by Alzheimer's disease.

Mon oncle Antoine has been rightly regarded as a central film in the output of an *auteur* known for films dealing with crises of identity in characters (often adolescents) faced with a culture whose values they find inadequate. Yet Jutra was not the film's sole author. The screenplay was originally written by Clément Perron, who had grown up in the asbestos-mining region, and the film could also be seen as the middle film of a trilogy devoted to Québec's recent history as reflected in small-town life. The other films, both directed by Perron himself, were *Taureau* (1973), set in the present, and *Partis pour le gloire* (1975), set during the conscription crisis in World War II. Perron had worked at the NFB since 1957 and was best known as the director of *Jour après jour* (1962), an innovative short documentary on working conditions in a paper mill. His contribution to *Mon oncle Antoine* is clearly evident in its autobiographical tone (as suggested by the title) and in the concern with the exploitation of the mine workers.

Jutra was involved in the final revisions to the screenplay, and the two authors seem to have worked well together. The tension in the film between involvement and detachment cannot be attributed simply to the differences between the visions of the authors, but the dual authorship was probably a

---

[5] Jutra had made a second feature film at the NFB with a group of young people who were interviewed in the film and who collaborated in the creation of fantasy sequences representing their dreams. The director referred to *Wow* (1970) as a film "born in the midst of waiting for something else" (*La Presse*, 28 March 1970). The significance of 1964 for Canadian cinema is discussed in Peter Harcourt, "1964: The Beginning of a Beginning," in ⇨Pierre Véronneau & Piers Handling, ed., *Self-Portrait*, 64–76.

factor in the development of the features which give the film its power and complexity.

Not only did the film have two authors; it also had two titles. At the time of the Thetford Mines party, it was to be called *Silent Night* (in English even for the French version), and this title still appears as a sub-title in the opening credits of some English-language prints. Jutra explained that Perron chose this title for several reasons: "first, *Silent Night* is Christmas Eve; secondly, it is an English title because, in this francophone community, English words slip in very easily and, thirdly, more than Christmas Eve, the English title would suggest the Québec night which had been so long."[6] This dark and ironic title was eventually abandoned because, as Jutra explained, it was becoming a "mannerism" to give English titles to works in French. A new title was chosen with the aim of encouraging the "phenomenon of spectator identification."[7]

As *Mon oncle Antoine*, the film achieved a greater popularity than any previous Canadian film and was able to create a sense of "solidarity" in its audiences just as it had in the community in which it was filmed.[8] However, the original title lingered as a reminder of the film's disturbing undercurrents. In his review in *Canadian Forum*, David Beard argued that, as *Mon oncle Antoine*, "it is a heart-warming film" but, as *Silent Night*, "it is a vibrant and subtle political statement by a mature film maker."[9] More recently, Jacqueline Viswanathan has made a similar point about the two titles: "on the one hand, *Mon oncle Antoine* is a light comedy, a 'Christmas film' suitable for the entire family. But on the other, it is also a film noir, an 'anti-celebration' with an 'anti-Father Christmas' [...] *Silent Night*, better than the inoffensive joviality of *Mon oncle Antoine*, evokes the double face of this work."[10] As Jean–Pierre Tadros noted in his review, the film's "simplicity" "attracts our adhesion," but the effects of identification are achieved in the face of aspects of the film's style which encourage a more detached critical perspective.[11]

---

6 ⇨ Léo Bonneville, ed. *Le Cinéma québécois par ceux qui le font*, 454.

7 ⇨ Bonneville, *Le cinéma québécois*, 459.

8 Henriette Fontaine, "Un moment de notre passé pour mieux voir notre présent," *Cinéma Québec* 1.10 (July–August 1972): 4.

9 David Beard, "*Mon Oncle Antoine: Silent Night*," *Canadian Forum* 52.1 (April 1972): 12.

10 Jacqueline Viswanathan, "Approche pédagogique d'un classique du cinéma québécois: *Mon oncle Antoine*," *French Review* 63.5 (April 1990): 856.

11 *Le Devoir* (20 novembre 1971).

I have already indicated that this 'double face' did prove disturbing to a few critics, especially in Québec. Although Jutra was a life-long separatist, the lack of explicit political themes in his films was disturbing to those who felt the need for films that would engage with the urgency of the present situation. The October crisis of 1970 occurred after the film had been shot but before its release, and *Mon oncle Antoine* seemed to have little relevance in this volatile political situation.[12] In the circumstances, it is hardly surprising that the general acclaim for the film, from both francophone and anglophone critics and audiences, should generate some resistance in Québec. By exploring the terms in which this resistance was articulated, however, I will argue that the film's 'double vision' allows it to develop a 'fable' which represents a complex response to the cultural context in which it was made.

Questions of form

At the end of a book of essays on Québec cinema, published in 1970, when Jutra was already working on *Mon oncle Antoine*, Dominique Noguez tentatively identified a movement away from the documentary-inflected realism of the direct cinema tradition towards what he called a "cinema of fable."[13] Noguez does not clearly define what he means by this term, but it seems to refer to films in which documentary observation and psychological involvement are subordinated to a more or less allegorical depiction of the complex cultural and political tensions shaping life in Québec. My appropriation of this term may not be quite in the spirit which Noguez intended, but I will use it to bring out the distinctive qualities which contributed to the success of *Mon oncle Antoine* and which help to situate the film within its cultural environment.

Although some critics did discuss *Mon oncle Antoine* in the context of direct cinema, there was widespread recognition that the film broke with a tradition with which Jutra had been closely associated. The significance of this break was, however, open to interpretation. Even before the film was

---

[12] The imposition of the War Measures Act, in response to the kidnapping of two diplomats by the FLQ, led to a wave of arrests which is the subject of *Les Ordres* (1974), directed by Michel Brault, Jutra's close friend and cinematographer on *Mon oncle Antoine* (see André Loiselle's essay on *Les Ordres*, below).

[13] Dominique Noguez, *Essais sur le cinéma québécois* (Montréal: Editions du jour, 1970): 207.

released, one reporter noted that it promised a return to "a more classical form of cinema," suggesting that the film told its story using the familiar methods of Hollywood cinema.[14] Jutra himself simply noted that the film's "simplicity" was dictated by the subject-matter, an explanation that accords well with Noguez's assessment of new developments.[15]

Canada's direct-cinema films had themselves met with considerable resistance from critics and audiences alike, and the unsettling blend of documentary and fiction in *A tout prendre* was often seen as a weakness. Now Jutra was accused by some critics of abandoning the qualities that made Québec cinema distinct, but at the same time condemned for failing to conform to the norms of the classical narrative cinema to which he was supposedly returning. The narrative structure created problems even for an enthusiastic reviewer like Tadros, who regretted that the spectator is lured down a number of "false trails."[16] It would seem that the 'story' constructed by Jutra and Perron, perceived by some as a return to a more traditional model, works in ways that cannot be fully explained in terms of this model.

Similar complaints that the narrative is "poorly balanced" and "badly constructed" continue to appear in assessments of *Mon oncle Antoine*.[17] However, there really is only one 'false trail' of any significance (the only one that Tadros mentioned and that many critics noted), and this occurs in the opening sequences, setting up a framework for the entire film. Since the film is largely concerned with the experiences of Benoît, an adolescent critically observing the adult world which he is about to enter, it seems strange that the first sequence and four of the first five sequences deal with the events

---

[14] *La Presse* (28 mars 1970).

[15] Geneviève Bujold, Michel Brault & Claude Jutra, "Interviews," *Cinema Canada* 7 (April–May 1973): 48.

[16] Although Tadros pointed to a lack of economy in plot construction, he argued that it would be wrong "to judge the film solely in terms of its dramatic structure" (*Le Devoir*, 20 novembre 1971). Herman Weinberg felt that "the implementation of an imposed 'story'" detracted from the film which would have worked even better as a "straight documentary on the Québécois" ("Reflections on the Current Scene," *Take One* 3.3 [April 1972]: 33). Jean Leduc argued that the film's treatment of its "story" lacked the clarity and efficiency expected of narrative cinema, "La Québécitude, maladie à virus?" *Cinéma Québec* 1.8 (mars–avril 1972): 13. These critics refuse even to consider the possibility that the film's deviations from the norms might suggest that it does not owe an uncomplicated allegiance to the 'simple' narrative conventions that it apparently adopts.

[17] ⇨Michel Houle & Alain Julien, ed. *Dictionnaire du cinéma québécois*, 191; ⇨Yves Lever, *Histoire générale du cinéma au Québec*, 249.

leading to the decision of a middle-aged man, Jos Poulin, to leave his home to work in a logging camp.

Our introduction to the world of the film comes through an argument between Jos and an anglophone foreman in the wasteland created by the asbestos mines. The colloquial Québécois French which Jos uses to swear at his broken-down truck contrasts with the foreman's use of English as the language of authority, although he insists that the truck does not belong to him and that he is merely protecting the company's property. Benoît is introduced in the second sequence, assisting his uncle Antoine at a communal wake. Yet Benoît's presence is only lightly stressed, the narrative soon returning to Jos. The next three sequences show him expressing his frustrations to a group of men in a tavern, saying farewell to his wife in the barn on their farm, and leaving for a logging camp with his axe.

At this point, the narrative focus shifts permanently to Benoît, who emerges as the bearer of "the dominant 'look' of the film."[18] Jos becomes a minor character, with only a few brief sequences devoted to him before he returns at the end of the film. This shift of attention is anticipated by the film's title, which suggests that the film will offer Benoît's view of his uncle, and there would thus seem to be some justification for the oft-repeated claim that the concern with the Poulins is a "distraction" from the film's central concern.[19]

The Poulin family does, however, have an important narrative function: it is the death on Christmas Eve of the eldest son, a youth of about Benoît's age, that sets in motion the events that lead to the film's denouement. These opening sequences also help to build up a sense of the community in which Benoît lives, and there are even some specific anticipations of later developments. Thus the case of beans which falls from a horse-drawn sleigh in the background as Jos says goodbye to his children may seem like a "distraction" within this sequence, but it is a macabre foreshadowing of a major event later in the film when the Poulin boy's coffin falls from the sleigh on which Benoît and Antoine are taking it to town. At a deeper level, as Jacqueline Viswanathan has pointed out, there are clearly thematic links between "two plots" which centre on "the death of one young boy and the maturing of another."[20]

The issue thus seems to be less the irrelevance of the Poulin material than the way in which it disrupts the patterns of identification on which classical

---

[18] Viswanathan, "Approche pédagogique," 855.

[19] ⇨Houle & Julien, *Dictionnaire du cinéma québécois*, 191.

[20] Viswanathan, "Approche pédagogique," 851.

narrative cinema supposedly depends. We are first asked to identify with Jos and then have to shift the focus of our attention to Benoît – an effect not unlike, although much less violent than, the way in which Alfred Hitchcock invites us to identify with Marion in *Psycho* (1960) and then kills her off part-way through the film. The difference is that Jos is still alive and thus available as a focus of identification; but, allowing for the major differences between the two films and their directors, the effects are quite similar.

The implications of the transfer of identification-figures in *Mon oncle Antoine* are suggested by Bruce Elder's argument that "for Jos Poulin, reality is too oppressive to be overcome," whereas Benoît, by the end of the film, "has seen the weakness of those who hold power and the stage is set for him to take revolutionary action."[21] Although the ending hardly points unequivocally towards revolution, Elder's interpretation does suggest the way in which the film's structure offers Benoît as a younger version of Jos. In other words, Jos represents what Benoît may become. The shift of the central consciousness from Jos to Benoît thus functions as a kind of flashback to an earlier stage of the process by which (male) identity is constructed in this culture.

As the title reminds us, a third male figure also looms large in the film. Antoine belongs to a yet older generation, but he remains the object of Benoît's increasingly critical gaze and is never offered as an identification-figure. Even though his store and undertaker's business place him at the centre of community affairs, he is finally revealed as a fearful and impotent old man. In a community in which the rituals of religious and social life seem to be wearing thin, Antoine's role as a patriarchal figure is undercut by tensions within his own 'family.' When he collapses in the snow after the coffin has fallen from the sleigh, he blames his alcoholism on his lack of children of his own and on Cécile's refusal to move with him to the USA. He and Cécile seem reluctant to formally adopt Carmen, who also lives at the store and who is exploited by her own father. Fernand, the other member of Antoine's 'family,' although he does not seem to be related to any of the others, really runs the store and eventually displaces Antoine in Cécile's bed.

Fernand himself exists outside the family and outside the generational sequence of males represented by Benoît, Jos, and Antoine.[22] At the end,

---

21 Bruce Elder, "Claude Jutra's *Mon oncle Antoine*," in ⇨Feldman & Nelson, ed., *Canadian Film Reader*, 198.

22 Jutra explained his decision to cast himself in this role by claiming that Fernand is a "director" within the film: "he is a character who effaces himself behind other more active

Cécile tells him that he is not yet ready to fill Antoine's boots, but the main point is that none of these men can provide an adequate substitute for Benoît's absent and unmentioned father. Although Antoine is Benoît's 'uncle,' there is no mention of the boy's parents or of how he came to be living at the store, and his critical gaze is used to expose a society whose supposedly patriarchal structure is a mask for impotence and fear.[23]

If the film introduces its concerns with masculinity and the family in a rather devious way, it also draws the processes of looking and desiring to the spectator's attention by devices which Jean Leduc condemned as "obvious weaknesses in the direction" precisely because they violate the dictum of classical cinema that style should not call attention to itself.[24] At the end of the first sequence, a zoom in on the asbestos tip is followed by a cut to a body in a coffin. A few moments later, a cut juxtaposes the coffin with beer on a table in the tavern. After Jos has declared his intention of quitting his job at the mine, another zoom brings the parish church into focus through the tavern window. This effect, obtrusive in itself, is rendered even more strange because it does not introduce a sequence in the church. Instead, the narrative takes us to the Poulins' farm, and only after Jos's departure do we see Benoît assisting the priest at morning mass, a sequence that is introduced by yet another zoom and by a montage effect that this time juxtaposes the church with the mine.

The unusual structure of the opening sequences thus establishes a number of links: between the oppression of Jos at the mine and the old man's corpse, between the fact of death and the drinking at the tavern, and between the tavern and the church as twin foci of community life. In drawing attention to its own activities, the film also reminds us of the processes of looking and making connections basic to all cinematic production and spectatorship and, at the same time, distances itself from those styles which imply that these processes do not depend on the activity of the filmmaker or spectator. While the spectator will soon be invited to identify with Benoît as he looks at and judges his surroundings, the opening sets up a distance that allows an ongoing awareness that the spectator is also looking at Benoît.

---

and more important characters but who, in a sense, manipulates and directs them" (⇨Bonneville, *Le cinéma québécois*, 457). Yet, the film stresses Fernand's self-effacement rather than his directorial skills.

[23] Another possible 'father'-figure is the priest, whose authority is, however, undercut when Benoît finds him secretly drinking the communion wine.

[24] Leduc, "La Québécitude, maladie à virus?" 13.

The funeral sequence, in which we are first introduced to Bênoit, is of crucial importance because it places the entire opening under the sign of death and links the intimations of mortality to the boy's sexual awakening. Benoît's observation of the corpse and its treatment anticipates his confrontation with another dead body at the end of the film. Death emerges as a natural event which makes Benoît aware of his own mortality and which is incorporated into communal life through religious and social rituals. Although these rituals grow out of the closeness to nature of traditional peasant culture, the film also links death to the effects of asbestosis, and thus to the exploitation of workers like Jos and to the death-in-life existence which is all that Québec apparently has to offer Benoît.

The natural and cultural meanings of death become entwined with a similar complexity of meanings surrounding sexuality. Although their love-making among the animals in the barn offers a brief physical relief to Jos and his wife, Benoît's emergence from adolescence into adulthood is troubled by the association in his mind of sexuality with death, an association which also has both a natural and a cultural basis. It first appears when he watches Antoine and Fernand strip the dead man's body: the formal suit is merely a façade which is removed to reveal the naked body beneath. This glimpse of the flesh hidden under a veneer of social decorum evokes Benoît's fascination with, and fear of, the sexuality and mortality of the human body.

Bênoit's observation of the activities in Antoine's store, during the central section of the film, also reveals the attraction and the constraints of a culture based on tradition. The store functions as a kind of community centre, occupying a space mid-way between the tavern and the church – at least metaphorically, since the film remains vague about the geographical layout of the village. The high-point of Christmas Eve is the annual unveiling of the manger-scene in the store window, and this is followed by an impromptu celebration of the engagement of a young couple. Yet there are hints that something is wrong with this traditional way of life: the Jesus figure is broken, the curtain collapses during the unveiling, and a large Father Christmas looms incongruously over the manger. The lack of privacy in a small community is also suggested by the way in which the celebration develops from a young woman's whispered request for a bridal veil, although this may be the couple's modest way of announcing their engagement.

Our increasing involvement with Benoît's perspective is closely related to his sexual awakening. When he sees Carmen trying on a bridal veil which she has been sent to fetch from the attic, the erotic chase that follows takes place among the coffins used in the undertaking business. A little later, he spies on Alexandrine, the glamorous wife of the notary, as she tries on her new girdle, her nudity a contrast to, but an uneasy reminder of, that of the dead man at the funeral reception.

The spectator is implicated in this act of voyeurism, which is shared by Maurice, another boy who works in the store. Their erotic pleasure seems to spill over into the one act of political defiance in the film. As the mine owner drives his sleigh through the village, solemnly throwing trinkets to the children of the workers he exploits every other day of the year, Benoît and Maurice pelt his horse with snowballs, causing it to bolt and the owner to beat an ignominious retreat. While the people seem to enjoy this spectacle, they fearfully close their doors to avoid being associated with the perpetrators. Only Carmen looks directly at them and smiles her approval. Since she has just been shocked by Benoît's sexual attentions and disgusted when she finds the two youths spying on Alexandrine, Carmen's smile seems to imply the possibility of a new sexual and political freedom.

But the snowball attack remains an isolated incident. The warmth of communal life in the store seems to depend on an acceptance of existing social conditions. That the narrative hardly progresses during these sequences accentuates the sense of inertia, while annoying critics who nevertheless accused the film of viewing the past nostalgically.

Jutra does, however, link these episodic sequences through a running gag that also highlights the impact of inertia and conditioned responses. It involves a keg of nails which Cécile asks Fernand to move because it has been left in the way at the foot of the stairs. Fernand in turn asks Benoît to move it, but he is unable to lift it because his arm is in a cast (the origin of which is never explained but implies the impotence of the adolescent male), and the keg repeatedly gets in the way of staff and customers. Eventually, Maurice picks up the keg just as Alexandrine makes her dramatic entrance, silhouetted in the doorway and accompanied by the noise of an explosion from the mine. Maurice is so stunned by this sight that he steps over the place where the keg has been standing as if it were still there. After carrying the keg to the attic, he puts it down to spy on Alexandrine, and Carmen trips over it and is sent sprawling when she bursts in on the voyeurs.

The gags involving the keg help to maintain a tone of ironic detachment from the happenings in the store. But there are now also an increasing number of shots of Benoît watching and judging the behaviour of his elders. Our involvement with Benoît's look reaches an even higher degree of intensity when he and Antoine arrive at the Poulin house to collect the son's body. This is the first time that Benoît has accompanied his uncle on such an errand, and his eyes are drawn irresistibly, as represented by another zoom shot, to the half-open door of the dead boy's room. However, his anxiety is most vividly conveyed by his revulsion at the sight of Antoine eating the food which the grieving mother has provided.

As Bruce Elder points out, the key shot in this sequence is "from the boy's point of view" and shows "his perception of Antoine as disgustingly piggish."[25] The (appropriate) use of the term "piggish" to describe how this shot presents Antoine's gluttony links Benoît's experience to Carmen's denunciation of the boys as "pigs" when she finds them spying on Alexandrine. However, since the "piggish" effect is created through the use of a fish-eye lens which distorts Antoine's appearance, there is clearly a process of 'double vision' involved here. When viewed 'normally,' Antoine's behaviour does not seem so inappropriate. He hugs Mme Poulin when he arrives and tells her that he has tried to contact her husband. Her provision of food and his acceptance of it, after a long and cold journey, are seen as expected behaviour in a traditional peasant culture in which mourning for the dead does not exclude a practical concern with the needs of the living. If this is the case, the distortion reflects Benoît's alienation from this culture as he grapples with his own fears and desires.

Benoît is similarly disgusted when, on returning to the store, he finds Fernand and Cécile together in the bedroom. Under the pressure of fatigue, drink, and the packed events of the day, Benoît falls asleep on a counter in the store and has a dream that derives from the powerful association of sexuality and death that has built up during the day. The visualization of this dream, which has been prepared for by the subjectivity of the distorted shot of Antoine eating, is the climax of the process by which the spectator is brought to share in Benoît's acts of spectatorship. In the dream, Benoît first sees himself, dressed in the costume he wore when assisting at mass, lying in a field with his hand on his crotch, echoing the position of the dead youth being placed in the coffin. He gets up, and there is a dissolve to a close-up of hands removing the suit from a body in a coffin, as in the film's second sequence, but the dream substitutes Alexandrine's body for that of the old man. She then rises from the dead and bounces in her girdle in front of an ecstatic Benoît.

---

[25] Elder, "Claude Jutra's *Mon oncle Antoine*," 197.

The dream is cut short when Fernand reaches into the frame to shake Benoît and draw him back into the real world to act as a guide in an attempt to retrieve the corpse. When they arrive at the Poulin house, having failed to find the coffin, the film ends with an effect that both underlines our complicity with Benoît's look and invites us to consider the implications of what he sees. After a long shot of Benoît following Fernand towards the house, there is a cut to a shot in which the camera, apparently hand-held, moves unsteadily forward. The instability of the moving camera and the sound of drumbeats on the soundtrack evoke the pressures weighing on Benoît, whose point of view the shot clearly represents, as he approaches the front window of the house. Three shots from inside, showing Benoît peering out the window, are now intercut with two shots of what he sees: the Poulin family gathered around the open coffin. The final shot of Benoît's face at the window is frozen, forming a background for the unrolling of the credits.[26]

The freeze-frame ending, like the famous freeze-frame on Antoine's face as he turns back from the sea at the end of François Truffaut's *Les 400 coups* (1959), functions as a challenge to the spectator to respond to the questions which have troubled the adolescent throughout the film. In both cases, the effect of the final image is difficult to decipher because of the virtual silence of the protagonist during the last part of the film. Benoît has not been granted the power of language to articulate his concerns, and these have emerged mainly through his observation of his community and our observation of his behaviour. What is read into the final image will thus be largely a projection of the spectator's response to the entire film.

One spectator on whom the final image had a powerful impact is Margaret Atwood, who used it as evidence for a sweeping claim about Canadian culture: "if the central European experience is sex and the central mystery 'what happens in the bedroom', and if the central American experience is killing and the central mystery is 'what goes on in the forest' (or

---

[26] A French critic described a version of the film which apparently included shots of Jos finding the coffin on his return from the logging camp and, mistaking it for a box like the one which fell from a sleigh just before his departure, taking it home to his family as a gift (*Le Devoir*, 10 février 1973). However, assuming that this grotesque image was not simply a product of the critic's imagination, the decision to completely eliminate the discovery of the body, and leave it to the spectator's imagination, reveals how far the plot has developed since its opening in which Jos's experiences introduced us to the world of the film. While we do see Jos make his decision to return home for Christmas, abandoning his job once again, and travelling home by train, the omission of a key event in the plot confirms that our involvement in the film is now completely bound up with Benoît.

in the slum streets), surely the central Canadian experience is death and
the central mystery is 'what goes on in the coffin'." From this perspective,
Atwood argues, the ending of the film implies that "the knowledge that is
important" in Canada is "not your first woman or your first murder but
your first dead person."[27]

Atwood suggests that the film's depiction of Benoît's initiation into
adulthood is an archetypal representation of a biological process shaped by
broad cultural forces. The ending can sustain this kind of reading, although
this is not really Benoît's "first dead person" and Atwood does not point out
that the film itself gives Benoît's vision of the mourning family overtones of
sexual voyeurism. Intimations of the Freudian 'primal scene' must remain
highly ambiguous, given the film's silence about Benoît's parents, but the
question of 'what happens in the bedroom' has just been raised by his intrusion on Fernand and Cécile; and its effect, heightened by Benoît's dream,
hovers over the final sequence.

The camera (Benoît, the spectator) is drawn irresistibly towards the window, evoking the mixture of fear and fascination with which Benoît has approached both death and sex throughout the film, and the look frozen in the
final shot may not be entirely innocent of erotic desire. In the previous shot,
the camera has moved across the faces of the family group and come to rest
on the daughter who showed an interest in Benoît on his earlier visit. While
the previous shots of Benoît at the window have placed him in the centre
and looking straight forward, his face has moved off-centre in the final shot,
and the direction of his eyes suggests that he may be looking at the young
woman. The ending thus echoes the tension in the dream sequence in which
Benoît, who identifies himself with the dead Poulin son, is drawn back to life
by Alexandrine's erotic attractions; and the freeze-frame may be equivalent
to the hand of Fernand (played by Jutra himself) waking up Benoît (the
spectator).

Atwood's reading also fails to mention the specific cultural associations
of the 'dead body' which Benoît witnesses. In effect, he is confronted with an
anti-nativity scene, with the son, crammed into a coffin that is too small for
his body, equivalent to the broken Jesus in the display in the store window.
This blatant allusion to an image central to Québec's Catholic tradition
allows the ending to be read as a cultural and not just a personal revelation:
"Benoît sees with horror what Québec glimpsed when it allowed itself to

---

[27] ⇨Margaret Atwood, *Survival*, 222–23.

Metaphone

look into the depths of its own experience: the spectre of its own 'disappearance', of its death [...] Québec, hallucinated, thus sees its own possible
death."[28] Whether this leads to the "revolutionary" implications which Elder
attributes to the ending is questionable, but a full assessment of the film's
possible cultural meanings requires that we attend to the effects of its historical setting.

Questions of history

When Jean Leduc attacked *Mon oncle Antoine* for its alleged formal weaknesses, he also condemned what he called its "folklore" image of Québec's
past and attributed its popularity to the effects of a viral infection called
"Québécitude."[29] Jutra responded by arguing that the only way to escape
from "folklore" in contemporary Québec was to make films like those produced by Cinépix – sex comedies and other genre films made with the international market in mind. He insisted that he had simply remained faithful to
his own "sociological and cultural reality."[30]

In returning to Québec's recent past, Jutra felt that he was in fact responding to current events, claiming that, like other members of his generation, he was playing "the role of intermediary between yesterday and tomor-
row."[31] The need for such an "intermediary" implied that Québec had lost
touch with its past and was thus vulnerable to the homogenizing influence
of multinational capitalism. Jutra saw his film as working against the forces
that were reducing Québec culture to the status of "folklore."[32]

There was some uncertainty, however, about exactly which past the film
depicts. A caption at the beginning identifies the period as "not so long ago,"
but this is a rather imprecise way to identify the time-period.[33] The name of

---

[28] ⇨Heinz Weinmann, *Cinéma de l'imaginaire québécois*, 88.

[29] Leduc, "La Québécitude, maladie à virus?" 13.

[30] ⇨Bonneville, *Le cinéma québécois*, 455.

[31] *Le Devoir* (6 juin 1970).

[32] Probably some spectators did experience the film in the "nostalgic" manner suggested by Léo Bonneville, when he attributed its "charm" to an "authenticity" which he
defined not in terms of historical accuracy but of likeness to the traditional image of
Québec life presented in the paintings of Cornelius Krieghoff and Clarence Gagnon
("Hommage à Claude Jutra," *Séquences* 131 [octobre 1987]: 14). As my analysis of the
film's structure will have suggested, however, this kind of reading ignores those elements
which work against the comfortable warmth expected of a nostalgia film.

[33] Weinberg ("Reflections on the Current Scene," 33) ignored the caption completely

Maurice Duplessis, glimpsed among the graffiti in the tavern washroom, would suggest that the film is set some time during his long tenure as Premier: that is, between 1936 and 1959 (unless we assume that these graffiti are themselves relics of the past). In an interview, Jutra noted that the action is set in the 1940s and pointed to the political significance of this period in "the asbestos country, one of the first hotbeds of political agitation and labour unrest" in the early stages of the Quiet Revolution.[34]

The question remains as to why Jutra could be so precise in this interview and yet choose to be so vague in the opening caption. In order to answer this question, we need to examine the film in relation to the two key questions which any historical fiction provokes. What kinds of 'signs of the past' does the film deploy? What relationship between past and present does it imply?

One familiar approach to the historical film, adopted by most classical Hollywood films set in the past, is to take advantage of the controlled environment of the studio to construct a replica, mainly through sets and costumes, of what the past is assumed to have looked like. With the emergence of more 'realist' styles of filmmaking in the wake of Italian neorealism, however, such versions of the past came to seem artificial. In order to make the past seem more immediate, many filmmakers (notably in Europe) used actual locations in their historical films, either making use of historical sites preserved under museum conditions or allocating a portion of the budget to remove signs of the present from the view of the camera.

In *Mon oncle Antoine*, the signs of the past are sufficient to place the action, for those familiar with Québec history, at a specific, significant juncture in the recent past; but they are relatively sparse, so that, even for spectators aware of that past, the experience of viewing the film involves a constant oscillation between impressions of past and present. There is a persistent tension between the historical fiction and an awareness that the film was filmed on location, testifying to the 'present' existence of what the camera shows and providing the basis for 'documentary' readings of the film.

In the opening credits-sequence, after a distant shot of people milling around on a school playing-field, the camera slowly pans across a misty

---

and treated the film as a virtual "documentary" on what he called present-day "French-Canadian (Québec) provincial life." ⇨Weinmann (*Cinéma de l'imaginaire québécois*, 73) took the caption literally and confidently situated the film's action in the recent past, during the "process of desacralization" which took place "at the end of the Sixties."

[34] *Le Devoir* (10 février 1973).

landscape, the green trees giving way to what appears to be a snow-covered hill. The idyllic effect is reinforced by the background music, which features a female voice humming to a guitar accompaniment. However, this initial impression is undercut when we see dust being spewed out on top of the hill and realize that it is a mound of waste from a mine, the product not of nature but of industry. The caption, which is superimposed on this shot, reveals that this is "the asbestos country" and that these images belong to the recent past.

But do we believe what we see or what we read? The uncertain temporality indicated by the caption struggles against an awareness that the school, the landscape, and the mine can only have been filmed in the present. While such a tension is endemic to all historical films, it becomes a structuring principle in *Mon oncle Antoine*. The blurring of past and present is perhaps most evident in the use of the inhabitants of the region in a number of sequences. As they stand outside the store, waiting for the unveiling of the manger-scene in the window, the eager spectators do not wear 'costumes' referring to a specific past but what appear to be their everyday clothes. There are no obvious anachronisms, but also very little attempt to historicize the image. It seems to be timeless, even as it testifies to the myths and rituals that shaped a particular period in Québec history.

Some of the implications of the fluid treatment of time in *Mon oncle Antoine* are caught in Martin Knelman's account of the film. Knelman correctly identifies the period as "the late forties," just before "the so-called Quiet Revolution." But he also notes that "the persuasively detailed milieu feels much more than thirty years in the past: the way of life it represents hardly seems to belong to the twentieth century." The film thus reaches back beyond the 1940s to a more remote past; but Knelman also argues that it looks forward to "the explosive public debates of the sixties" by catching "the way that grievances, not yet openly articulated, were expressed in private grumbling."[35]

What this suggests is that the film is both an accurate depiction of a period when resentments were actually confined to "private grumbling" and a representation of cultural forces in Québec which still have a powerful resonance in the present. From this perspective, the film's mixture of tenses invites the people of Québec "to assume our past, in order to better understand our present, the only guarantee of a possible future."[36]

---

[35] ⇨Knelman, *This Is Where We Came In*, 47–48.

[36] Fontaine, "Un moment de notre passé," 4–5.

Mon oncle Antoine thus develops a fluid and dreamlike time-scheme that allows it to function as an example of Noguez's "cinema of fable." The meaning of Jutra's fable, however, will depend on how the spectator reads the implied relationship between past and present. Jutra produced his own optimistic reading of the film by insisting on the difference between then and now, claiming that a new "cultural awareness" had eliminated the forces blocking Benoît's development.[37] (However, some of the actors in the film reportedly did not share this view and found that "this reality which is set in the past is not as old as all that and is still very much with us."[38])

In responding to an interviewer who thought that "at first sight [...] the story could take place today," Jutra could only define the signs of the past negatively through the absence of cars and television.[39] These absences point to the material changes in Québec society which accompanied and accelerated the Quiet Revolution. A 'nostalgic' reading of *Mon oncle Antoine* might blame the spread of television for the absence in the present of the communal life centred on Antoine's store, but the narrative certainly also demonstrates the hardships caused by the lack of modern communications and technology.[40]

If Jos's problems at the mine suggest that modern production methods do not necessarily entail a break with the oppressive ideological structures of the past, the depiction of the store seems to offer a more nostalgic view of the past. It belongs to a time preceding the coming of modern consumer society to Québec, although a Coca Cola sign is visible in several long shots of the main street. Jutra pointed out that such stores had been replaced by supermarkets, and he felt lucky to have found "a real general store of the period, perfectly preserved, which belonged to two old women."[41] As we have seen, the store is as much a community centre as a place of business and, unlike the mine, it is clearly not a capitalist enterprise. Yet, if the introduction of modern industrial relations hardly seems a blessing, the archaic

---

[37] *Le Devoir* (10 février 1973).

[38] *Le Devoir* (6 juin 1970).

[39] *Le Devoir* (10 février 1973).

[40] The absence of cars, and the corresponding presence of horse-drawn vehicles, creates the impression of a pre-industrial society which, as Knelman points out, seems to date back well beyond the 1940s. Yet the first sequence after the opening credits does feature two trucks operating in the wasteland surrounding the mine. These battered and broken-down vehicles seem to belong to the past but could conceivably be seen as relics of the 1940s still, more or less, functioning in the present.

[41] *Le Devoir* (10 février 1973).

past is by no means idealized, and Jutra claimed that industrial and cultural development had brought about improvements, so that most of the abuses associated with the mine no longer existed in the present.

It is certainly true that the film itself does not simply endorse such a 'progressive' view. The need for a political reading is to some extent masked by the focus on Benoît's passage from adolescence to adulthood, a psychological process that seems to record a 'universal' human experience. Yet the film's mode is not that of psychological realism, and the specific forms in which this experience manifests itself are clearly related to the inadequacies of Benoît's cultural context. Most critics were, in fact, prepared to see Benoît's story as emblematic of certain cultural developments; but there was widespread disagreement about the film's cultural implications.

The debate largely centred on the 'ambiguity' of the final freeze-frame, and Jutra seems to have been aware of the 'double vision' built into this image. In one interview, he argued that, "in the context of the period," Benoît's future seems "hopeless" because there is "no opening available to him."[42] However, as we have seen, "the context of the period" is very unstable in the film, and Jutra was also able to envisage Benoît's future as one in which he will be able to "exorcise" his past and "learn to live [...] collectively."[43]

The film thus questions the myth of the Quiet Revolution. If there is more of the past in the present than the myth acknowledges, the myth is itself an expression of utopian hope for the future which still allows for the possibility of change. The movement from the "not so long ago" of the opening caption to the freeze-frame of Benoît's face at the window suggests that the past lives on in the present, despite obvious changes and differences, and that the film functions as a documentary/fantasy about the past/present. As a 'fable,' *Mon oncle Antoine* invites the spectator to adopt both perspectives and to be prepared to move between them. Past and present, the real and the possible, "earthy realism" and "theatre of the absurd" (Leduc), *Silent Night* and *Mon oncle Antoine*, are equally activated and come into a critical relationship in the experience of watching the film.

ชอ

---

[42] *Le Devoir* (6 juin 1970).

[43] *Le Devoir* (10 février 1973).

Filmography

Features

1963   *A tout prendre* (99 mins., 16mm)
1969   *Wow* (95 mins., 16mm)
1971   *Mon oncle Antoine* (or: *Silent Night*; 104 mins.)
1973   *Kamouraska* (124 mins.; video release 173 mins.)
1975   *Pour le meilleur et pour le pire* (117 mins.)
1980   *Surfacing* (88 mins.)
1981   *By Design* (91 mins.)
1984   *La Dame en couleurs* (111 mins.)

Short films and television work

1948   *Le dément du Lac Jean–Jeunes* (44 mins., 16mm)
1949   *Mouvement perpétuel...* (15 mins., 16mm)
1956   *Chantons maintenant* (29 mins.)
1956   *Jeunesses musicales* (43 mins.)
1956   *Pierrot des bois* (9 mins., 16mm)
1956   *Rondo de Mozart* (3 mins.)
1957   *A Chairy Tale/Il etait une chaise* (with Norman McLaren; 10 mins.)
1958   *Les Mains nettes* (73 mins., 16mm/TV)
1959   *Anna la bonne* (10 mins.)
1959   *Félix Leclerc troubadour* (27 mins.)
1959   *Fred Barry comédien* (21 mins., 16mm/TV)
1961   *La Lutte* (with Michel Brault, Marcel Carrière and Claude Fournier; 28 mins., 16mm)
1961   *Le Niger, jeune république* (58 mins., 16mm/TV)
1962   *Les Enfants du silence* (with Michel Brault; 24 mins.)
1962   *Québec USA ou l'invasion pacifique* (with Michel Brault; 28 mins., 16mm)
1963   *Petit discours de la méthode* (with Pierre Patry; 27 mins., 16mm/TV)
1964   *Ciné-boum* (with Robert Russell; 54 mins., 16mm/TV)
1966   *Comment savoir...* (71 mins., 16mm)
1966   *Rouli-roulant* (15 mins., 16mm)
1969   *Au cœur de la ville* (4 mins.)
1970   *Marie-Christine* (10 mins.)
1976   *Ada* (58 mins., 16mm/TV)
1976   *Dreamspeaker* (75 mins., 16mm/TV)
1976   *Québec fête, juin '75* (with Jean–Claude Labrecque; 65 mins., 16mm)
1977   *Arts Cuba* (58 mins., 16mm/TV)
1978   *The Patriarch* 1 & 2 (episodes of *The Beachcombers*; 51 mins., video/TV)
1978   *Seer Was Here* (57 mins., 16mm/TV)
1979   *The Wordsmith* (72 mins., 16mm/TV)
1985   *My Father, My Rival* (50 mins., 16mm/TV)

Bibliography

Screenplay

Jutra, Claude, & Clément Perron. *Mon oncle Antoine*. Montréal: Art Global, 1979.

Perron, Clément. *Mon oncle Antoine*, tr. Wayne Grady, intro. Clément Perron, in ⇨Douglas Bowie & Tom Shoebridge, ed. *Best Canadian Screenplays*, 83–146.

Books and special journal issues

Cinémathèque québécoise. *Retrospective Jutra*, intro. Jean Chabot. Montréal: Cinémathèque québécoise, Musée du cinéma, 1973; 27pp. Survey by Chabot to 1973; extracts from interviews and articles.

Conseil québécois pour la diffusion du cinéma. *Claude Jutra*, intro. Jean Chabot. Cinéastes du Québec 4. Montréal: Conseil québécois pour la diffusion du cinéma, 1970. The introduction, a survey, is followed by excerpts from articles, an interview (9–18), and a filmography (19–26).

Jutras, Pierre, ed. *Claude Jutra*. Montréal: Cinémathèque québécoise, 1987. Reprints obituary memoirs from *Copie Zéro* 33 (septembre 1987): 4–35; of particular note are: filmography (4–14); Pierre Véronneau, "1956–1960: Entre l'espoir et la colère" (17); Fernand Dansereau, "Le grand savoir de Jutra" (18); Jean Cousineau, "Musique pour Jutra" (28); and Lorraine Du Hamel, "Claude nous devançait" (30).

Leach, Jim. *Claude Jutra, Filmmaker: Film in the National Context(s)*. Montréal: McGill–Queen's UP, 1999. Critical study of Jutra's feature films; filmography; bibliography.

Interviews

⇨Bonneville, Léo, ed. *Le cinéma québécois par ceux qui le font*, 440–66.

Camerlain, Jacques. "Entretien avec Claude Jutra," *Séquences* 67 (décembre 1971): 4–14.

Cox, Kirwan. "*Kamouraska*: Interview with Claude Jutra," *Cinema Canada* 7 (April–May 1973): 47–50.

Delahaye, Michel. "Le nouvel âge: Entretien avec Claude Jutra," *Cahiers du cinéma* 200–201 (avril–mai 1968): 109–13.

Evanchuk, P.M. "Claude Jutra: Filmmaker," *Motion* (January–February 1974): 32–34.

——. "Claude Jutra," *Motion* (March–May 1974): 17–18.

Freeman, Brian. "Parlez-vous CBC? Mais oui!," *Maclean's* 91.28 (November 1978): C16–D16.

⇨Hofsess, John. *Inner Views*, 39–52.

Kelman, Paul. "Jutra on the Tube," *Cinema Canada* 53 (March 1979): 21–24.

Koller, George Csaba, & Peter Wronski. "Jutra in Two Takes," *Cinema Canada* 23 (November 1975): 30–34.

Langlois, Gérard. "Une exploration dans une morale pathologique," *Cinéma 73* 172 (janvier 1973): 64–68.

Tadros, Jean-Pierre. "Claude Jutra," *Le Devoir* (21 mars 1970).

——. "A la découverte de Claude Jutra, acteur," *Le Devoir* (20 novembre 1971).

——. "Une Espèce de joie dans la création: Une interview avec Claude Jutra," *Cinéma Québec* 2.6–7 (mars–avril 1973): 15–19.

Articles, essays and sections in books

Anon. "Les Honneurs siéent bien à Claude Jutra," *Séquences* 121 (juillet 1985): 21.

Beaulieu, Janick. " ' À tout prendre': Les films de Claude Jutra sont là pour qu'on en garde mémoire," *Séquences* 131 (octobre 1987): 19–23.

Bonneville, Léo. "Le meilleur film québécois," *Séquences* 100 (avril 1980): 6–8.

——. "Pierre Lamy parle de Claude Jutra," *Séquences* 131 (octobre 1987): 15–18.

Brault, Michel. "Claude Jutra" (funeral oration), *Séquences* 131 (octobre 1987): 24.

Charney, Ann. "What's the Matter With Claude?," *Saturday Night* 103.5 (May 1988): 40–47.

Chase, Donald. "Eyes of the North," *Film Comment* 35.3 (May–June 1999): 76–78.

Cinema Canada. "Claude Jutra: 1930–1987," *Cinema Canada* 142 (June 1987): 28–29. Filmography and extracts from Jutra's writings.

Goyette, Louis. "Jutra's English Films in Focus," *Cinema Canada* 142 (June 1987): 25–27.

Hofsess, John. "The Emergence of Claude Jutra," *Maclean's* 86.8 (August 1973): 42–43, 66, 68, 70–71.

Knelman, Martin. "Claude Jutra in Exile," *Saturday Night* 92.2 (March 1977): 40–44, 49–51; repr. (with prefatory note) in ⇨Douglas Fetherling, ed., *Documents in Canadian Film*, 215–29.

——. ⇨*This Is Where We Came In*, esp. 47–63.

Lockerbie, Ian. "Regarder la mort en face," *Ciné-Bulles* 15.2 (Summer 1996): 46–49.

⇨Prédal, René. *Jeune cinéma canadien*, esp. 57–64.

Sheppard, Gordon, & Bernard Dansereau. "Anecdotes et complicités," *Lumières* 2.8 (juillet–août 1987): 8–9.

Socken, Paul G. "*Mon Oncle* Revisited," *Cinema Canada* 49–50 (September–October 1978): 26–27.

Tadros, Jean-Pierre. "Claude Jutra, Clément Perron et Thetford Mines," *Le Devoir* (6 juin 1970).

Viswanathan, Jacqueline. "Approche pédagogique d'un classique du cinéma québécois: *Mon oncle Antoine*," *French Review* 63.5 (April 1990): 849–58.

⇨Weinmann, Heinz. *Cinéma de l'imaginaire québécois*, 67–89.

Reviews

John Hofsess, "The Way Claude Jutra – Film Maker, Artist, Free Man – Sees Québec," *Maclean's* 84.3 (March 1971): 75, 77; Martin Knelman, *Globe & Mail* (25 September 1971); Ronald Blumer, *Take One* 3.1 (September–October 1971): 25; Dane Lanken, *Gazette* (Montreal; 19 November 1971); Jean-Pierre Tadros, *Le Devoir* (20 novembre 1971); Janick Beaulieu, *Séquences* 67 (décembre 1971): 14–18; Robert Fulford [as Marshall Delaney], "Coming of Age in Québec: Jutra Tells How It Was," *Saturday Night* 87.1 (January 1972): 41; repr. in ⇨Fulford, *Marshall Delaney at the Movies*, 52–53; Jean Leduc, "Libre opinion: La Québécitude, maladie à virus?," *Cinéma Québec* 1.8 (mars–avril 1972): 13; Penelope Gilliatt, "The Current Cinema: Story of a Man Who Is a Foreign Body in His Life," *New Yorker* 48.9 (22 April 1972): 125–27; David Beard, "*Mon oncle Antoine*: 'Silent Night'," *Canadian Forum* 52.1 (April 1972): 12–13; Herman G. Weinberg, *Take One* 3.3 (April 1972): 32–33; Robert Hatch, *The Nation* 214.18 (1 May 1972): 574; Stanley Kauffmann, *New Republic* 166.21 (20 May 1972): 33–34; Jay Cocks, "End of Innocence," *Time* 99 (Canada; 22 May 1972): 60–61; Henriette Fontaine, "Libre opinion: Un moment de notre passé pour mieux voir notre présent," *Cinéma Québec* 1.10 (juillet–août 1972): 4–5; Dilys Powell, *Sunday Times* (20 August 1972); Anon., "Film de Claude Jutra," *L'Avant-scène du cinéma* 130 (novembre

1972): 57, 59–62; Gerald Pratley, *International Film Guide* (1972): 72; Jacques Grant, *Cinéma 73* 172 (janvier 1973): 116–18; Marcel Martin, *Écran 73* 11 (janvier 1973): 80–81; F. Jeancolas, *Jeune Cinéma* 70 (avril–mai 1973): 13–16; Bruce Elder, *Descant* 6 (Spring 1973): 74–79, repr. in ⇨Feldman & Nelson, ed., *Canadian Film Reader*, 194–99; Richard Combs, *Monthly Film Bulletin* 40.479 (December 1973): 253–54.

◌

FIGURE 3

The Apprenticeship of Duddy Kravitz (Ted Kotcheff, 1974; produced by
John Kemeny) – Zvee Scooler (grandfather); Richard Dreyfuss
(Duddy Kravitz).

3 The Apprenticeship of Duddy Kravitz (Ted Kotcheff, 1974)

Production: produced 1972, released in Montreal and Toronto 12 April 1974. International Cinemedia Center Ltd. (Montreal), with the participation of the Canadian Film Development Corporation. **Director:** Ted Kotcheff. **Executive Producer:** Gerald Schneider. **Producer:** John Kemeny. **Associate Producer:** Don Duprey. **Screenplay:** Mordecai Richler, Lionel Chetwynd. **Cinematography:** Brian West and Miklos Lente. **Editor:** Thom Noble. **Music:** Stanley Myers. **Sound:** Patrick Rousseau. **Colour, 121 mins., 35mm.**

Cast: Richard Dreyfuss (Duddy Kravitz), **Micheline Lanctôt** (Yvette), **Jack Warden** (Max), **Randy Quaid** (Virgil), **Joseph Wiseman** (Uncle Benjy), **Denholm Elliott** (Friar), **Henry Ramer** (Dingleman), **Joe Silver** (Farber), **Zvee Scooler** (grandfather), **Robert Goodier** (Calder), **Alan Rosenthal** (Lennie), **Barrie Baldaro** (Paddy), **Allan Migicovsky** (Irwin), **Barry Pascal** (Bernie Farber), **Susan Friedman** (Linda), **Jacques Durette** (bodyguard), **Jonathan Robinson** (Rabbi), **Edward Resmini** (Bernie Altman), **Vincent Cole** (Moe), **Henry Gamer** (lawyer), **Lou Levitt** (Rubin), **Sonny Oppenheim** (Cohen), **Lionel Schwartz** (Arnie), **Mickey Eichen** (Cuckoo), **Robert DesRhes** (Laplante), **Judith Gault** (tarty woman), **Norman Taviss** (grandfather Farber).

Synopsis: In Montreal in 1948, nineteen-year-old Duddy Kravitz skips out of his military cadet parade and goes to Wilensky's Café, where he meets his father, Max. Max is singing the praises of Jerry Dingleman, the local "Boy Wonder" who escaped Montreal's Jewish ghetto and became rich. Duddy listens, and decides to become a somebody like Jerry. Shortly after, Duddy's grandfather tells him that "a man without land is nobody." Working at his Uncle Benjy's garment factory and then at an exclusive summer resort, Duddy is determined to buy some land. At the resort, he falls in love with Yvette, a French-Canadian. Visiting a nearby lake with her, he resolves to buy it and asks for her help. In a restless search to raise money, Duddy establishes a film production company, Dudley Kane Enterprises, and enlists a drunken English filmmaker, Peter John Friar, to make bar-mitzvah movies. His film business is soon struggling, so Duddy agrees to deliver a suitcase to New York for Dingleman. On the train there, he meets Virgil, a young epileptic who has ten pinball machines, which Duddy agrees to buy. On his return, Duddy, learning of his brother Lenny's involvement in an abortion scandal which threatens to get him expelled from medical school, intercedes with the girl's rich father. Virgil arrives; together they take the pinball machines into Québec's resort country to peddle them to local businessmen. Yvette is meanwhile having second thoughts about Duddy's financial dealings. When Virgil has an accident while driving for Duddy, Yvette leaves him. Alone and now desperate to buy the land that will make him a 'somebody,' Duddy secures a loan from his father, steals a cheque from Virgil's suitcase, and forges his signature, thus getting his deed to the property. Celebrating on the lakeshore with his father, Duddy rebuffs a partnership offer by Jerry Dingleman. His grandfather, who has since spoken to Yvette, expresses his disappointment in his grandson. Yvette, now tending to the paralyzed Virgil, tells Duddy she never wants to see him again. Back at Wilensky's, Duddy is finally given credit at the cafe and walks out on to the street alone while his father speaks glowingly of his son's success.

The Apprenticeship of Duddy Kravitz

Or, the anxiety of influence

——————————————— ૭૦

Tom McSorley

> To create a Canadian film industry, we first have to create Canada.[1]
>
> Well, you can make it the way you want if you make it with an American company. That's the advantage. You don't get tangled in all the nationalist roles.[2]
>
> Canadian culture contains so many stories of failure that it's pleasant to report on *Duddy Kravitz* as a success.[3]

The winner

I T COULDN'T LOSE. Adapted from Mordecai Richler's popular and critically acclaimed 1959 novel of the same name, *The Apprenticeship of Duddy Kravitz* had everything going for it. The screenplay was by Richler himself, it was shot on location near the novel's setting and Richler's boyhood home on St. Urbain Street in Montreal, it featured young and impressive American movie stars Richard Dreyfuss and Randy Quaid, it had a handsome budget by Canadian standards, and it was directed by an experienced filmmaker who was also a friend of Richler, Ted Kotcheff. The film was given a wide release in Canada, was received favourably, and went on to be one of the highest grossing films in Canadian box office history. *Duddy Kravitz* was also bought by Paramount and released in the USA, where it was modestly successful. It captured the 1974 Film of the Year award in Canada, was awarded the Golden Bear at the Berlin Film Festival that same year, and Richler won the Academy Award for best screenplay. After literally decades of struggle, it seemed, the Canadian cinema had finally produced a 'winner.'

---

[1] ⇨John Hofsess, *Inner Views*, 37.

[2] Mordecai Richler, "Mordecai Richler Now and Then," *Cinema Canada* 118 (May 1985): 20.

[3] ⇨Robert Fulford, *Marshall Delaney at the Movies*, 81 (repr. from *Saturday Night*).

Ten years later, in 1984, when the Canadian cinema was given its first 'official' pantheon, *Duddy Kravitz* was identified as the fourth-best Canadian film ever made. Eleven years later in 1995, the Canadian film magazine *Take One* conducted a similar poll and once again *Duddy Kravitz* made the top ten, though in the intervening years it had slipped from fourth to seventh place. More recently, in August 1996, it was one among ten special postage stamps commissioned by the Canadian government to commemorate 100 years of motion pictures in Canada.

Curiously, and in spite of a general increase in scholarly and popular writings on Canadian cinema during this period, there is a surprising lack of critical work, scholarly or otherwise, on *Duddy Kravitz*. For a film apparently so highly regarded that it consistently makes top ten lists even twenty years after its release, this is indeed a conspicuous absence. It also raises several questions: what are the possible reasons for its inclusion and retention on such a list if there is comparatively little abiding interest in the film? Has *Duddy Kravitz* been damned with no praise, or praised merely by virtue of respectful silence? Why this apparent ambivalence about one of Canada's repeatedly acknowledged 'ten best'?

Leaving aside for a moment the dubious and problematical processes of canon formation, it is intriguing to explore further the implications of this absence. To what can it be attributed? Is there unease about the film because of its subject matter, its predominantly American cast, its commercial success? Was too much expected of it by the Canadian film industry in the 1970s? Did we and do we regard the success of *Duddy Kravitz* the film as we do the success of Duddy Kravitz the character: as embarrassingly amoral and venal, as a 'winner' in only the worst possible sense? These questions necessarily inflect any serious analysis of what remains a fascinating film, for *Duddy Kravitz* both embodies and illuminates perhaps *the* archetypal tension in the troubled evolution of Canadian cinema specifically and, by extension, Canadian popular culture generally: our relationship with the USA. For our purposes here, this tension manifests itself at two fundamental levels in Kotcheff's film.

Outside the frame

The first level involves and implicates the troubled and marginalized Canadian film industry itself. It is here that, in cinematic terms, the American influence is monumental, as is the anxiety about it. For most of this century, the very century of cinema, Canada's screens have been occupied almost exclusively by American images. Indeed, the mere idea of a Canadian feature film appearing on American-controlled Canadian cinema screens was, and in large measure remains, unthinkable. One response to this situation, repeated in recent Canadian film history, is to make films deliberately designed to attract American distributors; that is, to make films in Canada in what is euphemistically termed the 'international style.' Such a style, of course, raises important questions for Canadian filmmakers: for whom do we and should we make films? What concessions to international, largely American, markets should we make? In other words, how do we reconcile the need to recoup financial investment with the desire to produce distinctive, indigenously Canadian films? It is a debate as old as filmmaking in Canada, and, perhaps predictably, the release and the grand success of *Duddy Kravitz* ignited it again, largely because of Kotcheff's casting of Americans in the principal roles: Richard Dreyfuss as Duddy, Jack Warden as Duddy's father Max, and Randy Quaid as Virgil. As Gerald Pratley would assert, the film is "one that takes the 'sell out' mentality of so many English-speaking producers to the limit since five of the main roles were played by American actors and the cameraman and the composer were British."[4]

Even Kotcheff himself was implicated in this tangled question of national pedigree as an 'émigré' director who worked in television in the UK before moving to Hollywood to direct films (*North Dallas Forty, Rambo: First Blood*) in the very camp of the enemy. As director of this 'international' version of *Duddy Kravitz*, Kotcheff was, not surprisingly, a subject of considerable criticism by cultural nationalists. For his part, Kotcheff, echoing Richler, dismissed the charges as Canadian parochialism: "I feel very prickly on the situation because people keep saying, 'You're not a Canadian.' I get furious [...] this country has a real identity problem [...] I think there *is* a Canadian quality and that I'm a Canadian and that we have to find out what it is. But we can't just say, 'As soon as you leave this country, you're not a Canadian'."[5] From writer to director to cast, then, *Duddy Kravitz* generated prodigious and various forms of national cultural anxiety.

The second level of this tension is rooted in broader Canadian cultural attitudes which shape how we interpret the ferocious individualism of Duddy Kravitz himself. Rightly or wrongly perceived as more American than Canadian, the drama of triumphant individualism enacted by Duddy can be

---

4 ⇨Gerald Pratley, *Torn Sprockets*, 112.
5 Ted Kotcheff, "Kotcheff and Lanctôt on *Kravitz*," *Cinema Canada* 14 (June–July 1974): 44.

regarded as evidence of the influence of an ideology not entirely foreign, but not entirely our own either. Appropriately enough, and this is the film's chief strength, it is also evident that Duddy's pursuit of success is itself driven by his own anxieties of influence: on the one hand, his myth-making father, who rhapsodizes about those successful men who escaped Montreal's Jewish ghetto through sheer force of will and ruthlessness; on the other, his grandfather (Zvee Scooler), who counsels young Duddy that, in the novel's most famous phrase, "a man without land is nobody." Conflating these two influences in his postwar world of expansion and opportunity, these two generations of immigrants articulating attitudes new and old, Duddy neurotically seeks approval from both.

In one sense, Duddy's personal predicament is not unlike any Canadian film wanting to remain true to its roots while at the same time being recognized by the big shots: not an easy task and not without serious consequences. The influence of the dominant American commercial filmmaking system fixed so firmly in Canada creates industrial and cultural anxieties about what kinds of films to produce here, echoing Duddy's own neurotic, scratching, desperate search for success as it is defined for him by others. In *Duddy Kravitz*, then, we have a remarkable mirror image of the film itself and its protagonist: both can be regarded as successful, but on what and on whose terms? Perhaps *this* can account for the critical ambivalence about an award-winning film that still claims membership in the Canadian canon.

It is important to remember that, upon its commercial release in April 1974, popular critical response to the film was anything but ambivalent. The *Montreal Star*'s Martin Malina enthused: "*The Apprenticeship of Duddy Kravitz* is a marvellously vital movie, wildly funny, brash and bittersweet, full of pungent realism and nostalgia. A first rate comedy."[6] In Toronto, the *Globe & Mail* trumpeted the film as "a first class piece of entertainment" and as "a sturdily built, irresistibly vital movie."[7] George Anthony at the *Toronto Sun* declared that "*Kravitz* is something to celebrate! A touching, memorable film, packed with powerful performances and some splendid emotional twisters."[8] The critic Clyde Gilmour of the *Toronto Star* described it as "a movie that tingles with the honest juices of life" and as "an almost continuously absorbing entertainment, crammed with lively characters and brim-

---

6 Martin Malina, *Montreal Star* (11 April 1974).

7 Betty Lee, "The Screen Enhances *Kravitz* Tale," *Globe & Mail* (13 April 1974).

8 George Anthony, *Toronto Sun* (11 April 1974).

ming with a totally convincing recaptured time-and-place."[9] Marshall Delaney in *Saturday Night* magazine wrote that "*Duddy Kravitz* is probably the best film ever made in English Canada, and it ranks as well with the best of the Québec films of the last few years."[10]

In Canadian cinema magazines, the film was received warmly as well, being even described in one as "the real big winner we were all waiting for."[11] *Cinema Canada* dedicated two reviews to it, and *Take One* was very enthusiastic about its arrival. In the former, Natalie Edwards enthused: "Duddy Kravitz is a winner. And so is the movie";[12] in the latter, Joe Medjuck called it a "dynamite movie," a film "so good you wish it were better."[13] *Motion* magazine brayed that "Like a thunderstorm after a drought, *Duddy Kravitz* has swept into Canadian movie houses," and offered the somewhat hysterical hypothesis, though completely understandable in the context of the passionate desire to champion a truly Canadian film industry, that, "*Kravitz* has almost singlehandedly revived faith in the viability of an indigenously Canadian feature film industry, although the hope had never died."[14] Of course, it did no such thing and, as some have argued, it did much worse: it laid the foundations for more 'international style' films to be produced in Canada.

French-Canadian critics were much more reserved in their response and, revealingly, identified immediately the Americanness of the film's pace and style. *Le Devoir*'s Robert Guy Scully, an admirer of the novel, bemoaned the film's visual banality and its conventional narrative structure.[15] In the Montreal-based cinema magazine *Séquences*, the critic Patrick Schupp, while he admired its energy, found the film to be overdetermined in its characterizations and lacking subtlety.[16]

International response to the film was equally mixed. After its triumph in Berlin, the British critic John Gillett expressed dismay that a major festival prize had been given to Kotcheff's "overheated and facile" film.[17] Derek

---

[9] Clyde Gilmour, "*Duddy Kravitz* Hits The Screen As A Gutsy, Funny Movie," *Toronto Star* (13 April 1974).

[10] ⇨Robert Fulford, *Marshall Delaney at the Movies*, 81.

[11] George Csaba Koller, "Canadian Film News," *Cinema Canada* 14 (June–July 1974): 7.

[12] Natalie Edwards, "Lunch with Randy Quaid," *Cinema Canada* 14 (June–July 1974): 72.

[13] Joe Medjuck, *Take One* 4.3 (May 1974): 31.

[14] James McLarty, "Let's Hear It For Duddy," *Motion* (July–August 1974): 30.

[15] Robert Guy Scully, "Duddy tout en os," *Le Devoir* (20 avril 1974): 15.

[16] Patrick Schupp, *Sequences: Revue de cinema* 77 (juillet 1974): 26.

[17] John Gillett, "Festivals 74," *Sight and Sound* (Autumn 1974): 228.

Elley described *Duddy Kravitz* as "more a film of single performances than a satisfying whole."[18] The French cinema journal *Positif*, however, was impressed, even likening the film to Otto Preminger's best work.[19] In the USA, critical response ranged from modest praise by Pauline Kael, John Simon, and William Avery, to outright contempt by Penelope Gilliatt, who snorted derisively that "The novel is not literature, it's book making, just as the Kotcheff picture of it is not film but a drive-in movie."[20] Unwittingly anticipating the debate which would emerge around Kotcheff's film is this aphoristic and apposite summation: "A Canadian film, with Richard Dreyfuss."[21]

Shortly after the initial and almost unanimously positive responses in English Canada, however, there were vociferous critics of the film's rather obvious un-Canadian attributes. The Canadian Film Institute's *Film Canadiana* 1975 editorial, that year written by Robert Fothergill, noted that "For English Canada the chief satisfaction [of the year] must have been *The Apprenticeship of Duddy Kravitz* – a satisfaction not without alloy as we contemplated the line-up of American stars and the émigré status of director Ted Kotcheff."[22] Len Klady in *Cinema Canada* suggested that the film "looks about as Canadian as a MacDonald's [sic] hamburger or a bottle of Canada Dry."[23] In the same article, critic Gerald Pratley lamented that the film "contains so many American players that most Canadian actors feel betrayed and rejected. It is likely that it will be financially successful, but at what cost to Canadian confidence?"[24] More concise and more devastating was Toronto writer John Hofsess's blunt pronouncement that *Duddy Kravitz* was "the best Canadian film the United States has yet produced."[25] He goes on observe: "Well, obviously one can make American films (in Canada) with American stars and do fair-to-good business: what's so remarkable about that? The fact that it was shot in Montreal does not make it Canadian."[26] Hofsess and others would argue that the film, despite also being financed entirely in

---

[18] Derek Elley, *Films and Filming* 21.6 (March 1975): 34.

[19] Christian Viviani, *Positif* 171–72 (juillet–août 1975): 59.

[20] Penelope Gilliatt, "Duddy-O," *New Yorker* 50.22 (22 July 1974): 65.

[21] "Goings On About Town," *New Yorker* 50.22 (22 July 1974): 13.

[22] Robert Fothergill, *Film Canadiana* 1974–75, 6.

[23] Len Klady, "Canada at Cannes 1974: A Second Look," *Cinema Canada* 15 (August–September 1974): 8.

[24] Gerald Pratley, quoted in "Canadian Film News," by George Csaba Koller, *Cinema Canada* 14 (June–July 1974): 7.

[25] ⇨Hofsess, *Inner Views*, 34.

[26] ⇨Hofsess, *Inner Views*, 35.

Canada, was not an indigenous Canadian product, but rather a film designed and assembled for the 'international' (read: US) market. Contrary to
most in the industry, Hofsess expressed no pride at the film being picked by
Paramount, arguing that "it was hardly any surprise when Paramount ac-
quired US distribution rights since the film could easily have been made by
Paramount to begin with."[27]

In and around its release, then, *Duddy Kravitz* received considerable
attention. Retrospectively, the film has met with ignorance, oblivion, or, in
the case of film historian Peter Morris, haughty dismissal. In 1984, the same
year *Duddy Kravitz* was named one of the Ten Best, Morris remarked that
"the novel's blatant theme seems even more so in the film, and the stiff
characterizations hover always on the edge of caricature. Its pastiche 'Hollywood North' style reflects (perhaps appropriately) Richler's own cultural
disaffection more than the milieu of the characters."[28] Advocates of the
film's 'greatness' are difficult to find, and the current critical consensus is
perhaps best summarized by the Toronto-based critic Geoff Pevere in describing the work of a generation of Canadian 'emigré' directors like Norman Jewison, Arthur Hiller, and Ted Kotcheff. As Pevere notes, "none have
made one [film] that more than a very few would ever call great."[29]

Nevertheless, the film version of Richler's distinctly Montreal tale was
highly regarded when released and was, indeed, thought of by many as
great. More importantly, it soon became the focus of a renewal of the ongoing debate in Canadian cultural history between, as the Canadian cinema
scholar Peter Harcourt identified them, cultural nationalists on the one hand
and continentalists on the other.[30] Who was more Canadian? Those who
wanted to appeal to the American market by choosing American performers, or those who cast only Canadians, in the hope of exposing home-
grown talent on our own cinema screens? In spite of its famous Canadian
literary source, its Canadian financing, and its Canadian box-office success,
was *Duddy Kravitz* actually a betrayal of the Canadian cinema, a colonial
gesture to the acknowledged and unassailable film power to the south? In
the early 1970s, with a nascent English-Canadian feature-film industry
struggling against almost total American domination of Canadian screens,

---

[27] ⇨Hofsess, *Inner Views*, 35.

[28] ⇨Peter Morris, *The Film Companion* (Toronto: Irwin, 1984): 16.

[29] Geoff Pevere, "Ghostbusting: 100 Years of Canadian Cinema, or Why My Canada
Includes *The Terminator*," *Take One* 5.12 (Summer 1996): 11.

[30] Peter Harcourt, *Movies and Mythologies*, 156.

these were potent, unavoidable questions that are rooted in broader debates about Canadian cultural sovereignty and the very idea of Canada itself. It is hardly surprising that these questions should organize themselves around such a high-profile and admittedly border-blurring production. (Similar debates about the work of David Cronenberg are rehearsed today.) Of course, in reviving the debate about the nature and contours of a truly indigenous cinema, *Duddy Kravitz* is undeniably and quintessentially Canadian. Perhaps it is the unavoidable presence of this intense, internal, insoluble debate that accounts for why so few scholars and critics have returned to examine this picaresque tale of St Urbain Street's *pusherke*, this amoral on-the-make character Duddy Kravitz, whose movie, for a short time, was a hit in his native country.

Inside the frame

With an official budget of $600,000 and a final cost of $910,000, Duddy Kravitz was an expensive Canadian production. In other words, it was a film that needed a strong box office to recover its costs. The controversial decision to cast American stars was based, according to Kotcheff and Richler, not on potential box-office appeal but on hiring the best available talent, irrespective of nationality. As we have seen, this was regarded as an affront to Canadian talent and as yet another submission to the US-controlled distribution system. While such arguments were dismissed by both Kotcheff and Richler as parochial ("tangled in all the nationalist roles"), the casting of *Duddy Kravitz* does raise questions about making films in Canada for a perceived 'international market.' It is also a telling manifestation of the powerful influence of American cinema in Canadian consciousness, and a moment that anticipates the notorious Tax Shelter Era films of the late 1970s, which designed their productions with the dubious prospect of appealing to the lucrative 'American market' by casting American actors, disguising Canadian locations, and imitating American film genres. While it is excessive to hold *Duddy Kravitz* responsible for the execrable films of the Tax Shelter Era, it is not unfair to regard it as a highly successful and therefore supremely seductive execution of that very production philosophy.

Beyond these specific historical circumstances and the gnarled cultural politics of its production, of course, there is the film itself. Set in the Jewish quarter of Montreal in 1948, it is an urgent, busy portrait of an ambitious character who is, as Dreyfuss described him, "a guy without an operating manual."[31] Chronicling Duddy's pursuit of land and status from his beginnings as a waiter to his abbreviated career as a film producer, it is a well-wrought Hollywood-style commercial realist film, briskly paced and crisply edited. As Kotcheff himself noted of the film's rhythm, "I want the film to have that kind of very staccato, partly frenetic, partly febrile texture to it so that somehow it mirrors the pace with which Duddy lives his life, the kind of jagged mosaic of the way he exists."[32] As a portrait of the Montreal Jewish community of the late 1940s, *Duddy Kravitz* is certainly energetic and effective, as it is in outlining the nature of power in postwar Duplessis-era Québec: industry, banking and high finance largely controlled by American and English-speaking Canadian Protestants, and land by the Catholic church and French-Canadian farmers. It is between these two forces that Duddy, an ambitious and awkward young man from the Jewish ghetto, must navigate his course to acquire land and become a 'somebody.'

In the Canadian cinema, Duddy is not alone. This quest to become a somebody is one undertaken by plenty of Canadian protagonists. In the largely fatalist and downbeat Canadian narrative cinema of the 1960s and 1970s, however, that quest almost always ends in failure. In one of Canadian film criticism's most influential and persistent paradigms, writer Robert Fothergill likened this tendency to concentrate on 'losers' as the cinematic articulation of Canada's inferiority complex, its "younger brother syndrome": a desire to please an older, more competent and able sibling, and an awareness of how impossible such a task is.[33] In cultural, political, and especially cinematic terms, that older brother is the USA. While American cinema celebrates its cultural myths (individualism, manifest destiny, success) with strong and confident protagonists, Canadian cinema offers up again and again anti-heroes who struggle against and fail to overcome their own limitations or the constrictions imposed on them by their society. In one sense, then, Duddy's success is very unusual and is, as Robert Fulford asserts above, something to celebrate; it is also somehow un-Canadian, and as a result the moral and ethical shortcomings of this successful character, this 'winner,' are, as we shall see, duly emphasized in Kotcheff's film. Beyond the level of plot and characterization, there is also the success of

---

[31] Richard Dreyfuss, "I just knew I wanted to be Duddy," *Globe & Mail* (13 April 1974): 17.

[32] Ted Kotcheff, "Kotcheff and Lanctôt on *Kravitz*," 42.

[33] Robert Fothergill, "Coward, Bully or Clown: The Dream-Life of a Younger Brother," in ⇨Feldman & Nelson, ed., *Canadian Film Reader*, 234–50.

Duddy Kravitz the movie, a commercial success which, as we have seen, was also regarded by some as a sign of the film's compromised nationality. Perhaps Richler himself put it best when he observed that "to be a Jew and a Canadian is to emerge from the ghetto twice";[34] to 'Canadian' one could easily add the word 'film.'

Duddy's companion and moral compass on this troubled journey towards success, this emergence from the ghetto, is a French-Canadian woman, Yvette, whom he meets while working at an exclusive Jewish summer resort in Québec's Eastern townships. As Thomas Waugh has pointed out, Duddy and Yvette represent a fascinating though not unique example of the Canadian cinema's 'multi-cultural couple,' in this instance an uneasy intersection of Québec's French-Catholic culture and the minority anglophone and predominantly urban Jewish presence.[35] While their relationship is based on sexual attraction, it is also, especially for Duddy, a convenient business arrangement. Through his partnership with Yvette, Duddy is able to negotiate with the Catholic and, as he discovers, anti-semitic rural Québec farmers to buy their land. Although she agrees to help Duddy realize his dream and endures several indignities of his making, Yvette finally cannot tolerate his exploitative cruelty towards his epileptic employee, Virgil; she leaves him after Virgil is paralyzed in an accident while driving a truck for Duddy's film-exhibition business. As Duddy's chaotic career trajectory can be seen to trace the emerging postwar materialist and capitalist consumer culture in North America, Yvette's embodiment of an older and more humane social order illuminates the personal and political consequences of uncritically embracing this new world. Like the grandfather, to whom she relates Duddy's underhanded dealings later in the film, Yvette is anchored to an ethical tradition which Duddy forsakes in pursuit of materialist gain which he mistakenly holds to be ethical in and of itself.

The role of Yvette is noteworthy for another reason: it is much more prominent in the film than in Richler's novel, and it reveals the fascinating process of adapting this popular novel to the screen. While the expanded role of Yvette in the film may demonstrate the film's concession to commercial cinema's demand for a 'love interest,' or reflect the fact that Micheline

---

[34] Mordecai Richler, in George Woodcock, *Mordecai Richler* (Toronto: McClelland & Stewart, 1971): 58.

[35] Thomas Waugh, "Cultivated Colonies: Notes on Queer Nationhood and the Erotic Image," *Canadian Journal of Film Studies* 2.2–3 (1993): 171.

Lanctôt and Kotcheff were lovers at that time, it is also appropriate and effective. As Kotcheff states,

> so much of the film is also the moral wrestling that goes on between Duddy and Yvette. In the book, you can ignore Yvette. But in the film she is *there*. I thought Yvette's character was much more interesting in the picture. Yvette is sketchily conceived and drawn in the book. Her whole development from a simple backwoods French-Canadian farm girl into a complicated, sophisticated person is one of the strands in the development of the film. The part was a great challenge because Yvette was underwritten – it was really starting from scratch. We had to give her a very definite substance which wasn't in either the book or the script.[36]

Indeed, throughout the production Richler and Kotcheff collaborated, expanding some aspects of the story while reducing others, cutting entire scenes. Among a number of scenes filmed but discarded is one in which Duddy licks the answers from his forearm when his teacher catches him cheating during a high-school exam. Seeing only a blue smear, the teacher says "you'll go far, Kravitz; you'll go far." Kotcheff recalls that

> the only other scene Mordecai regretted being cut was the scene when Duddy reads Uncle Benjy's letter by the lake [...] That was one of the first scenes I cut and the reason I cut it was because in the letter there's an overt statement of the theme. In the letter, Uncle Benjy says, "There are two sides to you Duddy. There's the behemoth – the nasty, opportunistic Duddy Kravitz that I saw – and there's the gentle intelligent boy that your grandfather saw, bless him. But you're becoming a man now and you have to choose which one you're going to be." And I hate those kinds of things in a picture, where you state the theme. To me, the whole theme is implicit in the structure of the film [...] .[37]

Whether the overall adaptation-process of *Duddy Kravitz* can be seen as successful or not (Richler and Kotcheff would collaborate a decade later on the film version of Richler's novel *Joshua Then And Now*, regarded by many as the second part of *Duddy Kravitz*), one aspect of the novel which did benefit enormously from Kotcheff's cinematic re-writing is Duddy's decision to become a filmmaker.

Arguably the most sophisticated and engaging section of the film, and one that reflects upon the complex question of the relationship between the cinema and the society which produces it, is Duddy's brief foray into the film business; and for Duddy, of course, it is *strictly* business. He sees film

---

[36] Kotcheff, "Kotcheff and Lanctôt on *Kravitz*," 42.

[37] Kotcheff, "Kotcheff and Lanctôt on *Kravitz*," 43.

exclusively as a way to make money in order to finance his land purchase, not to deliver cinematic artistry or even works of social or cultural significance. When he hires the once distinguished and now besotted British documentary filmmaker, Peter John Friar, who happens to be visiting Montreal at the request of the National Film Board of Canada, Duddy is interested only in cashing in by making wedding and bar-mitzvah movies. He even ignores Friar's warning about his documented affiliations with the Communist Party, which is no small admission in the late 1940s. Duddy the aspiring capitalist film producer, whose company he calls Dudley Kane Enterprises, sees only money, not manifestos.

As they plan their first and, as it turns out, only bar-mitzvah film, which Duddy finances via the rich and ruthless scrap-dealer Mr Farber, this unlikely producer-and-director team demonstrate hilariously two fundamentally divergent approaches to cinema. While Friar speaks of exploring "racial memory" in the film, Duddy's baldly pragmatic and decidedly empirical aesthetic code insists that any films made by Friar for him must be "in colour and have lots of shots of the family." Seldom have the twin faces of cinema, art and commerce, been juxtaposed with such candid humour than in the screening of Friar's bar-mitzvah movie to the Farber family patriarchs and their rabbi. As Friar's gloriously pretentious film is being screened, mixing images of young Bernie's circumcision with various 'earthy' tribal rites practised around the world in a dizzying montage worthy of a crazed Sergei Eisenstein, Duddy frets at the back of the theatre while Friar smiles knowingly at his work. When the bewildered silence which greets the film's conclusion is broken by a solemn pronouncement by the rabbi (who, shrewdly, has been given a prominent role) that it is "Most edifying, a work of art," everybody is happy: Duddy gets his money from the proud father, Friar is critically vindicated, and the sceptical backer Mr Farber has his son's bar mitzvah on film.

More than a marvellously self-reflexive moment in an otherwise stylistically conventional film, this remarkable sequence also interweaves *Duddy Kravitz*'s larger thematic tensions between materialism and morality with the politics of racial representation and the politics of film production in Canada. Invoking the documentary tradition in Canadian cinema, which includes the sponsored film as well as the NFB variety, Friar's bizarre exploration of 'racial memory' is also an unusual specimen of Canadian multiculturalist philosophy: its agit-prop editing reveals the similarities of Jewish rituals to those found in other parts of the world and, as such, functions as a challenge to narrow orthodox views of race and religion and as a plea for universal humanist values. Not unlike the NFB films under John Grierson, whom Friar may represent in some respects, the bar-mitzvah movie is, for all its formal panache, rooted in ideas of community, social duty and doctrines of improvement. It is a remarkable sequence in *Duddy Kravitz* because it does ventilate what is otherwise tightly controlled, conventional commercial filmmaking. As a commentary on the limited imaginations of those, like Duddy, who make films only to make money, it is a satirical delight; as a wry illustration of the mysterious relationship between spectator and screen, even in the most ludicrous and pedestrian films, it is inspired; as a concrete demonstration that the processes of human interpretation and judgement are unpredictable, it is incisive: significantly, it is this last lesson that quite escapes Duddy, a man obsessed with the judgements of others.

In a lively debate about *Duddy Kravitz* published in the *Canadian Forum* just after the film's successful release, the critics John Hofsess and Robert Fothergill take up the Friar film's challenge and discuss the relationship between representation and interpretation.[38] Was Duddy Kravitz's kind of greed being celebrated by the film and, if so, what would this say about contemporary values, or, more explosively, about contemporary Jewish culture? Was the film, as one critic from the *New York Times* charged,[39] virulently anti-semitic in its representation of Duddy? Using Stanley Kubrick's *A Clockwork Orange* (1971) as an example, they discuss how Duddy's amorality and venality are shaped by his cultural context and whether or not the film celebrates his triumph. While Kotcheff's film certainly lacks the formal rigour of Kubrick's, it does depict Duddy's rather brutish approach to capitalism not as something to be celebrated, but rather as the product in his life of what can be called, to borrow from Harold Bloom, the 'anxiety of influence.'[40]

---

[38] John Hofsess & Robert Fothergill, "The Rich Get Richer: A Dialogue On *Duddy Kravitz*," *Canadian Forum* 54 (October 1974): 32–36.

[39] Don Isaac, "Some Questions About the Depiction of Jews in New Films," *New York Times* (September 8 1974): 13–14. Isaac asserts: "Now that we have *The Apprenticeship of Duddy Kravitz*, we can forget about *The Merchant of Venice*." For a broader discussion of this theme, see Patricia Erens' *The Jew In American Cinema* (Bloomington: Indiana UP, 1984). The fact that Duddy appears in a book about Jews in 'American cinema' should not pass unnoticed.

[40] Harold Bloom, *The Anxiety of Influence: A Theory of Poetry* (New York: Oxford UP, 1973).

Indeed, the strength of Kotcheff's film resides precisely in its sketching of possible contextual explanations for Duddy's amoral, occasionally cruel behaviour. The film plays with our uncertainty about a protagonist who seems to have no code of ethics beyond crude self-interest. Although he is often startlingly ruthless, Duddy is also shown to suffer from the lack of a mother and from his father's emotional distance: he refuses Duddy's gift of a sport shirt, which moves his son to tears, and is constantly warning Duddy not to embarrass him. Moreover, in the early sections of the film, Max Kravitz also loudly professes his pride and his preference for Duddy's brother Lenny, a medical student. For his part, however, Duddy contributes money to the cost of Lenny's attending McGill University, and even intercedes in an abortion scandal on his brother's behalf. Duddy also perceives and articulates the hypocrisies of his own family, sparring verbally with his rich Uncle Benjy and demanding to know why he has become the pariah. Duddy works in Benjy's factory, mocks his old-fashioned tolerance of his employees, and points out that it is easy to be moral when you are affluent and influential in the community; simple moralizing is much tougher at the bottom. From his father to his uncle to his grandfather, then, Duddy is counselled, cajoled, advised, dissuaded, criticized, even dismissed. The influences are as many as they are contradictory. For a young man who wants to succeed, they produce considerable and unremitting anxiety.

On another level, though certainly related to the various pressures applied within his family, Duddy's relationship to elites in both Jewish and gentile Montreal offers a fascinating glimpse of the processes of assimilation, of how individuals can internalize the assumptions and aspirations of others. His desire to join their ranks is simple and evident, but his education on elite power is complex and obscure. As a Jew, he is already excluded from a whole section of elite society in Montreal. Duddy learns this first-hand when he goes to negotiate with the rich WASP patriarch, Mr Calder, with whose daughter Lenny was involved in an abortion scandal. Pleading for his brother not to be expelled from McGill, Duddy shoots pool with the bemused Calder and understands how efficient, corrupt, and exclusive self-interest can be at this rarefied level of the social order. Another lesson in the war of exclusion comes from Mr Farber, the scrap-dealer and film-investor, who tells Duddy that to be a Jewish businessman is to be at war: it's every man for himself. Within the Jewish community there are also class consciousness and elitism, as Duddy learns while working at the resort, encountering Irwin Schubert, who derides Duddy's acquisitive capitalism by sniff-

ing: "it's Jews like Kravitz who cause anti-semitism, you know." Ever observant and a quick study, Duddy, with his approach to capitalism, combines
the ruthless opportunism of Farber with the guile and duplicity of Calder.
Under these influences, not to mention the legendary narrative of Jerry
Dingleman that his father repeats like an incantation, Duddy wishes to be
assimilated into the emergent culture of triumphant individualist capitalism.
He wants to be a winner, or at least be seen to be on the winning side: the
side of the elites he encounters throughout the film.

So, while Max and Duddy Kravitz can take refuge in the master-narra-
tives of individual will and material success (the film opens with Max's
rhapsody about the Boy Wonder, Jerry Dingleman, and closes with a similar
encomium about his Duddy, who we see out on the street alone as we hear
Max's testimonial), Kotcheff's film does illustrate that such attitudes are
fraught with limitations and consequences. The anxiety of influence, for
Duddy, has motivated him to seek redemption before his father, but as a
consequence it has also delivered him as a failure to his beloved grandfather.
Duddy's longing for his deceased mother and his strained relationship with
his Uncle Benjy also complicate the portrait of this morally ambiguous protagonist. The film ultimately suggests that Duddy's capitalist dream of
Kravitzville, if it ever gets built, will be a very lonely place indeed. It also reveals that, if redemption is important, the terms under which it is granted
are a matter of considerable speculation: Who makes the rules of the game?
Who writes the terms of redemption? Who defines winning and losing?

Stubborn paradoxes

Paradoxically, *Duddy Kravitz* seems to be tentatively formulating these probing thematic questions for its audience while simultaneously ingratiating
itself in the finest commercial Hollywood film style. More complicating still
is the fact that it does so while quite self-consciously demonstrating its
awareness, however abbreviated, of how cinematic codes and conventions
can often be profoundly misunderstood, misapplied, and even made to
serve the interests of those it opposes philosophically: the Kravitz–Friar bar-
mitzvah co-production is an acute example of this. The richness of ambiguity does not, therefore, reside only in the protagonist of Kotcheff's film,
but also in the film's very style. Over and above these ambiguities we can
add, as we have seen in the responses to the film by many critics and cultural nationalists, the fiercely contested designation of it as a truly Canadian

film in the first place. In a broader sense, one can ask if our judgements of Duddy can be divorced from our judgements of ourselves and, perhaps, of postwar Canada itself, as we witness our economy, politics and popular culture slowly merge with models formed elsewhere. In terms of the Canadian film industry and the failure of our national governments to protect and nurture it against American domination, the parallels with Duddy are as obvious as they are disquieting.

Formally and thematically, then, is *Duddy Kravitz* finally a film about cultural assimilation, for Duddy, for the Canadian cinema, and for Canada itself? Is to speak about this film to speak also about our own anxieties of influence, our simultaneous attraction and resistance to an American ideology of triumphant individualism and its various dominant and seductive vehicles of popular culture? If it is, can this account for the relative absence of serious critical work on the film? Undeniably but probably unintentionally, Kotcheff's film does open up vast and thorny questions of delineating the anxious Canadian psyche within a pervasive and increasingly invasive American cultural influence. In its casting and its 'international style,' this film also raises complicated and politically charged questions about the shape and destiny of the Canadian film industry; if we extend the inquiry further to embrace John Hofsess's opening aphorism, perhaps even the shape and destiny of Canada as a nation.

As if anticipating these streams of critical response and discourse, when Astral released *The Apprenticeship of Duddy Kravitz* in Canada, it served up an ingenious and memorable advertising tag-line, one that still adorns the video packaging for the film. In a somewhat unsettling claim to audience identification, it proposes cheerfully that, "There's a little bit of Duddy Kravitz in all of us." As the century of cinema closes, the many and accurate resonances of this statement may be more than we would care to admit, given the context and history of our geographical, political and cultural development as a nation with claims to a national cinema. Indeed, the implications of this line address how we imagine ourselves as a society and as a nation, and, in the case of this particular celebrated film, how we organize our film industry under the constant, pressing influence of the world's most powerful cinematic model. Perhaps because it *is* such a convincing and complex cinematic irritant in this ongoing debate about ourselves as a film-producing nation, *The Apprenticeship of Duddy Kravitz* stubbornly and, despite its many detractors, even appropriately remains a 'somebody' in an ever-shifting and still fragile pantheon of great Canadian films.

Filmography

Features

1962	*Tiara Tahiti* (100 mins.)
1965	*Life At The Top* (117 mins.)
1969	*Two Gentlemen Sharing* (92 mins.)
1971	*Outback* (99 mins.)
1973	*Billy Two Hats* (80 mins.)
1973	*The Lady and the Outlaw* (80 mins.)
1974	*The Apprenticeship of Duddy Kravitz* (121 mins.)
1977	*Fun With Dick and Jane* (95 mins.)
1978	*Who Is Killing The Great Chefs of Europe?* (112 mins.)
1979	*North Dallas Forty* (120 mins.)
1982	*Rambo: First Blood* (95 mins.)
1982	*Split Image* (111 mins.)
1983	*Uncommon Valor* (100 mins.)
1985	*Joshua Then And Now* (127 mins.)
1986	*The Check Is In The Mail* (83 mins.)
1988	*Switching Channels* (108 mins.)
1989	*Weekend At Bernie's* (97 mins.)
1989	*Winter People* (110 mins.)
1992	*Folks!* (106 mins.)
1995	*Red Shoe Diaries 5: Weekend Pass* (97 mins.)
1996	*A Strange Affair* (97 mins.)
1996	*Family of Cops* (91 mins.)
1996	*Hidden Assassins* (89 mins.)
1997	*Borrowed Hearts: A Holiday Romance* (97 mins.)
1999	*Crime in Connecticut: The Story of Alex Kelly* (96 mins.)

Short films and television work

Ted Kotcheff's vast and diverse television work stretches over two continents, but precise information on his many productions is difficult to obtain, even from Kotcheff sites on the internet. He did work in the United States in the 1970s, directing *The Human Voice* and *Of Mice and Men*. Prior to his television work in the USA, Kotcheff began at the Canadian Broadcasting Corporation as a director of various television dramas from 1954 onward with producer Sydney Newman. He went with Newman to England and directed many television dramas and docudramas for ABC TV's "Armchair Theatre" from 1959 to 1962. In 1972, he captured a British Emmy for his docudrama *Edna, the Inebriate Woman*. For the past two years (2000-2002) he has been an Executive Producer on the series *Law and Order: Special Victims Unit*.

Mordecai Richler's screenplays

Richler (1931-2001) wrote the screenplay for the following films: *Room at the Top* (Jack Clayton, 1959; from John Braine's novel); *Life at the Top* (Ted Kotcheff, 1965; from John Braine's novel); *The Looking Glass War* (Frank Pierson, 1970; adapted, with Frank Pierson, from John Le Carré's novel). He also wrote the following adaptations of his own fiction: *The Apprenticeship of Duddy Kravitz* (1974); *Jacob Two-Two Meets the Hooded Fang* (1977); *Joshua Then and Now* (Ted Kotcheff, 1985); *St Urbain's Horseman* (for Alan Pakula; unproduced); and *The Incomparable Atuk* (for Norman Jewison; unproduced). An award-winning short animated movie (*The Street*) by Caroline Leaf was made from Richler's St Urbain story "The Summer My Grandmother Was Supposed to Die," and a delightful half-hour drama from his "Mortimer and Skolinsky."

Bibliography

Interviews

Castel, David. Interview with Kotcheff, *Films Illustrated* 4.42 (February 1975): 230-31.

Dreyfuss, Richard. "I just knew I wanted to be Duddy," *Globe & Mail* (13 April 1974): 17.

Edwards, Natalie. "Lunch with Randy Quaid," *Cinema Canada* 14 (June–July 1974): 50.

Ibrányi-Kiss, A., & Laurinda Hartt. "Kotcheff and Lanctôt on *Kravitz*," *Cinema Canada* 20 (July 1974): 42–44.

Katz, John. "Kotcheff: An Interview by John Katz," *Cinema Canada* 20 (July–August 1975): 60–63.

Knelman, Martin. "How Duddy's Movie Brings Us All Back Home," *Saturday Night* (March 1974): 17–24.

McLarty, James. "A View of Us: Richard Dreyfuss, Randy Quaid," *Motion* (July–August 1974): 58.

Richler, Mordecai. "Mordecai Richler Now and Then," *Cinema Canada* 118 (May 1985): 17–21.

Essays

Escott, Manuel. "Celebration of a Likable Fink," *Globe & Mail* 24.1 (16 February 1974), Weekend Magazine: 16–18.

Fuller, Arthur. "The Making of *Duddy Kravitz*," *Canadian Dimension* 10.4 (September 1974): 11, 50.

Golden, Daniel. "What Makes Duddy Run?," *Jump Cut* 5 (January–February 1975): 12–13; repr. in ⇨Feldman & Nelson, *Canadian Film Reader*, 258–62.

Hofsess, John, & Robert Fothergill. "The Rich Get Richler: A Dialogue On *Duddy Kravitz*," *Canadian Forum* 54 (October 1974): 32–36.

Isaac, Don. "Some Questions About the Depiction of Jews in New Films," *New York Times* (8 September 1974): D13–14.

⇨Knelman, Martin, in *This Is Where We Came In*, 131–34.

McLarty, James. "$1,000,000," *Motion* (July–August 1974): 30–32.

Richler, Mordecai. "Shooting *Duddy Kravitz*," *Globe & Mail* 24.7 (16 February 1974), Weekend Magazine: 2–4, 7–8.

——. "Waiting for the Movies," in Richler, *Notes on an Endangered Species and Others* (New York: Alfred A. Knopf, 1974): 86–94; repr. in Richler, *The Great Comic Book Heroes and other essays*, ed. Robert Fulford (Toronto: McClelland & Stewart, 1978): 130–48.

Scott, Jay. "From *Duddy* to *Rambo*," *Globe & Mail* (14 April 1989): A12.

Waugh, Thomas. "Cultivated Colonies: Notes on Queer Nationhood and the Exotic Image," *Canadian Journal of Film Studies* 2.2-3 (1993): 145-78.

Reviews

Alexander Hausvater, "A Day With *Duddy*," *Motion* (March–May 1974): 27; Anon., *Variety* 274.9 (10 April 1974): 17, 20; George Anthony, *Toronto Sun* (11 April 1974); Martin Malina, *Montreal Star* (11 April 1974); Serge Dussault, "Une Rue St-Urbain que je ne reconnais pas," *La Presse* (13 avril 1974): D13; Clyde Gilmour, "*Duddy Kravitz* Hits The Screen As A Gutsy, Funny Movie," *Toronto Star* (13 April 1974); Betty Lee, "The Screen Enhances Kravitz Tale," *Globe & Mail* (13 April 1974): 17; Jean-Pierre Tadros, "Le Canada entre mythologie et réalité," *Le Jour* (13 avril 1974); Robert Guy Scully, "*Duddy* tout en os," *Le Devoir* (20 April 1974): 15; Geoffrey James, "Loving *Duddy*," *Time* (Canada; 22 April 1974): 12; Francine Laurendeau, *Cinema Québec* 3.6-7 (avril-mai 1974): 43–44; Jean Leduc, "La Représentation d'un milieu donné," *Cinema Québec* 3.6-7 (avril-mai 1974): 43–44; Joe Medjuck, *Take One* 4.3 (3 May 1974): 32-33; Robert Fulford [as Marshall Delaney], "Duddy Kravitz as a fairly nice sort of guy," *Saturday Night* (June 1974), repr. in ⇨Fulford, *Marshall Delaney at the Movies*, 80–81; John Hofsess, *Maclean's* 87.6 (June 1974): 92; Natalie Edwards, *Cinema Canada* 14 (June–July 1974): 72–73; George Csaba Koller, *Cinema Canada* 14 (June–July 1974): 7; Mark Miller, *Cinema Canada* 14 (June–July 1974): 72–73; Penelope Gilliatt, "Duddy-O," *New Yorker* 50.22 (22 July 1974): 65–66, repr. in ⇨Douglas Fetherling, *Documents in Canadian Film*, 140–44; Paul Zimmerman, "Making It," *Newsweek* 84 (29 July 1974): 68; Patrick Schupp, *Séquences* 19.77 (juillet 1974): 25–26; James McLarty, "Let's Hear It For *Duddy*," *Motion* (July–August 1974): 72; Arthur Bell, "Dear Duddy Kravitz, face the future undaunted," *Village Voice* (15 August 1974): 70, 74, 76; Robert Hatch, *The Nation* 219.4 (17 August 1974): 123–24; Stanley Kauffmann, *New Republic* 171.8 (24 August 1974): 33; Len Klady, "Canada at Cannes 1974: A Second Look," *Cinema Canada* 15 (August-September 1974): 8; William Avery, *Films in Review* 25.8 (October 1974): 47; William Pechter, "The Importance of *Duddy Kravitz*," *Commentary* 58.5 (November 1974): 76–77; Caroline Leavis, *Monthly Film Bulletin* 41.491 (December 1974): 267–68; Douglas Marshall, "How *Duddy* Makes A Pip Of A Film," *Books in Canada* 3.5 (1974): 8–9; Derek Elley, *Films and Filming* 21.6 (March 1975): 34; Christian Viviani, *Positif* 171-72 (July–August 1975): 59.

ଈ

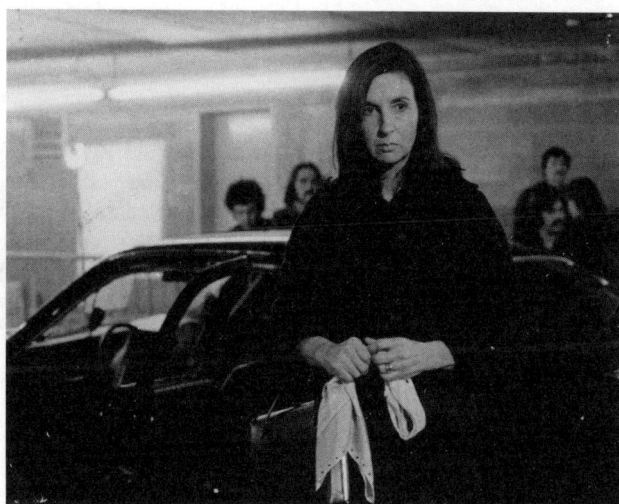

FIGURE 4

Les Ordres (Michel Brault, 1974) – Hélène Loiselle (Marie Boudreau).

4 *Les Ordres*
(Michel Brault, 1974)

Production: produced 1973, released in Québec 27 September 1974. Les Productions Prisma Inc. and Les Ordres Inc. (Montréal), with the participation of the Canadian Film Development Corporation. **Director:** Michel Brault. **Assistant directors:** Alain Chartrand and Suzanne Chiasson. **Producers:** Lise Abastado, Bernard Lalonde, Gui Caron. **Screenplay:** Michel Brault. **Editor:** Yves Dion. **Cinematography:** François Protat and Michel Brault. **Sound:** Serge Beauchemin. **Costumes:** Louise Jobin. **Set Design:** Michel Proulx. **Makeup:** Julio Piedra. **Colour/ black and white, 108 minutes, 35 mm.**

Cast: Hélène Loiselle (Marie Boudreau), **Jean Lapointe** (Clermont Boudreau), **Guy Provost** (Jean–Marie Beauchemin), **Claude Gauthier** (Richard Lavoie), **Louise Forestier** (Claudette Dusseault), **Louise, Martince** and **Monique Pratte** (Boudreau daughters).

Synopsis: In October 1970, the abduction of Québec labour minister Pierre Laporte and British diplomat James Cross, by factions of the terrorist group "Front de Libération du Québec" (FLQ), prompts Canadian Prime Minister Pierre Elliot Trudeau to proclaim the War Measures Act, suspending civil and legal procedures and giving the government unlimited emergency powers. Overnight, Montréal is put under siege by the Canadian army, and over 450 people are arrested and jailed without just cause. Based on interviews with real persons, the film tells the story of five fictional characters who are subjected to these arrests. The unpolitical housewife Marie Boudreau and her three daughters are awakened at home by police officers who barge in looking for her husband, Clermont. Because she cannot say precisely where her husband is, since he is driving a taxi, Marie is arrested on the spot and jailed for six days. Clermont, who has had to take up cab-driving after his suspension from work at a textile mill because of his union activities, is arrested upon his return home and spends the next sixteen days in jail. Meanwhile, Jean–Marie Beauchemin, a socialist physician who works in a free clinic, is taken away from his pregnant wife and kept from contacting her for over two weeks. The single parent Claudette Dussault, a social worker resisting an eviction order, and the unemployed Richard Lavoie, who takes care of children while his wife is at work, are also picked up by the police, who explain their actions by merely saying: "we've got orders." While in prison, the characters struggle to maintain a basic sense of dignity in the face of humiliation and physical abuse. Lavoie is an especially vulnerable target; sadistic guards regularly belittle him and even pretend to execute him. Clermont suffers because he is kept from visiting his dying father and is then allowed, handcuffed and in prison garb, to view the latter's corpse for only minutes. The worst torture inflicted is the authorities' refusal to give reasons for the arrests. Not knowing why they are jailed, when they will be released, or what is happening to their loved ones, the characters live in constant anguish. Even their eventual release remains unexplained. The film closes on words and images of resignation as the characters seek to reclaim their shattered existences.

Michel Brault's *Les Ordres*

Documenting the reality of experience and the fiction of history

———————————— ଚ୨

André Loiselle

Documentary and fiction

P ERHAPS MORE THAN any other French-Canadian filmmaker of his generation, Michel Brault (b. 1928) was instrumental in the development of *cinéma direct* or direct cinema, an ostensibly observational documentary style that emerged at the National Film Board of Canada (NFB) in the late 1950s and became one of the preferred modes of expression of nationalist artists in Québec. Brault's direct-cinema classics, especially *Les Raquetteurs* (1958, with Gilles Groulx) and *Pour la suite du monde* (1963, with Pierre Perrault), not only played an influential role in the evolution of French-Canadian cinema in the 1960s, but also helped represent and define the burgeoning Québécois culture that was just starting to escape the "Great Darkness" imposed by the ultra-conservative provincial government of Maurice Duplessis (in power from 1936 to 1959 with a brief interruption during World War II). Moreover, Brault's achievements as director of photography greatly influenced the *look* of nationalist narrative cinema in Québec in the 1960s and 1970s, as he shot some of the most important works of the period, from Claude Jutra's *A tout prendre* (1963), *Mon oncle Antoine* (1971) and *Kamouraska* (1973) to Anne Claire Poirier's *Mourir à tue-tête* (1979) and Francis Mankiewicz's *Le temps d'une chasse* (1972) and *Les bons débarras* (1980). Thus, because of his central contribution to the imaging of "la Nation québécoise" on screen, Brault, who was once described by his friend Jutra as Québec's "most present, most versatile, most prolific and most constant filmmaker,"[1] was arguably better suited than any other cinéaste to make *the*

---

[1] Claude Jutra, "Au Québec, c'est sûrement Michel Brault qui est le cinéaste le plus présent, le plus versatile, le plus prolifique, le plus constant," *Copie Zéro* 5 (Special issue on Brault; March 1980): 20. My own translation of the article's title. For details on Brault's

definitive film on the October crisis – this crucial event in the rise of Québec nationalism. Yet Brault decided to do neither an actual documentary on the events, like Robin Spry's *Action: The October Crisis of 1970* (1973), nor a wholly fictionalized rendition of the incidents, like Jean–Claude Lord's contemporary political thriller *Bingo* (1974), loosely based on the October crisis. Rather, he chose to merge fact and fabrication to produce a work that *is* and *is not* about the October crisis, a film that is at once strongly rooted in historical facts and highly dependent on imaginative transformations that transcend restrictive empiricism. This combination of fictional and documentary material, which cultivates ambiguity and unknowability, can be seen as either the greatest achievement of *Les Ordres* or as its most unforgivable flaw.

While Brault could have probably made a valid documentary on the October crisis, his decision to fictionalize events and characters appears as a logical choice given the nature of his material. As mentioned above, Brault's name is closely associated with direct cinema, a style that rejected the contrived narrative devices typical of the traditional documentary epitomized by John Grierson's NFB films of the 1940s, which were constructed around an authoritative voice-over commentary. Direct cinema, while remaining true to Grierson's focus on the victimized and unacknowledged, replaced the Griersonian interpretative 'voice of god' narration with immediacy, spontaneity and *direct* contact with its subjects, a practice facilitated by the light 16mm cameras and sound equipment that became available in the late 1950s. But direct cinema's avoidance of *a posteriori* explication in favour of seemingly unadulterated observation would make it almost impossible for Brault (or any other advocate of this mode of documentary) to realize a factual film on the October crisis, since the events he wished to depict had already come to an end when he started working on the project, and all he could capture with any sense of immediacy were *recollections* of the events. To make a film on the October crisis, Brault had to relinquish direct cinema's central principle of extemporaneity and adopt strategies of narrative reconstruction and manipulation.

But Brault never felt much inclination for narrative cinema. Indeed, while much of the Québec canon bears his visual signature, Brault paradoxically remains on the margins of narrative cinema. In terms of fiction film, although he has worked as cinematographer on dozens of projects, he has

---

career, see Gilles Marsolais, "Michel Brault," in ⇨Michel Coulombe & Marcel Jean, ed., *Le dictionnaire du cinéma québécois*, 67–70.

been much less productive as a director than other contemporary *auteurs* like Jutra, Gilles Carle and Claude Fournier, or even younger cinéastes like Jean–Pierre Lefebvre and Denys Arcand. In over forty years as a professional cinéaste, Brault has directed only five fiction feature films – *Entre la mer et l'eau douce* (1967), *Les Ordres*, *Les Noces de papier* (1989), *Sabbath Shalom* (1992) and *Mon amie Max* (1994). And although he is still the only Canadian filmmaker to have won the esteemed Best Director Award at Cannes, in 1975 for *Les Ordres*, his features have not enjoyed the popular success that Carle's and Arcand's have.[2] For, in spite of the honour bestowed on him at Cannes, Brault has always been less a movie director than a documentarian; he much prefers to record the subtle and equivocal variations of life unfolding before him than to choreograph car chases or sex scenes. In fact, he once described himself as a "cinéaste interested mainly in live document, [who feels] trapped with fiction."[3] When working on *Les Ordres*, Brault found himself caught between events that were no longer live and a form that he deems confining. He thus chose to blur the boundary between documentary and fiction, and capture the paradoxically spontaneous reality of reenacted events.

For reality is what matters to Brault, even if this is composed of fictionalized stories and imaginary characters played by professional actors. Brault is so "amorously and respectfully glued to reality," as Guy Borremans once phrased it, that even if his first fiction film, *Entre la mer et l'eau douce*, features several cultural icons of the 1960s such as the actress Geneviève Bujold, the rock-star Robert Charlebois, the poet–essayist Gérald Godin and the folk-singer Claude Gauthier, it is its remarkable use of direct-cinema techniques to depict 'real life' in the country and in the working-class neighbourhoods of Montréal that renders it one of the most important films of the period.[4]

---

[2] As Peter Harcourt once wrote, "the fine tribute paid there [at Cannes] last year to Michel Brault for *Les Ordres* has not helped the commercial life of the film in this country at all!"; Harcourt, "Introduction," in ⇨Feldman & Nelson, ed., *Canadian Film Reader*, 375. *Les Ordres* was not a flop, however. The film cost $250, 000, and recaptured a respectable $500,000 (*Copie Zéro*, 15–16). By comparison, Claude Fournier's *Deux femmes en or* (1970), one of the biggest successes of the 1970s, was produced for $218,000 and earned $4,000,000. See ⇨Yves Lever, *Histoire générale du cinéma au Québec*, 306.

[3] Michel Brault, "Un film sur l'humiliation," in Gilles Marsolais, ed., *Les Ordres: Un film de Michel Brault* (Montréal: L'Aurore, 1975) 18; "Cinéaste plutôt porté vers le document vécu je me sentais acculé à la fiction"; my translation.

[4] Guy Borremans, "La Morale à l'œil," in *Copie Zéro*, 29; "collé à la réalité, amoureusement et respectueusement"; my translation. On *Entre la mer et l'eau douce*, see Robert

Similarly, it is in great part the documentary quality of *Les Ordres* – markedly less flamboyant and sensationalistic than Lord's *Bingo* – that makes it such a gripping cinematic experience. Indeed, for the journalist Serge Dussault, the surprisingly captivating and disturbing impact of *Les Ordres* results precisely from the fact that it is "a sober film, presented almost as a documentary"; and film critic Jay Scott once called Brault's piece a "galvanizing documentary," completely passing over in silence the fact that *Les Ordres* is, strictly speaking, a fiction film with recognizable actors playing constructed personae.[5]

Scott's mistaken labelling of *Les Ordres* as a documentary is understandable, though, for Brault painstakingly incorporated in his screenplay factual details gathered from the testimonies of fifty individuals arrested on 16 October 1970, and worked with seasoned naturalist actors, like Hélène Loiselle as housewife Marie Boudreau, to attain the greatest degree of realism.[6] Critic Robert Lévesque actually argues that *Les Ordres*, in his view "the first true masterpiece of Québec cinema," is better acted than any other French-Canadian film ever produced.[7] Furthermore, Brault's camera-work, always attentive to the particulars of the milieu depicted and to the minutiae of idiosyncratic facial expressions, is clearly reminiscent of documentary cinematography. For example, a scene transpiring in the weaving mill where Clermont Boudreau works at the beginning of the film, seems so authentic that it could have been taken straight out of Denys Arcand's textile-industry documentary, *On est au coton* (1970, released in 1976). As a meticulously realistic reconstruction of the mortifying experiences suffered by those imprisoned during the October crisis, *Les Ordres* comes across as a striking example of what Bruce Elder calls "the empirical style which dominates the Canadian film tradition."[8]

Daudelin, "La Rencontre direct-fiction," in Pierre Véronneau, ed., *Les Cinémas canadiens*, 119–20.

[5] Serge Dussault, "Quand la réalité est insupportable, on n'y croit plus!" *La Presse* (9 novembre 1974); "Le film est sobre: Il se présente comme un documentaire"; my translation. Dussault's use of the term "sobre" recalls Bill Nichol's point that documentary is one of the "discourses of sobriety" (*Representing Reality*, [Bloomington: Indiana UP, 1991] 5). Jay Scott, "Burnout in the Great White North," in ⇨Seth Feldman, ed., *Take Two*, 33.

[6] René Prédal, "Entretien avec Michel Brault," *Jeune cinéma* 88 (juillet–août 1975): 22–24.

[7] Robert Lévesque, "Un très grand film sur un très grand sujet," *Québec-Presse* (29 septembre 1974).

[8] ⇨R. Bruce Elder, *Image and Identity*, 148.

Personal and political

But as much as Brault's documentary-style fiction or fictionalized documentary can be seen as one of the great achievements of Canadian realistic cinema, this strategy of hybridization also led to attacks on the part of certain Québécois critics who considered that by fictionalizing actual incidents the cinéaste failed in his attempt to relate the events of October 1970. Many commentators criticized Brault for hypostatizing the material, focusing on personal reactions rather than political actions.[9] For instance, the leader of the separatist Parti Québécois, René Lévesque, who actually enjoyed most of the film, deplored Brault's decision not to expose those who give "the orders," those who control what Althusser calls the ideological and repressive state apparatuses, limiting himself, instead, to showing the puppets who obey orders (police officers, prison guards, etc) and the innocent victims crushed by them (anyone with left-wing sympathies, no matter how temperate).[10] Somewhat more caustically, Jean–Marc Piotte accused Brault of having "reduced the October crisis, which is first and foremost a political phenomenon, to human problems. This leads him [...] to alter the meaning of the arrests by purging them of their political aspect."[11]

But the most vehement denunciation of *Les Ordres* came from Pierre Vallières, the author of the biting nationalist treatise *Les Nègres blancs d'Amérique* (1968) and himself a member of the FLQ. In his article, "Témoignage d'un otage privilégié des 'ordres': Brault a manqué son coup," Vallières denounces the film for failing to do what a valid documentary on the October crisis should have done: namely, "respecting the historical truth and facts" upon which it is based.[12] By claiming to use factual documentation, but hiding the truth "behind the screen of fiction and aestheticism," Brault made what Vallières considers to be a "politically and morally unacceptable" film.

---

[9] See, for instance, Michel Brûlé's summary of reviewers' responses to *Les Ordres* in "Un constat d'impuissance à l'égard des groupes d'opposition," *Cinéma/Québec* 4.1 (décembre 1974): 15.

[10] René Lévesque, "Pourquoi *Les Ordres*?" *Le Jour* (28 septembre 1974).

[11] Jean–Marc Piotte, "Et derrière?" *Le Devoir* (5 novembre 1974); "il réduit la Crise d'octobre, qui est un phénomène avant tout politique, à des problèmes humains. Ce qui l'entraîne, et ce, même au niveau du sujet traité, les emprisonnements, à déformer leur signification en les expurgeant de leur aspect politique"; my translation.

[12] Pierre Vallières, "Témoignage d'un otage privilégié des 'ordres': Brault a manqué son coup," *Cinéma/Québec* 4.1 (décembre 1974): 19. English translation: "An Account by a Privileged Hostage of Les Ordres: Brault Has Missed His Shot," tr. John Van Burek, in ⇨Feldman & Nelson, ed., *Canadian Film Reader*, 266.

Les Ordres, according to Vallières, is blind to the intricate deployment of power orchestrated by the right-wing bourgeoisie through the War Measures Act; thus it amounts to a mere "Kafkaesque melodrama" about a helpless existential struggle against some abstract, oppressive force. For Vallières, Brault is also guilty of having ignored the strong sense of collective outrage that actual detainees felt and expressed during the crisis, and of having focused instead on the individual trauma of five relatively non-politicized people who, in response to imprisonment, show more of a penchant for melancholy than for insurrection. "The revolt and disgust that was running from one floor to the next at the Parthenais [a Montréal jail] had nothing to do with the sobs of Jean Lapointe," says Vallières, referring to a scene in which Clermont, behind bars, sings a plaintive song that his recently deceased father sang for him. If Brault wanted to use his imagination, Vallières contends, he should not have made a film on the very real events of October 1970.[13]

Although many of his criticisms are legitimate, what Vallières simply won't accept is that Brault did not make a *documentary* about the October crisis but, rather, utilized direct cinema as a *filmic style* to convey his perspective on certain issues. Brault himself has stated that "[he] never wanted to make, with *Les Ordres*, a film on the October crisis in Québec in 1970. [He] wanted to make a film on humiliation based on the events that we experienced."[14] Indeed, more than documenting the specific incidents of 1970, the film reproduces the *personal experience* of utter humiliation suffered by the characters who are not only imprisoned without just cause, but are also mentally and physically tortured by petty officials during their incarceration. By showing his characters torn away from their homes, strip-searched, thrown in solitary confinement, deprived of proper food for days, victims of cruel pranks such as 'fake executions,' Brault not only exposes the situation in Québec in October 1970, but also denounces all fascist abuse of power either in Canada or elsewhere in the world.

In fact, the very first scene of the film suggests that abuse of power is not limited to the State but is also present in the microcosm of the household. As the film opens, Marie Boudreau is arguing with one of her daughters, Marine, who wants to visit her friend, Ginette. Not unlike governmental

---

13 Vallières, "Témoignage d'un otage privilégié des 'ordres'," 19, 20, 266–68 passim.

14 Brault, "Un film sur l'humiliation," 18; "je n'ai pas voulu faire avec *Les Ordres* un film sur la crise d'octobre au Québec en '70. J'ai voulu faire un film sur l'humiliation à partir des événements que nous avons connus"; my translation.

authorities, Marie imposes her will on the weaker members of the 'society' that she controls, by prohibiting Marine from going out after school. Significantly, the crux of the argument is not so much that Marie forbids Marine from seeing Ginette; rather it is the fact that the mother refuses to *justify her orders*. Marine's query, "*Comment ça, tu peux pas me l'expliquer?*" ("Why can't you explain it to me?"), the very first words spoken in the film, could very well be seen as the question that those imprisoned in October 1970 were dying to ask the government. Interestingly, when Marie replies that it would be too long to give her reasons, she, like governmental authorities throughout the film, is 'faceless,' being off-camera during the dialogue. Marine's frustration at being denied a rationale clearly parallels the situation of the victims of the War Measures Act, for the worst torture inflicted on Brault's main characters is doubtlessly to be refused explanations, communication and knowledge. Not allowed to phone family and friends after having been arrested, Marie remains without news of her daughters for several days; Clermont is only belatedly notified of his father's death; and Dr Beauchemin never receives reassurance concerning his wife's pregnancy. Kept uninformed about the crisis that precipitated their imprisonment, denied an explanation for their arrests, Brault's characters are bereaved not so much by physical torture as by the mental torture of an epistemological void. As David Clandfield has suggested, *Les Ordres* is about "the unsaid, the unacknowledged, and the unknown."[15]

Known and unknown

The condition of 'unknownness' depicted in the film does not refer only to the individual experience of the prisoners, but alludes as well to issues of cinematic style and politics of discourse. Those who, like Vallières, criticized Brault for not taking enough analytical distance from his material, ignored the influence of direct cinema on the cinéaste's approach. In rejecting traditional voice-over commentary in favour of immediacy, the direct-cinema style challenges the ascendancy of authoritative rhetoric, but by the same token also precludes *a posteriori* rationalization possible only through linguistic abstraction. In other words, direct cinema's defiance of the dominant discourse is achieved at the expense of explicit information. It does not come as a surprise, therefore, that the world of *Les Ordres* would not be presented

---

[15] From Clandfield's presentation at the 1990 American Council for Québec Studies quoted by Janis L. Pallister, "*Les Ordres*," in ⇨Pallister, *The Cinema of Québec*, 321.

as *objectively knowable* through abstraction. Rather, it must be experienced first-hand, viscerally, like the diegetic images and sounds that comprise direct-cinema documentaries. When Clermont vomits after having been served only cold porridge for five days, the spectators are not expected to theorize on the socio-economic import of oatmeal, but, rather, to feel sick to their stomachs. Similarly, when Richard Lavoie is taken to an isolated compartment by prison guards and 'executed' by a firing squad using blanks, the audience feels with utter immediacy the terror of death and might only much later reflect upon the ideological implications of conducting a fictional execution rather than a real one. As Luc Perrault writes, Brault "turns his back on ideological interpretations of October, and opts instead for a phenomenological description"[16] of the processes by which human beings are humiliated, crushed and denied knowledge.

Therefore, because of its reliance on direct-cinema stylistic devices, *Les Ordres* actually bears very little resemblance to a traditional, narrative documentary like Spry's *Action*, which situates the hostage crisis in a broad historical context, linking the incidents of 1970 to similar situations from the past and showing how political leaders interpreted the events. Given his chosen mode of representation, Brault's refusal to articulate a documented argument as Spry does is fully justified. But beyond stylistic imperatives, other, more expressly political concerns also dictate Brault's choice to emphasize the 'unknown.' Indeed, Brault's purpose, in 'withholding' information, is to make his audience experience phenomenologically the denial and perversion of knowledge characteristic of fascism – whether it be Trudeau's stately fascism, Marie's domestic authoritarianism or (as will be discussed later) cinema's own oppressive and controlling potential. While the premiss of the film is ostensibly the October crisis, the actual object of *Les Ordres* is not to set forth a straightforward history of the events that marked 1970. On the contrary: Brault exposes the very process of falsifying, altering or reconstructing history.

The authorities' refusal to communicate knowledge suggests a politically intricate logic of retribution, whereby withholding information operates as a punitive reaction against a perceived attack on the dominant ideological discourse, which is what all the main characters in *Les Ordres* can be accused of. In other words, any challenge to the 'master narrative' results in immediate

---

[16] Luc Perrault, "Portrait d'une humiliation," *La Presse* (30 septembre 1974); "tournant le dos à une interprétation sur le plan idéologique, [Brault] opte carrément pour une description phénoménologique"; my translation.

removal from the discursive field that supports it. As Lacanians might
phrase it, resistance against the Father's prohibitive language leads to ban-
ishment from the realm of the Symbolic.

Written and spoken

Unlike in *Action*, the voices of those who give the Orders, those who control
language, knowledge and history, are never *heard* in *Les Ordres*. Rather, their
messages have to be *read*; they are printed as a super-impression on the
screen. Brault prefaces the film with a typed comment by Trudeau from
1958, in which he declares that when a man is treated unjustly, all men are
responsible for this injustice through their apathy. In addition to the obviously ironic nexus between Trudeau's empty liberal rhetoric of 1958 and
his 1970 authoritarian actions, this introductory caption suggests that Trudeau has control over written, official language. Later in the film, a written
excerpt from Montréal's right-wing mayor, Jean Drapeau, requesting the
intervention of the Federal government to resolve the crisis is also superimposed on the screen, this time over a long-shot of a soldier with a
machine-gun. Even more than Trudeau's statement, Drapeau's written
words signify that the Orders and those who give them operate in the realm
of the Symbolic, the linguistic, the Law. Their control is exercised through
abstract rules that seek to contain subversive practices.

Conversely, those who are subjugated to the Law have little or no access
to written language, as a painfully mistake-ridden letter from Clermont's
mother clearly attests. From Richard Lavoie with his grade-10 education to
the social worker and even Dr Beauchemin, the victims of the Orders function almost exclusively in the sphere of fluid, unregulated but ineffectual
spoken language. They all speak various degrees of *Joual*, the bastardized
French-Canadian dialect that became emblematic of the alienation of Québec
people in the 1960s and 1970s, and was used as a political tool by artists like
playwright Michel Tremblay. Their testimonies are not written but spoken
in voice-over throughout the film, with all the mistakes, hesitations and stut-
ters characteristic of 'spontaneous' oral expression. Their words are heard
but not seen, except fleetingly near the end when Clermont writes in the
guest book, at the funeral parlour where he visits his father escorted by three
police officers, is the telegraphic phrase: "Clermont Boudreau. Injustice."

The endemic language problem that has long been at the core of
French-Canadian culture thus finds metaphoric expression in the fact that

the most tyrannical, punitive measure imposed by the written Orders is the prohibition of verbal communication among prisoners and, mainly, the denial of communication between the prisoners and the outside world. The written Orders contain and control spoken language as much as the prison bars, the jail cells, the aseptic corridors of the penitentiary, all that which comprises what Janis Pallister identifies as the film's "architectural expression of imposed order,"[17] contain and control Brault's characters. *Les Ordres* is thus as much (if not more so) about what Foucault might call "the effects of disciplinary power and knowledge"[18] as about the events of October 1970 in Québec.

In fact, at one point in the film, the audience is explicitly told that the action is *not* taking place in 1970 at all, but, rather, in 1973. Indeed, when Richard Lavoie is asked by the police to give his age and date of birth, he states: "I am 34. I was born on January 31, 1939." Here the putative truth of the 1970 context clashes with the actual truth of the film: ie, the actor, Claude Gauthier, who was born in 1939, and was 34 when *Les Ordres* was shot. This detail suggests that Brault, by juxtaposing the historical referent of the film and the actual truth of the actor's performance, by having the film 'misinform' the viewers, consciously draws the audience's attention to the different degrees and categories of reality that result from any process of representation, from authoritarian political discourse to cinema itself. If this were the only example of a discrepancy between the events that the movie is supposed to represent and the actual reality recorded on film (the actor's performance), one could argue that it is merely a mistake on Gauthier's part, and that Brault decided not to re-shoot the scene, thinking that no one would notice. But the film does contain other, much more unequivocal references to the true documentary quality of the film: namely, the recording of actors playing roles.

Actor and role

One of the most intriguing filmic strategies used by Brault in this regard is to have his five main actors, Jean Lapointe, Hélène Loiselle, Claude Gauthier, Guy Provost and Louise Forestier, introduce themselves as actors early in

---

[17] Pallister, "*Les Ordres*," 320.

[18] See, for instance, Michel Foucault's comments on sovereignty, discipline, knowledge and power in Colin Gordon, ed., *Power/Knowledge: Selected Interviews and Other Writings, 1972–1977* (New York: Pantheon, 1980): 108.

the film and explain briefly their characters' backgrounds. "I am called Jean Lapointe," says Lapointe in the first few minutes of the film, "and in the film I play Clermont Boudreau. I was born on a farm, like my wife Marie." Throughout the film, the actor–characters continue to appear in interview situations and comment on their ordeals, which are shown in flashbacks. This device creates an intricate blend of documentary and fiction. The 'interviews' remind the spectator of the actuality of Brault's material, yet the actors' self-presentation immediately undercuts the documentary effect of the recollections and contests the film's claim to authenticity. Simultaneously, the accounts of the characters, which emphasize the experience of imprisonment rather than the political and ideological implications of the government's actions, echo direct cinema's rejection of rationalized narration à la Grierson. But again, the issue of role playing, acknowledged by the actors, shifts the assertion of immediacy, alleged by the direct-cinema style of the film, from the experience of imprisonment itself to the corporeality of performance, for what the film truly captures are the idiosyncratic gestures, mannerisms and physiognomy of performers.

For contemporary reviewers speaking from the critical discourse of the 1970s, the actors' introduction of themselves and their roles was a straightforward example of "Brechtian distantiation," comparable to what Godard does in his contemporary "Dziga–Vertov Group" production, *Tout va bien* (1972). Gilles Marsolais, for instance, wrote in 1975 that "*Les Ordres* represents a perfect cinematic use of Brecht's theories," and Jan Uhde argued in 1979 that "Such 'stepping out of role' introduces into the film the distancing effect, first, in the temporary interruption of the narrative, the suspension of the dramatic action; the viewer is involuntarily brought back to the reality of his own projection room."[19] Some degree of distantiation or estrangement is doubtlessly achieved in certain parts of the film, especially with regard to the somewhat marginal character of Claudette Dussault, whom Louise Forestier plays with cool detachment. But it could also be suggested that, in other cases, far from distancing the actors from their roles, the technique used by Brault creates an uncanny correspondence between the performers

---

[19] Gilles Marsolais, "Démasquer les faux maîtres," in *Les Ordres: Un film de Michel Brault*, 13: "*Les Ordres* représente donc une parfaite application des théories de Brecht au cinéma"; my translation. Jan Uhde, "Estrangement Elements in Brault's *Les Ordres*," *Canadian Drama/L'Art dramatique canadien* 5.1 (Spring 1979): 54–55. For other references to the Brechtian distantiation effect created in *Les Ordres*, see Robert Lévesque, and Janick Beaulieu, "*Les Ordres*," *Séquences* 78 (octobre 1974): 26–27.

and their characters, as the fiction of the latter merges with the reality of the former. Only a few critics at the time recognized the high degree of identification generated by Brault's *mise-en-scène*. One of them was Marshal Delaney (aka Robert Fulford), who wrote with his usual insight:

> Brault's direction is so involving, and his use of the actors so skilful, that *our identification is complete*. We watch them wakened in the night, we hear the screams of the children as the police pound on the doors, we are stuffed into the backs seats of police cars, pushed, prodded, insulted, and humiliated. We identify with their degradation as they are stripped and examined, as their beards are cut off and their clothes taken away, as officious guards herd them like cattle.[emphasis added].[20]

The process of suture between actor, role and, by extension, spectator, is first and foremost verbal, as the "I" of Jean Lapointe becomes the "I" of Clermont Boudreau. The merger is also effected through a visual procedure. Brault once explained that "when the actors present themselves, they address the camera directly; and then, when they become the character, they speak beside the camera. In the same shot you have a transition from reality (the actor Jean Lapointe) to fiction (the character Clermont Boudreau)."[21] The spectators are thus made aware from the outset that the testimonies involve the personal history of the actors as much as, if not more than, the political history that *Les Ordres* is based upon. In this respect, the filmmaker's choice of actors is significant, for their extra-cinematic personae clearly impact on the spectators' reading of the film. Jean Lapointe probably presents the most illuminating case.

Lapointe was very well-known in the 1960s and 1970s as the funnier half of the stand-up comic duo "Les Jérolas" (with Jérôme Lemay), and for supporting roles verging on slapstick in Claude Fournier's early-1970s sex comedies (*Deux Femmes en or* [1970], *Les Chats bottés* [1971] and *La Pomme, la queue... et les pépins!* [1974]).[22] His most singular quality is arguably his ability, not unlike Chaplin, to maintain a backdrop of pathos behind even his most clownish numbers and irreverent impersonations. This results in

---

[20] Marshall Delaney [Robert Fulford], "Artists in the Shadows: Some Notable Canadian Movies," in ⇨Seth Feldman, ed., *Take Two*, 3.

[21] Prédal, "Entretien avec Michel Brault," 22: "Lorsque le comédien se présente, il parle face à la caméra puis, dès qu'il devient le personnage, il parle à côté de la caméra. Vous avez donc bien dans le même plan le passage du réel (le comédien Jean Lapointe) à la fiction (le personnage Clermont Boudreau)"; my translation.

[22] On Lapointe's career, see Michel Coulombe, "Jean Lapointe," in ⇨Michel Coulombe & Marcel Jean, ed., *Le dictionnaire du cinéma québécois*, 313–15.

part from his facial expressions, which always convey a dose of ambiguous fragility, and the pocked texture of his skin, which render him at once ridiculous and touching. In the role of Clermont Boudreau, Lapointe carries with him this laughable and pathetic quality long associated with comedy and injected into the middle of tragic circumstances. At least for a segment of the French-Canadian public in the 1970s, the impact of *Les Ordres* probably stemmed as much from their knowledge of the historical context depicted in the film as from their recognition of the unfair treatment inflicted upon an engaging 'little guy' like Lapointe.

At the end of the film, when Boudreau/Lapointe is finally released after sixteen days of unlawful imprisonment, he expresses his frustration towards the prison guards in a pathetic "conniption" about having been mentally and physically tortured. The comedian's twang and diminutive physique render his miserable verbal attack on the "screws" particularly effective in conveying not only the grief of the victims of the War Measures Act, but also the belittling of a people who had gone through a decade of enthusiastic and lively progress in the 1960s, and were now being crushed by their leaders. Lapointe, the stand-up comic who, during the 1960s, had embodied along with many other cultural figures, like Robert Charlebois and Michel Tremblay, the carnivalesque subversion made possible by the new-found freedom that the Quiet Revolution afforded,[23] was now performing a futile assault against forces that would hardly be shaken by such minuscule threats. The prolonged shot of two massive prison doors closed solidly behind Boudreau and Dr Beauchemin following their release sans apologies, asserts architecturally that even if they have now been liberated, freedom has forever lost its meaning. Those who give orders (Trudeau, Drapeau, Québec's premier Robert Bourassa, etc) have definitively put their foot down and will no longer allow the type of freedom previously enjoyed.

Freedom and repression

Michel Brault himself was a victim of the renewed repressiveness of the early 1970s, experiencing difficulty in securing financial backing for *Les Ordres*. Indeed, after having enjoyed the relative freedom that the NFB granted its filmmakers in the 1950s and 1960s, Brault saw his project to make a

---

[23] "The Quiet Revolution" was a period of great modernization and liberalism in Québec that started in 1960 with the election of Jean Lesage's Liberal Party to replace the conservative Union Nationale government of Maurice Duplessis (d. 1959).

film based on the October crisis interdicted by the newly appointed commissioner of the NFB, Sidney Newman who, besides forbidding the production of *Les Ordres*, also censured Arcand's *On est au coton*, and Gilles Groulx's *24 heures ou plus* ... (1971–72, released in 1976) for the subversive views they apparently promoted.[24] Brault thus had to make his film in the private sector and, although he eventually received the support of the Canadian Film Development Corporation (now Telefilm Canada), his budget ended up being much smaller than he expected, and he found himself unable to shoot all the film in colour as he had originally planned.[25]

Given the resistance that Brault encountered in his attempt to realize his project, it could be argued that in addition to its explicit criticism of the War Measures Act, *Les Ordres* actually represents an implicit attack on the kind of reactionary mentality, increasingly dominant in the 1970s, that condemns the very production of films like *Les Ordres*. In exactly the same way that the foreman of the textile mill suspends Clermont when he feels threatened by his union activities, the NFB commissioner censures films when they are deemed a menace to the ruling ideology. In a sense, Trudeau's proclamation of the War Measures Act is only the most powerful expression of a 1970s desire to put an end to the oppositional movements that had gained momentum in the 1960s. As Michel Brûlé suggests in his article on *Les Ordres*, the October crisis was neither a crisis for the general population of Québec nor even a crisis for the police force. Rather, it was a crisis for those who held power, both political and economic.[26] They felt the unity and cohesion of their (ruling) class threatened by subversive activities epitomized by the FLQ, but operating at various levels. For the authorities, the FLQ's acts of terrorism were only a radical magnification of more subtle, but more pervasive, threats to the system. Clermont Boudreau's altruistic involvement with the unions, Claudette Dussault's sarcastic defiance of a repossession order, Richard Lavoie's discreet support of the leftist party FRAP (Front d'action populaire), signalled only by a poster in his apartment, and even Michel Brault's project to make an ambiguous fictionalized documentary/docu-

---

[24] Gary Evans, "Censorship of French Production: Too Biased or Too Separatist?," in Evans, *In the National Interest*, 179–89. Not to paint too negative a portrait of Newman, however, it should be pointed out that he offered much support to the production of Jutra's *Mon oncle Antoine*. See Evans, 208.

[25] Prédal, "Entretien avec Michel Brault," 23.

[26] Michel Brûlé, "Un constat d'impuissance à l'égard des groupes d'opposition," *Cinéma Québec* 4.1 (décembre 1974): 16.

mented fiction on the crisis, are all blows against the monolithic, dominant power, hence cause for punishment. That *Les Ordres* was produced at all might very well be, in itself, a much stronger political statement than any ideological analysis Brault might have propounded.

Colour and black/white

Ironically, the financial restrictions resulting from NFB censorship led to one of Brault's most ingenious narrative strategies: namely, to shoot in black and white the scenes taking place before the arrests and after the releases, and to switch to colour for the scenes in prison. While it is the result of concerns as practical as a lack of funds, and has been seen by critics as otherwise perceptive as Delaney as "rather arbitrary,"[27] this procedure nonetheless supports remarkably well the overall structure of the film by intensifying the connection between the various categories of reality talked about earlier: ie, reconstructed historical reality and the reality of the performer in fiction film. At one level, the passage from black and white, traditionally associated with sober documentary, to colour, the chromatic signifier of Hollywoodian "Wizard of Oz" fantasy, can be read as a way for Brault to indicate to some of his more persnickety spectators, like Vallières, that he is fully aware that the prison scenes are, and could only be, fictive, for there is simply no authentic footage thoroughly documenting the forced confinement of the 450 victims of the War Measures Act. The only reality to which the filmmaker has access is *a posteriori* conversations (black and white) with those sensitized victims who remember (colour) the experience of being unjustly detained.

The particular syntagmatic arrangement of the film, however, suggests that the combination of colour and black and white not only stresses the degree of fictionalization present in film, but also comments on processes of identity-construction linked to both imprisonment and cinema. Brault first shifts from black and white to colour at a very significant point in the film – when Dr Beauchemin is given his prison clothes and bed sheets for the night. As the image becomes colourful, Beauchemin remarks in voice-over,

> Up till then I'd been hoping they'd let us go ... they'd see it was all a mistake. But then they gave us those uniforms. Christ! Looking down at yourself ... brown shirt, grey pants, boots ... you don't recognize yourself. You've got nothing of your own. That's when you realize how important clothes are.

---

[27] Delaney, "Artists in the Shadows," 4.

> They're who you are. And then the sheets. You wonder how long you'll be
> sleeping there. A year, two years? You have no way of knowing.

Thus it is not arbitrary that Brault chooses to switch from black and white to colour as the Doctor is reflecting on the importance of clothes for one's identity. The film's representation of the characters changes exactly at the same time as society's representation of the individual changes through the imposition of a certain required appearance. As much as the clothes that one wears codify her or his identity, cinema, even in its most 'direct' form, manipulates the appearance of its subject to force the performer's body to convey a certain meaning. By stressing not only the drabness of the men's prison uniforms, but also the excessive redness of the characters' complexions, the bilious green of the prison walls that surround the women, the squalid dun of the prison courtyard, colour is instrumental in the creating the experience of humiliation presented by the film.

Cinema and tyranny

Colour is used in combination with many other features of the cinematic apparatus to suggest that film *itself* partakes in the political, economic and domestic modes of tyranny that *Les Ordres* denounces. The camera's indiscreet invasion of the Boudreau's private space, early in the morning, not unlike the police force; the way the camera dollies 'freely' in the prison corridors *observing* the characters through bars, like animals in a cage; the ungrateful close-ups to which the actors are subjected throughout the movie; the scenes of strip-searching that position the spectator alongside prison guards as voyeurs – a position, incidently, that the invisible 'interviewer' also occupies; the illicit recording of conversations which correlates police wire-tapping equipment with the Nagra sound recorder used by filmmakers. All these examples testify to film's involvement in the processes of surveillance, confinement and oppression that *Les Ordres* paradoxically decries.

Such observations instantly remind one of discussions on the panopticonic nature of film – its ability to reproduce the function of prison architecture, which rests on invisible observation. Catherine Russell's commentaries on David Rimmer's films *Watching for the Queen* (1973) and *The Dance* (1970), for instance, immediately come to mind. She describes how Rimmer's films call attention to the fact that cinema is a technology of perception, control and power that entraps its subjects in closed frames where they must endlessly repeat the same movements.[28] It would probably be farfetched to claim that Brault was fully aware of cinema's kinship with the panopticon when he made *Les Ordres*. However, it would be even more preposterous to argue that a filmmaker who has always displayed such sensitivity to issues of documentary representation and who recognizes the terrifying impact that the director's *order* "Action!" can have on actors[29] could make a film on imprisonment and authoritarianism without making at least relatively conscious references to the role of the camera in the social mechanisms of surveillance. The closing shot of the film, when the camera rises from Clermont's humble apartment, passes by windows of other lodgings, reaches the roof, and stops there to invigilate the surrounding working-class neighbourhood, is a clear example of the cinéaste's acknowledgement that, in spite of his good intentions, honesty and sympathy for his characters, the medium that he uses remains an inhuman device of mechanical reproduction, whose essential function is to *capture* what it witnesses and deliver its catch to its masters.

Conclusions and speculations

These paradoxes between the humanist aspirations of the cinéaste and the mechanically detached nature of the medium, as well as the level of ambiguity inherent in the merger of narrative cinema and documentary, dissolve facile conclusions about *Les Ordres* and render Brault's piece one of the few truly inexhaustible works of the Canadian repertory. But the degree of intricacy and unknowability that the film displays might very well result less from the conflict between medium and artist or between fact and fiction, than from the very incidents that the narrative tries to come to terms with. The October crisis is perhaps too traumatic and too problematic an event to be tackled head-on, at least by a French-Canadian (note that *Action*, the best straightforward documentary on the Crisis, was produced by an anglophone). It has provoked too many conflicting reactions to allow a filmmaker to approach the issue with any claim to objectivity. Those who experienced this most disturbing moment in Québec history, even from a distance or even as children (like myself), remember October 1970 as a time when all the contradictions, inconsistencies, and dilemmas of French-Canadian society

---

[28] Catherine Russell, "Twilight in the Image Bank," in *David Rimmer: Films & Tapes 1967–1993* (Toronto: Art Gallery of Ontario, 1993): esp. 34–36.

[29] Pierre Jutras, "Entretien avec Michel Brault," *Copie Zéro*, 13.

collided in an explosion of confusion and disarray. While many separatists, as moderate as René Lévesque, expressed support for the demands of the FLQ in *early* October 1970, the unexpected murder of Pierre Laporte, on 17 October, had the effect of an ice-cold shower on many nationalists, leaving them in a state of utter bewilderment. Conversely, as much as Trudeau's show of power gained him support among the middle and upper classes, it also appalled, even horrified, segments of the population, in particular the intelligentsia, who would never forgive him for having so callously discarded civil liberties.[30]

To this day, it probably remains impossible for many Québécois to adopt a categorical position vis-à-vis October 1970. Even the openly separatist cinéaste, Pierre Falardeau, who, exactly twenty years after *Les Ordres*, released his own version of the October crisis, could not avoid ambiguity and paradox. Although looking at the events from a perspective totally different from Brault's – the experience of the hostage-takers themselves rather than the plight of the innocent outsiders – Falardeau's feature film *Octobre* (1994) still focuses on the personal pain caused by the events rather than analyzing the Machiavellian political mechanisms that orchestrated the unfolding of the drama.[31] It should not come as a surprise, therefore, that Falardeau decided to truncate the original title of the novel which inspired the film, Francis Simard's *Pour en finir avec octobre* (1982), for we are still very far from being able to 'get the October question over and done with.' Twenty years from now, perhaps, hindsight might permit a more forthright filmic depiction of the incidents. But, regardless of the increased understanding that time might afford, it is doubtful that any film could surpass *Les Ordres* in the immediacy of feeling that it offers its audience. For, beyond its subjection to the constantly shifting fiction of history, the lasting value of Brault's work remains its dedication to the reality of experience.

ಐ   *Bazin?*

---

[30] For a brief history of the October Crisis see, for instance, Craig Brown et al., *Histoire générale du Canada* (Montréal: Boréal, 1990): 642–44.

[31] Ironically enough, Falardeau's film – which is certainly more threatening to the 'authorities' than *Les Ordres* because of its sympathetic look at the terrorists, a position that resulted in some vehement criticism – was financed by both the NFB and Telefilm Canada. Perhaps this is a sign that, while individuals might remain perplexed by the October Crisis, institutions have managed to confine the events safely behind the distant veil of History.

Filmography

phenomenological approach — cinema direct — debate - fact/fiction — ambiguity

Features

1962   *Seul ou avec d'autres* (with Denys Arcand, Denis Héroux, Stéphane Venne and Gilles Groulx; 64 mins., 16mm)

1963   *Pour la suite du monde /The Moontrap* (with Pierre Perrault; + co-screenplay, cinematography; 105 mins./English version 84 mins., 16mm)

1967   *Entre la mer et l'eau douce /Drifting Upstream* (+ co-screenplay, co-cinematography, co-editor; 85 mins.)

1971   *L'Acadie, l'Acadie ?!?* (documentary; with Pierre Perrault, + co-screenplay, cinematography; 118 mins./English version 75 mins., 16mm)

1974   *Les Ordres* (108 mins.)

1989   *Les Noces de papier* (86 mins.)

1992   *Sabbath Shalom* (90 mins.)

1994   *Mon amie Max* (105 mins.)

1999   *Quand je serai parti…vous vivrez encore* (*The Long Winter*; 120 mins.)

Short films

1950   *Matin* (+ cinematography, editor; 6 mins 16mm)

1954   *Chèvres* (with Claude Sylvestre; 10 mins., 16mm)

1954   *La Mattawin, rivière sauvage* (with Claude Sylvestre; + cinematography; 58 mins., 16mm)

1958   *Les Raquetteurs* (with Gilles Groulx; + cinematography; 15 mins.)

1958   *Coup d'œil no 101* (10 mins., 16mm)

1961   *La Lutte/Wrestling* (with Claude Fournier, Claude Jutra, and Marcel Carrière; + co-cinematography; 28 mins., 16mm)

1962   *Les Enfants du silence* (with Claude Jutra; + cinematography; 24 mins., 16mm)

1962   *Québec USA ou l'invasion pacifique / Visit to a Foreign Country* (with Claude Jutra; + co-cinematography; 28 mins., 16mm)

1964   *Le temps perdu/The End of Summer* (+ cinematography; 27 mins., 16mm)

1965   *La Fleur de l'âge: Geneviève* (28 mins.)

1967   *Conflit/Settlement and Conflict* (for the Canadian pavilion at Expo 67; + cinematography; 4 mins.)

1967   *Québec …?* (collective work with Lise Abastado, Serge Beauchemin et al.; 28 mins.)

1968   *Les Enfants de Néant* (France, with Annie Tresgot; + cinematography; 45 mins.)

1968   *Le beau plaisir* (with Bernard Gosselin and Pierre Perrault; + co-cinematography; 15 mins.)

1969   *Éloge du chiac* (+ co-cinematography; 27 mins., 16mm)

1969   *René Lévesque vous parle: les 6 milliards* (25 mins., 16mm)

1972   *René Lévesque pour le vrai* (+ cinematography; 27 mins., 16mm)

1973   *Le bras de levier et la rivière* (+ screenplay, cinematography;.30 mins., 16mm)

1974–80   *Le son des Français d'Amérique* (series of 27 episodes with André Gladu; 28 mins. average; 16 mm)

1976   *René Lévesque, un vrai chef* (+ cinematography; 28 mins., 16mm)

1986   *A Freedom to Move*

1988   *L'Emprise* (with Suzanne Guy)

1990   *Diogène*
1991   *Montréal vu par... Six variations sur un thème* (*Montreal Sextet*, 123 mins. total run-
        ning length; third episode, titled *La Dernière partie*; 20 mins.)

Bibliography *

Books and special journal issues

Jutras, Pierre. *Michel Brault. Copie Zéro* 5. Montréal: Cinémathèque québécoise, mai 1980.
    Some contributions republished in *Ciné-Tracts* 3.2 (Spring 1980): 30–53. Includes: Jutras,
    Pierre, "Entretien avec Michel Brault"/"Interview with Michel Brault" (*Copie Zéro* 4–16;
    Ciné-Tracts 37–48); Raymond–Marie Léger, "Témoignages: Michel Brault ou la
    meilleure part," (*Copie Zéro* 17–19); Claude Jutra, "Au Québec, c'est sûrement Michel
    Brault qui est le cinéaste le plus présent, le plus versatile, le plus prolifique, le plus
    constant"/"In Québec, Michel Brault is certainly the most attentive, the most versatile,
    the most prolific, the most constant of filmmakers" (*Copie Zéro* 20–22; *Ciné-Tracts* 49–
    51); Pierre Perrault, "Michel Brault, cinéaste"/"Michel Brault, filmmaker" (*Copie Zéro*
    23–28; *Ciné-Tracts* 30–36); Guy Borremans, "La Morale à l'œil"/"The moral eye" (*Copie
    Zéro* 29; *Ciné-Tracts* 52–53); André Laflamme, "Filmographie" (*Copie Zéro* 30–51).
Marsolais, Gilles. *Michel Brault*. Collection Cinéastes du Québec 11. Montréal: Conseil
    québécois pour la diffusion du cinéma, 1972.
——, ed. « *Les Ordres* »: *Un film de Michel Brault*. Collection Le Cinématographe 1. Mont-
    réal: L'Aurore, 1975. Includes Gilles Marsolais, "Démasquer les faux maîtres" (11–15);
    François Protat, "Un défi" (15–17); Michel Brault, "Un film sur l'humiliation" (17–18);
    "Découpage technique et dialogue" (screenplay, copiously illustrated with stills; 19–
    111); and a selection of the reviews listed below.

Interviews and statements

Adams, Chalmers, "Michel Brault," *Cinema Canada* 7 (April–May 1973): 45–46.
Bonneville, Léo. "Michel Brault: Entretien," in ⇨Bonneville, ed., *Le Cinéma québécois par
    ceux qui le font*, 129–46.
——. "Entretient avec Michel Brault," *Séquences* 68 (février 1972): 4–14.
Boudreault, J.C. "A propos de 'Le combat des sourds' de Michel Moreau; Cinéma direct et
    cinéma pédagogique: Michel Brault et Michel Moreau," *Cinéma Québec* 4.3 (mai 1975):
    23–27.
Brault, Michel. "Le cinéma québécois en quelques mots," in ⇨Marie–Christine Abel,
    André Giguère & Luc Perrault, ed., *Le cinéma québécois à l'heure internationale*, 134–38.
——. "Un film sur l'humiliation," in Gilles Marsolais, ed., *Les Ordres*, 17–18.
——, & G. Hannebelle. "*Les Ordres*," *Écran 75* 38 (juillet–août 1975): 54–56.
Delmas, Jean, & René Prédal. "Entretien avec Michel Brault," *Jeune cinéma* 88 (juillet–août
    1975): 21–25.
Élia, Maurice. "Brève rencontre avec Michel Brault," *Écran 76* 44 (février 1976): 7–11.
Evanchuck, P.M., "An innerview of Michel Brault, filmmaker," and biography/filmo-
    graphy, *Motion* (January–March, 1975): 11–13 (filmography), 14–22 (interview).

---

* Compiled with the assistance of Jacqueline Lane and Glen Wood.

Jutras, Pierre. "Entretien avec Michel Brault," *Copie Zéro* 5 (1980): 5–16.

Maulucci, Anthony S. "Filming isn't writing," *Motion* 4.2 (January–March 1975): 32–33.

Wera, Françoise. "Entretien avec Michel Brault: 'La chance c'est d'avoir pu choisir'," *Ciné-Bulles* 6.4 (mai–juillet 1987): 4–8.

Articles, essays and sections in books

Bastien, Jean Pierre. *Québec 75: Cinéma/Textes et Documentation*. Montréal: Cinémathèque québécoise, Musée du cinéma; Institut d'art contemporain, 1975.

Bégin, J.P. "L'aventure du cinéma direct et *Les Ordres*," *Motion* 4.2 (janvier–mars 1975): 34–37.

Bonneville, Léo. "Michel Brault: aperçu critique, filmographie, bibliographie," in ⇨Bonneville, *Le Cinéma quécois par ceux qui le font*, 146–50.

Brûlé, Michel. "Un constat d'impuissance à l'égard des groupes d'opposition," *Cinéma Québec* 4.1 (décembre 1974): 13–17.

Clandfield, David. "From the Picturesque to the Familiar: Films of the French Unit at the NFB (1958–1964)," *Ciné-Tracts* 1.4 (Spring–Summer 1978): 50–62.

Daigneault, Claude. "De l'intolérance à l'humiliation; Le film de Michel Brault: Un événement capital dans l'histoire de notre cinéma," *Le Soleil* (29 septembre 1974): D3–4.

Delaney, Marshall. "Canada's Trauma Produces a Major Work of Art," *Saturday Night* 90.2 (June 1975): 78, 80; repr. as "Canada's Trauma and Michel Brault" (as part of Delaney, "Artists in the Shadows: Some Notable Canadian Movies," 2–17) in ⇨Seth Feldman, ed., *Take Two*, 2–5.

Delisle, Martin. "Spry et Brault," *Motion* (janvier–mars 1975): 38–39.

Eisler, K. "Doppler effect at the Dunbar," *Movietone* 43 (September 1975): 27–31.

Evanchuck, P.M. *Motion* 4.2 (January–March 1975): 39.

——. "The October Crisis: 'Action – Reaction'," *Motion* 4.2 (January–March 1975): 40–43.

Lamonde, Y. "Réflexions autour d'un cinéma: indirectement le cinéma direct," *Cinéma Québec* 4.1 (décembre 1974): 22–24.

Leach, James. "Second Images: Reflections on the Canadian Cinema(s) in the Seventies," in ⇨Seth Feldman, ed., *Take Two*, 100–10.

Marsolais, Gilles. "Michel Brault, cinéaste exemplaire," *Vie des arts* 20.78 (printemps 1975): 44–55.

——. "Démasquer les faux maîtres," Gilles Marsolais, ed., *Les Ordres*, 11–14.

Miller, Mark. "The Québec Crisis: Once More With Feeling," *Cinema Canada* 20 (July–August 1975): 64–65.

Morris, Peter. "Brault, Michel" and "*Les Ordres*," in ⇨Morris, *The Film Companion*, 40–42, 221–22.

⇨Pallister, Janis L., *The Cinema of Québec*, 319–24.

Poisson, Roch. "La Solitude va bien à Jean Lapointe" (interview with the actor), *Nous* 4.8 (janvier 1977): 18–19.

⇨Prédal, René. *Jeune cinéma canadien*, 19–32.

Rozon, René. *Take One* 4.9 (January–February 1974): 34.

Shuster, Nat. *Motion* 4.2(January–March 1975): 23–24.

Sotiaux, Daniel. "*Les Ordres*" (also includes interview with Brault), *Revue belge du cinéma* 13 (octobre 1979): 1–14.

Toubiana, Serge. "...mais qui raisonne (*Les Ordres*, Section speciale)," *Cahiers du cinéma* 258–59 (juillet–août 1975): 42–47.

Uhde, Jan. "Estrangement Elements in Brault's *Les Ordres*," *Canadian Drama/L'Art dramatique canadien* 5.1 (Spring 1979): 53–60.

Vallières, Pierre. "Témoignage d'un otage privilégié des *Ordres*: Brault a manqué son coup"/"An Account by a Privileged Hostage of *Les Ordres*: Brault Has Missed His Shot," *Cinéma Québec* 4.1 (décembre 1974): 18–20. English tr by John Van Burek repr. in ⇨Feldman & Nelson, ed., *Canadian Film Reader*, 264–68.

Reviews (see also *Les Ordres: Dossier de Presse* [Montréal: Collège Montmorency, 1975])

Jean-Marc Piotte, "Et derrière?" *Le Devoir* (5 mai 1974): 13, 17; repr. in Gilles Marsolais, ed., *Les Ordres*, 125–27; Jocelyne Dépatie, "Une vision partielle mais juste de la crise d'octobre," *Journal de Montréal* (27 septembre 1974); repr. in Gilles Marsolais, ed., *Les Ordres*, 121; René Lévesque, "Pourquoi *Les Ordres*?" *Le Jour* (28 septembre 1974); repr. in Gilles Marsolais, ed., *Les Ordres*, 124; Luc Perreault, "Portrait d'une humiliation; Montrer la crise d'octobre afin de l'exorciser," *La Presse* (28 septembre 1974): E15; repr. in Gilles Marsolais, ed., *Les Ordres*, 117; Robert Lévesque, "Un très grand film sur un très grand sujet," *Québec-Presse* (29 septembre 1974), repr. in Gilles Marsolais, ed., *Les Ordres*, 117–18; Jack Kapica, "War Measures revisited," *Gazette* (Montreal; 4 October 1974): 36; Jean Éthier-Blais, "Ordre et désordre," *Le Devoir* (5 octobre 1974): 13; Martin Knelman, "*Les Ordres* an eloquent response to shame of October 1970," *Globe & Mail* (5 October 1974): 29, rev. and repr. (as part of "Politics and Québec") in ⇨Knelman, *This Is Where We Came In*, 85–88; André Leroux, "Cri de coeur," *Le Devoir* (5 octobre 1974): 13, 19,; repr. in Gilles Marsolais, ed., *Les Ordres*, 119–20; Geoffrey James, "Night of the garbage bags," *Time* 104 (Canada; 7 October 1974): 12; Guy Milot, "Un rappel éloquent des événements d'octobre 1970," *Le Devoir* (7 octobre 1974): 5; Janick Beaulieu, *Séquences* 78 (octobre 1974): 26–28; Serge Dussault, "Quand la réalité est insupportable, on n'y croit plus!," *La Presse* (9 novembre 1974): C10, repr. in Gilles Marsolais, ed., *Les Ordres*, 121–24; Marc Blandford, "Un jour à l'aube, les forces de l'ordre...," *Le Maclean* 14 (16 novembre 1974): 12, 16; Jean-Pierre Tadros, *Variety* 257.2 (20 November 1974): 16; Ronald Blumer, "The Knock in the Middle of the Night: *Les Ordres*," *Cinema Canada* 17 (December 1974–January 1975): 77; Pierre Véronneau, "Lettre du Québec: Deux films, un évènement politique," *Cinéma 1975* 195 (février 1975): 16–17; John Hofsess, "Baring the Shame of 1970," *Maclean's* 88.4 (April 1975): 88; Gene Moskowitz, *Variety* 279 (21 May 1975): 22; Barry Thomson, *Pulse* 1.8 (May 1975): 12; Doug Fetherling, *Canadian Forum* 55 (June 1975): 48–49; repr. Fetherling, *The Blue Notebook: Reports on Canadian Culture* (Oakville, Ontario: Mosaic, 1985): 89–91; F. Maupin, *Revue du cinéma* 297 (juin–juillet 1975): 14; A. Cervoni, *Cinéma 1975* 200 (juillet–août 1975): 134–35; Michel Ciment, *Positif* 171–72 (juillet–août 1975): 106; Jean Delmas, *Jeune cinéma* 88 (juillet–août 1975): 20–21; François Gévaudan, "Une tendance à la démesure" (report on Cannes Film Festival 1975), *Cinéma 75* 200 (juillet–août 1975): 83–89; Sandra Hall, "Orders," *Cinema Papers* 2 (July–August 1975): 132; Olivier Serre, *Téléciné* 201 (July–August 1975): 24; Guy Gauthier, *Revue du cinéma: Image et Son* 298 (septembre 1975): 113–14; Penelope Houston, "Cannes 75," *Sight and Sound* 44.3 (Summer 1975): 151–52; Luc Perreault, "Sorrente: Une simple opération de marketing," *La Presse* (5 octobre 1974): D15; Jacques Chevallier, *Revue du Cinéma* 299 (octobre 1975): 274–75; R. Pede, *Film and TV* 223 (December 1975): 20–21; René Rozon, *Take One* 4.9 (1975): 34; David Wilson, *Monthly Film Bulletin* 43.510 (July 1976): 150–51.

ଛ

FIGURE 5

Les bons débarras (Francis Mankiewicz, 1980; produced by Claude
Godbout and Marcia Couëlle) – Marie Tifo (Michelle); Charlotte
Laurier (Manon).

5 Les bons débarras (Francis Mankiewicz, 1980)

Production: produced 1978, released in Montreal 29 February 1980. A production of Les Productions Prisma Inc. (Montréal), with the financial participation of the Canadian Film Development Corporation, L'Institut québécois du cinéma, and the Société de Radio-Télévision du Québec. **Director:** Francis Mankiewicz. **Producers:** Claude Godbout, Marcia Couëlle. **Screenplay:** Réjean Ducharme. **Cinematographer:** Michel Brault. **Editor:** André Corriveau. **Music:** Bernard Buisson. **Art Director:** Michel Proulx. **Sound:** Henri Blondeau. **Colour, 114 mins., 35mm.**

Cast: Charlotte Laurier (Manon), **Marie Tifo** (Michelle), **Germain Houde** (Guy), **Louise Marleau** (Mme Viau–Vachon), **Roger Lebel** (Maurice), **Gilbert Sicotte** (Gaëtan), **Jean–Pierre Bergeron** (Fernand), **Serge Thériault, Léo Ilial, Madeleine Chartrand, Louise Rinfret.**

Synopsis: In an isolated house near a small town in rural Québec, thirteen-year-old Manon lives with her unmarried mother, Michelle, and her mother's retarded brother, Guy. They survive by chopping firewood and selling it to customers in the area. Manon is a precocious and sensitive child, uninterested in school, deeply absorbed in her reading of the novel *Wuthering Heights*, and obsessed with obtaining her mother's absolute love. Guy lives in a world of his own, romantically roused by his response to the wealthy Madame Viau–Vachon, whom they provide with firewood. Michelle stands at the centre of several people who demand her affection: Manon, Guy, Maurice, her policeman boyfriend and Gaëtan, a mechanic and friend of Manon's. When Michelle discovers she is pregnant by Maurice, she attempts to share her joy with Manon, but it has the opposite effect. Manon leaves home, desperate to prove she is capable of caring for her mother in every possible way. After she returns, she drives Guy to suicide, prevents her mother from hearing the news, and cuts her mother's emotional ties to Maurice and the outside world.

∞

Canadian gothic and *Les bons débarras*
The night side of the soul

———————————— ℰꙮ

Peter Morris

B ASED ON A SCRIPT by the Québec novelist and dramatist Réjean Du-charme, *Les bons débarras* (Good Riddance) was made at a cost of $600,000 and released in the fall of 1980 to almost universal acclaim. When Francis Mankiewicz's tale of passion, jealousy, and all-embracing love was selected as Best Canadian Film of 1980 at the Academy of Canadian Cinema's Genie Awards, it capped a landslide of achievements. The film had earlier won seven other Genies – for best cinematography, editing, sound, original screenplay, actress, and supporting actor. Canadian critics had already been virtually unanimous in their reviews, praising the baroque poetry of the film's dialogue, its austere, evocative imagery, spare narrative action, and brilliant performances. In the USA, Stanley Kauffmann was the most receptive, noting that "seeing the film was like opening an unmarked door and finding a treasury."[1] Most critics noted the way in which Mankiewicz melded the various elements of the film in order to generate a sense of the menace of evil, building to a crescendo of horror. Barbara Samuels singled out the cinematography and screenplay: "Mankiewicz has created images of a powerfully dark beauty, visions that meld with rather than subordinate, the lean, eloquent script."[2] John Locke was more fulsome:

> Francis Mankiewicz's film has it all: it is a superbly crafted, beautifully acted, sensually and intellectually satisfying film reflecting its regional origins [...] The performances are uniformly excellent [...] While [Charlotte] Laurier's is the single most extraordinary performance [as Manon], she is not alone. Marie Tifo as Manon's mother, Germain Houde as the brother, and Gilbert Sicotte as Gaëtan (Manon's mechanic friend) are all remarkable. Marie Tifo has an intensity and presence perfect for her role.[3]

---

[1] Stanley Kauffmann, "Intimations of Mortality," *New Republic* 184 (7 February 1981): 24.

[2] Barbara Samuels, *Cinema Canada* 65 (May 1980): 33.

[3] John Locke, "Shooting for the Best," *Cinema Canada* 73 (April 1981): 25.

Locke went on to suggest that *Les bons débarras* "best represents the direction
our national cinema should take if it is to establish itself internationally as a
distinct cinema of quality" (25). But he was not alone. Robert Fulford, under
his pen-name Marshall Delaney, found the film "so eloquent and rooted in
current Québec realities that it revives all those hopes we felt for Canadian
movies only a few years ago."[4] Mankiewicz's film, building on the momentum it established in Canada, was this country's entry in the Hollywood
Academy Awards and since then has firmly established itself in the canon of
Canadian cinema.

A great director, sadly gone

The director Francis Mankiewicz is considered one of the best filmmakers
and writers of his generation in Québec. Born of Polish parents in Shanghai
on 15 March 1944,[5] he came to Canada when he was one year old. After
studying geology at McGill University and the Université de Montréal, he
went to England in 1966 to study filmmaking in London. When he returned
to Montreal in 1968, he worked as a cameraman and as an assistant director
on several sponsored films and features before directing his first film in
1972, *Le temps d'une chasse*. This remarkable debut feature is centered on the
picaresque adventures of three men and the young son of one of them on a
hunting expedition. Written also by Mankiewicz (and featuring unforget-
table camerawork by Michel Brault), it has a gentle sense of humour and,
though critical of the macho behaviour of the characters, presents them as
trapped by social myths. As with several of his best later films, it relies on
the perspective of a child as its central dramatic premiss and makes effective
use of natural landscape as a means of defining his characters.

Although he has written screenplays on his own (*Les vagues* and *Berthier
en bas*, both in 1975), Mankiewicz's mature films are based on adaptations. In
1978, after directing several short films and documentaries, he adapted to
film the theatrical comedy of manners, *Une Amie d'enfance*, written by Louis
Saia and Louise Roy – essentially a witty discussion among the four central
characters set entirely in a garden. *Les bons débarras* was the first of two col-

---

[4] Marshall Delaney [Robert Fulford], "Close to Home," *Saturday Night* (November
1980): 85, repr. in ⇨Seth Feldman, *Take Two* (Toronto: Irwin, 1984): 9–11.

[5] Francis Mankiewicz is also the nephew of the famous American filmmakers Herman
and Joseph Mankiewicz.

laborations with Réjean Ducharme. In speaking about their collaboration, Mankiewicz observed:

> When Ducharme sends you a script, he sends you a universe – a universe in which there are a number of levels of content and meaning [...] Though the film looks realistic, the characters often express themselves through a kind of poetry [...] Réjean's scenes always begin where drama begins and not where life begins.[6]

To help convey Ducharme's peculiar drama, Mankiewicz turned to one of Canada's great cinematographers, Michel Brault. Of their work together, Mankiewicz noted:

> We didn't want high contrasts. Even when the sun was out, we shot with back-light so as not to get sharp shadows across the face. We wanted a very textured picture, in which you could feel the earth, the leaves, the house and the texture of people's faces.[7]

They were also seeking to emulate the hard, flat planes and sense of loneliness and mystery associated with the American urban-realist paintings of Edward Hopper, inspired in particular by his *Chop Suey*.

> La lumière et l'atmosphere de solitude qui baignent le tableau de Hopper traduisaient parfaitment l'ambiance et la texture qu'on cherchait pour traduire l'univers à la fois personnel et nord-américain de Ducharme.[8]

In 1979 Ducharme wrote the screenplay for their follow-up film, *Les Beaux souvenirs* (Happy Memories). This film has a motherless family at its core in contrast to the fatherless family of the earlier film, but tragedy again arises out of the exclusivity of the family unit. It is, however, more transparent in its dramatic structure and lacks the tragic power of *Les bons débarras*.

His last film in French, *Les Portes tournantes* (1988), was adapted from the novel by Jacques Savoie and, again, is structured around the perspective of a child. Mankiewicz also directed three films in English for CBC television, two of which received wide critical praise and were considerable international successes: *Love and Hate* and *Conspiracy of Silence*. Both films were based on sensational Canadian crimes but bear little comparison to his best work in French. Mankiewicz died of cancer in Montreal, 14 August 1993.

---

6 Joan Irving, "Francis Mankiewicz: To Berlin with Love," *Cinema Canada* 63 (March 1980): 12–13.

7 Irving, "Francis Mankiewicz: To Berlin with Love," 14.

8 Quoted in Réal La Rochelle, *Cinéma en rouge et noir* (Montreal: Éditions Triptyque, 1994): 220.

A sinister dream

Les bons débarras begins deceptively as a naturalistic tale of the dispossessed, but develops inexorably into tragedy, a quasi-mythic tale of evil and of survival above all else. It is also the sinister dream of a child who wants nothing more, and nothing less, than to love her mother.

Such later critics as Ian Lockerbie[9] have analyzed the film as an allegory of Québec nationhood from the period following the 1980 Québec referendum. It is argued that this period in Québec cinema is marked by an aversion to overtly nationalist themes in favour of allegorical themes of subjugation and victimization, typically in stories in which the father is absent or ineffectual. While it might seem tempting to apply such a socio-symptomatic approach to this film featuring a fatherless child, one should note that it was, in fact, produced prior to the referendum and was one of several Canadian films, both English and French, to focus on children with absent or inadequate fathers. Given the film's style, tone and structure, other critical approaches might be more appropriate.

Throughout the film, the young daughter, Manon, is shown reading and quoting from Emily Brontë's classic novel *Wuthering Heights*. Though the filmmakers certainly did not offer the film as a parallel to the novel (the differences are perhaps more meaningful than the similarities), the novel does function as a kind of literary chorus, inviting us to consider the film's gothic structure. Certainly, many of the characteristic marks of the gothic are apparent. Not least among these are the claustrophobic atmosphere (the Yorkshire moors of the novel have their parallel in the rural Québec of the film), the use of different narrative voices, and the irruption of the monstrous, irrational id into rational society.

Canadian critic Margot Northey, in her book *The Haunted Wilderness*, argues that a variant of gothic fiction is apparent in the form of "Canadian Gothic."[10] She points out, for example, that, where the gothic novel typically prefers the irrational, passionate side of human nature over the civilized, Canadian Gothic stresses the threatening or negative side of both. There is "a pattern of double menace" (109). This sense of double menace is very

---

9 Ian Lockerbie, "Québec Cinema as an Allegory of Nationhood: The Example of *Les bons débarras*, " in *Image and Identity: Theatre and Cinema in Scotland and Québec*, ed. Ian Lockerbie (John Grierson Archive Occasional Papers 2; Stirling: Department of French, U of Stirling P, 1988): 120.

10 Margot Northey, *The Haunted Wilderness: The Gothic and Grotesque in Canadian Fiction* (Toronto: U of Toronto P, 1976): 109. Further page references are in the text.

much present in this film: society offers neither love nor support to the family, but Manon's irrational solution to her lack is viewed with equal horror. A second motif Northey characterizes as "the insistence upon evil despite an abandonment of any explicit religious dimension [...] God may be dead but the devil lives on"; in this film, it is difficult not to conclude that Manon is the manifestation "of a primal evil which goes beyond behaviourist or sociological explanations" (108).

Finally, Northey argues that "the dominance of one human over another is a prime contribution to the final doom or destructive action of the story"; that sexual conflict is a far from frequent cause of "the willful desire for domination," in contrast to the typical gothic novel (109). Although there are hints of a sexual conflict between Manon and her mother (in their interactions with Gaëtan), Northey's analysis of Canadian fiction fits *Les bons débarras* almost perfectly. Manon's urge to control or manipulate other people is a prime motivating force in the film, and it leads to a doom that resonates beyond the film's final images.

The tone of the film is set in the opening sequence. A high-angle camera shot depicts the Québec countryside in the fall, the leaves of the trees forming pretty patterns of red and gold – a not untypical Canadian film image. But the lush pastoral effect is undermined by the ominous sound of a chainsaw in the background; this world may not be as innocent as it seems. Indeed, it is an apt introduction to what Northey has characterized as a place that allows "the dark mysteries of life" to be brought to the fore. Another high-angle shot shows a typical small Québec town in the Laurentian hills north of Montreal. (Its name, Val des Vals [vale of vales], is itself somewhat ominous.) A police car does a U-turn in the middle of the street, its siren, momentarily and pointlessly, turned on. The car is driven by Michelle's policeman lover, Maurice, through an increasingly drab and wet countryside until it arrives, with another pointless use of the siren, at the isolated and equally drab home of Michelle, her retarded brother Guy, and her 13-year-old daughter Manon. The distance from town, the twisting roads, and the ramshackle house and yard all indicate that this family is clearly among the dispossessed. This is, in fact, familiar metaphoric terrain: the landscape of social victims so typical of the Canadian realist tradition.

Les bons débarras is meticulous in its observation of the social and physical environment: the gloomy fall landscape, from which the light seems to have been drained; the depressed small town; the seedy bars; and, not least, the contrasting lifestyle of the rich Mme Viau–Vachon. Like the Yorkshire

moors in Brontë's *Wuthering Heights* (the novel quoted often by Manon during the film), the landscape is an enveloping presence, taking on an almost
abstract symbolic character. The sense of observation is matched in the *mise-
en-scène*, which has a raw, casual, apparently unstaged quality. It appears to
offer simple vignettes from the lives of the three central characters, portraits
that range from the comic through the grotesque to the derisory and even
tragic. However, the film's naturalism and observational style are deceptive.
The gothic often uses a surface naturalism to better portray what Davendra
Varma has called "the night side of the soul," the sense of gloom and terror
lurking beneath the accepted surface of life, the mysterious non-rational
levels of existence.[11]

The film, indeed, projects a profound sense of ambiguity about the landscape. On the one hand, there is a fascination with its beauty, its excitement,
its vigour, its continuity amid change. At the same time, there is a tone of
danger, of nature as a claustrophobic trap, a place of psychic, if not physical,
danger. It might be noted that this ambiguity about nature has a long tradition in Canadian fiction. Northrop Frye, for example, has noted "the deep
tone of terror" associated with nature, adding that: "It is not a terror of the
danger or discomforts or even the mysteries of nature, but a terror of the
soul at something these things manifest."[12]

The sense of menace engendered by the film at first seems focused on
Guy, mentally retarded after suffering from meningitis as a child. He projects resentment in almost every early scene, whether rebelling against
orders, stealing money to get drunk, or fighting invisible opponents in the
street. Manon, initially, appears to be the usual peripheral child character, a
little wilful, perhaps, but understandably so, given her apparent powerlessness in social circumstances she did not choose. It is soon clear, however,
that Manon is more complex than she seems. As the film progresses and she
develops into the film's central character, Manon is shown with several different faces. Early in the film, there is Manon, the indulged, somewhat
spoiled brat, who orders her mother home before midnight or she "will lock
the door." (To which her mother affectionately responds, "Yes, boss.") There

---

[11] Devendra P. Varma, *The Gothic Flame: A History of the Gothic Novel in England* (London: Arthur Barker, 1957): 224.

[12] Northrop Frye, *The Bush Garden: Essays on the Canadian Imagination* (Toronto: Anansi,
1971): 225. See also: Gaile McGregor, *The Wacousta Syndrome: Explorations in the Canadian
Landscape* (Toronto: U of Toronto P, 1985), which offers a detailed discussion of this characteristic.

is the happy, flirtatious Manon shown with the mechanic Gaëtan, especially during the scene in his truck. Then there is the Manon who is contemptuous and insulting toward her uncle Guy – and who eventually provokes his death. There is the vicious Manon who orders her dog to bite Maurice and later falsely accuses Maurice of sexually molesting her. There is the manipulative, blackmailing Manon, resentful over her mother's pregnancy. And, above all, there is Manon as lover, obsessed with possessing her mother's love solely for herself.

Multiple perspectives

As already indicated, throughout the film Manon is shown reading *Wuthering Heights*. Whether this was intended as a hint by the writer and director about the film's gothic structure is perhaps irrelevant. The device acts as a kind of literary chorus, shifting our attention from the overt observational style to themes of evil and psychological obsession. Manon's readings often uncannily echo events we have just seen or are about to see. The novel sometimes seems like a text guiding her own transformation from powerlessness through evil manipulation to ultimate control over her love-object.

This transformation of Manon from precocious adolescent to possessive lover depends on a subtle and complex use of point of view. Indeed, the use of narrative point of view in *Wuthering Heights* also has its parallels in *Les bons débarras*. Manon may, so to speak, get the last word, but each of the family members provides a perspective on the events. The result is a multi-layered texture that emphasizes the film's tragic trajectory.

In the skein of multiple perspectives that weave the fabric of the film, Guy's point of view is minimal. His is best identified in terms of his staring through windows and his watching Mme Viau–Vachon in her swimming pool – scenes that are stylized, almost abstract, in their staging. Guy's fantasies are the only ones overtly expressed as such in the film. The image of Mme Viau–Vachon emerging from the swimming pool becomes his final dream-like vision as the woman, no longer appearing to sense a lurking threat, and accompanied by Puccini's "O Mio Bambino Caro," runs eagerly to Guy. His own obsession becomes his doom, but seems to offer him a better alternative than Manon's constant torments. The Manon seen through Guy's eyes is brutal and vicious, especially in the scene before his death; she cannot abide the fact that some of her mother's love must go toward protecting Guy.

Michelle's point of view dominates the first part of the film. Here Manon is seen as little different than most adolescent girls. She is sometimes cheeky, wilful, argumentative, self-centred, and disobedient. Her modest attempts at control over her mother seem to be no more than minor irritants. Michelle herself seems happy and well-balanced. Although she is poor, she is not powerless in her own environment and is clearly capable of making her own life-decisions, whether in her family, in her relationship with Maurice, or concerning her pregnancy. There are several scenes here in which Michelle is typically motherly: loving and protective, but also responsible and in control.

The first major shift in perspective occurs about fifteen minutes into the film, following the scene with Maurice and Michelle in the restaurant. Manon is reading *Wuthering Heights*; she looks up from her reading, but the reverse shot does not show what she is looking at – it shows another image of Manon reading. The effect is oddly disturbing – the first hint that the film will shift from naturalistic observation into the psychic life of Manon. Later, following the scene with Michelle and Maurice in bed (filmed in such a way that Maurice in bed does look like the "fat pig" Manon calls him), Manon herself is in bed alone with her book. She hears a dog crying, runs to the window, and looks out; this time, the reverse shot shows the dog. Obviously disturbed, Manon runs back to bed and pulls the covers over her head. This window shot is a reprise of an earlier shot of Manon at the window, and underlines the window/door motif that is so typical of the gothic narrative, with its overtones of penetration, of possibilities, yet of distance. This motif is used most revealingly in Guy's peering into the Viau–Vachon house, but it recurs constantly, though without emphasis, throughout the film. (Guy is often seen looking in windows at what others are doing.) Following Manon's return to bed, there is a cut to Guy in the street, fighting opponents only he can see. It is not too fanciful to suggest this scene is Manon's projection or wishful thinking. That it might be a projection is reinforced by the sequence that follows Guy's rescue by Michelle: a series of amorphous, almost disorienting shots in complete contrast to the naturalistic style earlier in the film. Back in the house, there is a sequence of shots: Manon and the sound of heavy breathing; Guy; Manon turning toward her mother in bed; Guy's hand in the frame; Manon's mother sitting by the bed; Manon and her mother, but this time with Manon turning away. The implication is that Manon sees Michelle's love for and protection of Guy as a threat, separating her from her mother.

The sequence that follows presents Manon's own self-image. Here, there are no moments when Manon's love for her mother seems threatened. In the scenes with Gaëtan in his truck and later in the woods rescuing Michelle and Guy, Manon is simply a happy kid, capable of jokes, games, laughter, and innocent flirting. Her mother, in contrast, seems like a nagging shrew, her face distorted into a caricature of the Michelle previously seen. Guy is absent from the last part of this sequence but, since Michelle earlier complained at his stupidity and ineffectiveness, he seems more pathetic than the potential threat of the previous sequence.

The key sequence marking the transition from an apparent focus on Michelle to one on Manon occurs about half-way through the film, following Michelle's return home from a spirited discussion with Maurice over her right to choose whether to keep the baby. Apart from one shot, the sequence is presented entirely from Michelle's point of view. Michelle comforts Manon, who has walked home after another vindictive confrontation with Guy. When Manon walks into her room, Michelle gently refuses to allow her to stay in her bed, and Manon storms out. The next shot is of Manon reading a passage from *Wuthering Heights* ("your veins are full of ice-water but mine are boiling hot") that uncannily reflects her sense that her mother does not share her passion. As Michelle comes into the room, we return to her point of view as Manon and her mother leave for a walk. During the walk, Manon passionately professes her love for her mother, adding: "I keep wishing the two of us were shipwrecked. Just you and me on a desert island, far away." Michelle seems more puzzled than moved by the declaration, but tries to extend the intimate moment by telling Manon about the baby. Instead of sharing her mother's joy, Manon reacts angrily, refers to "a baby cop, a baby Maurice," and tells her mother: "You disgust me." The final shot of the sequence is a close-up of Michelle's face, her eyes filled with tears.

Michelle's point of view is maintained in the next sequence. As she is preparing breakfast for Guy, Manon telephones; she has skipped school (not for the first time) and, as Michelle describes it, is "pouting." During the conversation, Michelle is evidently a responsible mother, sympathetic and comforting, yet authoritative. When Manon announces she is un-happy, Michelle asks her why; Manon does not answer; Michelle leaves the phone to get Guy out of bed – an action which itself confirms for Manon that she is not the sole possessor of her mother's love ("Just you and me alone"); she leaves the phone dangling and walks away. (One is reminded here of the famous line in *Wuthering Heights* about love being "a source of little visible delight, but necessary.")

Manon's second phone call goes unanswered. But the third call begins to shift the balance of control away from Michelle to Manon. Using the emotional blackmail that she will repeat following her return home, she accuses her mother of not loving her and threatens to steal her away if that is the only way she can have her. She announces she will wander around "like an old dog with no collar," before coming home. Michelle, in tight close-up throughout, is reduced to virtual speechlessness and, in the next scene, to tears. The largely one-sided conversation is more akin to one between estranged lovers than between daughter and mother.

Manon has discovered a source of control over her mother and, although Michelle acts nonchalantly when Manon returns home, Manon's control over events continues to escalate. The first conscious manifestation of her manipulation occurs during her birthday party. Behaving sulkily throughout, even over Maurice's generous gift of a bicycle, she then whispers to her mother that Maurice has touched her sexually. Michelle, understandably, reacts with horror. Tinged by guilt over Manon's earlier accusation of not caring about her, she violently forces Maurice to leave the party without giving him an opportunity to defend himself. After he leaves, a drunken Guy is brought home by police. The ominous scene that follows effectively introduces the climax of the film: Manon awakens in her mother's bed in the middle of the night to discover her mother is missing. In the beam of a flashlight she sees her mother protectively nursing Guy. When she asks her mother if she's coming back to bed, Michelle simply shushes her, and Manon's face tightens in a grimace.

The final third of the film, staged almost entirely from Manon's point of view, draws us into the depths of her obsession as she becomes aware of the threat to sole possession of her mother's love and determines to eliminate it. She first attempts to remove the threat represented by Maurice, and tries to tempt her mother back to the time "before Maurice," a time when she went out and enjoyed herself but had no love for any man in particular. Gaëtan is not a threat to Manon, since he seems to care only about fun and sex.

The morning following the scene with Guy and her mother seems to return to the earlier observational social-realist style. However, it soon becomes clear that this is still following Manon's point of view. Her mother is the same nagging shrew she was earlier in the woods, and Manon again tells her, "You sure are a pain," when Michelle fails to respond to her overtures of affectionate possession. (Later, in the town, there is a reprise of the woods scene, as Michelle chases Manon across the street.) In the truck, Manon tries a different approach, urging her mother to find herself "a rich guy" with a sports car. Her monologue then turns in a direction parallel to that of the 'desert island' one, but more ominous. She describes how they will drive fast in the car, have an accident and "your blood and mine would mingle" so that no one could tell them apart. As elsewhere in the film, Manon's desires become apparent reality when Michelle indeed meets a "rich guy" who rescues her after the truck's tire is punctured.

Manon continues to display her sulky, willful, side to Michelle and her flirtatious side to Gaëtan as they leave to spend the day drinking in a local hotel. During one interlude from Michelle's and Gaëtan's time in the hotel, Manon confides to Gaëtan: "If she's punishing me, she's in for a big surprise. Because I'm liable to outdo her." Manon's behaviour softens only when, late in the day, Michelle returns to the car, bursts into tears, and asks Manon why she treats her this way: "Why are you breaking my heart?" A tearful Manon, urging her not to cry, responds: "I'll never hurt you again."

The film retains, until the final tragic scenes, an almost playful tone. Yet it is now clear that Manon is the kind of character who carries in her unconscious what William Van O'Connor calls "not merely willfulness or the need to indulge [herself], but a deep bestiality and dark brutality."[13] During a meal in a restaurant, Manon again seems reassured that she has regained her mother's sole love. This is reinforced in the scene following, when Manon and her mother exchange a drink during a kiss, in the manner of lovers.

However, despite the reconciliation and the sense of Manon's apparent joy, there are constant reminders, through cutaways, of Guy's presence. He and his friend Ferdinand drink on a isolated roadway and are later thrown out of a beer hall; Guy remains the outsider, excluded from normal social intercourse.

Manon is immediately reminded of the threat Guy offers when Michelle insists on taking Guy ice-skating with them. She tells her mother: "You sure do turn into a pain fast." The threat Manon feels is presented visually in the next sequence. Michelle and Gaëtan are skating hand-in-hand, with a laughing Manon hanging on between them. Behind them, in the rear of the shot, is a slightly out-of-focus Guy, like a ghostly presence at the feast. Manon's

---

[13] William Van O'Connor, *The Grotesque: An American Genre and Other Essays* (Carbondale: U of Illinois P, 1962).

"dark brutality" takes control in the following scene, in a manner reminiscent of the scene in which she accuses Maurice of sexual molestation. Sent by Michelle to prevent Guy from driving the truck, Manon finds him already sitting in it. Her face twisted with hatred, Manon urges him to get drunk and leave: "Get out of here, moron. You make me sick." An obviously incapable Guy drives the truck away. His elimination as a threat is both terrifying and terrible. Guy is still haunted by his own obsessive vision of Mme Viau–Vachon. However, this time in his fantasy and to the music of Puccini's "O Mio Bambino Caro," she runs towards him; Guy drives off a cliff in order to meet her. Manon, meanwhile, casually tells her mother that Guy had already left.

The final scenes are chilling. Manon lies in bed beside her slightly tipsy and drowsy mother, reading from *Wuthering Heights* as Guy, pressured by Manon, plunges to his death. She tells her mother, "Listen to me and close your eyes. Everything will work out." When Maurice telephones to report Guy's death, Manon calmly responds that Michelle does not wish to speak to him. She returns to her mother in bed and reads from the novel's famous conclusion: "... listened to the soft wind breathing through the grass; and wondered how anyone could ever imagine unquiet slumbers for the sleepers in that quiet earth."

She turns to her mother, puts an arm around her in a manner that seems more possessive than protective, and says: "Mommy. Mommy. I'm finished. Goodnight." As the image fades to black, Michelle is sleeping while Manon's eyes are still open.

These final scenes are an almost self-reflexive reminder of the ability of the gothic tale to depict the awful powers of the unconscious and the ever-present threat of evil. Margot Northey argues that this threat in Canadian Gothic is often a shaking of the social order. If this is so, then *Les bons débarras* makes us wonder about the fragility of such social concepts as the nuclear family and home – wonder at their fragility in the face of a child's obsession; a child whose only wish is to be loved by her mother.

ଔ

where's the social analysis?
– description but not realised

Filmography

Features

1972   *Le temps d'une chasse* (98 mins.)
1978   *Une Amie d'enfance* (85 mins.)
1980   *Les bons débarras* (114 mins.)
1981   *Les beaux souvenirs* (114 mins.)
1988   *Les Portes tournantes* (101 mins.)

Shorts

1973   *Une Cause en civil* (17 mins.)
1973   *Un procès criminel* (23 mins.)
1973   *Valentin* (30 mins., 16 mm)
1974   *L'Orientation* (30 mins., 16 mm)
1975   *Expropriation* (57 mins., 16 mm)
1976   *Pointe Pelée* (10 mins., 16 mm)
1976   *What We Have Here is a People Problem* (57 mins., 16mm/TV)
1977   *Suicide en prison* (25 mins., 16mm)
1978   *A Matter of Choice* (57 mins., 16 mm/TV)
1984   Eleven commercials for Les Productions Téléscène (30 seconds each)
1985   *The Sight* (25 mins., 16mm)
1987   *And Then You Die* (105 mins., 16 mm/TV)
1989   *Love and Hate: The Story of Colin and Joanne Thatcher* (also known as *Love and Hate: A Marriage Made in Hell*; 200 mins., 16mm/TV)
1991   *Conspiracy of Silence* (200 mins., 16mm/TV)

Bibliography

Books

Marsolais, Gilles. «*Le temps d'une chasse*»: *Dossier sur le film de Francis Mankiewicz*. Collection Le Cinématographe 5. Montréal: Éditions Le Cinématographie/VLB editeur, 1978.

Interviews

Adilman, Sid. "Key Roles for Movie-World Couple," *Toronto Star* (17 September 1988).
Andrews, Mark. "Filmmaker Hooked on 'Family' Theme," *Vancouver Sun* (14 October 1988).
Bonneville, Léo. "Entretien avec Francis Mankiewicz," *Séquences* 70 (octobre 1972): 4–8.
——. "Francis Mankiewicz," *Séquences* 135–136 (septembre 1988): 15–21.
Boulad, Brenard. "Francis Mankiewicz: Je voudrais voir la mère," *Voir* (août 1988): 7.
Bourdeau, Roger. "Les autres qui vivent en nous," *Cinéma* 442 (18–24 mai 1988): 14–16.
——. "*Les Portes tournantes* de Francis Mankiewicz," *Lumières* 13.2 (mai–juin 1988): 14–16.

Demers, Edgar. "Francis Mankiewicz et Monique Spazziani: Une heureuse alliance," *Le Droit* (24 septembre 1988).

——. "Du cinéma universel ... et québécois," *Express* (Toronto) (13 septembre 1988): 7.

Dupré, Frédéric. "Mankiewicz prénom Francis: Le réalisateur des *Bons débarras* a un nom bien lourd à porter," *Le Matin de Paris* (9 novembre 1985).

Dussault, Serge. "« Entre Réjean Ducharme et moi, une complicité »," *La Presse* (9 août 1980): B11.

Fraser, Matthew. "Mankiewicz Ambivalent about Film Industry Changes," *Globe & Mail* (4 August 1987): A15.

Irving, Joan. "Francis Mankiewicz: To Berlin with Love, " *Cinema Canada* 63 (March 1980): 11–17.

Jean, Marcel. "Entretien avec Francis Mankiewicz," *24 Images* 38 (été 1988): 18–19.

Kelly, Brendan. "New Flick Clicks: Mankiewicz Back on Top," *Montreal Daily News* (13 August 1988).

Kiss–Koller, Ibrányi, & George Csaba Koller. "Francis Mankiewicz," *Cinema Canada* 7 (April–May 1973): 64–67.

Manceau, Jean–Louis. "Être cinéaste au Québec," *Cinéma 85* 328 (12 novembre 1985): 2.

Nuovo, Franco. "Francis Mankiewicz se rejouit d'avance," *Le Journal de Montréal* (14 mai 1988).

Petrowski, Nathalie. "Pourquoi nos films seraient-ils québécois?," *Le Devoir* (20 août 1988).

——. "Portrait," *Maclean's* 94 (23 March 1981): 58.

Richler, Daniel. "Home Movies," *Today* (30 May 1981): 8–10.

Roy, Pierrette. "Le rêve d'éveiller le rêve," *La Tribune* (22 septembre 1988).

Scott, Jay. "Canadian Renaissance at Cannes," *Globe & Mail* (17 May 1988).

Taylor, Noel. "Period Charm in Almonte," *The Citizen* (Ottawa; 14 September 1988).

Essays and sections in books

Anon. "Le sinueux itinéraire de Francis Mankiewicz," *Le Figaro* (16 novembre 1988): 41.

Beaulieu, Janick. "Un réalisateur," *Séquences* 100 (avril 1980): 10–29.

Euvard, Michel. "Quand la mer se retire," *Cinémaction* 40 (1986): 30.

Jean, Marcel. "Francis Mankiewicz: Itinéraire en forme d'enfance," *24 Images* 38 (été 1988): 42.

Langlois, Gérard. "Nouveaux cinéastes québécois," *Téléciné* (septembre 1973): 18–19.

Lockerbie, Ian. "Québec Cinema as an Allegory of Nationhood: The Example of *Les bons débarras*," in Lockerbie, ed., *Image and Identity: Theatre and Cinema in Scotland and Québec* (John Grierson Archive Occasional Papers 2; Stirling: Department of French, U of Stirling P, 1988): 120–30.

Pavlovic, Diane. "Réjean Ducharme scénariste: Les P(l)ans de l'illusion," *Revue d'histoire littéraire du Québec et du Canada français* 11 (hiver/printemps 1986): 85–92.

Pétrowski, Nathalie. "Le tendre cinéma de Mankiewicz," *L'Actualité* 7.1 (janvier 1982): 36–40.

Weinmann, Heinz. "*Les bons débarras*: La Revanche d'Aurore," in ⇨Weinmann, *Cinéma de l'imaginaire québécois*, 91–106.

Reviews

Anon., "La Réalité s'en va," *Le Devoir* (1 mars 1980): 19; Richard Gay, "Le cinéma des talents," *Le Devoir* (1 mars 1980): 25; Luc Perreault, "Le vieux cinéma est mort, bon débarras!," *La Presse* (1 mars 1980): D11; Gene Moskowitz, *Variety* 296.5 (5 March 1980): 26; Wayne Grigsby, "From Québec a Vintage Crop," *Maclean's* 93.17 (28 April 1980): 43; Janick Beaulieu, *Séquences* 100 (avril 1980): 151–54; Jean-Marie Poupart, "Deux grands films absolument merveilleux," *L'Actualité* 5.5 (mai 1980): 90; Barbara Samuels, *Cinema Canada* 65 (May 1980): 33–34; Carole David, "Histoire de filles," *Spirale* 10 (juin 1980): 14; Robert Fulford [as Marshall Delaney], "Close to Home," *Saturday Night* 95.9 (November 1980): 85; repr. in ⇨Seth Feldman, *Take Two*, 2–3, 9–11; Gilles Marsolais, "Un beau saccage d'amour," *Vie des arts* 25.101 (hiver 1980–81): 81; Howard Kissel, *Women's Wear Daily* (14 January 1981); Archer Winston, "*Les Bons* a good film," *New York Post* (14 January 1981); Janet Maslin, "Film *Les bons débarras* About Jealousy," *New York Times* (15 January 1981): C1; David Denby, "Enfant Terrible," *New Yorker* (26 January 1981): 47–48; Andrew Sarris, *Village Voice* 26.5 (28 January–3 February 1981); Stanley Kauffmann, "Intimations of Mortality," *New Republic* 184.6 (7 February 1981): 24–25; Robert Hatch, *The Nation* 232.6 (14 February 1981): 189; Anon., *Atlantic Insight* 3 (March 1981): 68–69, 71; Maurice Tourigny, "Une Carrière américaine qui s'annonce brillante," *Le Soleil* (4 avril 1981): E12; John Locke, "Shooting for the Best," *Cinema Canada* 73 (April 1981): 25;Robin Wood, "'Art' and Alligators," *Canadian Forum* 61.711 (August 1981): 38, 40; François Ramasse & Yann Tobin, "XVIIe Festival international du jeune cinéma: Hyères 1981," *Positif* 248 (novembre 1981): 51–53; Olivier Seguret, "Les très bons débarras," *Libération* (6 novembre 1985); Olivier Serre, "Ras-le-bol québécois," *Cinéma 85* 328 (6–12 novembre 1985): 5; Michel Perez, "Zazie des Laurentides," *Le Matin de Paris* (11 novembre 1985); Jacques Chevallier, *La Revue du cinéma* 410 (novembre 1985): 42; Vincent Ostria, "Terroriste d'amour," *Cahiers du cinéma* 378 (décembre 1985): 54–55; Anon., *Jeune Cinéma* 171 (décembre 1985–janvier 1986): 46–47; Jean–Pierre Jeancolas, "*Les bons débarras*: Maman je t'aime, je te tue...," *Positif* 229 (janvier 1986): 69.

છ

FIGURE 6

The Grey Fox (Phillip Borsos, 1982; produced by Peter O'Brian) –
David Petersen (Louis Colquhoun); Richard Farnsworth (Bill
Miner); Wayne Robson (Shorty Dunn).

6 The Grey Fox (Phillip Borsos, 1982)

Production: produced 1980, released 16 December 1982. Produced by Grey Fox Pictures Inc., for Mercury Pictures, with the participation of the Canadian Film Development Corporation and Famous Players Limited. **Director:** Phillip Borsos. **Producer:** Peter O'Brian. **Executive Producer:** David H. Brady. **Co-Producers:** Phillip Borsos, Barry Healey. **Screenplay:** John Hunter. **Cinematographer:** Frank Tidy. **Production Designer:** Bill Brodie. **Music:** Michael Conway Baker. **Editor:** Frank Irvine. **Consulting Editor:** Ralph Rosenblum.

Sound: Rob Young. **Colour, 91 mins., 35 mm.**

Cast: Richard Farnsworth (Bill Miner), **Jackie Burroughs** (Kate Flynn), **Ken Pogue** (Jack Budd), **Wayne Robson** (Shorty), **Timothy Webber** (Fernie), **Gary Reineke** (Detective Seavey), **David Petersen** (Louis Colquhoun), **Don Mackay** (Al Sims), **Samantha Langevin** (Jenny), **Tom Heaton** (Tom), **Ray Michal** (gunsmith), **Stephen E. Miller** (Danny Young), **Sean Sullivan** (newspaper editor), **Peter Jobin** (Sergeant Wilson), **Isaac Hislop** (town boy).

Synopsis: June 1901. After years in prison, stagecoach robber Bill Miner is released, as an intertitle puts it, "into the 20th century." A train takes him to Washington state, where he lives with his sister and brother-in-law, earning an unhappy living harvesting oysters. After seeing *The Great Train Robbery*, he buys a revolver and sets out for a new career holding up the railroad. In Oregon, the first job goes bad, leaving one accomplice dead and another wounded, who identifies Miner to Pinkerton agent Seavey. Miner meanwhile steals a horse and heads into Canada. Working in a British Columbia sawmill under the name George Edwards, he befriends Shorty Dunn, and they hold up a train at Mission Junction, getting away with thousands in gold and banknotes. Burying the money, they make their way to Kamloops, where Miner's old acquaintance Jack Budd puts them up in the hotel he manages. They work in his gold mine, where Louis Colquhoun, a consumptive former schoolteacher from the East, already labours for Budd.

Miner first encounters photographer Kate Flynn at the local newspaper office, then finds her as she practises golf in the hills while listening to a gramophone; their courtship follows. On Christmas morning, B.C. Provincial Police corporal Fernie fetches them so Kate may document a crime scene; a Chinese immigrant has murdered his family. Later Miner and Shorty rustle a herd of horses for Budd. The job goes awry when an unexpected train appears on the tracks they are using to move the herd. When Seavey tracks Miner to Kamloops, Fernie realizes that Miner is his friend George Edwards, and informs Kate. Realizing the Pinkertons are on his trail, Miner arranges to rendezvous with Kate in Chicago, and she leaves on a train.

Miner, Shorty, and Colquhoun embark on another robbery, at Ducks Crossing, but get away with only a few dollars and some patent medicine. North-West Mounted Police officers catch up with them and arrest them, shooting Shorty when he panics and runs. Returned to Kamloops, they are tried and convicted. Titles indicate that Miner escaped in 1907, and was never seen again in Canada; Kate Flynn relocated to Chicago, and in 1908 "visited Europe accompanied by a wealthy mining engineer known as George Anderson." In a final sequence Miner, in prison gear, finds a small boat and rows away.

The Grey Fox afoot in a modern world

———————————— ೞ

Blaine Allan

"Bill Miner was released into the 20th century"

A MOVING-PICTURE PROJECTOR, an automobile, a steam-powered locomotive, a revolver: all are modern, mechanical icons of a late-nineteenth-century industrial age, agents of propulsion that promise particular ideas about development and progress beyond the millennium. Objects encountered by Bill Miner and linked in an early sequence of *The Grey Fox*, they mark the transition of the stagecoach bandit from an agrarian age to a train robber in the age of steam. The change he undergoes – having rejected a life of wages, explaining to his sister, "I'm just no good at work that's planned by other heads" – underlines the significance of specialized work for a thief who considers himself a professional. Dramatic social and technological changes, including the rise of both the means and the will for industrialization, the movement from the country to the cities, and the refinement of the division of labour have marked this century. The historical setting for the tales of the West dissolved in the early 1900s, as Justus D. Barnes fired his revolver into the Edison Manufacturing Company's movie camera for *The Great Train Robbery*, the same year, 1903, that Bill Miner slipped into Canada. In other words, the West as a historical condition diminished at about the same time technological and industrial innovations – the cinema, then Hollywood – made the Western an internationally pervasive form of storytelling.

The Grey Fox, produced in the 1980s, constitutes a rare Canadian rendition of the Western movie at a moment when Hollywood had all but abandoned the Western, a fictional form that revolves around the transition from a rural, pioneering past in the latter decades of the nineteenth century to the modern moment from which the tale is told.[1] Such a temporal relation is

---

[1] In the early 1980s, few Westerns were produced and released, among them the financial and public-relations fiasco *Heaven's Gate* (Michael Cimino, 1980). See Edward Bus-

woven into the structure of *The Grey Fox*, which starts with images of the US Southwest drawn from *Stagecoach* and less readily identifiable stock footage. (John Ford's 1939 film offers a felicitous precedent for Borsos's, since it appeared at a moment when Hollywood considered Westerns unsuitable for A-features and by definition a lower class of production.[2]) Black-and-white images, anchored by intertitles, signify Miner's past as a stage robber and provide a background for the body of the film. Such images also suggest a cinematic past that connotes the time of early cinema at the turn of the century and the moment of Miner's release, and anticipate the moving-picture show that changes his destiny. A sequence later in the film reintroduces archival materials and resumes the look of early cinema, intercutting actual shots from *The Great Train Robbery* with 1980s footage of Miner and his cohorts escaping with the law in pursuit, printed and distressed to look antique, thus reviving a border between a present and a past. Archival footage, in particular the desert images indicating Miner's history, also marks contrast and difference in space and location. Drawing from examples in US literature and film, Jane Tompkins argues that "the desert is the classic Western landscape, rather than the rain forests of the Pacific Northwest or the valleys of California," but the Pacific Northwest and regions farther north in Canada are exactly the locations the film points Bill Miner towards.[3]

Although Pierre Berton has demonstrated that the Western has been one of the principal places to locate images of Canada in Hollywood cinema, stories of settlement and conflict in the West have formed only a small part of Canada's cinema.[4] Fostered in popular literature, as Keith Walden has outlined, the myth of the Mounted Police has circulated around the force's capacity to bring "stability and peace to a succession of frontiers, making these formerly wild areas habitable by ordinary settlers or at least amenable to the norms of white civilization," yet Mounties have been more prominent

---

combe, *The BFI Companion to the Western* (London: André Deutsch/British Film Institute, 1988): 52–54. In 1983 Phil Hardy recorded only four Westerns released in 1982, including *The Grey Fox* and another Canadian production, *Harry Tracy – Desperado* (William A. Graham, 1982). In 1991, with additional information, he revised the figure to seven. For 1972, by contrast, he lists 27. See his *The Film Encyclopedia: The Western* (New York: William Morrow, 1983), and *The Overlook Film Encyclopedia: The Western* (Woodstock NY: Overlook, 1991): 337–41, 362–64.

[2] Edward Buscombe, *Stagecoach* (London: BFI Publishing, 1993): 15.

[3] Jane Tompkins, *West of Everything: The Inner Life of Westerns* (New York: Oxford UP, 1992): 74.

[4] ⇨Pierre Berton, *Hollywood's Canada*.

in Hollywood films than in Canadian pictures.[5] Of the dozens of movies that feature Mounted Police in the frontier era, only a handful has issued from Canada itself.[6] Perhaps within Canada the ubiquity of the Mountie as a national symbol has stripped it of a novelty required of a feature film, or imbued it with the undesirable excess of stereotype.[7] Since the silent era and Ernest Shipman's adaptations of Ralph Connor and James Oliver Curwood, moreover, Canada's cinema has tended not to mine popular fiction about Canada – at least not genre fiction and series novels of the type Walden surveys and revives – for story ideas. While its backlots and other infrastructure enabled Hollywood to turn out a regular schedule of B-level oaters and frequent Westerns ranking higher on the production schedule, the sporadically active feature-film industry in Canada has tended to the contemporary, with period productions more exceptions and special efforts.

The Grey Fox was produced at the tail-end of the so-called Capital Cost Allowance period of Canadian film production, and in that era it is both symptomatic and exceptional. The year 1974 produced only three certified feature films with a total budget of just over $1.5 million, but the boom years that followed saw a sharp increase to a peak of sixty-six productions in 1979 at over a hundred times the cost. The year after, over fifty films were certified Canadian, among them *The Grey Fox*.[8] A commonplace holds that the

---

[5] Keith Walden, *Visions of Order: The Canadian Mounties in Symbol and Myth* (Toronto: Butterworths, 1982): 95.

[6] See Bernard A. Drew, *Lawmen in Scarlet: An Annotated Guide to Royal Canadian Mounted Police in Print and Performance* (Metuchen NJ: Scarecrow, 1990): 153–216. Of the approximately 200 titles listed, indisputably Canadian productions include *Alien Thunder/Dan Candy's Law* (Claude Fournier, 1974): *Back to God's Country* (David M. Hartford – and, uncredited, Bert Van Tuyle – 1919), *Cameron of the Royal Mounted* (Henry MacRae, 1921), *The Grey Fox*, *Policing the Plains* (A.D. Kean, 1927), and *Riel* (George Bloomfield, 1979). Drew notes, in addition, that "only a dozen such works (featuring Mounties, mind you) are listed among the 1,200 pictures described in D.J. Turner's *Canadian Feature Film Index/Index des films canadiens de long métrage 1913–1985*" (Ottawa: Public Archives Canada/National Film, Television and Sound Archives, 1987), presumably including such titles as *Paperback Hero* (Peter Pearson, 1973), *Goldenrod* (Harvey Hart, 1976), and *The Kidnapping of the President* (George Mendeluk, 1980). In 1959–60, CBC TV broadcast a filmed series, produced by Crawley Films, titled *R.C.M.P.* Aimed at young viewers, it revolved around the adventures of a post of contemporary Mounted Police.

[7] Christine Ramsay (on the first page of her essay elsewhere in the present volume) cites an example of the latter to be found in a review of *Goin' Down the Road* (Donald Shebib, 1970): "Canadian, though not excessively so (no Mounties or Eskimos)."

[8] ⇨Ted Magder, *Canada's Hollywood*, 168.

films associated with this period squandered the recognizably indigenous qualities of early-Seventies cinema in Canada and Québec.[9] The Capital Cost Allowance period was also arguably a point of significant change for Canadian film, when it transformed from cottage industry to a more intricate cultural business. At the very least, it adopted the trappings of a modern and more sophisticated industry, whether the infrastructure or the markets existed to sustain one. "When the boom ended in 1980," writes Ted Magder, "the industry was once again in the throes of a crisis, the victim of overproduction (a new phenomenon in Canadian film production to be sure), the loss of investor confidence, and uncertainty over the future of the capital cost allowance provisions."[10]

As part of its own creation myth, *The Grey Fox* represented a rare example of the system of Canadian film production working as it ought, in cultural terms and to some extent in industrial terms. Contemporary reports suggested that the project was underfinanced; the public offering closed with considerably fewer than the full slate of units sold to investors, and the producers had underestimated the administrative costs of financing.[11] Subsequent reports indicate that the problems were more severe, because of the monetary shortfalls threatening to shut down production.[12] Before production, *The Grey Fox* had also provoked some controversy internal to the Canadian film industry as it competed with Donald Brittain. A veteran and renowned documentary filmmaker, he had planned his first narrative film to be the Bill Miner story, and claimed to be developing the project with the Canadian Film Development Corporation's support, which subsequently turned away from Brittain's Bill Miner and toward Borsos's.[13]

Among films from Canada, *The Grey Fox* was perceived to be a high-quality film, the costs of which were evident on the screen. It told a story arising from one region of the country, drawn from the passions of an identifiable artist and facilitated by a committed and caring producer. With

---

[9] See, for example, Jay Scott, "The Burnout Factory: Canada's Hollywood," in his ⇨*Midnight Matinees*, 22–39.

[10] ⇨Magder, *Canada's Hollywood*, 170.

[11] "O'Brian On the Production of *The Grey Fox*," *CineMag* 55 (2 February 1981): 5; Ron Base, "A Car Accident Saved a Dream," *Toronto Star* (2 April 1983): C1.

[12] See Gordon Roback, "A Study of the English-Canadian Feature Film Industry, 1977–1981," dissertation, U of Southern California, 1987, 277–316.

[13] National Archives, MG 31, D222, vol. 3, 3–2, Draft letter, Donald Brittain to André [Lamy]; 16–15, "Silver and Gold. A Tale of the Oldest Outlaw. A Motion Picture Treatment by Donald Brittain."

the imprimatur of Francis Ford Coppola's Zoetrope Studios and a distribution deal with the boutique United Artists Classics, it promised to have international legs, and ultimately it circulated in much of the world to considerable admiration, if not vast fortunes.[14] A trade ad trumpeted the box-office figures in Canadian and US cities, and the picture earned over $6 million in 1983, although the next year reports claimed the investors would lose money.[15] While the film was in production, director Phillip Borsos was reported to have wanted to adapt Miner's adventures for several years; he had first encountered the story when he was a teenager in school not far from the site of one of Bill Miner's train robberies.[16] While cynicism about the capacity of the current Canadian cinema system to produce films of any quality pervaded, according to a report from the set, producer Peter O'Brian protested, "This isn't a deal movie [...] This is a film being made by an artist (Borsos) who has a vision of what it should be."[17] A later account suggested that O'Brian himself had a mission. During the tax-shelter period, according to Robert Fulford "one of the most fascinating and appalling episodes in our cultural history," the "whole [film] industry was rushing toward its destruction, and apparently nothing could be done to stop it." Fulford's narrative of cultural heroism recounted, "In the middle of this period, Peter O'Brian – an imaginative businessman with cultural ambitions – kept wondering whether a *good* film might be made under the tax allowance."[18]

Capital Cost Allowance productions summoned Canada-born actors of international status, most notably Donald Sutherland, to make points to-

[14] See, for example, Vincent Canby, "Movie: *The Grey Fox*, a Western," *New York Times* (13 July 1983): C17; Georgia Christgau, "Foxy," *Village Voice* (26 July 1983): 53; Stanley Kauffmann, "Holding Up," *New Republic* (1 August 1983): 22–23; George Robert Kimball, review of *The Grey Fox*, *Films and Filming* (November 1984): 37; Dilys Powell, review of *The Grey Fox*, *Punch* (22 May 1985): 66. For distinctly mixed response, see Pauline Kael, "The Current Cinema: Anybody Home?" *New Yorker* (8 August 1983): 87–89; and for a dissenting view, see Richard Combs, review of *The Grey Fox*, *Monthly Film Bulletin* (July 1985): 216–17.

[15] Advertisement, *Variety* (27 July 1983): 20; Robert Fulford, "The Apprenticeship of Phillip Borsos," *Saturday Night* 99.12 (December 1984): 36–37; Roback, 321–22; "Investors Will Lose on *The Grey Fox*," *Calgary Herald* (6 October 1984): H4.

[16] "Information about *The Grey Fox*," *The Grey Fox*: Production Notes, Grey Fox Pictures, Inc. [c1980], 2, Film Reference Library, Cinematheque Ontario; Glenda Bartosh, "In Progress: *The Grey Fox*," *Cinema Canada* 71 (January–February 1981): 5; Fulford, "Apprenticeship," 30.

[17] Ron Base, "First Train Robber Rides again," *Toronto Star* (6 December 1980): F3.

[18] Fulford, "Apprenticeship": 32, 33.

wards certification, but casts more often comprised Canadians in secondary roles and secondary imports in starring roles. For every true star, such as Jack Lemmon or Yves Montand, a dozen actors starred in Capital Cost Allowance productions – Michael Douglas, Bill Murray, Isabelle Huppert, Jodie Foster, Jamie Lee Curtis – although at the time in their own nations' industries their names would have remained under the title.[19] This was the case for *The Grey Fox*, which was originally planned to feature Harry Dean Stanton as Miner, and ultimately starred Richard Farnsworth. A veteran character actor, Stanton's name appeared under Miner's image in a full-page advertisement that promoted the production in the issue of *Variety* timed for the 1980 Cannes festival. He withdrew, however, to take a sixth-billed role in Francis Ford Coppola's stylized musical romance, *One From the Heart* (1982).[20] As a stuntman and veteran of some 300 pictures Farnsworth, born in 1920, had recently given up falling from horses and earned an Academy Award nomination for his breakout supporting role as a ranch-hand in the contemporary Western *Comes a Horseman* (Alan J. Pakula, 1978).[21]

Canadian films had regularly featured imported actors as characters who become a narrative focal point and, as Miner, Farnsworth followed the un-broken line. Such characters generally comprise the love interest and an object of fascination for a Canadian character, and by implication for Canadians in general. Farnsworth made a particular impression in his role, as did *The Grey Fox* at a moment of high-volume investment and low cultural return in the domestic film industry. The character and the film fore-shadowed a proliferation of such characters, as leads or in key supporting roles, in Canadian and Québec cinema of the 1980s. To take a number of prominent examples, *My American Cousin* (Sandy Wilson, 1985), *Canada's Sweetheart: The Saga of Hal C. Banks* (Donald Brittain, 1985), *Un zoo la nuit* (Jean–Claude Lauzon, 1987), *Bye Bye Blues* (Anne Wheeler, 1989), and *Perfectly Normal* (Yves Simoneau, 1990) all incorporate solitary males who, while in Canada, wield influence and indelibly imprint their lasting pres-

---

[19] Jack Lemmon starred in *Tribute* (Bob Clark, 1980), and Yves Montand in *La Menace/Backlash* (Alain Corneau, 1977). Michael Douglas, Bill Murray, Isabelle Huppert, Jodie Foster, and Jamie Lee Curtis headlined *Running* (Steven Hilliard Stern, 1979), *Meatballs* (Ivan Reitman 1979), *Violette Nozière* (Claude Chabrol, 1978), *Blood Relatives/Les Liens de sang* (Claude Chabrol, 1978), and *Prom Night* (Paul Lynch, 1980), respectively.

[20] Advertisement, *Variety* (7 May 1980): 115.

[21] See Ina Warren, "Real Cowboy Takes Limelight," *Winnipeg Free Press* (15 April 1983): 21.

ence on the Canadians they touch before they steal away, implicitly or explicitly, back to the USA.[22] Russell Brown has indicated that in prose fiction concerning Canada–US encounters, "the American has traditionally been portrayed as a potent, aggressive male seducing the feminine Canada."[23] To a considerable extent, this model holds true in film fiction. In *The Grey Fox* and several other films, an attractive character from the US charms or entices a female Canadian. A secondary character in *Un zoo la nuit* serves as bait to attract a corrupt, gay cop, and in *Perfectly Normal* the roguish endomorph Alonzo Turner lures the nebbish ectomorph Renzo Parachii to do his will, including investing in a theme restaurant and cross-dressing to perform in the floor show. While the relationships may not be strictly male–female or explicitly sexual, they nonetheless remain sexualized scenarios of power. More than just narratives of cultural seduction, these films situate their protagonists from the USA as mythical or magical figures, much like Bill Miner.

"A professional always specializes"

As the first feature-length narrative Phillip Borsos directed, *The Grey Fox* has had privileged status. It reconfigured an interest in the aesthetics and issues of traditional work in a modern world evident in his earlier films, and introduced fictional situations and character types that persisted through several more productions. Not least was the mysterious, solitary protagonist Miner embodies. Borsos's untimely death of pneumonia resulting from leukemia in 1995 at the age of forty-one amplified the promise with which his work was invested from an early age, and fixed the significance of his first theatrical feature. The Toronto International Film Festival had identified him in 1985 as Canada's representative among a group of ten directors "to watch," largely on the record of *The Grey Fox* and the handful of documentaries that had preceded it.[24]

---

[22] This is a point I introduce at greater length in "Canada's Sweethearts, or Our American Cousins," *Canadian Journal of Film Studies* 2.2–3 (1994): 67–80, with particular attention to *My American Cousin, Canada's Sweetheart, One Magic Christmas*, and *The Grey Fox*.

[23] Russell M. Brown, "A Search for America: Some Canadian Literary Responses," *Journal of American Culture* 2 (Winter 1980): 680.

[24] Graham Dowden, "Phillip Borsos," in *10 to Watch: Ten Filmmakers for the Future* (Toronto: Festival of Festivals, 1985): 12–15.

Cooperage, Spartree, and *Nails* all express fascination with people doing jobs of work. *Cooperage* profiles a barrel-making operation – the location for the factory where Bill Miner and Shorty Dunn meet – where the machinery and the methods hark back to the Victorian era. In *Spartree* a solitary lumber-jack climbs the first tree at a logging site, stripping and topping it as it sways to and fro. *Nails* describes three methods of nail-making, from the traditional work of a blacksmith to modern mass production. These films belong among documentaries that aestheticize industry and manufacturing. Al-though such films often rely on the regular rhythms and patterns of machines and assembly lines, Borsos's documentaries by contrast tend to concentrate on objects made, tools operated, and work done by hand. *Nails,* which depicts different ages of manufacturing, and which incorporates the lockstep of automated production, begins and ends with a smith forging nails one by one. Nothing concrete overtly indicates greater sympathy for this method of nail-making over mass production, but the smith's traditional practice does frame the picture and provides a conclusion that the film im-plicitly endorses.

Bill Miner clearly issues from these more contemporary predecessors, and *The Grey Fox* shares some of the documentaries' concerns with work and personal skill. Like the barrel-makers, the blacksmith, and the logger, Miner possesses skills and exhibits professionalism. The movie-to-gun sequence suggests the relations of those skills and standards to the changing world. Surrounded by the new technologies of a moving-picture, an automobile, and a train, he responds by reacquainting himself with the familiar machinery of a Colt. Framed in close-up and as the gun dealer witnesses, he handles the weapon confidently, analytically, and dexterously. Miner also specializes, as he points out; even though he has to adjust his specialty and retrain, he uses orthodox practices. Of the three train robberies he commits, one clearly pays off. For the Mission Junction robbery, he and his new trainee Shorty deploy the "Chapman method," separating the engine and cargo from passenger cars, a technique particular to trains and not pertinent to stagecoaches, and one that depends on a strict division of labour among the band of thieves. Although the changes of modernization envelop Miner, he modifies his methods and uses a new plan to assail a new target.

To some extent *tours de force* of technique, and aesthetic explorations of industry, Borsos's documentaries also suggest that the practices they docu-ment are noteworthy because they survive under duress. The nascent indus-trial production methods of the Sweeney cooperage may have sufficed into the late twentieth century, but, like the blacksmith's craft as a nail-maker, they are distinctive in large part because they are simultaneously viable and out of time, a phrase suggesting both displacement and nearness to an end that Borsos himself used: "These are people who are somehow a little bit out of time, isolated people using methods that are being left behind."[25] The *Spartree* logger uses contemporary equipment, but does his work in solitude, underlining the craft and skills he practices; capitalizing on that isolation, in the film the sounds of his chainsaw and labour seem the only sounds in the woods. As traditional and skilled as it might appear, however, his job is also a prologue to the greater task of removing vast tracts of timber to feed construction and paper industries, just as barrel-building and nail-making of any type have meaning only in relation to other industrial undertakings and the forces they invoke.

Borsos initiated three of the five feature films he directed, and each revolves around a figure who appears in the lives of ordinary people as an object of allure and an agent of change. Not insignificantly, of the three only Bill Miner is clearly human. Following *The Grey Fox*, Borsos had planned to collaborate again with Peter O'Brian on a seasonal fantasy, *Father Christmas*, but delays in financing caused him to take a job in Florida directing *The Mean Season*, a thriller,. He returned to Canada to pick up the holiday movie. Ultimately titled *One Magic Christmas*, and set in a place that bears traits of both the USA and Canada, it stars Borsos's original Bill Miner, Harry Dean Stanton, as an angel in the form of a cowboy who has a mission to reintroduce the seasonal joy into a woman whose husband has lost his job, and whose family is about to be evicted from their company-owned house and is forced to rely on her income from a dead-end job as a supermarket cashier. Literally a supernatural being, the angel Gideon puts the mother and family through a series of ordeals in order to win her over and restore well-being to the family. For what turned out to be his final film, Borsos again introduced into the lives of a family under stress a mysterious, external agent, this time a dog. In *Far From Home: The Adventures of Yellow Dog*, a Labrador simply appears and is adopted into a Vancouver Island family. When one of the children and the dog are cast adrift in a storm and lost in the island woods, the

---

[25] Rick Groen, "'If I Can See One Moment, I Can Make the Film Work'," *Globe & Mail* (12 April 1980): E5.

dog sacrifices himself to save the boy, later miraculously reappearing to resume a role in the restored order of the family.[26]

If the figure of a mysterious agent offers one consistency in Borsos's films, then the title of this last picture, *Far From Home*, suggests another, which also embraces a for-hire project that accounted for a large part of the director's activity in the 1980s, *Bethune: The Making of a Hero*. A biographical narrative produced as both a four-hour television film and two-hour theatrical feature (released outside Canada as *Dr Bethune*), it ended up a prolonged and troubled undertaking, not least of the reasons the remote locations in rural China.[27] Where Bill Miner, the angel Gideon, and Yellow Dog astonish the Canadians they encounter, the Montreal surgeon Norman Bethune, in a mirror-scenario, travels to revolutionary China and becomes the object of its people's adoration. Befitting their post-human and non-human status, Gideon and Yellow Dog simply appear and form allegiances to mortal, nuclear families. Like Miner, Bethune is more peripatetic. Miner's fictional journey starts in the Old West, and moves through a California prison, the Pacific Northwest, and into Canada, then back to the United States and beyond, after which his memory endures in British Columbia as local legend. Bethune's starts in Montreal of the 1930s and the rise of a domestic Communist Party. He pursues his radical ideals, first to the Spanish Civil War and then to revolutionary China, where his travels end in his death and grand funeral, a harbinger of the renown in which the Chinese hold his memory. Like Gideon and Yellow Dog, Miner and Bethune are both outsiders, but in situations determined by national difference and the circumstances of history and modernity – Bethune as a Canadian in a China gripped by the forces of political transformation, and Miner as a US citizen incognito in a changing Canada.

The cinema itself is an expressive invention of the modern, industrial age, so perhaps it is more likely than not to yield essays and stories that incorporate problems of that time. With few words, Borsos's three key documentaries explore methods of manufacturing and industry in contemporary

---

[26] Ron Base, "Director Comes of Age with New Thriller," *Toronto Star* (9 February 1985): F1, 5; Chris Dafoe, "Phillip Borsos' Two Miracles," *Globe & Mail* (12 January 1995): C1.

[27] See ⇨Knelman, *Home Movies*, 183–226; and his "Anatomy of a Fiasco," *Saturday Night* 103.9 (September 1988): 27–34. Journalist Bob McKeown also produced and directed *Strangers in a Strange Land: The Adventures of a Canadian Film Crew in China* (1988), a television documentary about the production that particularly concerned the difficulties the Canadian production unit encountered or made for themselves while working in China.

practice, which continue to bear traces of their artisanal pasts and traditional skills. The films analyze the intricacies of the handwork that goes into making barrels and nails or into logging. A lesser-known documentary strongly implies the connections between these forms of work and Borsos's own; *Spartree: Making the Film* demonstrates how Borsos's crew was able to gain the close-up view at dizzying heights that *Spartree* affords, and uses split-screen techniques to document the production's logistical and technical complexities. The feature films set the broader changes of society, typically for the narrative cinema, into the experiences of individuals and small groups of people. The families of *One Magic Christmas* and *Far From Home* experience the forces of economics and industry that threaten to pry apart or uproot stable, conventional families, while the protagonists of *Bethune* and *The Grey Fox* travel through maps of great social change.

"A country in transition, filled with beauty and pain"

Interviewed about *Nails* on the occasion of its nomination for an Academy Award, Borsos also introduced the Bill Miner project. "For Borsos," wrote the reporter, quoting the filmmaker, "the theme is a familiar one – 'It's about a guy who's being dragged kicking and screaming into the twentieth century'."[28] Formative forces that propel change circulate around Bill Miner. As a character released into a society from years of prison isolation, he remains an agent of reaction. Richard Farnsworth's placid characterization conveys restraint and dignity belying Miner's criminal status, but it also results from Miner's role as a person surrounded by changing conditions in which he has not participated. Apart from the black-and-white footage depicting in general terms his stage-robbing past in the Old West and the titles that briefly describe his background, *The Grey Fox* includes nothing of the young Bill Miner. The older Bill Miner faces significant differences. A simple apple peeler introduces him to technological change, soon amplified by more pervasive, new machines, such as steam locomotives, automobiles powered by internal combustion engines, and moving-picture projectors. He encounters differences in social composition, including the immigration of Asians into North America, many to build the railroads and settle after the construction

---

[28] Groen, "'If I Can See One Moment'," E5. Borsos apparently had also alluded to his development of a film about Canada's reputedly first train robbery when he was making *Spartree*, in Doug Herrick, "Clear and Independent," *Cinema Canada* 57 (August 1979): 20.

is done, and the identity of women. Among grander political and geographical changes he confronts the existence of a new frontier.

A prolonged pursuit, the narrative of *The Grey Fox* episodically follows its protagonist through a series of encounters. To consider the elderly Miner a Don Quixote of the West – as Phil Hardy does, combining Cervantes's hero with Robin Hood to encapsulate the character – with Shorty Dunn his squire, would misrepresent the characters, although invoking a picaresque may offer a useful frame for the film's loosely plotted narrative structure and its reflections on social, political, and cultural conditions.[29] John Hunter's final draft was selected for a volume of *Best Canadian Screenplays*, alongside four other, comparably episodic and evocative scripts. While, as the book's co-editor Douglas Bowie affirms, each contains "above all a structured story," structure in these screenplays tends to be oriented less around intricacies of plot and event, and the intrigue of enigma and solution, than around properties of situation and theme, suggesting a degree of esteem for such qualities.[30] Among Westerns, the episodic structure and the outlaw-hero of *Stagecoach* offer comparisons, although *The Grey Fox* lacks the revenge motive, characteristic of many, that drives Ford's film to its resolution. The story of Bill Miner might compare more favourably in general narrative terms to such late-era Westerns as *Butch Cassidy and the Sundance Kid* (George Roy Hill, 1969) or *The Wild Bunch* (Sam Peckinpah, 1969), in which the outlaw protagonists are propelled in part by their own criminal goals, but also by the posse or bounty hunters who dog them so persistently that the heroes, like Miner, have to flee the USA.

Once released from prison, Bill Miner heads for the Pacific Northwest, a region in which, Laurie Ricou points out,

> the borders run east–west [...] and north–south," including the both physical lines marked by rivers, mountains, and coastline and the conventional lines of latitude used as state and international boundaries.[31]

---

[29] Hardy, *Overlook Film Encyclopedia*, 363. See Peter Morris, "In Our Own Eyes: The Canonizing of Canadian Film," *Canadian Journal of Film Studies* 3.1 (Spring–Summer 1994): 27–44, repr. in ⇨Allan, Dorland & Pick, *Responses: In Honour of Peter Harcourt*, 159–60; see also my "Canada's Sweethearts," 70–71.

[30] ⇨Bowie & Shoebridge, 11. The other four screenplays are William Fruet, "Goin' Down the Road"; Clément Perron, "Mon oncle Antoine"; Sandy Wilson, "My American Cousin"; and Denys Arcand, "Jésus de Montréal."

[31] Laurie Ricou, "Crossing Borders in the Literature of the Pacific Northwest," in Robert Lecker, ed., *Borderlands: Essays in Canadian–American Relations* (Toronto: ECW, 1991): 288–89.

Among regions of Canada the West – understandably taken as the terrain of Western film and fiction – may have particular meaning. The closing frontier that historian Frederick Jackson Turner imagined and described in 1893, often cited to conceive the West of Western fiction in the USA, comprised a vast land mass in "continuous recession" as part of the process of "colonization of the Great West," to the Pacific.[32] By contrast, in studies of Canadian culture the West may well designate the Prairie provinces, and end at the Rocky Mountains. In 1949 Edward A. McCourt argumentatively introduced his literary study *The Canadian West in Fiction*, "British Columbia is a world apart from the prairies: regional unity begins near Kenora and ends in the foothills. To the native of the prairies Alberta is the far West; British Columbia the near East." Forty years later, historian R. Douglas Francis subtitled his book *Images of the West*, "Responses to the Canadian Prairies," although he does acknowledge British Columbia for the western access it provided David Thomson, for example, to the plains.[33]

Canada in *The Grey Fox* is British Columbia. When Miner crosses the border from the USA, he rides his stolen horse through snow-covered woodland (identifying national difference with the change in climate) and spies a stake driven in the ground to mark the international boundary, but a title superimposed over the following sequence identifies Miner's destination as the province. Allan Pritchard has argued that the literature of British Columbia may yield as a central myth "the legend of Eden or the earthly paradise."[34] Itself a constructive myth of the USA, the Eden myth pertains to this film as well, since Miner renames himself, eliminates history, and thus starts with a clean slate. The fetchingly picturesque visual treatment of the B.C. interior may further support a general sensation of the region as heaven on earth. The first place Miner lights, however, belies that impression and implies different properties in the constitution of the province, and in Miner's role in the place he has relocated.

---

[32] Turner, *The Significance of the Frontier in American History*, ed., Harold P. Simonson (New York: Frederick Ungar, 1963): 27. The most influential invocation of Turner's frontier hypothesis in relation to literature and thought is Henry Nash Smith, *Virgin Land: The American West as Symbol and Myth* (Cambridge MA: Harvard UP, 1950).

[33] Edward A. McCourt, *The Canadian West in Fiction* (Toronto: Ryerson, rev. ed. 1970): vi; R. Douglas Francis, *Images of the West: Responses to the Canadian Prairies* (Saskatoon: Western Producer Prairie Books, 1989): 4–5, 18–19.

[34] Allan Pritchard, "West of the Great Divide: A View of the Literature of British Columbia," *Canadian Literature* 94 (Autumn 1982): 97.

The film discovers Miner labouring incognito in a sawmill, once again "at work planned by other heads," delivering timber to Shorty Dunn, who operates a big, open circular saw. The film quickly establishes a greater frame for their situation when Miner complains about deductions from his wages for bed, board, and work clothes, which Shorty explains: "Hey, the railroad'll shave you six ways from Sunday, George. Who d'you think owns this factory? The railroad owns everything both sides of the track." Immediately thereafter, Miner talks Shorty into joining him in his first train robbery. Wielding considerable power and influence in British Columbia, the railroads formed a significant part of the myth of the historical Bill Miner. By the election of 1907, the year Miner escaped from prison in New Westminster, the Liberals and Conservatives each were able to accuse the other of undue identification with competing railroads. One of the principal issues was the Conservative government's subsidy and protection of the Canadian Pacific.[35] Anti-railroad sentiments fed a statement of the day that appears almost inevitably in accounts of Miner's career to suggest popular assent to his crimes: "Oh, Bill Miner's not so bad, he only robs the CPR once every two years, but the CPR robs us every day."[36]

Miner remains in this respect consistent with the outlaw-hero conventional to much popular fiction and, within the cinema, to the Western in particular. Mark Dugan and John Boessenecker's account of the historical Bill Miner concludes with a discussion that positions the outlaw more as "folk hero" than "social bandit." E.J. Hobsbawm uses the latter term to construct a cross-cultural and international account of "peasant outlaws [who] are considered by their people as heroes, as champions, avengers, fighters for justice, perhaps even leaders of liberation, and in any case as men to be admired, helped and supported." Dugan and Boessenecker, however, discern problems in applying the category to outlaws of the North American West in general, as well as to Miner in particular.[37] Hobsbawm's account draws few examples from the United States – Billy the Kid, Jesse James,

---

[35] Martin Robin, *The Rush for Spoils: The Company Province, 1871–1933* (Toronto: McClelland & Stewart, 1972): 102.

[36] See Frank Anderson, *Bill Miner...Stagecoach and Train Robber* (Surrey, B.C.: Heritage House, 1982): 41; Martin Robin, *The Bad and the Lonely* (Toronto: James Lorimer, 1976): 215; Mark Dugan & John Boessenecker, *The Grey Fox: The True Story of Bill Miner, Last of the Old-Time Bandits* (Norman: U of Oklahoma P, 1992): 130.

[37] Dugan & Boessenecker, *The Grey Fox: The True Story of Bill Miner*, 200–11; E.J. Hobsbawm, *Bandits* (Harmondsworth: Penguin, 1972): 17.

Stagolee – and clearly attributes the westerners' and other bandits' status as much to their historical legends as to their verifiable records.

If Miner is a hero to the people of the Kamloops area, few of those people appear actually to interact with him. The film includes very few of its citizens, apart from those who are important to Miner's story, and few public events – apart from a wedding party that Kate photographs – that might serve to bring out the town.

The only event to reveal the populace as a whole is Miner's own exile to prison. While Borsos's Miner is cheered by the townspeople, exactly why they come out in multitudes remains uncertain. Miner has done nothing to help the people of Kamloops, except be a working resident. The town turns out, but their celebration embodies an ambivalence appropriate to his status as an outlaw and hero, as the undeniable Bill Miner and the George Edwards he continues to insist he is. Cheering him on to incarceration, as the rail line he has plundered is about to carry him away, the townsfolk could be celebrating their protection from the criminal element and restoration of order that it implies, though their jubilance just as likely arises despite the capture of Miner. Among the people of Kamloops gathered at the train station, two individualised representatives of the law appear juxtaposed: Seavey, the Pinkerton op who follows Miner's path across the international border, who stands tall among the crowd, and Fernie, the B.C. Provincial Police officer who has had to compromise his trust both by succumbing to the coercion of the private-sector agent from the USA and by warning off the criminal he likes better. Turned to the background and partly masked by his collar, unlike Seavey, Fernie is more concealed; although not at all exultant like the rest of the crowd, his ambivalent status about Miner is consistent with his fellow Canadians'. The conviction of the outlaw from the United States could be discerned as a retrieval of Canada, but only as a subject of the Empire as the citizens gaily wave Union Jacks proclaiming their allegiance as they follow the train down the tracks. John Hunter's script indicates that the brass band plays the "British Grenadiers" for Miner's sendoff; in the film, however, they are playing the "Invercargill March," a tune – like the Irish airs played by the Chieftains identified with Miner throughout the film – associated more with the colonial margins than with the imperial centre, which suggests the tensions extend beyond the ambivalent positions of the Canadians in the picture.[38]

---

[38] John Hunter, "*The Grey Fox*," in ⇨Douglas Bowie & Tom Shoebridge, ed., *Best Canadian Screenplays*, 247. Jill Carfra suggested the colonial associations in the film's use of

The physical layout of the town differs from the conventionalised town of the Western movie. John Hunter's script describes it in typical enough terms: "A fairly settled, prosperous-looking small town that still bears a frontier appearance. There is a short main street flanked by stores and other establishments."[39] In the film's Kamloops, however, what main street exists is little-defined, and few businesses or institutions serve as familiar locations of social exchange. To be sure, Miner finds his old acquaintance in the Tulameen Hotel, which Jack Budd manages, first meets Kate in the local newspaper office, and chats with Fernie at the back of a church where Kate is photographing the wedding party. The three head down a board sidewalk to the scene of the Chinese family's murder, moreover, and Miner walks along a Kamloops street to the general store, where he acquires and then hands over an orange to a boy sitting outside. These are isolated incidents, however, which tend not to provide any coherent map of the town.

This dispersed sense of space to some extent corresponds to Miner's peripatetic status. After the release from prison that starts the film, Miner has been in motion and unable to settle down. Kamloops appeals to Miner (in a romantic and sexual liaison with Kate, befriended even by a representative of the law, Fernie) as a place to settle, despite Shorty's protests. Following one of their most misguided undertakings, Jack Budd's horse-rustling scheme that results in disaster when the herd is run off the railroad tracks by an unanticipated work train, Shorty complains about having to do Budd's bidding – "work planned by other heads," as Miner put it earlier – but Miner retreats into caution, claiming, "Well, it's safe here in Kamloops." Physically and socially, however, Kamloops appears only sketched.

In the broader context of Miner's cross-cultural adventure, turn-of-the-century Kamloops is British Columbia is Canada. If, as Borsos claimed, Miner's story involves drawing a resistant figure into the twentieth century, the twentieth-century Canada that *The Grey Fox* depicts bears clear traces of construction and change, but has not been completely transformed. The partial view of Kamloops suggests a settlement in the process of becoming a community. The Tulameen appears a fine, frontier hotel, with a clean, bright lobby where Miner and Jack Budd sit to conspire over a cup of coffee, but not much stands nearby to imply a town. A boardwalk indicates a dose of

---

Celtic music in her unpublished undergraduate paper, "Neglected Notes: A Study of the Use of Music in *The Grey Fox*" (1990).

[39] Hunter, "The Grey Fox," 184.

permanence, but Seavey's automobile – a machine apparently anomalous in the area – still has to rumble over the town's rutted dirt road.

The growth of such a community exemplifies only a conventional process of imposing culture on nature, which *The Grey Fox* underlines repeatedly. An opening-credit image taken from high above of a train snaking through mountainous woodland echoes the path of a river cutting through the same terrain. The imagery perhaps suggests the 'phantom ride' films of the period, which provided surrogate tourists with the thrill of a view from the front of a locomotive steaming through the wilds.[40] More vividly, associated particularly with the character of Kate Flynn, the film depicts the introduction of uniquely human activity into a terrain that may previously have been touched by people, but which had remained undisturbed. Sometimes anomalous, typically European in origin or connotation, such activities also exemplify the change of modernization. Some time after their first encounter Miner, for example, discovers Kate when in open fields he first hears the voice of a tenor singing an aria from Friedrich von Flotow's *Martha*, then spies her practising her golf and driving through the tall grass as her recording of Caruso plays on a Victrola. Of course much of the charm in the sequence trades on the incongruity of her actions to contemporary eyes, but only zoning, ownership, shaping, grooming, and naming – hallmarks of a modern, capitalist relation between human and earth – differentiate the land she occupies from an actual golf course. Kate, dressed in fine clothing, swinging at golf balls in the countryside, moreover, offers an image consistent with turn-of-the-century tourism in the western regions, fostered by the Canadian Pacific Railway.[41] The later, central sequence that links images of their courtship under the voice-over reverie of Miner singing in the bath concludes as they dance in a gazebo built on the open range, itself a physical manifestation of the appeal to the middle class to travel west for recreation. The architectural structure graphically echoes the mountains against which it is set, but it and their waltz again suggest the layering of rational and emotional organization onto hitherto undifferentiated physical terrain.

Miner may discover Kate in the open air, but, non-stereotypically, she is not principally associated with nature. From her earliest incarnation, the

---

[40] ⇨Peter Morris, *Embattled Shadows*, 29. An Edison picture, offering such a view of the Fraser River valley, is included in the opening minutes of *Dreamland: A History of Early Canadian Cinema* (Donald Brittain, 1974).

[41] See E.J. Hart, *The Selling of Canada: The CPR and the Beginnings of Canadian Tourism* (Banff: Altitude Publishing, 1983).

film's female lead was imagined as a woman of culture – in early versions of the script she was a piano teacher – and politically modern woman. Her transformation into a photographer may have resulted from a 1906 photo of Miner inscribed, "Miss M. Spencer, Kamloops, B.C."[42] As a photographer, of course, she herself is consistent with the film's motif of technological modernism, although she is further socially coded as a modern woman. A prior draft named her a Fabian, and in the film Kate introduces herself as sympathetic to the "National Women's Trade Union League."[43] Reflecting the conditions of contemporary female workers, while slightly anticipating the pre-World War I innovation of the Women's Labour Leagues, Kate's avowed political position marks out her position of difference.[44] In her initial set-to with the local newspaper editor, she protests, "We have a transcontinental railway on the edge of town, and it brings ideas here, Mr Wilkes, not just goods and supplies." Specifically, she later admits to Miner, the train also brought her west. Kate's story enacts a liberatory idea of frontier, combining her single-woman status, her work as an photographer, and her emigration from an unnamed eastern location to the West. That she remained unmarried "mortified" her parents but made her "ecstatic" for the difference and individualism it accorded her. In photography she "found [her] passion," and it provides the means for her to "make [her] own way in the world." Her allusions to family connote an East of class, refinement, compromise, and social convention well known in studies in fiction and film of the West. When Miner indicates he thinks "there isn't much out here to take pictures of," she disagrees, identifying a range and ambivalence in both place – though whether she means Canada, British Columbia and the Canadian West, or, in deference to an international audience, simply the West remains uncertain – and time: "This is a country in transition, filled with beauty and despair. You yourself might be shocked at some of the injustices I've recorded with my camera."

---

[42] Martin Robin, *The Bad and the Lonely: Seven Stories of the Best – and Worst – Canadian Outlaws* (Toronto: James Lorimer, 1976); Dugan & Boessnecker, *The Grey Fox: The True Story of Bill Miner*, 122.

[43] T.Y. Drake, "First Revised Draft…. Based on material written by Barry Healey. Additional story material by Christian Bruyere," 1 April 1980, CFDC Collection, Queen's University, Kingston, Ontario.

[44] On Women's Labour Leagues, see Joan Sangster, *Dreams of Equality: Women on the Canadian Left, 1920–1950* (Toronto: McClelland & Stewart, 1989).

Miner might, and so might the viewer, except that those photographs never actually appear in the film. She and Miner examine her pictures during the courtship sequence, and view them in their albums as much like domestic keepsakes as professional work, without any reverse angle to depict the photos they see. The closest example of such crusading work on Kate's part arises on Christmas Day, when she is called to make photos of a murder site. In an earlier sequence dropped from the script, Miner and Shorty ride into town and spy Kate at work photographing the Chinese settlement, "a squalid collection of shacks, huddled together outside the town proper."[45] The general conditions reflect British Columbian resistance to Asian immigration, the restrictive and deterrent entry taxes of the first years of the century, and the recent 1902 Royal Commission on Chinese and Japanese immigration, with which Ottawa responded to local racist sentiments. The commission report observed that the Chinese comprised

> a community within a community, separate and apart, a foreign substance within, but not of our body politic, with no love for our laws and institutions; a people that will not assimilate or become an integral part of our race and nation [...] They are not and will not become citizens in any sense of the term as we understand it. They are so nearly allied to a servile class that they are obnoxious to a free community and dangerous to the state.[46]

The finished film defers depicting the subcommunity until disaster strikes, and leaves reasons for the mass homicide in the background. Blood from the bodies of the Chinese family stains the walls of the tent they occupied. Barely sheltered from the cold and "a world away from home," as Miner sympathizes, they were presumably brought into their new country to build the same railroad that Kate extols, that Miner plunders, and that seems to have left the Chinese labour barely to subsist on the edges of the community.[47]

Initially a vocal trade unionist and champion of justice, over the course of the film Kate is tamed into submission. Even in the sequence where she first practises her trade as a professional photographer, she is not recording and

---

[45] Hunter, "The Grey Fox," 184.

[46] Government of Canada, *Report of the Royal Commission on Chinese and Japanese Immigration* (1902): 278, quoted in W. Peter Ward, *White Canada Forever: Popular Attitudes and Public Policy Toward Orientals in British Columbia* (Montreal: McGill–Queen's UP, 1978): 60–61.

[47] See Harry Con et al, *From China to Canada: A History of Chinese Communities in Canada* (Toronto: McClelland & Stewart, 1982): 20–24.

revealing the impoverished conditions of the Chinese immigrants, but compiling evidence of a crime for the Provincial Police. Introduced as an ambitious and articulate proto-feminist, moreover, she changes over the course of her relationship with Miner. While Shorty resentfully tells Miner, "I'd say she's just about made a gelding outa you," in fact Miner has involved her in his own scenario to the point where her future is determined by his. She makes travel plans for both of them when she learns that the law has caught on to him, but he sends her on ahead to Chicago, with the promise that he will join her. While Miner's Canadian sojourn constitutes an exile, so does Kate Flynn's fate. Perhaps, however, her fortune was suggested at an earlier point, when she interpreted a past of her own that intimately connected an individual freedom and fulfilment with a new frontier in the West, a relation more firmly associated with the myth of the US West than with the metropolitan myth of Canada's West.

As an account of an outlaw from the USA in Canada, as a story that crosses and re-crosses borders, *The Grey Fox* inevitably entails relations between Canada and the USA as nation-states "sharing the continent," to use Northrop Frye's phrase.[48] Although the film suggests distinct cultural differences, it does so with a tone that moderates stereotypes of the USA as a violent frontier republic and Canada as a peaceable kingdom. In the Washington region, Miner acquires his gun, solves a bar-room altercation with a whiskey bottle, and fouls up a robbery that results in violent death and injury. With the Chinese family's murder–suicide, however, Canada too represents a site of potential violence. To be sure, the film establishes mirror images of law enforcement – Fernie an amiable (and ultimately corruptible) public servant, and Seavey an efficient and intractable commercial operative. That Miner's story is situated in a border region suggests relative values rather than distinct difference, and the possibility of differential societal impact between the two adjoining parties.[49]

The Grey Fox is clearly imagined along axes of space and time, and plots coordinates of change. Spatially, it incorporates meaningful distinctions between Canada and the USA as nation-states. Bill Miner himself bears significance because he crosses the border. The film further incorporates meaningful distinctions between the past and the present, and that sense arises

[48] Northrop Frye, "Sharing the Continent," in his *Divisions on a Ground: Essays on Canadian Culture*, ed. James Polk (Toronto: Anansi, 1982): 57–70.

[49] See Roger Gibbins, *Canada as a Borderlands Society*, Borderlands Monograph 2 ([Orono]: Borderlands Project, University of Maine, 1989).

from its expression of change across time. Miner bears significance in part because he is old, or, in his sixties, old for his chosen line of work, at least. His age has meaning because he has spent most of it away from conventional society and instead in the alternative society of prison.

The trajectory of the film, however, leads from the material to the mythic. At its start, Miner is released from the confines of a prison, and encounters the technological changes represented by an automated apple peeler and a steam locomotive, which suggest not only the small and the large, but also the exotic – "the kind of products," proclaims kitchenware drummer Sims, "that are just gonna make your head spin" – and the mundane and everyday that they invariably become over the course of time, consumption, and use. Relocating from the USA to Canada, Miner adopts a new identity, which according to the film he never publicly sheds, and an aura that corresponds to his capacity to win the Canadians he encounters. Potent silence and summary aphorisms mark their consent when they are faced with his actual identity, confirming that aura and the power that it implies. Fernie, for example, keeps complicitly mum when Seavey mentions the bluebird tattoo that positively identifies George Edwards as Bill Miner. When the police officer then tries to pass along a warning to Miner via Kate, and she realizes what he is saying, she significantly cautions him, "Not another word, Sergeant." Arranging his Chicago rendezvous with Kate, Miner asks when he promises to meet her if she believes him, and she responds concisely, reassuringly, and prophetically, "I believe *in* you." On the way to their last job at Douglas Lake, in the mist and early morning light, he advises Shorty and Louis Colquhoun not to return to Kamloops, which, he says, "isn't safe for me any longer." In an exchange of medium close shots, Colquhoun guesses: "Yer Bill Miner, aren't ya?" In nearly scriptural tones Miner admits, "I am" – crossing out of frame, leaving disciple Shorty open-mouthed and dumbstruck.

"He eluded an intensive manhunt, and was never seen again in Canada"

The Grey Fox ends with a coda. Having been caught by the North-West Mounted Police after a bungled train robbery, Bill Miner is sentenced to twenty-five years in prison. Intertitles indicate that he escaped in 1907, and suggest that he fled Canada to make good on his plans to rejoin his Canadian love Kate Flynn in the USA, and that the next year they travelled to

Europe in wealth, presumably loot from an earlier, more lucrative robbery, perhaps the heist at Mission Junction. Under the final title crawl, however, after these intertitles, Miner wears a striped prison uniform and clambers along a shoreline to a rowing-boat. Climbing into the boat and rowing to open water, under an overcast sky and in the haze in the distance he fades from sight. No posse or hounds chase him as he slips away. The titles have already determined the success of Miner's escape. With a slow Irish air filling the sound-track, his flight is not dramatic, but evocative and figurative, less a picture of the evasion and more an imagined idea.

Like the preceding ninety, the last few minutes of the picture reveal aesthetic standards of the early 1980s, when *The Grey Fox* was produced, but also hark back to the first decade of the 1900s, when the story of Bill Miner is set, and its cinema. Carefully composed, the images are picturesque, still landscapes in muted tones, captured in protracted takes. The stillness of the scenes extends the restrained pictorial style of the film as a whole to its endpoint, but also incorporates features of early cinema, not least its still and inclusive frame. Miner's broadly striped clothes mark him conventionally as an escaped convict. His broad scuttling movements, unlike the poise and repose that physically characterize him through the film, may simply be the way he has to negotiate the reeds at the water's edge, but also suggest momentarily the expansive performance styles of early cinema. Formally and stylistically positioning the figure in two times, the film implies relations between its own and the moment the cinema started, when "the last machine," as a recent account names it, started to tell stories.[50]

The end of *The Grey Fox* condenses the fate of Bill Miner into a figurative conclusion. The historical Miner did break out of New Westminster Penitentiary in August 1907, precipitating suspicions that he had been helped from inside, and questions that reached as high as the House of Commons. The Royal North-West Mounted Police officer who had arrested him speculated at the time that Miner had been allowed to escape in return for the CPR bonds he had stolen, but the government refused to initiate an inquiry. Miner likely lived off his booty, not in Europe with a female photographer, but in the US Midwest and South, where in Georgia he returned to robbing trains. Caught and imprisoned in 1911, he escaped twice more before his death in September 1913.[51] While suggesting the outlaw's fate, by implying

---

[50] Ian Christie, *The Last Machine: Early Cinema and the Birth of the Modern World* (London: BBC Publications, 1994).

[51] Dugan & Boessenecker, *The Grey Fox: The True Story of Bill Miner*, 135–99.

his escape from the B.C. prison and associating his future with Kate's, the film's conclusion confers meaning on Miner only in relation to Canada.

Presumably illustrating Miner's flight from Canada, the imagery dissolves the border that he encountered on his way into the country. A series of three long shots, the sequence situates the character in relation to an indistinct space, with no far shore and few solid depth cues, into which he himself disappears as he rows away into both myth and history.

ɞ

Filmography *

Features

1982	*The Grey Fox* (91 mins.)
1984	*The Mean Season* (104 mins.)
1986	*One Magic Christmas* (88 mins.)
1990	*Bethune: The Making of a Hero* (*Dr Bethune*) (118 mins.)
1995	*Far From Home: The Adventures of Yellow Dog* (81 mins.)

Short films and television work

1974	*The Barking Dog* (5 mins., 16 mm)
1974	*Cadillac* (5 mins., 16 mm)
1975	*Cooperage* (17 mins., 16 mm)
1977	*Spartree* (15 mins., 16 mm)
1977	*Spartree: Making the Film* (17 mins., 16 mm)
1978	*Phase Three: Regeneration* (29 mins., 16 mm)
1979	*Nails* (13 mins., 35 mm)
1979	*Racquetball* (16 mins., 16 mm)
1979	*The Night Before the Morning After* (producer only; 14 mins., 16 mm)
1988	Ontario Hydro spots (16mm): *Business* (30 sec.); *Heating* (30 sec.); *Environment* (30 sec.); *Safety* (30 sec.)
1989	Wardair spots (16mm): *Restaurant* (30 sec.); *Advertising* (30 sec.)
1990	Ocean Spray spots (16mm): *Red Box* (30, 45 sec. versions)
1990	Canadian Tire spots (16mm): *Spaceship* (60 sec.); *Captain Thunder* (30 sec.); *Soapbox Derby* (60 sec.); *Race* (30 sec.); *Swing* (60 sec.); *Garden* (30 sec.)
1990	KFC spots (16mm): *Just Like Your Father* (30 sec.); *Growing Up* (30 sec.)
1990	Weston's spot (16mm): *Country Honesty* (30 sec.)
1990	Choclairs spot (16mm): *Restaurant* (30 sec.)

* I am grateful to Peter O'Brian; to Lina Della Serra and Brant Lambermont of Partners' Film Company; and to David Baxter and Dan Lee, both formerly of Partners', for providing details about Borsos's work as a director, including television commercials.

1990	Eckerd Drugs spots (16mm): *Grandpa's Camera* (30, 60 sec. versions; *First Steps* (30, 60 sec. versions)
1990	Dempster's spot (16mm): *Walk Home* (30 sec.)
1990	Pepsi spots (16mm): *Kitchen* (30 sec.); *Principal* (30 sec.); *Cinema* (30 sec.)
1990	Molson Take Care spot (16mm): *Colin James* (60 sec.)
1991	Canadian Unity spot (16mm): *Grandfather* (30 sec.)
1991	Anacin spot (16mm): *Mom & Dad* (15, 30 sec. versions)
1991	Canadian Tire spot (16mm): *Hockey* (30, 60 sec. versions)
1991	Campbell's Soup spot (16mm): *Daughters* (30 sec.)
1991	General Motors spots (16mm): *Au revoir* (30, 60 sec. versions); *Cavalier* (30 sec.)
1991	Pepsi spot (16mm): *Pizza Guys* (30, 60 sec. versions)
1991	Choclairs spot (16mm): *Delicious Liaisons* (30 sec.)
1991	Campbell's Soup spot (16mm): *Dad Makes Soup* (30 sec.)
1992	*Bethune: The Making of a Hero* (2 parts, 480 mins. broadcast length; 35 mm)

Bibliography

Screenplay

Hunter, John. "The Grey Fox," intro. John Hunter, in ⇨Douglas Bowie & Tom Shoe-bridge, ed., *Best Canadian Screenplays*, 147–249.

Interviews

Aisenberg, Linda. "Reel Talk: Film Directors Philip Borsos and David Cronenberg Try Commercials," *Applied Arts Quarterly* 5.1 (Spring 1990): 71–72.

Andrews, Marke. "Maker of an Upbeat Movie for Christmas," *Vancouver Sun* (23 November 1985): C3.

Anon. "Tax Plan Will Kill Our Movies, Director Says," *Toronto Star* (15 September 1987): F5.

Base, Ron. "A Car Accident Saved a Dream," *Toronto Star* (2 April 1983): C1.

——. "Director Comes of Age With New Thriller," *Toronto Star* (9 February 1985): F1, F5.

Godfrey, Stephen. "Killers, Crooks and Father Christmas," *Globe & Mail* (8 February 1985): E3.

Groen, Rick. "'If I Can See One Moment, I Can Make the Film Work'," *Globe & Mail* (12 April 1980): E5.

Herrick, Doug. "Clear and Independent," *Cinema Canada* 57 (August 1979): 17–20.

Portman, Jamie. "Fraser Valley Boy Borsos and his Dog," *Vancouver Sun* (11 January 1995): C7.

Shapcott, Catherine. "Borsos Weighs Canadian–US Pic Equation: If Work Calls, You Go," *Variety* (4 March 1983): 460, 464.

Articles, essays and sections in books

Adilman, Sid. "Cancer Claims One of 'Best Directors' Anywhere," *Toronto Star* (3 February 1995): D3.

Allan, Blaine. "Canada's Sweethearts, or Our American Cousins," *Canadian Journal of Film Studies* 2.2–3 (1993): 67–80.

——. "The Grey Fox," in *The Canadian Encyclopedia* (Toronto: McClelland & Stewart, 1999).

——. "Borsos and *Grey Fox* Ready Feature Debut," *Cinemag* 37–38 (1980): 75.

——. "Borsos Bows with 1st Feature," *Cinemag* 42 (21 July 1980): 6.

——. "O'Brian On the Production of *The Grey Fox*," *Cinemag* 55 (2 February 1981): 5.

——. "Placing the Past in Film Present," *Screen International* 292 (May 1981): 14.

——. "Healey Gives Advance Raves to *Grey Fox*," *Cinema Canada* 74 (May–June 1981): 23.

——. "U.A. Classics Gathers Strength in Canada, Picks Up *The Grey Fox*," *Cinema Canada* 83 (April 1982): 18.

——. "*Grey Fox* Bows at Taormina Festival," *Cinema Canada* 86 (July 1982): 5.

——. "*Grey Fox* Rides Off with Honors," *Vancouver Sun* (24 March 1983): D1.

——. "*Grey Fox* Builds from West Coast Premiere," *Cinema Canada* 95 (April 1983): 17.

——. "*The Grey Fox* Big in National Launch," *Cinema Canada* 96 (May 1983): 6.

——. "*Grey Fox* Still Strong," *Cinema Canada* 98 (July–August 1983): 7.

——. "*Grey Fox* Wins Good Press, Good Grosses in US Distribution," *Cinema Canada* 99 (September 1983): 16.

——. "*Grey Fox* Good Rating," *Cinema Canada* 106 (April 1984): 35.

——. "Investors Will Lose on *The Grey Fox*," *Calgary Herald* (6 October 1984): H4.

——. "Leukemia Claims Borsos in Director's Prime," *Montreal Gazette* (3 February 1995): C2.

Bailey, Bruce. "Grey Foy Tops Genie Contenders," *Montreal Gazette* (10 February 1983): D13.

Bartosh, Glenda. "In Progress: *The Grey Fox*," *Cinema Canada* 71 (January–February 1981): 5–6.

Birnie, Peter. "Borsos: He Took the Direct Approach to Films and People," *Vancouver Sun* (February 1995): H1.

Browne, Colin. "Il était une fois Hollywood North: Colombie britannique 1929–1986," in ⇨Garel & Pâquet, ed., *Les Cinémas du Canada*, 173–87.

Collins, Richard [as R.C.], "The Grey Fox," in *The BFI Companion to the Western*, ed. Edward Buscombe (London: André Deutsch/British Film Institute, 1988): 265.

Cuff, John Haslett, & Gillian McKay. "The Grey Flannel Kid," *Globe & Mail* (23 January 1986): 40–45, 54–55.

Dafoe, Chris. "Director Made 'Astonishing' Film Debut," *Globe & Mail* (3 February 1995): C1.

——. "Phillip Borsos' Two Miracles," *Globe & Mail* (12 January 1995): C1.

DeFelice, James. "Borsos, Phillip," *The Canadian Encylopedia*, 2nd edition (Edmonton, Alberta: Hurtig, 1988): 253–54; *The 1996 Canadian Encyclopedia Plus* (Toronto: McClelland & Stewart, 1995); *The 1999 Canadian Encyclopedia* (Toronto: McClelland & Stewart).

Dowden, Graham. "Phillip Borsos," in Piers Handling, ed., *10 to Watch: Ten Filmmakers for the Future* (Toronto: Festival of Festivals, 1985): 12–15.

Dowler, Andrew. "Borsos Becomes an International Force," *Screen International* 511 (24 August 1985): 45.

Dugan, Mark, & John Boessenecker, "Appendix: Synopsis and Photographs from the Motion Picture *The Grey Fox*," Dugan & Boessenecker, *The Grey Fox: The True Story of Bill Miner – Last of the Old-Time Bandits* (Norman: U of Oklahoma P, 1992): 219–24.

Fulford, Robert [as Marshall Delaney]. "The Apprenticeship of Phillip Borsos," *Saturday Night* (December 1984): 30, 32–40.

——. "A Startling Talent, Tragically Unfulfilled," *Globe & Mail* (4 February 1995): C1–2.

Hardy, Phil. "*The Grey Fox*," in *The Aurum Film Encyclopedia: The Western* (London: Aurum, 1983): 362–63; *The Film Encyclopedia: The Western* (New York: William Morrow,

1983): 362–63; *The Overlook Film Encyclopedia: The Western* (Woodstock NY: Overlook, 1991): 363.

Johnson, Brian D. "Bringing Canada's Soul to the Screen," *Maclean's* (11 August 1986): 53–55.

———. "Inspired Images," *Maclean's*. (13 February 1995): 85.

Kirkland, Bruce. "Crazy Like a Fox," *Toronto Sun* (22 November 1985): 97.

———. "Lovable Grey Fox Farnsworth Makes Heist a Thing of Beauty," *Toronto Sun* (8 April 1983): 83.

———. "A Means To an End," *Toronto Sun* (1 February 1985): 80.

———. "A New Start After Sixty: Farnsworth Finds Fame," Toronto *Sunday Sun* (31 March 1985): S10.

———. "Our Peter the Great!" Toronto *Sunday Sun* (6 April 1986): S12.

Klady, Leonard. "*Grey Fox* Leads Genie List," *Winnipeg Free Press* (10 February 1983): 22.

Knelman, Martin. "After *The Grey Fox*," *Toronto Life* (May 1985): 33–34, 36.

———. "Hollywood North: The Sequel," *Report on Business Magazine* (April 1987): 60–61, 64, 66, in *Globe & Mail* (13 March 1987).

———. "Telefilm Noir," *Toronto Life* (July 1985): 27–28.

Leckich, John. "Larger Lives," *Globe & Mail* (23 December 1995): D3.

Lownsborough, John. "Son of *Grey Fox*," *City and Country Home* (September 1986): 6, 10, 12.

Morgan, Joanne. "Borsos Leaves Film Legacy," *Playback* (13 February 1995): 5, 10.

Morris, Peter. "Borsos, Phillip," and "*The Grey Fox*," in ⇨Morris, *The Film Companion*, 39, 134.

O'Brian, Peter."Tribute: Phillip Borsos," *Take One* 8 (1995): 52.

Roback, Gordon. "A Study of the English-Canadian Feature Film Industry, 1977–1981," dissertation, U of Southern California, 1987.

Salem, Rob. "Stuntman Thrives on Second Career in Movies," *Toronto Star* (16 August 1983): E3.

Scott, Jay. "*Grey Fox* Runaway Winner with 7 Genies," *Globe & Mail* (24 March 1983): 21.

———. "A Moviemaking Maverick," *Globe & Mail* (23 November 1985): D3.

———. "Top Genie Prospects for Bill Miner Movie," *Globe & Mail* (10 February 1983): 23.

Studlar, Gaylyn. "*The Grey Fox*," in *Magill's Cinema Annual 1984: A Survey of 1983 Films*, ed. Frank N. Magill (Englewood Cliffs NJ: Salem, 1984): 168–73.

Thomson, David. "People We Like: Richard Farnsworth," *Film Comment* 19.4 (July–August 1983): 78–79.

Walsh, Michael. "From Stagecoach to Train Robbers," *Variety* (9 April 1980): 6, 34.

Warren, Ina. "*The Grey Fox* Bids for an Oscar," *Globe & Mail* (20 December 1983): 17.

———. "The Grey Fox Gets Some Help from U.S. Critics," *Globe & Mail* (27 July 1983): 16.

Wilson, Peter. "Asking Producer Questions Put O'Brian in the Picture," *Vancouver Sun* (16 July 1986): C3.

Reviews

Ron Base, "First Train Robber Rides Again," *Toronto Star* (6 December 1980): F3; D. Young [as Yung], *Variety* (18 August 1982): 14; George Martin Knelman, "The Bandit Who Always Said Please," *Atlantic Insight* (November 1982): 72, 74; Martin Knelman, "Nineteenth-Century Fox," *Toronto Life* (November 1982): 135–36, 139; John Harkness, *Cinema Canada* 93 (February 1983): 34; Peter Wilson, "*Grey Fox*: Movie for Romantics," *Vancouver Sun* (25 March 1983): C1; Ron Base, "*Grey Fox* Professionalism Wonderful to Behold,"

Toronto Star (7 April 1983): F1; Jay Scott, "*Grey Fox*: Winning Tale of Courtly Coot," *Globe & Mail* (8 April 1983): E3; repr. in Karen York, ed., *Great Scott!: The Best of Jay Scott's Movie Reviews* (Toronto: McClelland & Stewart, 1994): 123-26; Barbara Amiel, "*Grey Fox* is Haute NFB," *Toronto Sunday Sun* (10 April 1983): 12; Bruce Kirkland, "*The Grey Fox*: More than Just Another Movie!" *Toronto Sun* (10 April 1983): 97; George Anthony, "Terribly Pretty, but Pretty Terrible," *Toronto Sun* (11 April 1983): 32; David Macfarlane, "The Well-Mannered Outlaw," *Maclean's* 96 (11 April 1983): 70; Ina Warren, "Real Cowboy Takes Limelight," *Winnipeg Free Press* (15 April 1983): 21; Lyle Slack, "Genie Winner is Sweet – and Slow," *Hamilton Spectator* (16 April 1983); Bruce Bailey, "Old West Meets New in *Grey Fox*," *Gazette* (Montreal; 4 June 1983): D11; Richard Gay, "Deux productions primées, mais....," *Le Devoir* (4 juin 1983): 32; Robert Fulford [as Marshall Delaney], "Movies: Miner Mystery," *Saturday Night* 98.6 (June 1983): 77-78; repr. in ⇨Seth Feldman, ed., *Take Two*, 2-3, 15-17; Vincent Canby, "Movie: *The Grey Fox*, A Western," *New York Times* (13 July 1983): C17; repr. in *New York Times Film Reviews 1983-1984* (New York: Times Books/Garland, 1988): 84; D. Young [as Yung], *Variety* (13 July 1983): 22; Charles Ryweck, *Hollywood Reporter* 277.38 (14 July 1983): 4; Chris Chase, "At the Movies," *New York Times* (22 July 1983): C10; David Denby, "Movies: A Star Comes Back," *New York* (25 July 1983): 67-68; Georgia Christgau, "Foxy," *Village Voice* (26 July 1983): 53; Robert–Claude Bérubé, *Séquences* 113 (July 1983): 35-37; Graham Dowden, "The Quick Grey Fox," *Canadian Forum* 730 (July 1983): 12-13, 29; David Ansen [as D.A.], "Gentleman Bandit," *Newsweek* 102 (1 August 1983): 46, 49; Stanley Kauffmann, "Holding Up," *New Republic* 189.5 (1 August 1983): 22-23; Pauline Kael, "The Current Cinema: Anybody Home?" *New Yorker* 59.25 (8 August 1983): 87-89; Richard Schickel, *Time* 122.7 (15 August 1983): 64, 67; Michael Sragow, "Movies: *The Grey Fox*: Striking Gold with the Legend of an Old Miner," *Rolling Stone* (18 August 1983): 31; Roger Greenspun, "Films: Good Taste," *Penthouse* (August 1983): 54; R.D. Lawson [as R.D.L.], review of original soundtrack recording. *Cinemascope* 11–12 (Fall-Winter 1983): 59; Lloyd Billingsley, *Christianity Today* 27.16 (21 October 1983): 47; K.R. Hey, *USA Today* 112 (November 1983): 67; Kenneth L. Geist, *Films in Review* 34.10 (December 1983): 622; Colin L. Westerbeck, Jr., "Missed List: Catching Up," *Commonweal* (13 January 1984): 17-18; Robert Kimball, *Films and Filming* 362 (November 1984): 37; ; Vernon Young, "Of Mice and Wolves and Hounded Men," *Hudson Review* 37 (1984): 289-94John Coleman, "Crimes Past," *New Statesman* (17 May 1985): 36-37; Dilys Powell, *Punch* (22 May 1985): 66; Clancy Sigal, "Gentleman Bandit," *Listener* 113.2910 (23 May 1985): 37; Richard Combs, *Monthly Film Bulletin* 52.618 (July 1985): 216-17; Anon., *Film* (October 1985): 10.

ಬ

FIGURE 7

Videodrome (David Cronenberg, 1983; produced by Claude Héroux)
– James Woods (Max Renn); Deborah Harry (Nicki Brand).

7 Videodrome (David Cronenberg, 1983)

Production: produced 1981–82, released 4 February 1983 in Toronto; Filmplan International II Inc. (Montréal), Universal Pictures (Los Angeles), with the participation of the Canadian Film Development Corporation. **Director:** David Cronenberg **Executive Producers:** Pierre David, Victor Solnicki. **Producer:** Claude Héroux. **Screenplay and story:** David Cronenberg. **Cinematography:** Mark Irwin. **Editor:** Ron Sanders. **Sound:** Bryan Day.

Music: Howard Shore. **Art Director:** Carol Spier. **Special make-up design and creation:** Rick Baker. **Colour, 87 mins., 35mm.**

Cast: James Woods (Max Renn), **Sonja Smits** (Bianca O'Blivion), **Deborah Harry** (Nicki Brand), **Peter Dvorsky** (Harlan), **Les Carlson** (Barry Convex), **Jack Creley** (Brian O'Blivion), **Lynne Gorman** (Marsha), **Julie Khaner** (Bridey), **Reiner Shwarz** (Moses), **David Bolt** (Raphael), **and others.**

Synopsis: Max Renn, a purveyor of television pornography, becomes interested in a hardcore violent programme called "Videodrome" which his assistant, Harlan, apparently zaps from the satellite airwaves. It promises to add edge to the nightly programming of Max's cable station. His lover, Nicki Brand, watches "Videodrome" on their first date and loves it; she initiates him into sado-masochistic play, but then leaves for Pittsburgh, the headquarters of "Videodrome," to get on the show; we don't see her again except on TV. Max goes to see Professor Brian O'Blivion, media messiah and founder of "Videodrome," but meets only his daughter, Bianca, at the Cathode Ray Mission, where derelicts, diseased by insufficient exposure to cathode rays, go for their daily doses of TV to get, in Bianca's words, "patched back into the world's mixing board." Max learns that "Videodrome" contains signals which enable massive, pervasive, and personalized (hence, for Max, sado-masochistic) hallucinations; he also learns that it is the latter which cause a tumour in the brain (and not vice versa). Harlan is revealed to be really working for "Videodrome," which aims to control the world through brain-washing. Max appears to kiss Nicki while she is on (or in the?) TV, then apparently hits his secretary, Bridey James, murders the programme broker, Marsha, and develops a long opening in his stomach into which he loses, and from which he retrieves, a gun that later mysteriously grafts itself to the flesh of his right hand. The owner of "Videodrome," Barry Convex, has programmed Max to murder his partners at Civic TV (so that the station can be controlled by "Videodrome") and Bianca O'Blivion. Max kills his partners and is helped by ever-faithful Bridey to escape; he goes next to Bianca, but she distracts him with Nicki's image and murder on TV, then convinces him to re-programme himself to fight against "Videodrome"'s fascist agenda. He goes to Convex's optical store, Spectacular Vision, where he blows Harlan to bits; he then proceeds to the eye-wear trade-show, where he shoots Convex dead. Max retreats to a condemned vessel moored in the harbour, where he sees Nicki on TV. She tells him that, though his body has metamorphosed, he has reached the end in his old flesh, and that to reach the next stage, he must kill the old and embrace the New Flesh. Max sees himself shoot himself in the head on TV; then viscera (intestines, organs) explode from the TV. Max says, "Long Live the New Flesh!" and shoots himself in the head. We cut to a blank/black screen.

"Forget Baudrillard"

The horrors of 'pleasure' and the pleasures of 'horror' in David Cronenberg's *Videodrome*

———————————————————— ∞

Suzie Sau–Fong Young

D AVID CRONENBERG was born in 1943 in Toronto, where he went to school, wrote short stories, and started to make films in 1966 as a Literature and Philosophy student at the University of Toronto. Although some of his films are financed or distributed by American companies, he remains resolutely Canadian, living and working in Canada and shooting his films in and around Toronto. As Canadian film critic and prolific writer, Geoff Pevere, has noted, Cronenberg is not only Canada's best known film-maker but is "something of a dream" for auteurist criticism because he writes many of the screenplays of his films.[1] Of his thirteen feature-length films, six of them – including *Videodrome* – are adapted from his own stories; he wrote eight and co-wrote three of the screenplays.[2] The thirteen features have won some forty national and international awards, and Cronenberg has the distinction of winning the Canadian film award, the Genie, as 'Best Director' four times (once for *Videodrome*).[3] In 1990, the Canadian director was honoured with France's prestigious *Chevalier de l'ordre des arts et des lettres.*

Cronenberg was dubbed "the King of Venereal Horror" after his first feature-length film, *Shivers* (1975) (aka *They Came From Within* or *The Parasite*

---

[1] Geoff Pevere, "Cronenberg Tackles Dominant Videology," in Piers Handling, ed., *The Shape of Rage: The Films of David Cronenberg* (Toronto: Academy of Canadian Cinema/ General, 1983): 138.

[2] *Shivers* ('75), *Rabid* ('76), *The Brood* ('79), *Scanners* ('80), *Videodrome* ('82), and *eXistenZ* (1999) are Cronenberg's original screenplays. He wrote the screenplay for *Naked Lunch* ('91) and *Crash* ('96) and co-wrote the screenplays for *Fast Company* ('79), *The Fly* ('86) and *Dead Ringers* ('89).

[3] The Genies are the Canadian equivalents of the American Oscars. Cronenberg won the "Best Director" award for *Videodrome*, *Dead Ringers*, *Naked Lunch*, and *Crash*.

Murders);[4] since then, he has been called a "shock specialist"[5] and a "bondage freak."[6] One critic describes the *mise-en-scène* in his films as "shopful of flesh gobbets, slimy mutations and twisted sex,"[7] while another condemns his films for being "soaked with gloom and defeatism, with ugly images and worthless characters."[8] Martyn Steenbeck, a psychologist and cinéaste who had dedicated much of his academic life to analyzing the impact of violent sexual imagery, has labelled Cronenberg a "creative genius" and "mad scientist," and said of his cinema that "the pain is in the emergent melancholia; the pleasure is in its absolute integrity [...]; the joy is in its necessary and perverse sense of humour and play."[9] Robin Wood, a film theorist and culture critic who has condemned Cronenberg's cinema as "reactionary," nevertheless concedes that it "demands careful attention and even, in a certain limited sense, respect [for its] artistic authenticity [...] thematic and stylistic consistency, [and] integrity."[10] Kevin Thomas of the *Los Angeles Times* refers to Cronenberg as "the talented young Canadian film maker [who is] the dark obverse of Steven Spielberg," and he resolves that "there's no getting around it any more: David Cronenberg must be reckoned with."[11] Martin Scorsese, the American director of such critical successes as *Taxi Driver* and *Raging Bull*, says of the Canadian director that he is "twentieth century. Late twentieth century."[12]

Videodrome is Cronenberg's sixth feature film. It was shot in Toronto in the last two months of 1981 for a budget of CAD $5.95 million, and released in North America to 600 theatres about fourteen months later. *Videodrome* is arguably the most 'Canadian' of Cronenberg's films – the character Professor Brian O'Blivion is said to be modelled on the media guru Professor Marshall McLuhan (University of Toronto), and the porn-TV station

---

[4] Paul Taylor, review in *Monthly Film Bulletin* (November 1983): 310.

[5] David Sterritt, review in *Christian Science Monitor* (24 February 1983): 18.

[6] Paul Kael, *Hooked* (New York: E.P. Dutton, 1989): 212.

[7] John Coleman, review in *New Statesman* (25 November 1983): 30.

[8] Roger Ebert, "*Videodrome*," review from the *Chicago Sun–Times*, in *Cinemania '96* (CD, Microsoft, 1996).

[9] Martyn Steenbeck, "Foreword," in *Cronenberg on Cronenberg*, ed. Chris Rodley (Toronto: Alfred A. Knopf, 1992): xv. In 1988, Dr Steenbeck died mysteriously by self-immolation.

[10] Robin Wood, "Cronenberg: A Dissenting View," in Handling, ed., *The Shape of Rage*, 125.

[11] Kevin Thomas, review in *Los Angeles Times* (4 February 1983), Calendar: 1.

[12] Martin Scorsese, quoted in Rodley, ed., *Cronenberg on Cronenberg*, xxv.

president Max Renn is said to be modelled on Moses Znaimer, founder of City-TV (Toronto), infamous in the 1970s for showing late night "baby blues."[13] Secondly, the fact that the film is largely about television, and about the 'message' that needs television to reach the populace, can be seen as brazenly 'Canuck,' since Canada as an "imagined community" would not be possible without television. Thirdly and most importantly, the film's central concern is the border transgressions of technology and ideas into Canada from the South, and the subsequent breakdown of boundaries and previous ways of seeing and being. It is a theme familiar to all Canadians, whether or not we accept 'Canadian Content regulations'[14] as a solution, and it is only a slight step away from what Northrop Frye has famously called the "garrison mentality" – an acute awareness of an indifferent but always encroaching Other.[15]

But *Videodrome* is not a fascist film that warns against the infiltration of 'undesirable elements,' and it does not advocate a protectionist response to preserve 'purity' or to insulate against change. On the contrary: *Videodrome*

---

[13] Marshall McLuhan (1911–80) was a ubiquitous presence at the University of Toronto from 1946 to 1979 (where Cronenberg was an undergraduate student in the mid-1970s) and in the city of Toronto (where *Videodrome* was filmed in 1982). Moses Znaimer is the co-founder, president, and executive producer of several TV stations, including Toronto's radical and popular independent station, CITY-TV (1972), which in the 1970s was most famous for airing softcore porn movies late at night. It is likely that McLuhan and Znaimer's notoriety (in mass media theory and in porn-TV) had a strong influence on Cronenberg's conception and construction of "media prophet" Brian O'Blivion and porn-station president Max Renn in *Videodrome*. McLuhan was a professor of communications theory at the University of Toronto from 1946 to 1979; he was the founding director of the university's Centre for Culture and Technology, established in 1963. Like McLuhan – whose WorldWideWebsite (maintained by his daughters) invites us to "experience Mc-Luhan first-hand" and view all of his major theories "as he himself expressed them on camera" – Professor O'Blivion in *Videodrome* only appears on video-tape or on TV, "living," as he can, only in the videotapes (put together by his daughter from footage made before he died of a brain tumour; Professor McLuhan's brain tumour was removed in 1967). For the description of *The Video McLuhan*, a set of six tapes of the media prophet's interviews and lectures edited by Stephanie McLuhan, see online at www.VideoMcLuhan.com.

[14] *Videodrome* was filmed in Toronto, and the film's story identifies its setting as Toronto; Max was initially told that the snuff shows he wanted were beamed from Pittsburgh, and his assistant sarcastically explained that "that's in the States."

[15] Frye is speaking of a paradigm in Canadian painting which sees nature as an indifferent force that refuses to be assimilated with the human world; see his *Divisions on a Ground* (Toronto: Anansi, 1982).

is Canada's *Bacchae,* and just like Pentheus, the king of Thebes in Euripides' play,[16] Max in Cronenberg's film is both destroyed and released after he gives in to what he really wants and that which he had at first sneered at – femaleness. Perhaps it is small wonder, then, that when the film opened in New York in 1983, one critic called it "David Cronenberg's latest sickie,"[17] while another not only panned it but added that movie-goers who had not seen a Cronenberg film should consider themselves "lucky."[18] Roger Ebert denounced *Videodrome* as "one of the least entertaining movies ever made."[19] On the other hand, David Ansen's pan in *Newsweek* included high praise for the director, saying that even if the film fails, it does so "on a level that most of his colleagues wouldn't dare attempt,"[20] while Kevin Thomas reviewed it in the *Los Angeles Times* as "thoroughly compelling and terrify-ing" and as the director's "most accomplished film to date."[21] Andy Warhol praised it as "the *Clockwork Orange* of the 80's," and Phil Hardy's encyclo-paedia of science-fiction films puts it "into the distinguished company of works like Michael Powell's *Peeping Tom* (1959) and [Stanley] Kubrick's *A*

---

[16] Euripides, *The Bacchae*. tr. Geoffrey S. Kirk (Englewood Cliffs NJ: Prentice–Hall, 1970). Pentheus, the young king of Thebes and grandson of Cadmus who founded the city, is practically Apollo himself in human form. He is commanding, forthright, certain, and moralistic, and he has set his word against the god of wine, Dionysos, and his worshippers. When Dionysos comes to Pentheus disguised as a traveller, Pentheus imprisons the god on charges of immorality and drunkenness, but of course Dionysos cannot be held. Inspiring Pentheus – making him mad – Dionysos leads him out of the city, dressed as a woman, to go and spy on the bacchantes. Suddenly released, Pentheus is charmed by himself in his disguise, and carefully arranges curls and dress, even asking if he looks more like his mother or his aunt, a remarkable change from his initial refusal ("No, I could not put on female garb!" – l. 836, p.91) to have anything to do with the god's scheme to spy on the maenads. He had rejected the god's scheme several times before he gives in to what he really wants – to leave the ranks of men (that which he had, at first, sneered at). In the end, the women of his palace, with his mother Agaue leading, tear him to pieces in the (god-inspired) belief that he is a young lion (one of Apollo's. Like Pentheus, the Maxes of men have something that they hide and strenuously deny. For a brief re-telling, see "The Story of Pentheus and Bacchae" in Ovid, *Metamorphoses,* tr. Rolfe Humphries (Bloomington: Indiana UP, 1955): 73–80.

[17] Coleman, review in *New Statesman*, 30.

[18] Rex Reed, *New York Post* (4 February 1983): 43.

[19] Ebert, "*Videodrome*," in Microsoft *Cinemania*.

[20] David Ansen, *Newsweek* (14 February 1983): 85.

[21] Thomas, review in *Los Angeles Times*, 1.

Clockwork Orange (1971)."[22] After watching the film, Cronenberg's friend, Peter Rowe, told him: "You know, someday they're going to lock you up."[23]

Forget Baudrillard

Videodrome is not an easy film, and it is not an easily likeable film. It is a political film, though not of the sort of politics that CNN would/could 'cover' (or recognize). It is a film about the politics of the body, the body that disrupts 'business as usual.' And 'business' in the *Videodrome* world means the businesses of pornography (Max's "Civic TV, the one you take to bed with you"), of military weapons research (Barry Convex's "Spectacular Vision"), and of TV itself (the great, late-twentieth century's mind's eye); in fact, 'business' in David Cronenberg's films always means the business of oppression and the politics of hegemony. The politics of *Videodrome*, in a word, is the politics of everyday life, with all of its madness underscored. Jean Baudrillard says of cinema that it is "fascinated by itself as a lost object," that it plagiarizes itself, retells its myths, remaking its classics and its silent films more perfectly than the originals. What Baudrillard has in mind is the Hollywood machinery, for his indictment cannot be further from the truth for Cronenberg's cinema: although his films are typically found in the 'Horror' section in books and in video stores, they challenge rather than constitute much that is conventional in the genre. In the horror scene, what is terrifying is death and dying; in Cronenberg's (ob)scene, what is terrifying is life and living.

Perception, thought, and images in Cronenberg's narratives are far from Baudrillard's "simulacrum" – "endless enwrapping of images [with] no destiny but images."[24] Instead, video images cause hallucinations which then cause brain-tumours (*Videodrome*), telepathy penetrates nervous systems (human and electronic) and literally explodes them (*Scanners*), rage produces skin lacerations, boils, and even whole, humanoid creatures who exact revenge (*The Brood*). Far from being an intangible hyperreality, thought in Cronenberg's cinema creates, mutates, and exists as matter (*Naked Lunch*). Consistent with Tzvetan Todorov's treatise on the literary fantastic, every

---

[22] Phil Hardy, *Science Fiction* (London: Aurum, 1984): 379.

[23] Peter Rowe, quoted by Cronenberg (interview by Tim Lucas), in *The Shape of Rage*, ed. Handling, 175.

[24] Jean Baudrillard, *The Evil Demon of Images* (Annandale, Australia: Power Institute Publications, 1987): 28.

Cronenberg movie revels in "the fragility of the limit between matter and mind"; they all explore the "multiplication of the personality" as well as the "collapse of the limit between subject and object."[25]

Like the classic American horror movie,[26] Cronenberg's films exploit cultural fears of transgression across the boundaries of binary opposites: sometimes, the old, the weak, or the oppressed find in themselves a new energy to act, often aggressively; at other times, those in authority lose their senses and their command; always, the 'pillars of society' (scientists, doctors, and corporations) have hidden stresses (agendas), risking and/or costing the lives of the individuals who trust (in) them. But the impetus of the films is not a role- or power-'reversal' in which the underdogs install themselves atop the existing society. Unlike much in the horror genre, Cronenberg's films delineate cultural anxieties in ways which destabilize their logic and submit them to scrutiny.

One of Cronenberg's primary strategies is to examine the biological body as a continual source of anxiety in our culture, an anxiety which prompts a persistent production of malleable, manageable, social bodies to displace or disavow biological realities. But to understand 'the body' as a cultural entity, as Michel Foucault demonstrates in *Discipline and Punish*, does not require the disavowal of that body, which has "a number of natural requirements and functional constraints."[27] There is no 'pristine,' 'pre-cultural' and 'pre-discursive' body, but there are material contingencies to our bodies and in our lives, even if, as Judith Butler reminds us in *Bodies That Matter*, materiality is "bound up with signification from the start."[28] Indeed, posited as antecedent to discursive action, the material body is said to require (and deserve) our indifference most of the time. In health, we can 'forget' our bodies; in health, we have a reflex, unthinking relationship with our bodies – a healthy body is not a matter for concern. In Cronenberg's cinema, as in life, disease becomes an opportunity to think about the body, for it arrives as a violent

---

[25] Tzvetan Todorov, *The Fantastic: A Structural Approach to a Literary Genre* (Ithaca NY: Cornell UP, 1973): 25.

[26] See Robin Wood's "Introduction" to Wood & Richard Lippe, ed., *The American Nightmare* (Toronto: Festival of Festivals, 1979), repr. as "An Introduction to the American Horror Film," in Barry Keith Grant, ed., *Planks of Reason* (Metuchen NJ: Scarecrow, 1984): 164–200.

[27] Michel Foucault, *Discipline and Punish: The Birth of the Prison*, tr. Alan Sheridan (New York: Random House, 1979): 155.

[28] Judith Butler, *Bodies That Matter: On the Discursive Limits of 'Sex'* (New York: Routledge, 1993): 30.

interruption of our complacency; in pain, in shortness of breath, in cancerous decay, the body asserts itself as something material, organic, and it demands our full attention.

Cronenberg has always said that he is "on the side of the disease," and he asks that we try to see things from the disease's point of view; this has proven difficult for many critics. There is no doubt that Cronenberg exploits our cultural fears of the 'irrational body' – that unruly body which gets fat or sick or needy – but it is important to note that this is only where the films begin and never where they end; in other words, the cultural fears are a point of departure and the object of scrutiny, not a reinforced conclusion or the subject of discourse. In addition, while being a source of anxiety and transgression, the body in Cronenberg's cinema is simultaneously a source of pleasure; it is these things all at once and all together.

In Hollywood, the gaze that traverses another's body surveys it as spectacle and object of desire; this body is a common datum in American mainstream cinema and is variously massaged in film theory. Cronenberg's cinema is 'obscene' (against the scene), in that it calls our attention to that other body, the speaking body, for the erotic gaze of the other has the potential to transform the desired body into a desiring body: in love, the body listens and the body speaks. In erotic play, there is a fluidity between the body-for-the-other and the body-for-the-self; in other words, there is delight in being both object and subject of desire. A desiring body is a speaking subject, and a woman in this position makes 'civil society' sore (and cultural anxieties soar). In Cronenberg's films, women as desiring subjects threaten such ideological apparatuses of patriarchy as the research university, cosmetic surgery, psychotherapy, and gynaecology; in *Videodrome*, for example, they threaten porn/snuff TV.

This essay will look closely at the women in *Videodrome*. Something unusual is going on with all the female characters, and with concepts of femaleness in general, which both popular reviews and critical essays seem to have missed. This essay will carry out a different kind of film analysis – one that might be just as unpopular as the film itself, but that will address it at its creative centres; there is really no sense in repeating ad nauseam that *Videodrome* is offensive. What matters is why it gives offence and what is in there living beside those offending things, and to ask whether the world might not be better to acknowledge them. If everyone is offended by Cronenberg's images (to the point that only 'politically correct' criticism is possible), then, in the end, we've only said something about ourselves and not much at all about the film.

Some images in Cronenberg's cinema have gained so much notoriety that they are cited and condemned with little regard for the context in which they occur; a gaping vagina-like opening in a man's abdomen is one example in *Videodrome*. The present analysis is a re-vision, a "looking back [...] seeing again with fresh eyes [...] entering an old text from a new critical direction."[29] In "Anti-Porn: Soft Issue, Hard World," B. Ruby Rich tells the story of a friend who had modelled for a series of nude photographs and who was "tormented by the image of an unknown man jerking off" to one of her photographs which was stolen from the gallery exhibition. Rich asks, "was that photograph erotic or pornographic?" Other stories of interpretative confrontations led her to conclude that "surely it is not merely an *image* which is one thing or another, but equally (if not foremost) the *imagination* that employs the image in the service of its fantasy."[30]

'Tastes,' as Pierre Bourdieu argues in "The Aristocracy of Culture," are social constructs disguised as universal aesthetics; the training of the aesthetic sense is one of the cultural 'invisibilities' which reproduce the systems of power and assure the dominance of established relations.[31] What, in *Videodrome*, opposes 'good' (legitimate) taste, and what do the 'tasteless' things do to the existing systems of power relations? Julia Kristeva observes in *Powers of Horror* that the abhorrent signifier, the phobic object, is a means to call attention to "a drive economy in want of an object – that conglomerate of fear, deprivation, and nameless frustration, which, properly speaking, belongs to the unnameable."[32] What unspeakable images do we confront in *Videodrome*? How and why do they frighten or offend us? What desires do they name?

ഇ

[29] Adrienne Rich, "When We Dead Awaken: Writing as Re-Vision," in Rich, *On Lies, Secrets, and Silence: Selected Prose, 1966–1978* (New York: W.W. Norton, 1979): 35.

[30] B. Ruby Rich, "Anti-Porn: Soft Issue, Hard World" (1983), repr. in *Films for Women*, ed. Charlotte Brunsdon (London: British Film Institute, 1986): 36 (emphasis in the original).

[31] Pierre Bourdieu, "The Aristocracy of Culture," in *Media, Culture and Society* 2.3 (1980): 234–39.

[32] Julia Kristeva, *Powers of Horror: An Essay on Abjection*, tr. Leon S. Roudiez (New York: Columbia UP, 1982): 35.

I

The business of representing men is a precarious one indeed.[33]

Is *Videodrome* so obviously a re-working of the Christ myth that scant attention has been paid to the analogy? In the film, we hear of the "Video-Word
Made Flesh," we encounter an absent Father who is all-knowing but not of
this world, and, in the end, he who is the word-made-flesh accepts his own
end, in his own wasteland Gethsemane, in order that a new intelligence and
new aliveness (the new flesh) can be born into a world now without grace.
Yet, if we examine some of the important differences once the stories are put
side-by-side, we can see just how the film disrupts the older myth. As Cronenberg's narrative unfolds, it becomes clear that the undisturbed and
unquestionable authority of patriarchal society that was established in
Christ's name is not likely to emanate from the new doctrine of the New
Flesh. Rather than aiming to disembowel feminine authority (as Christianity
did throughout Europe and in much of the Third World), *Videodrome* is
about re-establishing it right at the centre – in the belly, if you will – of a
patriarchal world gone mad and destined to grow madder. This is the meaning of Max Renn's very odd new growth (a gash in his stomach); it is no
accident that it is women who guide him through the dark world of the
fathers to the vision of rebirth and renewal.

The Saviour

Max Renn, the male protagonist who becomes the "video-word made flesh"
through death and rebirth, is without self-knowledge, vision, or philosophy
through much of the film; time after time, his understanding of the new and
strange happenings is at a minimum rather than at a maximum. In fact, he is
the doubter since, like Thomas, who stuck his fingers inside Christ's wound
and so proved His return in the flesh,[34] Max also has to stick his fingers into
his own wound (the opening in the middle of his abdomen) to convince
himself that he has been transformed in the flesh. Throughout the film, Max
lacks insight, for he sees only with the pornographic vision that women can
be contained in photographs and video-images and that to possess the
image is to possess the woman. Marsha (the video broker) warns Max that

---

[33] Steven Cohan & Ina Rae Hark, "Introduction" to *Screening the Male: Exploring Masculinities in Hollywood Cinema*, ed. Cohan & Hark (London: Routledge, 1993): 3.

[34] For the story of doubting Thomas, see St. John's Gospel 20:27–29.

he is out of his league with "Videodrome" (the corporation which produces the snuff films and the tumour-inducing signal); even though she is a small-time porn broker who has to sell to the Maxes of the world, her comprehension of the world, her worldliness, is vastly superior to his, and this pattern holds true with all the women in the film. When she warns Max that "Videodrome" "is dangerous" because "it has something" – a philosophy – which Max lacks, she helps us understand a truth which Barry Convex and Harlan of "Videodrome" already know but which Max is yet to learn – that Max is empty, hence penetrable.

Judas and the Pharisees

Convex can shove a videocassette directly into Max's stomach; he can also programme Max's brain through TV. Convex owns a business conglomerate which dispenses inexpensive eye-glasses to the Third-World poor while it manufactures expensive missile guiding systems for NATO and produces "Videodrome" (the films and the signals) in the USA; the hypocrisies and contradictions are obvious. True to his name, Convex is outward rather than inward looking; he seeks to control the world rather than himself. He employs Harlan to infiltrate Max's Civic TV by becoming its technical assistant. Harlan is the traitor, the Judas, but for a (yet another) 'new world order' rather than for thirty pieces of silver. Arrogant and authoritarian, he complains to Max (whom he addresses, only half-jokingly, as "Pátron") that "North America is getting too soft" while the rest of the world is "hard"; he wants "Videodrome" to make North Americans "pure, erect, and strong." Like the Pharisees who seek power, Convex, Harlan, and the others who own Spectacular Vision and "Videodrome" aim to change the world for all citizens, but the power is self-serving and fascistoid, and the capitalist/free-enterprise jargon only encases and secures the usual greed for absolute power and control.

Heavenly Father

The only relationship that Max has with a man which doesn't absolutely justify a paranoic view of the world is, interestingly, with a dead man, Professor Brian O'Blivion. O'Blivion only appears on TV for a reason that neither he nor the director of the film gives away in the first few scenes: it is because TV is the only place in which he 'exists.' So, much like Hamlet's relationship with his dead father (or Luke Skywalker's with Obi-Wan-

Kenobi[35]), Max's relationship with his Symbolic Father (who art in Video) is a one-sided series of exchanges: Professor Brian O'Blivion instructs and poses in an attitude of wisdom; he really only talks at Max, not with him. Between the professor and Max, between screen and spectator, god and subject, the space is charged with expectation, emotion, and interpretation, but this god (who can be seen) is, contrary to the Judaeo-Christian Father-God, oblivious! He does not listen, and he cannot be 'reached,' though he can reach his disciples – through TV.

II

> [I]f we think physically rather than metaphysically, if we think the mind-body split through the body, it becomes an image of shocking violence.[36]

Men who behave like boys are more predictable and less discriminating, and in a society that is predominantly about consumption, boy-men are valued as better subjects because they are better consumers; boys buy more toys. Rites of passage are reduced to rites of consumption that go on for entire lifetimes and are never 'passed through' – first, toy guns, toy cars, adventure comics; then, real guns, real cars, and snuff TV. But normal life never lasts long in Cronenberg's films, and in *Videodrome*, Max cannot avoid his passage into the night (or the light, depending on your point of view). He has successfully met and surpassed the criteria set for manhood (he is King Peter Pan): he has money and the proper bottom line ("will it sell?"); he has, if you will, the 'balls,' though we can as easily see it is cockiness without courage or commitment or, so far as he knows, without much at stake.

Max's business is pornography, which relies on the fast and loose (il)logic that to possess the image is to possess the person. In *The Pornography of Representation*, Suzanne Kappeler suggests that "the fantasy of porn is not [...] identical with the 'content' of representation"; rather, it is "completed by the active subject, the viewer–hero [...], the doing-subject: what he is doing is watching, imagining, fantasizing, producing the feeling of life, delight and pleasure in himself."[37] At Civic TV, Max serves 'civil society' by containing

---

[35] Played by Mark Hamill and Alec Guinness, respectively, in George Lucas's 1977 mega-hit, *Star Wars*.

[36] Jane Gallop, *Thinking Through the Body* (New York: Columbia UP, 1988): 1.

[37] Suzanne Kappeler, *The Pornography of Representation* (Minneapolis: Minnesota UP, 1986): 59.

women, sex, and death in images of them in hard-core and snuff films; as he proudly declares on a TV talk-show, "it's a matter of economics."

Early in the film, he expresses his dissatisfaction with 'regular' porn: "I want something else, something harder." He doesn't know it for a long time, but he gets more than he bargains for, since the snuff in "Videodrome" is just the foreplay which makes another penetration possible: "Videodrome" enters his brain and deposits a tumour, and once it has done its work, once it is 'let in,' all kinds of things are 'let out' – things that must never get out of a man! The most horrific thing that 'gets out' is, of course, Max's vagina. He develops an opening in his abdomen in which he loses his gun; he later retrieves and reclaims it in a transformed state, but not before Convex commands him to "Open up" and then shoves a videocassette into him so that the programme will compel him to feel and do certain things.

Max has been raped into unconsciousness or, more accurately, he has been raped in the Unconscious. And to Max, this extremely phallocentric dealer in women's flesh as image, this 'patron' who wants containment and order above all else, nothing could be more horrific than to become what he tried to capture and hold and control in his years of controlling her – woman's – image. So, female genitalia is "the last outrage," as one critic writes in a review of another Cronenberg film (*The Fly*, 1986), but only because what is happening to Max is the ultimate betrayal: it is not that his body should do what he really didn't want but that it should do what he really did want – that he should become someone with this red, mucous opening, that what he'd always kept down, what he'd always feared and fought to control, should rise up and embrace him and be a part of him. He has become what he most fears and really most wants to be, and this, to Max, his culture, and ours, is Horror! Much has been written about the fear of the feminine or of feminization as a constant of the horror genre,[38] but it doesn't follow from the act of citing this fear that Cronenberg's film is itself paranoid (or, for that matter, that Cronenberg himself is). To say the least, Max's feminization is given ironic distance by the kind of man Max is; to say the most, he is clearly made better by it near the end of the film.

Max had said that he wanted "something else, something harder," a realer reality, a reality more powerful than the symbolic; through "Videodrome," he gets a reality of the flesh which culture and the symbolic labour

---

[38] See, for example, Barbara Creed's *The Monstrous-Feminine: Film, Feminism, Psychoanalysis* (London: Routledge, 1993) and Mary Russo's *The Female Grotesque: Risk, Excess and Modernity* (London: Routledge, 1994).

to contain. That Cronenberg focuses his camera on the body is only logical, for he knows it is this 'part' of the human being which is most anxiously apprehended in the West:

> The body must bear no trace of its debt to nature: it must be clear and proper in order to be fully symbolic. In order to confirm that, it should endure no gash other than that of circumcision, equivalent to sexual separation and/or separation from the mother. Any other mark would be the sign of belonging to the impure, the non-separate, the non-symbolic, the non-holy.[39]

In *Videodrome*, the male protagonist wants most what he frantically disavows and what he hysterically strives to control, but the problem with wanting something that he's always been led to believe isn't good for him is that he doesn't know how to go about getting it. He has to enter a world not his own, a world not of representing the flesh and containing it in images (the project of porn). When Harlan shoves his hand inside Max's new abdominal opening, it is ripped apart and transformed into a hand-grenade which blows a hole through Harlan and the brick wall behind him; when Convex is shot by Max, he literally turns inside-out, his viscera spilling to the ground. After he has killed these 'fathers,' Max heads for the harbour (literally into the sea of rebirth) and enters a condemned vessel (a no longer useful body). Nicki is there, magically speaking out of a TV set that has no electricity and no antenna; she talks to him, and shows him what he must do. With the sacred formula on his lips – "Death to Videodrome. Long Live the New Flesh!" – Max blows a hole through himself. He is not the despairing suicide; he is re-creating himself.

Critics have charged that Cronenberg's male protagonists (and, by extension, Cronenberg himself) suffer from womb-envy.[40] I see nothing wrong with this envy, since it it is not fantastic bliss but pain and the burdens of the womb, including the outrage that is rape, that the film shows Max has achieved. His realization of his dream of *jouissance* contains that nightmare which feminists have always said is a part of the day-to-day real of the maternal in a phallocentric world. It is only later, when Bianca switches the patriarchal programme for the womb (by changing the tape in Max's opening), that he gains in-sight, or a sight beyond his search in pornography for the naked Mother. He is no longer empty.

---

[39] Kristeva, *Powers of Horror*, 102.

[40] See, for example, Helen Robbins, "More Human Than I Am Alone," in Cohan & Hark, ed., *Screening the Male*.

In *Videodrome*, as in his other films, Cronenberg shows a reverence for the womb; that it is at least as powerful as the phallus is fully suggested. Except for the fact that the womb has been coded ad infinitum as undesirable, womb-envy would be an accusation in Cronenberg's favour.

III

> Humankind [is] composed of two equally creative genders, one of which is additionally a procreator in itself, in its body. That doesn't stop it from having the right to freedom, identity, and spirit.[41]

It is not possible to over-emphasize the fact that Max's spiritual guides are women, for, whichever way he looks, there is a woman with whom he has sympathy and who has sympathy, compassion, and understanding for him. It would be a male fantasy par excellence – save that Max, like Hamlet before him, "has dreams."

Bridey James: Secretary at Civic TV

The film opens to a TV screen with static interference; a red, white, and blue station-identification clip comes on: "Civic TV – the one you take to bed with you." Then, a woman's face appears in close-up and she beckons: "Max! It's that time again, time to slowly and painfully ease yourself back into consciousness...." The camera pans, and we eventually see a man in a messy bed: apparently, he sleeps with his watch on and in his street clothes. The woman's face on TV is the first face we see in the film, and hers is the first voice that he (Max) hears as he awakens; she is Bridey (pronounced "bride-dee") James, Max's secretary at Civic TV, and he has used all the electronic media at his disposal to have her there so that she can bring him into the world every day. She is polite and efficient, yes; but she is also loving and attentive, and she knows well what he needs.

Max's expectations and treatment of his secretary make clear her relationship with another cultural ideal – the loving Mother: both are expected to be motivated for the welfare of their 'boy' alone. They are there to wake him, serve him, admire him, and even to protect and cover for him when they, with motherly disappointment, 'catch him in the act' and recognize his guilt; so, like a mother who catches her boy using porn, Bridey later catches Max (with his hand in his shirt, holding the smoking gun that

---

[41] Luce Irigaray, *Je, Tu, Nous: Towards a Culture of Difference* (London: Routledge, 1993): 79.

killed his business partners), and she helps him get away. Secretaries and mothers stand in for one another so that men can run to them for mental and physical sustenance (a listening ear and a cup of hot coffee) at anxious moments, at home or at the office; women who have worked as secretaries know this, even if they have fought against the role. The nurturing care of the home/ private domain is expected to continue into the office/public domain, complete with the transference of the incest taboo: Bridey is the wonderful secretary who admires and loves but who doesn't cross the line; she has the discretion to 'hold back'; although she is bride-like (Bride-y), she remains 'bridled.'

Rather than reinforcing the relationship, *Videodrome*'s reiteration of the secretary/mother myth at the very start of the film draws critical attention to it so that a response more complex and thoughtful than "it's all misogyny" can be made to the film's male and female protagonists. On the one hand, we can hardly fail to despise Max, whose relationship with women consists entirely of buying and selling their images and seeking and requiring their service; here is someone who wants so much to be pampered by women all through life that he stands by patriarchy uncritically, expecting every female in every domain to cater to him. On the other hand, Max's yearning for the maternal is not in itself evil or always already hateful; on the contrary, to the extent that it is a kernel of fantasy which excludes the Fathers (Barry Convex, Harlan), who want only their version (the "Videodrome" ideal) of the world for all, it speaks a desire which disrupts phallocentric discourse.

In the history of the West, two master narratives typify theories on the genesis of human subjectivity: (a) initial oneness with the mother, and (b) necessary separation from, and renunciation of, her.[42] Normative development in these views requires both an original state of bliss and the subsequent forfeiture of that bliss, with both experiences presumed to give the infant's perspective; inasmuch as the mother is deemed the reason for both the plenitude and its loss, theoretical attention is paid to her physical presence, but her subjectivity is seldom considered. In fact, intrapsychic development during infancy is commonly discussed in terms which óbjectify the mother as 'breast,' 'food,' or some non-specific environmental source of relief for a physiologically dependent infant. In Sigmund Freud's model of psychic development (to use a large example), successful maturation requires that the initial closeness with, and desire for, the mother be replaced

---

[42] See, for example, classical psychoanalytic theory and its revisions, object relations theories, American ego psychology.

by psychic separation from, and rejection of, her; in this way, individual sovereignty is achieved only through psychological matricide. 'Separation' is especially critical for the male subject, who must identify with the Father and 'recover' the mother only through the future possession of women; this, we might say, is Freud's tragedy of heterosexuality – and Max's problem in *Videodrome*.

It may be that Max's obsessive use of porn is a struggle to capture the image of she who is lost; certainly, *Videodrome* identifies with the maternal voice the cultural fantasy of associating plenitude and bliss. However, in showing Max's extraordinary arrangement to be in that sonorous envelope in(to) which he awakens every morning (the daily video-call from Bridey), the film insists on the retroactivity of that bliss, or the "after-the-fact construction or reading of a situation which is fundamentally irrecoverable."[43] By rejecting the fantasy of initial oneness and idyllic unity of mother-and-child, *Videodrome* makes it possible to conceive of the mother as a subject in her own right so that "from the beginning there are always (at least) two subjects."[44] Cronenberg's film shows these qualities of desire for the maternal in Max, because only a protagonist with these desires could ever imagine a world in which something other than the Phallus could reign.

Nicki Brand & her "Emotional Rescue Show" on C–RAM Radio

Most immediately, Nicki Brand's name suggests 'name-brands,' or that device which disguises commercial homogeneity to give consumers the illusion of sovereignty and freedom of choice. At C–RAM Radio, where she is the 'personality' of the "Emotional Rescue Show," she is the 'brand' that distressed listeners choose; she dispenses advice on the air much as Max dispenses porn. In this way, both Nicki and Max feed on mainstream culture by first creating a need and then supplying the demand; they cannibalize and capitalize on the desperations of 'normal society.' However, Max's Civic TV ("the one you take to bed with you") cares only about the human being's over- and ever-represented surface (porn), while Nicki's "Emotional Rescue Show" at least tries to see into the depths of the human subject.

But that meaning of 'brand' is a recent derivation from the red-hot steel markers that sear the flesh of cattle, and Nicki's connection to this is

---

[43] Kaja Silverman, *The Acoustic Mirror: The Female Voice in Psychoanalysis and Cinema* (Bloomington: Indiana UP, 1988): 73.

[44] Jessica Benjamin, *The Bonds of Love: Psychoanalysis, Feminism, and the Problem of Domination* (New York: Random House, 1988): 24.

obvious; in a love-making scene with Max, she burns one breast and then offers him the lit cigarette and her other breast. With 'nicks' (knife-cuts) on her shoulders and 'brands' (cigarette burns) on her breasts, Nicki Brand lives also at the margins of 'civil society.'

Still an older association of 'brand' is with torches that guides carry to lead travellers through a benighted world, or that gods carry to lead souls through the caverns of the Underworld. When Persephone was snatched away (by Hades, the lord of the Underworld, who wanted her all to himself), her mother, Demeter, searched the earth day and night with a staff-like brand in each hand.[45] Likewise, Nicki – who is not the hostage (Persephone) but the light ('brand') that seeks – is burned up in the search for what's been lost and for what's been hidden, but she also illumines what the hiding means.

What has been lost in our world, as it was lost when Persephone was raped and abducted, was the power and glory of the feminine; for Persephone, the maiden, represented one-third of the triumvirate power of the Female Trinity (the maiden, nymph or matron, and crone). It is, of course, significant that it is at that point, with the first of the Trinity, that the Underworld god struck, for – now and from now on, and ever since then – matriarchal power was at an end: girls never get to their full power without symbolic abduction. Since the advent of the patriarchal world, women have typically been buried, robbed of integrity, freedom, and their rightful voice. Nicki's name and her playing with fire combine to suggest that light might be cast on things anew: as with Demeter, we might soon see what has been stolen, forgotten, and thought lost forever. And just as masochism is unseen and unseeable, except that Nicki makes Max see (and feel) it, so are other possibilities, other potentialities long buried and thought gone forever, about to arise again in the *Videodrome* world.

Nicki is also the 'Magdalene,' but unlike the whore of the New Testament, who has no voice beyond that of gratitude, adoration, and obedience, Nicki successfully seduces the male protagonist and initiates him into her desires. In fact, Max proves precisely unequal to Nicki in every way; even though he warns her and even tries to "forbid" her to do it, she ignores him and goes to Pittsburgh to join the "Videodrome" cast. Beginning with their first meeting ('on the air,' on TV), and throughout the film, not only is Nicki beyond his control, he is as often under her control; it is she who tells him to

---

[45] See Hesiod, *Theogony.*

hurt her and she who shows him how (with knives and pins and burning cigarettes). In the end, she also tells him to "give up his old flesh," and she shows him how to do it.

A common, strong objection to Videodrome has to do with the way it explores sado-masochistic play. As a culture, we cannot wholly shake off the idea that those who like such play (must) hate themselves; the 'modern' attitude – vis-à-vis, say, Madonna – is to regard it as a mere taste, even if it is a taste of the "true gourmand." I think it is at least arguable that sado-masochism is mostly beyond all but the most totalitarian control; more to the point is to ask what thrills the players. What does the pain tell them in both the giving and the getting of it, and what might it tell us about unspeakable desires?

Pain, as we know, is a feeling; it is felt through the body, and whatever the mind might do or wish to do to control it or deny it, the feeling is more powerful than the voice of reason, the voice that says "no!" Because pain makes the body speak louder than the controlling and containing mind, sado-masochistic pain enunciates desires that are muted by civil society and its repressive logos. What is revealed in Nicki and Max's play is a need for connection through pain, and an eroticism never to be admitted into the world of order. Sadism and masochism suffered willingly, this kind of hot-ness that Nicki Brand's name likewise suggests, a burn from a cigarette that is felt across the body so that 'normal' sexual zones are categorically dis-solved into one body (a whole-not-just-a-hole) – all of these disrupt the terms of violence and pain in the patriarchal world, or violence that is done in police or military order, by men. Nicki has stolen the fire of the gods.

Their sado-masochism pulls Max, by his own volition, into a new sym-pathy with his own flesh, by virtue of the new sympathy he gains through sympathy with and fear of Nicki – my sentence is long, but all the parts are critical. Sex is a habit that Max takes up and puts down; it is his business, and he stays 'on top of it.' So, as long as Max was involved in this static phallic-positioning (in which he considered himself the fucker vs the fucked), his flesh could never go beyond its self-containing and merely penetrative status; he would colonize the bodies of women, but never be-come one (as in the ecstasy of sex, identity 'barriers' are broken down). The point at which he cares for Nicki but cannot at all control or limit her – when Nicki takes the brand and sears her own flesh – is the point at which she sears him as well. It is important that when they're making love on the living room floor, apparently surrounded by a red sea, the camera shows those parts of them that are non-distinguishing; in other words, they are physically similar, and the flesh shown could be male or female. It is also important that when Nicki offers Max a lit cigarette and her other (as yet un-seared) breast, the camera does not show us his decision before the scene cuts; the conspicuous absence in the scene proves, beyond a shadow of a doubt, that our imaginary is alive with both the seen and the ob-scene.

Bianca O'Blivion & the Cathode Ray Mission

> For centuries, whatever has been valorized has been masculine in gender, whatever devalorized, feminine. [...] man becomes God by giving himself an invisible father, a father language. Man becomes God as the Word, then as the Word made flesh. Because the power of semen isn't immediately obvious in procreation, it's relayed by the linguistic code, the logos. Which wants to become the all-embracing truth.[46]

Bianca O'Blivion apparently works for her father – but only apparently, since her father, it turns out, is dead. As the displayer and controller of her father's tapes of himself, Bianca stands in for all the prophets, from Isaiah to John the Baptist. Like the prophets, Bianca is who is speaking, even though it is understood that she is the earthly priest who conveys the Word of God above (sitting on his Heavenly Throne). In fact, Bianca speaks for herself, and we can think this for two reasons. First, inasmuch as she constructs a living media guru (Brian O'Blivion) by manipulating the millions of possibi-lities in the thousands of videotapes of her dead father, it is she who is the professor, it is she who chooses the words, and it is she who is the religion. Secondly, the desk at which her father used to sit, in front of his camera on its tripod while it recorded his 'thoughts,' is now the rightful property of Bianca, for she is the prophet and high-priestess.

In ancient Delphi, a priestess called the Pythoness sat on a tripod and answered the questions of those who travelled far across Greece to seek her guidance; the tripod symbolized her three co-existing aspects (maiden, matron/nymph, hag) and their mutual dependency. At Cumae, the Sybil, a seer, dispensed oracles. The shrine at Delphi as well as the one at Cumae were founded in the name of Mother Earth; in fact, all oracles were "origi-nally delivered by the Earth-Goddess, whose authority was so great that patriarchal invaders made a practice of seizing her shrines and either ap-

---

[46] Irigaray, *Towards a Culture of Difference*, 68–69.

pointing priests or retaining the priestesses in their own service."[47] At Delphi, Apollo killed the Python that had lived there, and he took over the shrine for himself; he even installed a priest to distill the words of the Pythoness into hexameters.[48] At Cumae, Apollo fell in love with the Sibyl and, to gain her favours, he granted her eternal life – but without benefit of eternal youth, in effect making life for her only a burden and never a joy. Clearly, it spelt bad times ahead for any of the female seers of the ancient world whenever the gods of the invading patriarchal tribes came to love them (or, when love failed, to rob them of authority).

The oracular priestesses at Delphi and at Cumae were survivors of an older and almost-forgotten matriarchal age, and it is with these robbed wise ones that I rank Bianca, as their long-awaited successor. The pythonesses and sibyls were said to make the ghost of the dead speak, and Bianca is their equivalent as she shuffles the video-recorded words of her dead father so that he (mysteriously, if the truth be told) speaks. Women do not lose spiritual power simply because men say that they don't have it any more; to paraphrase Luce Irigaray, just because a woman is a procreator doesn't stop her from being a creator as well.[49] Bianca O'Blivion is the sibyl or the pythoness, the great prophetess biding her time, only pretending to serve the male god. Of course, this doesn't prevent Roger Ebert from referring to her as the professor's "sexy daughter."[50] The capacity of popular reviewers to see only what they want to see beggars description.

IV

There is a definitive immanence of the image [...] this endless enwrapping [...] (literally: without end, without destination) which leaves images no other destiny than images [...] What we have is the sign alone; [...] reality is the effect of the sign.[51]

Videodrome looks tailor-made for Jean Baudrillard – or it would seem so, had the film not come out well before the main body of Baudrillard's work on the culture of the sign. When the hallucination takes over after Max becomes

---

[47] Robert Graves, *The Greek Myths* (Pelican Books; Harmondsworth: Penguin, 1960), vol. 1: 180–81.

[48] Graves, *Greek Myths*, 181.

[49] Irigaray, *Towards a Culture of Difference*, 79.

[50] Ebert, "*Videodrome*," in Microsoft *Cinemania*.

[51] Baudrillard, *The Evil Demon of Images*, 30; and the "Interview" which follows the essay, by Ted Colless, David Kelly and Alan Cholodenko, tr. Philippe Tanguy, 47–48.

the property of Spectacular Optical and "Videodrome," the film achieves "the pure strategy of the sign."[52] When Baudrillard says of the TV image that it is "a miniaturized terminal located in your head and you are the screen,"[53] he is articulating Brian O'Blivion's doctrine that "the TV screen has become the retina of the mind's eye."

A key scene in *Videodrome* occurs when Harlan reaches inside Max's opening to insert a new programme but finds his hand chewed off and transformed into a hand-grenade; it is indexical because it shows us that Harlan himself witnesses the transformation. Of course, Harlan's reaction could still be a part of Max's hallucination, and when the grenade goes off and blows a hole through Harlan and a brick wall, and Max walks through the hole into the street, it could still be "just Max's hallucination"; perhaps Max is somewhere else, in a café, or at the TV station, or in bed. The point is, what difference does it make, at least within the world of the film? What if, conversely, it is the TV-station, or Max-at-the-TV-station, that is the hallucination? It all starts to break down – and this is Baudrillard's point, too: "[images] are the sites of the disappearance of meaning and representation, sites in which we are caught quite apart from any judgement of reality and of the reality principle."[54] Within this vision, and faced with the filmic images of vaginal openings in men's stomachs, of a whole new kind of 'hand-grenade,' and of guns that grow into and out of men's arms, we enter that breakdown, and have only the choice between not-seeing and accepting the hallucination as reality.

To be sure, if, in the final shots, Max were to click his heels together and find himself safe in his own bed on his farm in Kansas, critical responses to *Videodrome* might have been different (although I must hasten to add that it has never been wholly clear to me whether it is Oz or Kansas that occurs 'in Dorothy's head'[55]) In *Videodrome*, if it had been possible to accept Max's hallucinations as having no 'impact,' not just in the sense of blowing holes through walls but also as not infecting others with them, then a kind of closure in the film, and an innoculation against the film, would have been achieved. In other words, as things are, the open-endedness of *Videodrome* is its most irritating feature – but oughtn't it to be a strength as well? It is

---

[52] Baudrillard, *The Evil Demon of Images*, 47.

[53] Baudrillard, *The Evil Demon of Images*, 25.

[54] Baudrillard, *The Evil Demon of Images*, 28.

[55] Are we more willing to "accept" Kansas because it is so dull – filmed in black-and-white, unlike the Technicolor Oz?

precisely open-endedness that can carry a work of art beyond what it merely states. In the end, *Videodrome* adds up to more than the sum of its parts, because Max is somehow no longer an emptiness that can be used/ programmed/raped. There is something beyond for Max, just as there is for the film, because he can make the leap of faith – even through death – to fulfil the promises made by Bianca when she "changed his programme," and by Nicki Brand, who illuminated his dark desires.

Baudrillard suggests that to assert that the world is 'real' or 'unreal' is futile, that there is "no objectivity to the world"[56] in the "cool universe of digitality."[57] But what if digitality stops being "cool"? What if it becomes hot, as it does in *Videodrome*? We have clues to this warmth, this danger of burning and of being burnt, almost from the start of the film. It is true that Max is a pornographer, and porn, as Linda Williams has argued in *Hard Core*, is always working on the surface and for the visible, obsessed with "the confession of previously invisible 'truths' of bodies and pleasures."[58] It is also true that Brian O'Blivion is 'only on TV' and is destined to remain there all the days of his death (for his TV-life is still death, however else it appears, just as his TV-name isn't the one he was born with). Regardless of these various levels of madness and love of the captured and captive image, there remains in Cronenberg's *Videodrome* the uncontrollable and uncontained, the gift of vision reconstructed by Bianca out of ages forgotten, and in Nicki Brand, the lover of pain, whose very name means a burning by which we see.

Both Bianca and Nicki are seers. Bianca sees the suffering of countless unhoused, unwashed, discarded humans, and her mission (in both senses) is to save them. Nicki seeks suffering, the real pain of a cigarette burn, the kind of burn that throbs and stings for long days after the wounding, and she seeks her own immolation and annihilation in the "Videodrome" arena. Nicki doesn't just love pain, she needs it. Pain is the signifier that makes her the referent; it enables self-recognition in a world without referents and reference. Nicki Brand lives at the point where pain meets its opposite, pleasure, and this is why, in the end, Max prefers to leave the nightmare of the world and go where she beckons.

---

[56] Baudrillard, *The Evil Demon of Images*, 47-48.

[57] Baudrillard, "The Orders of Simulacra," in *Simulations*, tr. Paul Foss, Paul Patton & Philip Beitchman (New York: Semiotext(e), 1983): 152.

[58] Linda Williams, *Hard Core: Power, Pleasure, and the 'Frenzy of the Visible'* (Berkeley: U of California P, 1989): 7.

It is no longer a world of nothing but simulacra, where the dream or fantasy is as real as anything else, and the unreal is "a hallucinary resemblance of the real with itself."[59] The *Videodrome* world is caught by its pain, the only constant of human existence, the only experience that cannot wholly be contained with/in language. Suffering breaks the illusion of the world, nailing down existence and making reality speak itself, in words that are unutterable. In *Videodrome*, everything starts to show up in the body; the cool becomes hot, and TV gives you brain tumours that make you see the illusion as the illumination. The military–industrial complex, snuff-movies, and other 'matters of economics' are all there in a nightmare from which we can only be liberated by real pain. As Bianca, the wisewoman, tells us, "it hurts to change the programme."

There are times when pain has been so great, and suffering so immediate, so unrelieved, that on its farther shore the sufferer is without fear, not even of death. This is where Max exits at the end of *Videodrome* – very far, indeed, from where the film picks him up. He has left elsewhere his lust for power, his lust for money, and his lust for lust. Max's last words are "Long Live the New Flesh!", and he kills himself, in the flesh. What is this promise of the new flesh that carries him out of the world? A life-after-death, on TV? It is possible, but unlikely: the screen is at last black/blank when we hear the gun's report. The answer seems to lie elsewhere – in seeing and hearing while in the flesh, while alive, by being alive to life's irreducible pain. And this is a step beyond simulacrum, beyond Baudrillard.

⁎⁎

Filmography

Features

1975 *Shivers* (or: *They Came From Within*; or: *The Parasite Murders*; + screenplay; 87 mins.)
1976 *Rabid* (+ screenplay; 91 mins.)
1979 *Fast Company* (+ co-screenplay; from story by Alan Treen; 91 mins.)
1979 *The Brood* (+ screenplay; 91 mins.)
1980 *Scanners* (+ screenplay; 103 mins.)
1982 *Videodrome* (+ screenplay; 87 mins.)
1983 *The Dead Zone* (100 mins.)
1986 *The Fly* (+ co-screenplay; from story by George Langelaan; 92 mins.)

---

[59] Baudrillard, *Simulations*, 142.

1988   *Dead Ringers* (+ co-producer, co-screenplay; from *Twins*, by Bari Wood and Jack Geasland; 115 mins.)

1991   *Naked Lunch* (+ screenplay; from *The Naked Lunch*, by William S. Burroughs; 115 mins.)

1993   *M Butterfly* (+ screenplay; from play by David H. Hwang; 102 mins.)

1996   *Crash* (+ co-producer, screenplay; from novel by J.G. Ballard; 96 mins.)

1999   *eXistenZ* (+ screenplay; 90 mins.)

Short films and television work

1966   *Transfer* (+ cinematography, editor; screenplay; 7 mins., 16mm)

1967   *From the Drain* (+ cinematography, editor; screenplay; 14 mins., 16mm)

1969   *Stereo* (+ cinematography, editor, producer, screenplay; b/w, 65 mins.)

1970   *Crimes of the Future* (+ cinematography, editor, producer, screenplay; 65 mins.)

1971   *Jim Ritchie, Sculptor* (+ cinematography; no narration, music track only; short TV-filler, 16mm)

1971   *Letter from Michelangelo* (+ cinematography; short TV-filler, 16mm)

1971   *Tourettes* (+ cinematography; no narration; music track only; short TV-filler, 16mm)

1972   *Don Valley* (+ cinematography; no narration; music track only; TV-filler, 5 mins., 16mm)

1972   *Fort York* (+ cinematography; no narration; music track only; TV-filler, 5 mins., 16mm)

1972   *Lakeshore* (+ cinematography; no narration; music track only; TV-filler, 5 mins., 16mm)

1972   *Winter Garden* (+ cinematography; no narration; music track only; TV-filler, 5 mins., 16mm)

1972   *Scarborough Bluffs* (+ cinematography; no narration; music track only; TV-filler, 5 mins., 16mm)

1972   *In the Dirt* (+ cinematography; no narration; music track only; TV-filler, 5 mins., 16mm)

1972   *Secret Weapons* (+ cinematography; CBC-TV broadcast, 1 June 1972; 27 mins., 16mm)

1975   *The Victim* (CBC-TV broadcast, 22 January 1976; 27 mins., 2" VTR)

1975   *The Lie Chair* (CBC-TV broadcast, 12 February 1976; 27 mins., 2" VTR)

1976   *The Italian Machine* (+ screenplay; 28 mins., 16mm)

1990   *Regina versus Horvath* (CBC programme, "Scales of Justice" 48 mins., Betacam)

1990   *Regina versus Logan* (CBC programme, "Scales of Justice"; 44 mins., Betacam)

2000   *Camera* (5 mins.; 16mm)

Commercials

1989   Hydro (*Hot Showers, Laundry, Cleaners, Timers*; 4 @ 30 secs.)

1990   Caramilk (*Bistro, Surveillance*; 2 @ 30 secs.)

1990   Nike (*Transformation*; 1 @ 15 secs., 4 @ 30 secs.)

Bibliography

Books and special journal issues

Cinéfantastique 14.2 (December 1983–January 1984).

Beard, William. *The Artist As Monster: The Cinema of David Cronenberg*. Toronto: University of Toronto Press, 2001. 488pp, 20 illustrations.

——, & Piers Handling, ed. *The Shape of Rage: The Films of David Cronenberg*. Toronto: Academy of Canadian Cinema/General; New York: Zoetrope, 1983.

Dompierre, Louise. *Prent/Cronenberg: Crimes Against Nature*. Toronto: The Power Plant, 1987.

Drew, Wayne, ed. *David Cronenberg*. Dossier 21. London: British Film Institute, 1984.

Film Festival Rotterdam. *David Cronenberg: Transformatie van een horrorfilmer/A Horrorfilmer in Transformation*. Rotterdam, 1990, 74pp.

Grant, Michael, ed. *The Modern Fantastic: The Films of David Cronenberg*. Trowbridge: Flicks Books; Westport CT: Praeger, 2000.

Grünberg, Serge. *David Cronenberg*. Collection Auteurs. Paris: Editions de l'Étoile/Cahiers du cinéma, 1992.

Handling, Piers, & Pierre Véronneau. *L'Horreur intérieure: Les films de David Cronenberg*. 7e Art. Paris: Cerf; Montréal: Cinémathèque québécoise, 1990.

Morris, Peter. *David Cronenberg: A Delicate Balance*. Toronto: ECW, 1994.

Post script 15.2 (Winter–Spring 1996).

Rodley, Chris, ed. *Cronenberg on Cronenberg*. Toronto: Alfred A. Knopf, 1992.

Sinclair, Iain. *'Crash': David Cronenberg's Post-Mortem on J.G. Ballard's 'Trajectory of Fate'*. London: British Film Institute, 1999.

24 Images 59 (hiver 1992); 16pp.

Interviews

Ayscough, Susan. *Cinema Canada* (December 1983): 15-18.

Beard, William, & Piers Handling, in *The Shape of Rage*, 159–98.

Breskin, David. *Rolling Stone* (6 February 1992): 66+.

——, in *Inner Views: Filmmakers in Conversation* (London: Faber & Faber, 1992): 201–66.

Hickenlooper, George. *Cineaste* 17.2 (1989): 7.

Hookey, Robert. *Motion* 6.4-5 (1974): 16.

Porton, Richard. "The Film Director as Philosopher: An Interview with David Cronenberg," *Cineaste* 24.4 (1999): 4–9.

Rodley, Chris, *Cronenberg on Cronenberg* (London: Faber & Faber, 1992).

Rolfe, Lee. *Cinéfantastique* 6.3 (1977): 26–27.

Essays, film documentaries, and chapters in books

British Broadcasting Corporation. *Long Live the New Flesh: The Films of David Cronenberg*. London: BBC, 1986 (documentary film).

——. *Naked Making Lunch*. London: BBC, 1991 (documentary film).

Beard, William. "The Canadianness of David Cronenberg," *Mosaic* 27 (June 1994): 113–33.

Campbell, Mary B. "Biological Alchemy and the Films of David Cronenberg," in Grant, ed., *Planks of Reason*, 307–20.

Creed, Barbara. "Woman as Monstrous Womb: *The Brood*," in *The Monstrous Feminine: Film, Feminism, Psychoanalysis* (London: Routledge, 1993): 43–58.

Harkness, John. "The Word, the Flesh, and the Films of David Cronenberg," *Cinema Canada* (June 1983): 23–25.

Leach, Jim. "North of Pittsburgh: Genre and National Cinema from a Canadian Perspective," in Barry Keith Grant, ed., *Film Genre, Reader II* (Austin: U of Texas P, 1995): 474–98.

Lucas, Tim. "The Image as Virus: The Filming of *Videodrome*," in Handling, ed., *The Shape of Rage*, 149–58.

McGregor, Gaile. "Grounding the Counterfeit: David Cronenberg and the Ethno-Specificity of Horror," *Canadian Journal of Film Studies* 2.1 (1992): 43–62.

Pevere, Geoff. "Cliffhanger: Cronenberg and the Canadian Cultural Consciousness," *Take One* 3 (Fall 1995): 5–6.

Pomerance, Murray. "Considering Cronenberg: A Great Filmmaker Exposes the Dark Side of the Canadian Psyche," *Canadian Art* 9.2 (Summer 1992): 40–45.

Ramsay, Christine. "Male Horror: On David Cronenberg," in Paul Smith, ed., *Boys: Masculinities in Contemporary Culture* (Boulder CO: Westview, 1996): 81–95.

Robbins, Helen. "More Human Than I Am Alone: Womb Envy in David Cronenberg's *The Fly* and *Dead Ringers*," in Steven Cohan & Ina Rae Hark, ed., *Screening the Male: Exploring Masculinities in Hollywood Cinema* (London: Routledge, 1993): 134–47.

Rodley, Chris. "Game boy," *Sight and Sound* 9.4 (April 1999): 8–10.

Russo, Mary Russo. "Twins and Mutant Women: David Cronenberg's *Dead Ringers*," in *The Female Grotesque: Risk, Excess and Modernity* (London: Routledge, 1994): 107–27.

Sharrett, Christopher. "Myth and Ritual in the Post-Industrial Landscape: The Horror Films of David Cronenberg," *Persistence of Vision* 3–4 (1986): 124–28.

Shaviro, Steven. "Bodies of Fear: David Cronenberg," in *The Cinematic Body* (Minneapolis: U of Minnesota P, 1993): 127–56.

——. "Panic Pornography: *Videodrome* from Production to Seduction," *Canadian Journal of Political and Social Theory* 13.1-2 (1989): 56–72.

Testa, Bart. "Technology's Body: Cronenberg, Genre, and the Canadian Ethos," *Post script* 15.1 (Fall 1993): 39–56.

Wees, William. "From the Rearview Mirror to Twenty Minutes into the Future: The Video Image in *Videodrome* and *Max Headroom*," *Canadian Journal of Film Studies* 1.1 (1990): 29–35.

Wood, Robin. "An Introduction to the American Horror Film," in Barry Keith Grant, ed., *Planks of Reason: Essays on the Horror Film* (Metuchen NJ: Scarecrow, 1984): 164–200.

Reviews

Carrie Rickey, *Village Voice* (1 February 1983): 62–65; Rex Reed, *New York Post* (4 February 1983): 43; Kevin Thomas, *Los Angeles Times* (4 February 1983): Calendar, 1; David Ansen, *Newsweek* (14 February 1983): 85; Lawrence O'Toole, *Maclean's* (14 February 1983): 63; Jim Hoberman, *Village Voice* (15 February 1983): 50; David Sterrit, *Christian Science Monitor* (24 February 1983): 18; David Chute, *Rolling Stone* (17 March 1983): 33, 36; John Coleman, *New Statesman* (25 November 1983): 30; Paul Taylor, *Monthly Film Bulletin* (November 1983): 310; Tim Lucas, *Cinéfantastique* 14.2 (December 1983–January 1984): 24–31, 32–46.

Le déclin de l'empire américain (Denys Arcand, 1986; produced by
René Malo and Roger Frappier) – Yves Jacques (Claude); Geneviève
Rioux (Danielle); Pierre Curzi (Pierre); Dorothée Berryman (Louise);
Dominique Michel (Dominique); Daniel Brière (Alain); Rémy Girard
(Rémy).

8 Le déclin de l'empire américain (Denys Arcand, 1986)

Production: produced 1986, released 19 June 1986 in Montréal, 4 February 1987 in France. Produced by Corporate Image M and M and the National Film Board of Canada, with the financial participation of Telefilm Canada, the Société générale des industries culturelles, and Radio-Canada. **Director:** Denys Arcand. **Producers:** Roger Frappier, René Malo. **Screenplay:** Denys Arcand. **Assistant Director:** Jacques Wilbrod Benoît. **Cinematographer:** Guy Dufaux. **Script Director:** Johanne Prégent. **Art Director:** Gaudeline Sauriol. **Music:** François Dompierre, adaptation of music by Handel. **Editor:** Monique Fortier. **Costume:** Denis Sperdouklis. **Makeup:** Micheline Trépanier. **Sound:** Richard Besse. **Colour, 102 mins., 35 mm.**

Cast: Dominique Michel (Dominique), **Dorothée Berryman** (Louise), **Louise Portal** (Diane), **Geneviève Rioux** (Danielle), **Pierre Curzi** (Pierre), **Rémy Girard** (Rémy), **Yves Jacques** (Claude), **Daniel Brière** (Alain), **Gabriel Arcand** (man).

Synopsis: A history professor, Dominique, is being taped for Radio Canada about her new book by Diane, a junior colleague, in the corridors and on the staircases of the University of Montreal. Dominique explains her main thesis: concentration on personal happiness heralds the decline of a civilization. The next sequence intercuts between the university interior and a private house. Four women (Diane; Dominique; the middle-aged Louise; Danielle, a graduate student) exercise and converse at the university sports facility; simultaneously four men (the senior history professors Rémy and Pierre; Alain, a young graduate student; and Claude, a gay art-history professor, the gathering's host and main chef) assemble and prepare an elaborate dinner at a lake-side house, and also constantly converse. Both discussions are almost entirely about their sex lives, and are undercut ironically by flashbacks. A fifth man, Mario, intrudes briefly on the men's group looking for Diane, whose cottage is nearby, and then disappears. The women arrive at the house and join the men for dinner. Mario enters, and drags Diane away to her nearby cottage. After dinner, during a walk by the lake after dinner, Danielle tells Louise how she met Pierre, now her lover. A montage of nature images is then accompanied by a voice-over of Dominique's taped interview, developing the 'decline' theme to social elites. The whole group is now shown gathered in the living room and listening to the tape, the thesis of which is discussed. In the third movement, later that night, the group has broken up into couples. Pierre and Danielle talk about having a child. Rémy refuses to discuss what Louise now knows, and they retire in pained silence. Mario makes love to Diane in her cottage. Dominique meanwhile joins Alain on the veranda. Dominique expatiates sarcastically on Rémy's philandering. Overhearing the speech, Louise flees to Claude, who comforts her. In the fourth movement, Claude wakes at dawn with the sleeping Louise cradled in his arms. He rises, and joins Diane after she kisses Mario goodbye. As they walk by the lake, Claude tells her about his secret ailment. Rémy attempts reconciliation with Louise. Now lovers, Dominique and Alain make breakfast, and the group (save for Louise and Danielle) reassembles to resume their sexual banter. In the living room, Louise performs a piano duet with Danielle. The film closes with a winter shot of the lakeside house amidst snow.

The decline of frivolity
and Denys Arcand's American Empire

———————— ℬ

Bart Testa

T HE BRIEF SUMMARY of Denys Arcand's *Le déclin de l'empire américain* provided in the above synopsis serves mainly to reveal the slightness of the film's narrative interest. Proper synopsis must be rather more extended to be of much use. It is a film *à thèse*, and this affects even its most straightforward reception by the viewer. Arcand signals this thesis with a declarative prelude consisting of two theoretical statements bracketing the credit sequence. In the first, briefer one, Rémy, a history professor, tells his class that history knows no morality, but is a matter of "numbers... numbers... numbers" – specifically, that the calculations of demography constitute the core of historical knowledge. Rémy immediately provides an illustration: because of numbers it is unlikely that American blacks, a small US minority, "will ever make it," whereas South African blacks, a huge majority, eventually will. In addition to Rémy's intended lesson – the ethics of history dissolve into mathematical calculation – the pertinent echo of his generalization is obvious: exactly the same can be said for French Québec as for American blacks. Surrounded by an English-speaking North American continent, and internally experiencing a declining birth-rate (a modern reversal of its historical fertility), the Québécois are destined for gradual extinction by demographic absorption.[1]

The ensuing credit sequence consists of a single protracted dolly shot penetrating a wide and deep interior passageway at the University of Montreal. The cavernous space is empty. The shot gains a ceremonial feeling by its musical accompaniment, an adaptation from Handel by the film's

---

[1] This demographic prospect is recent. Until the Second World War, francophone Québec's birthrate was notably higher than in English Canada, leading to the expression, "revenge of the cradles" – revenge, that is, for the British Conquest of the Canadas in the eighteenth century. The falling birthrate in postwar Québec has combined with other demographic factors, most importantly the large-scale immigration to Canada from non-francophone countries (the so-called "allophones") that continues to the present day.

composer, François Dompierre. The credit sequence establishes a crucial thematic locale of the film. Although most of the story takes place in resort country, at a house beside Lake Memphremagog in Québec's Eastern Townships, the University of Montreal pivots the film ideologically. All but one of the characters (the wife) work in its history department, arguably the most important academic centre of Québec cultural and political nationalism.

Following the credits, there is a second declaration, this time theoretical and taking the form of a radio interview. Another professor, Dominique, is being interviewed for Radio Canada (the French-language branch of the Canadian national radio network) by her junior colleague, Diane. As they pass through the corridors and up the staircases of the university, Dominique explains, into Diane's tape recorder, the thesis of her new book. When a preoccupation with personal happiness pervades a civilization, she says, it is a symptom of its decline: Rome, the *ancien régime* of eighteenth-century France, and now "the American Empire" – all exemplify this historical truth. As the critic Denise Pérusse points out, Dominique "introduces this thesis which the remainder of the film seeks to demonstrate."[2] Before the interview concludes, on Diane's request that Dominique elaborate, specifically on what the latter terms "the decline of the elites," Arcand cuts away.

The rest of the film is divided into four narrative movements. The first, by far the longest, lasts over fifty minutes. Four women exercise, take a sauna and shower at the university sports facility while constantly conversing. Simultaneously, four men assemble and prepare a dinner of coulibiac, an elaborate dish of pastry and fish, at a lakeside house, and likewise constantly converse. Both discussions are almost entirely about their sex lives.

The men are Rémy and his colleague Pierre, senior history professors; Alain, a young graduate student, and Claude, a gay art-history professor and both host of the gathering and main cook. A fifth man, the rough-looking Mario, intrudes briefly on the men's group looking for Diane, whose cottage is nearby, then disappears until the dinner hour. In addition to Diane and Dominique, the women are the middle-aged Louise, Rémy's wife, and the young student Danielle, Pierre's lover.

Arcand constructs *Le déclin*'s first movement as a protracted alternation of short scenes between the men and women. There is only slight narrative

---

2 Denise Pérusse, "Gender Relations in *The Decline of the American Empire*," in *Auteur/Provocateur: the Films of Denys Arcand*, ed. André Loiselle & Brian McIlroy (Trowbridge, England: Flicks Books, 1995): 72.

progression in the zigzagging scenes of the two groups. The meal gets cooked, the women progress from weight machines to pool, to sauna, etc. The segment is cunningly edited so that the separate discussions are juxta-posed with each other. The talk is humorous and sophisticated, and the effect of the cutting – bits of dialogue act as commentary on what is said at the separate locations – makes it more so. Another effect of the cutting is to indicate how the two groups' perspectives differ according to gender, with the women enjoying a decided advantage in the superior quality of their sarcasm. But the perspectives are also symmetrical. For example, Rémy's facile excuses, lies, and theatricalized complaints (about having to give women orgasms, for example) peculiarly match his wife Louise's forced naivety and self-deceptions, and her insistence that everything about her marriage is basically fine.

A number of the intercut short scenes are supplemented by brief flash-backs to erotic episodes involving the characters. These flashbacks initially seem to illustrate the dialogues in straightforward fashion, but their purpose is soon revealed to be more elaborate: they qualify and colour them. More sombre in tone than the bantering dialogue alone might suggest, the flash-backs include information the characters might prefer to withhold. Domi-nique has bedded both Pierre and Rémy and found them disappointing lovers. The supposedly steadfast Louise actively anticipated an affair with her tennis instructor but was humiliated. The funny stories Rémy tells are accompanied by repeated shots in which he is ridiculed, in one case being literally caught with his pants down. And so on.

By the end of the long segment, Arcand has expanded knowledge of the characters, and tinged them with irony, since the viewer has become aware that little of what they say is straightforward. Rémy and Louise have been married fifteen years. While her husband is a habitual philanderer, Louise remains self-protectively naive, in the manner of a sheltered bourgeois housewife, and remains stubbornly unaware of Rémy's many adventures. Pierre is long divorced and pursues affairs that all seem to end in sourness and boredom. Claude describes himself as promiscuously gay (a flashback bears him out), which keeps him unattached. A brief scene shows that, unknown to his friends, Claude suffers from an ailment that causes him to urinate blood. Though she is a woman senior and brilliant enough to have become her department's chairperson, Dominique lives alone and has affairs and adventures that she regards with cynicism. A divorced mother of two, Diane's similar disillusionment with respect to sex seems, at this point at least, to be a younger version of Dominique's. However, her recent affair with Mario, as she explains to Dominique, possesses an intense – in fact, sado-masochistic – edge that the self-contained Dominique would never imagine for herself.

Both the women and the men thoroughly enjoy their witty erotic repartee, rather more than the viewers probably do. We cannot avoid noting that the talk is a series of well-worn erotic clichés – about penis size, the egregious requirement to dance at discos in order to pick up women, the old news that Italian men cry "Mama mia!" at orgasm, that men with mistresses must frequent suburban restaurants and hotels, etc. Moreover, much of the humour draws on scarcely hidden grievances and masked hurts on all sides. The exception to all this is Louise, but her feckless innocence and girlish emotionalism are, in a woman of her age, more irritating than endearing.

The second, shorter, movement of the film joins the two groups over dinner as soon as the women arrive at the house. After promisingly bustling opening moments – in which the women's arrival is jokingly shot and cut to look like a sort of male–female show-down – the meal scene slows and darkens noticeably. The childless Pierre declares the circle of friends to be his true family, then Pierre goes on too long with his speech and places everyone (including the viewer) at the edge of embarrassment. Diane complains bitterly about her limited professional prospects, that she will never become a professor – and will never, she says, enjoy "the best [teaching] contract in North America" – because she interrupted her academic career to fall in love, marry and have children. Finally, Mario intrudes on dinner with an unsettling display of sullen rudeness – especially toward inoffensive Claude – and, after cruelly pulling at her hair, drags Diane away from the conversation to her nearby cottage.

After dinner, during a walk by the lake that begins as a lyrical interlude in the film, a priggish remark from Louise prompts Danielle's story of how she met Pierre, now her lover, in the course of working at a body-rub parlour to support her history studies. From the flashback relating their initial encounter,[3] Arcand cuts immediately to a montage of nature images.

---

[3] This flashback abruptly reprises the comedy of the first long movement. While she is massaging Pierre, Danielle chats on about her main historical interest, the millennial movements of the medieval period. Pierre politely interrupts her to announce he is having his orgasm. The point of the flashback is that for all his expressions of cynicism about sex, Pierre is hardly a predatory male, and is peculiarly disposed to being moved,

There is no established point of view for these shots among the characters.[4] The montage is instead accompanied by the remainder of Dominique's taped interview, which develops the 'decline' theme begun as Arcand cut from the prelude at the moment that Dominique was applying her thesis specifically to social elites. Although most of this speech is a voice-over accompanying the nature images, there is a segue to a shot of Diane's tape recorder. It is followed by a wider establishing shot of the group gathered now in the living room to listen.

When the tape ends, Rémy and Pierre have nothing much to say about Dominique's book, leaving Louise an opportunity to dispute its pessimistic thesis. She claims that intellectuals project personal unhappiness onto the wider world. Dominique immediately and calmly takes her revenge – on just whom is ambiguous – by revealing to everyone that, in the past, she has slept with both Rémy and Pierre. It is the sort of revelation that stops conversation. It certainly does in this case, and ends the segment.

In the third movement, later that night, the group has broken up into couples. Before *not* making love – Pierre begs off, feigning tiredness – he and Danielle have a desultory conversation about having a child, which Danielle wants in order to remember this love affair she expects not to last. Rémy, who has dosed himself with tranquilizers borrowed from Pierre, refuses to discuss what Louise now knows. They retire in pained silence. Diane's face is shown from outside a window of her cottage ecstatically enduring Mario's rough attentions. Dominique meanwhile links up with the young Alain on the veranda and pours herself a Scotch. After making a further short round of shots revisiting the couples, Arcand's camera returns to Dominique, who laments her loneliness and chronic infuriation and then delivers a long, sarcastic speech about Rémy's sexual adventurism. Unknown to her, Louise overhears the speech from a balcony above. Louise then flees to Claude, who comforts her through the night on a couch.

The fourth and briefest movement is introduced by Claude, waking on the couch with the sleeping Louise cradled in his arms. He rises and silently

---

as he is by Danielle's rapt enthusiasm for her studies and utter disregard for the squalid setting of this, their first encounter.

[4] Arcand's intent with this montage seems deliberately to break away from the characters and their perspectives. Such an open break is rare in this film. In fact, this passage, as well as all the other montages of nature images (there are four all together) interpolated into the film after this point, were not shot by Arcand's crew, but by Roger Frappier, the film's producer and a notable Québec director–cinematographer in his own right.

(in a voice-over) speaks a poetic text accompanied by dawn-grey nature images. Claude is recalling his own classroom art lecture ("Who are the painters of dawn, the hour of death?" he says, and this could be its title) and Arcand modulates Claude's meditation into a flashback of him delivering it. After Diane kisses a now-subdued Mario goodbye, Claude joins her. Diane displays to him (that is, to the camera) Mario's gift, Michel Brunet's *Notre passé, le présent et nous* (the English subtitles call it *Perspectives in History*).[5] As Claude and Diane walk along the lake, he speaks anxiously of his ailment and reveals that it has not yet been diagnosed. A short scene shows Rémy on his knees trying to make it up with Louise by delivering a bathetic speech extolling family values. Now lovers, Dominique and Alain make breakfast, and the group is soon reassembled – though without Louise and Danielle – and back at their familiar sexual banter, this time with several conflicting versions of a story about a colleague who had a fling while abroad. In the living room, Louise, melodramatically wearing large sunglasses, solemnly descends the stairs for breakfast (the comic allusion to *Sunset Boulevard* is lightly made but unmistakable), and is invited by Danielle to the piano to play a duet, which she does.

There is a very short, wordless coda: images of nature, then a long shot of the house by the lake – but now it is winter, months after the story has ended, with snow gently falling.

A format of frivolity

Le déclin de l'empire américain was an astonishing success. The most popular Canadian film ever on the US and international market, it won nine Genies (Canadian Oscars) and the "Fipresci" (the Critics' Award at Cannes), and was nominated for best foreign-language Oscar.[6] All this occurred at a time when even the release of a subtitled Québec film in the USA was extraordinary. It should also be added that this was a period when Hollywood films had, in very large measure, abandoned 'dialogue drama' as a popular genre vehicle, even for comedy.[7]

---

[5] There has been some dispute over the title in commentary on the film; see Ben–Z Shek's clarification in "History as a Unifying Structure in *Le déclin de l'empire Américain*," *Québec Studies* (1989–90), notes 4 and 6. In this matter, I follow Professor Shek.

[6] The career of the film is well told by Michael Posner in his ⇨*Canadian Dreams*, 213–34.

[7] There are exceptions, notably the films of John Sayles and Woody Allen, but they must be regarded as American independents: ie, non-studio directors. This has changed to some degree in the 1990s, under pressure from independent directors, with such titles

As it happens, Arcand's career did not build toward the success of *Le déclin*, nor did it ride any strong 'wave' of Québec or Canadian cinema. On the contrary, the film came as a complete surprise. Arcand had not even made a feature film for over a decade and had directed just one documentary, *Le confort et l'indifférence* (1981), in this period.[8] He was making a living in television.[9] His reputation, moreover, persisted over this lag only on the strength of politically incisive documentaries made in the 1970s. His previous fiction films were quite tentative and not held in high regard by anyone.[10] So, despite his seniority as a Québec filmmaker, Arcand's role as a major feature director could be said to have overtaken him overnight. Moreover, *Le déclin* owes virtually nothing to English-Canadian or Québec film forms or tradition. Although Arcand has claimed a certain Canadian typicality for the film by arguing that "the quintessential Canadian situation is

as *How to Make an American Quilt, Driving Miss Daisy, Learning to Exhale*, and *The Brothers McMullen*. But at the time, one Hollywood studio, Paramount, was sufficiently impressed by *Le déclin*'s success to plan an English-language remake, to be scripted by American scenarist David Geiler. Arcand was hired as script consultant and given first refusal as director. Paramount imagined a re-tooled *Le déclin* along the lines of the series of remade French farces studios had been making since the late 1970s, for example *Three Men and a Baby* (Leonard Nimoy, 1987). This was Geiler's take on the re-write. It was just as likely, however, that Paramount saw the box-office potential of another *The Big Chill* (released in 1983), a comparison to be developed below. In any case, the project never materialized. More bemused by the experience than disappointed, Arcand returned to Québec and made *Jésus de Montréal* (1989), also a great popular and commercial success.

   [8] This last Arcand documentary to date earned him the enmity of many Québec intellectuals. For example, Lise Bissonette, writing in *Le Devoir* in February 1982, called the film "insulting" to the Québécois. Some have taken *Le confort et l'indifférence* as Arcand's last political film and have done so with the director's encouragement. This is a highly questionable assumption.

   [9] Arcand's previous fiction film, *Gina* (1975), was not a success. His television work was not especially distinguished and consisted mainly of directing three episodes of *Empire Inc.* (1983), a network mini-series. The cause of his absence from cinema can be traced to one of the periodic financial crises that beset Québec filmmaking. It was Roger Frappier, during his brief tenure as head of the National Film Board of Canada's Studio C, who rescued Arcand from his obscurity. In fact, Frappier quickly produced a dozen features in the mid-1980s and primed a major revival of Québec cinema.

   [10] Arcand's breakthrough as a documentarist was *On est au coton* (1970), a highly politicized depiction of the textile industry in Rural Québec. Arcand's reputation became legendary when the film was suppressed by the NFB, which had produced it. Two years later, Arcand was back at the NFB with another political documentary, *Québec: Duplessis et après* (1972). That year he began making fiction films, with *La Maudite galette* (1972), *Réjeanne Padovani* (1973) and *Gina*.

people sitting on a couch and talking,"[11] the implied contrast, with American 'action' drama, is misleading.

Sophisticated dialogue movies, and dramas placed within an elite or intellectual setting, are unheard of in Canadian filmmaking, English and Québécois alike. Stories about the sexual and psychological concerns of upwardly mobile middle-class characters are equally unknown. While Canadian fiction cinema is plausibly divisible into themes either of social–spatial imprisonment, or of a symmetrical mobility endured by displaced people 'on the road' who cannot fit in anywhere, these tendencies hardly connect such films with *Le déclin*. The characters in Canadian cinema are often social marginals or, at best, hapless, but Arcand's characters are well-off and comfortably situated at the centre of their society. If they can be described as in any sense entrapped, *Le déclin's* characters are entrapped paradoxically by their freedom: they are socially mobile and clearly control their work-sites, private spaces, and leisure, which is likewise a rare narrative premiss for Canadian filmmakers. While characters often have time on their hands, it is usually forced on them by unemployment, or experienced as an affliction of youth: ie, as mere idleness.

Although Québec cinema was once creatively oriented toward France (especially the *nouvelle vague* of the 1960s), French models have not had much influence on Québec filmmakers for a generation. Nonetheless, *Le déclin* does successfully play off against European precursors, particularly many of the films of Eric Rohmer, although to his works a long list could be added, including Fassbinder's *Chinese Roulette* (1976), Bergman's *Smiles of a Summer Night* (1955), Fellini's *8½* (1963), De Sica's *Il Giardino dei Finzi–Contini* (1970), and Tavernier's *Une Semaine de vacances* (1980). These films indicate the wide dispersal of what is, in effect, a highly variable European narrative format that stems from Jean Renoir's template-masterpiece, *La Règle du jeu* (1939).

The format – and we are speaking here of something hardly so definite as a genre – consists of a narrative gathering of characters at a remote locale (a spa, a resort, a retreat, country house, ancestral home) for an interval of leisure, conversation, and, frequently, erotic intrigues. Deliberately cast in a mode of civilized frivolity when regarded as a drama – little happens to disturb a situation passed at leisure – the format is, in consequence, rather a blank, dramatically speaking. This blankness is precisely its strength and

---

[11] Robert Sklar, "*Decline of the American Empire*: An Interview with Denys Arcand," *Cinéaste* 15.2 (1987): 50.

defines its serious usefulness. As Renoir so brilliantly understood, the format opens an interstitial social space on which the author can inscribe dialogue and character elaboration, often in the form of a social and affective diagrammaticism – young and old, upper class and lower, rural and urban(e), etc. Characters shape an emblematic group depicting the social order at large. The literary and dramatic background of the format, so obvious and intentional in *La Règle du jeu*, is social comedy.

Dialogue here enjoys a marked advantage over dramatic action, which is normally slight and serves largely as a formal marker for shifts in tone or rhythm. Earnestness is an intruder, but not always unwelcome or ruinous to the format. However, earnestness must never be allowed to puncture the necessary illusion of frivolity that provides such films with the occasion for their proper serious purpose. This purpose is a reflective and (usually) pessimistic recasting of the comedic idiom, most often under the sign of politics.

Although Arcand had earlier worked mixed-class gatherings in *Réjeanne Padovani* and *Gina*,[12] the director never before allowed such intellectuality, social elitism, comfort, and leisure as the characters of *Le déclin* enjoy. These are people, not unlike Rohmer's Parisians, Fellini's culturati, and Renoir's aristocrats, who exist at the heart of their society. Especially in a national cinema such as Canada's, largely populated by outsiders and marginal figures, *Le déclin*'s characters appear as consummate social and cultural insiders. Although the society whose intellectual elite they arguably form lies at the periphery of the "American Empire," this, as Dominique explains (and as many Canadian intellectuals would be inclined to explain), is only to their advantage. Critics have debated a good deal about the significance of the film's title, about the meaning of "the decline of the *American* empire."[13]

---

[12] Both films involve the gathering of socially diverse characters in an isolated setting – respectively, a dinner party and a film-shoot in a remote Québec textile town. However, the characters in these films are worlds apart from the privileged intellectuals of *Le déclin*. Both works fully indicate Arcand's diagrammatic tendencies, which are even more prominent in his highly structured documentaries. These tendencies serve his usual inclination to transmute narrative premises into opportunities for social allegory. I have discussed this feature of Arcand's filmmaking in two essays, "Denys Arcand's Sarcasm: A Reading of *Gina*," in ⇨Pierre Véronneau, Michael Dorland & Seth Feldman, ed., *Dialogue*, 203–22; and "Arcand's Double-Twist Allegory: *Jesus of Montreal*," in Loiselle & McIlroy, ed., *Auteur/Provocateur*, 90–112.

[13] For a selective account of these, see Peter Wilkins, "No Big Picture: Arcand and his US Critics," in Loiselle & McIlroy, ed., *Auteur/Provocateur*, 113 35.

This is a bit odd, since the meaning is explained clearly by Dominique.[14] The strife that accompanies *le déclin* elsewhere on the continent is muffled here. The peripheral position of Canada, and even more of Québec, with respect to the USA is itself a national matter of frivolity's serious privilege. Distance opens opportunity for calm, even comfortable, reflection upon the less dramatic, but perhaps deeper, features of political and social decline.[15] Michael Dorland smartly condenses this attitude of some Canadians, and many Canadian intellectuals, when he says:

> It's a fantasy of Canadian nationalism that, after so many years of being part of somebody else's empire, that empire's decline would not fatally entail ours – and our day could still come. In the margins we dream, as they fantasize in the film, that we can stand idly by watching the U.S. go up in a spectacular armageddon.[16]

The distance and reflectivity form a social privilege that Arcand's film seizes, but the grip is transformed by erotic satire. That satire, which especially forms the narrative and dialogic programme of the long opening movement, offers a relentless demonstration that these people are not living up to their social and intellectual position, of *thinking* the issues it is their privilege and profession to ponder. Just about all they do is talk about sex. But they are not even, for that matter, speaking very amusingly about sex,

---

[14] And by Arcand himself. See Sklar, "*Decline of the American Empire*: An Interview with Denys Arcand," 49. Confessing that practicalities led him to the thesis of the film, and not the reverse, Arcand explains that he began with the intention of making a film of sex talk, then decided that the characters would have to be articulate to make that talk interesting; he soon hit upon the idea that they should be professors, since talking is their job. It was only then, he says, that "I came out with my little theory that usually one sign of the decline of a civilization is that people are turned inward to their personal happiness, that it should be the most important thing in life to be happy, now, today, and it would be a sign of decline. Going from there, I implied that we're now beginning to live the decline of the American empire, but it's a long process." The film's title, therefore, came very late in the script-writing process.

[15] I should add that Wilkins does not accept or even mention this explanation in his discussion. He seems convinced that Arcand is interested in the relationship between American cultural imperialism and Canada. I view this interpretation as groundless, both within the film and in Arcand's commentary, and view Wilkins's own case for it as incoherent.

[16] Michael Dorland, "*Le déclin de l'empire américain*," *Cinema Canada* 134 (octobre 1986): 15. See also Dorland's theoretically expanded account in his "Denys Arcand et le ressentiment canadien ou (petite) lecture machiavelique d'Arcand," *Copie Zéro* 34–35 (décembre 1987–mars 1989): 40–41.

not even as amusingly as characters customarily do in Woody Allen's films. Pierre dismisses Allen as a taste indulged by the sillier women he pursues, but the comparison cuts two ways. His and Rémy's own jokes and observations are sillier yet. Their sex talk reduces these intellectuals crucially, so that they can only exemplify the political problem Dominique theorizes. Their preoccupations with personal happiness – with pleasure and gratification, sex and food – are symptomatic of systematic distraction from the serious political and moral issues which we might generalize as 'structural' concerns that it is their profession to think, talk, and write about. These are the matters that bind a society – or, better, an 'empire' – since that binding involves an organic substance, the tumescence of social power. In this respect, the American empire and its Québec periphery share the same condition. This condition, Dominique theorizes, is an equally *organic* detumescence of the empire's social power, and it has no moral or political solution, any more than it did in Rome or the court of the Sun King. Arcand's repetitive dialogue and his narrative arrangement articulate, in highly reiterative form, the thesis on this condition, making this cell of exemplary intellectuals stand for the social body as a whole. Pérusse is right when she adds to her observation cited above:

> Beyond the conventional structure of plot, the narrative progresses through the repetition of the question of decline that Dominique raises at the start of the film. The demonstration is pitiless, irrevocable and relentless. If we may observe a certain linearity in the construction of the narrative [...] it is also accompanied by a discursive element which betrays the filmmaker's point of view.[17]

It happens that pessimism is common coin for this format of films in postwar cinema, and especially as *La Règle du jeu* established its favoured thematic purpose. Renoir essentially overturned the expectations of the dramatic situation as conceived, for example, in classic dramatic comedy. This is the expectation – as old as the plays of Plautus and as recent as Hollywood screwball comedies – that the comedy's outcome will be a renewal of the social organism. The comic chaos of confused identities, romantic entanglements, rude reversals and so on invert or disrupt the social order. By the end, however, the order is righted; further, it is renewed by its descent into refreshing energies (which are often erotic) and tonic confusions (which often involve breaking up rigid class positions). This renewal never occurs in Renoir's film. Order is simply reinstated and chaos ends with a murder.

---

[17] Pérusse, "Gender Relations," 73.

Nonetheless, the overturning of comedic expectation proceeds throughout
La Règle du jeu without Renoir abandoning comedy's energetic cadences and
apparent generosity.[18] The discord between the film's pessimistic significance and its frivolous and comedic aspect opens the space for Renoir's
highly cultivated political ironies. In Arcand's case, however, the adaptation
of the Renoirian format affords blunter opportunities for a political intellectual with an inclination toward sarcasm serving a barbed thesis.

In Arcand's film, the pessimism takes an emphatically discursive turn, as
Pérusse rightly emphasizes. Directly voiced by Rémy and Dominique in the
film's prelude and in the film's postprandial remainder, the thesis-narrative
of *Le déclin* crayons a diagram of attitudes and feelings that are both admitted to and partly hidden, but that, all the same, amount to the way in which
a preoccupation with personal happiness has displaced political and intellectual concern for the fabric of the social that should properly provide a
focus for the energies of these representatives of Québec's intellectual elite.
Moreover, this is openly admitted, most bluntly by Pierre in a private conversation with Alain. He says he knows he will never be "a Toynbee or a
Braudel," and so – "I only have sex left." This attitude is hardly his alone. It
pervades the characters, reaching back to Rémy's glib denial that history
knows a morality. So it is all the more powerfully accented by the return to
Dominique's interview in the passage just before the film's slight drama –
the brutally simple (and satisfying) demolition of Louise's self-protective,
sentimental illusions. It is important to realize that this episode is in itself not
the antithesis of comedy and to recall that the disenchantment of marriage
is, on the contrary, a comedic commonplace. Louise's demolition is satisfying in Arcand's film initially because Louise represents *petit-bourgeois* mis-
trust of the intelligentsia and its pessimism. Her own wilful illusions about
marriage encapsulate the preferred assumptions of her class. These rhyme
with her criticism of Dominique's ideas for projecting a personal unhappi-

---

[18] See Christopher Faulkner, *The Social Cinema of Jean Renoir* (Princeton NJ: Princeton
UP, 1986): 105–22, for an astute discussion of the political pessimism of *La Règle du jeu*. It
was a film made with a perfect awareness of the collapse of French political will in 1938–
39 and the national catastrophe it would entail in only a few months. Some post-war
filmmakers – notably, (and incongruously, given the main tendencies of his cinema)
Ingmar Bergman in his *Smiles of a Summer Night* – do restore the comedic significance of
the format, in Bergman's case through marvellous recourse to Shakespearean romance.
More typical is the pessimism that undercuts the outbursts of gaiety in Fellini's *8½* and, in
a much more facile register, of Bertolucci's *Stealing Beauty* (1996). Bergman's reversion to
comedic significance is comparatively rare in modern films.

ness into theoretical pessimism, and both echo the Pollyanna-ish belief, currently pandemic on the Right in North America, that 'family values' can renew the 'American empire.' These illusions require destroying, or else *Le déclin* would make Louise a sentimental alternative to the film's central thesis. In a way, Mario, potential emblem of working-class directness, might also have been a vital alternative. Mario cannot be this, however, since he is an erotic sadist (ie, more erotic desublimation, not less) and, even more than this, he is Diane's boy-toy. She says she runs their sado-masochistic game, and there is no reason not to believe her, since it fits so well with her sexual cynicism that she should enjoy playing the sexual victim.

Nonetheless, it is also true that comedies familiarly require the resurrection of romantic love from the ashes of marriage through the erotic energies of the young. Here, however, in the aftermath of Louise's demolition, Arcand withholds any prospect of the classic comedic resurrection, the renewal of social life through the students Danielle and Alain. They do *not* find each other – not even a glance is exchanged between them. Instead, they embrace Pierre and Dominique, and do so immediately after speeches in which these elders testify to their exhaustion of spirit, Pierre to his deepest disappointments, and Dominique to her desperately harnessed bitterness. The figures of youth, Danielle and Alain, are generally feeble and tentative personalities and, more pointedly, they possess little erotic charge. Accordingly, they barely protest before surrendering to the authority of their elders, exhausted as it may be. Even Renoir felt compelled to kill off the young hero André at his film's climax before folding his young heroine Christine back into the old, doomed social order. Arcand's young are not erotically alive to start with.

Pessimism is the other side of the frivolity that the format inspires an author to cultivate. In Arcand's case, however, neither pessimism nor frivolity is left unweighted by political critique. Take, for example, the brittle gaiety of the opening movement, which lacks all but clichéd wit, and is critically shaded by the flashbacks. The characters' pessimism resides in their distraction from thinking in earnest, not in the grimmer wisdom that ratiocination has provided them with. Arcand's critique is everywhere coloured by the director's unwavering deployment of snapshots of the characters' sexual mores, focused through the constant recurrence of allusions to a life spent in preoccupations with furtive, pointless, and even nasty pleasures that distract his characters and diffuse their intelligence. Eventually, these snapshots fall into place in a diagram centred on the film's inaugural thesis, and no zone is left in which an alternative conception can arise.

In the respects just outlined – its atypicality within Canadian cinema, its insistence on the irrecuperable potencies of its privileged characters, its reliance on frivolity as a vehicle for political critique diagrammed *à thèse*, and finally its refusal to extend any branch of comedic redemption to its characters – *Le déclin* is an idiosyncratic film.

Narrative without drama: Politics of a generation

As a roundabout approach to appreciating that idiosyncrasy, let me offer my own comparison of *Le déclin* with Lawrence Kasdan's *The Big Chill* (1983). This is the film to which Arcand's work is often compared by American critics.[19]

Although the social and professional settings of the two films are superficially different, the characters' situations are basically similar. *The Big Chill* concerns a group of six American 'ex-radical' students, now in their late thirties and well underway in careers. They gather at a couple's house, significantly in the American South (American culture's favoured pastoral retreat) on the occasion of the never-explained suicide of one of their circle. Although the occasion, it is insisted, proves to be initially a painful one for the group, the gathering soon relaxes. Frequently humorous and even fun, with much horseplay, several convivial meals, and even a game of touch-football, the weekend unfolds as a nostalgic retreat for friends. It colours the tone of *The Big Chill* that Kasdan has assembled some of the most attractive and engaging actors of their Hollywood generation at a moment before the gloss of stardom has thickened too heavily on them. Kasdan has also taken every opportunity to lyricize his group encounter, something the director is supremely skilled at realizing. And, during this retreat, the characters enjoy pleasures that, for people coded by common journalistic convention as members of the 'baby-boom generation' (implying urban sophistication and fashionability), must be regarded as adolescently idyllic and pastoral.

---

[19] That comparison is, as far as I can determine, rather casually drawn and offered without analysis. Canadian film critics' abhorrence of any association of respected Canadian films with Hollywood productions means that such comparisons are much less frequent among them. Exceptionally, Posner uses American critic Molly Haskell's *Vogue* magazine review for his chapter title, "*The Big Chill* with a Ph.D."; see Posner, 213.

Le déclin's six main characters are slightly older than those in *The Big Chill*, and enjoy themselves much less easily or innocently. It matters less that Arcand has likewise assembled a cast of leading Québec actors, since their reputations are obscure to the wider world and, in any case, their charms are considerably more limited. Socially, Arcand's characters are members of the "*génération lyrique*," those who, in the 1960s, were the first to enjoy the rapid cultural and political modernization of Québec following the Quiet Revolution.[20] While also 'baby-boomers' in the broad journalistic sense, their social position within Québec is more specific than this term suggests in US discussions.

In 1986, at about forty years of age, they form the elite made possible by an unfinished (but still ongoing) revolution. In the 1950s and 1960s, Québec underwent a transformation in which the francophone quarters of the province were rapidly – and belatedly – modernized, both culturally and economically. This broad development, called "The Quiet Revolution," had taken a militant form during the next decade and, by the late 1960s, Québec separatism led to a Canadian national crisis. Unlike the militant phase of American student 'radicalism,' which was born of opposition to the Vietnam War and promptly died after its cessation, Québec separatism survived its radical-action phase to become a respectable political option for the Québécois, with its own strong Parti Québécois, whose power was consolidated through the 1970s. The party was soon elected to power in Québec and held a separatist referendum in 1980 that failed.

Arcand made *Le déclin* during the mid-1980s lull in separatist energies. In his interview with Robert Sklar about the film, Arcand declared of the 1980 referendum, "This settled the question ... So the political movement is dead."[21] *Le déclin* is sometimes regarded as a companion piece to the documentary *Le confort et l'indifférence*, which was made after the 1980 referendum and has as its thesis the claim that a consumerist culture successfully

---

[20] On these points, I am indebted to Professor Ben–Z Shek for his lectures on Arcand at the University of Toronto. See his "History as a Unifying Structure in *Le déclin de l'empire américain*," *Québec Studies* 9 (Autumn 1989–Winter 1990): 9-15. See also Pérusse, "Gender Relations in *The Decline of the American Empire*," passim.

[21] Sklar, "Interview," 50. Arcand could not have been more mistaken. The 1980 referendum's failure did deflate the Parti Québécois for a while, but a series of complicated Canadian constitutional wrangles during the 1980s and 1990s strengthened its hand. It regained power and mounted another referendum in 1995, which also failed, though with a much narrower margin. This time, the party retained firm control of the province and maintained its separatist programme, and has done so to the present.

militates against political consciousness among the general population. In *Le déclin*, the intellectual leaders of Québec, exemplified by this group of historians, have likewise surrendered their political consciousness, albeit to a more sophisticated style of *confort* available to senior tenured academics – a combination of permissible narcissism, international travel, and erotic adventurism.

The essence of their malaise, according to Dominique, is what journalists and some social critics (notably Christopher Lasch and Allan Bloom[22]) often accuse the American 'baby boom' generation of falling into – a loss of serious consciousness itself, by which they mean a wholesale loss of purposive commitment to their society. Lasch terms it "the revolt of the elites." Unlike the concerns of the Americans in *The Big Chill*, however, the political stakes are more specific in the case of Québécois intellectuals. They have a much more pointed and important political position in the social process. These academics emerged from within a fully defined ideological situation into the context of an organized party politics with nationalist aspirations, and these things determined their scholarly projects, debates and purpose. The University of Montreal, whose central atrium appears under the credits, has long been the centre of that national–intellectual project, and Arcand's professors are central representatives of its prospects. When the rough Mario gives Diane Michel Brunet's *Notre passé, le présent et nous*, Arcand is introducing into the film a barbed reminder of the politico-academic responsibilities of the already articulated consciousness that accompanies the role of the historian in Québec.[23]

---

[22] See Christopher Lasch, *The Revolt of the Elites and the Betrayal of Democracy* (New York: W.W. Norton, 1995) and Allan Bloom, *The Closing of the American Mind* (New York: Simon & Schuster, 1987). One must note that both these books were published well after *Le déclin* and, for that matter, *The Big Chill*. These books are, however, academic elaborations on themes already quite common among journalistic critics during the late-1970s and early 1980s.

[23] Ben–Z Shek discusses this aspect of *Le déclin* in detail in his "History as Unifying Structure," *passim*. For such reasons as I have outlined here and Shek documents, a critic should avoid the temptation to interpret Arcand's films in terms of those strands of contemporary theory often termed 'postmodernism.'

The French philosopher Jean–François Lyotard's famous thesis would seem to apply to the film in a broad sense. Lyotard claims that our era has seen the dissolution of the *grands récits* ('master narratives') of modernity, and with them the authoritative structures of political history. It is also true that Lyotard's influential thesis was initially formulated in a book commissioned by the Québec government in the late-1970s, *La Condition postmoderne: rapport sur le savoir* (Paris: Editions de Minuit, 1979), tr. as *The Postmodern Condi-*

A telling piece of what Pérusse calls Arcand's "discursive" point of view in this connection is the story of "Mustafa" told by Rémy and alluded to by other characters. It might seem just another excursus leading to a sour sexual punch-line, as with other anecdotes of Rémy's. Mustafa was an African academic, a historian, visiting Montreal on an exchange programme. During his several months stay at the university he failed to have any sexual encounters. Rémy jokingly explains that apparently the "Third World" has fallen out of fashion with female undergraduates. So, just before his departure (and this Arcand now shows in flashback) Mustafa's considerate colleague Rémy takes him to the Montreal streets (in fact, to St Catherine's Street, the city's run-down main drag) to procure a prostitute. First, they encounter a transvestite who politely identifies himself as such to an embarrassed Rémy while Mustafa shuffles nervously just out of sight. No matter, Rémy says (here the flashback ends), we found two fine brunettes –"I took one myself"; and Mustafa returned to Africa well satisfied.

The connotations involved in this story are several: the identification of Québec as another 'postcolonial' nation, which is what makes Mustafa so readily an emblematic colleague; the assumption of the Québec intellectual's expertise in and sympathy for the developing world; the role of history as a political tool that African and Québécois academics share. A similar scene would be scarcely conceivable in an American (or English-Canadian) film and, if one could imagine it, its significance would be entirely different. It would certainly not be made available as one of a long series of humorous stories professors tell one another while preparing an elaborate meal, as it is so easily in *Le déclin*, nor would its political associations be the same. But Arcand's critique, while subdued in its expression (and diffused by the bit with the transvestite), is that this collegiality of the African and the Québec

---

tion: A Report on Knowledge (Minneapolis: Minnesota UP, 1984). Picking up on Lyotard, the American theorist Fredric Jameson, who provided the preface to the English translation of the book, has proposed that the consumerist culture has displaced modern culture, as in his "Postmodernism and Consumer Culture," in Hal Foster, *The Anti-Aesthetic: Essays on Postmodern Culture* (Port Townshend WA: Bay Press, 1983): 111–25. Central to Jameson's interpretation of postmodernism is the claim of a loss of that historical imagination and capability that was so much a hallmark of modern culture.

My own view is that Arcand believes in a 'science of history' very much of modern conception, and that the moralism and sarcasm of *Le déclin*, as well as the political ethos of all his other films, arise from that conception, to which the director is still firmly committed. In this respect, Arcand is very much a sternly old-fashioned filmmaker when compared with his contemporaries, and he is anything but a postmodernist.

intellectual has tipped away from ideological significance (the type of identification that exists between two not wholly dissimilar national struggles)
into an anecdote about the horniness of two middle-aged professors looking
for a good time out in a run-down Montreal shopping street.

The characters in *The Big Chill* do ask one another, in passing, whether
they have not betrayed the ideals of their youth, which they assume to have
been political. Perhaps they were political while they were students, but the
film significantly provides them with no defined or articulated politics even
to remember. As *The Big Chill* proceeds through its concatenation of short
scenes and group meals and discussions, not wholly unlike those in *Le
déclin*,[24] the political question rapidly dissolves into issues of sincerity and
love – in short, the unfinished personal business of their youth. These concerns are never measured against any lost political consciousness. Unlike
what occurs in *Le déclin*, when sex and happiness displace the shared intellectual and political past of *The Big Chill*'s characters, sex and happiness appear in an entirely different light, as the most serious concerns of human life.

The preoccupation in *The Big Chill* with personal happiness is coded as a
concern with authenticity, the end or purpose of the film's narrative direction. Three of the group form erotic liaisons with their old friends, a fourth
beds the husband of another (it is the wife's idea) in order to conceive a
child, and a fifth, emotionally troubled and sexually incapable owing to a
war injury, takes up with Chloe, the young woman who had been the lover
of the suicide. He effectively displaces the painful enigma of the friend's
death onto a chaste love, and replaces the troubled, despairing friend with
himself, even taking over his small house nearby. Only the hosting couple
and the journalist remain as they were when they arrived.

The Big Chill, then, actually exemplifies what *Le déclin* brings under critique, the dissolution of politics into personal happiness. Kasdan's issues, his
narrative tone, and his solutions are all unabashedly sentimental. The political questions that are briefly raised may be decorated with the "music of
the Sixties," but this is all that remains, a nebulous synecdoche, of the aspirations of that decade. No one remotely comparable to Mario ever appears,
and certainly no one carting a book into the film. What would the book be,
anyway? Herbert Marcuse's *Eros and Civilization*, Norman O. Brown's *Love*

---

[24] Kasdan even begins with a protracted alternating segment cutting among the partici-
pants and, after a somewhat odd funeral, proceeds to another long alternating passage at
the wake-party until the characters are finally gathered in a large country house. So, even
the editing structures of the two films bears comparison.

Against Death, Marshall McLuhan's *Understanding Media,* or Abby Hoffman's *Steal This Book?* These plausible candidates, key books of the American youth revolt of the 1960s, all sound ridiculous enough to indicate the amorphous state of political discourse on which their original radicalism rested. Such observations generate two obvious points of comparison with *Le déclin.* There is also a third, less obvious point that requires elaboration.

The first is that, since the characters in *The Big Chill* have nothing substantial to recall from their radical youth, Kasdan feels no compulsion to provide them with a remembered political tradition – nor should he, given the emotional economy of his film. The radicalism of the 1960s stands as the generic experience of being young, and of being emotionally close to one's friends. This is why the Sixties' putatively intellectual culture can be credibly reduced to its emotional accompaniment (ie, to rock music). It is likewise noteworthy that none of the group became intellectuals and it is hardly incidental that two of the group now have – and another did have – careers in the mass media. One was an on-air radio therapist, another is a TV action star, and a third is a writer for *People* magazine, a frothy celebrity weekly,. Only the last is made a fool of, and lightly at that. There is no intellectual or social space opened in *The Big Chill* for imagining, much less discussing, a collective political responsibility in the past or the present. Kasdan sees no reason to lament this fact, or even to raise it as an issue.

The second point is that, while the characters in *The Big Chill* are, like those of *Le déclin,* preoccupied with sex, sex does not appear under the sign of a substitute-gratification, as it does expressly for Rémy and Pierre and implicitly for other of Arcand's characters. Rather, sex appears in Kasdan's film as the ideal and proper object of what becomes, as the story progresses, a traditional comedic quest. The women in *The Big Chill* do make some wry remarks about men in general, but they love their men in this circle of friends unqualifiedly, and speak of them very kindly. The men, in turn, are positively courtly in their talk about women.

These are surface details pointing to the pervasive narrative strategy of *The Big Chill.* Kasdan restores the classical dramatic linearity behind the Renoirian format discussed above, and he greatly attenuates its pessimism. The sexuality of *The Big Chill* is never risqué or predatory, but is instead perfectly puritanical and chaste. Where, in a single instance of erotic adventurism, the journalist makes a move on Chloe, mocking disapproval lands on him and, when he persists, a trick involving drugs dispatches the hapless character. No – in this film, sex operates under the sign of a recuperation of youthful sincerity, and serves the characters as a means for renewal of sentiment. This is of a piece with the director's generosity; he allows most of the characters to redeem the blankness of their historical memory, and to forget even the initially painful enigma of their friend's suicide by equipping them with renewed naivety about love, which they now realize romantically during this pause in their lives.

The frivolity of *The Big Chill* is, then, is more thoroughgoing than that of *Le déclin*, yet is completely overturned by the end. Leisure attains a serious end without the fun abating, by taking on the atmosphere of romance. These characters become, in effect, their own renewed erotic young selves through the vehicle of nostalgia. Sentiment becomes the serious engine of the narrative and comedic optimism overwhelms an initially despairing film (which, after all, opened with the funeral, as it were, of a generation). It ends with a sort of casual group marriage of friends to their youthful past.

It is precisely Kasdan's facile generosity that Arcand radically refuses. Both directors make their characters clearly exemplify the political and intellectual aspirations of their historical generation. Arcand posits a thesis about their civilization's decline being exemplified by their fall – indeed, hedonistic escape – from those aspirations into the obsessive pursuit of personal happiness. Kasdan permits his characters to regain their aspirations by successfully replaying this pursuit, but now under the non-historical aspects of sexual love and sweet sentiment. The characters' separation from their political and intellectual aspirations in *Le déclin* has caused them to slide permanently into an impossible quest for satisfaction through pursuits that are shown to be a poor substitute – frivolity as a sign of social decline. Arcand's characters freely admit that they are frozen in patterns, and this the film both reports out of their own mouths and has them enact over again before our eyes. Sentiment is beyond them – save for Louise, the most irritating of all of them, and the proper object of demolition during the slight drama.

This leads to the third point. Kasdan's film was instantly a cliché, a popular but fundamentally unattractive mirroring of a generation that had reduced itself to a cult of self-fulfilment, and the film was itself an exemplification of cultural decline. But the basic, even determining feature of the film whose effects I have just surveyed is its Hollywood classicism. The broadest feature here is the requirement that a drama be enacted with goals set and plausibly achieved by its characters. For all the anecdotal qualities of its surface structure, *The Big Chill* drives toward narrative solutions to the problems that the characters express near the start. The meaning of the film is constrained, and also constituted, by classical Hollywood cinema's requirement to keep filmic discourse immanent to its narrative.

In Hollywood cinema, narration strictly maintains the pretence that narrative structure arises and is resolved within its own terms. This can be explained by drawing on the distinction in narrative theory between *histoire* (story), in which the narrative seems to 'tell itself,' and *discours* (discourse), where the enunciation is marked (and often positioned) at some remove from the diegesis, or represented whole. Hollywood cinema's so-called 'realistic' commitments to its type of psychological characterization – which involve marked traits and desires, and clearly stated goals – are not only suited to *histoire* but involve a mutual dependency with this narrational mode. Narrative classicism cannot allow determinations about desires and goals to remain permanently in suspense. They must be realized, or definitively frustrated.

It follows that, in Hollywood films, principal characters very rarely, and almost never knowingly, initiate patterns of behaviour that are compulsive or circular. Their behaviour, as the story's immanent engine, must move the narrative, and move it toward resolution. What cannot be striven for and potentially reached narratively must be abandoned, transformed, displaced, or replaced. *The Big Chill* conforms ideally to this pattern. All of the characters indicate desires that they achieve, or simply (in one case) fail to achieve. This is no less true of the most damaged character, whose goals are the most ambiguous initially, but who takes up with Chloe (whose goals are totally unformed) for an undetermined period of healing, the solution they both require and find. As for the other characters, they struggle in scene after scene, even though these are rather elliptically arranged, to achieve ends that are clear to them from near the start, and are then realized. In each case, the stated questions of the film – political radicalism, the dead friend, their own youth – are replaced by romantic desires because these can drive the story toward resolutions immanent to the film's diegesis. Sixties politics, death, youth – these are not, nor could be, immanent to the type of classically 'realistic' film. The option Kasdan selects – to recast the Renoirian format *back* into a quite traditional comedic mode (as I have just suggested, by claiming that lost youth's sentiments are recuperated in *The Big Chill*) – was facile in the extreme. But taking a dramatic narrative option of this type was, in a sense, forced upon him as a Hollywood-classical film director. If, after the funeral, Kasdan had chosen to turn *The Big Chill* into ninety minutes of

discussions among his ex-radicals on, for instance, the grim unfolding of
Marcuse's thesis on "repressive desublimation" (even though this would
have been a perfectly relevant topic for a film made in 1983), the director
would have had to break the canonical rules of Hollywood classicism.

This is akin to what Louis Malle opted to do when he made *My Dinner
with Andre* (1981) and what Arcand decided to do in *Le déclin*. Arcand subordinates psychology to ideology, emotionalism to intellectualism, and
classical narrative to diagrammatic illustration – in this case, illustration of
Dominique's thesis. This is why I have to differ with Pérusse over his claim,
among many that are so insightful, that *Le déclin* has a linear structure and
that the drama of Rémy and Louise is at its heart. Of these two, she claims
that "the couple is torn away and thrown [...] in the maelstrom grinder of
decline, crumbling, entropy."[25] Nothing nearly so dramatic as these words
indicate occurs or is even suggested by the film. In fact, such drama would
be antithetical to Arcand's strategy. It is much more probable that, after an
interval of acting the hurt wife, as suggested by her descent down the stairs
to breakfast at the end, Louise will forgive Rémy, who will, just as probably,
continue his sexual adventures after resolving to keep them outside the
university history department. In a similar fashion, Pérusse claims that the
events depicted in flashbacks "explain the characters' current behaviour."

In fact, there is no *explanation* provided, though this critic makes three
further claims about the flashbacks: that they "haunt," provide clues for
intrigues, and reveal contradictions in what the characters say. All of these
claims depend upon a classical-cinema narrative psychology. Pérusse seems
to want to place *Le déclin* comfortably within the protocols of *histoire*, of a
story immanent to itself and mediated by characters whose traits and desires
drive the narrative. The likely reason she wants to do this is that Pérusse,
like other critics, believes *Le déclin* is really a film about gender relations,
hence amenable to feminist analysis. The best path into such an analysis is
through the psychology of the characters, especially the women, and the
sexual politics of the couple. As the interpretation that has been pursued
here should indicate, there is very little in *Le déclin* that sustains such a reading. For instance, rather than offering psychological insight, the flashbacks
are both more restricted in their operation and more idiosyncratic. They do
not explain but, in their brevity and bluntness, illustrate points of dialogue,
often ironically. They do not "haunt" the narrative; this word suggests that

---

[25] Pérusse, "Gender Relations in *The Decline of the American Empire*," 71.

the film has expressionist overtones. Rather, in their strategic ironies they qualify and colour the characters' dialogue. They show the viewer what the character would rather not say to the others, which is substantially less than a contradiction of what they do say, but enough for the viewer to begin qualifying the truth of anything they say. Finally, the flashbacks do not provide clues to intrigues. First of all, there are no intrigues in *Le déclin*, because there is scarcely any narrative complexity that would permit intrigues to develop. In this respect, *The Big Chill* is a much more complex film, with many more revelations and intrigues. *Le déclin* offers the viewer only one revelation, and it is made to just one character. Dominique's revelation to Louise comes from nowhere but her own vengeful and just perversity in choosing this moment to let go with her news.

What I am suggesting about the flashbacks – and this should be extended to characterize Arcand's narrational procedure in other respects as well – is how literally they function as narrational *informants*. They function not on behalf of the characters' psychological makeup but on behalf of the viewers' knowledge of their behaviour: in effect, to ironize their dialogue and, most importantly, to humiliate their stated desires and render them ignoble. Rémy and Pierre, Louise, Dominique, Diane, Claude and even Mario each deliver speeches in which they lay out the "philosophy" of their behaviour. But these speeches are sometimes at cross purposes – we are told this by Arcand's alternating montages, by the flashbacks, and by a few sudden strategic cutaways. The consequence of these narrational tactics is to expose the characters more thoroughly to the viewer's interpretation than Kasdan allows; in turn, the viewer's interpretation is channelled quite strictly along the 'discursive' lines of Arcand's political critique, just as Pérusse observes in the remarks quoted above.

All this is to specify instances of how Arcand keeps the comedic register of the Renoirian format, how he insists on frivolities (pertaining to sex, adultery, erotic adventurism) and on what they signify in this film – Arcand's/Dominique's thesis of decline. What is idiosyncratic about the flashbacks, and about Arcand's process of narration in general, is his strong tendency toward *discours,* toward a marked enunciation that causes the narration itself to transcend (in the sense of overseeing) the diegesis. In each flashback and instance of montage, the ironization of the character signifies that we know what is spoken by the narration, above and beyond what anyone inside the narrative knows except for those whose past this is. And we know as well from their talking that this supplementary knowledge humiliates them – humiliates them even more than their brittle banter about sex does. Arcand's flashbacks, then, are not there chiefly to perform the familiar 'expressionist' service of delving into characters' inner psychology. Quite the opposite: they serve as a commentative instrument that comes from outside the characters, from Arcand's 'discursive' design of *Le déclin*. While we may sympathize with certain characters at times – especially with Claude's dawn meditations on death and art – this is not the principal effect of the film's structure. *Le déclin* is not a film driven toward an end by characters' desires and goals, but a film that remains with this or that piece of knowledge, only one piece of which achieves dramatization, Dominique's revelation to Louise.

This is, however, also true in *Le déclin* of Arcand's overall narration, whose montage, its main mode of channelling information, generally operates not *with* the characters, either individually or collectively, but at their narrational expense. I referred to Arcand above as a diagrammatic director and this applies particularly to his editing, which constantly shifts away from characters and the immanence of the drama and, through their own words and statements, approaches a different site of narration where what is shown, and especially what is said, is fitted into a theoretical structure. In the case of *Le déclin*, it is a massively redundant assemblage whose significance (as Pérusse argues) is a declared thesis, pitilessly demonstrated. This cannot arguably be a feminist thesis, nor does Pérusse claim that it is. Instead, she believes that the film can simultaneously be regarded as some sort of psychological drama, a drama of women, and as a film *à thèse*. But all of the film's drama – or narrative, rather – is composed of narrational linkings to its *discours*, as distinct from the immanent narrative flow of *histoire*. Therefore, what distinguishes *Le déclin* from *The Big Chill* is not just a social or ideological textual difference, or one of aesthetic design, but the determinations of the kinds of significance each narrative mode may generate; and this is a matter of each film's method of cinematic discourse. Kasdan has opted for a method harnessed to a psychology of the sentiments; Arcand has systematically opted to disqualify his characters from psychological truth in favour of a political and historical thesis. So the meaning of the first long movement, for example, does not inhere chiefly in the dialogue, which consists, when all is said and done, in a long series of cheap shots delivered by brittle people, but in their assemblage through montage. In other more isolated cases, Arcand detaches the filmic discourse from the characters entirely, even to the point of constructing montages of images without an internal diegetic viewpoint. The credit sequence, the natural montages, the swift transitions among the characters in the night segments, and so on, are constructed in order that comparisons and inferences can be made by viewers at a discursive level beyond diegetic immanence – indeed, beyond normal narrativity itself. *Le déclin* passes into the discursive order of political critique offered unapologetically *à thèse*; that thesis and its elaboration are what this interpretation has sought to track down.

ॐ

Filmography

Features

1970	*On est au coton* (released 1976; + editor; b/w, 159 mins., 16mm)
1971	*La Maudite galette* (released 1972; 100 mins.)
1972	*Québec: Duplessis et après...* (Québec: Duplessis and After; b/w, 115 mins., 16mm)
1972	*Réjeanne Padovani* (released 1973; + co-screenplay, co-editor; 94 mins.)
1974	*Gina* (released 1975; + screenplay, editor; 94 mins.)
1981	*Le confort et l'indifférence* (109 mins., 16mm)
1984	*Le crime d'Ovide Plouffe*
1986	*Le déclin de l'empire américain* (+ screenplay; 102 mins.)
1989	*Jésus de Montréal* (+ screenplay; 119 mins.)
1993	*Love and Human Remains* (+ screenplay; 98 mins.)
1996	*Joyeux Calvaire* (*Poverty and Other Delights*; + screenplay; 90 mins.)
2000	*Stardom* (*15 Moments*; + screenplay; 88 mins.)

Short films and television work

1959	*A l'est d'Eaton* (student film; with Stéphane Venne; 20 mins., 16 mm)
1962	*Seul ou avec d'autres* (student film; with Denis Héroux and Stéphane Venne; co-director and co-screenplay; b/w, 64 mins., 16mm)
1963	*Champlain* (released 1964; + screenplay; 28 mins., 16 mm)
1964	*La Route de l'Ouest* (+ screenplay)
1965	*Les Montréalistes* (+ screenplay; 27 mins., 16 mm)
1966	*Volley-ball* (+ editor; 13 mins.)
1967	*Montréal, un jour d'été* (+ editor; 12 mins.)
1967	*Atlantic Parks/Parcs atlantiques* (+ editor; 17 mins.)
1976	*La Lutte des travailleurs d'hôpitaux* (28 mins., 16 mm)
1982	*Empire, Inc.* (released 1983; episodes 2: *Brother, can you spare $17 million?*, 5: *Titans Don't Cry*, and 6: *The Last Waltz*; Douglas Jackson directed episodes 1, 3 and 4; 51 mins. each, 16mm; CBC/TV)
1991	*Les Lettres de la religieuse portugaise* (88 mins.; video)
1991	*Montréal vu par... Six variations sur un thème* (*Montreal Sextet*, 123 mins. total running length; sixth and last episode, titled *Vue d'ailleurs*; 29 mins.)

Bibliography

Screenplays

Arcand, Denys. *Le déclin de l'empire américain*. Montréal: Boréal, 1986.
——. *Duplessis*. Montréal: Éditions Le Cinématographie/VLB éditeur, 1978. [Television series.]
——. *Jésus de Montréal*. Montréal: Boréal, 1989
——. "Jesus of Montreal," tr. Matt Cohen, intro. Denys Arcand, in ⇨Douglas Bowie & Tom Shoebridge, ed., *Best Canadian Screenplays*, 339–429.
Latour, Pierre, ed. *«La Maudite galette»: Dossier établi par Pierre Latour sur un film de Denys Arcand*. Montréal: Éditions Le Cinématographie/VLB editeur, 1979.
——, ed. *«Gina» : Dossier établi par Pierre Latour sun un film de Denys Arcand*. Montréal: L'Aurore, 1976. [Available only at the Cinémathèque Québécoise.]
Lévesque, Robert, ed. *«Réjeanne Padovini»: Dossier étabili par Robert Lévesque sur un film par Denys Arcand*. Montréal: L'Aurore, 1976. [Available only at the Cinémathèque Québécoise.]

Documentary

De l'art et la manière chez Denys Arcand, dir. Georges Dufaux (Canada 2000, 60 mins.).

Books and special journal issues

Chevrier, Henri–Paul. "La Distanciation au cinéma (application dans les films de fiction de Denys Arcand)," Master's thesis, Montréal: Université de Montréal, août 1982.
Coulombe, Michel. See under: Interviews.
La Rochelle, Réal, ed. *Denys Arcand*. Cinéastes de Québec 8. Montréal: Conseil québécois pour la diffusion de cinéma, 1971. Contains: Réal La Rochelle, "Présentation," 3–9; "Points de Vue" [extracts from Arcand's writings], 10–11; "Entretien" [interview with Arcand by Michel Houle, Jacques Leduc and Lucien Hamelin], 12–31; Michel Houle, Jacques Leduc and Lucien Hamelin, "Post Scriptum: *On est au coton*" [interview with cinematographer Alain Dostie, researcher Gérald Godin and textile worker Bertrand St–Onge], 32–39; "Paroles" [extracts from *On est au coton*], 40–46; "Filmographie," 47–48; "Bibliographie," 49.
Loiselle, André, & Brian McIlroy, ed. *Auteur/provocateur: The Films of Denys Arcand*. Trowbridge, England: Flicks Books/Westport CT: Greenwood, 1995. Contains: Pierre Veronneau, "Alone And With Others: Denys Arcand's Destiny within the Quebec Cinematic and Cultural Context," 10–31; Réal La Rochelle, "Sound Design and Music as *tragédie en musique*: The Documentary Practice of Denys Arcand," 32–51; Gene Walz, "A Cinema of Radical Incompatibilities: Arcand's Early Fiction Films," 52–68; Denise Pérusse, "Gender Relations in *The Decline of the American Empire*," 69–89; Bart Testa, "Arcand's Double-Twist Allegory: *Jesus of Montreal*," 90–112; Peter Wilkins, "No Big Picture: Arcand and his US Critics," 113–35; André Loiselle, "I only know where I come from, not where I am going" [interview], 136-60; André Loiselle, "Denys Arcand: Filmography;" and Brian McIlroy, "Denys Arcand: Selected Bibliography," 170–82.
Véronneau, Pierre, & Pierre Jutras, ed. *Denys Arcand: Entretien, points de vue et filmographie*. *Copie Zéro* 34–35 (décembre 1987–mars 1988). Montréal: Cinémathèque québécoise, 1987 (74 pp.). Contains: Pierre Véronneau, "Présentation," 3; Pierre Jutras, Réal La

Rochelle and Pierre Véronneau, "Entretien: Conversation autour d'un plaisir solitaire," 4–12; Réal La Rochelle "Denys Arcand: La tentation du lyrisme," 13–17; "Fin de siècle" [synopsis of unperformed opera], 18–19; "La fin du voyage" [extract from a sketch], 20–21; "Maria Chapdelaine" [extract from unproduced film project written by André Ricard and Denys Arcand], 22–23; Pierre Véronneau, "De l'incertitude au paradoxe: De l'histoire, ou la singularité originelle d'Arcand," 24–26; Marcel Jean, "L'histoire chez Denys Arcand: la marque du passé sur le temps présents," 27–28; Roger Bourdeau, "Le Québec, Machiavel et Arcand...," 29–31; Michel Larouche, "De *On est au coton* à *Gina*," 32–33; Henri-Paul Chevrier, "La Lucidité et le désespoir," 34–36; Claire Dion, "La Série *Duplessis* dix ans plus tard," 37–39; Michael Dorland, "Denys Arcand et le ressentiment canadien ou (petite) lecture machiavélique d'Arcand," 40–41; Marc DeGryse, "Arcand ou la vie d'artiste," 42–44; Gérald Godin, "Les origines: *On est au coton*," 45; Luce Guilbeault, "I lost it at *La maudite galette*," 46; Monique Fortier, "Le pré-vu et l'imprévu ou les charmes discrets du montage," 47; André Pâquet, "Du comportement du cinéaste," 48; Denise Pérusse, "*Le Déclin*: Une stratégie filmique oscillant entre le cliché et l'ironie," 49–51; Denis Bellemare, "Retournement et duplicité," 52–54; Fulvio Caccia, "La Vérité perdue," 55; Véronique Dassas, "La Critique féministe et *Le déclin de l'empire américain*," 56–57; Marguerite Lemay, "Réflexion sur un succès," 58–59; "Les hauts et les bas d'un scénario devenu diva: Rapports de lectures du scénario du *Déclin de l'empire américain*," 60; "Textes critiques de Denys Arcand," 61–63; Pierre Véronneau, "Filmographie," 64–70; Nicole Laurin and Carmen Palardy, "Repères bibliographiques," 71–74.

24 Images 44–45 (automne 1989). 68pp., "Dossier Denys Arcand," 38–68. Contains: Marcel Jean, "Dossier Denys Arcand [Introduction]," 39; Gilles Marsolais, "Du spirituel dans l'art: Critique de *Jésus de Montreal*," 40–43; André Roy, "Jésus des médias: Critique de *Jésus de Montreal*," 44–45; Marcel Jean, "Entretien avec Denys Arcand," 46–53; Michel Euvrard, "Homo Ludens," 54–55; Louis Goyette, "Quand le cinéma devient un spectacle," 56–59; Henri-Paul Chevrier, "Cet obscur objet du documentaire," 60–61; Marcel Jean, "L'Éternel retour," 62–63; Michel Beauchamp, "L'Éloquence contre la forme," 64–65; Claude Racine, "Le metteur en scène, par ses acteurs" [interview with Rémy Girard, Paule Baillargeon and Johanne-Marie Tremblay], 66–68.

Interviews and statements

Allon, Yves. "Entretien avec Denys Arcand," *La Revue du cinéma* 424 (février 1987): 16–17.

Amiel, Mireille. "Denys Arcand," *Cinéma 73* 180 (septembre–octobre 1973): 102–105.

Andrew, Geoff. "Messiah's handle," *Time Out* 1011 (3–10 January 1990): 22–23.

Anon. "Denys Arcand: Le confort sans indifférence," *Séquences* 171 (avril 1994): 14–16.

——. "Des évidences," *Parti Pris* 7 (avril 1964).

——. "Le cinéma et l'argent," *Lumières* 12 (mars–avril 1988): 6–7.

——. "For Arcand, It's Back to Business As Usual," *Globe & Mail* (28 March, 1990): C11.

——. "Le réalisateur d'un film est-il un auteur? Une bataille pour le respect de l'auteur du film et de ses droits," *Lumières* 16 (novembre–décembre 1988): 5–7.

Arcand, Denys. "Denys Arcand," in ➪Marie-Christine Abel, André Giguère & Luc Perreault, ed., *Le cinéma québecois à l'heure internationale*, 109–14.

——. "Être acteur," *Copie Zéro* 22 (octobre 1984): 24–25.

——. "L'Historien silencieux," in Robert Comeau, ed., *Maurice Séguin, historien du Pays québécois* (Montréal: VLB, 1987): 256–57.

——. "Speaking of Canadian Film," in André Pâquet, ed., *How to Make or Not to Make a Canadian Film* (Montréal: Cinématheque canadienne, 1967): 17.

——. "Waiting For the Barbarians," *Profile* 6 (September 1986): 4.

Barker, Adam. "Actors, magicians & the little apocalypse," *Monthly Film Bulletin* 57.672 (January 1990): 4.

Bergeron, Johanne. "Denys Arcand, scénariste," *Séquences* 153–54 (septembre 1991): 80–83.

Bonneville, Léo. "Denys Arcand," in ⇨Bonneville, *Le cinéma québecois par ceux qui le font*, 33–52.

——. "Entretien avec Denys Arcand," *Séquences* 74 (octobre 1973): 5–11.

——. "Interview Denys Arcand," *Séquences* 140 (juin 1989): 12–19.

Bouthillier-Lévesque, Jeannine. "Entrevue avec Denys Arcand," *Positif* 187 (vovembre 1976): 20–22.

Chabot, Jean. "Cheminements d'une écriture," *Lumières* 22 (printemps 1990): 17–21.

——, & Paul Tana. "Le cinéma et l'argent (5): La face cachée de Jésus," *Lumières* 19 (été 1989): 44–48.

Charboneau, Alain. "Entretien avec Denys Arcand," *24 Images* 72 (printemps 1994): 6–11.

Ciment, Michel. "Entretien avec Denys Arcand sur *Le déclin de l'empire américain*," *Positif* 312 (février 1987): 16–20.

Corbeil, Norman. "Ma solitude diminue," *Philosopher* 3 (1987): 7–17.

Coulombe, Michel. *Denys Arcand: La vraie nature du cinéaste* (Montréal: Boréal, 1993). [A collection of interviews with Arcand, and a few introductory comments by Coulombe.]

Demers, Pierre. "Denys Arcand, cinéaste," *Mouvements* 4.1 (septembre–octobre 1986): 46–50.

Dorland, Michael. "Renaissance Man," *Cinema Canada* 134 (October 1986): 15–19, 21.

Fortin, Marie Claude. "Denys Arcand chasseur d'images," *Vous* (septembre 1989): 28, 30, 32–33.

Harris, Christopher. "'Success is the strangest thing to explain'," *Globe & Mail* (4 November 1991): A1.

Hennebelle, Guy. "Brève rencontre ... avec Denys Arcand," *Écran* 72.9 (novembre 1972): 26–28.

——. "Entretien avec Denys Arcand," *Écran* 19 (novembre 1973): 61–3.

Hofsess, John. "Denys Arcand," in ⇨Hofsess, *Inner Views*, 145–57.

Lachance, Micheline. "Saint Denys Arcand," *Châtelaine* (August 1989): 29–30, 32, 34.

Lionet, G., & N. Ghali. "Denys Arcand: le chemin d'un cinéaste québéois," *Jeune Cinéma* 73 (september–octobre 1973): 23–26.

Loiselle, André. See above, Loiselle & McIlroy, ed., *Auteur/Provocateur*, 136–61.

McSorley, Tom. "Between Desire and Design: The Passionate, Sceptical Cinema of Denys Arcand," *Take One* 4 (Winter 1994): 6–13.

Mahon, Kevin. "*Jesus of Montreal* and the Culture of Nihilism," *Take One* 8 (1995): 42–43.

Marcel, Jean. "Entretien avec Denys Arcand: Je me souviens," *24 Images* 44–45 (automne 1989): 46–53.

Marcorelles, Louis. "Entretien avec Denys Arcand," *Revue du cinéma: Image et Son* 270 (mars 1973): 81–94.

Marsolais, Gilles, & Claude Racine. "Entretien avec Denys Arcand: A propos de *Jésus de Montréal*," *24 Images* 43 (1989): 4–9.

Nuovo, Franco. "Denys Arcand un an après le déclin...," *Hommes* 5 (printemps 1987): 50–51.

Ramasse, François. "Être tendre malgré tout: entretien avec Denys Arcand," *Positif* 340 (juin 1989): 12–17.

Racine, Claude. "Denys Arcand: Le confort après l'indifference," *24 Images* 28–30 (automne 1986): 27–32.

Rousseau, Yves. "*Jésus de Montréal*, c'est aussi l'histoire de ma vie," *Ciné Bulles* 8.4 (juin-août 1989): 4–7.

Sklar, Robert. "*Decline of the American Empire*: An Interview with Denys Arcand," *Cinéaste* 15.2 (1987): 46–50.

——. "Of Warm and Sunny Tragedies: An Interview with Denys Arcand," *Cinéaste* 18.1 (1990): 14–16.

Tadros, Jean Pierre. "The second coming of Denys Arcand? *Jésus de Montréal* in Official Competition at Cannes," *Cinema Canada* 162 (April–May 1989): 11–12.

——. "Un film dramatique pour provoquer une série de sentiments: *Réjeanne Padovani*," *Cinéma/Québec* 3.1 (septembre 1973): 17–23.

Toumarkine, Doris. "Post-*Decline* Satire and Drama in Arcand's *Jesus of Montreal*," *Film Journal* 93.5 (June 1990): 14, 28.

Vigeant, Louise. "Adaptation des lettres écrites, jouées, filmées: Entretien avec Denys Arcand," *Cahiers de théâtre Jeu* 60 (1991): 93–99. [interview concerning Arcand's staged adaptation of *Les lettres de la religieuse portugaise*, text attributed to Guilleragues [1669] performed at the Théâtre de Quat'Sous in Montreal from 12 November to 8 December 1990.]

Warren, Ina. "It Started With an Apology," *Halifax Chronicle Herald* (12 May, 1989): 4E.

Wera, Françoise. "Entretiens avec Denys Arcand: 'Je voulais que la caméra trahisse les personnages'," *Ciné-Bulles* 5.3 (février–mars 1986): 28–30.

Wright, Judy, & Debbie Magidson, "Making Films for Your Own People: An Interview with Denys Arcand," repr. in ⇨Feldman & Nelson, ed., *Canadian Film Reader*, 217–34.

Journal articles and essays in books

Beaulieu, Janick. "*Jésus de Montréal*," *Séquences* 141–42 (septembre 1989): 67–72.

Bellemare, Denis. "Les négativités," *Revue belge du cinéma* 27 (automne 1989): 55–58.

Bombardier, Denise. "Le succès a-t-il changé Denys Arcand?," *L'Actualité* 13.4 (avril 1988): 176–79.

Collins, Richard. "Duplessis," *Culture, Communications and National Identity: The Case of Canadian Television* (Toronto: U of Toronto P, 1990): 318–26.

Garel, Sylvain, & Michel Coulombe. "Denys Arcand: Prophète et son pays," *Cinéma 90* 465 (mars 1990): 11–12.

Garneau, Michèle. "Du pays de rêve au Québec prêt-à-porter," *24 Images* 52 (novembre-décembre 1990): 32–35.

Goyette, Louis. "L'opéra revisité: *Réjeanne Padovani* et *Au Pays de Zom*," *Copie Zéro* (octobre 1988): 27–30.

Harkness, John. "The Improbable Rise of Denys Arcand," *Sight and Sound* 58.4 (Autumn 1989): 234–38.

Hoven, Adrian Van Den. "*The Decline of the American Empire* in a North-American Perspective," in ⇨Joseph I. Donohoe, Jr., ed., *Essays on Québec Cinema*, 145–55.

James, Caryn. "Postmodernism Goes to the Movies," *New York Times* (23 July 1990): C11.

Jean, Marcel. "Denys Arcand," in ⇨Michel Coulombe & Marcel Jean, ed., *Le dictionnaire de cinéma québecois*, 9–12.

——. "L'histoire chez Denys Arcand: La marque de présent sur les temps passés," *Cinema et histoire: Bilan des études en cinéma dans les universitiés québécoises*. Montréal: Association québécoise des études cinématagraphiques, 1987: 49–53.

Johnson, Brian D. "Savage thrusts from a satirist's blade," *Maclean's* (15 September 1986): 48–49.

Knelman, Martin. "Triumphant Loser," *Saturday Night* (November 1989): 103, repr. in ⇨Knelman, Martin. *This Is Where We Came In*, 72–80.

Lamontagne, Gilles G. [untitled] *City Magazine International* 30 (March 1987): 124–25.

Larose, Jean. "Savoir et sens dans *Le déclin de l'empire américain*," in *La Petite Noirceur* (Montréal: Boréal, 1987): 9–17.

Leblond, Daniel. "Symbolisme retrouvé, mais ...," *Relations* 553 (septembre 1989): 213–14.

Major, Ginette. "*Réjeanne Padovani*," *Le cinéma québécois à la recherche d'un public: Bilan d'une décennie, 1970–1980* (Montréal: Presses de l'Université de Montréal, 1982): 91–97.

Martel, Angéline. "Le déclin du patriarcat et l'impresario féministe dans *Le Déclin de l'empire américain* de Denys Arcand," *Les Cahiers de la femme / Canadian Woman Studies* 8.1 (printemps 1987): 91–93.

Montal, Fabrice. "Histoire d'absence," *Revue belge du cinéma* 27 (automne 1989): 17–21.

Patar, B. "Denys Arcand: Le refus de la ligne juste," *24 Images* 22–23 (automne–hiver 1984–85): 70–71.

Pérusse, Denise. "Analyse spectrale autour de la réprésentation des femmes," in Claude Chabot, Michel Larouche, Denise Pérusse & Pierre Véronneau, ed., *Le cinéma québécois des années 80* (Montréal: Cinémathèque Québécoise, 1989): 22–37.

Posner, Michael. "*The Big Chill* with a Ph.D: *The Decline of the American Empire*," in ⇨Posner, *Canadian Dreams*, 213–34.

Rochais, Gérard. "Dire Jésus au présent: Point de vue d'un exégète," *Relations* 553 (septembre 1989): 209–12.

Salmon, Paul. "*Jesus of Montreal*: A Review," in *Magill's Cinema Annual 1990: A Survey of 1989 Films*, ed. Frank N. Magill (Englewood Cliffs NJ: Salem, 1990): 201–204.

Shek, Ben–Z. "History as a Unifying Structure in *Le déclin de l'empire américain*," *Québec Studies* 9 (Autumn 1989–Winter 1990): 9–15.

——. "*Jésus de Montréal*," *University of Toronto Quarterly* 60 (1990): 210–15.

Snyman, J.J., & H.P.P. Lotter. "The Saving of Appearances: Denys Arcand's *Jesus of Montreal*," *Journal of Literary Criticism* (November 1992): 83–91.

Testa, Bart. "Denys Arcand's Sarcasm: A Reading of *Gina*," in ⇨Pierre Véronneau, Michael Dorland & Seth Feldman, ed., *Dialogue*, 203–22.

Véronneau, Pierre. "Quebec Documentary in Perspective," in *Image and Identity: Theatre and Cinema in Scotland and Quebec*, ed. Ian Lockerbie (Stirling: The John Grierson Archive: University of Stirling, Department of French, 1988): 109–19.

Warren, Paul. "Le style de Denys Arcand," *Québec français* 75 (automne 1989): 94–95.

⇨Weinmann, Heinz. *Cinéma de l'imaginaire québécois*, 139–71 (*Le déclin*) and 177–261 (*Jésus de Montréal*).

Reviews

Robert Sklar, *Cineaste* 15.2 (1986): 46–47; Gilbert Guez, "Denys Arcand libère le Québec," *Le Figaro* (13 mai 1986): 37; Len Klady, *Variety* 323.3 (14 May 1986): 20; Fabrice Revault d'Allonnes, *Cinéma 86* 354 (14 mai 1986): 10; Guillaume Malaurie, "L'empire des sens," *L'Express* 1819 (23 mai 1986): 55; Guy Pinard, "Son dernier film est porté aux nues par la critique," *La Presse* (25 mai 1986): 9; Nathalie Pétrowski, "La renaissance de l'empire québécois," *Le Devoir* (31 mai 1986): C1; Bruce Bailey, "Don't decline an invitation to view this Cannes critics' award-winner," *Montreal Gazette* (20 June 1986): F12; Marcel Jean, "Words are cheap, Baby!" *Le Devoir* (21 juin 1986): D6; Louis–Guy Lernieux, "Une histoire superbe et des comédiens bien dirigés," *Le Soleil* (21 juin 1986): C5; Leo Bonneville, *Séquences* 125 (juillet 1986): 18–20; René Prédal, *Jeune Cinéma* 175 (juillet 1986): 22–23; François Chevassu, *La Revue du cinéma* 418 (juillet–août 1986): 18; Michel Ciment, *Positif* 305–306 (juillet–août 1986): 28–30; Bernard Autet, "Les différents sens du déclin," *Le Devoir* (22 août 1986): C2, 4; François Fournier, Jean–François Thuot & Daniel Villeneuve, "Déclin d'un empire ou échec d'une génération?" *Le Devoir* (25 août 1986): 5; Robert Lévesque, "L'affiche du *Déclin* ou Tartuffe à New York," *Le Devoir* (25 août 1986): 11; Marie–France Bazzo, "Le syndrome de la table de cuisine," *Québec Rock* (août 1986): 74–75; Jay Scott, "Sex and Canada's solitudes," *Globe & Mail* (3 September 1986): A14; Christopher Harris, "Quebec masterpiece that talks and talks of sex," *Ottawa Citizen* (5 September 1986): D7; Anon., "Talking frankly of sex – and empires in the '80s," *Toronto Star* (12 September 1986): C7; Anon., "Here she is, the last good woman," *Vancouver Sun* (19 September 1986): H1; Marko Andrews, "Sex, sex and still more sex: Movie's based on one theme," *Vancouver Sun* (26 September 1986): E2; Vincent Canby, "'Decline' a comedy by French–Canadians," *New York Times* (27 September 1986): 11; Claude Robert, "Dialogues crus mais jamais vulgaires," *Le Journal de Québec* (27 septembre 1986): A2; Marie–Christine Abel, "Le déclin des historiens n'aura pas lieu," *Québec Rock* 109 (septembre 1986): 14; Anon., *Toronto Life* 20 (September 1986): 30; Susan Barrowclough, *Monthly Film Bulletin* 53.632 (September 1986): 268; Brian Baxter, *Films and Filming* 384 (September 1986): 32–33; René Homier–Roy, "*Le Déclin de l'empire américain...* et le début d'un temps nouveau," *Châtelaine* 27.9 (septembre 1986): 25–26; Francine Pelletier, *La Vie en rose* 38 (septembre 1986): 45–46; Paul McKie, "Sex sole topic of *Decline* dialogue: Arcand's superb new movie exposes emptiness of sexual conquests," *Winnipeg Free Press* (10 October 1986): 29; John Lownsbrough, "Hot talk and chilly scenes of autumn," *Medical Post* (14 October 1986): 47; Lise Lacasse, "Plutôt le déclin d'une génération," *Le Quotidien* (25 octobre 1986): 24; Louis–Marie Lapointe, "Le sexe en paroles plutôt qu'en images," *Progrès Dimanche* (26 octobre 1986): 56; Jean–Marc Beaudoin, "Un langage cru... mais jamais vulgaire," *Le Nouvelliste* (31 octobre 1986): 19; Marshall Delaney, "The joy of sex," *Saturday Night* 101.10 (October 1986): 71–72, 74; Michael Dorland, *Cinema Canada* 134 (October 1986): 20; Leslie Bennetts, "A Film About Sex That's All Talk," *New York Times* (9 November 1986): 17, 20; David Ansen, "Everything you wanted to know....," *Newsweek* 108 (17 November 1986): 89; Roger Ebert, *Chicago Sun–Times* (21 November, 1986); Anon., *Los Angeles Times* 6 (21 November 1986): 1; Anon., *Chicago Tribune* 5 (26 November 1986): 3; Anon., "Les blues de la classe moyenne," *Le Courier francais* (novembre 1986): 13; Molly Haskell, *Vogue* 186 (November 1986): 86+; Andrew Sarris, "Arcand and his academics," *Village Voice* (2 December 1986): 99; Stanley Kauffmann, *New Republic* 193 (8 December 1986): 28; Pauline Kael, "Families," *New Yorker* 62.43 (15 December 1986): 85–87; Paul Attanasio, "A night at the talkies," *Washington Post* (25 December 1986): C9; Rita Kempley, *Washington Post* (26 December, 1986); Peter Stoler, "Sex and Success in Montreal: Director Denys Arcand scores with a small but spicy film," *Time* (Canada; 29 December 1986): 53; E. Kissin, "Two Canadian directors," *Films in Review* 37.12 (December 1986): 608–10; Wendy Weinstein, *Film Journal* 89.11 (December 1986): 41; Henry Heller, "The autumn of empire," *Canadian Dimension* 20.7 (December 1986–January 1987): 21; Louise Vandelac, *Resources for Feminist Research / Documentation sur la recherche féministe* 15.4 (décembre 1986–janvier 1987): 59–60; Marie–Claude Arbaudie, "La triomphe du *Déclin*," *Le Film francais* 2125 (23 janvier 1987):

3; John Simon, "Worst declension," *National Review* 39.1 (30 January 1987): 61–63; Jean-Pierre Deschamps, *Fiches du cinéma* 905 (4 février 1987): 5; Marie–Dominique Jamet, "Oh, Canada!" *Le Quotidien* (4 février 1987): 28; François Quenin, *Cinéma 87* 386 (4 février 1987): 7; Elizabeth Rouchy & Raphaël Sorin, "La chaire est triste, hélas, en Occident: *Le Déclin de l'empire américain*, de Denys Arcand, sort aujourd'hui," *Le Matin* (4 février 1987): 22; Guy Teisseire, "Profs d'histoire et histoires de cul," *Le Matin* (4 février 1987): 22; Anne Andreu, "Les Québécois sont des parasites logés sur le dos de la baleine américaine," *L'Evénement du Jeudi* (5–11 février 1987): 82–83; Michel Braudeau, "La langue verte et le cœur juste," *Le Monde* (5 février 1987): 15; Alain Riou, "Le premier film qui ne parle que de sexe," *Le Nouvel Observateur* (5 février 1987): 66–67; Joshka Schidlow & Pierre Murat, "Le dérive des incontinents: les avis sont partagés sur *Le Déclin de l'empire américain*," *Télérama* 1934 (7–13 février 1987): 20–21; Denise Bombardier, "Le divan québécois: un film dissèque, avec le sourire, les échecs de la libération sexuelle," *Le Point* 751 (9 février 1987): 74; Claude Baignières, "Délicieuse décadence," *Le Figaro* (10 février 1987): 33; Lysiane Gagnon, "Les illusions retombées," *La Presse* (12 février 1987): B3–4; Guillaume Malaurie, "Les mensonges de l'amour," *L'Express* 1857 (13 février 1987): 52–53; Jacques Bernard, *Première* 119 (février 1987): 16; François Chevassu, "Le bonheur est pour hier," *La Revue du cinéma* 424 (février 1987): 14–15; Karen Kreps, *Boxoffice* 123.2 (February 1987): 19–20; Alain Masson, "Gailonla lurette, gailonla gaiement!" *Positif* 312 (février 1987): 14–15; Denis Parent, "Le nouveau désordre amoureux," *Première* 119 (février 1987): 24; Anon., "Critique et cinéma," *Jeune Cinéma* 179 (février–mars 1987): 3–9; Frédéric Sabouraud, "Le téléphone rose," *Cahiers du cinéma* 393 (mars 1987): 48–49; Anon., *Canadian Churchman* 113.4 (April 1987): 22; Anon., *Visions International* 3 (avril 1987): 18.

∞

FIGURE 9

I've Heard the Mermaids Singing (Patricia Rozema, 1987; produced by
Alexandra Raffé and Patricia Rozema) – Sheila McCarthy (Polly
Vandersma).

9 I've Heard the Mermaids Singing (Patricia Rozema, 1987)

Production: produced 1986, released 11 September 1987. A Cinéphile release of a Vos Productions film, made with the participation of Telefilm Canada, the Ontario Film Development Corporation, the Canada Council, the Ontario Arts Council, and the National Film Board (PAFFPS). **Director:** Patricia Rozema. **Executive Producer:** Don Haig. **Producers:** Alexandra Raffé, Patricia Rozema. **Screenplay:** Patricia Rozema. **Cinematographer:** Douglas Koch. **Editor:** Patricia Rozema. **Music:** Mark Korven. **Art Director:** Valanne Ridgeway. **Sound:** Gordon Thompson, Michele Moses. **Colour, 81 mins., 35 mm.**

Cast: Sheila McCarthy (Polly Vandersma), **Paule Baillargeon** (Gabrielle St. Peres), **Ann–Marie MacDonald** (Mary Joseph), **John Evans** (Warren), **Brenda Kamino** (Japanese Waitress), **Richard Monette** (Clive).

Synopsis: Graceless, naive, and 'organizationally impaired,' Polly Vandersma takes a job as temporary secretary to Gabrielle St. Peres, the owner of a Toronto art gallery. Gabrielle finds Polly amusing and easy to be with; Polly is immediately smitten by the Swiss curator's continental sophistication. Polly expresses her feelings in one of her self-videotaped confessions: "I just loved how she talked and wanted her to teach me everything." Away from the gallery, Polly takes photographs and lives alone in a cramped apartment, where she has visions of climbing up buildings and flying like Superwoman. Another young woman, Mary Joseph, appears one day in the gallery to see Gabrielle. Polly spies on their intimate conversation and learns of their lesbian relationship. Artistic complications follow from personal ones: drunk and morose at her birthday party (in an art class her work has been described as "simple-minded"), Gabrielle shows Polly a room full of 'paintings,' framed glowing shapes, as examples of her art work. Polly smuggles one piece home, and then takes it to the gallery, where a local art critic sees it, and writes a rapturous review, much to Gabrielle's embarrassment. Gabrielle's drunken confession of despair and artistic inadequacy gives Polly the confidence to submit her own photographs, which she takes of people and things that appeal to her, to the Gallery under a pseudonym. Gabrielle dismisses the work as "the trite made flesh." Stricken, Polly burns her pictures, smashes her camera, and withdraws into sullenness at work. Meanwhile, Gabrielle has found the fame she longed for, and with it, less time to spend at the gallery with Polly. The film's crisis occurs when Polly overhears Gabrielle and Mary discussing their 'victimless crime': the luminous paintings Gabrielle has presented as her own are actually Mary's. At the peak of the ensuing confrontation, Polly throws hot tea in Gabrielle's face. In the aftermath, Polly takes a surveillance camera from the gallery to her apartment, where she narrates the events the film has depicted up to then, and awaits the consequences of her assault on Gabrielle. As she concludes her video-narrative, Gabrielle and Mary turn up to explain themselves. While there, they recognize Polly's photographs on the walls as those sent to the gallery anonymously. Polly invites the two women to see more of her work, ushering them through a door that opens onto an impossible landscape of trees and light. Polly turns, walks back to the video camera, and turns it off, presumably to follow her guests to a place where the camera, and the spectator, cannot follow.

"Gender is irrelevant"

I've Heard the Mermaids Singing as women's cinema

———————————————————— &

Brenda Austin–Smith

Beating the odds

I'VE HEARD THE MERMAIDS SINGING was Patricia Rozema's first feature, financed by the Canadian Film Development Corporation, Telefilm Canada, the Canada Council, and the Arts Council of Ontario. Rozema, born in 1958 and raised in a Dutch immigrant family in Sarnia, Southern Ontario, received a Dutch Calvinist school education and graduated in philosophy and English from Calvin College (Michigan). After trying journalism (in New York for NBC, on the CBC's *The Journal*, as well as on other television shows), she became a third and second assistant director on David Cronenberg's *The Fly*.[1] In 1985 (after completing a five-week crash-course on filmmaking), she made a 26-minute black and white film called *Passion: A Letter in 16 mm*, which was included in the Festival of Festivals first Perspective Canada programme and won a Silver Plaque at the Chicago International Film Festival.[2] Still, she and her partner–producer Alex Raffe had had no experience writing, producing, or directing a feature-length film. In the end, *Mermaids* cost less than $400,000 to make, and beat all odds by winning the Prix de la Jeunesse at Cannes in 1987. The unexpected international reaction to this off-centre comedy resulted in a flurry of sales, and *Mermaids* turned a profit six months later. As Michael Posner writes in *Canadian Dreams*, "In the 1980s, the number of quality Canadian films that did that could be counted on the fingers of one hand."[3] In the fall of 1987, *Mermaids* opened the Toronto Festival of Festivals, accompanied by much hype

---

[1] Details of Rozema's work experience and of *Mermaids'* production history are taken from Bruce McDonald's essay "Scaling the Heights," *Cinema Canada* 141 (May 1987): 12–15, and ⇨Michael Posner's *Canadian Dreams*.

[2] ⇨Michael Posner, *Canadian Dreams*; 2–3.

[3] ⇨Posner, *Canadian Dreams*; 2:

and circumstance, and soon afterwards, began its theatrical run in New York City. The film did well in both the United States and Canada wherever it was shown. Posner, though, identifies American control of Canadian theatres as an obstacle to *Mermaid's* domestic success; like other Canadian films, it was often passed over as a screening choice by the major cinema chains.[4] He quotes Andre Bennett, *Mermaids'* distributor, on the irony of the film not showing in Rozema's home town, "because there were no independent cinemas. It was either Cineplex or Famous Players and they prefer American schlock"; yet Posner reports that *Mermaids* earned approximately 2.5 million in the USA, and $644,000 in Canada, by the early 1990s.[5]

Reactions to the film, both negative and positive, were unanimous in their perception of the movie as "whimsical," and "wacky." Mainstream reviews of *Mermaids* were especially ecstatic about Sheila McCarthy's performance as Polly. In a pre-release review in the *New York Times*, Ron Graham described McCarthy as a "Chaplinesque Everyman." Vincent Canby called her "a find," even though he faulted the film for its reliance on the whimsy referred to above. *The Globe & Mail's* Jay Scott wrote that McCarthy was "almost too good – too magnetic, too funny, too *much* – to be believable as a nerdette." Nevertheless, he thought her performance elevated the film "to the level of sheer delight." Even strongly negative responses to the film, such as Lawrence O'Toole's in *Maclean's* and Michael O'Pray's in the *Monthly Film Bulletin*, singled out McCarthy as "impeccable" (O'Pray) and "marvellously expressive" (O'Toole).[6] Positive notices appeared in magazines such as *Commonweal*, *Cineaste*, and the French-language *Séquences*. The last two publications featured interviews with the director as well.

Criticism of the film indicated the low tolerance some viewers had for Polly's off-beat character, and centred on what they saw as the film's clumsy symbolism and simplistic feel-good message. O'Pray mentioned the film's "facile cuteness," and O'Toole deemed its whimsy "leaden." According to *Time's* Richard Corliss, *Mermaids* was "a desperate audition for endearment," and falling for the film was, like adopting an orphan

---

[4] ⇨Posner, *Canadian Dreams*; 20:

[5] ⇨Posner, *Canadian Dreams*; 19–21:

[6] Ron Graham, "For Patricia Rozema, Mermaids Sing," *New York Times* (6 September 1987): Sec.2: 15+; Vincent Canby, *New York Times* (11 September 1987): C8; Jay Scott, "McCarthy Makes a Splash in *Mermaids*," *Globe & Mail* (10 September 1987): D1; Lawrence O'Toole, "Murmurs of the Heart," *Maclean's* (28 September 1987): 48; Michael O'Pray, *Monthly Film Bulletin* 55.650 (March 1988): 81.

puppy, "an act of humane surrender."[7] For all his admiration of Mc-Carthy's performance, Canby wrote that after the first forty minutes, "Polly's innocence loses its charm, and watching this movie is like being cornered by a whimsical, 500-pound elf," while O'Toole thought that Polly had been turned into "a bumbling idiot" by the director's condescension towards her. Some reviewers thought the film's themes of the religious status of art, the relativity of beauty, and the triumph of the subjective imagination over the dictates of authority were trite. Others saw them as secondary to the attractions of the main character. The allegorical reverberations of the characters' names in the context of a setting called the Church Gallery were also criticized as heavy-handed.

In its incarnation as script, *Mermaids* had what Posner describes as the "improbable" title *Oh, The Things I've Seen*, which was changed by Rozema and Raffe at some time during financing discussions with Telefilm.[8] In an interview with Karen Jaehne of *Cineaste*, Rozema said she settled on the final title primarily because Polly was "modeled on Prufrock," the speaker of T.S. Eliot's poem "The Love Song of J. Alfred Prufrock."[9] Rozema saw in Polly, whom she compares to Eliot's anti-hero and herself in this regard, an awareness "that there is something out there beautiful beyond belief and ethereal" that she will never be able to capture or re-create.[10] However, as Roger Ebert mentions in his review of the film, it is Gabrielle who voices a fear of being able to sense but not create beautiful things, not Polly.[11]

Responses to Polly, and to the structure and themes of *Mermaids*, deepen in essays and articles that take up the multiple intersections of art, technology, gender, and sexuality that lie at the heart of the film. In its emphasis on an eccentric woman, its representation of lesbianism, and its use of video-in-film in connection with matters of identity, *I've Heard the Mermaids Singing*

---

[7] Richard Corliss, "Terms of Endearment: *I've Heard the Mermaids Singing*," *Time* (14 September 1987): 96.

[8] ⇨Posner, *Canadian Dreams*; 5, 9:

[9] Karen Jaehne, "Independents: *I've Heard the Mermaids Singing*," *Cineaste* 16.3 (1988): 22.

[10] Jaehne, "Independents;" 22.

[11] Roger Ebert's review of the film, originally published in the *Chicago Sun Times* (4 March 1988) and available online through the Internet Movie Database, addresses this point in some detail, pointing out that the speaker of "Prufrock" is very much like the Curator, "who has measured out her life in coffee spoons, who has seen the moment of her greatness flicker, who lacks the strength to force the moment to its crisis, who grows old." Nevertheless, in one of her fantasies Polly sits on rocks near water, apparently listening to singing mermaids.

presents itself as an example of alternative "women's cinema."[12] Critics looking to this film for astringent social critique based on its independent status, its female director, or its lesbian content face disappointment, however. *Mermaids* veers away from direct and sustained criticism of dominant class, social and sexual relations that many so-called women's films embody. Though it shares ingredients and strategies with contemporary feminist film practice, *I've Heard the Mermaids Singing* does not marshal these elements towards profound or challenging ends. Though its narrative form is innovative, and its characters engaging, its content is curiously conventional. The film is concerned with the validation of private dreams and private visions, rather than interested in how, or if, these affect the public eye. These humble intentions have secured the film its international legions of charmed viewers, but have also limited its territory of effect. Modest and likeable, *Mermaids* is what Teresa De Lauretis would call a "weak" alternative film.[13]

In an essay on "women's cinema" – a term "whose definition or field of meaning is almost as problematic and contested as the term 'feminism' itself"[14] – De Lauretis refers to alternative cinema as taking both "strong" and "weak" forms. Strong alternative films are oppositional, in the sense of challenging "the System," the status quo of power relations in the extra-cinematic world. "Weak" alternative films, in contrast, "would only be alternative with regard to very specific and local contexts of reception."[15] For example, they may be alternative in form rather than in content, or in content rather than in form. Thus, "strong" women's cinema uses both its form and its content to question sexual and gender relations. It is cinema "*by and for women*" that includes critical discourses and practices bound up "with the history of feminism and the development of a feminist sociopolitical and aesthetic consciousness."[16] As Annette Kuhn also argues, to be considered

---

[12] For detailed discussion of the history of 'women's cinema' as a critical term and a body of work, see B. Ruby Rich, "In the Name of Feminist Film Theory," and Teresa De Lauretis, "Rethinking Women's Cinema: Aesthetics and Feminist Theory," in Patricia Erens, ed., *Issues in Feminist Film Criticism* (Bloomington: Indiana UP, 1990): 268–87 and 288–308, respectively.

[13] Teresa De Lauretis, "Guerilla in the Midst: Women's Cinema in the 80s," *Screen* 31.1 (Spring 1990): 6. De Lauretis places *Mermaids* in the "weak" category, but does not discuss in detail the elements of the film which lead her to do so.

[14] De Lauretis, "Guerilla in the Midst," 6:

[15] De Lauretis, "Guerilla in the Midst," 11.

[16] De Lauretis, "Guerilla in the Midst," 7, 9.

alternative or oppositional and not merely novel, women's cinema needs to match "oppositional forms with oppositional contents."[17] Evidence for *Mermaids'* status as a weak form of alternative women's cinema can be found in the elements mentioned above: the characterization of Polly Vandersma, the sub-text of lesbianism, and the role of photographic and video technology. In each of these areas, *I've Heard the Mermaids Singing* hedges its political bets, challenging some of the conventions of dominant cinema while leaving the socio-political implications of those challenges un- or under-addressed.[18]

Polly, the prelapsarian innocent

The most remarkable element of the film, and the one with immediate feminist potential, is its main character. Polly Vandersma is in several ways an unlikely film heroine. She is not particularly attractive, she is excruciatingly self-conscious, and she lacks even the verbal wit that might have been attached to her character in a more conventional film about a slightly unconventional woman. Rozema, weary of 'successful women' images in film, wanted to develop a protagonist who was unsuccessful in worldly, professional terms, but who lived an intense fantasy life.[19] Thus the film concentrates on Polly's subjectivity, her flaky inner world of shape and sound, which finds its exterior counterpart in the awkwardly composed pictures she takes of people and things that 'give her a kick.' Polly is an orphan and an only child; she lives alone except for a cat, has no social or institutional ties, no lover, and no close friends. Her daydreams and the subjects of her pictures – children playing street hockey, a mother and child on a city bench, workers cleaning windows – are her sources of spiritual and social nourishment. It is a life apparently bereft of significance and form, except, of course, for the person who lives it. This is in large measure part of Polly's appeal as a protagonist. She may be living a rather solitary life, but she is doing so in a contentedly loopy way, in which no trauma or disabling pathology is apparent. Polly is not the usual dressed-for-success female

---

[17] Annette Kuhn, "Textual Politics," in Patricia Erens, ed., *Issues in Feminist Criticism* (Bloomington: Indiana UP, 1990): 254.

[18] Marion Harrison, in *"Mermaids*: Singing Off Key?" *CineAction* 16 (May 1989), goes so far as to say the film *"only fools* us into thinking it is a feminist film; attention to the filming technique, the narrative construction, the characterization and the treatment of voyeurism and sexuality all reveal that the so-called positive images of women in this film are undermined" (25).

[19] ⇨Posner, *Canadian Dreams*; 3.

protagonist, but a rather insecure, frumpy waif with a magically radiant face. Her physical appearance guarantees that the relationship of the spectator to her screen image is not one of erotic longing or hopeless envy. This alone is marvelously refreshing, and in keeping with a feminist critique of the cinema's historically unrealistic depiction of women.

In her interview with Rozema, Karen Jaehne identifies something particularly Canadian in Polly's characterization as "unassuming, polite, and subservient, but secretly fantasizing about superhuman feats."[20] By this view, Polly is a Canadian and female Walter Mitty, a figure lacking potency in the real world, but triumphant and invincible in the imagination. Polly's marginal relationship to the conventional world of work and social interaction has also been read as evidence of serious dysfunction, and again connected to issues of national cinema. Geoff Pevere, for example, describes *Mermaids* as "essentially" a story of "social alienation" and "psychological withdrawal" despite its comedic effects.[21] He notes the film's reliance on voice-over narration, its "emphasis on tightly sealed environments," and the "preeminence of psychological over social realism" as a shift away from the realism once taken as the hallmark of Canadianism in film; however, *Mermaids* is still a film about a "chronically disenfranchised" person, and so participates in an even more deeply ingrained Canadian preoccupation with "alienation and failure":[22]

> Rozema's film takes the state of chronic delusion that once represented failure and alienation and renders it as something practically worth crowing about. The condition is the same, but the lens is rose-tinted. Polly's still an archetypically Canadian loser, the difference is this film is *proud* of her for it.[23]

Reading Polly only by the light of national cinematic traditions in this way does her a disservice. Polly does share a lack of self-confidence with some of her cinematic compatriots. The fact of her gender, though, has at least as much to do with the film's settings and focus on her psychology as national cinematic habits of mind do, since women's cinema has often tended to concentrate on women's domestic lives and inner worlds. Rozema herself noted that "the case with many women is that their adventures are

---

[20] Jaehne, "Independents;" 23.

[21] Geoff Pevere, "In Others' Eyes: Four Canadian Films Come Home from Cannes," *CineAction* 11 (Winter 1987–88): 22.

[22] Geoff Pevere, "In Others' Eyes," 23, 24.

[23] Geoff Pevere, "In Others' Eyes," 27.

internal, which does not make for action-packed screens."[24] If one relies too heavily on what Pevere admits are rough terms of analysis, it would be possible to dismiss Canadian films centred on female subjectivity as *de facto* films about losers. Polly is not at all a loser, either at the beginning or at the end of the film. The ingredients of her solitary life do not add up to a portrait of isolated despair, even though the potential for pathos is there, particularly in scenes of Polly dressed in her flannel nightgown, eating a dinner of canned peas at night in her kitchen. While affording the spectator a view of Polly's circumscribed life and circumstances, such scenes do not evoke pity for the character, perhaps because Polly does not pity herself; instead, she is "decidedly content."[25] This is a significant achievement, as film critic Kathi Maio acknowledges in her review of *Mermaids*, lauding the film's break with the usual portrayal of a single woman as a "Shriveled-Up Spinster [...] a symbol of society's contempt for nonconforming (unmarried, child-free) women."[26]

In positive contrast to Pevere, Mike Gasher discusses Polly's Canadianness in terms of her creativity, claiming that "creation and representation are recurrent themes in Canadian feature film."[27] Gasher connects the fragility of the Canadian film industry, and the attendant marginalization of the artist in that industry, to the tendency of Canadian films to present artists or would-be artists like Polly as protagonists.[28] In tracing Polly's journey of self-discovery, a film like *Mermaids* enacts the movement of Canadian (film) culture itself, seeking a sense of its own place, its own value, in the shadow of American-inspired definitions of what "good films" are. *Mermaids'* send-up of art conventions and criticism, and its defence of personal vision in the face of 'objective' judgement, constitute for Gasher an allegory of the struggles of Canadian filmmakers. The "Canadian film paradox" which Gasher points out is that the very exclusion of Canadian film from the "industrial infrastructure" dominated by the USA contributes to the political potential of Canadian film; what Pevere regards

---

[24] Jaehne, "Independents;" 23.

[25] Shirley Peterson, "Devaluing the 'Ornamental Pot': Voyeurism, Marginality, and Women's Cinema in *I've Heard the Mermaids Singing*," *West Virginia University Philological Papers* 38 (1992): 306.

[26] Kathi Maio, *Feminist in the Dark: Reviewing the Movies* (Freedom CA: Crossing Press, 1988): 128.

[27] Mike Gasher, "Decolonizing the Imagination: Cultural Expression as Vehicle of Self-Discovery," *Canadian Journal of Film Studies* 2. 2–3 (1993): 99.

[28] Gasher, "Decolonizing the Imagination," 99.

in Polly's characterization as evidence of failure, Gasher links to the film's "social engagement" and "social possibility."[29]

Polly is an unusual and attractive protagonist in many ways, but there are disturbing vacancies in her characterization that undermine the full feminist potential of the film. While her loner status is uncomplicated by any signs of acute emotional distress, it also places her in a curious void regarding class and sexuality. We know, for example, that her parents died ten years before her job at the gallery began, but we do not know anything about what they did for a living. Unlike Gabrielle, whose parents did well in the "bittersweet market" of chocolate and bought her the art gallery, Polly seems to have come from the working class, and does not have much money. Just as Polly seems unaffected by her solitude, so she also seems unmarked by her background, her family circumstances, and her economic situation. Polly appears to have sprung up out of nothing and nowhere, and to have an unnervingly affect-less relationship to her world. Polly's lack of consciousness about her own and other people's class locations seems intended as a sweet and admirable character trait. She is a Blakean figure of prelapsarian innocence who is simply unaware of injustice or inequality on a scale larger than the personal. The effect of this class naivety is not to make her association with Gabrielle an example of female friendship in the face of socio-economic difference. Rather, it becomes a relationship based on Polly's – but not Gabrielle's – ignorance of this difference. For Gabrielle is obviously aware of her distance from Polly, not only in terms of employer-employee distinctions, but also in terms of class. The differences between the two women, visible onscreen in forms such as Gabrielle's stylish clothing and sophisticated, confident manner, are at once acknowledged and denied by the film, as if they need not have any significant real-world effects. The film conjures up this class inequality, only to set it aside as finally inconsequential.

Early in the film, providing background for her video confession, Polly mentions that she has had boyfriends, but that she could not talk to them about what she really thought and felt. There is no indication in these remarks that Polly has had any sexual experiences at all. Neither is there unambiguous evidence that she feels sexual desire for anyone, not even for Gabrielle, whom she declares she loves, but not in a way that involves "kissing and all that stuff." Polly's null sexuality was apparently a deliberate

---

[29] Gasher, "Decolonizing the Imagination," 104.

choice on the part of the director, who wanted "a rather nonsexual, universal character" so that men could identify with her "without romantic baggage."[30] Polly's physical portrayal is without question a departure from the much-analyzed eroticization of female figures in conventional cinema. She is never an object of the cinematic gaze in the sense of being fetishized by a camera acting as a stand-in for a male heterosexual character in the film, or a male heterosexual spectator in the audience. *Mermaids'* departure from this pattern, though, is aimed at securing broad-based audience identification rather than grounded in a critical response to the history of sexual and gender representation in film. While this results in a protagonist who is treated as something more than eye candy, it also means that Polly's characterization is stunted. The connection between Polly's subjectivity, sexuality, and creativity remains obscure, and her interactions with other presumably sexually aware adult characters become problematical. This is particularly the case in the film's depiction and treatment of lesbianism.

Sexuality or no sexuality

Mermaids' hesitancy to present lesbianism as something more than incidental to its characters has earned the film and its director both praise and criticism. Rozema has been complimented by viewers who see her treatment of lesbianism as appropriately understated. She has also been accused of cowardice, and her film of "more or less overt homophobia."[31] In an interview with Chris Bearchell, Rozema discusses the film's balance of feminist and gay-positive attitudes on the one hand, and its gender-neutral anti-authority theme on the other.[32] This balancing act may also have been related to the realities of the market-place, which act against the successful production of first films which are sexually and politically courageous, particularly when made in Canada by a woman. Rozema did have US examples to follow in both John Sayles's 1983 *Lianna* (with Linda Griffiths, who appeared later in Rozema's *Passion*) and Donna Deitch's 1985 *Desert Hearts* (also a first film) when she made *Mermaids*. It was not until 1995, however, five years after her second feature, *White Room*, and three years after the National Film Board's *Forbidden Love*, that Rozema returned to the subject of lesbianism in *When Night is Falling*. In that film, the protagonist, Camille,

---

30 Jaehne, "Independents;" 23.
31 De Lauretis, "Guerilla in the Midst," 19.
32 Chris Bearchell, "A Canadian Fairytale," *Epicene* 1 (October 1987): 26.

falls in love with a circus performer named Petra. The film features three love scenes: one between Camille and her fiancé, Martin, and two between Camille and Petra. The two lesbian love scenes earned the film a rating of NC–17 in the USA, which Rozema regarded as "a homophobic move on the part of the MPAA [Motion Picture Association of America]."[33] Rozema's remarks about *Night* as a story about a woman's introduction to "the whole wonderful world of lesbianism" and her reactions to its rating address the political as well as artistic implications of representing lesbian sexuality much more directly than any comments she has made about *Mermaids*.[34]

Barbara Koenig Quart describes *I've Heard the Mermaids Singing* as a "celebration of lesbian love and love for women," achieved "with barely an explicit show of physicality."[35] Kathi Maio agrees, seeing the film as "a joyous portrayal of the spinster and the lesbian," despite its narrative flaws.[36] Cindy Fuchs refers to Polly's "emerging sexuality" and "potential sexual arousal," while Kay Armatage writes of the film as "a truly Edenic vision of lesbian sexuality" in which Polly experiences a "sexual awakening" that connects erotic awareness to "creative commitment."[37] Among those critics who have been dissatisfied with the film's portrayal of lesbianism is Robin Wood, who contends that Polly's lesbianism "is never in the least threatening, largely because she herself appears not to wish to put it into practice."[38] Given the ambiguities in the film, it is not at all certain that Polly achieves the lesbian consciousness that Armatage and Wood credit her with, let alone that she feels or acknowledges lesbian desire.

---

[33] This remark by Rozema appears in an interview with Trudy Ring, "*Mermaids* Filmmaker Makes Another Lesbian Treat," online posting (8 July 1996): http://suba.com/ "outlines" 1.

[34] Rozema made this comment in conversation with Edward Guthman in "Director Finds Gender Does Matter," *San Francisco Chronicle* (25 November 1995): C1. Rozema is also paraphrased in the feminist magazine *Herizons* 10.2 (Spring 1996): 24–27 as saying of *Night* that it is her definitive lesbian film (25).

[35] Barbara Koenig Quart, *Women Directors: The Emergence of a New Cinema* (New York: Praeger, 1988): 82.

[36] Maio, *Feminist in the Dark*, 132.

[37] Cindy Fuchs, *Cineaste* 16.3 (1988): 54–55; Kay Armatage, "'All That Lovin' Stuff': Sexuality and Sexual Representation in Some Recent Films by Women," *CineAction* 10 (Fall 1987): 37.

[38] Robin Wood, "Towards a Canadian (Inter)National Cinema," *CineAction* 16 (Spring 1989): 61.

Polly's initial fascination with Gabrielle is a function of the Curator's difference from her.[39] Gabrielle is self-possessed, beautiful, articulate, and rich, everything Polly is not. Gabrielle's ease with the intellectual world, for which the art gallery is a metonym, is indicated in Polly's mind by her accent, a sign of culture, and establishes Gabrielle as an exotic 'Other' for the Anglo Polly.[40] Gabrielle is also lesbian, although Polly is not aware of this.[41] Indeed, Polly is unaware of any aspect of Gabrielle's personal or sexual life until Mary Joseph appears at the gallery, and Polly spies on the two of them touching. Polly has by this time admitted to herself that she is in love with Gabrielle, though she quickly adds that her love had nothing to do with anything physical. "I just loved her," says Polly. Interestingly, even as Polly voices this disavowal, the camera traces the body of Gabrielle in a tilt-pan as she stands looking away from Polly into the middle distance. The contradiction between what is said and what is shown is so perfectly ambiguous that it is difficult to say whether or not Polly has actually felt stirrings of sexual desire for Gabrielle. The shot of Gabrielle's body from Polly's point of view is in flashback. It is thus conceivable that Polly does not want to admit that she ever felt anything but the most uncomplicated affection for Gabrielle. It is also possible that Polly simply does not recognize her own potential sexuality. Whatever the case, it is clear that Polly is intrigued, though not

---

[39] Peterson, "Devaluing the 'Ornamental Pot'," 305.

[40] It is possible that in casting Paule Baillargeon as the Curator, the woman whom Polly finds so fascinating, Rozema may also be paying homage to Léa Pool's *La Femme de l'hôtel*. In that film, Baillargeon was cast as the film director who was "haunted" by the image of Estelle, the "femme" of the title, who is for the director "the embodiment of [...] her model, her dream and her alter ago, the elusive woman 'star'" (Janis L. Pallister, "Léa Pool's Gynefilms," in ⇨Joseph I. Donohoe, Jr., ed., *Essays on Québec Cinema*, 112). Pallister mentions the haunting of "one woman by another" as "not an uncommon scenario in feminist films," and mentions as well *Femme*'s concerns with questions of filmmaking (112). Pool's film was released in 1984, which would have made it available to Rozema during the planning stages of *Mermaids*. My thanks to Gene Walz for drawing this example of intertextuality to my attention. In her use of music from Léo Delibes' opera *Lakmé* in Polly's fantasy of flying, Rozema may also be nodding in the direction of Tony Scott's 1983 film *The Hunger*, in which the same duet scores the famous love scene between Catherine Deneuve and Susan Sarandon.

[41] Gabrielle personifies 'lesbian chic,' and is a lesbian variant of the "artist–intellectual" figure Tom Waugh traces in his article "The Third Body: Patterns in the Construction of the Subject in Gay Male Narrative Film," in *Queer Looks: Perspectives on Lesbian and Gay Film and Video*, ed. Gever, Greyson & Parmar (Toronto: Between The Lines, 1993): 141–61. In fact, Gabrielle and Polly divide aspects of this figure between them, suggesting the filmmaker's ambivalence toward the embodiment of these tendencies in one person.

particularly shocked, by the evidence of sexual intimacy she sees between Mary Joseph and Gabrielle on the video monitor.

Judith Mayne writes of this scene that "it is not just lesbianism that provokes her curiosity, but rather the sheer facts of sexuality and personal lives themselves."[42] But it is oddly as if the specificity of lesbian desire is lost on Polly, so innocent is she of desire in general. In the next scene she is following couples around parks, trying to take pictures of them making out. They are heterosexual couples, though, rather than lesbian ones. Mayne's comment is that Polly's "position on the outside, looking in, is emphasized insofar as all sexual relations – and not just lesbian ones – are concerned."[43] This may be true, but Polly's, and the film's, innocent equation of lesbianism and heterosexual activity robs Gabrielle and Mary Joseph's relationship of its full social and narrative significance. Why else would Gabrielle, resisting Mary Joseph's attractions in the gallery, mention the "Baptist ministers" who could cause trouble for her, if not because their relationship could be professionally dangerous? And what else allows Gabrielle to misrepresent the glowing artworks as her own, and doubles the jeopardy of revealing the truth about their creation, if not the intimacy of lovers?

In the *Epicene* interview with Chris Bearchell, Rozema says that the curator character "could have been a man, or a straight woman, but the fact that she is a lesbian is meant to blow Polly's mind."[44] Bearchell notes in a later comment on the film that "Rozema doesn't let the audience see that which is 'meant to blow Polly's mind.' Whenever the two women who are supposed to be lovers kiss or embrace, the camera slides away."[45] "It is difficult to see what lesbianism has to do with this story," writes Teresa De Lauretis of *Mermaids*, "which features it so prominently in theme (and so stereotypically in characterization)."[46] Quoting extensively from the *Epicene* interview with Bearchell, De Lauretis identifies Rozema's contradictory stance towards feminism and lesbianism, seeing both as "appropriated and legitimated" by the film, and at the same time "preempted of their sociopolitical and subjective power."[47] She locates this contradiction in Polly herself, described by Rozema as "an asexual polymorphous–perverse 'every-

---

[42] Judith Mayne, *The Woman at the Keyhole* (Bloomington: Indiana UP, 1990): 70.

[43] Mayne, *The Woman at the Keyhole*, 70.

[44] Chris Bearchell, "A Canadian Fairytale," 26.

[45] Chris Bearchell, "A Canadian Fairytale," 26.

[46] De Lauretis, "Guerilla in the Midst," 19.

[47] De Lauretis, "Guerilla in the Midst," 20.

woman'."[48] De Lauretis objects that "the two adjectives are mutually incompatible, that the subjectivity they would describe is unimaginable, and that such a privileged and omnipotent universal female subject is, at best, improbable."[49] Marion Harrison also criticizes the film's failure "to comment on or even hint at the social pressures that act on lesbians," and to "confront any lesbian issues."[50] Polly declares in one of her fantasy sequences that "gender is irrelevant."[51] The comment is liberal wishful thinking masquerading as innocent open-mindedness, and would be disingenuous coming from any other character in the film. Gender is definitely relevant, as the camera's uneasiness in recording even one kiss between Gabrielle and Mary betrays.

Though the non-sensational representation of lesbians is a progressive cinematic move in this film, it has been achieved in denial of lesbianism's social valences, and at the expense of the protagonist's own sexual definition. Though *Mermaids* has been read by reviewers and critics as a feminist 'coming of age' film, Marion Harrison remarks that Polly is thirty-one, "an age by which one would expect a woman to have already come of age."[52] The point is well-taken, as Polly's characterization throughout the film – including her childish fantasies of flying like Superwoman, her impulsiveness in destroying her camera, her fit of sulkiness in the gallery office following the rejection of her pictures – reeks of adolescent, or even pre-adolescent, emotional development. Even her feelings for Gabrielle resemble a schoolgirl crush rather than a nascent sexual passion. Harrison's discussion of lesbianism and sexuality concurs with that of Judith Mayne, that the film remains ambiguous about Polly's recognition of sexuality, whether in relation to herself or to anyone else: "Polly's fantasy of polymorphous perver-

---

[48] Chris Bearchell, "A Canadian Fairytale," 26.

[49] De Lauretis, "Guerilla in the Midst," 19.

[50] Harrison,"*Mermaids*: Singing Off Key?," 29.

[51] In interviews with Chris Bearchell in *Epicene*, Cindy Fuchs in *Cineaste*, and Edward Guthmann in the *San Francisco Chronicle*, Rozema makes similar remarks, stressing that for her, "gender is such an insignificant category"; Guthmann, "Director Finds Gender Does Matter," *San Francisco Chronicle* (25 November 1995): C1, 2. This outlook may account for why Linda Lopez McAlister (in a positive review of the film) calls *Mermaids* "post-feminist," in the sense that it takes the achievements of feminism for granted. In Joanne Latimer's article "Lesbian Chic Goes to Hollywood," *Herizons* 10.2 (Spring 1996): 24–27, Rozema also looks forward to the end of homophobia: "Call me Pollyanna, but all this homophobia's going to be passé very soon" (27).

[52] Harrison, "*Mermaids:* Singing Off Key?," 29.

sity suggests simultaneously a desire for a different sexuality and a desire for no sexuality at all."[53]

Technology, narration, and the gaze

While *Mermaids* can be faulted for a failure of nerve in its attempts to portray lesbian sexuality onscreen, its formal and thematic use of visual technology is in keeping with the oppositional intentions of women's cinema as a form of counter-cinema. In this film, the machines of technologized looking – the still, video, and film camera – read by some theorists as ultimate versions of a Duchampian 'bachelor machine,' are in the hands of a 'bachelorette' who uses them for her own purposes, to present and illustrate her own narrative. Structured as a partly retrospective narration, *Mermaids* opens with an image of Polly adjusting herself in front of a video camera that she has set up as an electronic confessor. Treating the video camera as if it were a diary, Polly participates in a venerable documentary tradition associated with feminism, feminist filmmaking, and Canadian film practice.[54] As Timothy Shary observes, the association of video with "'realness'" lends to the appearance of video-in-film "a presence in time that seems more immediate than does that of the film images."[55] Thus we are inclined to read the video images of the film as "something *real*, something *true*"[56] as well as something *now*.

Polly's video narration is embedded in the film narration of *Mermaids* as a character's immediate first-person utterances are embedded in the apparently objective and omniscient discourse of the narrating film camera. Two Pollys are created by this technique. There is the 'present' Polly who speaks hesitantly but earnestly to the video camera, and the 'past' Polly who appears on film courtesy of retrospection.[57] The complexities and ambiguities of this retrospective narration (including the matter of reliability and the potential for critical reflection on past events) are discussed by Harrison.[58]

---

[53] Mayne, *The Woman at the Keyhole*, 74.

[54] Harrison, "*Mermaids*: Singing Off Key?," 26.

[55] Timothy Shary, "Present Personal Truths: The Alternative Phenomenology of Video in *I've Heard the Mermaids Singing*," *Wide Angle* 15.3 (July 1993): 42.

[56] Harrison, "*Mermaids*: Singing Off Key?," 26.

[57] Peterson, "Devaluing the 'Ornamental Pot'," 304.

[58] Harrison, "*Mermaids*: Singing Off Key?," 26.

Rarely, though, does the film exploit the potential dissonance between narrative levels for dramatic effect.

One example of such a disjunction occurs when we shift from Polly's video narration to the flashback scene in which Polly's voice-over describes her platonic love for Gabrielle, even as the camera caresses Gabrielle's body in a remarkably non-platonic way. Timothy Shary astutely points out crucial differences between video and film which are relevant to this scene. Shary writes that the video camera which Polly sets up and speaks to provides the spectator of this film with "a limited field of vision," controlled by Polly herself, while film portrays "an omniscient 'reality' of Polly's past."[59] This particular scene is presented through film, the narrative authority of which, by Shary's argument, suggests that Polly was indeed sexually aware of Gabrielle. A psychoanalytic reading of this scene, prompted by Polly's orphan status and unqualified adoration of Gabrielle at this point in the film, could identify too the desiring gaze of an infant at the body of its mother.[60]

Within the scenes of flashback that depict the events leading up to the present moment of Polly's video narration, there are two other "ways of seeing" that belong to Polly. One is represented by Polly's still photos of people and buildings in the city. The other is represented through the convention of the 'mindscreen,' which shows us how Polly sees herself in fantasies of flying, walking on water, and conducting an orchestra.[61] The portrayal of Polly's fantasies adds a third level to the narrative, as Mayne and Shary note. *Mermaids* shifts deftly from one level of narration and insight to the next and back again. As it does so, it also moves forward in the direction of a final confluence of past with present, and an integration of internal fantasy and external reality.

On the way to a merging of time frames and narrative perspectives, the film departs from conventional renderings of women, technology, and the power relations of looking. At the same time, Polly's vulnerability to images, indicated by her darkroom fantasies, places her squarely in the realm of

---

[59] Shary, "Present Personal Truths," 44.

[60] Shirley Peterson refers to the later scene in which Polly witnesses the intimacy of Gabrielle and Mary Joseph as "quasi primal" ("Devaluing the 'Ornamental Pot'," 305), while Teresa De Lauretis calls Gabrielle a "female man and a bad phallic mother" ("Guerilla in the Midst," 19). Marion Harrison also mentions that Polly tries to create "a mother/daughter bond in order to deal with her love for Gabrielle" ("*Mermaids:* Singing Off Key?," 29).

[61] Mayne, *The Woman at the Keyhole*, 74.

what psychoanalytic theorists have termed 'the imaginary.'[62] This qualifies critical enthusiasm over her status as consciously creating subject in the film's final frames, "fully in control of the apparatus and its potential."[63]

A substantial body of work on the nature, intention, and effect of 'the gaze' has dominated critical discussion of women and cinema since the mid-1970s. This material has diagnosed in mainstream commercial narrative film an imbalance of both narrative and political power between the male possessor of 'the gaze' and the female object of that gaze.[64] As a consequence of this imbalance, commercial narrative cinema has filled screens with eroticized images of women for the pleasure of the (presumably) male heterosexual spectator. Further, this theory of looking relations stresses the analogy between spectators in a movie theatre and sexual voyeurs: in both situations, individuals indulge in "surreptitious observation" of others, which produces pleasure.[65] Although the force of this argument, first articulated by Laura Mulvey, has been modified in recent decades, the notion of the 'sadistic' male gaze, and of looking as an exercise of political and sexual power, remains influential. *Mermaids* interrupts this nasty economy by focusing on a female protagonist who is de-eroticized to a fault, and by challenging the negative associations between technology, voyeurism, and control that obtain in mainstream narrative film.

Against mainstream cinema's positioning of women as passive objects of an aggressive male gaze, *I've Heard the Mermaids Singing* is a film that places

---

[62] Mary Ann Doane's book on 1940s melodrama, *The Desire to Desire* (Bloomington: Indiana UP, 1987) and her article, "Film and the Masquerade" in Patricia Erens, ed., *Issues in Feminist Film Criticism*, 41–57, both explore women, the imaginary, and film in great detail. The assumption that women are more 'taken in' by images than men are is a staple of melodramatic film, not to mention popular culture. To be seduced by images into mistaking them for reality often connotes emotional or sexual immaturity, especially in women.

[63] This claim about Polly, which suggests that she is a fully-fledged artist figure by the film's conclusion, is made by George Godwin in "Reclaiming the Subject: A Feminist Reading of *I've Heard the Mermaids Singing,*" *Cinema Canada* 152 (May 1988): 25.

[64] See Laura Mulvey's "Visual Pleasure and Narrative Cinema," in Patricia Erens, ed., *Issues in Feminist Film Criticism*, 28–41. Mulvey's article, originally published in *Screen* 16.3 (Autumn 1975): 6–18, is responsible for over twenty years of discussion and debate. For extensions and rebuttals of Mulvey's argument in connection with women and film, see also E. Ann Kaplan, *Women and Film* (London: Routledge, 1983), *Feminism and Film Theory*, ed. Constance Penley (New York: Routledge, 1988), and Judith Mayne, *The Woman at the Keyhole* (Bloomington: Indiana UP, 1990).

[65] Mulvey, "Visual Pleasure and Narrative Cinema," 31.

female 'looking' at its centre. From the opening frames of the film, Polly is characterized as "controller of the image."[66] Indeed, throughout the film Polly is consistently at ease with the technology of looking that is conventionally intimidating, and even dangerous, to women in classical narrative film. Polly is a spirited amateur photographer, committed enough to her hobby to have given over her bathroom as a darkroom. When the surveillance video camera arrives at the gallery, it is Polly who examines it with an easy shrug, and says it is already assembled, while Gabrielle pores over the instructions that come with it. This is the same camera Polly switches on when Gabrielle and Mary retreat for some privacy to the gallery, and the one she will later appropriate and "adapt to her own storytelling ends."[67] Polly may not be a very good typist, but she displays none of the stereotypical female fear of technology, and she does not assume the usual role of woman as victim of the apparatus. Polly's particular facility with cameras leads directly to the issues of voyeurism and power that have given reviewers and critics of *Mermaids* pause.

That Polly is a species of voyeur is obvious. Whether she is guilty of "disturbing and obsessive voyeurism,"[68] or possesses what Godwin calls a "probing look" that can be read in a more positive light, is another matter. Marion Harrison, for example, sees Polly's interest in photography as invasive. She writes that "Polly invades private worlds by watching and looking, either directly or through a lens, objectifying these worlds in the process." Polly is a "spy" and "an obsessive voyeur whose looking becomes a perversion." For Harrison, Polly's pictures of boys playing street hockey, of a mother holding a child, and of workers waving at her are a sign that her "look" is as "aggressive as the male look."[69] Harrison sees Polly as an example of Mulvey's voyeur, a viewer who objectifies others through the mechanism of the camera for her own pleasure.

It is hard to agree with this extreme point of view. The image of a woman using a camera in a film does not automatically denote control-seeking perversion, and there is definitely something about Polly's kind of voyeurism that unsettles its usual operation in the complex of dominance and power. One has only to compare *Mermaids* to such films as *Peeping Tom*, *Rear*

---

[66] Peterson, "Devaluing the 'Ornamental Pot'," 303.

[67] Mayne, *The Woman at the Keyhole*, 74.

[68] Michael O'Pray, "I've Heard the Mermaids Singing," *Monthly Film Bulletin* 55.650 (March 1988): 81.

[69] Harrison, "*Mermaids*: Singing Off Key?," 30.

Window, Blow-Up, and *The Conversation,* as George Godwin has suggested,[70] to realize the difference between an unethical use of technology as a means of controlling others, particularly from a safe, distant, or invisible position, and Polly's use of her camera in the pursuit of much more innocent pleasures.[71]

One aspect of Polly's voyeurism that argues against the aggression and sadism associated with 'the gaze' is the way in which she exposes herself in the process of taking pictures as she rides around the city. She even waves to the people she photographs, treating them as subjects, rather than as dehumanized objects of a controlling, technologized look. The only time she acts like a conventional sexual voyeur, spying on an amorous straight couple in the park, she is spotted, and awkwardly pretends to be watching birds. Another is the process of the video narration itself. Rather than take up or maintain a safe position on the powerful side of the viewfinder, Polly occupies "both the subjective and objective positions" in her narrative.[72] In settling herself in front of the lens, and then addressing the spectator, Polly dispenses not only with her own photographic immunity, but with ours as well. When she speaks to us through the double set of lenses that separates our world from hers, she prevents us from escaping into the anonymity we usually enjoy as "meta-voyeurs" of film.[73] Peterson also remarks on the way in which Polly's direct reproach addressed to the video camera – "But you don't want to hear about that. You just want to know what happens" – "indicts the spectators for their well-conditioned reflexes to conventional cinematic patterns."[74] Polly "*invites* us to look at her, and more importantly, to look *with* her" in a way that demonstrates the harmlessness of her look; her look

> is not pathological: it is not essentially linear and focused, but rather is diffuse and exploratory. As a woman lacking in confidence, she is seeking an understanding of the world and a way of being in it. She is looking to learn, not to secretly possess.[75]

---

[70] Godwin, "Reclaiming the Subject," 23.

[71] Shirley Peterson identifies Polly as part of a "short tradition of feminist heroines who vicariously dramatize their directors' passion for the camera" through their characterization as photographers. Peterson mentions Susan Weinblatt in *Girlfriends,* and Molly in *Working Girls* as other examples of this tradition ("Devaluing the 'Ornamental Pot'," 303).

[72] Peterson, "Devaluing the 'Ornamental Pot'," 303.

[73] Godwin, "Reclaiming the Subject," 23.

[74] Peterson, "Devaluing the 'Ornamental Pot'," 307.

[75] Godwin, "Reclaiming the Subject," 24.

Another element that distinguishes Polly's look from more sinister celluloid voyeurism is her position within the film as a powerless person. A significant part of the power in looking relations flows from the social position inhabited by the possessor of the gaze as well as from the voyeur's hiddenness from the gaze of others. Polly has none of the power associated with being male and looking at women, or being white and looking at people of colour. Though the two people she watches most often are lesbian, Polly does not spy on them from the socially sanctioned position of a heterosexual. She looks and watches from a marginalized position as asexual, or even pre-sexual child. She is a dowdy, working-class woman who looks up to, never down on, almost everyone and everything – even the video camera in her living-room, as Harrison notes.[76]

Even as *Mermaids* takes on voyeurism and the technology of looking from an apparently feminist perspective, it relies heavily on a cliché about women in its presentation of Polly as an adorable dreamer. The fantasy sequences in which Polly flies, walks on water with Gabrielle, and hears the voices of the mermaids near the Scarborough bluffs, are all triggered by the process of gazing, alone in her apartment, at the pictures she herself has taken. Polly does not actually fall asleep in these sequences, though Shary refers to the "red-light slumbers of her darkroom."[77] Rather, she slips into trances in which she enters the image she is looking at. These scenes are perfect illustrations of women's habitual association, in dominant film practice, with 'the imaginary,' a state of psycho-social development suggestive of an inability to separate oneself from others, and to distinguish between reality and images. Kaja Silverman describes 'the imaginary' from a Lacanian perspective as the realm of a subject's experience "which is dominated by identification and duality."[78] The imaginary is a psychological relationship to the world which is reminiscent of an infant's identification with "the mother's breast, voice, gaze, or whatever other object is perceived as its missing complement."[79] Polly's relationship to Gabrielle is strongly coloured by elements of the imaginary. She envies and identifies with Gabrielle, imitating her accent, and wanting Gabrielle to teach her everything. A subject "trapped" in the imaginary "will fluctuate between extremes of love and hate," and "be capable of identifying alternately with diametrically opposed

---

[76] Harrison,"*Mermaids*: Singing Off Key?," 26.

[77] Shary, "Present Personal Truths," 43.

[78] Kaja Silverman, *The Subject of Semiotics* (Oxford: Oxford UP, 1983): 157.

[79] Silverman, *The Subject of Semiotics*, 158.

positions."[80] Polly, too, experiences swings of emotion toward Gabrielle over the course of the film, and, in one of her fantasies, occupies the position of articulate companion to an impressed and attentive Gabrielle.

Polly's tendency to over-identify with images produces the fantasies that make her so endearing a figure. It also enacts a closed circuit, since Polly is seduced by images she herself has created. This inclination toward immersion in fantasy contradicts the movement of the film toward a conclusion Armatage reads as "a vision of feminine sexuality in full possession of its own knowledge."[81] *Mermaids'* final scenes struggle unsuccessfully to reconcile these competing characterizations of Polly. From one perspective she is an innocent, childlike, asexual dreamer, vulnerable to complete identification with images. From another, she is a self-aware artist who subordinates images, and image-making devices, to her conscious vision.

The contradiction between these two ways of dramatizing Polly repeats the contradiction between Polly as asexual and Polly as polymorphously perverse. The conflict provokes a narrative crisis that reaches a literal vanishing-point in the film's last moments, in which Polly's fantasies, her first-person narration, and the retrospective film images merge.[82] Shary, Armatage, Peterson and Godwin all read the concluding reconciliation of the three women as a vision of an artistic and sexual utopia in which all differences and difficulties are transcended in a feminist burst of colour and foliage. The ending looks very much, though, like an extension of Polly's fantasizing, an example of wish-fulfilment. The opening of the fantastic door suggests that Polly is not conquering her "desire for anonymity,"[83] or replacing her "private look" with a more public one,[84] but instead retreating even further into her home, her privacy, and her imagination. Escaping the world of artspeak and critical judgement, not by venturing out or standing one's ground, but by burrowing deeper into dreams, is a rather weak move for a feminist film to make.

Both the beginning and the ending of this film spill over into opening and closing credit sequences, reminding viewers of the constructedness of the narrative, and of the arbitrary forces which declare certain moments 'beginnings' or 'endings.' Violating the contours of conventional narrative

---

[80] Silverman, *The Subject of Semiotics*, 158.

[81] Armatage, " ' All That Lovin' Stuff'," 37.

[82] Mayne, *The Woman at the Keyhole*, 72.

[83] Peterson, "Devaluing the 'Ornamental Pot'," 308.

[84] Godwin, "Reclaiming the Subject," 24.

this way is related to the on-screen representations of Polly's flights of fantasy, which again intrude in a highly-wrought way into the progression of her reminiscence. Even as these filmic manoeuvres accentuate self-consciousness, the main target of the film's satire is the world of commercial art, and the inflated, self-conscious verbiage that passes as criticism within it, as when Clive and Gabrielle debate the merits of a particular work hanging on the Church Gallery wall:

CLIVE   There is a hopefulness in his contextual destruction, and the lack
            of resolution of his themes almost adds to a vaguely literal
            internal transformation of his subject.
GABRIELLE   It's an external transformation.
CLIVE   Internal.
GABRIELLE   External. Look at the lemon.
CLIVE   What about the fork?

In contrast to this is Polly's own rapt speechlessness in front of the glowing 'paintings' she sees in Gabrielle's apartment. In voice-over we hear Polly recall her reaction: "I didn't even have to pretend to like them." The squares of light on the walls of the apartment and the gallery are perfect blank screens upon which critics and other viewers can project any meaning at all. In this way they are indeed the universally 'good' works of art that Gabrielle has confessed a desire to create, even though the film debunks the notion of universal or objective standards of value in art.

I've Heard the Mermaids Singing leaves the clean, well-lighted path of typical narrative progression and heterosexual romance for a structure and a story that promise more maverick pleasures than they finally deliver. It is a funny and lightly satirical film, with an engaging and imaginative heroine who combines aspects of Giulietta Masina with Anne of Green Gables. What is unusual about the film's form and characterization is, however, muted by its attempts to address significant issues about artistic value while at the same time trying to forestall its own potential critics. It does this by offering itself, finally, as a filmic equivalent of Mary Joseph's radiant paintings, as a work that means whatever the viewer wants it to. All other issues – of sexuality, technology, politics and plagiarism – are subject to the film's use of charm and whimsy to make its case for the supremacy of subjective responses to art over the dictates of convention and the pronouncements of criticism. These inoffensive tactics are *Mermaids'* modest way of addressing what it sees as the big picture.

ℰ०

Filmography

Features

1987	*I've Heard the Mermaids Singing* (or: *Le chant des sirènes*; 81 mins.)
1990	*White Room* (+ co-producer; 90 mins.)
1995	*When Night is Falling* (+ screenplay; 94 mins.)
1999	*Mansfield Park* (+ screenplay; from Jane Austen's novel; 112 mins.)

Short films and television work

1985	*Passion: A Letter in 16mm.* (+ producer, screenplay; 26 mins., b/w, 16mm)
1986	*Urban Menace* (3 mins.)
1991	*Montréal vu par... Six variations sur un thème* (*Montreal Sextet*, 123 mins. total running length; first episode, titled *Desperanto*)
1997	*But At My Back I Always Hear* (episode of TV series *The Hunger*)
1997	*Bach Cello Suite #6: Six Gestures* (one of six CBC programmes collectively titled *Yo Yo Ma Inspired by Bach*; TV, 90 mins.)
2000	*This Must Be Good* (+ screenplay; 7 mins., b/w, 16mm)
2000	*Happy Days* (from play by Samuel Beckett; TV, 79 mins.)

Bibliography

Background readings

de Lauretis, Teresa. "Rethinking Women's Cinema: Aesthetics and Feminist Theory," in Erens, ed., *Issues in Feminist Film Criticism*, 288–308.

Doane, Mary Ann. *The Desire to Desire*. Bloomington: Indiana UP, 1987.

———. "Film and the Masquerade," in Erens, ed., *Issues in Feminist Film Criticism*, 41–57.

Erens, Patricia, ed., *Issues in Feminist Film Criticism*. Bloomington: Indiana UP, 1990.

Kaplan, E. Ann. *Women and Film: Both Sides of the Camera*. London: Routledge, 1983.

Kuhn, Annette. "Textual Politics," in Erens, ed., *Issues in Feminist Film Criticism*, 250–67.

Maio, Kathi. *Feminist in the Dark: Reviewing the Movies*. Freedom CA: Crossing Press, 1988.

Mayne, Judith. *The Woman at the Keyhole*. Bloomington: Indiana UP, 1990.

Mulvey, Laura. "Visual Pleasure and Narrative Cinema," in Erens, ed., *Issues in Feminist Film Criticism*, 28–40.

Pallister, Janis L. "Léa Pool's Gynefilms," in ⌊Joseph I. Donohoe, ed., *Essays on Québec Cinema*, 111–34.

Penley, Constance, ed. *Feminism and Film Theory*. New York: Routledge, 1988.

Rich, B. Ruby. "In the Name of Feminist Film Criticism," in Erens, ed., *Issues in Feminist Film Criticism*, 268–87.

Quart, Barbara Koenig. *Women Directors: The Emergence of a New Cinema*. New York: Frederick J. Praeger, 1988.

Silverman, Kaja. *The Subject of Semiotics*. Oxford: Oxford UP, 1983.

Waugh, Tom. "The Third Body: Patterns in the Construction of the Subject in Gay Male Narrative Film," in *Queer Looks: Perspectives on Lesbian and Gay Film and Video*, ed. Gever, Greyson & Parmar (Toronto: Between the Lines, 1993). 141–61.

Interviews and statements

Andrews, Marke. "*Mermaids* Star to Sing Lullaby," *Vancouver Sun* (17 October 1987): C1.

Anon. "Press is caught up in *Mermaids*' spell," *Globe & Mail* (12 May 1987): A17.

Ayscough, Susan. "Sushi and the *Mermaids*," *Mirror* (Montreal; 16 October 1987).

Bailey, Bruce. "Swimming in praises: *Mermaids* film-maker is taking it all in stride," *Gazette* (Montreal; 23 October 1987): 248.

Bearchell, Chris. "A Canadian Fairytale," *Epicene* 1 (October 1987): 24–26.

Bourdain, G.S. "Sheila McCarthy: *Mermaids* Heroine," *New York Times* (2 October 1987): C32.

Carr, Jay. "Filmmaker hits with *Mermaids*," *Boston Globe* (16 September 1987).

Delisle, Martin. "Entretien avec Patricia Rozema," *24 Images* 36 (hiver 1987): 22–23.

Elia, Maurice. "Patricia Rozema," *Séquences* 132 (janvier 1988): 24–27.

Guthmann, Edward. "Director Finds Gender Does Matter," *San Francisco Chronicle* (25 November 1995): C1.

Haeseker, Fred. "Canadian film-maker wins instant fame at festival," *Calgary Herald* (12 September 1987): C4.

Henley, Gail. "Quality filmmaking on a shoestring budget," *Playback* (7 September 1987); interview with Alexandra Raffe.

Jaehne, Karen. "Independents: *I've Heard the Mermaids Singing*; An Interview with Patricia Rozema," *Cineaste* 16.3 (1988): 22–23.

McCarthy, Sheila. "Sheila McCarthy Interview" [10 July 1996], online posting: Www.e–commerce.com/ shift/qanda/mccarthy/html.

Nacache, Jacqueline, & Jean Rabinovici. "Une Rencontre avec Patricia Rozema," *Cinéma* 87 410 (30 septembre 1987): 2.

Ring, Trudy. "*Mermaids* Filmmaker Makes Another Lesbian Treat" [November 1995, 8 July 1996]; online posting: http://suba.com/"outlines".

Rozema, Patricia. "Pourquoi filmez-vous?," *Cinema Canada* 156 (October 1988): 6–7.

Warren, Ina. "Film-maker finds herself in the big time," *Winnipeg Free Press* (8 May 1987): 25.

——. "Toronto film-maker prepares to take on Cannes festival," *Edmonton Journal* (8 May 1987): D4.

Essays

Alemany–Galway, Mary. "Postmodernism in Canadian Film: *I've Heard the Mermaids Singing*," *Post script* 18.2 (Winter/Spring 1999): 25–36.

Armatage, Kay. "'All That Lovin' Stuff': Sexuality and Sexual Representation in Some Recent Films by Women," *CineAction* 10 (October 1987): 35–37.

Cagle, Robert. "Canadian Filmmaking in the Face of Cultural Imperialism," *Reverse Shot* 1.2 (Summer 1994: 8–12 (on *White Room*).

De Lauretis, Teresa. "Guerilla in the Midst: Women's Cinema in the 80s," *Screen* 31.1 (Spring 1990): 6–25.

Gasher, Mike. "Decolonizing the Imagination: Cultural Expression as Vehicle of Self-Discovery," *Canadian Journal of Film Studies* 2.2–3 (1993): 95–106.

Godwin, George. "Reclaiming the Subject: A Feminist Reading of *I've Heard the Mermaids Singing*," *Cinema Canada* 152 (May 1988): 23–25.

Gray, Louise. Review of *When Night is Falling*, *Sight and Sound* 5.11 (November 1995): 54–55.

Harrison, Marion. "*Mermaids*: Singing Off Key?," *CineAction* 16 (May 1989): 25–30.

Latimer, Joanne. "Lesbian Chic Goes to Hollywood," *Herizons* 10.2 (Spring 1996): 24–27.

McDonald, Bruce. "Scaling the Heights," *Cinema Canada* 141 (Spring 1987): 12–15.

Peterson, Shirley. "Devaluing the 'Ornamental Pot': Voyeurism, Marginality, and Women's Cinema in *I've Heard the Mermaids Singing*," *West Virginia University Philological Papers* 38 (1992): 302–309.

Pevere, Geoff. "In Others' Eyes: Four Canadian Films Come Home from Cannes," *Cine Action* 11 (Winter 1987–88): 20–29.

——. "What is an Independent Film?," *Cinema Canada* 145 (October 1987): 21–22.

Posner, Michael. "The Little Movie That Did: *I've Heard the Mermaids Singing*," in ⇨Posner, *Canadian Dreams*, 1–21.

Shary, Timothy. "Present Personal Truths: The Alternative Phenomenology of Video in *I've Heard the Mermaids Singing*," *Wide Angle* 15.3 (July 1993): 37–55.

Tanner, L. "Adrian Lyne and Patricia Rozema," *Films in Review* 38.12 (December 1987): 597–602.

Wood, Robin. "Towards a Canadian (Inter)National Cinema," *CineAction* 16 (Spring 1989): 59–63.

Reviews

Ina Warren, "Film-Maker Finds Herself in the Big Time," *Winnipeg Free Press* (8 May 1987): 25; Ron Base, "*Mermaids'* Siren Song Seduces Cannes Critics," *Toronto Star* (12 May 1987): F1; Sid Adilman, *Variety* 327.4 (20 May 1987): 18, 24; Fred Haeseker, *Calgary Herald* (11 June 1987): E10; Gérard Legrand, *Positif* 317–18 (juillet–août 1987): 73; Ron Graham, "For Patricia Rozema, Mermaids Sing," *New York Times* (6 September 1987), sec. 2: 15+; Jay Scott, "McCarthy Makes a Splash in *Mermaids*," *Globe & Mail* (10 September 1987): A18; Jami Bernard, *New York Post* (11 September 1987): 25; Vincent Canby, *New York Times* (11 September 1987): C8; Joseph Gelmis, *Newsday* (11 September 1987): 3; Tom O'Brien, "Three Women: *Mermaids*, *Wish*, and *Nadine*," *Commonweal* 114 (11 September 1987): 498–99; Noel Taylor, "*Mermaids* and its fair star get festival off to great beginning," *Ottawa Citizen* (11 September 1987): F6; Richard Corliss, "Terms of Endearment: *I've Heard the Mermaids Singing*," *Time* 130.11 (14 September 1987): 77; Jay Carr, "*Mermaids*: Humane, engaging," *Boston Globe* (17 September 1987): 89; Joel Weinberg, "Angels in the Architecture," *New York Native* (21 September 1987); Katherine Dieckman, *Village Voice* (22 September 1987): 76; David Sterritt, *Christian Science Monitor* (23 September 1987): 21; Kevin Thomas, *Los Angeles Times* (25 September 1987): Calendar 24; Lawrence O'Toole & Edward Trapunski, "Murmurs of the Heart," *Maclean's* 100.39 (28 September 1987): 48; Jean Rabinovici, *Cinéma 87* 410 (30 septembre 1987): 1; Jay Scott, "Outrageous Fortune: Sheila McCarthy's Triumph in *I've Heard the Mermaids Singing* Proves That You Can Be Goofy and Glamorous at the Same Time," *Toronto* 2.6 (September 1987): 32–37, 90–91; Desson Howe, *Washington Post* (16 October 1987): Weekend, 33; Marke Andrews, "Holey Moley!: Pretentious Polly was Better as an Airhead," *Vancouver Sun* (17 October 1987): C2; Anon., "Singing Mermaids Possible," *Cinema Canada* 145 (October 1987): 69; John Simon, "All in the Allegory," *National Review* 39.20 (October 1987): 60–61; Jacques Zimmer & Danièle Parra, *Revue du cinéma* 431 (octobre 1987): 43–46; Anon., "*Mermaids* Sing Sweet Song of Success in Foreign Sales," *Cinema Canada* 146 (November 1987): 37; Cameron Bailey, *Cinema Canada* 146 (November 1987): 25; Anon., "Exploration of a Dreamer," *Maclean's* 100.52 (28 December 1987): 34–35; Richard Gay, "L'Année du *Zoo* et des *Sirènes*," *L'Actualité* 12.12 (décembre 1987): 151; Gérard Grugeau, *24 Images* 36 (hiver 1987):

24-25; Marie-Christine Abel, *Séquences* 132 (janvier 1988): 60–61; S. Sdraulig, *Cinema Papers* 67 (January 1988): 47–48; Simon Cunliffe, *New Statesman* (26 February 1988): 32; Roger Ebert, *Chicago Sun Times* (4 March 1988): n.p. Online. Internet Movie Database. 8 July, 1996; Michael O'Pray, *Monthly Film Bulletin* 55.650 (March 1988): 81; Beth Spring, *Christianity Today* 32.4 (March 1988): 57; David Wilkinson, "No One Expected *I've Heard the Mermaids Singing* to be Such a Hit, Least of All its Director," *Chatelaine* 61.4 (April 1988): 78, 288+; Cindy Fuchs, *Cineaste* 16.3 (1988): 54–55; Linda Lopez McAlister, 22 September 1990. Online posting. Http://www.inform.umd.edu. 14 August 1996.

ॐ

FIGURE 10

The Company of Strangers (Cynthia Scott, 1990) – Alice Diabo (Alice);
Constance Garneau (Constance); Winfred Holden (Winnie); Cissy
Meddings (Cissy); Mary Meigs (Mary); Catherine Roche
(Catherine); Beth Webber (Beth).

10 The Company of Strangers (Cynthia Scott, 1990)

Production: 1990. A National Film Board of Canada Production. **Director:** Cynthia Scott. **Executive Producers:** Colin Neale, Rina Fraticelli, Peter Katadotis. **Producer:** David Wilson. **Screenplay:** Gloria Demers, Cynthia Scott, David Wilson, Sally Bochner. **Cinematography:** David de Volpi. **Editor:** David Wilson.

Music: Marie Bernard. **Colour, 101 mins., 35mm.**

Cast: Alice Diabo (Alice), **Constance Garneau** (Constance), **Winfred Holden** (Winnie), **Cissy Meddings** (Cissy), **Mary Meigs** (Mary), **Catherine Roche** (Catherine), **Michelle Sweeney** (Michelle), **Beth Webber** (Beth).

Synopsis: Seven elderly women and their 27-year-old bus driver, Michelle, are stranded in Québec's Mont Tremblant region when their small bus breaks down. Abandoning the bus, the group finds refuge in a deserted farm house. For three days and two nights the strangers join forces and skills to survive within a picturesque, benign wilderness. They go fishing, catch and cook frogs, bathe in the lake, and send out SOS messages. They also pass the time by walking to a nearby lake, painting, bird-watching, singing and dancing, and playing cards. The urgency and potential life-threatening danger of the situation is minimized, most notably, by shifting attention away from the crisis situation and towards casual conversations which are the centrepiece of the film. The women recount the trials and tribulations of their personal histories: Mary (71) tells of coming out as a lesbian, Beth (80) mourns the early death of her only child and obsesses over the deterioration of her physical body, Constance (88) speaks of her fear of dying, Alice (74) reminisces about life on the Indian reserve and single-motherhood, Cissy (76) confesses to fears of being abandoned by her son, and Winnie (76) speaks of the promises of the future. Catherine (65), a lay nun, attempts to fix the bus and, when that fails, volunteers to walk twenty miles to find help; she succeeds, returning in a sea-plane to rescue the others. Each of the women's histories is punctuated by a series of family photographs which, along with the use of non-actresses who retain their real names and real lives, convey the authenticity of the women's stories. In the tradition of the National Film Board of Canada's Alternative Drama programme, however, this documentary material is blended with dramatic elements which include a narrative premiss, a loose dialogue script, and a fictional setting.

߅

Pictures of age and ageing

in Cynthia Scott's *The Company of Strangers*

———————————————— ℰↃ

Angela Stukator

I N A PRESS RELEASE for *The Company of Strangers*, Cynthia Scott states
that her objective was "not to make a film about 'old people' but about
people who are old ... the distinction is crucial."[1] To that end, Scott has
crafted a film which foregrounds discrete and distinguishing qualities that
exist within and between eight women, seven of whom are over the age of
sixty-five. The film also draws attention to the commonality amongst them
but without allowing the points of connection to suggest that the group constitute a stable category of old women or that they attest to a terminal, fixed
point of human subjectivity. *The Company of Strangers* frames the parallelism
and variance that belong to the women in relation to a complex amalgama-
tion of personal histories and memories. Collectively, the women's stories
function as a disquisition on the process of female ageing, on the coexistence
of past and present, and on the experience of physical deterioration and the
intractability of death.

This representation of people who are old is not insignificant, given the
conspicuous absence of images of the elderly in our Western cultural landscape. The absence speaks of a persistent form of prejudice, communicated
through a network of intersecting discourses, with cultural discourses such
as advertising, television, film, and fashion functioning as exceptionally ob-
stinate messengers. Ageism, the fear of and discrimination against old
people, is conveyed through the marketing of fantasies of halting the ageing
process and through negative stereotypes of old women and men. Ageism is
also evident in the cult of youth, which situates age as the anxiety-provoking
'other.' In its exclusive concern with old women, *The Company of Strangers*
suggests that the 'problem' of age and the agents of ageism have particular
relevance for feminists. The perception of age has to be understood as bound
to gender:

---

[1] Press release, *The Company of Strangers*, 1990.

If the feminine is other, marginal and chaos, and therefore socially disruptive, then the old(er) woman in her obscene and ugly wretched excess, is even more threatening.[2]

Germaine Greer offers an explanation for why old women are viewed in this manner. Greer links ageing to menopause, which occurs around the age of fifty; since the mid-nineteenth-century, menopause has been perceived as a tragedy because it marked the "death of the womb."[3] The conflation of woman and womb in medical and psychoanalytic discourses has led, among other things, to the designation of women as the "arbiters of birth" and of old (post- menopausal) women as the "managers of death"; Greer highlights the intersection of ageism and sexism in our culture, labelling it 'anophobia,' the irrational fear of the old woman.[4] Critical theorist Mary Russo makes a similar point in her definition of "ordinary female trouble," a sub-category of the grotesque, which is defined by conditions such as illness, non-reproduction, and ageing.[5] But anophobia is perhaps most emphatically transmitted through "stereotypical grotesques," notably hags, nags, witches and crones. They have historically imparted contradictory meanings, yet in contemporary cultural discourses they are usually invoked to demarcate negative and contemptuous sentiments: the terms conjure up female ugliness, defilement, monstrosity, maliciousness, and depravity.

The mechanisms which define and shape these kinds of stereotypes of old women and the ageing female body are manifestations of anxieties fostered within our culture. In other words, poststructuralist theorists have demonstrated that the body is both a "text of culture and a practical locus of control."[6] Dominant representations of old women (like dominant representations of women in general) purport to imagine the body as a site of individual self-determination, but they are, in fact, representations of the body as it is culturally and socially moulded and as it has been historically constituted. It is, therefore, crucial to acknowledge that *The Company of Strangers* is

---

[2] Joanna Frueh, "Visible Difference: Women Artists and Aging," in *New Feminist Criticism*, ed. Joanna Frueh, Cassandra Langer & Arlene Raven (New York: HarperCollins, 1994): 277.

[3] Germaine Greer, *The Change: Women, Aging and the Menopause* (New York: Fawcett Columbine, 1991): 3.

[4] Greer, *The Change*, 4–5.

[5] Mary Russo, *The Female Grotesque: Risk, Excess and Modernity* (New York: Routledge, 1994): 14.

[6] See, for example, Susan Bordo, *Unbearable Weight: Feminism, Western Culture, and the Body* (Berkeley: U of California P, 1993): 165.

informed by the discursive terms which regulate the popular and sanctioned
representational norms. The film, however, reclaims seven old women who
refuse to fade away, and, in their visibility, distinctiveness and adaptability,
they disturb the mechanisms that normalize and legitimize anophobia.

The intricate and heterogeneous details in the film's representation of
"people who are old" are possibly obscured by the film's deceptive simplicity. *The Company of Strangers* has a skeletal fictional narrative, topical
subject-matter, and a rambling, leisurely pace; it is, in a word, a 'typical'
product of the National Film Board, and, specifically, of the Board's Alternative Drama programme. Alternative Drama refers to seven films produced
by the NFB during the 1980s and early 1990s.[7] Contract filmmakers at the
NFB, most notably John N. Smith and Giles Walker, used the resources at
the Board to develop films which began as documentaries and evolved into
fictional dramas.[8] Each film is, therefore, distinguished by its combination of
conventions of fiction – dramatic narrative premiss, functional characterization, and fictional setting – with those that belong to documentary film: non-
actors playing themselves in natural situations, open-framing, and two
camera set-ups. The conventions of alternative drama function in *The Company of Strangers* as a strategy for reclaiming and making representable old
women as subjects; further, they expose the relationship between age,
gender, and subjectivity.

The project is clearly aligned with the objectives of women's cinema.
According to Teresa De Lauretis, contemporary women's cinema aims "to
effect another vision: to construct other objects and subjects and to formu-

---

[7] The first alternative drama was *Masculine Mystique* (John N. Smith, Giles Walker,
1984), followed by *90 Days* (Giles Walker, 1985), *The Last Straw*, Giles Walker, 1987), *Sitting
in Limbo* (John N. Smith, 1986), *Train of Dreams* (John N. Smith, 1987), *Welcome to Canada*
(John N. Smith, 1989) and *The Company of Strangers* (Cynthia Scott, 1990). With the exception of *The Company of Strangers*, the Alternative drama films were made on minimal
budgets using mainly in-house resources (personnel, equipment, film stock, etc). The
films were met with mixed critical reactions, in large part because the first three, which
constitute a trilogy of sorts, were considered to exemplify the authority of white, male,
conservative, heterosexist and sexist representations sanctioned by the NFB.

[8] This is, in fact, a return to some of the original dramas made by the NFB in the 1960s,
most notably *Nobody Waved Goodbye* (Don Owen, 1964). Cynthia Scott explains that this
type of drama combines the strengths of entertainment and documentary: "you get an
authenticity of experience which cannot be duplicated by actors, while at the same time
you get closer to the women than would be possible in a straightforward documentary";
George Godwin, "*The Company of Strangers*," in *Border Crossings* (1991): 40.

late the conditions of representability of another social subject."[9] Scott achieves this objective through the use and abuse of fiction and documentary conventions authorized by the alternative drama genre. It is a strategy which contests the authority and authenticity of the representational norms, particularly those which contain and constrain old women to the paradigms of "stereotypical grotesques." But equally significantly, the use and abuse of fiction and documentary function, within the film, to challenge a number of related distinctions: between story and history, fabrication and 'truth,' performance and being, and concealment and appearance. As I shall go on to explicate, the collapse of these terms and categories is tied to the formal features of the film's two narrative trajectories: the fictional story of women stranded for three days in the 'wilds' of Northern Québec; and the individual and personal histories of the old women, which span a period of 88 years.

The (non)drama of the company

The film opens with a shot of extended duration; it precedes the title credit sequence and is temporally, spatially and graphically discontinuous with the first narrative event. One of its functions is to establish economically the terms by which the film will reclaim age. The image is of a thick, white mist that fills the frame. In the distance the faint traces of six figures appear, and move slowly forward towards the camera (Beth and Constance are not included in the shot.; the narrative explanation for their absence is that they stayed behind to fix the bus.) Their anonymity and their unity are visually reinforced by the muted colours of the costumes and the ghost-like appearance effected by the whitewash. As they cut through the mist and move from extreme long shot to medium long shot, the women become individuated by details such as eye-glasses, carefully coiffed hair, a cane, body-size, and skin-colour. They are then linked to distinctive voices: Michelle's loud complaints, Cissy's high-pitched laughter, Constance's thin, yearning voice, and Mary's dry–flat tone. The film, significantly, ends with a reverse of this shot: the women move from foreground to background, disappearing into the mist. The narrative between these framing shots expands on this process of generality and individualization, oscillating between the project of portraying them as a 'company' and the project of stressing how their differences – of class, race, ethnicity, education, and sexual orientation – render

---

[9] Teresa De Lauretis, *Technologies of Gender* (Bloomington: Indiana UP, 1987): 135.

them intrinsically 'strangers.'[10] The framing device has other implications, which I will return to; it establishes the film's style as inconstant – mixing together sublime and prosaic images – and it frustrates narrative closure, since the closing shot, which repeats the discontinuities of the opening shot, can also be read as a double ending.

The first narrative event – the breakdown of the bus – establishes the premiss of the film, that of the stranded group. It is a fairly conventional paradigm, in both documentary and fiction films, for exploring the effects of being cast out of routine life. Documentary films are often structured around a 'crisis' of this sort where ordinary people are put to a test. In particular, this is an anthropological strategy, a way of recording the conduct of individuals under pressure. There is also a genre of mainstream narrative films (eg, *Stagecoach* [John Ford, 1939], *Lord of the Flies* [Peter Brook, 1963], *Lifeboat* [Alfred Hitchcock, 1944]) which uses the crisis scenario to expose and explore the dynamics of interpersonal relationships, human endurance, gender production, and the like. But *The Company of Strangers* is no *Nanook of the North* (Robert Flaherty, 1922) or *Deliverance* (John Boorman, 1972). The catalytic event that leads to the women being stranded (with no hope of being found, since they have detoured from the planned route and their bus is hidden within a dense forest grove) is rendered anti-dramatic: the break-down is acoustically signaled by a unimpressive bang and the initial responses from the women to the crisis are apathetic and unconcerned. And while the film includes the conventional tasks performed by the stranded group – finding supplies, searching for food, sending SOS messages – these activities are also marked by a pronounced absence of urgency or conflict. They are activities which gain no more import than bird-watching, exercising, painting, or singing and dancing. They mark time passing, time waiting.

The chronology of mundane events is echoed and reinforced by the dialogue; in a mix of loosely scripted and improvisational conversations, the women discuss nothing of great significance and no topic is dealt with in-depth. Moreover, there are a number of prolonged periods when the women are silent and the sound shifts to melancholic tunes on piano, violin and cello, or to jazz music. In these scenes, the landscape and the women framed within it are exceedingly aestheticized. Catherine Russell, in her illuminating analysis of the film, interprets the music and painterly landscapes as "exces-

---

[10] Significantly, the American title of the film, *Strangers in Good Company*, retained this oscillation.

sive signifiers" that belong to the woman's film and function to evoke melo-dramatic pathos.[11]

I would suggest that these images also have implications with respect to the film's project of challenging fixed, stable terms of identity. The exceed-ingly aestheticized images provide intensely contemplative moments of un-mediated vision which punctuate the narrative and delay its temporal flow. They also interrupt and disturb the dominant style of the film, which is marked by a commitment to the codes of observational cinema, a sub-category of the documentary film. Observational cinema is commonly defined by its 'fly on the wall' approach, an analogy which serves to define the movement's (delusive) commitment to objectivity and distance from the subject. To that end, observational cinema is distinguished by techniques such as long takes, the use of long lenses, location sound, cut-aways, and a lack of reverse shots and point-of-view shots. In *The Company of Strangers*, the juxtaposition of 'painterly' images of nature and observational tech-niques used to 'document' the narrative events functions to challenge the film's potentially essentialist representation of women and nature, or more precisely, women *as* nature. Thus, on the one hand, the film calls up, in its aesthetic excesses, nature as allegorical, cathartic, and feminized. This is a reading which is reinforced by a comment made by one of the actresses/subjects, a painter and writer whose book, *In the Company of Strangers*, details the process of making the film and elaborates on the histories of the women. On the subject of the setting, Meigs states that

> the landscape was not the backdrop [...] it was a multiple metaphor for age, memory and death. We became company with each other and with our landscape.[12]

Alternatively, it can be argued that the wilderness setting is depicted as a 'strange' space, an external and 'other' space. It decontextualizes the women, separating them off from their homes, belongings and communities. The strangeness of the space is manifest through the excessive signifiers wherein the women become compositional elements. For example, there are numer-ous occasions when the women are doubly framed, within the frame itself and then again within the architecture of the farmhouse or other compo-nents of the environment. By employing the frame as an aesthetic and meta-

---

[11] Catherine Russell, "Mourning the Woman's Film: The Dislocated Spectator of *The Company of Strangers*," *Canadian Journal of Film Studies* 3.2 (Fall 1994): 34.

[12] Mary Meigs, *In the Company of Strangers* (Vancouver: Talonbooks, 1991): 12–13. Meigs also includes her personal interpretation of the representation of age.

phoric code, the film places the women in the space rather than using them to support some natural, innate synergy between women and nature. This is particularly evident in the discontinuities of representational codes in the opening and closing shots, as well as the discontinuities in the narrative proper. These discontinuities speak of the construction of the space and) ⯑ signal the parenthetical scenes as passage into and out of the fictional world. Finally, the setting is a 'strange' place because, as Janine Marchessault notes, it is depicted as devoid of power relations, and men are absent.[13] The point is that the space has to be read as a utopian place within the norms of gender representation and, in particular, the representation of old women. Only in a "strange" place, a place that exists outside of the centre, are they able to assert: "We're alive...We're all alive"; it is a declaration of their presence, identity, and subjectivity.

The film also calls up the generational divide between the women as a potential point of friction, only to systematically efface it. The divide is most evident in the discrepancy between Michelle's youth and the women's age; but it also exists between Catherine who, at age 65, is a generation apart from the 88-year-old Constance. The dichotomy between youth and age, Meigs writes, designates Michelle as the one who sounds life and Constance as the one who sounds death.[14] Superficially, this is true: Michelle is vivacious, energetic, and associated with soul and jazz music. Constance is silent, contemplative, suicidal (evident in her obsession with death and the spurious act of throwing her pills into the lake); and she is associated with classical music. However, this dichotomy is challenged from the first image of the film. It is Michelle who, having sprained her ankle immediately following the breakdown of the bus, must rely on a cane to walk. And as Michelle is crippled by the experience in the wilderness, Constance is markedly rejuvenated. As the narrative progresses, the association of Constance with death is undermined by her dialogue (asserting to Winnie that she has never felt so happy, so calm) and her involvement in group activities such as killing the frogs with Cissy and playing cards. Likewise, the jazz music originally associated with Michelle invades numerous scenes with the older women. In one of the final scenes, the women are inside the farmhouse playing cards, laughing and singing. Michelle's voice, which early in the narra-

---

[13] Janine Marchessault, "Writing Feminist Histories: *The Burning Times* and *The Company of Strangers*," *CineAction* 23 (Winter 1990-91): 73. In its planning stages, the film did include men.

[14] Meigs, *In the Company of Strangers*, 121.

tive was marked as domineering, is now challenged by the equally hardy voices of Constance, Winnie, and Alice. The camera cuts to an exterior of the house at night and the soundtrack fills with the sound of their laughter and voices. Here again, Scott exploits the power of the frame; the off-screen, hence disembodied, sounds of the women heighten the capacity of aural signs to signify vitality and rapture against images which convey decay and evoke pathos.

Thus, the representation of generational difference, like the synergy between woman and nature, collapses. In this case, however, the collapse is less a result of making use of normative codes for representing youth as distinct from age than it is a function of narrative. The ironic character traits, incongruous dialogue, and inappropriate or inconsistent character actions gain meaning within the context of a fictional trajectory. In other words, the narrative thwarts any sense of fixing the women's identities to ideals of 'women,' or of binding them to the cultural dictate of age as hopelessly in opposition to youth. Rather, narrative, with its investment in transformations over time, is the strategy for rendering a fluid and dynamic relationship between gender, identity, and age.

Histories of strangers

Re-conceptualizing the terms that communicate conventional notions of gender identity functions to frustrate our desire to establish the 'truth' about age and ageing. This is reinforced by the other narrative trajectory in the film, the histories of the old women, which are inextricably bound to the governing fictional narrative. The women tell their histories to each other over the course of three days. They are not coherent stories but, rather, fragments of their past which reveal unique as well as comparable experiences. Formally, the histories are distinguished by two features: they are conveyed by interviews concealed as conversation; secondly, they are accompanied by photo-montages which punctuate the fictional narrative.

I have concentrated so far on examining how the film establishes itself as a fictional narrative, and how it uses and subverts narrative codes to challenge conventional representations of age and ageing. Yet, given that the film is part of the alternative-drama programme, it is also crucial to examine the way in which the film's fictional premiss is mediated by documentary conventions. The mediation is reciprocal, meaning that the documentary codes are likewise modified by their encounter with fiction. For example, the women are both ethnographic, historical individuals and characters in a drama. This dual status is established by the credits: the names of the actresses correspond to the names of the characters. It is also apparent in the construction of the dialogue sequences, wherein two or more of the women engage in casual conversations or, more accurately, "masked interviews"; the term is Bill Nichols' and is used to identify conversations in documentary films which are implanted or prearranged.[15] In *The Company of Strangers* the interviews are post-arranged into conversation, evident in the repeated use of cut-aways to conceal the construction of answers into conversation. The stamp of "masked interviews" is also applied through the characters' rhetorical questions (eg, "you were paralyzed [from a stroke], weren't you?"), which reveal that the film is not documenting in real time the women as strangers moving towards becoming company; rather, they are company re-creating and performing an earlier, pre-diegetic, experience of being strangers.

The form of the interviews raises the question of the function and value of recording women's personal histories. Are the histories we hear truthful documents of the women's pasts and evidence of their status as historical subjects? Or, given their contrived formal structure, do the histories simply reinforce the film's fictional narrative, and if so, to what end? Russell draws attention to the similarities among the histories, noting that, like the genre of the woman's film, they trace "tales of sacrifice and loneliness"; and she sees Mary Meigs, because of her rejection of "compulsory heterosexuality," as "luckier than the others to have been able to resist the prescribed fates of so many women her age."[16] Thus, Russell highlights how the histories are aligned with the generic project of unveiling women's status as 'Other' within patriarchal culture. Yet the women's stories are not dismal, depressing accounts of female oppression any more than they are stories of domestic contentment and symbiotic bliss. Each of the stories traces the ambivalence of lived experience within existing social institutions and class relations, and this ambivalence, which is represented as complex and multi-faceted,

---

[15] Bill Nichols, *Representing Reality* (Bloomington: Indiana UP, 1991): 50. As George Godwin explains, because the women were not actors it was impossible to get them to repeat anything. As a result, Scott shot with two cameras, filming as much as 25 minutes to gather enough material for what would become a three-minute scene in the finished film; Godwin, "*The Company of Strangers,*" in *Border Crossings*, 39.

[16] Russell, "Mourning the Woman's Film," 32. One wonders if Winnie also escapes the fate of the other women. Does Winnie's single status carry the same 'freedom' and 'liberation' that Russell attributes to Meigs' lesbianism?

affords a fluidity in the spectator's identification with the film's divergent subjects.

This is not to argue against the importance of common themes attributed to the domain of women: the women speak of the fear of 'coming out,' the thrill of falling in love, and the joys and pains of marriage and motherhood. In this way, there is a consciousness-raising quality generated by the women's simple, unexceptional histories; apropos of this mode of feminist documentation, the spectator is invited to identify with their humbling discourses of individual spirit, endurance and survival.

It is worth digressing slightly to situate the consciousness-raising tract of the film in relation to Cynthia Scott's background, directing documentary films under the auspices of Studio D, the Women's studio at the National Film Board of Canada. Gloria Demers, who was responsible for writing the script for *The Company of Strangers* also worked at Studio D, writing and narrating, among other projects, *Behind the Veil: Nuns* (1984). From 1974 until its demise in 1995, Studio D was committed to producing films about women and their experiences, providing the audiences with glimpses into other women's lives. Some of the more renowned films, such as *If You Love This Planet* (Terri Nash, 1984), *Abortions: Stories from the North and South* (Gail Singer, 1984), and *Not a Love Story* (Bonnie Sherr–Klein, 1984), adopted the issue-oriented Griersonian approach of social criticism and infused it with a woman's perspective. Other films, including Scott's Academy Award-winning *Flamenco at 5:15* (1983), hearken back to the observational strategies of the mid-1950s and through the 1960s that developed from the efforts of Studio B, the famed English Unit, and in particular the Candid-Eye films such as *Lonely Boy* (Roman Kroitor, Wolf Koenig, 1962), *Paul Tomkowicz, Street Railway Switchman* (Roman Kroitor, 1954) *Corral* (Colin Low, 1954), and *The Back-Breaking Leaf* (Terence McCartney–Filgate, 1959). It has been argued that the Candid-Eye films were influenced by the photography of Henri Cartier–Bresson, and are distinct from the American direct-cinema documentaries, which are indebted to *Life* magazine's photographic tradition, with its 'key' (read: dramatic) images.[17] As such, Candid-Eye films are marked by an absence of drama, focusing as they did on the everyday, the ordinary, the intimate, and the private.[18] It is an approach which seems to have found its way into many of the films produced by Studio D, where the

---

[17] See Bruce Elder, "On the Candid-Eye Movement," in ⇨Feldman & Nelson, ed., *Canadian Film Reader*, 86–94.

[18] ⇨Elder, "On the Candid-Eye Movement," 92–93.

female experience and, in particular, personal politics are rendered complex and contradictory.[19] Furthermore, the influence of the Candid Eye's nuanced political tone is arguably marked in *The Company of Strangers*, where compelling feminist issues are raised in a detached and cautious manner. The film's concern with women and age, race, ethnicity, class, sexual preference, and patriarchal oppression (which, the film suggests, includes everything from the institution of marriage to a 'pornographic' boot-horn), is rendered non-threatening although pervasive, through the film's commitment to de-dramatized, poetic and, most significantly, heterogeneous representations of what it means to be old and to be a woman.

Most notably, the consciousness-raising quality of the women's stories includes giving voice and representational space to the convergence of race, ethnicity, class and sexual orientation in the production of identity, and thus to the inevitable disparity among the women. However, with the inclusion of a Roman Catholic nun, a lesbian, a black woman, and a Native Indian, the film rides the fine line between affirming a field of difference and the tokenism that belongs to the politically correct.[20] But perhaps most critical to a political plurality is the film's attempt to explain how gender and identity intersect with age. The women claim the repressed discourse of the ageing body: they speak of death and dying, of bodies in perpetual pain, of physical deterioration, of illness and convalescence, and of post-menopausal sex and sexuality. In so doing, they recover corporeal experiences which have been silenced within the authorized discourses of the centre. The recovery of these prohibited discourses is matched by the film's attempt to resurrect what bell hooks has termed "outlawed" representations.[21] In the casting and in the narrative representation of the seven women, the film effectively evokes the positive attributes of mythic female archetypes; Mary, Beth and Constance are sages: wise, discreet, and judicious; Winnie and Cissy are cantankerous and mischievous crones; and Catherine, with her link to God, and Alice, with her Mohawk remedies, are modern-day witches, female magicians.

---

[19] Chris Sherbarth, "Why not D? An historical look at the NFB's Woman's Studio," *Cinema Canada* 139 (March 1987): 9–10.

[20] It is important to note that the group does not include a francophone woman. This is remarkable, since it is implied that the tour group's point of departure is Montreal.

[21] *Outlaw Culture: Resisting Representation* (New York: Routledge, 1994).

The second feature of the histories that I want to consider is the inclusion of photo-montages.[22] At some point within the unfolding of each of the women's stories, the present-tense narrative is disrupted by a series of still photographs of the women. The photographs feature the individual woman in the distant past, with children, a partner, or alone. Bruce Elder has argued that, in Canadian cinema, both experimental and non-experimental films "seem to rest on the assumption that film is a photographically based medium."[23] The incorporation of still photographs into film is just one strategy for raising questions about links between film and photography in general and the nature of representation in particular. Thus, we find in *The Company of Strangers* that the inclusion of the photographic images is crucial to the representation of the women as historical subjects and subjects of ethnographic enquiry. Moreover, the photographs heighten the question of performance and being, or fabrication and truth, raised by the double status of the women and the 'masked interviews'; for, in juxtaposition with the fictional narrative, the photographs augment the project of re-establishing age against epistemological certainty. The photographs, like the verbal histories, are insufficient, inconclusive testimonies of human existence and experience. The spectator is not certain what is real and what is artificial; are they authentic photographs of the actresses or contrived inserts? Why these ones and not others? Who chose them and what were the criteria? These questions have far-reaching implications in theorizing modes of rendering accessible and communicable the complexities of identity wherein the external body functions as the visible vehicle of other 'invisible' constituents of identity.

The photo-montages also insist on the film's commitment to drawing the relationship between present and past, life and death. It is a complex relationship, for, as Bill Nichols explains,

> A photographic likeness offers evidence of a life as it was lived and experienced in the flesh, within the constraints of the historical, physical body itself. And yet that likeness in and of itself is insufficient evidence. It is but a frozen

---

[22] Martin Duckworth's *The Wish* (1970) also uses still photographs as part of its attempt to 'document' its subjects. Peter Harcourt's analysis of the photographs within this documentary attends to some theories of photography which, I am arguing, are also applicable to the photomontages of *The Company of Strangers*. See "The Photographic Trace," in ⇨Seth Feldman, ed., *Take Two*, 229–35.

[23] Bruce Elder, "Image: Representation and Object: The Photographic Image in Canadian Avant-Garde Film," in ⇨Seth Feldman, ed., *Take Two*, 252.

moment, an artifact that requires the animating force of time, narrative and history to gain experiential meaning.[24]

The crisis narrative and the histories of the women together provide this animation. They render the photographs both potent in their capacity as signifiers of presence and absence, most notably the absence of youth, and also in their function as signifiers of time passing, and the processes of ageing.

Photographs are a form of history, in that they are concrete, material evidence of the past. Moreover, photographs allow us to understand that "history is hysterical": history "is constituted only if we consider it, only if we look at it – and in order to look at it we must be excluded from it."[25] The photographs in *The Company of Strangers* doubly exclude the spectator from the history of the women: they are not only still photographs of a 'dead time,' they are also photographs contained and circumscribed by cinematic properties. While they are visual artifacts of histories which are spoken, the brevity in which the photographs are held, within the temporal structure of the narrative, intensifies the spectator's confrontation with, but detachment from, the past. The photographs of youth are fixed and posed: "nothing can be added; [the photograph] is without a future."[26] These fleeting moments of a time that has gone by thus function as a cogent reminder of the precariousness of the present. Yet they also suggest, through their function as memories, coexistence with the present. They work within the double narrative form to render ageing as a flowing process of perseverance.

It is, ultimately, the fictional narrative trajectory, coupled with the documentary histories of the old women, that reclaims age as a generative process with distinct and heterogeneous individual manifestations: the old women, through the unfolding of the narrative, become women who are old, and white or black, educated or not, heterosexual or lesbian. There are a number of consequences of this kind of representation of age. It frustrates the illusory pleasure of knowing afforded by culturally sanctioned fantasies of escape from age and, indeed, from death. 'Death-denying' narratives, and narratives that feature old stars passing as young stars, define the bulk of popular representations of old women; they are products of both an ageist society and an era which places its faith in technological mastery. While

[24] Nichols, *Representing Reality*, 233.

[25] Roland Barthes, *Camera Lucida: Reflections on Photography*, tr. Richard Howard (New York: Hill & Wang, 1981): 65.

[26] Barthes, *Camera Lucida*, 89.

science and medicine provide real, if not outlandish, ways of evading the ageing process, photographic illusionism and the rhetoric of Hollywood narratives offer the consolation that was once the domain of traditional religions. *The Company of Strangers* positions itself as anterior to the technological era and uses this site to posit another response to age. The film carves out a space for old women who refuse to become invisible in our culture and who, in their association with thresholds, passages, and margins, are rendered, above all, figures of ambivalence. Finally, the film expands the discursive boundaries of representing human existence by insisting on the intractability of death that, as Constance casually notes, "is always around us." The film thus avows the aged female body as a visible sign of degeneration and impending death; but it does so by reconnecting that same body with the tenacity and vitality that 'belong' to life.

∾

Filmography

Features

1990   *The Company of Strangers* (*Strangers in Good Company*, US title; + co-screenplay; 101 mins.; 35mm)

2002   *The Stone Diaries* (+ co-screenplay; from novel by Carol Shields)

Short films and television work

1972   *The Ungrateful Land: Roch Carrier Remembers Ste. Justine* (27 mins., 40 secs.)
1973   *Some Natives of Churchill* (+ producer; 27 mins., 20 secs.)
1973   *I Don't Have To Work That Big* (+ producer; 27 mins., 20 secs.)
1973   *Ruth and Harriet: Two Women of Peace* (30 mins.)
1973/74 *West* series (12 films; associate producer)
1974   *Scoggle* (30 mins.)
1974   *Hector* (10 mins.)
1976   *Listen Listen Listen* (producer; 82 mins., 35 secs.)
1976   *Road Test* clip (producer; 1 min.)
1978/79 *Fitness and Nutrition* (11 clips; producer)
1978   *Canadian Vignettes: The 30s* (producer; 1 min.)
1979   *Holidays* (producer; 1 min.)
1981   *The First Winter* (co-writer; 26 mins., 37 secs.)
1981   *For the Love of Dance* (co-producer, co-director with Michael McKennirey, John M. Smith and David Wilson; 57 mins., 46 secs.)
1982   *Gala* (backstage-director; 90 mins., 48 secs.)
1983   *Flamenco at 5:15* (+ producer; 29 mins., 22 secs.)
1985   *Discussions in Bioethics: A Chronic Problem* (12 mins., 3 secs.)
1986   *Jack of Hearts* (24 mins.)

1994   *David Hockney* (part of 90-minute TV special *Vision of Five*)
1997   *A Lover's Lament* (30 mins.)

Bibliography

Interviews

"Cynthia Scott and *The Company of Strangers*," *Canadian Women's Studies* 12:2 (Winter 1992): 109–13.

Cloutier, Anne. "Serine complicité: entretien de Anne Cloutier avec Cynthia Scott," *24 Images* 54 (printemps 1991): 22–24.

Essays

D'Arcy, Jan. "Cynthia Scott: The Art of Portraying the Human Condition on Screen," *Canadian Forum* 71.810 (June 1992): 109–13.

George, Diana. "Semi-Documentary/Semi-Fiction: An Examination of Genre in *Strangers in Good Company*," *Journal of Film and Video* 45.4 (Winter 1995): 24–30.

Godwin, K. George. "*The Company of Strangers*," *Border Crossing* 10.2 (April 1991): 38–41.

Marchessault, Janine. "Writing Feminist Histories: *The Burning Times* and *The Company of Strangers*," *CineAction* 23 (Winter 1990–91): 70–73.

Russell, Catherine. "Mourning the Woman's Film: The Dislocated Spectator of *The Company of Strangers*," *Canadian Journal of Film Studies* 3.2 (Fall 1994): 25–40.

Stukator, Angela. "Hags, Nags, Witches and Crones: Reframing Age in *The Company of Strangers*," *Canadian Journal of Film Studies* 5.2 (Fall 1996): 51–65.

Reviews

Suze, *Variety* (10 September 1990); Jay Scott, "A celebration of friendship," *Globe & Mail* (21 September 1990); Brian D. Johnson, "Voices in the Wilderness," *Maclean's* (24 September 1990); Janet Coutts, *Westmount (Québec) Examiner* (18 October 1990); Marc Horton, *Edmonton Journal* (5 and 9 November 1990); Noel Taylor, "A slow, quiet film worth five stars," *Ottawa Citizen* (17 November 1990); Luc Perrault, "La Mondiale de Québec: Dix jours de cinéma des femmes," *La Presse* (17 April 1991); Philip French, "Magic bus stop-off," *Observer* (London; 5 May 1991); Janet Maslin, *New York Times* (10 May 1991): col. 8:1; Linda Nelson, *Village Voice* (28 May 1991); Jill McGreal, *Sight and Sound* (May 1991): 44; Peter Goddard, "Elderly amateurs save film in woods," *Toronto Star* (21 September 1991); N. Provencher, *Séquences* 153–54 (September 1991): 81–82; F. Richard, "Parfums de femmes," *Positif* (décembre 1992).

୫

FIGURE 11

Masala (Srinivas Krishna, 1991; produced by Camelia Frieberg and Srinivas Krishna) – Zohra Segal (Grandma Tikkoo); Saeed Jaffrey (Lallu Bhai); Madhuri Bhatia (Bibi).

11 *Masala*
(Srinivas Krishna, 1991)

Production: A Strand release of a Divani Films presentation. **Director:** Srinivas Krishna. **Producers:** Camelia Frieberg, Srinivas Krishna. **Screenplay:** Srinivas Krishna. **Cinematographer:** Paul Sarossy. **Editor:** Michael Munn. **Music:** The West India Company, Leslie Winston. **Production Designer, Art Director:** Tamara Deverell. **Costumes:** Beth Pasternak. **Sound:** Ross Redfern. **Choreography:**
Johanika Roth. **Colour, 105 mins., 35mm.**

Cast: Saeed Jaffrey (Lallu Bhai Solanki, Hariprasad Tikkoo and Lord Krishna), **Sakina Jaffrey** (Rita Tikkoo), **Zohra Segal** (Grandma Tikkoo), **Srinivas Krishna** (Krishna), **Jennifer Armstrong** (Lisa), **Madhuri Bhatia** (Bibi), **Herjit Singh Johal** (Anil), **Ronica Sajnani** (Sashi), **Raju Ahsan** (Babu)

Synopsis: This dark comedy set in Toronto's present-day South Asian community follows many narrative threads, all winding out of the Air India disaster of 1985 (a never-solved mid-Atlantic explosion allegedly perpetrated by Sikh nationalist terrorists). Among the hundreds of Indo-Canadian orphans of the explosion is Krishna, an angry young anti-hero who emerges from prison and a detox programme five years later, complete with James-Dean-inspired leather jacket and dangling cigarette, tormented by identity confusion and survivor guilt. Now estranged from his white girlfriend Lisa, a fellow addict, Krishna regains the extended family circle of his uncle, Lallu Bhai, a wealthy sari merchant, the latter's aerobics-obsessed wife, Bibi, and their passive, not-too-bright medical student son, Anil. Krishna gets along better with another more sympathetic household of relatives headed by modest postman and stamp collector Tikkoo: two sympathetic daughters, Rita, an aspiring pilot pressured by her family into a more conventional medical career, and Sashi, disillusioned with Indian men; their elderly Grandma, devout but spunky; and the youngest brother, Babu, who wants to be a real estate agent when he grows up but for now is the frequent butt of racist neighbourhood hooligans. Meanwhile, the epicene and superannuated Hindu god Krishna (painted in traditional divine blue) presides restlessly over this extended family network and develops a special relationship with Grandma through her VCR, intervening just in time to arrange for Tikkoo to acquire a priceless Canadian threepenny beaver stamp that will solve all the family's problems. These problems get worse, however, despite anti-hero Krishna's and Rita's passionate romance, for the former can't find a job, Lord Krishna is faced with increasing irrelevance, the Canadian multi-culturalism ministry harasses the Tikkoos to get back the stamp, Anil's arranged betrothal to a sultry and wealthy prospective bride, complete with MBA, unravels, and the Mounties close in on Lallu Bhai's lucrative business relationship with suspected Sikh terrorists. This already intricate narrative web is further complicated by interludes of song and dance, eroticism, and fantasy, inspired by Bombay cinema. All the plots come together in a law-and-order standoff at the sari shop, and all would end happily with Tikkoo's donation of his treasure to the first National Canadian Centre of Philately but for anti-hero Krishna's tragic death at the hands of racists.

80

Home is not the place one has left

Or *Masala* as 'a multi-cultural culinary treat'?*

———————————————— ১৩

Thomas Waugh

> Help us, Bhagwan [God]. We are outsiders here. Make life the way it was before we came to this land of supply-side economics and no-money-down real estate. (Grandma Tikkoo)

> What happens to Indians when they go to foreign lands? They lose their grace, their composure and they`re constantly pestering me for explanations. (Lord Krishna)

Spice and fantasy

MASALA, the versatile foundational spice mixture of South Asian cooking, provides the title for Srinivas Krishna's first feature film about media, home and exile, ethnic authenticity and hybridity. Masala also establishes a piquant metaphor system for his postmodern fable and, indeed, for many of the discourses of South Asian culture and cinema, both diasporic and metropolitan. A more famous South-Asian diasporic director, Mira Nair, chose an almost identical title for her American film debut, *Mississippi Masala*, earlier the same year. But the metaphor is powerful 'at home' on the subcontinent as well, as in Ketan Mehta's 1985 *Mirch Masala* (literally chillies-masala; the film was distributed unsuccessfully in North America as *Spices*), the liveliest and most irreverent of the Brechtian genre hybrids to have emerged from the Indian New Cinema in the 1980s, a tongue-in-cheek bandit potboiler. Masala is also a common Indian generic handle for much of the spicy box-office fare of Bombay commercial cinema, "kitsch," as Krishna calls it (see Appendix below, 271–72), "Bollywood," as the fan magazines call it. Masala, then, means not only the pungent blends of pepper, turmeric, cardamom, cumin, cinnamon, chillies and cloves, etc,

* Thanks to Srinivas Krishna, Ameen Merchant and Marisa Rossy for their generous help.

that vary according to region, family, recipe, and availability: it also has all of the added connotations of popularity, excess, hybridity, and distinctive South-Asian ethnicity.

Krishna's fascination with masala movies, with Bollywood spectacle, and his absorption of their glitz, energy, and eclecticism constitute one of his most original injections into Toronto's solemn film landscape, a clear signal that, as dozens of critics pronounced, a promising new sensibility had spoken. If, as Rosie Thomas puts it, Bombay films offer

> an emphasis on emotion and spectacle rather than tight narrative, on *how* things will happen rather than *what* will happen next, on a succession of modes rather than linear denouement, on familiarity and repeated viewings rather than `originality' and novelty, on a moral disordering to be (temporarily) resolved rather than an enigma to be solved.[1]

then the kinship of Krishna's film is clear. Interwoven with his dizzying plot meanderings about plane crashes, visiting deities, terrorist intrigue, government perfidy, and teenage love are full-blown fantasy interludes which intermittently take over the screen and dispel any spectator attachment to character motivation and narrative enigma. In interviews, Krishna was frank about the origins of these narrative eruptions:

> In my film there's always a kind of free slippage between the characters' interior life and their objective realities. They intermingle all the time. At any minute a character's interior life could have expression as a fantasy. It's very free-form that way, and a lot of it is inspired by the musical tradition of Hindi films and Indian storytelling. That's part of the information that I carry around in my head.[2]

> I wanted to describe what was going on in [Rita's] head. But how do you give a representation of subjective thoughts? Then, I came up with the idea of expressing her thoughts and emotions by suddenly having her sing and dance [...] I had her talk about her visions of herself, using an American and an Indian musical context, but also a Music Video context [... Bombay cinema] can show you how to open up a dream space, a space of projections and fantasies in the narrative.[3]

---

[1] Rosie Thomas, "Indian Cinema: Pleasures and Popularity," *Screen* 26.3–4 (May–August 1985): 130.

[2] Cameron Bailey, "Indian film spices Canada's ethnic mix," *Now*, undated clipping, 1990.

[3] Grundmann, "Where Is This Place Called Home?," *Cinemaya* 23 (Spring 1994): 25–26.

In fact, the interior lives of all of the major characters are articulated in these non-narrative sequences, whose logic is less psychological than the "dream space" of "emotion and spectacle." Ingenue Rita, for example, expresses her ambition to fly in a sliding series of musical numbers: she leads a troupe of chorines, first past a carousel that somehow evokes both Busby Berkeley and Roy Rogers, then through a kitsch grove of ornate plaster pillars; the chorus line oscillate their lamé bodices and lithe necks in nautch-girl gyrations, then finally leave Rita and Anil on a cloud-borne airplane set. Rita seductively lip-syncs, first in English, then in Hindi, a syrupy playback number (sung by Bombay playback star Asha Bhosle) about the romance of aviation. Anil may be a bit too much of a bumpkin in his hayseed overalls and aviator costumes to be an effective romantic partner, but not for lack of posturings amid the mists swirling about the tacky set. Poor Anil, who in real life spends much of his time masturbating to his mother's aerobics videos and usually looks stunned, gets his own erotic fantasy, which is less celestial than Rita's: a cross-fertilization of Bombay and *Playboy*, in which he deflates the luscious centrefold idol he has constructed of his betrothed with his desperate missionary-position thrusting. Uncle Lallu Bhai's performance is both more mercenary and more carnal, a boisterous rendition of "I Did It My Way," sung amid garment racks, topless models and flouncing saris, the self-made merchant's dream. As for antihero Krishna, his fantasy-number also involves sari pieces, but this time swirling down from the plane explosion, escaping his grasp as he somersaults through the night sky, orientalized in gold pyjamas, necklace and earrings, his chest gleaming, trying to get his bearings in the updrafts of his loss, guilt, and alienation. Grandma's fantasy is anchored electronically in her VCR, a key link in her environment of contemporary domestic technology (her compulsive drive throughout the film is to accumulate the electric masala grinders and blenders that every diasporic housewife is entitled to): Krishna the god appears flirtatiously on her screen, brokering his favours to this transplanted worshipper who won't let him alone. Her down-to-earth stamp-collector son Tikkoo seems to be the only character deprived of a subjective Bollywood fantasy. Tikkoo settles instead for a wish-fulfilment induction into Canadian success-mythology, the inauguration of his stamp museum monument, a fantasy that is pure staid Ottawa rather than glitzy Bollywood. Is it any wonder that every Canadian reviewer stressed how un-Canadian this heady mix of non-narrative fantasy and spectacle is?

As if his departures from the logical coherence of English-Canadian cinematic realism were not enough, director Krishna looks beyond the Grierson
heritage for his broad style of performance excess and characterization as
well. *Masala* is a performers' film par excellence, a star-driven work exulting
in bald and erratic caricature, double and triple takes, disguises and prat-
falls, throwaway one-liners deliriously overwritten and triumphantly de-
claimed (seldom have critics of Canadian films so regularly quoted the
delectable lines of a script – the present author no exception). In this sense,
though John Waters and Pedro Almodóvar are names often invoked in the
literature, *Masala* owes as much to the histrionic excess of popular cinemas
around the world, especially Bollywood, as to the black comedies of the
Western postmodern: none of Egoyan's and Cronenberg's artfilm zombies
dare cross its frameline. Saeed Jaffrey, the Indo-British actor, plays an inspired triple role that was decided on the spur of the moment during his first
encounter with the young director. Jaffrey's participation reportedly assured
the $1.5 million financing from Telefilm Canada bureaucrats apparently
dazzled by his roles in Merchant–Ivory classics and in *Gandhi, The Man Who
Would Be King,* and *My Beautiful Laundrette,* and he especially carries the film
with the gleeful scenery-chomping that critics unanimously praised. (Inevitably compared to Peter Sellers for his zany comic disguises, Jaffrey was
nominated for a Genie, but lost out to the Academy-friendly psychological
realism of Tom McCamus, starring in *I Love a Man in Uniform* – another
Toronto film, interestingly enough, where fantasy impinges on reality but is
a marker of social pathology, not of dream space.) Nevertheless, Zohra
Segal, a well-known elderly theatre and screen performer, also recruited
from England, steals the film, according to several other critics, with her eye-
popping and heart-warming presence, Hindu matriarchy triumphant. Director Krishna's own performance as the rebel of diasporic Generation X (a role
undertaken, his arm twisted by his co-producer Camelia Frieberg, only after
other casting efforts failed) is the other essential ingredient in this perfect
mix: his sultry brooding and erotic intensity, as immobile as the others are
hyper, provides just the right note of balance. Grafting a Wellesian authorial
charisma onto the film, an egotistical sublime previously unknown in Canadian film (even in the work of Bruce LaBruce, Toronto's other actor-writer-
director), Krishna left a few reviewers uncomfortable, sputtering about "stiff
as a board" acting[4] or his "vanity production" (as *Variety* phobically de-

---

[4] Karen Kreps, "*Masala,*" *Boxoffice* (June 1993): R38.

clared at the sight of the authorial penis[5]) but left everyone else gushing. (Has any other English-Canadian performer ever prompted critics to terms like "sexy"[6] and "drop dead gorgeous"?[7]) The death scene, somehow seeming as de rigueur for Krishna as for a Jean Gabin, had an abrupt heaviness that many found out of sync with the tone of the rest of film, but, in a film that every single critic identified as a masala clash of genres, why not? If anti-hero Krishna's street martyrdom provides the accent that is most in stride with traditional mythologies of masculinity in English-Canadian cinema: namely, in the hoary loser-rebel genre from *Nobody Waved Goodbye* through *Paperback Hero* to *I Love a Man in Uniform* – its histrionic excess and pop glitz signal the auspicious departure of director Krishna from the underplayed realism of Canadian cinematic tradition.

Ethnoscapes

The excess of *metteur-en-scène* and performers joins with the flair of the production designer to cement *Masala*'s universe of ethnicity, the film's operation as a visualization of what Indo-American anthropologist Arjun Appadurai would call the "ethnoscapes" and "mediascapes" of the diaspora.[8] Appadurai conceives of "modernity" as a globalized regime increasingly shaped by migrations and media. Its proliferating, deterritorialized populations, affiliated through "ethnicity," language and religion rather than space, are plugged into the "imagined worlds" of ethnoscapes, or what he calls "flows along which cultural materials may be seen to be moving across national boundaries,"[9] landscapes of invented homelands and real or virtual mobilities. This diagnosis lends special resonance to Krishna's repertoire not only of musical and erotic fantasies and performance excess but also of the colours, fabrics, foods, and objects by which his diasporic community constitute themselves, and which were assembled with dazzling authority by his costumers and decorators.

---

[5] Lawrence Cohn, "*Masala*," *Variety* (22 March 1993).

[6] Lawrence Chua, "Passage from India," *Village Voice* (30 March 1993): 63.

[7] Ella Taylor, "Splitting Image: *Masala* celebrates fragmentation," *LA Weekly* (21–27 May 1993): 27.

[8] Arjun Appadurai, *Modernity at Large: Cultural Dimensions of Globalization* (Minneapolis: U of Minnesota P, 1996).

[9] Appadurai, *Modernity at Large*, 45.

Masala's ethnoscape is both volatile and dense, cumulatively layered from many different orders of the iconography of diasporic culture and politics:

1. Culinary, as the title of course suggests. This is a universe where tables are laden with chapatis and tropical fruit, with Grandma's kitchen at the centre, redolent with the spattering of onions in hot oil and lined with cupboards full of spices that burst out at anti-hero Krishna when he tries to make Western-style filter coffee (Anil, another culinary sellout, has mushroom cup-a-soup for lunch). But it is not so much the textures and flavours of foods that are cinematically rendered (as in *Like Water for Chocolate* and *Eat Drink Man Woman*, those other 1990s explorations of the postcolonial interface of food with family and ethnicity), but their apparatus and technology. "What's wrong with this curry?" Grandma demands rhetorically of her family. What's wrong is the primitive mortar and pestle she has had to use to grind the masala, instead of the latest electric gadget. "Good enough in India," Rita tells her, shrugging off Grandma's conviction that machinery is necessary for her matriarchal authority in the diasporic world kitchen. One of the more poignant images in the film is Babu's lunch container, which clatters across the pavement when he is chased by the Paki-bashers: it is the characteristic multi-tiered 'tiffin,' a marker of ethnic nourishment and portability, but Grandma wants to replace it with a Western lunch-pail. Grandma's dream of westernized food technology comes true in the end, for the catering area of the new stamp museum, where a "multi-cultural culinary treat" is being prepared, is alive with whirring motors.

2. Transportation. *Masala*'s ubiquitous jetliners – real planes, sets, toys, and models, exploding not once but twice – are repeatedly captured in the same frame with the anxious, upward-looking Krishna and Rita, who naturally both end up booking air travel at the same South-Asian travel agency. Krishna has explained on several occasions why airplanes are everywhere in his film:

> [The Air India explosion] was really a momentous, horrible event in the history of Indians who live outside of India [...] a turning point, or crossing a point of no return [...] What it began to mean to me was that there is no going home. Here are these people going home, some of them returning permanently, and the plane blows up [...] So I thought, there really is no going home. And you realize it's not the home that you left. And you, having left, are not the same person. So the home that you thought was home only exists in memory.[10]

---

[10] Cameron Bailey, "What the Story Is: An Interview with Cameron Bailey," *CineAction* 28 (1992): 43.

> I believe it may partially be a question of age – that those people who hated the
> film may inhabit an airplane in a way that is very different from the way I
> inhabit an airplane [...] You see we see space and time in a very different way.
> This comes as much from a multitude of transmigrations as from having
> televisions and telephones. The way my film looks and feels comes directly
> from the problems of a rootless life – too much travel, too much technology.[11]

The planes are not objects of national construction and acquisition called for
in Canadian cultural tradition, but fragile symbols of territorial loss, of
transmigration and uprootedness. Interestingly, one of the most 'Canadian'
moments in the film comes not out of planes or from the recurring Mountie
gags scattered through the film, but from an American-style Greyhound:
when anti-hero Krishna boards a bus for Vancouver, a night-time moment
of melancholy fatigue follows and the formulaic Fryean mythologies of
place-names and cross-continental trajectories reassert themselves in this
unlikeliest of conveyances and films.

   3. Electronics. *Masala*'s fantasy spaces of song and movement are inevitably juxtaposed with the more mundane mediascapes of North American
television. Rita's musical interlude is sparked by the boring ethnic commu-
nity-cable show she has playing in front of her. Each of the other characters
has a characteristic electronic fixation as well – Bibi and Anil their aerobics
shows, Babu his real estate infomercial, other characters the glib, superficial
and intrusive newscasting of the "BCB" network. Director Krishna thus provides a seemingly custom-made exemplification of Appadurai's sense of the
mediascape as a fundamental flow of the modern world: "image-centered,
narrative-based accounts of strips of reality." As Appadurai explains, these
accounts

> offer to those who experience and transform them [...] a series of elements
> (such as characters, plots, and textual forms) out of which scripts can be
> formed of imagined lives, their own as well as those of others living in other
> places. These scripts can and do get disaggregated in to complex sets of meta-
> phors by which people live as they help to constitute narratives of the Other
> and protonarratives of possible lives, fantasies that could become prolegomena
> to the desire for acquisition and movement. (35)

The Vancouver critic Yasmin Jiwani has a complementary inside take on the
mediascape scripts specific to the experience of ethnic isolation and its racist
context:

---

[11] Noah Cowan, "Srinivas Krishna, Writer/Director, *Masala*," *Independent* (April
1993): 15.

For the rest of us, who have lived in this country for 20, 30 or 50 years, or for those of us born here, the import of the VCR and television set is anchored in the cultural social reality that surrounds us. Excluded from participation in many of the institutions in the larger society, encouraged to retain our ethnicity but only in a privatized form, we have come to rely on the technologies of communication to maintain a symbolic connection to the `homeland.' We use these technologies to see popular Indian films; we use the TV set so we can access information about the wider society, learn how to get by, learn the symbolic rules and strategies that will enable our survival.[12]

Lord Krishna's VCR *darshan*[13] to Grandma is at the centre of the *Masala* mediascape – he also appears to the doomed Air India passengers thanks to the inflight video monitors, a symbolic connection to the 'homeland' soon to be shattered. Significantly, Lord Krishna's final appearance is not via video, but through a traditional dissolve effect in the midst of the film's standoff climax: what we see is not the triumphant deus ex machina of Hindu mythological films but the tragedy of a decrepit and fading god. The film's transplanted mortals don't need him and tell him to "scram," but he exits, despite the over-the-top burlesque of the scene, with an unexpectedly affecting dignity. The divine presence on the mediascape has yielded to the infomercial.

4. Textiles. An important technology of the mediascapes of pre-industrial India, textiles give *Masala* an iconography that is perhaps closest in spirit to Bollywood. That industry's genius in expressing desire through fabric is the reflection of its host culture, and the model for, among other things, director Krishna's three complete costume changes in a single musical number. As for the sari, that two-metre bolt of printed or woven luxury is the fetish object of *Masala*'s ethnoscape. The sari operates polysemously as an erotic tease in Anil's wet dream, as commodity of world economic domination in Lallu Bhai's, as memento of maternal loss in anti-hero Krishna's. In the latter, in the film's single most haunting image, repeated from the pre-credits crash scene, the Air India saris sift eerily down from the starry site of separation, eluding the anti-hero's outstretched hands. The sari is also the volatile register of tradition in the ethnoscape, which Rita and Sashi grace-

---

[12] Yasmin Jiwani, "*Masala* Take One: The Audience that Didn't Count," *Rungh: South Asian Quarterly of Culture, Comment, and Criticism* 1.3 (1992): 11.

[13] '*Darshan*' literally means 'seeing,' but also more loosely, in the sense of its religious ritual connotation within Hinduism, 'unveiling,' 'presence,' or '[divine] revelation.'

fully alternate with their miniskirts but which the ostentatious matrons of 'multicultural' opportunism brandish like a weapon.

Fundamentally, of course, the sari is a basic sign of gender and sexual difference. As Appadurai remarks in passing, the process of deterritorialization exacerbates the stresses and conflicts, often intergenerational, around family, gender, and sexuality amid the diasporic culture.[14] One suspects that director Krishna's irrepressible prodding of the minefields of sexuality and gender earn him even more detractors in the diasporic communities than his sacrilege about obsolescent gods and sensitive religious minorities. Witness the symptomatic confusion in Jiwani's denunciation of *Masala* for replacing Bollywood virgin-mother-vamp stereotypes with those of the Western 'vamp,' and in other women spectators standing up after screenings to protest that not all Indian women are "like that."[15] (Like what? like the blatantly "promiscuous" centrefold, a walk-on role clearly marked as a fantasy of the alienated Anil? like three of the film's most sympathetic, sincere, and memorable characterizations, Rita, Sashi and Grandma, all of whom operate more or less like sexual agents? like the women meant by Anil and anti-hero Krishna when they agree that "[Pakis] don't fuck, eh?" or those described by Lallu Bhai, who want security out of marriage in contrast to their bridegrooms, who just want a "fuck"?) Needless to say, the sari has an inescapable mythological resonance as well in this ethnoscape of destabilized gender roles: in the Hindu epic *Mahabharata*, Lord Krishna deploys an endless sari to save the honour of heroine Draupadi in the epochal rape scene, when her tormentors try vainly to unwind her sari.[16] Honour has, of course, accrued additional meanings in the late-twentieth-century ethnoscape, but the sari is still inextricably connected to it. *Masala*'s imaging of masculinity engaged other naysayers in an anti-stereotype discourse against the film's males, who sell and fetishize saris rather than wear them. Several misrecognized Sashi's bitter tirade against "mealy-mouthed, mother-loving, woman-hating, self-serving, self-loving, weakminded, yellow-bellied ... limp-dicked, chickenshit" Indian men as the official thesis of a film in which a whole spectrum of surprisingly subtle male characterizations are on offer, charged above all with an uncondescending tenderness for the vulnerability of Anil and Tikkoo alike – and even of the sexist sari merchant.

---

[14] Appadurai, *Modernity*, 44–45.

[15] Jiwani, "Audience," 11.

[16] I am grateful to Ameen Merchant for reminding me of this scene from the *Mahabharata* and for suggesting the resonance.

Sexuality is clearly as politically charged in the ethnoscape as elsewhere, the site of irreconcilable intergenerational stresses in both film and constituency. No wonder that some of the most creative of young South-Asian diasporic artists – the Canadians Deepa Mehta, Ian Iqbal Rashid, and Shyam Selvadurai, the British Pratibha Parmar, Sunil Gupta, and Hanif Kureishi – have focused on sexual orientation as the special field of ferment and creativity in the ethnoscape, an additional marginality layering over all the others. Mehta's *Sam and Me*, offering as one of its high points a sari-drag performance by one of its macho migrants, was frequently mentioned in *Masala* reviews, and Kureishi's ground-breaking *My Beautiful Laundrette* was the universal reference-point for critics coming to terms with *Masala* (and not only because of Jaffrey's virtuoso performance in both). Director Krishna has an undeniable homoerotic tinge to his sensibility – though he is not gay – not only in the campy manner in which he constructs his deity, but also in the frankly erotic way in which he constructs male-bimbo Anil and especially his own sensuous rebel-martyr persona. He certainly has more in common with the young sexual transgressors I have mentioned – and with other non-South-Asian diasporic queer artists such as Gregg Araki or Isaac Julien, with whom he has acknowledged a kinship – than with the Salman Rushdies to whom he's normally compared.[17] Krishna has filmed an ethnoscape in which gender and sexuality are troubled and in flux, and where traditional male heroics yield to the ambiguity of the anti-hero and to the strength, sensuality and authenticity of heroines Grandma and Rita.[18]

Receptions

The rich and irreverent narrative excess of *Masala*, its exuberance in confronting sexual, cultural, and political taboos – above all its reckless surfing along the interface of ethnoscape and mediascape – were no doubt responsible for the wide and dynamic range of official, critical, and audience responses the film triggered as it moved across Canada and around the world. Whether positive or negative, the response was always immediate and forceful. Early on, film-festival bureaucrats in Delhi, fearful for their jobs, abruptly cancelled its featured slot in the 1992 International Film Festival of India, in no mood to accommodate a film that dealt lightly or otherwise with

---

[17] Bailey, Interview, 46.

[18] By no coincidence, Zohra Segal is also the star of the Indo-British *Bhaji at the Beach*, another film depicting a diasporic ethnoscape revitalized through feminine resilience.

Sikh terrorism, especially from the Canada regularly accused by Delhi of harbouring Khalistani extremists. Of course, it didn't help that Krishna at the same time teased Indian excretory phobias with his climactic joke about Sikh history written on rolls of toilet paper, and baited sectarian sensitivities with his unsanctimonious representation of Hindu deities (in a society where films have been known to spark communal riots as well as new Hindu cults and old electoral careers). The situation was certainly not helped by the sexual iconoclasm involved in showing real naked South Asians with genitals, having simulated sex. (Indian film festivals specialize in Western simulated sex and nudity, but uphold the country's fanatically neurotic censorship conventions around the homegrown variety.) The London Film Festival was hardly more enlightened in its own cancellation the previous year, for reasons of "racism" reportedly detected by a white programmer.[19]

This latter Festival's fear of offending its Indo-British constituency was nevertheless justified at least in terms of some spectators, for, as we have seen, the film sparked protests within diasporic audiences wherever it was shown, from literal-minded concerns about blasphemy (the probably untrue contention that Canadians would never allow tax dollars to portray Christ in the same manner as Lord Krishna), to more reasoned arguments about what has come to be known as the burden of representation of minority artists. Jiwani was particularly articulate about her disappointment in this South-Asian diasporic artist who failed to address "our realities as a marginalized community in Canada" with " a story to tell," who "we hoped would articulate some of the experiences that have structured our lives in the west:"

> [*Masala*] violated us, made a mockery of our sense of being, and betrayed us to the wider society. For it was a masala that combined the ingredients of an internalized racism mixed with a postmodernist discourse of identity, sexuality and race, all of which were re-cast in the ahistorical plane of Krishna's vision of himself and his reality. Differences dislocated from their social, cultural and economic grounding floated in the spectacular plane of unreality taking fantastic shapes and grotesque forms.[20]

Jiwani was particularly concerned because she saw the film as a "reluctant ambassador" doing "more harm than good" in full view of the majority Canadian public:

---

[19] Reported regularly in interviews and reviews, eg, Taylor, "Splitting Image," 27.
[20] Jiwani, "Audience," 11.

> [Krishna] has just trashed his culture in a public arena which has no sympathy
> for the South Asian reality. As with the discourse of the mainstream media,
> *Masala* reduces us to a monolith, our differences become merely inflections in
> the great mix of symbols, customs and traditions; a mere fragment in the tiered
> mosaic that is Canada; we are one dimensional yet again.[21]

Interestingly, "one dimensional" is often a term of criticism brought to
bear on Bollywood narratives and characters by elitist South-Asian intellectuals at home and abroad, unconsciously applying unquestioned assumptions about the moral mission and formal structure of 'stories.' It is a
perspective that merges with the 'role model' and 'positive image' aesthetic
that minority critics have repeatedly demanded of 'their' writers and artists
since the 1960s, in Canada and elsewhere, from Mordecai Richler to Hanif
Kureishi and Isaac Julien. The escalating economy of minority invisibility,
disenfranchisement and identity politics in the West is such that minority
artists will probably never escape from this impossible burden of having to
choose between community accountability and individual vision, between
an aesthetic of communal therapy akin to socialist realism and the gamut of
personal expressive styles and imageries that majority artists have had unquestioned access to in the modern and postmodern eras. Some knee-jerk
non-diasporic critics dutifully adhered to Jiwani's position, subjecting Krishna's merciless internal satire to a literal-minded, stereotype-centred critique,
implausibly worrying that spectators might be swayed by anti-hero Krishna's angry dismissal of Hindi as "gibberish"[22] and interpreting the film as
"attacking a culture."[23]

Fortunately, *Masala*'s reception was far from one-dimensional, even
within the diasporic constituency. Director Krishna, no doubt naive in his
unpreparedness for the extreme reactions his iconoclasm would spark, was
reassured by encounters with many young people who repeatedly would
whisper post-screening disavowals of their elders' disapprovals.[24] Critics in
progressive English-language media in India itself also tended to be favourable, disparaging resignedly the censorship that the film encountered in the

[21] Jiwani, "Audience," 13.

[22] The Indian national language, Hindi, is of course a North-Indian lingua franca that
the South-Indian-born director Krishna does not know.

[23] Jacob Levich, "*Masala*," *Cineaste* 20.1 (1993):46.

[24] Described by director Krishna in Sanjay Khanna, "*Masala* Take Two: Cutting Your
Own Deals," *Rungh: South Asian Quarterly of Culture, Comment, and Criticism* 1.3 (1992): 15.

'homeland.' Diasporic critics such as Sanjay Khanna were also fully sympathetic, distancing themselves from

> the insecurity of a community that expects 'its' artists and filmmakers – which it only claims when they are successful – to represent them in a way that will necessarily ennoble them.[25]

Even the dissenters who joined *Variety* in identifying *Masala*'s "first film-itis" for the most part saw the film's lack of discipline and enthusiastically ragged edges as an asset, an index of brilliant energy and assurance of future achievements rather than the market liability diagnosed by the box-office bible. Almost without exception, critics rushed to participate in the culinary metaphor set up by the film and provided headers and verdicts about spices, curries, stews and ingredients, ad infinitum. As for audiences at diasporic crossroads, from London to Los Angeles, all voted at the box office and helped make *Masala* one of Canada's sleeper export successes of the first half of the 1990s, garlanded with laurels and raves.

No matter that Krishna was thereby set up for the notorious "first film syndrome" of Canadian cinema. As they did for the second films of Shebib and Rozema – to mention other first-film directors included in this anthology – critics were waiting with sharpened teeth outside of the 1996 Cannes premiere of Krishna's second feature, *Lulu*,[26] a film in which he took the risk of breaking out of the confining South Asian ethnoscape, all the while maintaining his interest in the culture and politics of race, migration, and sex. But that is another story. What was clear to anyone was that a Canadian filmmaker of the early 1990s who was waking audiences and reviewers out of their stupor around the world must be, like sprinter Donovan Bailey, a local hero to claim.

Nations and canons

Is *Masala* a 'great' film? As a member of an obsessively revisionist, canon-shattering generation, I would question both the relevance and the terminology of the straitjacket question of 'great'-ness. Yet to abstain from Andy Warhol's favourite word does not prevent me from intemperately loving

---

[25] Khanna, "*Masala* Take Two," 16.

[26] For example, the following intemperate pans in two of Canada's largest dailies: Huguette Roberge, "Ca commence bien mal... *Lulu* le premier titre canadien présenté ennuie," *La Presse* (11 mai 1996): C3; Peter Goddard, "Arid still-life sells *Lulu* short," *Toronto Star* (11 October 1996): D13.

Masala for all of its excesses, for all kinds of right and wrong personal as well as professional reasons. Still, the general question of the applicability of critical evaluation and canons to emerging colonized and disenfranchised cinemas, whether diasporic or 'Canadian,' cannot be escaped – nor the specific question of the place of a virtuoso, low-budget, minority-authored first film like *Masala* in the context of a 'national cinema' based in the metropolitan centres of Montreal and Toronto, with all their politics of inclusion and exclusion. How often has the burden of representation been forced upon the various films emerging from the surge of alterity felt in Toronto in the early 1990s that brought Clement Virgo, Midi Onodera, Stephen Williams, Deepa Mehta (and Vancouver's Mina Shum) all into the Telefilm feature film stable! No matter that this surge came long after even more important emergences in short, documentary, experimental and video production, inaugurated as early as the 1960s and featuring names as disparate as Duke Redbird, Helen Lee, Tahani Rached, Richard Fung, Alanis Obomsawin, Julian Samuel, and Paul Wong.

So, rather than wondering if *Masala* is one of *Canada*'s greatest films, we must ask whether the boundaries of national canons are porous enough to accommodate the Ottawa-financed work of this Madras-born, Philadelphia-trained Torontonian,[27] peopled by performers from London, Delhi and Bombay, New York and even Toronto itself. Does the nation enrich or dilute the ethnoscape? Can one address the nation without being subsumed/consumed by it? Even though Robert Fulford may have seen *Masala* as a cure for the ills of Canadian filmmaking and Jim Hoberman recognized the film as "a kind of social experiment *as un-Indian as it is un-Canadian* (and, yet, a film that could have only been made by an Indian in Canada),"[28] it is far from clear that the national uniform fits this outsized work any better than the Toronto Maple Leafs hockey jersey fits the divinely corpulent Krishna. In answer to Cameron Bailey's question about his unease with the Canadian label, director Krishna reflected:

> We all know who controls the stories in Canada, what the story is, and why no one, still, talks about the plane that blew up over the Atlantic, why the ship of Sikhs a hundred years ago is never talked about in history.

---

[27] Who, at the time of writing, alas, had recently obtained his US green card.

[28] Robert Fulford, "The impious film *Masala*: a daring shot at multiculturalism," *Financial Times* (24 February 1992): 34; Jim Hoberman, "Multi Culti," *Village Voice* (30 March 1993): 51.

Fine, I have a Canadian passport. I've spent a lot of time here. But there is no Canadian cinema with reference to my film. It doesn't exist. Canadian cinema comes out of documentary, the observational way of looking at the world. And it's a big lie. Every way of looking at the world is a vested way. So I don't really find a tradition of Canadian cinema to come out of [...] Whether I'm a Canadian or an Indian is irrelevant. That kind of nation-state way of dividing culture is irrelevant to my personal experience. If you can't subscribe to the dominant definition, then either you spend your life banging away at that door, or it becomes irrelevant to you [...] I wrote this script to be set in England, too. And it was cricket, and the Bobbies instead of the Mounties. So the film deals with the icons of Canada. I still feel as alienated as I ever did.

How different is Canada from America than Texas is from the rest of America? It's very hard to say this is Canadian when that whole idea, that whole metanarrative has just crumbled miserably. I don't know. I don't have a soundbite for that.[29]

If you come from India and you live here, and you live everywhere – I've lived in the States, in India and here – then you can't claim any kind of essentialist ground. You can't say, "I am an Indian," or an American or a Canadian. You become some kind of colonial hybrid. You become like a weed in the garden. The only comforting thing about that feeling is that it's going to increase, because more and more of the world is becoming like that.[30]

In a 'national' cinema in which national belonging is officially defined at Telefilm Canada through financing, casting, and technical credit points, in which it is accompanied by box-office invisibility, and in which the hegemony of the coproduction drains away all colour from locality and identity, perhaps the inclusion of a post-national film that asks all of Srinivas Krishna's questions is essential. Perhaps *Masala* can also challenge the presumptions and complacencies of passports throughout the fourteen other oases of 'greatness' in this volume. Or, perhaps its inclusion will simply engender the kind of compromise that Krishna so mercilessly savages with his satire of a cynical and tokenistic multi-culturalism, a compromise in which a fiery masala turns into Tikkoo's 'multi-cultural culinary treat,' a faded yellow, and bitterly stale, machine-ground, supermarket 'curry powder.'

❧

---

[29] Bailey, Interview, 47.
[30] Bailey, Interview, 47.

Filmography

Features

1991   *Masala* (+ screenplay; 105 mins.)
1995   *Lulu* (+ producer, co-screenplay; 89 mins.)
1998   *Waiting for the Mahatma* (+ screenplay; from novel by R.K. Narayan)

Short films and television work

1988   *Fingered!* (15 mins., 16mm)
1989   *The Turned Head* (21 mins., 16mm)
1994   *Burning Skin* (22 mins., CBC TV)
1994   *Tell Me What You Saw* (7 mins., 16mm)
1997   *Terminal, Lyekka,* and *Stan's Trial* (3 episodes from TV series *Lexx: The Dark Zone Stories* [Canada] / *Tales from a Parallel Universe* [USA, released 2000]; 62 mins. each)

Bibliography

Interviews

Amarshi, Hussain. "Power/Knowledge or a new meaning for agency," discussion by Srinivas Krishna and Vic Sarin, moderated by Hussain Amarshi, *Take One* 5 (Summer 1994): 12–15.

Bailey, Cameron. "Indian film spices Canada's ethnic mix," *Now* (1990; Srinivas Krishna collection).

——. "Srinivas Krishna: *Masala* filmmaker's heady hybrid redesigns standards of style," *Now* (6–12 February 1992): 26.

——. "What the Story Is: An Interview with Srinivas Krishna," *CineAction* 28 (1992): 38, 41–47.

Chua, Lawrence. "Passage from India," *Village Voice* (30 March 1993): 51, 63.

Cowan, Noah. "Srinivas Krishna, Writer/Director, *Masala*," *Independent* (April 1993): 15–16.

Grundmann, Roy. "Where Is This Place Called Home?," *Cinemaya* 23 (Spring 1994): 22–27.

MacInnis, Craig. "Why no one is serving Krishna's *Masala*," *Toronto Star* (11 February 1992).

O'Shaughnessy, Catriona. "Storm Warning," *Time Out* (London; 5 August 1992).

Padmanabhan, Chitra. "A Canadian *Masala*," *The Pioneer* (Delhi; 6 May 1992): 13.

Scott, Jay. "A spicy metaphor for a mixed-up messed-up world," *Globe & Mail* (14 February 1992): C5.

Srivastava, Vinita. "Leather, Sex, and *Masala*," *Rungh: South Asian Quarterly of Culture, Comment, and Criticism* 1.1–2 (1992): 15–18.

Essays

Lee, Helen. "Coming Attractions: A Brief History of Canada's Nether-Cinema," *Take One* 5 (Summer 1994): 4–11 (brief survey of ethnic and Aboriginal filmmaking).

Szeman, Imre. "Tracing Patterns of Flight: Ethnicity, Multiculturalism, and *Masala*," *Reverse Shot* 1.2 (Summer 1994): 13–17.

Reviews

Louise Blanchard, "*Masala* de Krishna: un film 'combinaison'," *Journal de Montréal* (26 août 1991); Elizabeth Aird, "*Masala* is one multi-ethnic stew with a few too many ingredients," *Vancouver Sun* (16 October 1991): C5; Craig MacInnis, "Krishna satire ranges from Hindus to hockey," *Toronto Star* (7 February 1992): D10; Robert Fulford, "The impious film *Masala*: a daring shot at multiculturalism," *Financial Times* (24 February 1992): 34; Brian D. Johnson, "The spice of life: Cultures clash in two pungent new movies," *Maclean's* 105.10 (9 March 1992): 52; Paul Delean, "Wry and energetic *Masala* dares to be different," *Gazette* (Montreal; 19 March 1992); Geneviève Picard, "Du film à retordre," *Voir* (Montréal; 19 mars 1992); Martin Siberok, "Spicy Mix: Indian Madness, Toronto-Style," *Mirror* (Montreal; 19 March 1992); Noel Taylor, "New *Masala* film as spicy as they come," *Ottawa Citizen* (3 April 1992); Madhu Jain, "Spicy Stuff: Whacky, inventive look at Indian life in the West," *India Today* (11 May 1992): 149; Ajit Duara, "Hot Stuff," *Illustrated Weekly of India* (9–15 May 1992): 34; Paul McKie, "Spicy *Masala* mixes moods, ideas," *Winnipeg Free Press* (7 June 1992); Élie Castiel, *Séquences* 158 (juin 1992): 49; Derek Malcolm, "Derek Malcolm on a revival of a savage Buñuel and a cheeky new Indian film he would have applauded," *Guardian* (6 August 1992); Farrah Anwar, *Sight and Sound* 2.4 (August 1992): 58; Yasmin Jiwani, "*Masala* Take One: The Audience That Didn't Count," *Rungh: South Asian Quarterly of Culture, Comment, and Criticism* 1.3 (1992): 10–13, repr. as "The Audience That Didn't Count" in *Reverse Shot* 1.2 (Summer 1994): 18–21; Sanjay Khanna, "*Masala* Take Two: Cutting Your Own Deals," *Rungh: South Asian Quarterly of Culture, Comment, and Criticism* 1.3 (Vancouver; 1992): 14–16; Lawrence Cohn, *Variety* (22 March 1993); Stephen Holden, *New York Times* (26 March 1993): C10:1; Stuart Klawans, "Films," *The Nation* (29 March 1993): 427–28; Jim Hoberman, "Multi Culti," *Village Voice* (30 March 1993): 51, 63; David Noh, *Film Journal* 96.3 (April 1993): 33; Ella Taylor, "Splitting Image: *Masala* celebrates fragmentation," *LA Weekly* (21–27 May 1993): 27; Karen Kreps, *Box Office* (June 1993): R38; Jacob Levich, *Cinéaste* 20.1 (1993): 44–46; Carrie Rickey, "Krishna, the kid and life's comedy," *Philadelphia Inquirer* (c1993; Srinivas Krihna collection); Rick Groen, "Elevating the M-word," *Globe & Mail* (7 February 1997); Howard Kissel, "*Masala* tastefully mixes it up," *New York Daily News* (26 March 1997): 52.

Appendix: A Statement by Srinivas Krishna

Masala is a mixture. All these different spices come together in Indian cooking, forming a flavour that wasn't there before: neither is it there in any one of the particular spices – one of the things that is greater than the sum of its parts. But it's a very tenuous unity. Mixture to me is about purity and impurity, authenticity and inauthenticity, truth of self, loss of self, particularly revolving around the idea of kitsch. Because things that are impure are often kitsch. Therefore, the other meaning of the word in the film refers to Bombay kitsch films. By contrast, the pure things, the tradition of purity itself, are both classically Western. [... In] the vast media boom [...] the levels of mediation are so great that they in fact impede memory [...] If you want to keep your identity and your soul, you have to stick to something that is authentic, that will keep you away from nihilism. For migrants, the authentic place is usually the place they've left. If you've been away from that place too long, you try to find the authentic in other themes: rain forests, whales, native cultures, all kinds of primitivisms, or in supporting the rights of minorities – some kind of cause. TV and video, which transmit these themes, become places where identities turn into artefacts of identity. Although those are preposterous identities, they are authentic in and of themselves – it's what people watch. For example, you can't render the entire history of India through movies – you can only claim a very reactionary mass media-, mass culture-oriented set of values from them. [...] I started thinking about [the Air India explosion] in terms of the question, "Can one really go home?" Home, it seems, is not the place one has left. The problem is the search for authenticity and origin. Upon returning to where one has come from, one won't find these things, because one is already destabilised. That got me thinking about Masala as a word.[31]

ɞ

---

[31] Roy Grundmann, "Where Is This Place Called Home?," *Cinemaya* (Spring 1994): 23–24.

FIGURE 12

Léolo (Jean–Claude Lauzon, 1992; produced by Lyse Lafontaine and
Aimée Danis) – Lorne Brass (Fernand's enemy); Yves
Montmarquette (Fernand); Maxime Collin (Léolo).

12 Léolo
(Jean–Claude Lauzon, 1992)

Production: produced 1992, released in Mont-réal 5 June 1992 and in Paris 16 September 1992. Les Productions du Verseau/ Flauch Films/ Le Studio Canal Plus with the partici-pation of the NFB, Telefilm Canada/Societé Générale des Industries Culturelles Québec/ Radio-Québec/ Super Écran/Procirep/ Ministre de la Culture et de la Communication. **Director:** Jean–Claude Lauzon. **Executive Producers:** Aimée Danis, Claudette Viau. **Producers:** Lyse Lafontaine, Aimée Danis. **Co-Producers:** Isabelle Fauvel, Jean–François Lepetit. **Assistant Director:** Jacques W. Benoît. **Screenplay:** Jean–Claude Lauzon. **Cinematography:** Guy Dufaux. **Editor:** Michel Arcand. **Art Director:** François Séguin. **Special**

Effects: Peter Lucraft. **Costume:** François Barbeau. **Colour, 107 mins., 35mm.**

Cast: Maxime Collin (Léolo), **Ginette Reno** (mother), **Julien Guiomar** (grandfather), **Pierre Bourgault** (the Word Tamer), **Giuditta del Vecchio** (Bianca), **Andrée Lachapelle** (psychiatrist), **Denys Arcand** (career adviser), **Germain Houde** (teacher), **Yves Montmarquette** (Fernand), **Lorne Brass** (Fernand's enemy), **Roland Blouin** (father), **Geneviève Samson** (Rita), **Marie–Hélène Montpetit** (Nanette), **Francis Saint–Onge** (Léolo, age six), **Alex Nadeau** (Fernand, age 16), **Gilbert Sicotte** (narrator).

Synopsis: Leo lives with his parents, grandfather, brother and two sisters in a cramped tenement in East Montreal. Save for Leo and his mother, the family is afflicted with a severe catatonia-like mental disorder which necessitates periods of psychiatric confine-ment. Leo's father, brutish and numb from his foundry job, is obsessed by the bowel movements he prescribes for the family's health problems. Leo's first memories are of his mother toilet-training him, and of his painful inability to satisfy her wishes. Renaming himself Léolo to mark the onset of self-awareness, Leo shouts his new name to the winter night sky while peeing from the balcony. As a very small child, he tries to dissociate him-self from his family. Inspired by the only book that has made its way into his home, Leo plans his escape from the wretched genetic fate of the Lauzons heredity and environment through writing, committing his thoughts and impressions to any scrap of paper he can find. He is sustained by his vision of a perfect reader, whom he calls the Word Tamer. A derelict by day, picking through garbage bins, the Word Tamer lives by night in a candle-lit heaven of lost and forgotten art objects, where he savours and stores Leo's scraps of writing. Leo is also drawn to Bianca, a neighbouring Italian teenager who embodies for him the innocent peasant vitality of Sicily, a mythical spiritual homeland to which he dreams of going with the girl. Leo's older brother, Fernand, escapes daily humiliations through body-building. Leo witnesses him being given a beating by the same bully who had laid into him as a child. Approaching adolescence, Leo becomes increasingly rash, heartless and self-destructive, and joins a group of boys who experiment with drugs, sex, and animal torture. Leo tries to kill his grandfather (who has been sexually exploiting Bianca) by hanging him while he bathes. Finally, Leo falls into a coma, and is transferred to a hospital-asylum. The Word Tamer continues to preserve the fragments of Leo's efforts – as a writer – to give form and meaning to his tumultuous childhood experience.

Drowning for love
Jean–Claude Lauzon's *Léolo*

———————————— ∞

George Toles

" the image is fast fading out. The light that made it now dismantles
it." (Robin Robertson, "Camera Obscura")

W ITH HIS DEATH IN A PLANE CRASH IN 1998, Jean–Claude Lauzon's brilliant film directing career came to a premature end after
only two feature films. Lauzon's only other feature, *Un zoo la nuit* (1987),
combines two stories. The first (and more compelling) is a quasi-autobiogra-
phical account of a son's relationship with his dying father; the second
follows a *policier* plot in which this same son, in his profession as a drug
dealer, attempts to evade capture by repellent law officers. The film has
received numerous awards (including nominations in thirteen of the fourteen categories in the Genie Awards – the Canadian Oscar – and best-film
prizes in Montréal, Québec, Toronto, and Belgium), as well as a *Quinzaine*
invitation to Cannes. While still a teenager, Lauzon admits, he had led a
freewheeling life on the criminal fringes of the streets of Montreal, before
returning to finish school and enrol in film studies courses at university. His
youthful experience of "plunging up to my neck in violence without really
knowing why,"[1] his first-hand familiarity with the urban punk-squatter
scene, and his defiant experiments with homosexuality all inform Lauzon's
first feature. The film's propensity towards the dark extremes of human
behaviour and its exploration of the sensuous surfaces of the decaying
material world are characteristics that Lauzon carries over into *Léolo*, where
the focus turns sharply inward, into the community of a single family.

---

[1] Jean–Claude Lauzon, "Le Zoo: C'était ma raison de vivre," in ⌊Marie–Christine Abel,
André Giguère & Luc Perreault, ed., *Le cinéma québécois à l'heure internationale*, 207–209.

Imagining memory

Léolo is the record of a struggle between two desires: the desire to face brave-
ly and without shame all the ways in which Lauzon belongs to his strangely
cursed family, and the desire to withdraw from membership in this family.
Lauzon revisits his childhood because this is the place where his memories
of both subjection and love are strongest and least dismissable. Within
memory, as Luis Buñuel once suggested, we find, if anywhere, "our coherence, our reason, our feeling, even our action."[2] The idea of our memory
disappearing is terrifying because we know that our most intimate selfhood,
salvaged bit by bit from the wreckage of our days, will vanish with it. Yet
memories are never merely our benefactor. Holding painful ones at a
manageable distance takes up much of our mental energy. Those that can't
be moved from the glare of full consciousness or the dark of absolute denial
are like tumours, and it seems scarcely an exaggeration to speak of their
lethal power. Part of Lauzon's reason for making *Léolo*, then, is to make
memory into a controllable structure, to become its author, as it were, so that
it will somehow reconcile rather than exacerbate his warring desires.

Lauzon's method of looking back at his childhood reminds us that
memory does not enjoy being literal, or taking even the most dire situations
at face value. Memory does not move in straight lines, nor does it assemble
things in proper sequence. Who among us absorbs our daily life straight,
without steady supplements of differently pitched emotional responses? We
imagine what we experience, not only after the fact but while it is going on.
That capacity is what steers whatever we undergo in a personal direction.
Imagination, our best survival mechanism, refines the raw materials of our
outward plight. As a conserving force, it helps memory decide what is
worth holding on to when so much that happens passes so swiftly into
oblivion. And, as a curative, imagination lightens forms of affliction that
would, in an unaltered state, prove unbearable.

For Lauzon, an imagination that operates passively and unrebelliously in
collaboration with external forces will very early on lose its power to make a
difference. The child, to put it simply, will stop seeing. Lauzon conceives the
child that he was as balancing on the tightrope that imagination has given
him. This rope is stretched across a mind forever in danger of sinking into
numbness or idiocy. If the rope breaks (an ever-present possibility), there
will be no other. Lauzon believes he can only keep his imagination alive and

---

[2] Luis Buñuel, *My Last Sigh*, tr. Abigail Israel (New York: Vintage, 1984): 5.

strong by occupying it like a warrior. In order to take control of memory and construct anew his still festering childhood environment, he must begin by setting himself at odds with all the elements of reality that have been assigned to him by others. The world he inhabits shall be reduced to as few givens as possible.

For Lauzon, what counts as a given is anything that undermines the transforming power of dream and fantasy. The presumably natural first facts that set most life histories in motion – one's biological parents, the name on one's birth certificate – are, in Lauzon's view, so treacherous and steeped in fate that to concede their truth (as a settled matter) is already a death warrant. Lauzon's origin is as much a quandary and a playground for conjecture as Tristram Shandy's.

The first story presented in *Léolo* tells us that Leo's true father is an anonymous Italian peasant who once upon a time insolently masturbated on a tomato marked for shipment to Canada. Some days later, this same tomato, by happy accident, became lodged in Leo's mother's womb long enough for her to be impregnated. Lauzon presents this buffoonish, squalid alternative to the 'known facts' of his birth with as much giddy pride in his new status as if he had been revealed, fairy-tale fashion, to be the lost son of a king. It is as though any more extravagant wish for a different lineage would be denied fulfilment because the imagination proved too greedy. The prospect of connecting himself to a better place (Sicily), and to a father who is at least sane, is so appealing to the child-author Lauzon that he willingly foregoes all thought of a higher class or any increase in privileges. In the kingdom of the unfortunate, the attention of the gods is not easily won, and one must keep one's demands not only modest but amusing to tempt their generosity. Lauzon revises his ancestry by placing himself as far beyond his father's genetic reach as a hard-nosed, peasant fable will permit. The semen-splattered tomato can be viewed as a temperamental recoil from romantic gestures that are too high-flown, too withdrawn from the wormy, lower earth that powerfully feeds Lauzon's dream life. Though there is a fierce romantic strain in Lauzon's work, there is an equally intense need to weight every transcendent impulse with the mean refuse of poverty. However much contempt he feels for his family's enslavement to a life without curiosity, comfort or art, Lauzon cannot betray that life by distancing himself, for any length of time, from its harsh materials. His heart lies down amidst harrowing things, and knows itself to be at home there, despite the spirit's yearning to pitch its tent on higher ground.

Léolo is a film haunted by the difficulty of beginning. Lauzon doesn't want to think of his beginning as an irreversible first step, one which duplicates the mechanism of heredity and commits him (just by the nature of stories) to a determinist view of things. He aspires to dissolve, as much as possible, the constraints of filmic time and space, so that he can hover above his life for a while, like an aircraft, and not belong to any image which too decisively identifies him. The effort to avoid discovery and naming suggests a fear of not being sufficiently protean in his sense of himself. To be discovered seems to carry with it the threat of being seen through and dismissed. And yet, Lauzon's drive to reveal himself – totally – is as great as his dread of being trapped in a too-limited identity. To possess yourself with any force, he repeatedly suggests, you must not be afraid of losing anything to others' zeal for judging by appearances. So, how to begin?

Beginning properly means clearing a space large and indeterminate and fluid enough to allow the film's young protagonist to manoeuvre freely. The opening must not feel like a settled place, giving spectators the confidence to attach Leo to a background with certain tidy meanings. Lauzon is determined to outwit potential jailers of all sorts, whether they present themselves as family members or moviegoers who assume that their decision to watch *Léolo* grants them some authority over its subject. Lauzon's anxiety about fixed starting-points can only be relieved by the decision to have his narrative begin not once but many times – so often, in fact, that one quickly loses track of sequential order. Each new beginning, by the force of its images and sounds, attempts to loosen the grip of what has preceded it.

Lauzon protects his surrogate's own first appearances within the fearsome house of childhood by making the viewers' points of entry to this dwelling confusing and provisional, implying that every room comes equipped with a secret escape route. (The unstable narrative time-frame, which overlaps several different periods of Lauzon's childhood with no obvious system, creates temporal escape routes to go along with the enticing domestic passageways the camera reveals to us.) The rhythm of the film is established immediately as a tug-of-war between images of enlargement and images of compression. The sudden expansion of conventional boundaries keeps pace with a ruthless litany of privations. Cramped rooms enlarge, natural vistas open up, time hangs luxuriously suspended in the dusty, somnolent air whenever freedom of any kind seems attainable. In those blessed intervals when the child's solitude appears like a fantastic jewel unmenaced by the clamour and contagious stupor of his kin, or by the sheer hardness of the world outside, Lauzon shows him effortlessly entering into realms bright with revelation. Light pours through an open closet door, a girl's voice rises in welcoming song, and Leo, like Saul on the road to Damascus, is shaken by visions fragrant with love and ecstatic surrender – the rending nearness of fulfilment. Solitude, in its productive hours, is, in Bruno Schulz's phrase, "the catalyst that brings reality to fermentation."[3] But Lauzon is compelled to add: take care that you don't withdraw too deeply inside it. Ineluctably joined to solitude's beautiful fever is the steady threat of his family's hereditary madness. Haunting the heroic solitary in Lauzon is the spectre of tiny, enfeebled destinies, beckoning him in chains.

"Yes" and "No"

The rhythmic alternation between views of things opening up and closing down is tied to Lauzon's belief in reversal as the first law of narrative movement. I use the word 'reversal' in the hope that it can be readily distinguished from its frequent companion, 'negation.' Unlike many reviewers of *Léolo* who were repelled by the film's apparent coldness and self-absorbed despair, I do not see Lauzon's main concern as the negation of possibilities. The frank depiction of childhood horrors might initially suggest an angry survivor's settling of accounts with those who have made him suffer. But vengeance recovers nothing of interest from reactivated 'time past,' as Lauzon well knows. Every window and door that memory yields to the man bent on retaliation turns out to be a wrong entrance. The rooms have no colour, the air is poisonous, the time that he would re-live is used-up time, where nothing but frozen, hyperbolic gestures remain.

To regard memory as the scene of a vast crime against yourself – even when the impulse seems justified – tends to make everything one retrieves impervious to clear light. Getting at the truth is confused with a fixation on wrongdoing. The moment of revelation is likely to mean catching someone in an unforgivable act – where the truth-teller plays the part of the blameless victim. One of the terrible facts of life is that real victims, like persecutors, must live in time, which means moving past the moment where an event has a pure, unmistakable shape. Perhaps such moments are never fully available to consciousness. Going back to the evil done against you, however necessary in a court of justice or in a therapy session, requires one to play a role

---

[3] Bruno Schulz, *The Street of Crocodiles*, tr. Celina Wieniewska, intro. Philip Roth (New York: Penguin, 1977): 22.

personalized account

that was formerly lived messily, and it is never an exact fit. Often we damage ourselves, and our memory, by trying to make the fit exact. Remembered acts of cruelty and neglect on the part of others can so easily become all-encompassing. A person who has done us injury can be reduced in memory to a single, defining gesture, performed by rote, like a mechanical figure on a clock who appears through a certain door whenever the hour strikes.

Reversal, as Lauzon employs it, is an attempt to keep the possibilities of "yes" and "no" equally in play at all times, by moving us back and forth between the two poles with bewildering rapidity. "Yes" and "no" – what can be affirmed and negated in every situation – are pressed very close to each other throughout *Léolo*. Lauzon's framing, camera movement, editing and elaborate voice-over narration all work to set antithetical values side-by-side, in intimate, quarrelsome relation, like the two brothers in the film (Leo and the mountainous Fernand) forced to share a single bed. Reversal, of course, is one of the most common devices in drama, and is fundamental to any successful film technique. What does Lauzon's formal and ethical approach to reversal require of us in this film?

Just as it is impossible for an actor to play two contrary intentions or feelings at the same moment, it is impossible for a movie spectator to occupy strong "yes" and "no" emotional positions (relative to a character) simultaneously. Both actors and spectators, however, have the ability to shift from one feeling to another very quickly. Only an instant or two is required to traverse large emotional distances, and to do so with remarkable precision. Every good film editor knows that the main function of a cut is to keep the emotion of a scene flowing, by fair means or foul, and that flow demands, paradoxically, a certain clash and tension between the images. One adds an image of 'something else' to set what has come just before in relief. The 'something else' applies some sort of 'reversal' pressure to the preceding image that keeps viewer-expectation alive and very often builds up a need to get back to what has been taken away from us, so we can see (and, the editor hopes, feel) what has altered in our brief absence from it. Prolonged camera movement is editing by other means, removing things from view to reveal other things, ideally in a manner that turns spectator-feeling in a different direction. Things must forcefully strike the viewer's eye in passing to register at all on film. Each new element that appears should seem to separate sharply from what it replaces, so that it will gain some of its impact through its relation to what is no

longer visible. In other words, one can be led to feel what is left behind as
the camera goes forward, so that successive disclosures rustle with trans-
ience. There is a continual subtle revision of the emotional landscape in a
well-planned tracking shot, like sunlight moving in and out of cloud-cover.
And the idea of objects taking over the light from other objects reminds us
of photography's close kinship with death's slow dissolve. ✕

Lauzon clearly understands how a camera's movement can remove
things from view in an emotionally charged way. For him, the removal is
most often allied with death and loss. When his camera tracks through the
unfastened, banging windows of his parents' bedroom on a lightning-filled
night, trying to make contact with his earliest memories, we seem to be
floating through a kind of funeral in the brain. Instead of having the sense of
a scene being restored to life, one feels that all signs speak of life slipping
away. The room is lit by banks of candles; an angelic hymn swells up like a
tide to make mourners of us as we slowly advance. Father is sprawled
motionless on a bed, fully clothed, almost an apparition on the more solid
mass of rumpled bedding. What is our destination? A cavernous bathroom,
in which a small wailing child is held prisoner on a makeshift potty. All the
forces conspiring against growth, freedom, rescue of any sort seem to greet
the desolate camera-visitor as it closes in on the bathroom. The fantastic
array of candles with their permeating warm light do not work against the
oppressiveness or provide any real shelter from the thunderstorm atmosphere. The candles seem tied to the crooning voice of the mother, who faces
her child – huge and inescapable as a church service – from her own toilet
seat, urging him to "push, my love" and to stop crying. She holds a flashlight, which she points at him like a prison searchlight. Here we have an
honest but profoundly misguided expression of love, whose capacity to
injure is vastly increased by its well-meaningness. Who can measure the
price of love? "Kind, gentle mama nails me to this pot each night, and if I am
to please her I must empty myself. Whatever I give up, let go of, she tells me
she can replenish with her hugs."

This episode, and others like it, introduce soft, gleaming, lavishly beautiful materials and then promptly reverse their pleasurable associations. A
ravishing visual surface becomes our channel into bitter, corporeal hells.
Horrific images, in Robert Lowell's celebrated line, "meat-hooked from the
living steer,"[4] erupt from openings where something benevolent and healing

---

[4] Robert Lowell, quoted in Mark Rudman, *Robert Lowell: An Introduction to the Poetry*
(New York: Columbia UP, 1983): 144.

philosophical musings

seems poised to reveal itself. Occasions such as these bring forth the desperate, negative vein in Lauzon's visionary style; imagination and memory
seem helplessly in thrall here to repudiation. The act of recollecting can so
easily leave one stunned by the sheer quantity of things in life that cannot be
undone. But if the camera, in its strange devil's pact with the world of
appearances, can continually discover the monstrous within the beautiful, it
also has an uncanny gift for resurrecting whatever it so firmly places in
death's hands. The camera restores hope by the same means that it takes it
away – once again, the simple act of *reversing* direction.

The time of a film is reversible time. Anything that enters the time-sphere
of a moving picture can be returned to, reclaimed for the attention 'just as it
was' (through a repeating shot) or slightly but crucially transformed (as an
alternate take). The reversal and pliability of time's motion is film's way of
proclaiming, potently, that whatever is destroyed now is gone only condi-
tionally. The whole of time, insofar as film can apprehend it, is "a mass of
conjoint possibilities"[5] whose editing order again and again averts the inevitable. A camera's farewell to an image can be final or momentary. Movement away may eventually come full circle, and give anything back to us,
shining with the full light of our first beholding. The dead can be restored to
life, so that we may watch them turn their attention once more to interrupted tasks: washing themselves, opening the blinds to check the weather,
coming down to breakfast. A gesture or phrase that never found its 'proper'
moment completes itself. Missing pieces are magically found; the child or
parent given up for lost suddenly appears, moving up the path toward
home. Robert Graves's lovely phrase, "past all hope where the kind lamp
shone,"[6] evokes the emotional space in any shot sequence where the forces
of "no" unaccountably yield to expanded boundaries of life.

In *Léolo*, scenes are often re-played with slight variations, at a later point
in the narrative, reversing the significance of our first reading. Repetition can
be traumatic, in film narratives as in nightmares, but it can also provide
chances to approach the same set of binding conditions by different routes,
and gradually to make them manageable. Repetition in *Léolo* also deliberately assumes the character of religious rituals. Brutal and profane elements
are lifted – on their second and third appearances – into the realm of the
sacred, and not merely for the sake of parody. Toxic images, which initially

---

[5] Jean Cocteau, *Cocteau on the Film: Conversations with Jean Cocteau*, tr. Vera Traill (New
York: Dover, 1972): 129.

[6] Robert Graves, *Collected Poems* (London: Cassell, 1975): 133.

seem to express a scalding hopelessness, often come back to us as a place of renewal. Total prostration is often the nesting ground for rapturous mystery.

Answered prayers

How does Lauzon intercede on behalf of the infant wailing on his potty in the depths of night? How does he turn the mother who regards her son's shit as the proof – indeed, the very image – of his love for her into a credible provider of freedom, emotional ease, and self-possession? He accomplishes this transformation in two stages. While we are still looking at the distressed infant in close-up and listening to his cries, a space beside him opens in the frame, revealing the head of an elderly man, radiating benevolence, who is reading in his study. The camera moves into this new environment with such a smooth, gentle motion that the study becomes a wing of the bathroom, continuous with it in space and time. Candlelight of a less ominous sort is also the source of illumination here. The mother's grotesquely abortive efforts to soothe and encourage are translated in the old man's features into the quality of loving acceptance that they mean to be. The old man's voice repeats the fragment of narration that we have just heard spoken by Leo's adult self, who throughout the film softly reads to us from the child Leo's journal – his book of memory. The old man has somehow come into possession of the scraps of paper on which the toilet-training memory was first set down. He is a *second* reader, an ideal reader, one fully responsive both to what the writing directly conveys and to what it aims to express, without quite knowing how. He echoes the phrase "the smells and the light that solidified my first memories." He laughs with appreciation at Leo's reference to his grandmother's fervent belief in daily bowel movements as a cure-all.

Our brief contact with this sympathetic eavesdropper on Leo's anguished first memory begins to reverse its emotional meaning. We are reminded that the rawness and chill of the primal suffering are, to some degree, ameliorated by their passage into another medium – written language. More important, however, is the suggestion that the struggle to make sense of what happened is not merely another form of isolation. The rough notes the boy has composed, no matter how disjointed or incomplete, have found their way into safe hands. The old man, whom the narrator will later identify as the Word Tamer, takes each of Leo's tangled messages into his luminous understanding, and surrounds them with his own healing quiet-

ness. He 'tames words' in the same spirit that one might calm a frightened
animal – stroking every phrase with his gentle voice, keeping close watch
over Leo's feverish outpourings until the agitation shows signs of abating.

Lauzon's other attempt to redeem the endless night of potty captivity
(stage two of the transformation) comes several scenes later, after we have
watched an older Leo refuse to swallow the laxative that he and every
member of his family gather to receive, like communion wafers, each day.
When we return to the crying infant on his pot, lit by the same thunderstorm, with mother still intoning her grim instructions about "pushing" and
"not crying," another observer has entered the scene. Resting in an adjoining
bathtub is a turkey, which, the narrator tells us, Leo's mother has won at a
movie theatre. The turkey's head rises above the rim of the tub and meets
the child's gaze with what feels like vehement alertness. Though the bird's
foulness is stressed in the narration ("its remaining feathers were damp and
stinky"), it functions in this context like an emissary from some delectable
golden isle. It distracts the child from its misery enough so that he stops
crying. The turkey then raises itself to an imposing height, becoming
through this act of resplendent, unchallengeable wildness the strongest presence in the room. Mother instantly loses her capacity to hold her son's mind
'in custody' to his ordeal.

As she repeats the injunction "Do like mama," the camera follows the
child's freshly liberated gaze into the dark mystery between her outspread
legs on the toilet. Lauzon seems initially to have chosen an escape route
from the scene that will only compound the obscenity of what transpires. It
feels as though the child's eye is carrying us toward a destination that is
clammily taboo: an engulfing womb steaming with the odor of defecation.
But on the far side of this stygian corridor an unexpected realm of marvels
awaits us. A joyful tribal chant suddenly rings out on the soundtrack,
summoning us to a celebration in the underworld. Two figures wearing illuminated miners' helmets move toward the camera from the far distance, in
what appears to be a gigantic, drizzling cavern. The darkness glistens with
light flaming up from free-standing torches. We soon identify Leo – here a
young boy – as one of the two fearless travellers in the night world. His
older companion is the Word Tamer. Both carry identical buckets, which
serve, like the matching helmets, to link the pair together on a shared mission. Their breath is visible in the cold, but no discomfort registers. Adversity has turned magical, as it so often does for children included in a grown-
up adventure.

We cut away from this walking scene for a view of the Word Tamer's private museum, the camera tracking through a collection of beautiful art objects, in pleasing disarray. The Word Tamer is once again silently reading a manuscript. Who exactly is this man? What sort of reality does he inhabit, and how is it connected to the child's? The narrator tells us here that the old man spends his nights "digging in the garbage of the world. Only letters and photographs interest him." (In other words, he is drawn to documents imbued with feeling which actively seek out fellowship, along with pictures preserving odd bits of memory from extinction.) The narration continues: "He carried every smile, every glance, every word of love, every separation as if it was his own story." The Word Tamer's identity, as it gradually fills out for us, is that dimension of Leo's imagination which says "yes" to the world, despite all evidence of the world's frightening unresponsiveness. The Word Tamer keeps alive the dream that there is some presence on earth, however hidden from sight, that is passionately *for* us. He is the imagination's answer to prayer, a kindred soul who sees and sustains and encourages us in the very depths of our solitude. Our actions and thoughts do not rebound back on themselves like the remains of some idle fantasy. The power of our attentiveness to the world elicits a similar force of attentiveness in things themselves. The process of opening ourselves unreservedly to an object may strengthen its ability to direct an answering light back to us. As in Rilke, the answering presence, or Word Tamer, moves closest to Leo when he is least acquisitive, when he is prepared to let everything, fear as well as security, go. "The serene/countenance dissolved in night makes room for yours."[7]

When we leave the Word Tamer's museum we are once more outdoors, facing a bonfire before which Leo and the Tamer, still in their miners' helmets, are sitting. Leo takes an armful of irreplaceable letters and photographs that the old man offers him and, as he has been directed, drops them into the blaze. The camera – called to witness the death of its own powers – closes in as a number of poignantly old portrait photographs are consumed. How quickly the preserved, singular faces blur together, blacken, and vanish. The narration accompanying this sacrificial ceremony declares the Word Tamer's belief that "images and words must mingle with the ashes of the worms to be reborn in the imaginations of men." The fight with isolation that Leo wages throughout the film receives its purest, but most difficult

---

[7] Rainer Maria Rilke, *Uncollected Poems*, tr. Edward Snow (New York: Farrar, Straus & Giroux, 1996): 57.

visualization of remedy in this scene. Only once in *Léolo* are Leo and the Word Tamer able to be together, as comrades unseparated by distance. While the narrator speaks of the Word Tamer's desire to be Leo's protector, we are granted a stunning long-shot view of the two of them on a tiny bit of dry land, tending their fire with a solitary tree behind them. On all sides are roaring cataracts, plunging to unseen depths. The sky above the lonely watchfire is threateningly dark. The narration links the torrential flow of water with the 'black hole' of Leo's family, reminding us that this entire fantasy segment commenced as a journey 'backward' into the mother's womb. The final image of the two of them yields many revelations at once. The forces of freedom have been mobilized; a child blossoms forth as an entity capable of withstanding the terrors of helplessness, able to make his own peace with a world that is not impossibly distant, not closed off. Leo entrusts his homelessness and habitual dread to someone fully attached to life and warmth, an old man who shares the boy's burden and shows him how to set it down, shows him that every external sign of his being *becomes* more real when it is moved inside him. Passing through fire and ashes does not necessarily result in death. The imagination needs to disintegrate the forms that it will later resurrect and consecrate. It is a secular version of Christ's summons: he who would save his life must first lose it.

In *Léolo* the camera takes instruction in how to see from the quiet, end-lessly attentive and patient Word Tamer. Its vision strives to acknowledge "every smile, every glance, every word of love, every separation" as vital to its "own story," and regards every instance of neglect as a failure of the moral imagination. (I think it is fair to say that there is a will to coldness in Lauzon himself which he *needs* the camera to oppose.) When the Word Tamer dimension of Lauzon is in command, the camera endeavours neither to flatter nor to abuse what it holds in view. Lauzon often seems to catch himself slighting the value of small, positive gestures in those scenes where cruelty and pathetic compulsions so fully dominate viewer attention that meaningful compassion seems unthinkable. If Lauzon's family history often runs the risk of becoming a sterile, repetitive mechanism, the Word Tamer is the ethical force that moves this history *beyond* the mechanical. He divines the pause-space in every stretch of filmic time when love or its possibility can manifest itself. He – and his camera surrogate – are forever on the look-out for "the space a man was meant for," as Brad Leithauser has termed it, "wrested from the drowning green and blue."[8]

---

8 Brad Leithauser, *The Mail from Anywhere* (New York: Alfred A. Knopf, 1990): 6.

We are made mindful of this space, and its spiritual contours, as early as the film's opening shot. The camera begins by showing us the top of a building with the year of its construction (1909) engraved like a headstone-marking at its highest point. (Lauzon has acknowledged in interviews that the building is the actual house he grew up in.) As the narrator addresses us for the first time, identifying what we are seeing as "*my* place," in Mile End, Montreal, Canada, the camera gradually descends, passing a shabby-looking upstairs balcony containing some aluminium lawn chairs, and a long set of steps leading up to the house's entrance. Without pausing to settle on him, the camera notices a young boy in a cowboy hat seated on one of the steps, taking aim with a toy rifle at some unseen target in the distance, and firing. It is crucial to the design of this shot that the camera passes over the boy and his initial flourish of bored, make-believe aggression, as though he were not what the viewer should focus on and validate. Before we go back to him, something larger than the child's immediate hostility needs to be located and embraced.

After Leo disappears from the frame – so casually observed that he cannot achieve point-of-view authority – our gaze comes to rest, and seemingly widens out, at ground level. We pause, in a way that feels effortless, in a space that is alive with ordinary beauty, altogether different from the drab markers of poverty and confinement with which the shot commenced. An open downstairs window catches our attention in the middle distance because its curtains ripple in the morning breeze with a lacy delicacy. Two bicycles rest in the grass, conveying a hopeful summons to adventure from the warmest summer recesses of childhood memory. When the camera halts in this enchanted corner of the yard and cleanly lifts us out of the shot's original feeling of stale hemmed-in-ness, one is reminded of how much the play of contingency determines the mood of vision. The duration of the camera's hold on this view is necessary for its soothing quality of interiority to sink in. Only in this spot, and perhaps only from this exact angle, can the setting release its power to console, and possibly improve the lot of the child 'doing time' here. But a tension arises from the fact that the boy with the rifle is so strikingly cut off from the camera's healing vantage-point.

How does Leo partake of this authoritative first 'outspreading' of vision? The answer arrives in the highlighted transition from this shot to the one that succeeds it. A slow lap-dissolve causes the mystery of the softly billowing curtains to generate a spectral after-image, as if in reply to the question: "What good thing might lie within such an enticing window frame?" We sense almost a rustle of dim objects before we are able to make out an older version of the first child labouring at his writing desk. The voice-over phrase, "Because I dream, I am not," is introduced as a knife-edge dividing line between the two realms – exterior and interior. The second moving-camera shot (boy at writing desk) is subtly proposed as the creative source of the 'memory' shot preceding it. Note once again how the camera reverses the direction (and meaning) of the earlier shot while seeming to expand upon it. The place of seeing becomes the boy who is committing words to paper. It is as though he were the hidden presence in the curtained window who is imaginatively recovering the one, easily overlooked point of equilibrium in his environment: the rescue point. It is the point at which the scattered, unpromising materials of the boy's world come together and form a whole. We are granted access, as he is, to the ideal dreaming space, and thus have the sense of fitting the right key to the right door of the past. For the moment, at any rate.

Dreams in cold storage

"Because I dream, I am not." This oracular pronouncement returns again and again in the film's narration, as though Lauzon had managed to find just once his true home "in one sentence, concise, as if hammered in metal." (Czesław Miłosz regards this securing of 'home' in an unforfeitable 'sentence' as the chief aim of his poetry, his best chance against "chaos and nothingness."[9]) How large does the "not" loom in Lauzon's trim credo, and what is left over when the force of negation has spent itself? The "not," I have argued, attaches itself to all the limiting labels and coercive alliances that form around the child without his consent and seek to hold him hostage. "I am *not* this man's son; I am *not* the same as these others; I am *not* mad; I am *not* ruled by fear or shame; I am *not* alone." The assertive "I dream" opposes itself to these and other ambushes of the vulnerable psyche. The waking dream resembles in its activity the routine survival mechanisms of most afflicted children: blotting out the source of distress by turning the inner gaze elsewhere, it hardly matters where. A television screen will serve as well as a drug, a favourite piece of music, a computer game, or a pet one might alternately hug and torture. Children, like everyone else, require a

---

[9] Czesław Miłosz, *The Collected Poems 1931–1987* (Hopewell NJ: Ecco, 1988): author's note on back cover.

'beyond,' and most of the time, again like their elders, they reach automatically for the one that lies closest.

The important questions to ask about escape routes, as Ernest Becker recommends in *The Denial of Death*, are: "What kind of beyond does [the] person try to expand in; and how much individuation does he achieve in it?"[10] Reading and, preeminently, imaginative writing are, of course, Leo/Léolo's chosen methods of attaining a meaningful beyond, but what kind of 'beyond' do they afford access to, once denial and escape have done their utmost? Let us extend Becker's list of questions. Once Leo has found the courage to say "NO in thunder"[11] to the soul-shrivelling options others set before him, what does he find within and outside himself to accept and make his peace with? Are the glimpses of beauty that the observant child encounters in the most unlikely places and 'catches' in language for the Word Tamer (as his sister catches pleasing insects in a jar) – are these glimpses adding up to some sort of progress of love? Is his rage against authority an insurmountable impediment to his desire to lay himself open to things? Does his longing for freedom move him (compulsively, self-protectively) in a different direction from his longing to love? Is there any chance of the two longings being revealed, in a gratifying denouement, as the same thing?

Surely the oddest feature of *Léolo*'s structure is its ultimate insistence that the child has failed in his project, that he has not proven strong enough to evade the 'living death' sentence that has claimed most of the others in his family. Our last view of the boy in the film's *present* tense shows him harrowingly afloat in a hospital ice-bath, his precious consciousness gone in a form of coma. The room he ends up in is a literal cage, as we viscerally discover when an attendant pulls a gate of bars across our field of vision to lock him in. This fiercely punitive end-point seems to sever not only the spectator's empathic connection with Leo's heroic struggle (declaring it, to all intents and purposes, *over*), but Lauzon's as well. I think Lauzon is implying that whatever he has become in his own right as an adult cannot be made continuous with the radiant, perished potential of his former life as a child. The very existence of the film *Léolo* would seem to testify powerfully against such a view, but Lauzon refuses to see this gathering of words and images as a reconciling bridge between worlds. He conceives his film,

---

[10] Ernest Becker, *The Denial of Death* (New York: Free Press, 1975): 170.

[11] Herman Melville, "Letter to Nathaniel Hawthorne, April 16?, 1851," in *The Norton Anthology of American Literature* (New York: W.W. Norton, 1979), vol. 1: 2072.

rather, as "a strange half-bridge," in Jeanette Winterson's words, "drawn up [like the Rialto in Venice] to stop one half of this city from warring with the other [...] Bridges join, but they also separate."[12]

The self-possessed, adult voice of *Léolo*'s narrator has misled us from the first. The mature survivor 'looking back' is exposed as a counterfeit. It is not Leo we have been listening to in voice-over, but a phantom reader of Leo's recorded thoughts. Where does this leave Leo himself, suddenly shorn of his grown-up perspective and authority? Robert Lowell writes in "The Dolphin": "Change I earth or sky I am the same,"[13] which painfully applies to the last images of the 'dreaming' Leo, running in search of something he is not destined to find in the vast openness of a picture-book Italian countryside.

Lauzon expressed genuine perplexity in a 1992 interview with Carole Corbeil about why he included a line of narration, close to the end of the film, that links Leo's defeat (the disintegration of his dreaming self) with his failure to love.[14] I confess that the out-of-left-field jolt of this emphatic judgement, so at variance with my overall impression of Leo's sensitivity and indulgence of others' failings (especially within his family), seemed, at a level I could not immediately come to terms with, precisely the intuition required to bring my whole experience of the film together. Lauzon's effort to depict his childhood resilience in the face of towering adversity is not the dimension of his work that distinguishes it from other 'portrait of the artist as a young man' narratives. What does seem unprecedented in *Léolo* is Lauzon's concern to balance the daily challenges of a turbulent, near-hopeless environment with the dismaying idea that one's growth in love, even as a child, is finally one's own responsibility.

No amount of kindness received from others can ensure that love will find deep enough roots in one's heart to make the emotion thrive. No amount of hardship relieves one of the obligation to press forward in whatever possible direction love's reality can be felt, in order to increase its presence in our inner life. It is truly a matter of survival. Love is the place where Lauzon's argument about childhood survival secretly begins and ends. In love's absence, surviving is reduced to what Eudora Welty once mockingly

---

[12] Jeanette Winterson, *The Passion* (New York: Vintage, 1989): 61.

[13] Quoted in David Laskin, *A Common Life: Four Generations of American Literary Friendship and Influence* (New York: Simon & Schuster, 1994): 346.

[14] Carole Corbeil, "The Indiscreet Charm of Jean–Claude Lauzon," *Saturday Night* 107 (December 1992): 60.

termed it: "perhaps the strangest fantasy of them all."[15] The creative dream-state only makes headway as a form of authentic revelation when its self-aggrandizing power-plays, its natural impulse to possess and rule what it 'takes in,' are held in check by love's gift of patient surrender. Why does the voice of love so often counsel us to reduce our defences, to relinquish our best hiding-places, and to present ourselves to our enemies steeped in visible imperfections (learned by heart, as it were)? It is as though we were enjoined to consent repeatedly to our own unmasking, with no assurance of safety.

Lauzon's film asks to be judged, along with its child hero, according to the degree of 'felt life' that has been attained in the right spirit. While it may sound unreasonable at first for the narrator to conclude that there was perhaps too little generosity and decency inside Leo, as well as outside him, to keep him 'alive,' in the full sense of that word, there is something memo-rably chastening about the thought that the child, as much or as little as anyone, is capable of crushing the heart's best gifts before they have ever been opened. Leo, like everyone, can give up on tenderness, and come ab-ruptly to the end of trust. The child, as fully as the adult, can be a collabo-rator in world-emptying betrayals.

This is the key to the almost unwatchable scene when Leo makes com-mon cause with a group of merciless boys at 'play' who encourage the most unformed and insensible of their party to rape a de-clawed cat. The narra-tion accompanying this hideous ceremony coldly attempts to thrust the responsibility for what is done and passively witnessed onto another party. The mother of the rapist is addressed (in her absence) as one who does not know her son or have any notion what he is capable of doing. The narrator's voice swells, rather uncharacteristically, with contempt at her shameful blindness and the sheer quantity of facts she has kept herself ignorant of, as though this woman, and the society that she is accused of personifying, were the true agents of evil here. But the words that are generated to shed light on the offence fail to carry us away from what takes place before our eyes, and the awful fact that Leo, at some deep, knowing level, embraces the deed that an outcast surrogate performs on his behalf. He says "yes" to the full flood of viciousness while pretending to stand back from it, as someone not there with the same *kind* of moral awareness as those 'others' who crowd forward to get a good, close look. For the moment, he experiments with the glassy

---

[15] Laskin, *A Common Life*, 265.

excitement to be found in asphyxiating empathy, as though it were a justified response to everything he has himself been made to suffer.

The cat scene subtly parallels the earlier episode in which Leo's older brother Fernand has his long-awaited chance to get even with the street tough who terrorized him and broke his nose years earlier, when he was too weak and inexperienced to defend himself. Fernand's chief purpose in life, after the hour he is beaten up, is to make certain that he is never again found cowering in tears before an aggressor. He must never again be in a position of physical disadvantage. Fernand believes he has a sure means of putting himself beyond the reach of ordinary physical fear. With ferocious single-mindedness, he devotes every spare moment to body-building. In little more than a blink of film-time, he has replaced his lean frame with one so massively imposing that it is comic. (The transformation is conveyed by Lauzon through another remarkable tracking shot, in which years dissolve as a camera slowly circles a room, entranced by the deceptive play of a mirror reflection.) When Fernand is finally given his second chance, the chance to prove that he is larger than fear and to turn the tables on his by now mythic childhood adversary, he has his nose broken once again, and again collapses against a wall, his useless bulk shaken by sobs.

Leo is the sole witness to both fights, and on each occasion reaches out with a pure sympathy for his brother, in which we detect no trace of shame or aversion, no inner recoil, no self-protective need to dissociate himself from the contagion of another's failure. The narrator declares as we watch Leo's commiseration that Fernand's core identity is fear, and that no amount of physical remoulding could change what he was. It strikes me that in this instance, as in the cat-scene, the narrator's emphasis is troublingly misplaced. His partial and bleak summing-up of Fernand's emotional cave-in is reasonable as far as it goes, but it does not touch on the most important of the camera's revelations. The great mystery of the encounter, one that movies too seldom take up, has to do with how Fernand could prevail against the bully and not, in the process, become more like him. Brutality unimpeded by reflection is the natural vocabulary of the ruffian. It is the advantage he holds in conflicts like the one in *Léolo*. Fernand's adversary has his narrowly focused survivor's truth, and manages to live by it without the intrusion of competing instincts or sympathies. After his initial surprise at Fernand's muscle-flexing immensity, he moves into closer range and performs a quick, dispassionate assessment of Fernand's face and eyes. "Do I *see* in this expression someone resolved to take pleasure in harming me, someone who has practice in landing blows without flinching and who can rejoice at the sight of a victim's blood and pain?"

The alley-fighter's brief time of calculation is the spectator's as well, though for the spectator the calculation may acquire a surprising moral weight. In the space of a few moments, we must decide not only whether Fernand has the resolve to demolish his foe (an outcome we have likely anticipated with some relish), but also whether we want him revealed to our gaze as the limited sort of creature who is 'made for the job.' To be this creature, he must let nothing appear on his face that compromises the will to vengeance, and we are lured, in a sense, into collaborating in the erasure of any giveaway signs of indecisiveness or softness. While it is undoubtedly horrifying to watch Fernand crumble in the ensuing assault, Lauzon makes it possible for us to see that what is best in Fernand (and most worth saving) is also what dictates the negative outcome and ensures his paralysis. Fear plays a significant part, to be sure, in preventing him from striking back, but beyond that we are allowed to observe that he is not, in spite of all his efforts to achieve a fighter's appearance and mentality, a person who can *find himself* in acts of violence. The images of this gigantic child–man weeping have far more cathartic power, I would venture to say, than the freeze-dried mechanics of successful retaliation.

The main parallel with the cat-scene I'd like to trace out has to do with the linked meanings of body-building (for Fernand) and the building-up of Leo's imagination through his daily immersion in writing and dreaming. Both Fernand and Leo suffer a major defeat, but Leo's is worse in the cat-episode because it is soul-eroding – what Robert Lowell once called "dust in the blood."[16] It would be better for him to give himself over to fear in this setting than to harden himself against it. The violation of the cat marks the defeat of the whole imaginative process through an internal numbing that is somehow *chosen*. It also signals the imagination's complete severance from the discipline of love. What is the imagination good for, ultimately, if one arrives at such a testing-ground and finds nothing more to dwell on than children repaying their families for failing to safeguard their innocence? Leo forgets that the justification for "dreaming" that he found with the Word Tamer's help has to do with the conduct of life. One dreams to keep alive the courage to act, in a manner that allows some triumph over one's baleful surroundings. One dreams to expand one's heart-language and to hold on to

---

[16] Laskin, *A Common Life*, 320.

images of what one's fellow-prisoners have it in them to be, through a perception infused with love – and clemency. Flannery O'Connor once memo-
rably defined evil as the defective use of good,[17] which seems to put evil
firmly in the realm of negligence, where a responsive spirit withers through
lack of exercise. Confusing power relationships with the effort to love and
assuming that the greater clarity of power proves it is more real than love
can easily foul the wellspring of action and art.

Léolo pulses with the anxiety that the boy's proper love-energy may be
lethally contaminated by the energy of sexuality, aggression, and death. If
there is a dominant fear in the film, it is that of an ever-encroaching coldness,
fulfilled, if you like, by Leo's final coma-bed of ice. The film's riotous profusion of candles is like a supplicant's appeal to every available visible
expression of warmth. But candles, in such mournful, suffocating quantity,
can equally attest (as we have seen) to a light without adequate heat – as
though no amount of imported fire could assuage the child's core shivering.
I am always struck by the image early in the film of Leo huddling in the
darkness to read his first serious book. The secret light he finds to read by
late at night is shed by an open refrigerator. He must pull a tuque over his
head to protect himself from the chill that seems (here and elsewhere) the
cost of illumination. What most intrigues me in this image is the suggestion
that Leo is as much drawn to the refrigerator's bracing cold as to the light
that accompanies it. It is the right temperature to learn by. As the narrator
intones the passage from Réjean Ducharme's L'Avalée des avalés[18] that Leo is
struggling to comprehend – "I find my only real joy is solitude. Solitude is
my castle" – we see the boy feeling the icy integrity of this tempting fortress
which, with the refrigerator as its gateway, rises up in fantasy against a bare,
northern sky.

The quest for love gains its urgency in Léolo from Lauzon's equally
strong attraction to a self-sufficient remoteness that will not thaw in the
face of others' repellent needs and expectations. The film maps out devious
pathways that momentarily link extremes of loving relationship with

---

[17] Flannery O'Connor, *The Habit of Being: Letters*, sel. & ed. Sally Fitzgerald (New York:
Farrar, Straus & Giroux, 1979): 144.

[18] Réjean Ducharme, *L'Avalée des avalés* (Paris: Gallimard, 1966), tr. Barbara Bray as *The
Swallower Swallowed* (London: Hamish Hamilton, 1968). The Jewish–Catholic child-
heroine of this novel self-protectively takes on the callous manipulativeness of her quar-
relling parents, transferring her love from her mother to her brother, and escaping the
pain of the world and the illusoriness of normal language by "swallowing" it in the form
of a farcically private language that she invents.

extremes of withdrawal, the latter very often bringing Leo close to death. This variation of "yes" and "no" fusion is most memorably accomplished in the film's two underwater scenes, where Leo is shown swimming effortlessly at a great depth, trying to put his hands on treasure no one else can see or reach. In the first scene, Leo experiences an ecstatic vision of a gleaming pirate's hoard at the bottom of the sea (with himself closing in on it) while his grandfather attempts to drown him in a plastic wading pool. Images of the boy pressing forward in slow motion closer and closer to the open sea-chest gleaming with gold and jewels are intercut with shots of Leo's face struggling for air in the pool and shots of his mother leading him on visiting day through the dark corridors of the mental hospital. Candles from the Word Tamer's library are briefly superimposed on one image of the sunken treasure, and the Word Tamer becomes the final component of Leo's vision, reading in his safe haven about the boy's lack of fear as he approached the 'white light' of death.

The various pieces of this 'stop-time' circling of death and beauty and love are held in suspension for a long interval until Leo's mother finally breaks it apart by her last-minute rescue of her flailing child. (She knocks his grandfather unconscious with a single blow to the head from an iron frying pan.) The strange bridge in the editing that is offered to us right *before* this resolution links up Leo's swimming toward death's alluring riches with a heartfelt declaration of the power of his mother's love for him. He reaches out to the jewels, and to his mother's living hand in the hospital corridor, as though the two movements could somehow be reconciled into a single gesture. Leo kisses his mother's hand, which, in pulling him back from an intensely desired death, had replaced one sort of plenitude with another. In a lovely, unforced way, his mother is all at once transformed into the treasure. The metaphor of the underwater heaven, by the end of the sequence, seems as attached to her and the mystery of her simple, unalienated affection as it is to death's siren song. The gift of love – what humans can be and do for one another when they shake off their confusion – beckons Leo to 'swim deeper' even more compellingly than the mirage at the furthest limit of solitude does. And the Word Tamer, who appears to live in some halfway house between the countries of the living and the dead, gently presides over Leo's struggle, hoping always that he will choose life but patient with each dark swerve and frantic mistake, as only one who lives beyond the reach of human turmoil can be.

So much of the visual design of *Léolo* is planned in terms of verticality. Leo's swimming to the bottom of the sea echoes or magnifies such pleasurable penetrations as the descent by stair and basement tunnel to sister Rita's insect and reptile sanctuary, or the dizzying climb, by secret airshaft, to a high bathroom window, through which Leo, disguised in a diver's mask, spies on his grandfather in the tub as he solicits peculiar sexual favours from the 'girl next door.' The Word Tamer's living quarters are eventually shown to include a maze of stairways, extending to a vast depth, where he keeps all his most precious documents and art objects in storage. Italy, Leo's "Fatherland" in his reveries of escape, is a verdant countryside with soaring hills and declivities, all warmly inviting a boy who dreams of unimpeded motion: endless climbing up and racing down. Finally, in a kind of parody of the transcendental urge, we are given a bird's-eye view of Leo stretched out on the floor of his bathroom, having fantasy sex with a raw chunk of liver he has sliced open, while he pages through a grimily earthbound skin magazine. The autoerotic is appropriately viewed here in terms of lifting and sinking: both a furious descent into the flesh and a vertiginous dream of sailing above it.

In the second underwater scene, Leo, once again outfitted in diving gear, is dropped from a high wall into a filthy Montreal canal, in order to retrieve fishing lures from the seldom visited, infectious murk of its lower regions. As we have seen so often, the *event* of the scene consists largely of contrasts between an apparent will-to-die and a hunger for 'deeper' life, gleaming intimations of which Leo snatches with Arabian Nights zest from a host of danger-filled hiding places. The fishing lures possess a palpable starlight power in the poisonous gloom of the stagnant canal. Everywhere the viewer's eye ventures here it is assailed by animal carcasses, rusty, slicing edges of things, and slime-coated consumer goods absurdly announcing their weighty uselessness. Bathtubs, refrigerators, and automobile torsos have usurped the places that rightfully belong to sunken galleons and the fabled spoils of piracy. The discarded possessions are somehow leprously imprinted with the rage and destitution of their former owners, who heaved them into the water as testimony of failure.

The operation that Leo performs, cutting each glittering lure loose from the object that has snagged it, is a re-play of his routine scavenging of his graceless home for suitable poetic material. And just as his writing self prefers jumble to logical ordering and ephemera to what endures, so too his diving expedition builds its case for beauty on the recognition that the risk is pointless: the trifles collected have next to no value, and the impression of enchantment will not survive a return to land. In fact, the very act of cutting a lure loose and taking possession of it 'kills' the precious image on the spot. What one owns is not the thing that filled one's gaze.

Wendy Lesser has found a nice term for the dramatic space of Lauzon's scenes that I am most interested in. She speaks of her predilection for "strange middle grounds because they help [one find] what's going on in seeming oppositions."[19] In the underwater search for lures, the middle ground is Leo's resourceful, swift-moving body, undaunted by all impediments, asserting its dignity in the very midst of hell. The body seems so vulnerable to infection and wound, yet its refusal to take notice of, to be the least bit intimidated by, the encircling poisons feels like a remarkable shield against harm. The lures come out from hiding, like tiny lamps, as if to acknowledge and reward the sight of such exuberant, un-selfconscious motion. And yet the impulse to dream our way into this landscape and make the young swimmer's freedom our own is held in check by some gathering pressure – perhaps something frightening in the *need* to stay under or the idea that vision is once more purchased at the expense of breathing.

The imagination is angling toward death (as in the first swimming scene). Death is the catalyst that will make things stand clear and glow with a pure light. Only in the danger zone, close to the bottom of the canal, do the lures come into magical focus, and hold a value one can see and give one's heart to. Why return to the surface, where one knows the light is wrong, and one's jewels will fade to rubbish? Like a pendulum, Leo's body – in this episode and many others – *overdoes* its movement because of an underlying drive to bring itself to rest. The pendulum's movement gives no outward sign that its basic desire is stillness. Leo's progressively more alarming physical excesses – by turns sexual and violent – seem impelled by the need to find a *point of no return*, which is a negative way of saying 'coming to rest.'

Bodily harm

Follow the arc of most of Leo's fantasies, and the end-point is a version of being crushed under an enormous weight, or being suffocated. To cite one of my favourite examples: he lies in bed one morning working his toe through a small hole in his blanket. He then imagines the amount of effort it will

---

19 Wendy Lesser, "Bodies at Motion and Bodies at Rest," *Threepenny Review* 66 (Summer 1996): 23.

require to make the hole big enough for his whole body to fit through. (Once again, the route to freedom involves willing oneself into the cold; it is no small thing to make gaping holes in one's only blanket.) Yet as soon as Leo's imagination carries his twisting body, feet first, all the way through the rent fabric, he becomes convinced that his head won't make it. The hole will tighten to a noose around his neck at the moment of Houdini-triumphant getaway. The noose isn't simply posited as the last barrier to freedom; it insinuates itself, here and elsewhere, as freedom's most inviting purpose. *Léolo* manages to locate a common denominator of 'gasping for breath' in nearly every form of love embrace, and leads our attention inexorably back to the painful squeeze without release in Leo's Prussian school toilet training.

How does love get so mixed up with the body's most imperious and dismaying compulsions? Why is it so often the case that the urge to mistreat a loved one can coexist with a lucid awareness of the intended victim's appealing qualities? A clear-eyed sympathy is no guarantee that one will forswear vengeance or the bracing pleasures of cruelty. "What swells impels" is a medieval expression that proclaims the casual despotism of the libido in channelling male action, and, as Guido Ceronetti has noted, links the drive to procreate with the less exalted work of abscesses and pimples.[20] I can think of no film that lays greater stress on the body's peculiar and relentless demands for obedience than *Léolo*, but Lauzon's vision of the corporeal life neither celebrates nor grieves over our common servility. Thankfully, there is no recourse to the empty utopianism of Bakhtin's 'carnivalesque,' a concept whose seemingly endless applications suggest not so much a daring and difficult regard for our subversive animal instincts as a sentimental replay of late-Sixties "let it all hang out" merrymaking. (For Bakhtin's Rabelais, substitute Woodstock and Elizabethan-style weddings in a meadow, and most of the pieces fall into place.)

When Leo makes his own version of the discovery that all our mansions are built on excrement, Lauzon resists the double temptation to declare the mansions illusory and to convert the excrement into something metaphorically (and metaphysically) more congenial. Lauzon stubbornly holds to the idea that if his imagination is to retain its faith in love as the highest human good, he must not seek to cleanse this love of its bodily embarrassments. Nor does he deny that his hunger for excess and pain may proceed from the same source as love's selfless expressions. Love finds its most compelling

---

[20] Guido Ceronetti, *The Silence of the Body*, tr. Michael Moore (New York: Farrar, Straus & Giroux, 1993): 8.

reflections in a mirror that also includes the body's stern will and love's mysterious Faustian wagers with death. The intimations of glory Lauzon shows to us are intermixed with uncouth discharges of all sorts, which declare their own truth without entering into some futile competition with the spiritual. The film, in other words, does not force us to choose between the Word Tamer and images of the out-of-control body. The authority of one does not emerge through the vanquishing of the other.

There is a cheap, potent glamour in all film assertions of the primacy of instinct and the exotic risks of surrendering to it. *Léolo* pursues the danger without believing for an instant that sexuality by itself is redemptive or a heroic response to chaos. Lauzon lacks any D.H. Lawrence-style crush on the male body's significance. He does not burden it with any more meaning than it deserves to carry. If Leo's body behaves immoderately, it is not because he lives within it more intensely or authentically than others, but because immoderacy is the natural fate of every emotion the body freely accepts: grief, dread, love. In our dreams and in our creaturely behavior, melodrama is our emotional realism.

Leo's drive to burst out of himself is what alternately moves him to enter compassionately the turmoil and despair of others, and to court annihilation. Whether he presses in one direction or the other, he always comes up against the same inner tightness, as though love and dying both demanded the snapping of the same iron band. What he can never seem to attain, though he longs for it, is the spontaneous lightheartedness of young Bianca, a next-door neighbour who performs simple actions like hanging up laundry with such satisfaction that she can't help singing. Bianca faces at least as many difficulties in her life as Leo does. (Among other indignities, she is preyed upon sexually by Leo's grandfather.) And yet, whatever she has suffered, she holds on to an exuberance and a capacity for joy that Leo has barely touched in his life. Leo finds ample occasions for love, but he cannot sing about them. He consistently tries to secure images of beauty so strong that they will allow him to defy (briefly) the laws of gravity. But there is always a flaw that oppressively reminds him of what cannot be escaped, like the single flower in his bedroom with its "made in Hong Kong" sticker that he cannot bear to remove for fear of *improving* the illusion.

One last view of Leo as pure potential: he sits in his kitchen window overlooking the courtyard, watching Bianca sing with her unkillable delight, while behind him sits his family – miserably together – at supper. Leo cannot fully join Bianca, either physically or in largeness of spirit. Still, the reality of her presence in his world and the possibility of a "better heart" that her song awakens in him allow him to turn his attention back to his family not merely with regret, but with a renewed interest in drawing near to them and finding out who they are. Bianca's music lowers the barriers to love, not through its ideas or some quality of effort in its unfolding. Her song is "simply there, with no prior notice [...] Nothing prepares for it," as if there could *be* preparation for the "pure poetry of good."[21] The song is not in search of love; it has found it, even if the form of love's object is not clear. All the accumulated tensions of Leo's mind and body, including the fact of his romantic longing for Bianca, are dissolved in the music, without the necessity of anything having to be denied. Momentarily unstuck from his usual place, between rebellion and shame, he begins to breathe. He looks at the members of his family one by one, not as figures to whom he is chained, but as beings who will almost certainly be lost to him before they have even once come into proper focus. See them now, the film and the music call out to him. Until you learn how, you will be unable to see anything that lies beyond them.

ଧ

Filmography

Features

1987	*Un zoo la nuit* (115 mins.)
1992	*Léolo* (107 mins.)

Short films

1976/79	*Le secret du colonel* (student film; 16mm)
1979	*Super Maire: L'homme de 3 milliards* (student film; 16mm)
1981	*Piwi* (16mm)

Bibliography

Interviews and statements

Alioff, Maurie. "Jean–Claude Lauzon's *Léolo,*" *Take One* 1 (1992): 15–19.
Brownstein, Bill. "Filmmaker Lauzon braces for Cannes zoo," *Gazette* (Montreal; 20 April 1992): E 6.

---

[21] Irving Massey, *Find You the Virtue: Ethics, Image, and Desire in Literature* (Fairfax VA: George Mason UP, 1987): 115, 127.

Brunette, Peter. "With *Léolo*, It is Better to Feel Than to Understand, " *New York Times* (26 March 1992): H22.

Conlogue, Ray. "Ray Conlogue Finds Mixed Emotions in Québec over Lauzon's *Léolo*," *Globe & Mail* (9 July 1992): C1.

Corbeil, Carole. "The Indiscreet Charm of Jean–Claude Lauzon," *Saturday Night* 107:10 (December 1992): 58–61, 86–90.

Johnson, Brian D., "A Canadian Maverick," *World Press Review* (August 1992): 51.

Lauzon, Jean–Claude. "*Le Zoo*: C'était ma raison de vivre," in ⇨Marie–Christine Abel, André Giguère & Luc Perreault, ed., *Le cinéma québécois à l'heure internationale*, 207–209.

Scott, Jay. "If I Wasn't Creative, I Would Be Crazy," *Globe & Mail* (16 May 1992): C1, C8.

Biopic

Belanger, Louis, & Isabelle Hébert, dir. *Lauzon/Lauzone*. Produced by Lyse Lafontaine & Pierre Latour for Lyla Films, 2001.

Essays and articles

Bonneville, Léo. "Jean–Claude Lauzon," *Séquences* (August 1987): 11–21.

Garrity, Henry. "True Lies: Autobiography, Fiction and Politics in Jean–Claude Lauzon's *Léolo*," *Québec Studies* (Spring–Summer 1995): 80–85.

Petrowski, Nathalie. "Lauzon by Petrowski," *Actualité* 17.11 (juillet 1992): 90–94.

Ramsay, Christine. "Léo Who? Questions of Identity and Culture in Jean–Claude Lauzon's *Léolo*," *Post script* 15.1 (Fall 1995): 23–37.

Reines, Philip. "The Emergence of Québec Cinema: An Historical Overview," in Joseph I. Donohue, Jr., ed., *Essays on Québec Cinema*, 15–36.

Weinmann, Heinz. "*Un zoo la nuit*: le Québec amnésique," in ⇨Weinmann, *Cinéma de l'imaginaire québécois*, 107–20.

Reviews

Brian D. Johnson, "Rebel Masterpiece: A Provocative Québec Movie Arrives in Cannes," *Maclean's* 105:21 (25 May 1992): 51–52; David Stratton, *Variety* (1 June 1992): 67; Bill Brownstein, "Montreal Director Offers a Disturbing Coming-of-Age Movie," *Gazette* (Montreal; 6 June 1992): E1, E8; Rick Groen, *Globe & Mail* (10 September 1992): C1; Janet Maslin, "Fleeing Youthful Misery With Feats of the Mind," *New York Times* (29 September 1992); Maurie Alioff, *Take One* 1 (1992): 33–35; Geoff Pevere, "Family Ties: Québécois Filmmaker Already Knows Canada is a Dysfunctional Family," *Canadian Forum* 71. 815 (1992): 23–24; Rod Lurie, *Los Angeles* 38 (March 1993): 90; David Ansen, *Newsweek* 121 (5 April 1993): 56–58; Richard Corliss, *Time* 141 (5 April 1993): 60–61; David Denby, *New York* 26 (5 April 1993): 60; Anthony Lane, *New Yorker* 69 (12 April 1993): 114; Peter Travers, *Rolling Stone* (15 April 1993): 72; Philip Strick, *Sight and Sound* 3.5 (May 1993): 51; Bert Cardullo, "Forbidden Games," *Hudson Review* 46.5 (Autumn 1993): 547–50.

FIGURE 13

Careful (Guy Maddin, 1992) – Gosla Dobrowolska (Zenaida); Kyle McCulloch (Grigorss).

13 Careful
(Guy Maddin, 1992)

Production: produced 1991, released 25 January 1992. Careful Pictures, with the participation of Telefilm Canada and CIDO (Canada–Manitoba Cultural Industries Development Office), the Arts Council of Canada, the Manitoba Arts Council, and Cinephile Ltd. **Director:** Guy Maddin. **Executive producer,** Andre Bennett. **Producers:** Greg Klymkiw, Tracy Traeger. **Screenplay:** Guy Maddin, Georges Toles, from Toles' story. **Cinematographer:** Guy Maddin. **Editor:** Guy Maddin. **Music:** John McCulloch. **Production Design:** Guy Maddin. **Art Director:** Jeff Solylo. **Costumes:** Donna Szoke. **Sound:** Russ Dyck. **Assistant Sound Director:** Liz Jarvis. **Casting:** Greg Klymkiw. **Colour, 101 mins., 35mm.**

Cast: Kyle McCulloch (Grigorss), **Gosla Dobrowolska** (Zenaida), **Sarah Neville** (Klara), **Brent Neale** (Johann), **Paul Cox** (Count Knotgers), **Victor Cowie** (Herr Trotta), **Michael O'Sullivan** (Blind Ghost), **Vince Rimmer** (Franz), **Katya Gardner** (Sigleinde), **Jackie Burroughs** (Frau Teacher), **Ross McMillan** (chief steward), **Leith Clark** (Butler Blore), **Glen Hubich** (Butler Schrammel), **Brendan Carruthers** (mortician), **George Toles** (Countess Knotgers), **Greg Klymkiw** (Shower Meister), **Kelli Shinfield** (Gerda the Mountain Girl).

Synopsis: In the Alpine village of Tolzbad, the ever-present danger of avalanches requires that people live their lives according to the rules of quiet and propriety. Among the residents of the village are a youthful widow, Zenaida, and her three sons, Grigorss, Johann, and Franz. Franz, an invalid, reminds his mother of her unhappy first marriage and is confined to an upstairs room. His brothers are studying to become butlers, hoping to enter into service with the local Count. Johann becomes engaged to Klara, daughter of Herr Trotta, but a dream reveals Johann's erotic attachment to his mother. One night, having drugged his mother, he cuts open her garments and kisses her breast. Horrified at his deed, he mutilates himself, then jumps to his death. Grigorss completes butler school, and goes to work for the Count. One day, the Count admits to a youthful romance with Grigorss' mother, and announces his intention to woo her once again. The Count meets with Zenaida, and they renew their romance, but Grigorss cannot bear this, and challenges the Count to a duel. The count is killed. Meanwhile, Grigorss' own budding romance with Klara is thwarted by her own love for her father, who himself is involved sexually with his other daughter. In grief, Zenaida hangs herself. Klara convinces Grigorss to kill her father, and they plot to set off an avalanche in which he will die. The avalanche kills Klara and her father, and Grigorss freezes to death in the mountain hideaway in which he and Klara had planned to live.

Reinhabiting lost languages
Guy Maddin's *Careful* *

———————— &

Will Straw

G UY MADDIN CLAIMS that his interest in making movies (he never
calls them films) was born at a screening of *The Obsession of Billie
Botski*, an early short film by fellow Winnipegger John Paizs.[1] No one would
confuse the films of Paizs and Maddin, but in the affinities which link their
respective bodies of work, one sees why the films of the Winnipeg Film
Group, and of those directors associated with it, have been sentimental
favourites among Canadian critics and film scholars. Profoundly grounded
in film history, these films nevertheless resist the precocious marshalling of
insider references typical of so many upstart schools, from the French New
Wave to post-Tarantino independent American cinema. The Winnipeg films
are ambitious in their painstaking reconstruction of lost or minor filmic
styles, yet endearingly free of provocative displays of *auteurist* bravura.
While first-time directors of independent features are typically drawn to re-
working the tradition of film noir, or to making loose, Cassavetes-ish documents of their friends and social circles, Maddin (like Paizs before him)
prefers the patient discipline of reconstructing obsolete colour processes or
mimicking the solemn pretension of late-silent credit sequences.

Careful was released in 1992 to critical acclaim, garnering reviews which
hailed it as the most accomplished of Guy Maddin's three feature films. By
then, the story of Maddin's career had become well-known in the relevant
film-critical circles, and would be repeated from one journalistic profile to
another. Much would be made of the fact that Maddin's first feature, *Tales*

* I would like to express my thanks to Gene Walz for invaluable suggestions and
meticulous editing. George Toles was an amazingly generous source of background information, materials and inspiration. Thanks as well to Rebecca Poff, for her assistance in
tracking down reviews and articles.

[1] "Far from the Maddin Crowd: An Interview with Guy Maddin," *Border Crossings* 9.3
(July 1990): 36.

From the Gimli Hospital (1988), had been rejected by the Toronto Festival of Festivals, then turned into a midnight-screening cult attraction in New York City by distributor Ben Barenholtz. (Barenholtz had earlier made David Lynch's *Eraserhead* into an underground hit in similar fashion.) For this, the film's history has entered the canon of cautionary tales about the failure of Canadians to acknowledge talent within their midst and the need for artists to seek their fortunes elsewhere. The film's success in midnight screenings in the USA would fuel comparisons between Maddin and the US director David Lynch, comparisons which Maddin consistently refused. (Indeed, 'Lynchian' would recur as often as the term 'surrealistic' in early attempts to describe Maddin's style.)

Maddin's first film was a 28-minute short, *The Dead Father* (1986), set in the Dominion of Forgetfulness – a place whose name suggests both Canada and somewhere else, and is thus like so many elements of the films which followed. *Tales From The Gimli Hospital* was made for only $22,000, and set in "a Gimli we never knew." Its story focuses on the rivalries and frustrations of two men confined to hospital during a smallpox-like epidemic in an Icelandic immigrant community in Manitoba's Interlake region. The film's real strengths, however, are less in its narrative than in the set pieces, stunning exercises of reconstructed style. In one of these, three young women dance in the forest as wood-nymphs, lit and shot through filters that evoke the lush look of a late-silent MGM film. In another, more absurdist moment, rivals in love engage in a ritualized duel of butt-cheek pinching, a piece of bogus ethnography that has entered cult-film legend.

Maddin received $375,000 to make his second feature, *Archangel* (released in 1990). That film's hero is an amnesiac Canadian soldier wandering, lost, in the north of Russia, amidst the carnage of the Revolution and Civil War. Its sets are minimal, and its scenes of battlefields or flight lack even the low-rent support of back-projection (they are simply filled with fog and snow), but it is endearing in part because it imagines itself an epic. Its hero is meant to wander across a vast, tragic landscape, fulfilling the formulaic destiny of the lovesick shell-shocked amnesiac. This landscape, however, is somehow claustrophobic, with a handful of ethnic stereotypes standing in for the immense mobilization of multinational forces described to us in inter-titles. Likewise, the hero's forgetfulness is less tragic than a pretext for his obliviousness, a trait he shares with so many of Maddin's heroes.

Archangel clarified Maddin's cinematic allegiances, making it clear that his chief points of reference were the lost codes of late-silent/early-sound

cinema, not the dissident traditions of surrealism or an American underground. While well-received, and voted Best Experimental Film of its year
by the US National Society of Film Critics, *Archangel* would come to be considered a failure of sorts by many – a jumbled, inaccessible second film in
the tradition of sophomore jinxes (like Orson Welles's *Magnificent Amber-
sons*.) Maddin himself, in interviews, encouraged the view that *Archangel*
was ill-conceived, and that its problems were ones which his next film
would resolve.[2] Indeed, reviews of *Careful* have helped solidify the view that
it rectifies the weaknesses of its predecessor. The *Sight and Sound* reviewer
noted approvingly that *Careful* was "more audience-friendly than *Archangel*,
in which a dying man strangles a Bolshevik by yanking out his own
intestines."[3]

Despite its $1,000,000 budget, two-strip Technicolor look, and at least
three performers with significant careers outside Maddin's stock company
(Dubrowolska, Burroughs and Cox), the production conditions of *Careful* do
not seem a qualitative leap over those of the films which preceded it. *Tales
from the Gimli Hospital* was shot in a building which had once been a beauty
salon belonging to Maddin's mother, and *Archangel* in an "empty warehouse
in front of papier-mâché sets."[4] Like its predecessors, *Careful* was filmed in
the Winnipeg area, this time in an abandoned silo, with McCain's potato
flakes standing in for real snow in the film's climactic sequences. According
to Don Gillmor, *Careful* was "presold [...] to German television based on a
screenplay that promised mountains, German names (Frau Teacher, Herr
Trotta) and 'a lot of Germanic death'."[5] Tolzbad, the Alpine village in which
Careful takes place is, in Clare Monk's words, "at once instantly recognizable
and like no place on earth."[6]

Rehearsing film history

Part of the triumph of *Careful*, then, stems from the fact that, while a much
more coherent, accessible film than the first two, it sacrifices none of the
painstaking reconstruction of obscure past film styles which made Martin

[2] Paul McKie, "Maddin reaps praise in New York," *Winnipeg Free Press* (13 October
1992): C11.

[3] Clare Monk, "*Careful*," *Sight and Sound* 3.10 (New Series; 1992): 42.

[4] Paul McKie, "Maddin tackles career movie," *Winnipeg Free Press* (4 September 1991): 33.

[5] Don Gillmor, "Start Making Sense," *Saturday Night* (September 1992): 36.

[6] Monk, "*Careful*," 41.

Scorsese and *Village Voice* critic Jim Hoberman early champions of Maddin's work. Indeed, the move to colour and a narrative moved along by dialogue and an almost conventional story-line might be best understood through Don Gillmor's suggestion that the development from *Tales* to *Careful* replicates the history of cinema itself:

> Maddin's oeuvre, viewed in sequence, is like the first term of a film-history course, beginning in the silent-film era: spare, unsynched dialogue, odd movements, black-and-white stock, claustrophobic sets. [...] With *Careful* we are moving into the 1930s, using the two-strip Technicolor of Maddin's childhood, colour that didn't look real. Everything looked like a movie.[7]

This view of Maddin's career suggests a passing comparison to another filmmaker whose work, in its own development, has been seen to repeat the historical development of the cinema. As Bob Colacello has noted, Andy Warhol's films, from the 1960s through the 1970s, "started at ground zero, and re-created the history of film as he went, adding motion, music, talking, scripted dialogue, plot, color, 35mm and 3D step-by-step."[8] Like Warhol, Maddin is obsessed with the secondary trappings of older modes of production: with the credit sequences and studio logos, the stock companies and star-effects which link even the most minor of classical films to a monumental system. Where this comparison breaks down, of course, is when the painstaking discipline of Maddin's filmmaking practice is set against the wilfully loose, chaotically playful procedures of Warhol and his Factory. An even more apt analogy, perhaps, is with the German director Rainer Werner Fassbinder, who, like Maddin, is preoccupied with "receremonializing" the cinema, restoring those ritualistic elements which postwar modernism had worked so hard to expel.[9] Both Maddin and Fassbinder work to ensure that the lead characters of the cheapest of films are lit and framed like movie stars, and that the most hackneyed of plot twists are made to creak with the weight of divine purpose.

From this perspective, *Careful* might be seen as an example of what Guy Scarpetta, writing in the mid-1980s, called the new baroque, an aesthetic favouring the ceremonial and the artificial over the referential.[10] Certainly, some of the audacity of Maddin's films stems from the fact that, although

---

[7] Gillmor, "Start Making Sense," 36.

[8] Bob Colacello, *Holy Terror: Andy Warhol Close Up* (New York: HarperCollins, 1990): 29.

[9] I take this use of the term 'receremonialization' from the work of Guy Scarpetta. See Scarpetta, *L'Impureté* (Paris: Grasset, 1985): 146.

[10] Scarpetta, *L'Impureté*, 92.

they are Canadian, regional, and independent – in other words, minor in all kinds of ways – they nevertheless revel in the rituals of more official and monumental cinemas: the studio title cards, the didactic pre-narrative sequences, the credits sequences in which performers, in posed shots, flutter and blink at a film's beginning or end. This investment in the ponderous rituals of classical cinema is one of the qualities of Maddin's films which work against the interpretation of them as surrealist. They are texts wilfully weighed down by the accessories of rigidly codified schools and genres rather than uncontrolled eruptions of the fantastic and oneiric. *Tales from the Gimli Hospital* and *Archangel* contain scenes that are, admittedly, 'weird,' but these seem surrealistic only to those unfamiliar with their antecedents in the improbable contrivances and baroque cosmologies of early melodrama.

Imagined traditions

The drive to clarify Maddin's stylistic ancestry is one of the ways in which critics have grappled with the difficulty of knowing what to say about his films. *Careful* confronted critics with what Jim Hoberman, discussing Maddin's work in *Premiere* magazine, called its "'*huh?*' quotient," and Geoff Pevere has written of the tendency of Maddin's films to resist interpretation.[11] Reviews of *Careful* have almost invariably floundered in the quest to describe it, breaking down into scattershot inventories of its stylistic and historical reference-points. For Graham Fuller, *Careful* is defined by "scenes of Caspar [David] Friedrich spectrality, Grimm enchantment, and Cronenbergian nastiness."[12] To another reviewer, it offers a "kitschhell of giant flugelhorns, flaxen-haired maidens and flower-bedecked funiculars."[13] Robert Horton, writing in *Film Comment*, described *Careful* as offering "the look of an overstuffed UFA film from the Twenties, the tone of an SCTV version of a Wagner opera, and the overall aesthetics of Dr Seuss."[14]

Lists such as these are often effective in suggesting the variety of resonances which *Careful* sets in play. They do injustice, however, to the discipline and consistency with which Maddin patiently unearths and reinhabits the lost languages of minor, transitional moments in film history. These lost

---

[11] See Jim Hoberman, "The Children of David Lynch," *Premiere* (February 1991): 36; and Geoff Pevere, "Guy Maddin: True to Form," *Take One* 1.1 (New Series; Fall 1992): 6.

[12] Graham Fuller, "Shots in the Dark," *Interview* 22.12 (December 1992): 53.

[13] Monk, "*Careful*," 42.

[14] Robert Horton, "New Bridges," *Film Comment* 28.6 (November–December 1992): 68.

languages are, most of the time, historically authentic, but the peculiar paradox of Maddin's films (and of *Careful* in particular) is that the stylistic predecessors of which they so successfully seem to remind us may, in fact, be ones we have never experienced to any significant degree. Reviewers who applaud Maddin's insight into the Bavarian mountain film are unlikely to have seen a great number of these, but that is the point. Maddin's films are both inventive revisitings of genuine past styles and imagined versions of such styles, seemingly drawn (in *Careful*'s case) from such ephemera as the illustrations of children's fairy-tale books or early sound-era operetta. The coherence of *Careful*'s world is not solely an effect of Maddin's careful reconstrucion of already existing generic traditions; it springs, as well, from the convincing completeness with which he has imagined such worlds.

Maddin's script for *Careful* was co-written with George Toles, the University of Manitoba film and drama professor with whom he had collaborated on *Archangel*. Toles' contribution to *Careful* is punningly acknowledged in the name of the town in which it is set ("Tolzbad"), and is evident in a set of thematic concerns which link both collaborations with Maddin and run through Toles' other work. Toles has produced stage versions of *Who's Afraid of Virginia Woolf*, *A Streetcar Named Desire* and *Long Day's Journey Into Night*, modern theatrical cauldrons of constricted or explosive emotion and desire. While the tortured relationships of these works pale beside the intergenerational incest rampant within *Careful* or the bewildering romantic triangles of *Archangel*, all centre on strange, dysfunctional familial and romantic arrangements. Toles has also co-written Maddin's latest feature, *Twilight of the Ice Nymphs*, a film described by its publicist as being "about three men and three women who pursue romantic happiness in a remote region. These residents of an ostrich bestiary encounter the delirium of unrequited love during a summer when the sun won't set." At the film's conclusion, a brother and sister, frustrated in their romantic longings, settle down with each other. As Toles himself has indicated,

> It frankly has puzzled me that next to no one who has reviewed *Careful* has been willing to say that the movie may be dealing seriously with the two topics it loudly announced as its main narrative concerns: repression and incest. Incest, when mentioned, is swiftly passed over as a by-product of the German influence. In point of fact, *Careful* is what it is because of our efforts to enter, unglibly and mysteriously, into a terrain that felt laden with genuine peril. What we *didn't* want was anything that would be dramatized – even a decade down the road – in a movie-of-the-week, high-earnestness fashion. All of our choices were made to make the incest theme somehow manageable and approachable. The moun-

tain movie genre was revised because mountain movies always seemed to gravitate toward uncontrollable family attachments. We created a town in which repression is the only available form of character oxygen. We chose to write in the manner of opera librettos and German Romantic tales because that language seemed to carry the authentic flash of fever. Everyone who speaks at any length resembles Hamlet's "sicklied o'er with the pale cast of thought" condition.[15]

The claim that Maddin's films are absurdly perverse often stems from the misperception that he is corrupting innocent genres through the insinuation, within them, of deviant relationships or aberrant, 'modern' desires. Neither the Central European fairy-tale nor the silent melodrama were as innocent as we now remember them, however, and one effect of Maddin's films is to restore to these forms the sense of grotesque violence or unholy passion which sanitized up-datings or selective memory have erased. As in Lauzon's *Léolo* (one of Toles' favourite films), the family in *Careful* is the dysfunctional centre from which cataclysmic narrative events are generated, rather than a place safe from such events. As *Careful* unfolds, the attic confining the invalid Franz comes to seem less a prison and more a refuge from the horrific events happening among the rest of the family below.

Careful and Canadian

If Maddin's films challenge interpretation, they have proved even more resistant to distinctly Canadian traditions of critical analysis. More specifically, Maddin's films have been poor fodder for a criticism which seeks to trace links between characteristics of works and the condition of life in English Canada. When the elements which normally ground thematic analysis – character predicament, psychological motivation, narrative worlds – come already built into the historical genres and styles being evoked, it is difficult to see such elements as responding directly to Maddin's lived experience or social background.

Yet critical commentary has laboured to suggest ways in which Maddin's films manifest a Canadian sensibility at the level of theme and story. It is sometimes claimed, for example, that the amnesiac hero in *Archangel* is quintessentially Canadian, his chief trauma being loss of identity.[16] This seems at once a forced reading and an apt explanation of why the bumbling,

---

[15] Personal letter from George Toles, 17 April 1997.

[16] This argument was made in a number of papers produced for a film course which I taught at Carleton University.

naive idealism of the film's protagonist seems to ring so true. A full account of this naivety, however, requires that we take into account the uni-dimensional, stereotypical nature of almost all of Maddin's characters. If, as Geoff Pevere suggests, each of Maddin's films is, at some level, a funda-mentally Canadian tale of "radical alienation," this is in part because they all unfold within styles and generic traditions which offer little room for psychological depth or for narrative trajectories leading to complex self-knowledge.[17] Similarly, the humility and collective acquiescence to rules of polite comportment which are enforced in the world of *Careful* have been taken as emblematic of a national character marked, in Kieran Keohone's insightful analysis, by the fear that others might be enjoying themselves too much.[18] This, too, rings true, but the film's elaborate recounting of these rules, and its staging of didactic episodes in which we are shown the deadly consequences of non-compliance, are also stylistic conceits, mannerist games which evoke a whole history of filmic prologues and moralizing tableaux.

In other writings, the link is made between Maddin's stylistic exercises and a distinct regionalist, prairie aesthetic. One interviewer, citing Terry Heath, suggests that Maddin's films demonstrate the essentially surrealistic quality of prairie culture, an interpretation with which Maddin concurs only partially.[19] Marie–Josée Minassian has asserted that the composite, pastiche quality of Maddin's films reflects the composite nature of prairie identity.[20] Her argument is convergent with Linda Hutcheon's claims about the ex-centric, decentred qualities of Canadian postmodernism.[21] It is now a com-monplace of English-Canadian cultural criticism that many of our most revealing works are characterized by the ironic appropriation of those cul-tures which dominate us. While this clearly helps illuminate the films of John Paizs, so many of which engage with the para-cinemas of US industrial films and 1950s cartoons, Maddin's work has little to do with Hollywood or any other major villain in the drama of Canadian cultural dependency. The Icelandic saga, the Soviet montage film, and the Bavarian mountain melo-drama are all almost as minor as Canadian film itself. It is almost as if, by

---

[17] Pevere, "Guy Maddin: True to form," 7.

[18] Kieran Keohone, "Symptoms of Canada: National Identity and the Theft of Enjoy-ment," *CinéAction* 28 (Spring 1992): 23.

[19] "Far from the Maddin Crowd: An Interview with Guy Maddin," 38.

[20] Marie–José Minassian, "Prairie Films in Paris," *Newest Review* (June–July 1993): 5.

[21] Linda Hutcheon, *The Canadian Postmodern: A Study of Contemporary English-Canadian Fiction* (Toronto: Oxford UP, 1988): 3.

rewriting the history of movies so as to privilege these minor, marginal movements, Maddin has helped to create a new constellation of styles and schools in which Canadian cinema itself might occupy a place.

Maddin's own responses to analyses of his work carry no automatic claim to truth. However, his insistence that his main allegiances are generational, rather than national or regional, is at least as useful as other accounts in explaining the impulses which fuel his films. Responding to the suggestion that the prairie experience is one of isolation, and that his films express this isolation, Maddin says:

> So maybe there is something geographical and demographic that makes people from Winnipeg make the same kind of film. I have another theory, though. When you attend film festivals worldwide you realize there's a type of film that comes from an age group. There are films from Sweden and Denmark that remind you of films from Winnipeg. So this undercurrent is less geographical or cultural than chronological.[22]

Like John Paizs, Guy Maddin has grown up in a world where, arguably, differences in stylized renderings of the world spring less from regional or national experiences than from the specific combinations of film stock, period style and colour process which shape each generation's experience of images. We are all subject to what Susan Stewart has called "the self-periodization of popular culture" – to the ways in which changes in the technologies with which films are made and the channels through which we see them shift the meanings of stylistic languages and shape our sense of historical time.[23] The codes of late-silent melodrama or two-strip Technicolor are, at one level, part of the collective cultural archive of the West as a whole. Only for a particular generation, however, will these also resonate with memories of childhood television viewing, or be marked with the sense of peculiar obscurity conveyed by washed-out prints of movies shown late at night on independent television stations.

As films which are principally about style and sensibility, Maddin's works are open to the criticism that they are merely clever, that he would rather rework discarded conventions with cold distance than develop a stylistic vocabulary through which he might express his own condition. Hal Foster is one of several critics who, over the last fifteen years, have bemoaned tendencies towards pastiche in the visual arts:

---

[22] "Far from the Maddin Crowd," 33.

[23] Susan Stewart, *On Longing: Narratives of the Miniature, the Gigantic, the Souvenir, the Collection* (Baltimore MD: Johns Hopkins UP, 1984): 167.

Modern art *engaged* historical forms, often in order to deconstruct them. Our new art tends to *assume* historical forms – out of context and reified.

[...] This 'return to history' is ahistorical for three reasons: the context of history is disregarded, its continuum is disavowed, and conflictual forms of art and modes of production are falsely resolved in pastiche. Neither the specificity of the past nor the necessity of the present is heeded.[24]

The choice offered here is between an excavation of historical styles which functions to criticize them, and an uncritical adoption of such styles which drains them of their historical meaningfulness. Clearly, the marginal status of those styles Maddin has chosen to revisit is such that there would be little point in seeking to 'critique' them: as suggested, the Bavarian mountain film is hardly a significant foundation of cultural power in Canada in the 1990s. What other purpose, then, might we ascribe to the sort of exercise in which Maddin is engaged? Keir Keightley has suggested that we must learn to see certain works of pastiche as, in effect, historical essays on style. Writing about movements in popular music which strain to capture the sensibility of past styles and moments, Keightley notes that this "is an example of a growing trend for musicians and filmmakers to 'do the work' scholars apparently have abandoned, i.e. archaeologically recuperating occulted histories."[25] Maddin is clearly engaged in this archaeology, making careful calculations about how to best convey the sense of being inside certain historical styles, offering implicit claims about what is central or important within them. The maddeningly interminable scene in *Careful* in which Grigorss fusses with the makeup of the Count's dead mother, risking discovery and reprimand from the head butler, is a meditation on historical constructions of cinematic time as profound as any produced by theoretical reflection on the subject.

Peculiar pleasures

While *Careful* offers more narrative coherence than Maddin's previous films, it would be disingenuous to claim that the film's pleasure comes from our being drawn into its story and narrative world to any significant degree. *Careful*'s delights, like those of *Tales from the Gimli Hospital* or *Archangel*, come in those moments when the mechanics of lost forms are both meticu-

---

[24] Hal Foster, *Recordings: Art, Spectacle, Cultural Politics* (Port Townsend WA: Bay Press, 1985): 16.

[25] Keir Keightley, "The History and Exegesis of Pop: Reading *All Summer Long*," M.A. thesis, Montreal: Graduate Program in Communications, McGill University, 1991: 80.

lously reproduced and innocently offered up. The exchange of glances between Johann and his fiancée as Johann anticipates, then completes, his flugelhorn solo is blissful at a number of levels. It pleases because the film is so highly invested in the idea of the young, ruddy-cheeked romantic lead, and in the formal rituals (of cross-cutting and pacing) through which the bonds between the couple are highlighted within the broader, community context of the sequence. In this respect, the scene is so obviously over-determined by generic and historical convention that we cannot be drawn fully into its emotion or drama. Neither, however, do we simply revel, as connoisseurs, in the careful perfection with which this exercise of stylistic reconstruction is carried off. The pleasure of the scene is also elsewhere, in our admiration for a film which would indulge itself in mounting, so pains-takingly, such a ludicrous set of events and images.

A more striking example of the densely affective appeal of *Careful* comes when Frau Teacher leads the students at Butler school through an exercise in which they read instructions from flash cards and carry out the actions written upon them. The hurried montage of shots here is meant to signal busy, choreographed activity, even as the minimal resources with which the scene is mounted render it, at a profound level, pitifully forlorn. At the same time, the disembodied voices and rhythms of speech and action all evoke the sense of a musical number in which songs are somehow not possible. The sequence is exhilarating, as musical numbers conventionally are, in the way it breaks loose from the careful control of the rest of the film. More impor-tantly, however, in its desperate and clunky attempt to crank the film into another, more extravagant mode, the sequence evokes the proud lineage of all those moments in film history marked by pathetic, failed ambition.

Here, as throughout Maddin's films, we are won over by the discipline and principle with which he resists opportunities for facile effect. In his choice of marginal, transitional moments in film history to revisit, Maddin has closed off the temptations of easy parody, of simply extending or exag-gerating the decadent campiness with which more prominent styles from the past already come laden. Maddin's filmmaking is wilfully 'minor,' not only in the modesty of the means employed, but in the obscurity of the historical sensibilities with which his films engage. Like John Paizs' feature *Crime Wave*, which wants nothing more than to be a "colour crime movie," *Careful* is happy being a part-talky, two-colour mountain tragedy of doomed love.

ဆ

Filmography

Features

1988   *Tales from the Gimli Hospital* (or *Gimli Saga*; or *Pestilence*; + screenplay; 72 mins., b/w, 16 mm)

1990   *Archangel* (+ co-screenplay; 90 mins., 16 mm)

1991   *Indigo High-Hatters* (+ screenplay; 34 mins., b/w)

1992   *Careful* (+ screenplay; 100 mins.)

1995   *The Hands of Ida* (TV movie, 30 mins.)

1997   *Twilight of the Ice Nymphs* (based on work by Knut Hamsun; 94 mins.)

2001   *Dracula: Pages from a Virgin's Diary*

Shorts

1986   *The Dead Father* (+ screenplay; 28 mins., b/w, 16 mm)

1989   *BBB* (+ screenplay; 12 cmins., b/w, 16mm)

1989   *Mauve Decade* (+ screenplay; 7 mins., b/w, 16mm)

1990   *Tyro* (+ screenplay; 4 mins., b/w, 16mm)

1993   *The Pomps of Satan* (+ screenplay; 5 mins., b/w, 16mm)

1994   *Sea Beggars* (7 mins., 16mm)

1995   *The Eye Like a Bizarre Balloon Mounts Towards Infinity* (or *The Eye Like a Strange Balloon*; + screenplay; on an 1882 lithograph, *Balloon Eye*, by Odilon Redon; 5/10 mins., b/w, 16 mm)

1995   *Sissy Boy Slap Party* (+ screenplay; 2 mins., b/w, 16mm)

1996   *Imperial Orgies* (+ screenplay; 3 mins., b/w, 16mm)

1998   *The Hoyden* (+ screenplay; 4 mins., b/w, 16mm)

1999   *Hospital Fragment* (+ screenplay; 3 mins., 30 seconds, b/w, 16mm)

2000   *The Cock Crew* (co-screenplay; 5/10 mins., 16mm)

2000   *Maldoror: Tygers* (+ screenplay; 3 mins., 40 seconds., b/w & colour, 16mm)

2000   *The Heart of the World* (+ screenplay; 5 mins., b/w, 16mm)

2000   *Fleshpots of Antiquity* (+ screenplay; 3 mins., b/w, 16mm)

Bibliography

Screenplay excerpts and storyboards

Toles, George, & Guy Maddin. "Dikemaster's Daughter," *Border Crossings* 16.4 (Fall 1997): 34–41.

Documentary

Guy Maddin: Waiting for Twilight, dir. Noam Gonick, screenplay by Caelum Vatnsdal (Canada 1997, 60 mins.).

Book

Vatnsdal, Caelum. *Kino Delirium: The Films of Guy Maddin*. Winnipeg: Arbeiter Ring, 2000.

Interview

"Far from the Maddin Crowd: An Interview with Guy Maddin," *Border Crossings* 9.3 (July 1990): 33–41.

Essays

Anderson, Robert. "Guy Maddin," *Film Comment* 34.2 (March–April 1998): 63–67.

DeWalt, Robert. "Play It Again, Sigmund: A Careful Inquiry into Guy Maddin's Tabooland," *Border Crossings* 12.2 (May 1993): 9–11.

Gembarsky, Bohdan. "Maddin's films create a stir," *Winnipeg Free Press* (15 March 1991): 33.

Gillmor, Don. "Start Making Sense," *Saturday Night* (September 1992): 34–37.

Gerstel, Judy. "A Gimli State of Mind," *Toronto Star* (30 August 1997): H1, H5.

Harris, Christopher. "Maddin and his careful touch," *Globe & Mail* (9 October 1992): D3.

Hoberman, Jim. "The Children of David Lynch," *Premiere* (February 1991): 34–35, 39.

Jones, Alan. "It's a Mad, Mad, Maddin World! Winnipeg cult director Guy Maddin continues his brand of weird and wonderful surrealism," *Cinéfantastique* 21.6 (June 1991): 44–45, 61.

MacInnis, Craig. "Off-beat Winnipegger in danger of being famous," *Toronto Star* (9 October 1992): C3.

McKie, Paul. "New York critics applaud Winnipegger's movie," *Winnipeg Free Press* (23 July 1991): 18.

———. "Maddin tackles career movie," *Winnipeg Free Press* (4 September 1991): 18.

———. "Maddin reaps praise in New York," *Winnipeg Free Press* (13 October 1992): C11.

McSorley, Tom. "In the Hour of Twilight: Guy Maddin Gets Melodramatic in *Twilight of the Ice Nymphs*," *Take One* 6.1 (New Series; Fall 1997): 12–16.

Minassian, Marie-José. "Prairie Films in Paris," *Newest Review* (June–July, 1993): 5–6.

Nicholls, Stephen. "Maddin film to open festival," *Winnipeg Free Press* (31 July 1992): C31.

Pevere, Geoff. "Guy Maddin: True to Form," *Take One* 1.1 (New Series; Fall 1992): 4–11.

Varga, Darrell, "Desire in Bondage: Guy Maddin's *Careful*," *Canadian Journal of Film Studies* 8.1 (Fall 1999): 56–70.

Reviews

David Stratton, *Variety* (18 May 1992): 44; Rick Groen, "Stealing with Panache," *Globe & Mail* (10 October 1992): C7; Jim Hoberman,"The Heights," *Village Voice* 37.41 (13 October 1992): 57; John Griffin,"Gothic film is *Careful* and fun," *Gazette* (Montreal; 18 October 1992): F3; Stephen Holden, *New York Times* (20 October 1992): C20; Graham Fuller, "Shots in the Dark," *Interview* 22.12 (December 1992): 53; Clare Monk, *Sight and Sound* 3.10 (October 1993): 41–42.

FIGURE 14

Exotica (Atom Egoyan, 1994) – Mia Kirshner (Christina); Bruce
Greenwood (Francis).

14 Exotica
(Atom Egoyan, 1994)

Production: produced 1991–93, released 1994. Ego Film Arts, with the financial participation of Telefilm Canada and the Ontario Film Development Corporation. **Director:** Atom Egoyan. **Producer:** Atom Egoyan. **Co-Producer:** Camelia Frieberg. **Associate Producer:** David Webb. **Production Coordinator:** Roland W. Schlimme. **Production Manager:** Sandra Cunningham. **Screenplay:** Atom Egoyan. **Script Supervisor:** Joanne Harwood. **Cinematographer:** Paul Sarossy. **Production Design:** Linda Del Rosario, Richard Paris. **Costume Design:** Linda Muir. **Editor:** Susan Shipton.

Music: Mychael Danna. **Choreography:** Claudia Moore. **Sound Design:** Steven Munro. **Sound Mixer:** Daniel Pellerin. **Colour, 103mins., 35 mm.**

Cast: Bruce Greenwood (Francis), **Elias Koteas** (Eric), **Don McKellar** (Thomas), **Mia Kirshner** (Christina), **Arsinée Khanjian** (Zoe), **Sarah Polley** (Tracey), **David Hemblen** (inspector), **Calvin Green** (customs officer), **Peter Krantz** (man in taxi), **Damon D'Oliveira, Billy Merasty** (men at opera), **Jack Blum** (scalper), **Ken McDougal** (doorman), **Victor Garber** (Harold).

Synopsis: In an airport, Thomas, a traveller who has come off a flight, is being examined by customs officers as he looks at himself unsuspectingly in a one-way mirror. His subsequent taxi ride, the removal of a cache of rare eggs smuggled into the country for his petshop, and his trip to a ballet performance are intercut with the activities of several people at a lushly decorated strip club called the Exotica, which features lap-dancing. Francis Brown regularly visits the Exotica. But he is only interested in watching one particular girl, named Christina, dance for him. It is gradually revealed that Christina used to baby-sit Francis's daughter Lisa, who Francis was at one time suspected of killing. Photos and home video indicate that his wife was black and his daughter of mixed race. Francis also pays his niece, Tracey, to house-sit for him when he visits the club, and we learn that Tracey's father, Harold (Francis's brother), once had an affair with Francis's wife before she was killed in a car accident. Harold was also injured in the accident; now wheelchair-bound, he lives in an apartment above a strip-mall in a black neighbourhood.

In a second narrative line, Christina's ex-lover Eric is the MC at the Exotica. They met while searching for Francis's daughter (her corpse is found in a field), but their relationship has fallen apart. Eric has fathered a child, by contract, with the club's owner Zoe, who is seven months pregnant. Jealous of Francis's attraction to Christina, Eric provokes him into breaking a strict club rule by touching her while she dances for him at his table, then throws him out.

A third storyline involves Thomas, whose petshop specializes in exotic species of birds and fish. He develops a ritual of picking up men (especially men of colour) at the ballet, but the only one who comes home with him turns out to be a customs officer who steals some rare eggs that Thomas had smuggled into the country. Francis, who works for Revenue Canada and comes to audit Thomas's books, discovers his smuggling operation and blackmails him into helping take revenge against Eric. Thomas complies by visiting Christina at the Exotica, but the confrontation between Francis and Eric ends with an embrace when Eric tells Francis that it was he who found his child in the field.

Role playing and the white male imaginary in Atom Egoyan's *Exotica*

———————————————— ℬ

Catherine Russell

> I really like Clint Eastwood. It was kind of odd when he was on the jury in Cannes when *Exotica* was in competition. It was one of the few times when someone saw a movie of mine and I really wanted to be beside that person as they were watching it. But I guess he didn't like it that much. (Atom Egoyan)

> You film "in reverse gear," with the risks of invisibility that implies, with the fall into oblivion [...] Are you the one who brings about the disappearance of the cameraman in favour of the machine, or are you the first cineaste of the new filmic representation? (Paul Virilio, video letter to Atom Egoyan)

W INNING THE CRITICS' PRIZE IN CANNES IN 1994, along with eight Genies and a few other prestigious awards,[1] *Exotica* put Atom Egoyan on the map of international cinema. His sixth feature film, *Exotica* appeared uncannily familiar to Canadian audiences who had followed his career since 1984. Egoyan is a director who continues to write and produce his own films, returning again and again to a particular set of themes, a network of actors, a consistent stylization of performance and design, and a complex narrative structure. This material is orchestrated somewhat differently in each instance, but the tone remains consistent. Many critics have described his films as having a certain "coldness," and while they do indeed have a dispassionate aspect to them, it does not detract from the visceral impact of his investigation of emotions, relationships and behaviour framed by contemporary urban Canadian culture.

---

[1] *Exotica* was also declared best foreign film in the 1994 Prix de la Critique in France; and best Canadian feature at the Toronto Festival of Festivals.

Of all the writing that has been produced on Egoyan's films, none is as insightful as Egoyan's own testimony. In numerous interviews, he analyzes and contextualizes his work without necessarily 'explaining what it means.' The films, in fact, defy such explanatory interpretation, working more as complex processes of layering, juxtaposition, and reflexive commentary on visual culture. Egoyan is especially conscious of his reliance on Canadian funding bodies, particularly Telefilm Canada and the Ontario Film Development Corporation, which supported *Exotica*. The Canadian arts-funding system has enabled him to develop his experimental narrative style without the constraints of commercial funding pressures.

Egoyan is one of the more prominent filmmakers of an emergent group of independent directors, including Patricia Rozema, Bruce McDonald, Peter Mettler and Guy Maddin, and is very supportive of younger filmmakers and the development of a Canadian art cinema. Moreover, he has been positioned within a kind of international *auteur*-chain; one of the well-known stories about him has Wim Wenders handing him his Montreal Festival prize in 1987, and Egoyan subsequently handing over his Toronto Festival prize to up-and-coming filmmaker John Pozer in 1991. The international success of the film prompted at least one critic to claim it as "a coming of age of English-Canadian filmmaking – a marker, a point of reference,"[2] indicating Egoyan's central role in the development of a Canadian art cinema.

Egoyan's films are also very Canadian in other, unexpected, ways:

> I see my films as being set in a particular society [...] I know the films are set in Toronto. They couldn't be set anywhere else [...] To me there's something essentially funny about a can-do mentality with dysfunctional people.[3]

But Egoyan's depiction of Toronto is not always funny. Within the ironies of his first six feature films is a startling psychological profile of a 'world-class city' that is gradually spinning out of control. From the inflated real-estate market to diasporic cultural communities, from the repressive dynamics of the WASP family to lap-dancing, Egoyan's Toronto is not the image found in tourist brochures. It is an image that may be very familiar to Torontonians, though, and one of the rewards of Egoyan's films is his depiction of the emotional landscape of the city. The 'coldness' of the films is not un-

---

[2] Wyndham Wise, "The True Meaning of Exotica," *Take One* 4.9 (1995). Wise goes on to say that it represents "the success of the Ontario Film Development Corp. [and] the Perspective Canada programme at the Toronto International Film Festival."

[3] "Difficult to Say: Atom Egoyan Interviewed by Geoff Pevere," in Atom Egoyan, *Exotica* screenplay (Toronto: Coach House, 1995): 62.

related to the Canadian climate, which forces people into enclosed spaces for so many months of the year. These are the spaces where Egoyan's characters subsist.

Egoyan himself grew up in Victoria B.C. and moved to Toronto in 1979 at the age of eighteen; this may account for his ability to see through the city's sheen. In each of his films except *Exotica*, he has dealt on some level with his Armenian heritage. Cultural identity is figured as a complex structure of memory, family, and representation, so that ethnicity and race cease to be 'issues' and become familiar features of urban Canadian life. This is only one of the ways in which Egoyan's work has begun to expand the parameters of Canadian cinema.

The style of filmmaking that Egoyan has forged falls somewhere between Hollywood and Europe, drawing on a range of generic and dramatic tendencies. The family melodrama constitutes the generic background for many of his films (especially *Next of Kin, Family Viewing,* and *The Adjuster*), but although he is preoccupied with emotions and psychological struggles, his work is not melodramatic in the conventional sense. The films indulge very little hysteria, and avoid the highs and lows of dramatic excess, along with manichaean forces of good and evil. Egoyan replaces the passion of despair with the coolness of characters who cannot communicate. His films are existential in their preoccupation with alienation, death, and states of being. At the same time, they are beautifully stylized and photographed, in keeping with the excessive *mise-en-scène* of film melodrama.

The frequent incorporation of video footage – with all of its conflicting connotations of surveillance and home movies – punctuates the filmic spectacle, propelling the existential subject into a postmodern image-culture. In *Family Viewing, Speaking Parts,* and *Calendar,* video mediates most of the relationships between characters and comes to stand in for significant memories and experiences.

Of all the auteurist elements in Egoyan's work (the constellation of effects that denote 'an Egoyan film'), it is perhaps the performance-technique that is most distinctive. In all of his filmmaking, from *Next of Kin* to *The Sweet Hereafter,* the actors seem slightly distanced from their characters, as if they were playing roles. His anti-illusionistic technique of having actors appear to quote their lines is a tradition well-established in French cinema; directors such as Robert Bresson, Eric Rohmer, and Chantal Akerman have worked extensively with a disjunction between script and speech, directing actors to double themselves as actor and character. Each has developed a distinctive performance style that evokes different kinds of tensions.[4]

Egoyan may be the most Brechtian of Canadian directors; but where Brecht advocated alienation-effects for a politicized form of theatre, in Egoyan's cinema it is not only the spectator who is alienated. The viewer is indeed distanced and provoked into 'thinking,' but the characters themselves are alienated from each other. And they are alienated from their own identities. Thus, the political dimensions of the films have far more to do with questions of cultural and sexual identity than with class struggle. The spectator's alienation is in turn a doubling of body and machine, as characters appear to be performing their identities for the camera.

Exotica is in many respects the culmination of the work on visual culture, performance and characterization that Egoyan has carried out in his previous films. He accounts for its unprecedented success by suggesting that "the characters seem more aware of the state they're in. They're able to articulate their pain, and for that reason seem to be more classically identifiable [...] people are able to trust that these characters are more responsible for their actions."[5] In fact, the acting in *Exotica* is still quite stylized, but perhaps just a little more relaxed – enough to encourage the impression that the characters have gained some independence from their creator. Egoyan thinks of *Exotica* as a "break," and, as his two subsequent films *The Sweet Hereafter* and *Felicia's Journey* indicate, it was a turning point in his career.

Exotica is, in any case, the product of a filmmaking style that is extraordinarily mature and confident, and able to tackle the dangerous and explosive subject of transgressive desire. If in conventional melodrama oedipal desires are deep structural components of familial relationships, for Egoyan, illicit desire is a starting-point for the exploration of everyday relationships. Pornography and voyeurism are omnipresent in the films, but they are almost always people's jobs (for example, the phone-sex operator in *Family Viewing*, the censor in *The Adjuster*). Boundaries between private and public are as fuzzy as those between viewers amd viewed. Desire infiltrates all relationships, as the voyeuristic structures of cinema and video come to characterize everyday life for most Egoyan characters.

If the characters in *Exotica* are somewhat more 'believable' than those of Egoyan's other films, it may be because the formal performance techniques

---

[4] See Ivone Margulies, *Nothing Happens: Chantal Akerman's Hyperrealist Everyday* (Durham NC: Duke UP, 1996): 42–64.

[5] "Difficult to Say," 43.

are echoed in the film's narrative premisses. Role-playing is a form of therapy for the characters, who are all driven by some kind of psychological torment. The examination of emotions in *Exotica* constitutes a treatment of character as a set of visible traits – costume, behaviour, race – that don't have an 'essential' fixed identity supporting them. Emotions are not deeply buried, but are legible in the surface traits of the characters. Egoyan's scripts don't waste words, and each fragment of dialogue is carefully spoken, heavy with meaning, so that the viewer is always aware of there being a script, a level of writing or textuality. that needs to be read. Point of view in *Exotica* is thus never that of the characters, but remains outside them, often literally looking down on them, watching the actors play characters playing roles.

A *haunted film*

The network of narrative lines, flashbacks, and images of which *Exotica* is constructed circulates around an absent centre. A nexus of paedophilia, abduction, incest, and murder informs the film without quite being dramatized, so that the spectator is left to imagine the unimaginable. The film ends with a scene that occurs years before the rest of the action takes place: Francis drives Christina home and pays her for babysitting his daughter. Its position as a kind of originary flashback tends to force an explanation of some kind for the preceding action, yet it fails to actually explain anything. It nevertheless calls for an analysis that starts from the end and works backwards to the beginning of the film.

Francis drives Christina home and pulls up in front of a house that is strangely forbidding – an 'ordinary' middle-class Toronto house set back from the road amidst dense shrubbery, back from the road, framed in a terrible symmetry. It is the kind of house that has a prim and well-painted face turned out to the world, but all is hidden behind it. Francis tells Christina how much his daughter appreciates her, and their final conversation outside the house goes as follows:

> FRANCIS   She thinks you're not very happy. Listen, Christina, if there is ever
> anything you want to talk about, about what might be going on at
> home, or whatever, you know that I'm here, okay?
> CHRISTINA Okay... okay.

He pays her, they say goodbye, and the film ends.

This ending is profoundly disturbing on a number of levels, not the least of which is the disorientation caused by closing the film in flashback.

It's also the first and final clue to Christina's psychological profile, which has been far less developed than those of the other characters. Her past, her home, has never been mentioned until this point. Egoyan is very revealing in an interview with Geoff Pevere when he explains the original idea behind *Exotica*:

> This film, more than any other, was an attempt to work out the charade of sexuality and the possibility of creating a sexual environment in which the relationships were quite platonic. Plus dealing with things outside of that, like how somebody who is abused makes a parody of their own sexual identity as a means of trying to convince themselves that that part of themselves which has been destroyed is somehow not as vital as it is. Somehow they have to reduce it to something more grotesque than it can be, otherwise it becomes too painful to deal with.[6]

We may well want to ask why, given this interest in the consequences of sexual abuse, the film ends up being focused on the psychology of the abuser (or possible abuser, Francis), rather than the abused. In the concluding flashback Christina wears braids, braces and glasses, in contrast to her more 'mature' appearance throughout the rest of the film. This suggests the limitations of the director's ability to investigate female psychic space, falling back on clichés of physical appearance. In contrast, Francis is much more developed psychologically, torn between conflicting feelings of loss, guilt, and desire. The film is in many ways focused on the male imaginary. Yet all the characters, especially Christina and Francis, are really extensions of the home, allegories of 'family,' and are ultimately subsumed within the shot of the house, which is haunted by oedipal desires.

A Freudian drama lurks within the film, and Egoyan exploits the structure of the primal scene for his own purposes precisely by withholding it. Transgressive desire is, moreover, doubled and redoubled within the film, and even the central, embedded scene of a green sunlit field, wide and empty, is returned to several times but is never clearly established. Its vastness is disorienting and uncentred. Ironically, this site of violent desire is the single pastoral image in the film. Periodic flashbacks show a group of people searching for the body of a young girl, Francis's daughter Lisa. Christina and Eric fall in love while searching, but the body they finally discover wears the same white blouse and tartan skirt that signifies 'schoolgirl' in Christina's striptease act. This central image of the eroticized schoolgirl, a commodified form of a 'loss of innocence,' is tied, by way of suggestion and

---

6 "Difficult to Say," 48.

implication, to the incestuous and abusive form of desire that the film circumnavigates. By alluding to it without ever naming it, the film incorporates a complex structure of denial, guilt, and repression that is the inevitable counterpart to paedophilia.

Towards the end of the film, Christina tells Thomas (and the viewer) what she says is "the full story," which is that Francis was a suspect in his daughter's murder, and even though he was released, he is still disturbed by it. He and Christina have an arrangement that is essentially a form of therapy for Francis, a special relationship in which she performs for him at the Exotica club.[7] She also says that he does something special for her; but her needs are much less clear. The concluding flashback may give a clue to her 'real' identity, beneath the sexual veneer, but it is merely a counterimage of repressed adolescence.

The empty centre of the film might be described as having three separate evocative images: the beautiful green field; the threatening façade of the 'home'; and a short video-taped sequence of Francis's wife and daughter. In the video, the girl, framed in tight closeup, smiles broadly at the camera until her mother's hand reaches in and covers the camera lens. This short sequence is repeated three times in the film, the first triggered by Tracey's memory while house-sitting, the second by Francis in the men's room of the Exotica while Eric is persuading him to touch Christina. In this context especially, the image becomes loaded with connotations of transgressive desire and its prohibition.

The third time the sequence plays, Francis is revealed as the camera operator, and it leads into the final, concluding flashback when Christina, dressed 'down,' rings the door-bell. As in so many sequences in *Exotica*, the editing situates this video imagery within chains of signifiers that impinge on one another to produce lateral, surface meanings lacking depth and certainty. Tracey, Christina, and Lisa, Francis's dead daughter, become linked as duplicates and stand-ins for each other. 'The schoolgirl' is the image that links them as fetishistic replacements for the lost daughter and for the 'lost innocence' of adolescent sexuality.

---

[7] Egoyan is quite explicit about the therapeutic aspects of his stories. "There's a group of analysts in Toronto who have looked at all my films. They've told me that from their point of view, all my films deal with a process called 'faulty mourning' – when a patient builds a ritual of mourning which only accentuates and exaggerates the sense of loss which they think they're dealing with"; interview with Jonathan Romney, *Sight and Sound* 5.5 (May 1995): 8.

All of Egoyan's films contain video imagery, and although *Exotica* uses it much less, its resonance as a kind of mediated access to memory remains the same. Video images often embody a level of truth that is otherwise unavailable to Egoyan's characters, and *Exotica* is no different in this respect.[8] At the same time, the status of the video image as 'image' (its difference from the filmic reality) points to the constructed nature of all images and the unreliability of memory. The role of video in Egoyan's films is instrumental to their fragmented, diffracted point of view, to the way in which he has modulated melodramatic narrative within a technological environment.[9] Francis may be the main character in *Exotica*, but he is also a link in an image-chain over which he really has no control, despite his 'possession' of the camera and the memory it has preserved.

The video fragment in *Exotica* stands as a buried fragment of Francis's memory, a clue to his behaviour. Its domestic format – its connection with the family home – is vitally linked to the act of censorship embodied in the covering-up of the image. In this way, the video imagery acts as a textual comment on the spectacle of the film, particularly the scenes set in the Exotica club and the pleasures of the gaze. Suddenly the innocuous act of filming one's daughter takes on subversive overtones. And, like the scenes in the meadow, the video footage is the locus of a memory that is both a romantic ideal and an ominous site of hidden dangers.

The sexual spectacle

Lap-dancing is one of North America's more peculiar rituals, a practice that encapsulates and makes literal those tensions of desire and prohibition that haunt *Exotica*. The Exotica club, where many of the film's key scenes are played out, is a place where men come to have semi-dressed women dance at their tables. They can look but not touch. A central stage showcases the individual women doing striptease acts, as Eric, speaking from a high voice-of-god podium above the floor, sells them off for $5.00 a dance. The set is darkly lit with glitter-ball effects; the music is heavy on the bass, unconventionally laden with Arabian melodies; the exotic effect is further enhanced by a forest of tropical plants. The space has a very womb-like atmosphere,

---

[8] Timothy Shary, "Video as Accessible Artifact and Artificial Access: The Early Films of Atom Egoyan," *Film Criticism* 19 (Spring 1995): 2.

[9] See the essays by Jacinto Lageira and Paul Virilio in *Atom Egoyan* (Paris: Editions Dis Voir, 1993).

and our first entry into the club is by way of a birth-canal-like passage; Zoe's office is a bohemian comfort zone, softly lit with tent-like walls. In all respects, the Exotica is a stylized, exaggerated play on the idea of a sex club, and not a realistic attempt to re-create such a place.

To Egoyan's credit, he has managed to orchestrate this film around the sexual spectacle without adopting a pornographic gaze. Women in various stages of undress writhe and undulate in the background of many of the shots, but they are basically scenery, part of the decor. Their counterparts, silent single men grasping highballs, are equally omnipresent. Except when it frames the main characters, the camera is in constant motion, describing long tracks through the space. Even more important is the absence of any reverse-shot editing that might suture the spectator's gaze into the erotic spectacle. Instead, we are slightly distanced from it, able to grasp the slightly pathetic and riciculous scene of women wiggling their bums in men's faces. The exoticness of exotic dancers is rendered somewhat banal through redundancy. The scene is less exciting than oddly comforting, offering warmth and darkness to lonely men and working women.

Christina doesn't really fit into the Exotica scene. Her schoolgirl routine, performed onstage to Leonard Cohen's "Everybody Knows," is even more contrived than the rest of the club. Egoyan takes advantage of the excess permitted by the lap dancing/striptease conceit to push the anti-naturalism in this film to a point of extreme stylization. Christina undoes her white blouse and occasionally shows her panties, but always wears more clothes than the other (background) women, and tends to carry on heavy conversations while dancing at Francis's table. Eric's introductions are often monologues, commenting on the effect of the dancers and his obsession with Christina. On one occasion, his monologue is really only a voice-over of his thoughts – not miked into the club's PA system. The Exotica scenes are not really a parody of a strip-club, but constitute a cinematic commentary on the darker, more melancholy aspects of the sex-industry.

Arsinée Khanjian's performance as Zoe, the pregnant Madam, is even more out of keeping with the clichés of the milieu. Seven months pregnant, she exudes a kind of maternal aura and tries to run her business like a family tradition. While touching is *verboten* out in the club, within her office/boudoir she encourages both Christina and Eric to touch her swollen belly. The camera seems to linger more on her semi-dressed, voluptuous body than on any of the strippers, in yet another departure from the conventions of the sexual spectacle. Zoe speaks in a half-voice, which other actors also adopt in scenes with her. Khanjian's performance in this film allows her pregnant body to stand in for her character. She depends heavily on an exotic repertoire of wigs and dresses, but wears them without irony. Despite Egoyan's care in circumventing an erotic gaze, the film nevertheless falls into the perennial trap of giving men minds and women bodies.

The Exotica is not the only site of performance and spectatorship in *Exotica*. Within the film's complex narrative structure is an elaborate series of matches between the club and an opera house where Thomas, the gay pet-shop owner, picks up men. Thomas is, in effect, the missing spectator of Christina's striptease. Shots of him in the ballet audience are intercut with her act, and in one instance we even get a shot of him gazing at his companion's crotch. The conjunction of opera house and strip-club is an ironic juxtaposition of 'high' and 'low' culture, but it also drives home the strict division between spectacle and spectator that the erotic gaze depends on. Lap-dancing is a ritualistic test of the pleasure implicit in the separation of viewer and performer, a kind of inverted voyeurism. Spectating is a theme that Egoyan has repeatedly come back to, but his approach is far from a Hitchcockian exploitation of the voyeuristic structure of cinema. In *Exotica*, spectating is an activity that has its own sexual component, quite distinct from the spectacle: we never do see any of the ballets that Thomas sees.

Don McKellar's performance as Thomas exploits the ironies of Egoyan's script for comedic effect without adopting any campy clichés of gay characterization.[10] Egoyan has confessed to an admiration for Woody Allen,[11] and Thomas is perhaps his best rendering of an Allen character – sexually inhibited, racked with guilt, and drawn deeply into other peoples' problems. As a gay character, he is very much out of place at the Exotica, where he goes wearing a wire to find out why Francis was kicked out the night before. Francis is outside in the car listening to his conversation with Christina. Thomas eventually goes to the men's room to talk privately with Francis, but when he's in the stall Eric comes in and starts talking to him, exactly as he had done with Francis. Eric confesses to Thomas that he was once Christina's lover, which explains his jealousy and his mistreatment of Francis.

---

[10] McKellar won a Genie for his supporting role in *Exotica*. It is surprising that this could be possible in an Egoyan film, given the tight control demanded by the script, and it may well be McKellar's use of comedy to highlight the ironies of his performance that brought it close enough to a conventional star performance to win an award.

[11] Lesley Ellen Harris, "Atom Egoyan: Laughter in the Dark," *Canadian Forum* 70.5 (December 1991): 17.

The men's room is an important part of the club, lushly decorated and underlit, the place where the real privacy of masturbation follows the private dance in the public space. Francis rushes in here a couple of times after Christina's private dance with him. Shot from an overhead angle, the men's room is the site of the film's most emotional moments. It is symptomatic that neither Francis nor Thomas sees Eric or knows his identity when they each, on separate occasions, speak to him from inside the stall. The men's room is, in this sense, the troubled heart of the club and of the film itself, a place where, in the absence of women, men confess to their tormenting desires. *Pulp Fiction* won the Palme d'Or at Cannes in the same year that *Exotica* won the Critics Prize, and while it is interesting that both films use the men's room so extensively, it is equally significant that Egoyan's bathroom is a site of alienation and psychological struggle, while Tarantino's is one of violence.[12]

The only consummated sexual act in the film takes place between Thomas and Ian, a man he meets at the ballet. It doesn't go well, as Ian teases Thomas about his hairy chest and then steals his precious hyacinth macaw eggs. The viewer may recognize Ian as a customs officer from the opening scene, in which he watches Thomas from behind a one-way mirror. Very little is actually shown, as the sex scene is abruptly curtailed, and the next scene in Thomas's apartment finds him alone in bed, "the morning after." The omission of the men's love-making may be interpreted as an instance of self-censorship, or as another evasion of the full sexual spectacle that is consistently circumvented despite the film's exotic/erotic promise. The inclusion of this scene is nevertheless an important means by which the thematics of sexual fantasy, ritual, and power are explored beyond the central paedophiliac narrative. By contrast, homosexual desire seems far less complicated, lacking the terrifying family dynamic that informs the other, heterosexual relations in the film. The effect is a kind of normalizing of gay culture, and in this respect the film makes an ironic break with the conventions of exoticizing homosexuality.

ဆ

---

12 Sharon Willis has analyzed the men's room as a space of violent confrontation and homosocial fear in Quentin Tarantino' films: "The Father's Watch the Boys' Room," *Camera Obscura* 32 (September 1993–January 1994): 41–74.

"It's a jungle out there"

Ian, like Francis's wife, and like Thomas's other dates at the ballet, is black. The notion of the exotic in *Exotica* goes beyond sexuality to incorporate a latent sense of colonial desire in contemporary Canadian culture. This broader sense of 'the exotic' is already referred to in the club's 'oriental' music and tropical vegetation, and by Thomas's trafficking in rare species of birds. It is in a scene in Thomas's shop that Francis remarks, "It's a jungle out there." The jungle is a space of fantasy, a place where 'the Other' takes precedence and where one's own identity can be redefined, repositioned, or masked. The most vivid inscription of this sense of the exotic in the film is Francis's brother, Harold, who lives in a West Indian neighbourhood and wears Bob Marley and Black Power T-shirts.

With the discourse of race in *Exotica*, Egoyan wanders into the treacherous waters of cultural politics. The black neighbourhood is represented in his typically ironic style, but here it verges on the ethnic stereotype: a hulking black man walks directly into the camera, signifying the threat and danger of the neighbourhood with a single (other) body. Egoyan's own explanation for his characters' attempts at integration is that

> both Thomas and Francis' brother would like to believe that those [black] cultures are at their disposal; but in each case there is something colonial about their approach, because both are going into that milieu to seek out something about themselves.[13]

In another interview, he comments on the relationship between Francis and his deceased wife, of whom we catch only a few brief images:

> I loved the idea that his separation from his family was reinforced by his having a wife of colour. You have a sense, a suspicion, of the nature of his attraction in the first place, of sowing the seeds of that alienation through the very reason by which that relationship was formed. It's very salient in the film. It's not really drawn out, but I think there is that sense that he consciously transported his wife into his culture and created this home that she never identified with.[14]

Egoyan's comments convey a sense (equally strong in the film) of a deep cultural divide, where the bridging function promised by the existence of interracial couples is merely a façade of racial harmony. This may be yet

---

[13] "Urban Angst," Scott Lewis interview with Egoyan, *Reverse Shot* (Spring 1995): 25.
[14] "Atom's Id: Lawrence Chua talks with Atom Egoyan," *Artforum* 33 (March 1995): 26.

another symptom of the urban setting of the film, as Toronto is a city that boasts of its exotic multiculturalism but is in fact riven by racial tensions.

By incorporating race into a film that is concerned primarily with the psychology and emotions of desire, Egoyan is able to incorporate racism and racialist desire into his psychological landscape. He does this by relegating people of colour to the status of secondary characters who are little more than the objects of desire for white characters. In his shorthand style of representation, Francis's wife, Thomas's dates and Harold's neighbours are reduced to the colour of their skin. We know nothing more about them, so the visual signifier of race constitutes their only distinguishing feature. As a superficial discourse of images, race is depicted as a visual language that is rendered exotic in a predominantly white society.

If the jungle is a place where the white man goes to discover himself, interracial encounters are crucial to the way in which the male characters in *Exotica* try to understand themselves through fantasy. This is what the Exotica provides for its clients: an imaginary zone where fantasy supersedes reality. Egoyan's incorporation of race as a discourse which is strictly visual is a means of analyzing latent forms of colonialism by way of the structure of the stereotype.

Homi Bhabha, a theorist of postcolonial culture, has analyzed the racial stereotype as a colonial fetish that needs to be deconstructed:

> The stereotype is not a simplification because it is a false representation of a given reality. It is a simplification because it is an arrested, fixated form of representation that, in denying the play of difference [...] constitutes a problem for the *representation* of the subject in signification of psychic and social relations.[15]

Bhabha advocates an analysis of the visual aspect of race within the fantasy of colonial power, an understanding of the racial stereotype as a fetish. "Fetish" is a psychoanalytical term for the fixing of difference, an imagistic containment of a threatening lack, or a guilty desire. It is a site of contra-dictory identification, of believing and disbelieving. In deconstructing the racial stereotype it "becomes easier to see the bind of knowledge and

---

[15] Homi K. Bhabha, "The Other Question: Difference, Discrimination and the Discourse of Colonialism," in *Out There: Marginalization and Contemporary Cultures*, ed. Russell Ferguson, Martha Gever, Trinh T. Minh–ha & Cornel West (New York & Cambridge MA: New Museum of Contemporary Art and MIT Press, 1990): 80.

fantasy, power and pleasure, that informs the particular regime of visibility deployed in colonial discourse."[16]

The 'Other' is a fantastic construction of colonial culture, an imaginary representation that depends on an imagistic, visual component to confirm an identity of mastery. Most importantly for Bhabha, the stereotype, as an allegory of racial fantasies, bears its deconstruction within it. Bhabha is not defending racial stereotyping, but reading it differently, from the understanding of its constructedness, its impossibility as an object or as a person. Egoyan essentially gets away with racial stereotyping because of the anti-naturalistic, slightly ironic, and distanced style of the entire film. As objects of desire, people of colour in *Exotica* play a role in the white imaginary that the film explores. It is not a 'real world,' but one that is thoroughly informed by desires, fantasies, and imaginary identities. The roles of the black characters are strictly limited to a discourse of images and representation: they are thus legible as visual constructs, or 'impossible characters.'

The un-homelike home

The discourse of race in *Exotica* is in many ways an extension of the role-playing that the characters engage in; it is merely a surface attribute beneath which identity is fluid and mobile. The opening scene of *Exotica* introduces the play of image and identity that underscores the various narrative threads of the film – the great rift between outer appearances and inner truths that is negotiated. Thomas is going through customs at Toronto airport. He is being observed by Ian and his superior officer from behind a one-way mirror. The superior officer is performed by David Hemblen, who plays cold, dominant authority figures in three of Egoyan's previous films (*Family Viewing*, *Speaking Parts*, and *The Adjuster*), an intertextual reference that contributes to his powerful image of authoritarian surveillance in this scene. His voice actually opens the film, speaking over a shot of the lush, throbbing, Exotica club. He is instructing Ian, saying "You have to convince yourself that this person has something hidden that you have to find. You check his bags, but it's his face, his gestures, that you are really watching." Thomas then walks up to the one-way mirror and stares directly at Ian on the other side, without realizing it. As Thomas examines his own face, Hemblen says to Ian: "He's staring straight at you. Look at him carefully. What do you see?"

---

[16] Bhabha, "The Other Question," 84.

In another one-way mirror in the Exotica, Francis stares at Eric in the same way. The device of the one-way mirror takes on a complex set of connotations as a metaphor for psychic splitting. Thomas looking at Ian is a powerful image of the arbitrariness of racial identity, the shared psychic space across the racial divide, and the crucial role of the image in the construction of racial difference. Francis looking at Eric invokes a different kind of splitting. Eric, like Hemblen's character, is in a position of central control at the Exotica, although his role as super-ego is radically inverted: he encourages Francis and the other clients to immerse themselves in their wildest fantasies.

These fantasies, however, are rendered inadequate – sad stories built up from tired clichés that girls like Christina are able to impersonate. The narrative strategies of the film itself are equally drained of their passion and their believability, withholding many images and truths that would potentially 'fill in' a true narrative. Egoyan's storytelling technique involves another level of splitting between images and events. The film's sense of doubling performance and script, like the doubling effect of the one-way mirror device, is best described as an uncanniness that can always be traced back to the ghostly aura of the dead schoolgirl in the great green meadow.

Around the central dynamic of illicit desire are woven the various threads of narrative that constitute *Exotica*. Within the film's weave are at least two collapsed stories, scenes in which a great deal of narrative information is compressed into a brief summary. An extreme instance is when Francis fills in the details of Christina's version of 'the full story.' He tells Thomas that the police told *him* that his wife was having an affair with his brother Harold; that he thought Lisa wasn't his own daughter; and that he could harm her. Framing the story in this way, Francis distances himself from it, and we don't really know whether he thought these things or not, let alone whether they're true. He goes on to say:

> And then they found the man that did it and they let him go. And I went home. And then my wife was killed in a car accident a couple of months later. Harold was in the car. He lived.

This speech exemplifies Egoyan's ability to separate characters from their actions and give them a certain self-consciousness that removes them from the narrative in which they are written. It also supplies a masterplot of hysterical melodrama of which the film is merely a moment, an exploration of the psychic energy implicit in a larger story that is not, in itself, dramatized.

Another compressed story concerns the relationship between Eric and Christina. Cross-cutting between the two of them searching in the green meadow (in the past) and Eric's apartment in the Exotica club (in the present), the découpage has them effectively meet and break up at the same time. The conversation taking place in the field is carried over into the later scenes, in which we merely see them meet and glare at each other. Eric seems to be lonely and discontented with his life at the Exotica, while on the soundtrack – the meadow conversation – they have both just graduated and do not yet work in the club. We never know what brought them to the Exotica or why their relationship goes sour. The implication, though, is obvious from the visuals: that Christina has lost the innocence that first attracted Eric to her. The irony is that Eric's principal spiel as the Exotica MC is to exploit Christina's schoolgirl act:

> Let me ask you gentlemen. What is it that gives a schoolgirl her special innocence? Her sweet fragrance? [...] Or is it her firm, young flesh inviting your every caress [...] Please join me in welcoming a sassy bit of jailbait to our stage. Yes indeed. Come out sweet Chrissy. Wherever you are baby, come on out.

The nagging sense of lack created by this splitting of image and identity, storytelling and event is finally figured as a form of homelessness. Eric's apartment somewhere in the Exotica is no more than a mattress on the floor. Thomas's chic high-rise apartment where he incubates exotic eggs is equally un-homelike, apparently under perpetual repair. Tracey and Harold's apartment is cramped and noisy. The only fully realized home-like environment in the film is Francis's well-appointed living-room. This space is, however, haunted by the mantlepiece photos of his wife and daughter, who, together with Francis, play out the roles of a perfect family in the film's concluding flashback in that very living-room. The videotaped version of this family scene contradicts its perfection, but the film's conclusion pushes past the difficult 'image' of family trauma to the fantasy of domestic bliss – which is in turn undermined by Francis's conversation with Christina in front of her imposing home. No character is, finally, 'at home' in the film, except perhaps Zoe, who has ensconced herself in the beating heart of the strip-club.

Home may be the ultimate object of desire, but it is also ultimately mysterious. Like the face that Ian is instructed to search, the image of home has hidden secrets. Penetrating the façade, inside the Exotica, the forbidden still remains out of reach, a mere show. And so the film works out a complex series of circular forms of desire that remain incomplete, unsatisfied, and exotic. The uncanny (literally un-homelike, *unheimlich*) is the term most appropriate to the recurring sense of apparent identity and coincidence that always marks the return of repressed desires.

Contractual emotions

In an essay related to *Speaking Parts*, Egoyan writes:

> The idea of surface, when associated with the depiction of character, suggests superficiality and lack of dimension. We tend to think of a surface as something that is without depth, something that offers nothing more than what is immediately visible. On closer reading, however, the concept of surface proves to be the most complex and intriguing aspect of any rendering of personality.[17]

Egoyan's use of video imagery in so much of his work is testimony to this fascination with the surface aspects of what he calls "psychological territory." In *Exotica*, the idea of surface is investigated by way of the theatrical dimensions of personalities split between guilt, desire, loss, and jealousy. Emotions in this film are occasionally released in hysterical gestures (Francis in the men's room; Christina kicking and screaming in Zoe's office), but for the most part they are channelled into ritualistic behaviour – Francis visiting the club, Thomas scalping tickets to the ballet, Eric emceeing Christina's show, Zoe dressing up, Christina playing a sexy schoolgirl.

The roles that the characters play are further bound by financial transactions, enabling a certain distancing of the emotional content of their social performances. Eric admits to not being allowed to feel anything for the baby Zoe is carrying, precisely because he was paid to father it. Francis pays Tracey to babysit for him, but Egoyan teases the viewer with their first exchange in Francis's car by making it look as though he is paying her for sex. After auditing Thomas's books (another form of voyeurism), Francis blackmails Thomas into infiltrating the Exotica. The contracts in the film are all various forms of social prostitution, people paying and receiving money for playing roles – from dating (at the ballet) to lap-dancing.

Only one character in the film is able to distinguish between reality and fantasy, and she ultimately refuses to play a role. After an unspecified number of times that she has been hired to babysit for her uncle Francis, Tracey finally points out that "there's no baby to sit." She wants to be released from her paid participation in his fantasy, but she's the only character willing to face facts. Tracey remains outside the vortex of desire that grips the other

---

[17] Atom Egoyan, "Surface Tension," in *Speaking Parts* (Toronto: Coach House, 1993): 25.

characters, but, even more importantly, she lacks their guilt. And it is precisely the symbiotic tension between desire and guilt that inflects the sexual and racial fantasies of *Exotica*.

The spectator of *Exotica* is equally affected by the emotional distancing and role-playing. Identification with these characters who buy and sell their identities and their feelings is made very difficult. While the spectacle of the film draws the viewer in with the lushness of the visuals and the lure of the music, we are nevertheless affected on some level by the characters' psychological struggles – what Egoyan calls "their pain." The distancing and seduction create a complex push–pull effect as the film balances careful observation of character with a sympathetic understanding of their plight.

As Egoyan points out, the interest in surfaces does not preclude depth of emotional content. Nor does it result in any superficiality. His dramatic technique detaches the outward behaviour of characters from a 'naturalized' conception of personality. His characters are neither villains nor angels, but symptoms of deeply felt social tensions and conflicts.

Egoyan's anti-naturalism is brought to bear on material that was fairly topical in Canada at the time of the film's release. To lap-dancing and racism, we could add the horror-story of the Kristen French and Leslie Mahafey murders, which took place in Southern Ontario in 1991 and 1992. In the media coverage of the subsequent arrest of Karla Homolka and Paul Bernardo, the victims were consistently referred to as "schoolgirls." It is not a term in common use, so in the cultural imaginary it has come to stand for a certain dangerous, threatened sexuality attached to young women. While such pathological material often lends itself to exploitation, Egoyan's denaturalized narrative technique is a means of deconstructing and analyzing the forms of desire that make such stories amenable to the media.

The attraction of exotic dancers and the racist overtones of exotic lovers are likewise thrown into relief and twisted into new shapes. The film offers a perspective on the white male imaginary that seeks to understand rather than to either criticize or exploit the dynamic of sexual and scopophilic desire. Egoyan is a dramatist who comprehends the dynamic of narrative pleasure and spectacular *mise-en-scène* well enough to distort them and invert them and throw them back at the viewer. Despite its deconstructive bent, *Exotica* is not without its own erotic pleasures; but they are not what one might expect, even from Egoyan.

∞

Filmography

Features

1984   *Next of Kin* (+ screenplay, editor; 72 mins., 16mm)
1987   *Family Viewing* (+ screenplay, co-editor; 86 mins., 16mm)
1989   *Speaking Parts* (Armenia/Canada/Germany; + screenplay; 92 mins.)
1991   *The Adjuster* (+ screenplay; 102 mins.)
1993   *Calendar* (+ screenplay, editor; 75 mins., 16mm)
1994   *Exotica* (+ screenplay; 103 mins)
1997   *The Sweet Hereafter* (+ screenplay, editor; 112 mins.)
1999   *Felicia's Journey* (+ screenplay; 116 mins.)
2002   *Ararat* (+ screenplay) [18]
2002   *The Blind Assassin* (from novel by Margaret Atwood) [18]

Shorts and television work

1979   *Howard in Particular* (+ screenplay, cinematography, editor; 14 mins., b/w, 16mm)
1980   *After Grad with Dad* (+ screenplay, cinematography, editor; 25 mins., 16mm)
1981   *Peep Show* (+ screenplay, cinematography, editor; 7 mins., b/w and col, 16mm)
1982   *Open House* (+ screenplay, editor; 25 mins., 16mm)
1983   *Ceremony and Allegory of the Medieval Hunt*
1984   *Spat*
1985   *Men: A Passion Playground* (+ cinematography, editor; 7 mins., 16mm)
1985   *In this Corner* (60 mins., 16mm/TV)
1985   *The Twilight Zone* (episode titled *The Wall*)
1987   *Alfred Hitchcock Presents* (episode titled *The Final Twist*, transmitted 28 March 1987, produced 1985; 30 mins., 16mm/TV)
1988   *Looking for Nothing* (+ screenplay; 30 mins., 16mm/TV)
1991   *Montréal vu par... Six variations sur un thème* (*Montreal Sextet*, 123 mins. total running length; fourth episode, titled *En passant*; 20 mins.)
1992   *Gross Misconduct* (120 mins., 16mm/TV)
1993   *Armenian Home Movies*
1995   *A Portrait of Arshile* (4 mins.; TV)
1997   *Yo-Yo Ma Inspired by Bach* (episode titled *Bach Cello Suite #4: Sarabande*; + screenplay; 56 mins.; TV)
2000   *The Line* (5 mins., 16mm)
2000   *Krapp's Last Tape* (from play by Samuel Beckett; TV, 58 mins.)

ಐ

---

[18] *Ararat* and *The Blind Assassin:* post- and pre-production note respectively (November 2001).

Bibliography

Screenplays

Egoyan, Atom. *Speaking Parts*. Toronto: Coach House, 1993. Includes an introduction, "Speaking of Parts," by Ron Burnett, 9–24; an essay, "Surface Tension," by the film-maker, 25–40; an interview with Egoyan, "Emotional Logic," by Marc Glassman, 41–58; and a filmography, 167–75.

———. *Exotica* (screenplay with essays). Toronto: Coach House, 1995. Includes an introduction, "No Place Like Home: The Films of Atom Egoyan," by Geoff Pevere, 9–42; an interview with Egoyan, "Difficult to Say," by Pevere, 43–68; and a filmography.

Documentary

Formulas for Seduction: The Cinema of Atom Egoyan, dir. Eileen Anipare and Jason Wood (UK 1999, 52 mins.).

Vinyl, dir. Alan Zweig (Canada 1997; discussion of and appearances by Egoyan, along with Don McKellar, Harvey Pekar, Guy Maddin et al.).

Books

Atom Egoyan. Paris: Editions de Jeu de Paume/Hérouville-St-Clair: Café des Images, 1993.

Desbarats, Carole, Jacinto Lageira, Daniele Rivière & Paul Virilio. *Atom Egoyan*, tr. Brian Holmes. Paris: Editions Dis Voir, 1993. Also available in French. This is the most analytic work available on Egoyan, drawing heavily on French critical theory and discussing all of the films up to and including *Calendar*. The translation and editing are somewhat deficient. Includes "Conquering What They Tell Us Is 'Natural'," by Carole Desbarats, 9–32; "The Recollection of Scattered Parts," by Jacinto Lageira, 33–82; "The Place of the Spectator," by Daniele Rivière, 83–104; "Video Letters," by Paul Virilio and Atom Egoyan, 105–17; and a filmography and bibliography, 118–22.

Kraus, Matthias. *Bild – Erinnerung – Identität: Die Filme des Kanadiers Atom Egoyan*. ARTE Edition; Marburg: Schüren Verlag, 2000. Large and comprehensive; first German study.

Sandrini, Luca, & Alberto Scandola, ed. *Solitudini troppo silenziose: Il cinema di Atom Egoyan*. Verona: Centro Mazziano di Studi e Ricerche, 1999. Brief essays, in Italian, on Egoyan's films up to *Bach Suite No. 4: Sarabande*, by Scandola, Giuseppe Gariazzo, Manlio Piva, Stefano Fascetti and others, with filmography.

Interviews and statements

Arroyo, José. "The Alienated Affections of Atom Egoyan," *Cinema Canada* 145 (October 1987): 14–19.

Blumenthal, Samuel. "Théorie de l'Atom," *Les Introckutibles* 46 (juin 1993).

Castiel, Elie. "Atom Egoyan," *Séquences* 144 (janvier 1990).

Ciment, Michel, & Philippe Rouyer. "Nous créons des rituels pour gérer nos névroses: Entretien avec Atom Egoyan," *Positif* 406 (1994): 79–81.

———. "Cette expérience représente pour moi une ouverture: Entretien avec Atom Egoyan," *Positif* 440 (1997): 16–18.

Chua, Lawrence. "Atom's Id," *Artforum* 33 (March 1995): 25–26, 104.

Cooper, Douglas. Interview with Egoyan and Arsinée Khanjian. *Sundance Filmmaker Focus* (1996). http://www.sundancechannel.com/focus/egoyan/

The Egoyan Nucleus: Web Guide to Atom Egoyan. http://www2.cruzio.com-.akreyche/atom. html.

Egoyan, Atom. "Ladies and Gentlemen of the Jury," *Cinema Canada* 156 (October 1988): 35.

——. "Recovery" (on *The Sweet Hereafter*), *Sight and Sound* 7.10 (November 1997): 21–23.

Falsetto, Mario. Interview with Atom Egoyan, in *Personal Visions: Conversations with Independent Filmmakers*, ed. Falsetto (London: Constable, 1999): 97–125.

Grugeau, Gérard. "Entretien avec Atom Egoyan: Les élans du cœur," *24 Images* 46 (novembre–décembre 1989): 6–9.

Lewis, Scott. "Urban Angst," *Reverse Shot* (Spring 1995): 23–25.

Porton, Richard. "Family Romances: An Interview with Atom Egoyan," *Cineaste* 23.2 (1997): 8–15.

——. "The Politics of Denial: An Interview with Atom Egoyan," *Cineaste* 25.1 (1999): 39–41.

Racine, Claude. "Entretien avec Atom Egoyan: Les affres de l'image," *24 Images* 43 (été 1989): 10–11.

Romney, Jonathan. "Exploitations," *Sight and Sound* 5.5 (May 1995): 6–8.

Rouyer, Philippe. "Jeux de miroirs: Entretien avec Atom Egoyan," *Positif* 370 (1991): 23–25.

Essays

Bailey, Cameron. "Scanning Egoyan," *CineAction* 16 (May 1989).

Banning, Kass. "Lookin' in All the Wrong Places: The Pleasures and Dangers of *Exotica*," *Take One* 6 (Fall 1994): 14–20.

Coates, Paul. "Protecting the Exotic: Atom Egoyan and Fantasy," *Canadian Journal of Film Studies* 6.2 (Fall 1997): 21–33.

Ellis, Scott. "Creepily Canadian: Atom Egoyan's Critical Cinema," *Prairie Fire* 20.4 (Winter 2000): 26–31.

Harcourt, Peter. "Imaginary Images: An Examination of Atom Egoyan's Films," *Film Quarterly* 48.3 (Spring 1995): 2–14.

Ramasse, François. "Atom Egoyan: La vidéo mode d'emploi," *Positif* 343 (septembre 1989): 13–15.

Rollet, Sylvie. "Le cinéma d'Atom Egoyan," *Positif* 406 (1994): 85.

Shary, Timothy. "Video as Accessible Artifact and Artificial Access: The Early Films of Atom Egoyan," *Film Criticism* 19 (Spring 1995): 2–29.

Taubin, Amy. "Up and Atom," *Film Comment* (November–December 1989).

——. "Burning Down the House" (*The Adjuster*), *Sight and Sound* 2.2 (June 1992): 18–19.

Reviews

As *Exotica* remains probably the most extensively reported Canadian film of all time, with well over a hundred reviews, the following listing is restricted to the more useful items.

Shlomo Schwartzberg, *Performing Arts* (Fall 1994); Gary Michael Dault, "Naked on the Inside: Atom Egoyan strips bare our dark desires," *Eye Weekly* (Toronto; 22 September 1994): 30; Ken Eisner, "Atom Egoyan Found *Exotica* Liberating," *Georgia Straight* (14 October 1994); Deirdre Kelly, "Bruce Greenwood is a Winner," *Globe & Mail* (9 December 1994); David Armstrong, "*Exotica* Weaves a Complex Web," *San Francisco Examiner* (3 March 1995): C3; Jay Carr, "Erotic *Exotica* Tantalizes," *Boston Globe* (3 March 1995); Roger

Ebert, *Chicago Sun-Times* (3 March 1995); Mick LaSalle, "Strange *Exotica* Won't Sit Well With Everyone," *San Francisco Chronicle* (3 March 1995): C16; Kevin Thomas, "*Exotica* Offers a Metaphor for Contemporary Sexuality," *Los Angeles Times* (3 March 1995); Hal Hinson, *Washington Post* (10 March 1995); Owen Gleiberman, "Extraordinary Peephole: Amid Strippers, *Exotica* Glimpses Innocence," *Entertainment Weekly* (24 March 1995); Amanda Lipman, *Sight and Sound* 5.5 (May 1995): 45; Tony Rayns, "Everybody Knows," *Sight and Sound* 5.5 (May 1995): 9; Wyndham Wise, "The True Meaning of *Exotica*," *Take One* 4.9 (1995).

ଚ

FIGURE 15

The Red Violin (François Girard, 1998; produced by Niv Fichman) –
Jason Flemyng (Frederick Pope); Greta Scacchi (Victoria Byrd).

15 The Red Violin (François Girard, 1998)

Production: produced 1998, released September 1998. A Rhombus Media/Mikado production in association with New Line International Releasing / Channel Four Films / Canada Television and Cable Production Fund / Telefilm Canada – Equity Investment Program / CityTV / Bravo! New Style Arts Channel and Sony Classical. With the assistance of the Canadian Film or Video Tax Credit. **Director:** François Girard. **Producer:** Niv Fichman. **Co-Producers:** Daniel Iron and Giannandrea Pecorelli. **Screenplay:** Don McKellar and François Girard. **Cinematography:** Alain Dostie. **Editor:** Gaëtan Huot. **Production Designer:** François Séguin. **Art Director:** Susan Quendler. **Set Decorator:** Maria Blumel. **Casting:** Deirdre Bowen. **Sound:** Claude La Haye, Marcel Mothier and Hans Peter Strobl. **Costumes:** Renée April. **Make-Up:** Adolf Urmcher. **Music / Orchestrations:** John Corigliano.

Cast (partial listing): CREMONA: **Carlo Cecchi** (Nicolò Bussotti), **Irene Grazioli** (Anna Bussotti), **Anita Laurenzi** (Cesca), **Tommaso Puntelli** (Apprentice), **Aldo Brugnini** (Assistant), **Samuele Amighetti** (Boy); VIENNA: **Jean–Luc Bideau** (Georges Poussin), **Cristoph Koncz** (Kaspar Weiss), **Clothilde Mollet** (Antoinette Poussin), **Florentin Groll** (Anton von Spielmann), **Arthur Denberg** (Prince Mansfeld), **Rainer Egger** (Brother Christophe), **Wolfgang Boeck** (Brother Michael); OXFORD: **Jason Flemyng** (Frederick Pope), **Greta Scacchi** (Victoria Byrd), **Eva Marie Bryer** (Sara), **David Gant** (Conductor), **Stuart Ong** (Manservant); SHANGHAI: **Sylvia Chang** (Xiang Pei), **Liu Zi Feng** (Chou Yuan), **Tao Hong** (Comrade Chan Gong), **Han Xio Fei** (young Ming); MONTREAL: **Ireneusz Bogajewicz** (Mr. Ruselsky), **Samuel L. Jackson** (Charles Morritz), **Colm Freore** (Auctioneer), **Monique Mercure** (Madame Leroux), **Don McKellar** (Evan Williams), **Paula De Vasconcelos** (Suzanne), **Russell Yuen** (Older Ming), **Sandra Oh** (Madame Ming).

Synopsis: In seventeenth-century Italy, the master violinmaker Nicolò Bussotti creates his greatest masterpiece, a violin inscribed "with all my love" and intended for his soon-to-be-born child. His pregnant wife Anna gets her fortune read by the gypsy servant Cesca, but as the film unfolds, the fortune told is revealed to be that of the violin. When Anna dies in childbirth with the baby stillborn, the violin leaves Bussotti's workshop. We follow the violin as it passes through the hands of its different owners, each episode opening with Cesca's predictions and ending with a return to the scene of a modern auction in Montreal, where the various descendants of the violin's owners bid for the instrument.

In the first episode, set in eighteenth-century Austria, the violin, now in the possession of monks, comes into the hands of Kaspar Weiss, an orphan musical prodigy with a heart condition. The monks summon the music teacher Georges Poussin, who takes the child to live with himself and his wife in Vienna to prepare for an audition. Poussin introduces the child to his invention, an early metronome, teaching the child to play his difficult audition-piece to the machine's fastest tempo. The machine's ticking ominously echoes the beating of the child's weak heart. The child, in taking his violin to bed, seems to be becoming enslaved to it; Poussin tries to make him sleep alone. When Kaspar suffers a "heart attack," the violin is returned to him. At the audition, a count offers to buy his violin, touching the instrument frighteningly with his claw-like fingernails. Urged to perform, Kaspar raises his bow, only to collapse and die before he can play the first note. At the monastery, the violin is buried with the child so that "he can play it in heaven."

Gypsies steal the violin from the child's grave, taking it across the ocean and time to nineteenth-century England, where its beautiful sound draws the virtuoso player and composer Frederick Pope "across the moor." Pope invites the gypsies to his concert after buying the instrument from them; backstage, he plays it (inspired by his "muse") while making love to Victoria, a romance-novel writer. Entering the stage late, he plays one of his own gypsy-tinged compositions rather than the programmed music. Victoria travels to Russia in pursuit of her hero, Jack; Pope, bereft of his muse, becomes despondent. Refusing to answer Victoria's letters, he starts smoking opium, given to him by his Chinese servant, and lounges in bed caressing the violin like a lover. Victoria returns, regretting their separation, but as she enters the house she hears the violin playing. Seizing a gun, she enters the bedroom to find Pope making love to a gypsy girl. Blaming the violin, she shoots at the instrument and runs from the house.

Pope, in a suicide note, leaves her his estate, with the notable exception of the violin, which is taken to China by Pope's servant, who sells it; the antique dealer strips the battered instrument of its ornamental jewels. It is finally bought by a beautiful well-dressed woman for her daughter, Xiang Pei, a member of the Communist party. During the Cultural Revolution, the latter, attends a demonstration where Chou Yuan is denounced for teaching Western composers, despite his claims that they are revolutionaries. Xiang Pei steps in, arguing that because Chou Yuan also teaches traditional Chinese music, he should be spared. Yuan is taken outside, where the violin he is holding is burned. Returning to her house, Xiang Pei frantically destroys her records and sheet music. Moving a heavy cabinet, she reaches under the floorboards, bringing out the "red violin" from where it lies hidden. As she holds its, her son Ming enters the disordered house. Xiang Pei plays the violin for him, urging him to keep it secret. Confused and scared, the child fetches his father, who bursts into the house with guards to find a record playing violin music and piles of music burning everywhere, but Xiang Pei gone. Her husband also finds pictures of her beautiful mother holding a violin. Meanwhile, Xiang Pei carries the violin to Chou Yuan, who takes it to prevent its destruction.

The violin is located years later among the deceased Chou Yuan's other violins, and sent to Montreal for auction. The assessor Charles Morritz, suspecting that the battered instrument is Bussotti's famed last, "red violin," undertakes research in secret. During his testing, the "strangely opaque" varnish of the violin which gives it its red colour is examined, and revealed to be "an organic compound." The film returns to Bussotti's workshop in Italy: after his wife's death, Bussotti mixed her blood with the violin's varnish. Convinced that this is indeed the "red violin" and the apex of beauty and perfection, Morritz plots to prevent it from being discovered and sold at the auction. Mr Ruselsky, a rich potential buyer, tries out the instrument, but does not recognize its beauty. Despite Morritz's secrecy, the auction house discovers the violin's identity and puts it up for auction. Purchasing a replica made in Pope's time, Morritz attends the auction, where he substitutes the false violin, which is purchased by Ruselsky, and takes the real one home as a gift for his daughter.

∾

Reconstructing the past
Memory's enchantment in *The Red Violin*

———————— ⅋

Eluned Jones

T HE RED VIOLIN continues 38-year old director Francois Girard's interest in music-themed work. Previously he co-directed (with Robert Lepage) a performance documentary of a Peter Gabriel concert called *Secret World Live* (1994) and directed one episode of a six-part television series in which Yo Yo Ma compared Bach suites to various other art-forms. (Other directors were Atom Egoyan, Niv Fichman, Kevin McMahon, Patricia Rozema, and Barbara Willis Sweete; Girard's episode compared the second cello suite to architecture.) Collaborators from Girard's 1993 feature film *Thirty-Two Short Films about Glenn Gould,* a biopic about the Canadian classical pianist, also worked on *The Red Violin*: Don McKellar, co-writer on the 1993 project, also co-wrote *The Red Violin;* Colm Freore, who plays the auctioneer in the latter picture, played Glenn Gould in the former film, while cinematographer Alain Dostie and editor Gaëtan Huot also worked on both films. *Thirty-Two Short Films,* presented as a gala in the 1993 Toronto Festival of Festivals, was subsequently nominated for seven Genie awards for 1993, winning four awards for Best Picture, Best Director, Best Editing and Best Cinematography. The fragmented structure of *Thirty-Two Short Films,* where 32 pieces of Gould's life are "mathematically" pieced together,[1] suggests that the apparently seamless movement of *The Red Violin* masks as deep a disruption in the film's structure as in the earlier film.

An international co-production, costing anywhere from 9 to 15 million dollars, depending on whose figures are believed, and filmed in German, French and Chinese with English subtitles as well as in English, *The Red Violin* is appropriately epic not just in its narrative, but in its production as well, with filming on three continents. The production was deftly publicized, emphasizing the complicated financial arrangements, the composer

---

[1] Bruce Kirkland, *Canadian Movie Guide* (online).

and the "Octopus" scene. The composer is a highly regarded American, John Corigliano, who rarely works in movies but won an Academy Award for his music for *Altered States*. His sound-track was entirely pre-recorded, which necessitated the elaborate mechanism called the "Octopus" for the concert scenes with Frederick Pope. The actor Jason Flemyng tucked the red violin under his own chin but let his arms droop at his sides. The violinist Joshua Bell, from behind and left of Flemyng, fingered the fingerboard while another professional at off-screen right bowed the strings. The three of them together looked like an octopus. This kind of publicity generated more reviews than usual for a Canadian film and eventually resulted in a successful campaign for an Oscar nomination (and the Academy Award) for best composition. The sound-track CD helped promote the movie, also unusual in Canada. The film was amply rewarded, receiving numerous national and international awards including eight Genies (Best Motion Picture, Direction, Screenplay, Cinematography, Art Direction / Production Design, Costume Design, Original Score, Overall Sound) in addition to nominations for Editing and Sound Editing.

Critics were mainly positive in their reviews of *The Red Violin*, though only a few were wholly laudatory. Music, acting, and cinematography were regularly singled out for praise. Jay Carr of the *Boston Globe*, for instance, noted that "there is a visual richness equivalent to the luscious tone of the fabled instrument itself." Eric Harrison in the *Los Angeles Times* praised it for being "intensely cinematic" and "symphonic in both scale and concept." Eleanor Gillespie of the *Atlanta Constitution* characterized it as "florid, expansive and emotional," a neat contrast to Girard's Glenn Gould movie, which she found "playful, spare and sophisticated." David Gillmor's review in *Saturday Night* magazine also compared it to Girard's previous feature, indicating that "*The Red Violin* amounts to more than Five Short Films about a Fiddle" because of its "rhapsodic power."

Many of the critics who found fault with the movie did so in the context of a favourable or mixed review. Their misgivings concerned *The Red Violin*'s anthology format and plotting. David Denby, the *New Yorker*'s critic, complained of the "awkward combination of vaunting pictorial ambition and feeble dramatic skills." He also claimed that it had a "busy, over-articulated construction." Mike Clark, in a mixed review in *USA Today*, found the narrative gimmick, the tracing of the violin's history, "oppressively inert" and not up to the standards of *Tales of Manhattan* (1942) and *The Pennywhistle Blues* (1952), both of which employed the same device.

Of the two lengthier examinations of *The Red Violin*, by Maurice Yacowar in *Queen's Quarterly* and Brenda Longfellow in the *Canadian Journal of Film Studies*, one is conventional and the other political – both leaving more than adequate room for my own interpretation.

Yacowar looks at *The Red Violin* alongside producer Robert Lantos's *Sunshine* – two "Canadian epics of passion." At the root of each of them he finds "a simple desire to rediscover and restore passion and purity in a world of deceit and compromise." He then recounts the story straightforwardly, noting the comparisons and contrasts that are part of *The Red Violin*'s smooth intricacy. Characters, cultures, times are carefully accounted for, implying that each story is of equal heft and value.

> Though each of the figures of genuine passion – Kaspar, Xian, Peng, and Morritz – represents but a single distinct facet of Bussottti's love and anguish, they nobly contrast to the characters who see in the Red Violin only a tool of self-aggrandisement – Pussin, Ruselsky, perhaps Williams.

Jacowar concludes, rather enigmatically, that "*The Red Violin* explores passions directed outwards."

Brenda Longfellow uses a Jamesonian approach in her reading, criticizing the film for its commodity fetishism and its misguided "tribute to Europe's glorious and irretrievably past cultural hegemony." She claims, mistakenly, that *The Red Violin* is the most expensive Canadian film ever and notes that it is "completely over-determined by the market, not only because of its status as an economic commodity but through its textual practices," which "represent and narrativize the commodification of aesthetic objects and their circuit within an international system of monetary exchange." While she goes on to admit that on a superficial level *The Red Violin* is a "critique of market hegemony" (through the auction scenes), in the final analysis the film is built on the hoariest of romantic clichés: the sacrifice of a woman on the altar of art." Such a cliché once offered, as Jameson put it, "a 'sanctuary' from the depredations and vulgar materialism of the marketplace," but here, in *The Red Violin*, "romanticism exists only as a nostalgic cliché for the ubiquitous and overweening power of money."

Enchanted Children

> 'That, at least, is behind us,' we say, 'but what still lies ahead?' The way we word it, it's as if our backs were turned to the past as we look towards the future; and that is, in fact, how we think of it: the future in front, the past behind. [...]

Besides, whoever keeps the future in front of him and the past at his back is doing something else that is hard to imagine. For the image implies that events somehow already exist in the future, reach the present at a determined moment, and finally come to rest in the past. But nothing exists in the future; it is empty; one might die at any minute. Therefore such a person has his face turned towards the void, whereas it is the past behind him that is visible, stored in the memory.

That is why when the Greeks speak of the future, they say, 'What do we still have behind us?' And in this sense Anton Steenwijk was a Greek. He too stood with his back to the future and his face toward the past. Whenever he thought about time, which he did once in a while, he did not conceive of events as coming out of the future to move through the present into the past. Instead, they developed out of the past in the present on their way to an unknown future.[2]

There is a shot towards the end of the movie *Gods and Monsters* (about *Frankenstein*'s director James Whale) that understands exactly what it is that Whale must have meant by his monster. The unmistakable silhouette of the monster emerges into the frame of a World War One battlefield, leading another shadowed figure by the hand. As the figures step into the light, the monster transforms into Whale's gardener, Clay Boone. The monster / gardner points the second figure, Whale, towards a trench filled with corpses, and Whale, letting go of his hand, climbs into the trench, lying down gratefully among the dead bodies. The shot recalls strikingly the scene in the *Frankenstein* movie where the monster, in a frame suddenly filled with light, plays with a little girl, tossing flowers into the water. If that scene ends with the girl's drowning death, because the monster is somehow unable to tell the little girl from the flowers, the scene in *Gods and Monsters* seems gently to give the monster a second chance. But now Whale is the girl/ flower, and the trench full of corpses has, because of the monster, become an enchanted sunlit lake. Everything that is so beautiful in the scene with the little girl is made grotesque in the shot, the drowned body of the little girl becoming hundreds of bloated bodies, the battlefield replacing the stillness of the lake. Suddenly the monster, the ugly thing who could almost have become beautiful in the child's presence, is the thing that could transform all that is terrible simply by gesturing Whale towards his longed-for death. The ending, where Whale's corpse, like the drowned little girl, floats in his swimming-pool, finally redeems the monster for his earlier mistake by the

---

[2] Harry Mulisch, *The Assault*, tr. Claire Nicolas White (*De Aanslag*, 1982; tr. 1985; Harmondsworth: Penguin, 1986): 167–68.

water. But this time the monster has led the way through death, through the bloated corpses whose dead limbs make up the monster's own body, and has guided us back to that magic place full of light that we thought the monster had forfeited forever.

Most affectingly, *Gods and Monsters* finds a place to return to which escapes memory. By gently easing its way into the scene from the movie *Frankenstein*, memory's increasingly horrific returns can finally be eluded. Memory, like Frankenstein, brings the dead back to life, into a world that can offer no place of welcome. Only the monster can be so surefooted on the battlefield of memory; the movie's most beautiful transformation is that which allows Clay, although unable to kill Whale as he has been requested, to become the monster anyway. The fact that he will pull Whale from the swimming-pool becomes enough. Memory in the film belongs not to the living, but to the dead. Although time's greatest threat so often is forgetfulness, the movie posits the return of all that had been buried as equally, if not more, terrifying. The trench filled with distorted dead bodies opens up the welcome light of the lake's enchanted space because the monster offers the entry point at which memory metamorphoses into imagination. The ending of *Gods and Monsters* reminds us of the ways in which we can make contact with the monster: how, like the little girl, we can hold the monster's hand and find it not dangerous but transforming.

The Red Violin, like the *Frankenstein* story, seeks to bring the dead back to life. The "red violin" is turned by its blood-varnish into a kind of Frankenstein's monster, a grotesque replacement for the life of the stillborn child. The thing that rescues the violin from monstrosity is that it can be held, that one cradles it, and in return is rewarded with beautiful music. Love in the movie, literally contained within the violin, makes its way precariously between the beautiful and the grotesque, just as Frankenstein's monster with the child in the sunlit stillness of the lake pauses between enchantment and death. One comes to understand this pause, in *The Red Violin*, as the condition of art. One thinks of the child Kaspar, bow arm raised, poised to begin playing, the film held briefly still between the anticipated music and the pounding heartbeat of his imminent collapse. That moment when the expectation of the music overlaps with our sense of the child's death, so that we seem to anticipate both at the same time as though his death were in some way the musical performance, captures perfectly what is at issue in Bussotti's making of the violin itself. A parent's wonder at a child's presence in his life must always be accompanied by a sense of the child's impermanence there. As Andrew W. Metcalfe writes,

> On their way through, children/texts remind you sharply of your mortal condition, of love's intermingling with the inevitability of separation and loss [...] A parent sees the trace of the child's heavenly condition in the downy light of their skin, but, though they try, they know they can never touch it. Parents embrace their children so closely because they know, from the moment of the child's birth, that they can *never* hold the child: it is always and already beyond them.[3]

The terrible thing about the violin in the film is the fact that it cannot die; that it can make its way through hundreds of years. All damage to it can eventually be repaired, yet it remains perfect and beautiful despite that damage, while the child himself is terribly mortal. Bussotti cannot protect his child from death: he can only create a violin that imitates the child's life or substitutes for it. One understands that the violin's beautiful music counterfeits, or mimics, a parent's joy in his child. This sense of the violin is expressed in George Steiner's view of art:

> if much of poetry, music and the arts aims to "enchant" – and we must never strip that word of its aura of magical summons – much also [...] aims to make strangeness in certain respects stranger. It would instruct us of the inviolate enigma of the otherness in things and in animate presences. [... Serious art makes palpable to us] the unassuaged, unhoused stability and estrangement of our condition. We are, at key instants, strangers to ourselves....[4]

Steiner's view is striking because it conceives of strangeness as being the necessary, and even desired, condition of enchantment. I am reminded of the magic book in C.S. Lewis's novel *The Voyage of the Dawn Treader*, where the pages turn forward, but not backwards, so that the reader can never return to anything previously viewed. The child reader of the book, Lucy, encounters a spell for the refreshment of the spirit that is "more like a story than a spell." It is the "loveliest story I've ever read or ever shall read in my whole life."[5] But she cannot turn the pages back, nor can she remember what the story was about; only the felt sense of its loveliness remains. Lewis concludes the episode by saying, "And she never could remember; and ever since that day what Lucy means by a good story is a story which reminds

---

[3] Andrew W. Metcalfe, "Inspiration," *Canadian Review of Sociology and Anthropology* 36.2 (1999): 238.

[4] Quoted in Metcalfe, "Inspiration," 237.

[5] C.S. Lewis, *The Voyage of the Dawn Treader* (Harmondsworth: Penguin, 1972): 134.

her of the forgotten story in the Magician's Book."[6] In Lewis' magical world, forgetting is the enchantment; a "good story" is one that casts a spell on memory. The magic of a "good story" is made possible only because the original spell has been forgotten. If Steiner understands the enchantment of art as casting a spell of estrangement, for Lewis, too, that vital act of becoming a stranger to oneself is contained within the instant of forgetting. The "magical summons" of art that so enraptures Steiner is present in memory, for memory at its most surprising and unexpected reveals to us moments that have remained hidden within us, possessing the power constantly to make us "a stranger to ourselves," to remind us of how much of us remains entirely unknown.

Lewis's sense of good art as fulfilling in some way the impossible longing to "turn the pages backwards" is echoed in the film. In *The Red Violin,* the centrality of the auction scene reveals the true flow of time in the movie to be not forwards, but backwards. If the movie's narrative seems to move forward, so that the future follows the gypsy woman Cesca's magical prophecies, the auction scene (as well as the sequences with Charles Morritz) suggests that it is not the future but rather the past that the movie's narrative truly seeks to construct. The narrative should be viewed not as moving forward from the point when Bussotti's wife and child die, but, in one sense, as moving backwards towards that point. The final sequence's focus on the violin's reconstruction offers a model for the movie's reconstruction of the past. The forward movement of the film's narrative is available to us only because of the violin's reconstruction, which is to say that the movie is not a tale of the violin's becoming lost and unknown, but of its magical discovery.

Memory and prophecy become strangely linked in the film. The same faith that prophecy exhibits in the film's forward movement is present in the film's retrograde movement as well. If the film progresses forward with each episode in step with one of the predictions of Cesca the gypsy, the movie's truer movement is the hidden backwards one. The auction scene recurring throughout the movie acts as a gathering-point for memory. Our repeated returns to the scene after each episode reveal a deeper longing within the film: that one could somehow go back in memory, that there might be a second chance. The presence of the adult Ming at the auction is particularly moving, for one senses his feeling that by reclaiming the violin he could erase his unintended betrayal of his mother. If the past has proved itself

---

[6] Lewis, *The Voyage of the Dawn Treader,* 135.

physically impossible to enter, the ability to lay claim to a part of the past offers the possibility of some kind of reparation, perhaps if only by acknowledging one's intent to hold onto the past tightly. One could imagine the scene as a version of an open-casket funeral viewing, with the violin having been repeatedly rescued from so many real and metaphoric graves. The movie's faith is that the past could somehow be collected, that everyone could return in some form to reclaim the violin, that no part of the past would become lost or go missing. The film reveals a longing to fit the past together as perfectly as one would create a violin. The auction acts as the site of return, as though, by finding the lost violin, the lost past would automatically follow.

But if the film longs for memory, it is most compelling within what Lewis might term "enchanted forgetfulness." It is a small instant of forgetting that I find most moving. In the Shanghai sequence, Xiang Pei plays the violin for her son, and suddenly the music sounds awkward and small, the virtuoso performances of the film replaced by an endearing clumsiness. The scene strains to try to find the ways in which we might begin to lay hold of the things missing from us for so long. That image of fingers recalling in the act of playing how it is that they should move is perfectly tuned to the presence of the son in the room. The scene suddenly recalls to us how awkwardly large Bussotti's violin is in its creation, a gift impossible to place in a baby's hands. Too often our most cherished gifts are the wrong size, perfectly fitted to our own hands, to our own self, but somehow all wrong when placed into the hands of another. When the child dies in birth, it is too easy to imagine the violin passing from hand to hand, somehow suiting each, as though one could locate that missing child within the hands of others, as though there were never any doubt that the gift would produce beautiful music, that the child could effortlessly produce exactly the right sound, find exactly the intended tone for the gift, and that none of the clumsiness so unavoidable in a child's relationship to his parents would be evident. If Bussotti can only create the perfect violin, if the parent can only package perfectly everything that is important in his life in a tangible way, then surely all the error, all the mistakes, all the imperfectly given and imperfectly received expressions of love between parent and child will miraculously disappear. Then one could present oneself to a child and say, "here I am," and the child, understanding, could lay hold and produce exactly the right response, could beautifully reproduce for the parent exactly what was meant by the gift.

So much of what appears seamless in the movie in the passing of the violin from hand to hand, even as it mimics the gestures of recovery that mark memory, is surely based in forgetting, in erasing the figure of the intended child, and replacing him with other eager hands. For where *The Red Violin* intentionally misleads us is in pretending that it is the perfect form of the violin that matters, and not the imperfectly expressed love, the love that forms itself as too large and can only hope that the child will grow into it, that the child will one day be able to seize that love and find it exactly the right size. If the film seems to believe wholeheartedly that everything lost can be recovered, that things which seem to be missing are only hidden like the violin under the floorboards, in fact the movie can only desperately reconstruct the wrong things: the violin can be played beautifully by others, but this can never make up for the fact that it cannot be played by the child himself. It is only in that moment when the Chinese mother picks up the violin, which she cannot have touched for a long while – perhaps for years – and finds those notes in their forgotten places, hidden in her hands just as the violin is hidden under the floor, and offers it to her child not as a completed and flawlessly executed performance but as a gently fumbling act of discovery – for a child who cannot understand the gift, who can only grasp that somehow the mother's secrets must be wrong, who can only be confused by this strange part of herself that the mother reveals – that the original gift of the violin is recalled to us, in all the clumsiness of love.

The mother's loving removal of the violin from its place of concealment beneath the floorboards subtly recalls the child Kaspar's grave. In a lovely and tender way, the mother is unburying that small child, and placing him again in her hands. If *The Red Violin* seems rather transparently to be replacing Bussotti's dead child with the violin, it in fact situates the violin not as child, but as something that is neither child nor mother. The violin comes to "adulthood" in China not so much because it is owned by a mature woman as because, like adulthood itself, the object has become incomprehensible to the child. To Xiang Pei's son, the violin is as mysterious and strange as his mother, a sense he attempts to combat by reporting her to his father in the hope that the latter will somehow be able to banish the disarray that the child feels his mother has brought to the house. Xiang Pei plays the violin for her son to make this disorder go away. To the son, however, the frightening disorder of his home must be somehow the fault of the strange instrument his mother holds in her hands. The child cannot understand his mother, so he turns to his father for explanation and rectification. The violin becomes the improperly understood adult world, a world the child can never hope to negotiate correctly. Faced with the strangeness of this world, with his mother's secret music, the child tries to put the adult world back into the hands of his father, "I do not understand this, but my father will, and he will know what to do."

To the child, the violin represents all that is frighteningly other about the adult world. However, to the mother the violin offers a return to the long-lost childhood world. She offers the violin as comfort to her son, unable to understand how culturally alien the violin is, because to her playing the violin places her back in childhood. The mother sees playing the violin in one sense as passing to her child the gift her mother bestowed on her. In this sense, she plays the violin to her son as a mother – as her own mother; at the same time, the remembered presence of her mother returns her to childhood, for some part of us is always a child in our parent's eyes. By conjuring the image of her mother, by conceiving of herself again as a child, Xiang Pei believes herself to be in companionship with her child. To her, the secret is not so much the violin itself as the secret knowledge, shared with her son, that she too is a child. The melody from her childhood is played as an offering of that childhood to her son, in the hope that the remembered phrase will reveal to him everything that her motherhood has hidden from him. The secret Xiang Pei wishes her son to keep is not that of concealing, not of the things that must remain hidden from view, but that of revealing. She wishes her son to be able to see her as a child and to understand that childhood; the shared knowledge of that childhood that only she and he possess would then forge a special companionship between them. The son cannot see this but, painfully, the father can; for the irony of the son's fetching his father is that, although the father, like all the adult world, is forced to destroy, at the same time it is he, holding the photographs of her mother, who can see the figure of Xiang Pei as a child, who can understand how the act of playing the violin sets her as that longed-for child against the impossibly beautiful figure of her mother, in the same way that the child Kaspar takes the violin to bed as a comforting adult presence rather than as a comforting doll-substitute.

If the violin is simultaneously both child and mother, it is because it has its roots not so much in the mother's blood marking its surface as in the stillborn child. The blood varnishes the violin as a mother's blood covers a child at birth; but a stillborn child is both of the mother and other to her. The child has no existence outside the mother, as it is born dead, but it is also not entirely of the mother, for it is perfectly, if lifelessly, formed as its own being. Somewhat disturbingly, Bussotti's wife seems to become the violin as he caresses her arm to draw the blood from her wrist, like a violinist shifting the position of his fingers on the neck of the instrument. The image might serve to remind us of the way a violinist must hold a violin by not holding on at all: the hand must be loose on the neck in order for the fingers to move properly. The hand that plays is therefore always letting go. The violin is created as both mother and child, never able to free itself entirely from either one, to become either one, as though a stillbirth were somehow animated, making its way through life as a kind of Frankenstein's monster.

The largeness of the violin is matched by its inscription, "with all my love." Sadly, the same hope that the child will grow into the violin is present in that impossible "all" – as if one could ever collect all one's love. The implication is: if the love presented is incomprehensibly large enough, the child might be able to grow into it. That initial largeness is gradually reduced, until the violin is referred to as "this little violin." Suddenly the movie has enough room to encompass the once unimaginably large love. One is reassured by the child Kaspar's sure grip on the violin, despite its awkward size, so that the largeness of the instrument becomes the thing that makes it exactly right, suggesting that the reason he plays so beautifully is that he can lay hold of the largeness. Kaspar the child's greatest gift is not that he can play beautiful music – rather, that he can grasp onto the immensity of Bussotti's love effortlessly, without needing to somehow grow into it, until one could imagine that love was not such an impossible gift after all. The smallness of the child seems suddenly to place everything in its right size; for it seems a wonderful thing that one should approach a world where one is made small in relation to the things one touches. If art's revelatory power is, in the words of Steiner, the power of the annunciating angel entering "the small house of our cautionary being," surely the "wingbeat" that alters us irrevocably is so transforming precisely because it reminds us of our smallness in relation to the felt immensity of the work of art.

One might see in Kaspar's grip exactly what was at work in *Last Night*,[7] where Patrick receives the box of old Christmas presents rewrapped by his

---

[7] A film written and directed by and starring Don McKellar released in the same year as *Red Violin*, *Last Night* is set in Toronto in the last hours before the annihilation of the world. The film follows a number of characters, including McKellar, who plays the cynical Patrick, as they prepare for death. The characters grope for some form of meaningful contact, faced with a void which seems to nullify any gesture that does not reach

mother. The inclusion of his sister's diving trophy amid the presents – as if his mother believes he won't notice that it is not his, that she could have the power to offer him a better version of himself, which could become his simply in the act of unwrapping – indicates to us how much of our parent's gifts to us are directed at our often elusive best self, just as Bussotti's refusal to create a smaller violin contains the faith that the child will be adequate to his best effort at perfection. By creating a perfect violin, he offers his faith that the child will possess a perfection equal to or beyond that of the violin. The mother's gift of the box with "Patrick" written on it, seeming to enclose all the things she holds most precious about him, at first offers to Patrick only a reminder of all the ways in which we cannot re-open memory. But the exact thing that the mother's gift offers, the thing that is most needed, is that it professes faith in memory, a faith in a past that is independent of any expectation of the future – a past that lives, full and precious, as itself. The oblivion threatened at the film's end is not so much physical annihilation as the destruction of any context in which memory can survive. If the mother's gift finds ways, however clumsily, to bring the past forward, to literally re-open it, the gift itself seems to open itself to Patrick's grief for his wife, as a place that understands and values memory.

A parent sees in her child a largeness, a breadth of soul, that the child himself cannot yet comprehend. The gift of Patrick's mother anticipates a perfect fit with a Patrick who opens himself to love, a Patrick who can find a place for grief, and within that grief find a way to make meaningful contact. The presents in the box are all about re-opening, for the mother understands that Patrick must unwrap his love for his wife, and within it find a new context for that love with Sandra. What is so beautiful about Bussotti's violin is that we must understand that the child Kaspar is not the child that the violin anticipates. Bussotti does not conceive of his child as a musical prodigy who would automatically do justice to such a perfect violin. Rather, the perfect violin is made for the child because he is not a genius, a gift given simply because it is perfect and the child is imagined as equal to that perfection. It is a gift far beyond what the child's own talents must rationally deserve, but a gift that resolutely contains the belief that

---

forward into the void itself. Any context for a private emotional response appears to have been eliminated: the absence of a future strangely destroys not only any sense of the present, but also dislocates the past. Much of what is compelling in the movie deals with the characters' fumbling attempts to maintain a place for memory where love and contact can exist, finding a site for the past that is not dependent on the future.

nothing is beyond the child's deserving. It is not the ability to play the violin that is most important at all: and if the child Kaspar seems like the perfect recipient of the violin, the perfect substitute for the dead child for whom the violin was intended, one also understands that it is not perhaps his ability to play the violin that is most important, but his ability to love the violin, so that one could almost imagine that by loving the violin he loves Bussotti – the best of Bussotti – in the same way that a child loves the imagined perfection of his parents.

Early in *The Red Violin*, Bussotti berates one of his apprentices for creating a violin fit only for a "priest or courtesan." He then smashes the apprentice's inadequate, imperfect violin to bits. The fact that he later gives his precious red violin to a monastery must therefore be a deliberate sacrifice, done more out of despair than devotion or faith. That act of taking the violin, now varnished with the mother's blood – as though the violin is so precious as to become almost grotesque, as if too much love distorts itself into monstrosity – and delivering it into the most worthless hands that Bussotti can conceive of, must be his way of killing the violin. Among priests, surely the violin will never be played beautifully. The music, which throughout the movie seems contained inside the violin (for the violin plays the same song in everyone's hands; one simply makes the right form of contact, and the violin produces the music), will never be released. My own father tells me that the best violins seem formed for a particular type of player. If owned for a long time by one violinist, in the hands of another the violin will simply not play properly; anthropomorphically, it becomes accustomed to the style of its owner, and cannot respond to a different one. It is only in the hands of a violinist who plays similarly to the first that the violin will play beautifully. One could imagine that, in the hands of Kaspar, the violin recognizes a love equal to Bussotti's, and so responds, re-opening itself, as it were, to release the music inside.

Frederick Pope's handling of the violin like a lover, however, is comically absurd, acknowledging too overtly the importance that love plays in the violin itself. It is likely for this very reason that the violin is counterfeited in the "Pope replica." Pope's performances, for all their virtuosity, never achieve the resonance of Xiang Pei's quiet performance for her son. The child Kaspar's collapse on the brink of his first performance in some ways shadows all of Pope's subsequent performances, which are somehow stolen from death just as the violin has been taken from Kaspar's open grave. Xiang Pei's playing of the violin, by contrast, is always accompanied by that act of removing the instrument from its hiding-place, of reaching into the open grave and receiving the violin directly from Kaspar's hands. In Xiang Pei's playing for her son, one senses the weight of another hiding-place, the place where love is kept secret, revealing itself tentatively in the playing of the violin. By playing the violin, the strange child, whom she does not understand at all, can be drawn nearer, as in Pope's wonderful line, appropriated from *Secret Garden*, where he says the sound of the violin "drew him across the moor." One imagines in Pope's line the image of a traveller pulled out of the mist, but perhaps this emergence from concealment is precisely the wrong thing. The violin repeatedly returns to places of obscurity – a grave, an antique shop, an attic – as if it demands to be found, to be rescued over and over. Mr. Ruselsky is clearly unworthy of possessing the violin, because he cannot recognize its beauty when it is first placed in his hands. He is blind to what is hidden below the battered exterior. "Worthiness" is therefore conceived of in the movie as being the ability to find that hidden beauty. This sense of the hidden is quite absent from Pope's performances – it is not virtuosity that the violin most values – and so it is perhaps a natural consequence that the fraudulent violin should be created as a result of his possession.

At the very end of *The Red Violin*, the instrument appears to come full circle. But there is something troubling in Morritz's gift of the violin to his daughter; it is encapsulated in his perception of the violin as "little." If Bussotti's gift anticipates a child who will hold easily onto the largeness, Morritz's gift to his small daughter challenges the child, unconsciously perhaps, to equal the surpassing perfection of the violin. Morritz's belief that the violin itself is the most perfect and beautiful thing that fulfils his search is at odds with Bussotti's conception of what he has made. For Morritz, it is the child who must be the perfect and beautiful thing; the violin is simply an approximation of the parent's wonder at his child. By putting the violin in the child's hand, the parent is saying, "this is the best way I have to show you how I conceive of you." One wonders if Morritz's child can ever hope to equal for him what he sees in the violin. Perhaps the gift of the violin hands the child a perfection that she can never hope to achieve. If the violin has become small to Morritz, it is because it contains everything most precious to him in itself; for the largeness of the violin expressed all that the violin could not contain, but that was present in the child. The violin becomes small like a child to Morritz. Is it the child he would most like to have?

The introduction of the counterfeit violin into the final scenes recalls to us rather ominously the violin's own existence as an imitation child. That the violin can be replaced unnoticed, and another violin carry on in its place, in a very real way returns the violin to death. It is terrifying to think that another could publicly assume our identity, and we could vanish without anyone noticing our disappearance. If forgetting can be equated with death, as a figurative movement underground, replacing the violin with a false version of itself consigns the violin to an obscure grave. What Morritz must come to understand as he watches the violin being publicly displayed at the auction is that the only remaining hiding-place for the violin is within death. In this sense, he is making a gift of death to his daughter. In the end, this is perhaps the best gift a parent has to offer a child. The violin becomes a "stranger to itself," replaced by a false violin; thus the final enchantment must be located within death. If the violin became a replacement for Bussotti's dead child, that the instrument can be returned to death in some way rescues the figure of the child, allowing him to resume his place in memory once the replacement figure is gone. We remember the monks, burying the violin with Kaspar so that he can "play it in heaven." By figuratively killing the violin, Morritz returns it to Bussotti's child, and the loving gift is once more placed securely in the child's hands.

ဆ

Filmography

Features

1993   *Thirty-Two Short Films about Glenn Gould* (+ screenplay; 94 mins.)
1998   *The Red Violin* (or: *Le violon rouge*; + screenplay; 131 mins.)

Short Films and Television Work

1983   *Das Brunch*
1984   *Human Scope*
1985   *Le train*
1986   *Tango, Tango*
1988   *Montréal danse*
1990   *Cargo* (+ screenplay)
1991   *Le dortoir*
1993   *Le jardin des ombres*
1994   *Secret World Live* (or: *Peter Gabriel's Secret World Live*; co-directed with Robert Lepage; TV; 90 mins.)

1997   *Bach Cello Suite #2: The Sound of Carceri* (+ editor; one of six CBC programmes
         collectively titled *Yo Yo Ma Inspired by Bach* ; TV; 90 mins.)

Bibliography

Essays

Longfellow, Brenda. "*Red Violin*, Commodity Fetishism and Globalization," *Canadian Jour-
    nal of Film Studies* (forthcoming).
Yacowar, Maurice. "Canadian Epics of Passion: *The Red Violin* and *Sunshine*," *Queen's
    Quarterly* 107.1 (Spring 2000): 86–100.

Reviews

Don Gillmor, "Fiddling Abroad," *Saturday Night* 113.7 (June 1998): 47–48; Brian D.
Johnson, *Maclean's* 111.37 (14 September 1998): 59; Rick Groen, *Toronto Globe & Mail* (13
November 1998): C5; Nick Kimberley, *Sight and Sound* (March 1999): 50–51; Steven
Hunter, "Filmfest DC's *Red Violin*: 3-part Harmony," *Washington Post* (21 April 1999): C1;
Richard Alleva, *Commonweal* 126.11 (4 June 1999): 19–20; Mike Clark, "*Red Violin* Fiddles
Flatly with Anthology Concept," *USA Today* (11 June 1999): E6; Eric Harrison, "Stringing
Together the Lives in Soulful, Moving *Red Violin*," *Los Angeles Times* (11 June 1999): F8;
Steven Holden, "That Old Fiddle Sure Got Around," *New York Times* (11 June 1999): E12;
Betsy Sherman, "A Violin Takes the Bows: François Girard Orchestrates a Time-Travel
Adventure Starring a 17th Century Instrument," *Boston Globe* (13 June 1999): N9; David
Denby, *New Yorker* 75.15 (14 June 1999): 90–91; Jay Carr, "Visual Treats give *Red Violin* its
Rich Tones," *Boston Globe* (18 June 1999): D10; L. Rozen, *People* (21 June 1999): 36; Eleanor
Ringel Gillespie, "*Violin* Plays Up Artistic Impulse," *Atlanta Constitution* (25 June 1999): 8;
David Sterritt, "Music Drives *Red Violin*," *Christian Science Monitor* (25 June 1999): 15; John
Von Rhein, "Bowing to Pressure: *Red Violin* Crosses Three Continents in Three Centuries
in Melodic Tale," *Chicago Tribune* (27 June 1999): 7–8; John Nordlinger, *National Review* (12
July 1999): 57–59.

ᛒ

Canadian film
A select annotated bibliography

———————————— ℰℴ

John Scholes
with Gordon Collier and Gene Walz

Books

Abel, Marie–Christine, André Giguère & Luc Perreault. *Le cinéma québécois à l'heure internationale*. Montréal: Alain Stanké, 1990. 340 pp.
General essays by Giguère and Abel are followed by a photo-gallery and by brief or extended statements by fifty-six figures centrally involved in francophone Canadian cinema; appendices cover filmography and awards (at Cannes and in Québec). The collection has an entertaining magpie inquisitiveness, and includes tables listing dates of birth, subjects studied at university and non-cinematic occupations, and a poll-survey of the best Québécois films.

Allan, Blaine, Michael Dorland & Zuzana M. Pick, ed. *Responses: In Honour of Peter Harcourt*. Kingston, Ontario: Responsibility Press, 1992. 290 pp.
A festschrift honouring Canadian cinema's original and most enduring champion, this anthology of twenty essays features homages by Harcourt's favourite filmmakers (Jean Pierre Lefebvre and Bill MacGillivray) and by fellow academics. It also contains essays on individual films and on film pedagogy (including Harcourt's own plea "Canadian Film Studies and Canadian Film: The Education We Need") and is highlighted by Peter Morris's insightful "In Our Own Eyes: The Canonizing of Canadian Film," which challenges long-held notions about feature films, especially in the 1950s and 1960s. There is also a bibliography of Harcourt's own writings.

Atwood, Margaret. *Survival: A Thematic Guide to Canadian Literature*. Toronto: Anansi, 1972. 161 pp.
While Atwood's book is more a guide to the conceptual concerns of Canadian literature, her discussion extends to the archetypes which pervade the Canadian imagination in general. Her commentary on *Goin' Down the Road* as representative of the themes of alienation and failure (which are so common in Canadian creative discourse) is a useful starting-point for any analysis of Shebib's film or a host of others (*Nobody Waved Goodbye* , *Les bons débarras*, and *Mon oncle Antoine*, to name a few).

Beattie, Eleanor. *A Handbook of Canadian Film.* Take One Film Book 4. Toronto: Peter Martin Associates & Take One, 1977. 355 pp.

For film students, this "Introduction to Canadian Film" provides historical background, offers a perspective, and catalogues some general works on Canadian cinema. The "Film Study" section offers suggestions for setting up a film society, and for locating film study opportunities. The "Making Films" section lists sources for film financing as well as technical services and assistance. "Using Films," "Film Publications," and the Bibliography list useful books, catalogues, periodicals and directories. (New sections in this revised second edition are: "Community Film and Video," "Native People and Film," "Political and Third World Films," and "Women in Film.")

Berton, Pierre. *Hollywood's Canada: The Americanization of Our National Image.* Don Mills, Ontario: McClelland & Stewart, 1975. 303 pp.

This bestseller reveals just how badly Canada has been misinterpreted and presented in Hollywood movies. Revealing devastating examples of Hollywood's mistakes of history, politics and landscape, Berton says: "If Canadians continue to hold the belief that there is no such thing as a national identity – and who can deny that many hold it? – it is because [Hollywood] movies have frequently blurred, distorted and hidden that identity under a celluloid mountain of misconceptions."

Bonneville, Léo, ed. *Le cinéma québécois par ceux qui le font.* Montréal: Editions Paulines, 1979. 738 pp.

Brief interviews with, and short critical appraisals of, thirty young Quebec filmmakers of the 1970s including Paul Almond, Denys Arcand, Jean Beaudin, Michel Brault, Gilles Carle, Mireille Dansereau, Andre Forcier, Gilles Groulx, Claude Jutra, Jean–Pierre Lefebvre, Francis Mankiewicz, Pierre Perrault, and Anne–Claire Poirier. Includes bibliographies and filmographies.

Browne, Colin. *Motion Picture Production in British Columbia, 1898–1940: A Brief Historical Background and Catalogue.* Victoria, B.C.: British Columbia Provincial Museum, 1979. 381 pp.

A background to the film industry's growth and development in British Columbia. This study includes a catalogue of over 1,000 films made in or about B.C. up to the time of World War II.

Bowie, Douglas, & Tom Shoebridge, ed. *Best Canadian Screenplays.* Kingston, Ontario: Quarry, 1992. 439 pp.

An anthology of five award-winning Canadian screenplays: *Goin' Down the Road* (William Fruet); *Mon oncle Antoine* (Clément Perron); *The Grey Fox* (John Hunter); *My American Cousin* (Sandy Wilson); and *Jésus de Montréal* (Denys Arcand).

Buxton, William J., ed. *Canada's Film Century: Traditions, Transitions, Transcendence.* Lonergan Review 6. Montreal: Lonergan University College, 2000. 240 pp.

A diverse collection of essays based on a year-long series of lectures, mainly by Concordia University academics, that begins with an examination of the first movie reviews in Canada and a look at an early Canadian theatre chain, contrasts the regional cinemas of British Columbia and Atlantic Canada, highlights films by three overlooked contemporary Quebec filmmakers (Richard Boutet, Paul Tana, and Esther Valiquette), and features an amiable, Harcourtian categorization of Canadian experimental films and a more serious analysis of two classics from the same genre, plus a study of how technology in NFB films mediates our national sense of space.

Carrière, Louise. *Femmes et cinéma québécois.* Montréal: Boréal, 1983. 282 pp.
Fourteen essays by Quebec women on subjects as diverse as images of women in masculine cinema and female spectatorship, women at the ONF/NFB, in animation, as editors, directors, and documentarians. Contains a useful index of directors and film titles.

Chadderton, H. Clifford. *Hanging A Legend.* Ottawa: War Amputations of Canada, 1986. 371 pp.
A collection of personal commentaries by the author is integrated with Senate subcommittee documents, correspondence, various background articles, and research papers all concerning the military career of Billy Bishop and its apparently slanderous depiction in the NFB production *The Kid Who Couldn't Miss.*

Clandfield, David. *Canadian Film.* Perspectives on Canadian Culture. Toronto: Oxford UP, 1987. 136 pp.
A rapid-fire survey of Canadian film origins and directions, Clandfield's study of both French- and English-Canadian cinema offers a brisk tour through national filmmaking history as well as a critical stance that points (as Bruce Elder does in his influential essay "The Cinema We Need," in Fetherling's *Documents*) toward the possibilities afforded by new categories of filmmaking. Of particular interest is the section on Pierre Perrault and *cinéma direct* (46–50).

Coulombe, Michel, & Marcel Jean, ed. *Le dictionnaire du cinéma québécois.* Montréal: Boréal, 1991. 603 pp.
Updated from 1988 (and due for another update), this standard dictionary contains over 700 entries beginning with ACPAV (Association coopérative de productions audio-visuel) and ending with film producer Yuri Yoshimura. It covers more than just directors, is a very good, terse introduction to various subjects, and is not restricted to francophones, including in its ranks many anglophone ONF/NFB filmmakers who worked in Montreal.

Dean, Malcolm. *Censored! Only in Canada: The History of Film Censorship – The Scandal Off the Screen.* Toronto: Virgo Press, 1981. 276 pp.
A convert to freedom from censorship because of the secrecy and political machinations he discovered, Dean writes about the history of film censorship in Canada (which does not have a national censor board or classification system) from early war and boxing films to *Damaged Goods* (1916) and – notoriously – *Les Enfants du Paradis* (1947), as well as *Pretty Baby* and *The Tin Drum* (1980). Full of the absurdities of intraprovincial contradictions and bizarre 'eliminations.'

Donohoe, Joseph I., Jr., ed. *Essays on Québec Cinema.* East Lansing: Michigan State UP, 1991. 194 pp.
The result of a symposium on Québécois cinema at the Canadian Studies Center at Michigan State University, these essays "range in substance from the technical to the philo-

sophical, from the sociological to the aesthetic," representing in roughly equal propor-
tions Québécois and anglophone authors. By dividing the collection into "Overviews of
Québec," "Filmmakers on Film," "Essays on Themes/Directors," and "Perspectives on
Individual Films," Donohoe delineates the quintessence of Québécois cinema.

Dorland, Michael. *So Close to the State/s: The Emergence of Canadian Feature Film
Policy*. Toronto: Toronto UP, 1998. 199 pp.
Sharing a continent with the USA, Canada has developed a feature-film industry mainly
because of a series of federal studies and policy decisions made in the face of American
intrusions. Using Foucault's 'governmentality' as a rubric, Dorland traces the ideological
discourses through which the film industry was conceived, argued, legislated, put into
practice and altered from the 1950s to today.

Drabinsky, Garth. *Motion Pictures and the Arts in Canada*. Toronto: McGraw–Hill
Ryerson, 1976. 201 pp.
One of Canada's foremost entertainment moguls discusses the "business and law" of the
film industry in Canada. Chapters include: "The Principles of Contract Law," "The Cana-
dian Law of Copyright," "The Role of the Agent," "Financing the Motion Picture," "The
Distribution Agreement," and "Obscenity, Censorship and Film Classification."

Elder, Bruce. *Image and Identity: Reflections on Canadian Film and Culture*. Waterloo:
Wilfrid Laurier UP; Toronto: Academy of Canadian Cinema, 1989. 483 pp.
Avant-garde filmmaker and theorist Elder performs important experiments on Canadian
cinema by way of contemporary film theory. Part One is a description of Canadian philosophical heritages; Part Two examines the Realistic tradition; and Part Three inquires into
the nature and future of avant-garde cinema in Canada. Elder's book is essential reading
for anyone wishing to examine Canadian cinema from a theoretical standpoint.

Elder, Kathryn, ed. *The Films of Joyce Wieland*. Toronto: Cinematheque Ontario,
2000.
A collection of essays, some previously unpublished (with illustrations) by, among others,
P. Adams Sitney, experimental filmmaker R. Bruce Elder and reviewer Jay Scott covering
the career of this great Canadian feminist artist and experimental filmmaker.

Evans, Gary. *John Grierson and the National Film Board: The Politics of Wartime
Propaganda*. Toronto: U of Toronto P, 1984. 329 pp.
Evans' study of Grierson's work with the NFB is yet another fascinating portrait of the
man largely responsible for Canadian prominence in the field of documentary film.

———. *In The National Interest: A Chronicle of the National Film Board from 1949 to
1989*. Toronto: U of Toronto P, 1991. 464 pp.
The NFB's mandate to serve "the national interest" has not been easy, Evans points out,
but it has been rewarding. In this volume, the author examines the role that the NFB has
played in assisting the diverse voices and visions of Canadians. This follow-up to *John
Grierson and the National Film Board* focuses primarily on the relationship between the
government film commissioners and the ministers they answered to. The interaction
between art and politics, then, is the ideological investigation that the book ultimately
undertakes.

Feldman, Seth, ed. *Take Two: A Tribute to Film in Canada.* Toronto: Irwin, 1984. 310 pp.
Like its predecessor, the *Canadian Film Reader, Take Two* represents a range of important articles in the field of Canadian film studies. Ranging from industry issues to in-depth discussions of individual films and filmmakers, articles include: Marshall Delaney (Robert Fulford) on *The Grey Fox*, Jay Scott on tax-shelter films, Piers Handling on David Cronenberg, Bruce Elder on *Not A Love Story*, and Lianne McLarty on Bruce Elder.

Feldman, Seth, & Joyce Nelson, ed. *Canadian Film Reader.* Take One Film Book 5. Toronto: Peter Martin Associates/Take One, 1977. 405 pp.
Feldman and Nelson's compilation of important essays is "designed as a source book [...] a gathering place of ideas, a dialogue, an exploratory tool, a reference work and a preserve for an endangered species of criticism." While the bulk of attention is directed toward 'establishment' English-Canadian cinema, the collection is as well-rounded as any attempt to investigate a 'national cinema' in Canada can hope to be. Featuring 'must-read' pieces by Gordon Sparling, Robert Fothergill, Bruce Elder, Peter Harcourt, Natalie Edwards, Alan Rosenthal, and others, the *Canadian Film Reader* continues to be an invaluable part of the Canadian film studies corpus.

Fetherling, Douglas, ed. *Documents in Canadian Film.* Peterborough, Ontario: Broadview, 1988. 343 pp.
A collection of seminal essays that focus on both English and French cinema, as well as experimental, narrative and documentary work, and on the debate surrounding the attractions and limitations of each. Of particular importance is Bruce Elder's 'manifesto' entitled "The Cinema We Need" and the responses it elicited from some of Canada's preeminent film scholars.

Forrester, James A. *Budge: F.R. Crawley and Crawley Films, 1939–1982.* Lakefield, Ontario: Independent Research Systems, 1998. 112 pp.
Following the format established by the Canadian Film Institute Publications Programme, this independently produced work features an excellent introduction by Munroe Scott, two illuminating articles, an extensive series of interviews, observations from the Crawley Films History project and a chronology of F.R. Crawley and Crawley films.

Foster, Charles. *Stardust and Shadows: Canadians in Early Hollywood.* Toronto: Dundurn Press, 2000.
Non-inclusive collection of sixteen anecdotal portraits of stars who formed an informal ex-pat community and whom the author met in the 1940s, including Marie Dressler, Allan Dwan, Louis B. Mayer, Mack Sennett, Jack and Mary Pickford, Norma Shearer and others who were born in or spent their formative years in Canada.

Fulford, Robert. *Marshall Delaney at the Movies: The Contemporary World As Seen on Film.* Toronto: Peter Martin Associates, 1974. 244 pp.
Fulford's book gathers together the reviews, mainly of Canadian features, which he published in *Saturday Night* and elsewhere under his non-de-plume of "Marshall Delaney."

Garel, Sylvain, & André Pâquet, ed. *Les Cinémas du Canada: Québec, Ontario, Prairies, côte Ouest, Atlantique.* Cinéma/pluriel. Paris: Editions Centre Georges Pompidou, 1992. 384 pp.

This volume is one of an extensive series on regional and national cinemas under the auspices of the Centre Pompidou, and on the occasion of retrospectives held at the Centre. Two introductory essays by the editors are followed by a seven-item section on Québec, ten essays under the provocative title "Les autres provinces," and a clutch of three reflections on animation, IMAX, and the development of the Canadian film industry as a regulated institution. Contributors include Pierre Véronneau, Peter Harcourt, Marcel Jean, Peter Morris, David Clandfield, Geoff Pevere, Tom McSorley, Bart Testa, and Brenda Longfellow. Thematic essays dominate (documentary, feminist cinema, experimental film) alongside regional coverage (Ontario, British Columbia, the prairies and the Atlantic provinces), and these limitations prevent the contributors from providing any depth of focus on individual filmmakers and films. This lack is partly remedied by factual 'dictionaries' of Canadian and Québécois directors and by chronological filmographies – first, Québec-financed productions, 1944–92, then films produced outside Québec, 1919–91; this latter parochial division results in Scott's *Company of Strangers* and films by John Smith, Robin Spry and others being prised out of the anglophone camp. This is a curiosity rather than a blemish in a highly useful compendium, which closes with a comprehensive bibliography and an alphabetical set of full definitions for historical, political, and cultural concepts and institutions of relevance to Canadian film.

Graham, Gerald. *Canadian Film Technology 1896–1986.* Newark: U of Delaware P & London: Associated UP, 1989. 272 pp.

A detailed and illustrated survey of historical developments in film techniques and technologies pertaining to Canadian filmmaking since 1896.

Gutteridge, Robert W. *Magic Moments: First 20 Years of Moving Pictures in Toronto (1894–1914).* Toronto: Gutteridge–Pratley Publications, 2000. 258 pp.

Packed with old photos and ads, this history of the film industry in Toronto is mainly about the machines, buildings and people associated with screening and distributing film. Only the final ten pages of this dry and limited study are about early filmmaking.

Harcourt, Peter. *Movies and Mythologies.* Toronto: CBC, 1977. 171 pp.

A transcript of eight CBC broadcasts concerning developments in international film. Of pertinence to Canadian contributions to cinema: VII: "The Canadian Cinema: the years of promise"; VIII: "The Canadian Cinema: the challenge of the present."

Hardy, Forsyth, ed. *Grierson On Documentary.* London: Collins, 1946; New York: Frederick J. Praeger, 1971. 256 pp.

Along with an introduction that provides a linkage between the development of the realist film movement and Grierson's "lucid and compelling exposition of its aims," this volume of Grierson's writing includes not only his statements on documentary principles but also film reviews, wartime writings, annual surveys of world documentary, and analyses of the early effects of television.

———. *Grierson on the Movies.* London: Faber & Faber, 1981. 200 pp.

The companion volume to *Grierson On Documentary*, this time concerned with the fiction film and its responsibilities.

Hebert, Gilles, ed. *Dislocations*. Winnipeg: Winnipeg Film Group, 1995. 79 pp.
A catalogue of an exhibition on motion picture production in Manitoba and the Winnipeg Film Group premiered at the Winnipeg Art Gallery on 13 February 1995.

Hehner, Barbara, & Andrea Sheffer, ed. *Making It: The Business of Film and Television Production in Canada*. Toronto: Doubleday/Canadian Academy of Film and Television, 1995. 374 pp.
Written by leading experts in the film and television industry, this volume (first edition, edited by Hehner, 1987), along with its companion, Joan Irving's *Selling It*, provides information on everything from finding actors to the production of theatrical trailers and posters. Essays by some of Canada's top producers, distributors, publicists, and marketing managers offer a complete guide to how to make and market feature films in Canada.

Hofsess, John. *Inner Views: Ten Canadian Film-Makers*. Toronto & New York: McGraw–Hill Ryerson, 1975. 171 pp.
An introduction by the author entitled "What is this thing called Canadian film?" followed by interviews with Claude Jutra, Alan King, Don Shebib, Jack Darcus, Graeme Ferguson, Frank Vitale, William Fruet, Paul Almond, Denys Arcand, and Pierre Berton.

Hoolboom, Mike. *Inside the Pleasure Dome: Fringe Film in Canada*. Toronto: Gutter Press, 1997. 181 pp.
Interviews with sixteen Canadian experimental filmmakers representing "a small sampling from each of Canada's five 'generations' of film artists." This collection begins with Michael Snow and includes such familiar names as Al Razutis, Patricia Gruben, Barbara Sternberg, Richard Kerr, and Mike Cartmell. Hoolboom himself is an experimental filmmaker.

Irving, Joan, ed. *Selling It: The Marketing of Canadian Feature Flms*. Toronto: Doubleday & The Canadian Academy of Film and Television, 1995. 252 pp.
This companion volume to *Making It* (ed. Hehner & Sheffer) contains sixteen essays by Canadian experts in everything from poster-making and market-testing to government grants and publicity.

James, C. Rodney. *Film as a National Art: The National Film Board of Canada and the Film Board Idea*. Dissertations on Film Series. New York: Arno, 1977. 762 pp.
An "expanded history" of the NFB as an "organic entity," commencing with a discussion of documentary itself, then turning to a chronological history of the Board – in both individual areas as well as types of productions – before concluding with a look at how the Film Board has acted as a model for other nationalist cinema projects.

Jean, Marcel. *Le cinéma québécois*. Collection Boréal express 2. Montréal: Boréal, 1991. 124 pp.
This is a concise historical survey of cinema in Québec, somewhat more substantial than Clandfield's Oxford book on Canadian film as a whole. Jean places the expected emphasis

on documentary approaches, and includes a chapter on the development of women's cinema.

Johnson, Brian D. *Brave Films, Wild Nights: 25 Years of Festival Fever*. Toronto: Random Canada, 2000.
Movie critic Johnson brings an enthusiast's perspective to this insider's view of the Toronto International Film Festival, the most important showcase for Canadian filmmakers in the world with almost 1,500 Canadian films screened in its first twenty-four years.

Jones, David Barker. *Movies and Memoranda: An Interpretative History of the National Film Board of Canada*. Canadian Film Series. Ottawa: Canadian Film Institute/ Deneau, 1981. 240 pp.
The book version of Jones's Stanford University doctorate, this is an "interpretation" of the NFB "based on pieces of evidence [...] relevant to answering one question: how did the National Film Board of Canada, a government organization, achieve leadership in documentary film so early and maintain it through decades of production – a feat unmatched in the world."

Knelman, Martin. *This Is Where We Came In: The Career and Character of Canadian Film*. Toronto: McClelland & Stewart, 1977. 248 pp.
A series of reviews on Canadian films and filmmakers which offers a journalist and movie critic's take on the relationship between Canadian film and Canadian character. "The first and definitive commentary on how Canada's 'instant' feature industry took shape after decades of producing documentary shorts."

——. *Home Movies: Tales from the Canadian Film World*. Toronto: Key Porter, 1987. 248 pp.
A follow-up to Knelman's *This Is Where We Came In*, this book follows the same procedure, whereby the author skilfully incorporates individual reviews and survey statements from *Saturday Night*, the *Globe & Mail* and elsewhere into a continuous narrative.

Lamonde, Yvan, & Pierre–François Hébert. *Le cinéma au Quebec: essai de statistique historique (1896 à nos jours)*. Saint–Pierre, Québec: IQRC, 1981. 478 pp.
Mainly graphs and diagrams that present comparative statistics of the commercial aspects of Quebec cinema – number of movie houses, receipts, percentage of Canadian films shown, gender of employees, taxes, etc. Fascinating and useful for other provinces as well as Canada as a whole.

Lerner, Loren R. *Canadian Film and Video: A Bibliography and Guide to the Literature*. 2 vols. Toronto: U of Toronto P, 1997. 1,811 pp.
A comprehensive reference source for literature on Canadian film and video up to 1989. With a foreword by Pierre Véronneau, this two-volume set includes sections on General Studies; Genres; Film and Government; Festivals and Awards; Industry; Production, Distribution and Exhibition Companies; Film and Video Associations and Organizations; Related Studies (ie, Film and Censorship; Film and Women) in Volume I; and People in Film and Video in Volume II. Also included is a chronology of the Canadian film industry from 1893 to 1989.

Lever, Yves. *Histoire générale du cinéma au Québec*. Montréal: Boréal, 1988. 551 pp.
A four-part sociological and historical perspective on the development of Québécois cinema. 1: "L'Époque du muet Québécois: 1896-1938"; 2: "Les Rêves tranquilles: 1939-1955"; 3: "La Révolution par l'album: 1956-1968"; 4: "Vers la maturité: 1969-1987."

Litt, Paul. *The Muses, the Masses, and the Massey Commission*. Toronto: U of Toronto P, 1992. 331 pp.
An in-depth examination of "the watershed event in Canadian cultural history," Litt's chronicle of the Massey Report's origins, politics, and the responses it generated reveals how its legacy continues to influence governmental policies on culture and media. Of particular interest to film analysts will be Part Three, which discusses the ways in which the report proposed the bringing of 'culture' to the people through forms of mass media such as the feature film.

Magder, Ted. *Canada's Hollywood: The Canadian State and Feature Films*. Toronto: U of Toronto P, 1993. 327 pp.
Beginning with an analysis of "media imperialism and its relationship to the activities of the Canadian state in the sphere of cultural policy," Magder then chronicles such land-mark developments as the formation of the Canadian Government Motion Picture Bureau and its successor, the National Film Board; the release of the Massey Report; and the establishment of the Canadian Film Development Corporation (subsequently renamed Telefilm Canada). Concluding with a chapter entitled "Culture, Nation, Dependency, and Beyond," Magder discards the question of "what is or is not Canadian," and asks for a re-evaluation of nationalism as a sufficient and unifying impetus for our cinema. "We need," he says, "public support for cultural production to explore the manifold and contra-dictory ways in which we exist as social beings in our every day lives."

Major, Ginette. *Le cinema québécois à la recherche d'un public: bilan d'une décennie: 1970-1980*. Montréal: Les Presses de l'Université de Montréal, 1982. 164 pp.
A sociological examination, indebted to Barthes and Julien Greimas and replete with graphs and diagrams, of ten representative Quebec films from the 1970s, this odd book is more pragmatic than theoretical. Its purpose is to determine just how the films are out of touch with their potential audience by carefully mapping over two dozen categories (from "l'ailleurs" to "spacialité," "bonheur" to "alimentation"). Among the films covered are *L'Amour blessé* by Lefebvre, *Pour le meilleur et pour le pire* by Jutra, *Rejeanne Padovani* by Arcand, and *J.A. Martin, photographe* by Beaudoin.

Marshall, Bill. *Quebec National Cinema*. Montreal: McGill–Queen's UP, 2001. 371 pp.
Acknowledging that "Quebec film texts tend to be vehicles for competing (as opposed to totalizing) discourses of the nation," Marshall examines the major fiction films made in French since the 1960s with Quebec financing and personnel, in order to explore "the faultlines of the national idea and project." Films are grouped according to social topics: Popular Cinema, Women's Cinema, The Indigenous Other, and The Immigrant Other; no English-language films receive mention.

Massey, Vincent. *On Being Canadian*. Toronto: Dent, 1948. 198 pp.

Vincent Massey's assessment of what it means to 'be Canadian' is of profound importance to any understanding of the 'business' of culture in Canada. While his chapter entitled "The Projection of Canada" is primarily concerned with the function of publicity on the inernational stage, the filmic metaphor cannot be overlooked. Massey's discussion of the role of the NFB in the chapter "Threads in the Fabric of Unity" makes special note of the Film Board's mandate: "to help Canadians in all parts of Canada to understand the ways of living and the problems of Canadians in other parts."

Mazurkewich, Karen. *Cartoon Capers: The History of Canadian Animators*. Toronto: McArthur, 1999. 320 pp.

Because this is a history of animators rather than animation, this lavishly illustrated book places undue emphasis on Canadians working in the USA and England. Thus renegades like Richard Williams and John Kricfalusi are given far more attention than Norman McLaren or Frederick Back. In addition, the book's organization is skewed, its insights banal, and its omissions too numerous to make it truly authoritative. But it is the first (and long overdue) study of an important area of Canadian cinematic accomplishment.

Morris, Peter. *Embattled Shadows: A History of Canadian Cinema 1895–1939*. Montreal: McGill–Queen's UP, 1978, repr. 1992. 350 pp..

Morris's exquisite chronology of Canadian cinema between the years 1895 and 1939 tells the stories of such Canadian film pioneers as Andrew and George Holland (the enterprising Ottawa brothers who brought Edison's Kinetoscope to Canada); James Freer (the Manitoba farmer who became Canada's first film producer); "Ten Percent" Ernie Shipman (the "Diamond Jim" of Canada) and his actress wife Nell; the outspoken Ontario Film Bureau head Ray Peck; and Varick Frisell, who lost his life while filming *The Viking*, his ironic portrayal of "the Newfoundland people's dramatic struggle for existence." Morris's "Postscript" discusses the way in which the strengths and weaknesses that emerge from the simultaneously conflicting and harmonizing forces of "liberal economics, regionalism and nationalism" work to together to provide a "dialectic of the Canadian ethos." Chronological appendices cover the developmental infancy of Canadian film 1894–1913 and a selected production filmography 1913–1939. The 1992 paperback reprint includes a new two-page preface, but no revisions have been undertaken.

———. *The Film Companion*. Toronto: Irwin, 1984. 335 pp.

A comprehensive guide to more than 650 Canadian films and filmmakers, Morris's *vade mecum* (recently updated by Wyndham Wise, qv) was issued to coincide with the Toronto Festival of Festival's Retrospective of Canadian Cinema. Morris, though claiming to have been selective, provides an astonishingly complete alphabetical account of Canadian film. The entries on individual films and filmmakers provide near-complete filmographical data, a general evaluation (with cross-references), a listing of interviews, an efficient plot-summary and selection of first reviews (in the case of film entries), articles, and sections in books. There are also entries on specific topics (for example, under "C": the Canadian Cooperation Project, Candid Eye, capital cost allowance films, the NFB's Challenge for Change programmes, Cinematography, Cooperatives). The dictionary format occasionally encourages an excess of elegant concision, as in the entry on State Production, in which the National Film Board and the CBC perhaps receive less than their due.

Moscovitch, Arlene. *Constructing Reality: Exploring Media Issues in Documentary.* Montreal: National Film Board of Canada, 1993. 288 pp.

Produced primarily as an educational resource, this catalogue of documentaries, interviews and essay excerpts provides an 'image bank' rather than a structured teaching method. Important techniques in documentary are addressed in both question and answer form. The author's chief aim is to assist students in developing a means of looking at documentary with a critical eye.

Nelson, Joyce. *The Colonized Eye: Rethinking the Grierson Legend.* Toronto: Between the Lines, 1988. 197 pp.

Nelson's controversial take on the motivations and ideology behind John Grierson's role as founder and head of the NFB. Focusing on the relations between film, big business, and politics, Nelson raises questions about what she calls Grierson's "sponsorship formula for documentary," as well as his "commitment to the expansion of the multinational corporation" and his "imperialist stance towards Canada and its filmmaking possibilities."

Pallister, Janis L. *The Cinema of Quebec: Masters in Their Own House.* Madison WI & Teaneck NJ: Fairleigh Dickinson UP, 1995. 599 pp.

Pallister covers the ground, thoroughly if not profoundly, to the end of the 1980s, discussing both documentaries and fiction films and grouping the individual films she covers into five subject categories: those that deal with Quebec's past, films by women directors, Quebecois literary adaptations, films on contemporary political and social institutions, and those by anglophone Quebeckers.

Pendakur, Manjunath. *Canadian Dreams and American Control: The Political Economy of the Canadian Film Industry.* Detroit MI: Wayne State UP, 1990 & Toronto: Garamond, 1992. 347 pp.

In part an analysis of Canada's dependency on imported feature films, Pendakur's study is a historical documentation of the Canadian feature film industry as a by-product of the interactions of political and economic institutions in Canadian and American society. Addressing the debate "over the vital issue of developing a national film industry with a policy devoted to producing films for the American and international market," Pendakur argues that "the fundamental contradiction between the needs of capital and the needs of the people – workers, audiences, and artists – has determined the nature and course of Canada's film industry."

Pevere, Geoff, & Greig Dymond. *Mondo Canuck.* Scarborough, Ontario: Prentice-Hall, 1996. 244 pp.

This "scrapbook" of Canadian pop culture provides all sorts of starting-points for more light-hearted discussions of the question "who and what is Canadian?"

Posner, Michael. *Canadian Dreams: The Making and Marketing of Independent Films.* Vancouver, B.C.: Douglas & McIntyre, 1993. 250 pp.

Featuring an inspiring foreword from Norman Jewison, Posner's study provides synopses of, and behind-the-scenes looks at, ten important Canadian independent film productions: *I've Heard the Mermaids Singing* (Patricia Rozema); *The Outside Chance of*

Maximilian Glick (Allan Goldstein); *A Rustling of Leaves* (Nettie Wild); *Les Noces de papier* (Michel Brault); *Diplomatic Immunity* (Sturla Gunnarson); *Comic Book Confidential* (Ron Mann); *Perfectly Normal* (Yves Simoneau); *Tales from the Gimli Hospital* (Guy Maddin); *Deadly Currents* (Simcha Jacobovici); *Le déclin de l'empire américain* (Denys Arcand).

Pratley, Gerald. *Torn Sprockets: The Uncertain Projection of the Canadian Film.* Newark NJ: U of Delaware P & London/Toronto: Associated UP, 1987. 330 pp.

Pratley's history of Canadian cinema is aptly subtitled: "Film becomes the medium through which an understanding of changing social attitudes becomes possible – but this is not the case in Canada. We have never made enough feature films about the various aspects of life to provide historians, researchers, sociologists, even audiences, with the evidence that can plainly be found in the films of other countries. Will this situation ever change? It has yet to change in over eighty years of motion picture history" (157) Divided into three parts: One: "Early Canadian Filmmaking – 1900-1939"; Two: "Success and Struggle – 1940-1984"; and Three: "The Credits – 1945-1984." Also includes an index to the films of the NFB Producers and Directors.

Reid, Alison, & Louisa Dupres, ed. *Who's Who in Canadian Film and Television.* Toronto: Academy of Canadian Film and Television, 1989. 811 pp.

Lists addresses, biographies, and filmographies of more than 2,000 writers, producers, directors, production managers, art directors, cinematographers, editors, composers, costume designers, and other behind-the-camera professionals in the Canadian film and television industries.

Reid, Alison, & P.M. Evanchuk. *Richard Leiterman.* Ottawa: Canadian Film Institute. 1981. 120 pp.

Leiterman might well be called the "eyes of Canada," for it is through the lens of his cameras that much of what has been called classic Canadian cinema has come to us. Reid's book is a useful introduction to Leiterman's work.

Rist, Peter Harry, ed. *Guide to the Cinema(s) of Canada.* Westport CT & London: Greenwood, 2001. 303 pp.

An alphabetical listing of Canadian films, directors, actors, and producers similar to the Wyndham Wise's Take One Guide but with (sometimes) more perceptive descriptions and spotty bibliographies.

Rose, Barbara Wade. *Budge: What Happened to Canada's King of Film.* Toronto: ECW, 1998. 260 pp.

A 'star bio' of Canada's most prolific (and by no means regal) filmmaker which highlights the contributions of F.R. Crawley's wives and the pecularities of his personal life, the book is hampered by its lack of a filmography and any attempt to examine, much less appraise, his films.

Scott, Jay. *Midnight Matinees.* Toronto: Oxford UP, 1985. 266 pp.

The only Canadian journalist to win the National Newspaper Award for criticism three times, Jay Scott was appointed film critic of the *Globe & Mail* in 1978. This collection of commentaries and reviews includes a chapter on "The Burnout Factory: Canada's Hollywood."

Steven, Peter. *Brink of Reality*. Toronto: Between the Lines, 1993. 287 pp.

A study of the "new documentary": work that is "stylistically innovative and daring, committed to social change, and often produced in collaboration with social groups and movements." Additional topics include an exploration of the Canadian film and video system and the role and responsibilities of audiences. As well, fourteen Canadian documentary producers are interviewed.

Testa, Bart. *Spirit in the Landscape*. Toronto: Art Gallery of Ontario, 1989. 71 pp.

Published in conjunction with a circulated program of outstanding Canadian experimental films (by David Rimmer, Rick Hancox, Joyce Weiland, Jack Chambers, Michael Snow, Bruce Elder, and others), this catalogue relies on the ideas of Northrop Frye and Gaile McGregor (in *The Wacousta Syndrome*) to show how these filmmakers are closer to the traditions of Canadian painting than to documentary or narrative cinema in their use of landscape.

Tremblay–Daviault, Christiane. *Un cinéma orphelin: structures mentals et sociales du cinéma québécois (1942–1953)*. Montréal: Editions Québec/Amérique, 1981. 355 pp.

Analyzes twelve important films to show how cinema reflected the contradictions in Quebec society between the traditional agricultural, Catholic values and new industrial, urban realities. The book also contains a chronological table of events important to Quebec film history from 1914 to 1954.

Uhde, Jan. *Vision and Persistence: Twenty Years of the Ontario Film Institute*. Waterloo: U of Waterloo P, 1990. 236 pp.

As much a tribute to OFI guru Gerald Pratley as it is to the "amazing profusion of activities" undertaken by the Ontario Film Institute since its inception in 1969, Uhde's book discusses the past, the present and the future possibilities of the international film community and Canada's place, responsibilities and opportunities within it.

Véronneau, Pierre. *Cinéma de l'époque duplessiste (Histoire du cinema au Québec II)*. Montréal: La Cinémathèque québécoise, 1979. 164 pp.

Volume 7 of "Les dossiers de la cinémathèque" contains photos, documents, cast and crew lists, review excerpts and other background information as well as this master chronicler's insights into films made in Quebec between 1944 and 1954.

Véronneau, Pierre, & Piers Handling, ed. *Self Portrait: Essays on the Canadian and Québec Cinemas*. Canadian Film 4. Ottawa: Canadian Film Institute, 1980. 257 pp.

Originally edited by Véronneau alone under the title *Les cinémas canadiens* (Montréal: Cinémathèque québécoise; Paris: Pierre Lhermier éditeur, 1978), this translated and expanded anthology raises important questions about the impact of regionalism and elusiveness of a defining centre for Canadian film. "This perpetual movement, this apparent coming and going," as Veronneau calls it," is amplified by the diverse points of view within the essays themselves. Twelve essays: "Canadian Cinema: The First Six Decades" (Morris); "Hollywood's Empire in Canada" (Cox); "The National Film Board of Canada: 1939–1959" (Handling); "The First Wave of Québec Feature Films: 1944–1953" (Véronneau); "1964: The Beginning of a Beginning" (Harcourt); "Direct Cinema" (Euvrard & Véronneau); "The Encounter Between Fiction and Direct Cinema" (Daudelin); "Animation" (Beaudet); "West Coast Filmmaking" (Tougas); "A Survey of the Commercial Cinema, 1963–1977" (Pageau); "Some Ideological and Thematic Aspects of the Québec Cinema" (Houle); and "A Chronology of Canadian and Québec Cinema, 1896–1979." Also includes a survey of 75 films and filmmakers.

Véronneau, Pierre, Michael Dorland & Seth Feldman, ed. *Dialogue: Canadian and Québec Cinema/Cinéma canadien et québécois.* Canadian Film Studies 3. Montréal: Médiatexte/Cinémathèque québécoise, 1987. 330 pp.

Divided into four parts (Cinema and Nation; Pierre Perrault, cineaste; Today's Cinema; and Conclusions), this is a representative selection of papers presented at the first joint conference of the Film Studies Association of Canada (FSAC), and l'Association québé-coise des études cinématographiques (AQEC) held at Laval University in 1986. Speakers included Peter Morris, Yves Lever, Pierre Perrault, Denise Perusse, and Michael Dorland.

Walz, Gene, ed. *Flashback: People and Institutions in Canadian Film History.* Canadian Film Studies 2. Montréal: Médiatexte, 1986. 171 pp.

A diverse collection of essays focusing on important but little-known aspects of Canadian film: "Backwards to the Future: John Grierson's Film Policy for Canada" (Peter Morris); "Action Stations!: Joris Ivens and the NFB" (Thomas Waugh); "A Canadian Film Critic in Malcolm Lowry's Cambridge" (Paul Tiessen); "The British Columbia Travel Bureau and Motion Picture Production, 1937–1947" (David Mattison); "Regionalization of a Federal Cultural Institution: The Experience of the NFB in Canada 1965–1979" (Ronald Dick); and "The National Film Society of Canada 1935–1951: Its Origins and Development" (Yvette Hackett).

Wees, William C., & Michael Dorland, ed. *Words and Moving Images.* Canadian Film Studies 1. Montréal: Médiatexte, 1983. 215 pp.

Previously unpublished essays by Canadian filmmakers and scholars regarding the complex interplay between images and texts, especially in relation to cinema. Specific topics include: avant-garde film; pornography and censorship; film and literature; voice-over narration; and cultural influences on the languages of French- and English-Canadian film and television.

Weinmann, Heinz. *Cinéma de l'imaginaire québécois: De « La petite Aurore » à «Jésus de Montréal ».* Montréal: l'Hexagone, 1990. 273 pp.

Weinmann, who teaches literature at Rosemont in Montreal and reviews for *Le Devoir*, has here written a psycho-sociological study of the Québécois 'personality' in its development since 1950, by locating its 'imaginary' through a meticulous analysis of representative films. Shorter sections deal with the films *La petite Aurore, Tit-Coq, Mon oncle Antoine, Les bons débarras,* and *Un zoo la nuit;* over half the study is devoted to Denys Arcand's *Le déclin de l'empire américain* and *Jésus de Montréal.*

Wise, Wyndham, ed. *Take One's Essential Guide to Films and Filmmakers in Canada.* Toronto: Take One, 1999. 144 pp. *Take One's Essential Guide to Canadian Film.* Toronto: Toronto UP, 2001. 272 pp.

The 1999 issue is an update of *The Film Companion* which expands Peter Morris's mandate by not just listing major Canadian talent (writers, directors, producers, actors) and films (features, documentaries, animation) but by also including Canadians working in Hollywood (from Mary Pickford and Mack Sennett to Jim Carrey and James Cameron), this guide begins with Geoff Pevere's apologia "Ghostbusting: 100 Years of Canadian Cinema, or Why My Canada Includes *The Terminator*," and contains a useful chronology of cinema in Canada from 1894, a year-by-year list of Canadian Film Awards, the Genies that replaced them in 1980, and the Golden Reel Awards (for the highest-grossing Canadian films), plus Academy Awards and nominations for Canadian films. The 2001 edition is a re-titled, greatly expanded and exhaustive update with over 700 entries and a more detailed chronology of the major events in Canadian film and television history.

ა

Periodicals

Current

ASIFA ა A well-illustrated, newsy magazine for members of ASIFA, covering the animation industry across Canada. Address: 10707, Grande Allée, Suite 3, Montréal, Québec H3L 2M8.

Cahiers du cinéma ა This famous Paris-based journal has regularly reviewed Canadian films, and is of historical importance for its engagement with Québec cinema during the 1960s.

Canadian Journal of Film Studies ა Established by the Film Studies Association of Canada in 1990, this is the only regular source of scholarly and academic writing on Canadian film. Address: Film Studies Association of Canada, York University, Department of Film and Video, North York, Ontario M3J 1P3.

CineAction ა A Toronto-based, Marxist-oriented journal (3 issues a year) which is usually focused on genre, popular American fare and international cinema, but contains regular essays on Canadian films plus periodic special issues (no. 16: "Canadian Cinema"; no. 28: "Canadas: cinema and criticism"). Address: 40 Alexander Street, Suite 705, Toronto, Ontario M4Y 1B5.

Ciné-Bulles ა Founded in 1981, this is the bimonthly journal of the Association des cinémas parallèles du Québec. Address: 4545, ave. Pierre-de-Coubertin, C.P. 1000, Succursale M, Montréal, Québec H1V 3R2.

Cinemas [Cinémas] ა Published by the University of Montreal in both French and English (3 issues a year since 1990), this learned journal covers different themes ("Nouvelles technologies," for instance) every issue, and often focuses on Canadian cinema. Address: Revue Cinémas, Programme d'études cinématographiques, Département d'histoire de l'art, Université de Montréal, Pavillon Jean–Brillant C–2130, Montréal, Québec H3C 3J7.

Cinema Scope ა A quarterly begun in 1999 with articles on Canadian and world cinema plus book reviews, festival reports, interviews and features. The Winter 2000 issue was on the best films of the 1990s, including *Exotica*, *Hard Core Logo* and ten other Canadian films.

Copie Zéro ᴤ This is an irregularly periodical publication, founded in 1979, of the Cinémathèque québécoise in Montréal devoted to monographs and collections of essays on Québécois filmmakers.

Film Canada Yearbook ᴤ Published by Patricia Thompson in Toronto since 1985, this industry-slanted annual provides up-to-date commercial information on Canadian film, television, and video.

fps (Frames per Second) ᴤ A recent addition to the burgeoning world of animation, this glossy magazine from Montreal has a definite Canadian bias.

Post script ᴤ Two special issues of this American scholarly journal have been devoted to Canadian cinema: 15.1 (Fall 1995) contains essays on recent Ontario movies and on the works of Lauzon, Cronenberg, McMahon, and Egoyan; 18.2 (Winter–Spring 1999) has essays on *Crash, Porky's, I've Heard the Mermaids Singing*, and on Quebec lowbrow comedies, independent Quebecois cinema, and on 'lost bodies' in recent Canadian film. Issue 15:2 (Winter–Spring 1996) was dedicated to the films of David Cronenberg..

POV (Point of View) ᴤ Ten-year-old magazine (3 issues per year) on the business of art and the politics of independent documentary film and video. Address: The Canadian Independent Film Caucus, 387 Bloor Street East, 5th Floor, Toronto, Ontario M4W 1H7.

Reverse Shot ᴤ Published three times a year since 1994 by the Education Committee of the Pacific Cinémathèque (Vancouver), this slim magazine with a multicultural bias concentrates on "film and video in contemporary [Canadian] culture." Address: Pacific Cinémathèque, Suite 200, 1131 Howe Street, Vancouver, B.C. V6Z 2L7.

Séquences ᴤ A quarterly magazine begun in the 1950s in Montreal. Useful special issues include "Animation at the NFB" (October 1978). Address: 4005, rue de Bellechasse, Montréal, Québec H1X 1J6.

Sight and Sound. ᴤ The monthly journal of the British Film Institute, this has since the early 1990s incorporated the Institute's *Film Bulletin*, and thus provides full production data on every Canadian feature to receive theatrical release in the United Kingdom.

Take One (new series) ᴤ Launched in 1992, this magazine on "Film in Canada" (3 issues per year) has occasional special issues and many literate but popularized examinations (sometimes too brief and superficial) of trends, genres, and personalities. It included, in 1994, a reprise of the first series' instructive 1984 poll-listing, from Canadian and international film journalists, of "Canada's ten best" films. Address: Canadian Independent Film & Television Publishing Association, 151 Golfview Avenue, Toronto, Ontario M4E 2K6.

24 Images ᴤ A quarterly in French from Québec which provides invaluable interviews and analyses of Canadian films. Address: 3781, rue Laval, Montréal, Québec H2W 2H8.

Defunct

Cinema Canada ಏ While it was in operation (from 1972 to 1989), this magazine provided essential reading on the Canadian film industry with especially useful reviews, background pieces and profiles.

Cinema Québec ಏ Published in Montreal from 1971 to 1978, this was an invaluable source of literature on québécois cinema.

Lumières ಏ This journal ran from 1988 to 1993 and, although it had a Quebec content, its mandate was international, having to do mainly with marginalized cinema from all over the world.

Monthly Film Bulletin. ಏ This long-established organ of the British Film Institute was founded in the early 1930s and provided, along with brief articles, interviews and production histories, the now-classic tripartite format, for all films with theatrical release in the United Kingdom, of technical / cast data, plot summary, and brief evaluation. The *Bulletin* has, since the early 1990s, been incorporated into the journal *Sight and Sound*.

Motion ಏ Published bi-monthly in Toronto from 1972 to 1979, this black and white magazine addressed issues related to Canadian film, theatre and television.

Take One (first series) ಏ Published in Montreal from 1966 to 1979, this popular magazine provided an important forum for the beginnings of writing about Canadian film.

ಏ

Websites

www.canadianfilm.com (history of Canadian film)

www.onf.ca (National Film Board of Canada)

www.telefilm.gc.ca (Telefilm Canada)

www.bell.ca/filmfest (Toronto International Film Festival)

www.bell.ca/filmfest/cinematheque (Cinematheque Ontario)

www.cinematheque.qc.ca (cinémathèque québécoise)

www.film.queensu.ca/FSAC/Home.html (Film Studies Association of Canada)

ಏ

Contributors

———————————— &

BLAINE ALLAN teaches in the Department of Film Studies, Queen's University. He is author of *Nicholas Ray: A Guide to References and Resources* (G.K. Hall, 1984) and co-editor, with Michael Dorland and Zuzana M. Pick, of *Responses: In Honour of Peter Harcourt* (1991). His *Directory of CBC Television Series, 1952–1982* is accessible on the World Wide Web (www.film.queensu.ca/CBC/index.html), and he has published on film and television in *Film Quarterly*, *Film History*, the *Journal of Canadian Studies*, and the *Historical Journal of Film, Radio, and Television*. His most recent film is the short feature *You Are Not Alone* (1991).

BRENDA AUSTIN–SMITH is an assistant professor of Film Studies at the University of Manitoba in Winnipeg. Her publications include essays on Marlene Gorris and Henry James. She is currently working on inter-generational responses to the women's film.

ELUNED JONES is a graduate student in English at the University of Manitoba. A poet and winner of the Nathan Rothstein Prize as the Outstanding Student in Film Studies, El played the violin for many years with the Winnipeg Youth Orchestras.

JIM LEACH is a Professor in the Department of Communications, Popular Culture and Film at Brock University in St. Catharines, Ontario. He is the author of several articles on Canadian cinema as well as *Claude Jutra, Filmmaker: Film in the National Context(s)* (1999) and the Canadian edition of *Understanding Movies* (with Louis Giannetti).

ANDRÉ LOISELLE is Assistant Professor of Film Studies at the School for Studies in Art and Culture at Carleton University in Ottawa. He also teaches in the Theatre Department of the Université du Québec in Montreal. He is the co-editor, with Brian McIlroy, of *Auteur/Provocateur: The Films of Denys Arcand* (1995), and has recently completed the manuscript for a book on Anne Claire Poirier's *Mourir à tue-tête* (forthcoming from Flick Books). He has published several articles on Canadian and Quebec film and drama in such journals as *Quebec Studies*, *The Canadian Journal of Film Studies*, *Post script*, *Essays in Theatre*, and *L'Annuaire théâtral*.

TOM MCSORLEY is Executive Director of the Canadian Film Institute in Ottawa. He is also a Contributing Editor at *Take One*, Canada's national cinema magazine, a Sessional Lecturer in Film Studies at Carleton University, and a freelance theatre, television, and film critic for CBC Radio One. He has contributed articles and book chapters to various Canadian and international cinema publications.

PETER MORRIS is a professor in the Film and Video Department and Coordinator of the Fine Arts Cultural Studies Programme at York University in Toronto. Books he has written include: *Embattled Shadows: A History of Canadian Cinema 1895–1935; The Film Companion;* and, most recently, *David Cronenberg: A Delicate Balance.* He has also published numerous articles and monographs on Canadian and international cinema, and edited and translated Georges Sadoul's *Dictionary of Films* and *Dictionary of Film Makers.* Past President of the Film Studies Association of Canada, he served as the editor of the *Canadian Journal of Film Studies* in 1991 and 1992.

CHRISTINE RAMSAY is Assistant Professor in the Department of Film and Video at the University of Regina, Saskatchewan. Canadian cinema and masculinities in contemporary cinemas are her currrent areas of research; her essays on these topics have been published in the *Canadian Journal of Film Studies,* in *Post script,* and in an anthology entitled *Boys: Masculinities in Contemporary Culture.*

CATHERINE RUSSELL is an Associate Professor of Film Studies at Concordia University in Montreal. She has published two books: *Narrative Mortality: Death, Closure and New Wave Cinemas* (University of Minnesota Press, 1995); and *Experimental Ethnography: The Work of Film in the Age of Video* (Duke University Press, 1999).

SUZIE SAU–FONG YOUNG teaches Cultural Studies and Feminist Theory at Trent University in Peterborough, Ontario. She lectures and publishes on Chinese cinemas and on horror films.

JOHN SCHOLES is a writer and filmmaker; he recently completed an MA degree in English at the University of Manitoba.

WILL STRAW is Director of the Graduate Program in Communications at McGill University in Montreal. Incoming President of the Canadian Communications Association for 1999–2000, he is also on the editorial boards of *Screen, Cultural Studies, Convergences, Perfect Beat, Social Semiotics,* and the *Journal of Musicological Research.* His articles on film and popular music have appeared in numerous anthologies and journals.

ANGELA STUKATOR is an Assistant Professor in the Film Program at the University of Western Ontario in London. She is currently completing a manuscript, *Into the Other: Beyond the Ideal Woman in Film.*

BART TESTA is senior tutor in Cinema Studies and Semiotics at the University of Toronto. He has written and lectured extensively on Canadian avant-garde film. His publications include a book, *Spirit in the Landscape,* the catalogue-essay "Richard Kerr: Overlapping Entries" as well as "Presence/Absense: The Films of Michael Snow," and "The Book of All the Dead," on Bruce Elder. Two previous essays on Denys Arcand appeared in *Dialogue* and *Auteur/Provocateur: The Films of Denys Arcand* (1995).

GEORGE TOLES, Professor of Film Studies at the University of Manitoba, has written the original screenplay for Guy Maddin's *Twilight of the Ice Nymphs* and co-authored *Archangel* and *Careful*. His essay on *Psycho* has been chosen by the BFI for its centenary anthology on Hitchcock. He is currently completing a book on family matters in literature and film.

GENE WALZ is the author of *Francois Truffaut: A Guide to References and Resources*, *Cartoon Charlie: The Life and Art of Animation Pioneer Charles Thorson*, and many essays on animation and Canadian film. He has written *Birding for Kids* for PBS-TV and *The Washing Machine*, a comedy-drama for CBC-TV which he also directed. Past president of the Film Studies Association of Canada, he is Associate Professor of Film Studies and Provost of University College at the University of Manitoba.

THOMAS WAUGH is Professor of Film Studies and Coordinator of the Programme in Interdisciplinary Studies in Sexuality at Concordia University in Montreal. His has three books to his credit: the anthology *Show Us Life: Toward a History and Aesthetics of the Committed Documentary* (1984), *Hard to Imagine: Gay Male Eroticism in Photography and Cinema From Their Beginnings to Stonewall* (1996), "Sexual Revolution, Canadian Cinema, and Other Queer Paradoxes," *Spectator* (Los Angeles) 19.2 (Spring–Summer 2000): 26–39, and the forthcoming *The Fruit Machine: 20 Years of Writing on Queer Cinema*. He has published widely on Canadian and Indian film and video, contributing to periodicals such as *The Body Politic*, *Cinema Canada*, and *Cineaction!*

ᘒ